JUVENILE
DELINQUENCY
AND JUSTICE

JUVENILE
DELINQUENCY
AND JUSTICE

Sociological Perspectives

edited by
Ronald J. Berger
Paul D. Gregory

LYNNE
RIENNER
PUBLISHERS

BOULDER
LONDON

Published in the United States of America in 2009 by
Lynne Rienner Publishers, Inc.
1800 30th Street, Boulder, Colorado 80301
www.rienner.com

and in the United Kingdom by
Lynne Rienner Publishers, Inc.
3 Henrietta Street, Covent Garden, London WC2E 8LU

© 2009 by Lynne Rienner Publishers, Inc. All rights reserved

Library of Congress Cataloging-in-Publication Data
Juvenile delinquency and justice : sociological perspectives / edited by
    Ronald J. Berger and Paul D. Gregory.
    p.   cm.
    Includes index.
    ISBN 978-1-58826-631-6 (pbk. : alk. paper)
    1. Juvenile delinquency—United States. 2. Juvenile justice,
Administration of—United States. I. Berger, Ronald J. II. Gregory,
Paul D., 1970–
HV9104.J843   2009
364.360973—dc22

                                                    2008054167

British Cataloguing in Publication Data
A Cataloguing in Publication record for this book
is available from the British Library.

Printed and bound in the United States of America

The paper used in this publication meets the requirements
of the American National Standard for Permanence of
Paper for Printed Library Materials Z39.48-1992.

5 4 3 2 1

To the flings and infatuations of adolescence,
its trials and tribulations,
and the hope that you don't stray too far
from the path that will lead to your dreams

Contents

Preface   xi

Part 1 Juvenile Justice and Delinquency
        in Historical Perspective

   Introduction to Part 1, *the Editors*   1

1 The Child-Saving Movement and the Origins of the
   Juvenile Justice System   9
   Anthony Platt

2 Best-Laid Plans: The Ideal Juvenile Court   27
   Ellen Ryerson

3 History Overtakes the Juvenile Justice System   45
   Theodore N. Ferdinand

Part 2 The Measurement and
        Social Distribution of Delinquency

   Introduction to Part 2, *the Editors*   65

4 Gangs, Drugs, and Delinquency in a Survey of Urban Youth   79
   Finn-Aage Esbensen and David Huizinga

5 The Impact of Sex Composition on Gangs and
   Gang Member Delinquency   101
   Dana Peterson, Jody Miller, and Finn-Aage Esbensen

Part 3 The Social Psychology of Delinquency

   Introduction to Part 3, *the Editors*   127

6 Scared Straight: A Question of Deterrence   149
   Richard J. Lundman

7 Social Learning Theory, Drug Use, and American Indian Youths:
A Cross-Cultural Test 161
L. Thomas Winfree, Jr., Curt T. Griffiths, and Christine S. Sellers

8 Delinquents' Perspectives on the Role of the Victim 183
*Cheryl Carpenter, Barry Glassner, Bruce D. Johnson,
Julia Loughlin, and Margret Ksander*

9 Self-Definition by Rejection: The Case of Gang Girls 199
Anne Campbell

10 Explaining School Shooters:
The View from General Strain and Gender Theory 219
Ronald J. Berger

Part 4 Social Structure and Delinquency:
Family, Schools, Community, and Work

Introduction to Part 4, *the Editors* 231

11 Family Relationships and Delinquency 239
Stephen A. Cernkovich and Peggy C. Giordano

12 Players and Ho's 263
Terry Williams and William Kornblum

13 Getting Rid of Troublemakers: High School Disciplinary
Procedures and the Production of Dropouts 275
Christine Bowditch

14 Organizing the Community for Delinquency Prevention 297
Ronald J. Berger

15 Juvenile Involvement in Occupational Delinquency 323
John Paul Wright and Francis T. Cullen

Part 5 Law-Violating Youth Groups
and Gang Delinquency

Introduction to Part 5, *the Editors* 351

16 The Saints and the Roughnecks 355
William J. Chambliss

17 Adolescent Subcultures, Social Type Metaphors, and
Group Delinquency: Continuity and Change 369
Ronald J. Berger

18 Urban Street Gangs: Class, Race/Ethnicity, and Gender   393
    Ronald J. Berger

19 Gangstas, Thugs, and Hustlas:
    Identity and the Code of the Street in Rap Music   407
    Charis E. Kubrin

20 Community Tolerance of Gang Violence   433
    Ruth Horowitz

Part 6 The Contemporary Juvenile Justice System

    Introduction to Part 6, *the Editors*   453

21 Legal and Extralegal Factors in Police and
    Court Processing of Juveniles   463
    Ronald J. Berger

22 Gang Members and the Police   477
    Carl Werthman and Irving Piliavin

23 Judging Delinquents   487
    Robert M. Emerson

24 A Comparative Analysis of Organizational Structure and
    Inmate Subcultures in Institutions for Juvenile Offenders   501
    Barry C. Feld

25 Viable Options: Intensive Supervision Programs for
    Juvenile Delinquents   523
    William H. Barton and Jeffrey A. Butts

26 Evaluating Juvenile Drug Courts:
    Shedding Light into the Theoretical Black Box   541
    Paul D. Gregory, Kristen E. DeVall, and David J. Hartmann

Appendix: Note on Statistical Techniques   563
Index   565
About the Book   593

Preface

THIS BOOK OFFERS STUDENTS A COMPREHENSIVE AND SYSTEMATIC examination of the phenomena of juvenile delinquency and the juvenile justice system from a sociological perspective. The articles have been selected with an eye toward exposing students to the theoretical and methodological diversity of the field (i.e., historical, survey, ethnographic, and evaluation research), as well as to the diversity of the delinquent experience and how this experience is influenced by the social statuses of class, race, ethnicity, and gender. The articles are both insightful and relevant, and students will find the ethnographic accounts especially interesting to read. The introductions to each of the six parts situate the readings in broader perspective and highlight the ways in which a sociological approach can deepen students' understanding of the topics under consideration. As such, the book may be used either as a core or supplemental text. In either case, students reading this book will acquire a thorough and substantive grounding in the sociology of delinquency and justice.

We thank Lynne Rienner, Leanne Anderson, Andrew Berzanskis, Lesli Brooks Athanasoulis, and the rest of the staff at Lynne Rienner Publishers for their support of this project and fine work in bringing the book to publication. We also thank Ruthy Berger and Kari Borne, who provided valuable assistance in preparing the manuscript, and our students, who have inspired us to find ways to enlighten and enliven their educational experience.

—R. J. B. and P. D. G.

PART 1

Juvenile Justice and Delinquency
in Historical Perspective

ADULTS OF EVERY GENERATION OFTEN HAVE COMPLAINED ABOUT THE unruly conduct of youths. Even the ancient Greek philosopher Aristotle remarked that the young are "apt to be carried away by their impulses . . . [and] carry everything too far . . . [and] every desire into action" (quoted in Hall 1905:523). But even though youths have long been known for the tendency to be rowdy, to fight with one another, to drink excessively, and to be sexually active, the concept of "juvenile delinquency" as a phenomenon distinct from adult criminality is a relatively recent historical invention. In fact, the first specialized juvenile court in the United States was not created until 1899, when the state of Illinois developed a legal code designed specifically to deal with juvenile misconduct (Aries 1962; Binder, Geis, and Bruce 1988; Empey 1982).

Earlier societies did not make the distinctions among childhood, adolescence, and adulthood that we make today. Children were believed to be miniature adults, as was illustrated by early paintings and sculptures that portrayed them as "mature midgets" (Aries 1962; Empey 1982:37). Moreover, the many years of schooling required by modern societies have extended the period of adolescence—the ages between the onset of puberty and full adult status—into the late teens and early twenties.

Modern families are expected to be child centered and protective of children. This was not the case in earlier times. Infanticide, the deliberate killing of unwanted infants, particularly females, was not uncommon and was viewed by some as casually as some may view abortion today. Unwanted children were also abandoned and sold into slavery, indentured servitude, and prostitution;

1

and children in general were both economically and sexually exploited. In addition, mothers with the economic means hired wet nurses to feed their babies, who consequently died at higher rates than mother-fed infants because wet nurses were often malnourished. Swaddling, a method of wrapping children entirely in bandages (feces and all) so that they could not move, was a common practice. A large number of children also could be considered "battered" in light of the harsh physical punishment they received. Thus, children often lived under difficult and unhealthy conditions and suffered much from disease. The average life expectancy as late as the seventeenth century was about 30 years (Bremner 1970; DeMause 1974; Empey 1982; Gillis 1974).

As Western civilization emerged from the Middle Ages, many of these practices began to fade. By the late sixteenth to seventeenth centuries, reformers became critical of the way children were treated, and in colonial America a modern conception of childhood began to take hold. Religious moralists believed that even though children were inherently sinful (original sin), they were also fragile and innocent. Since they were easily corrupted, they needed to receive special training from the family, church, and school. In other words, children were viewed as both "wicked and worth saving" (Aries 1962: Empey 1982:39). According to Puritan reformers, the **ideal child*** had to be extensively supervised and disciplined ("spare the rod and spoil the child"), absolutely obedient to authority ("children should be seen and not heard"), sexually chaste, and impressed with the moral virtues of hard work ("idle hands are the devil's workshop") (Bremner 1970).

The Puritans, however, continued to believe in the apprenticeship, which was considered a normal part of a child's upbringing until the eighteenth century. Although apprenticeships were highly exploitative, they were seen as offering "safeguard[s] against parental overindulgence" (Binder, Geis, and Bruce 1988:51–52). Under this system, young men and women were bound to "masters" for a designated period of time, "during which they would work for their masters and learn their trades. In return, the masters were expected to provide their apprentices with food, shelter, and clothing." But the life of an apprentice was not easy. "Though a youth, he or she was still expected to work hard . . . and was quite harshly treated and subjected to brutal punishments."

Gradually, however, a more nurturing attitude toward children emerged. Good behavior in children was increasingly viewed as a product of parental affection rather than of fear and punishment. The family was perceived more as an emotional unit and as a refuge from the outside world. Obedient children were still the ideal, but they were obedient "not because they were forced to behave" but because they wanted to behave (Binder, Geis, and Bruce 1988:55).

---

*Key terms are indicated in **boldface** the first time they appear in the part introductions of the book.

This social construction of the "ideal child" and the changes in family life set the stage for the concept of juvenile delinquency. But until the end of the nineteenth century, there was still no distinct legal category of "delinquency." Americans relied on English common law, which specified that children under age 7 were incapable of criminal intent and thus absolved of guilt for serious crimes. Children age 7 to 13 were presumed innocent unless proven otherwise, but children 14 and older were treated as adults. A separate juvenile justice system to deal with the crimes and derelictions of young people did not yet exist (Empey 1982; Thornton, Voigt, and Doerner 1987).

In colonial America, the community had been tightly knit and organized around the church, which "set strict standards . . . and related obedience to eternal rewards and punishments" (Empey 1982:55). By the nineteenth century, however, life in the United States had undergone dramatic change with the rise of industrialization and urbanization. Foreign immigration and rural-urban migration increased the size of city populations, and people were concentrated under conditions of considerable poverty in urban slums. Under these circumstances, the social controls characteristic of traditional community arrangements were less effective in controlling deviant behavior. Middle-class Protestant Americans were increasingly troubled by these changes and concerned that immigrant and lower-class families were failing their children (Binder, Geis, and Bruce 1988).

Institutional confinement emerged as the preferred method of dealing with both youthful and adult offenders, replacing earlier methods of swift corporal punishment such as "public whippings, confinement in stocks or pillories, . . . mutilation such as cropping the ears, . . . [and] death" (Binder, Geis, and Bruce 1988:209). Incarceration was considered to be a progressive and humanitarian alternative to the brutality of earlier approaches, and for the first time special places of confinement for juveniles were created in **houses of refuge.** Reformers supported houses of refuge in order to prevent children from being exposed to the corrupting influence of adult criminals.

The first houses of refuge appeared in New York and Pennsylvania in the 1820s and were designed not just for youthful criminals but also for a variety of problem children including runaways, vagrants, and other disobedient youths who were vulnerable to the corrupting influences of urban life. Houses of refuge became institutions designed to induce ungracious and unruly lower-class children to conform to the niceties of the "ideal child." They operated on the basis of strict discipline, hard work, and "tight daily schedules, with regular hours for rising and retiring, meals at set times, and regular periods set aside for workshop training, . . . schooling . . . [and] religious observances and prayers" (Binder, Geis, and Bruce 1988:211; Bremner 1970; Empey 1982; Schlossman 1977).

By the nineteenth century, however, houses of refuge, along with orphan asylums, began to be perceived as prisonlike warehouses that often bred criminality rather than preventing it. Reformers also were critical of the use of corporal punishment in these institutions and began to look for alternative methods of reforming problem youths. One of the most important of the new inventions was the **cottage system.** First introduced in Massachusetts and Ohio in the 1850s, the cottage system placed juveniles in small family-like environments of from one dozen to three dozen occupants under the supervision of a surrogate parent. The cottage system was believed superior to more congregate systems of confinement because it provided closer and presumably higher quality supervision (Binder, Geis, and Bruce 1988).

The modern system of juvenile justice was the most significant event in the development of alternative institutional approaches to delinquency. In the United States its emergence was associated with the **Progressive Era** of the late nineteenth and early twentieth centuries. Progressivism can be characterized as a liberal political movement designed to clean up some of the social problems and injustices associated with the early stages of industrialization and urbanization. As Siegel and Senna describe it:

> The Progressive Era was marked by a great deal of social change prompted by appeals to the conscience of the nation. Reformers were shocked by exposés of how society treated its less fortunate members. They were particularly concerned about what was going on in prisons and mental institutions. The poor, ill, and unfortunate were living in squalor, beaten, and mistreated by their "keepers." Progressive reformers lobbied legislators and appealed to public opinion in order to force better conditions. Their efforts helped establish the probation and parole system and other liberal correctional reforms. (1988:371; see also Rothman 1980)

Sociologists and historians have debated whether progressivism was, in fact, a movement of humanitarian reform or, rather, a means by which dominant groups in the United States began to consolidate their economic and political power and attempt to regulate people and social practices that threatened the orderly transition of society from an unregulated competitive laissez-faire capitalist system to an economy increasingly dominated by large powerful corporations. In Chapter 1, "The Child-Saving Movement and the Origins of the Juvenile Justice System," Anthony Platt discusses the emergence of the **child-saving movement** that was ostensibly designed to ameliorate the plight of underprivileged children. In the area of juvenile justice reform, Platt argues, the child-saving movement "tried to do for the criminal justice system what industrialists and corporate leaders were trying to do for the economy—that is, achieve order, stability and control while preserving the existing class system and distribution of wealth." Platt believes that the child-saving reformers could not have succeeded "without the financial and political support of the wealthy and powerful," and he suggests that the informality associated with the new juvenile court system was a means by which the state expanded its jurisdiction over an increasing number of youths without providing them with constitutional due process protections against unwarranted governmental intrusion in their lives. According to the legal doctrine of ***parens patriae*** adopted from English common law—which refers to the role of the king as the father or guardian of his country—the state could act in the "best interests" of children and take control of their lives *before* they committed a crime.[1] It is important to note that the new system of juvenile justice established a range of **status offenses**—behaviors that were illegal only because the individual was under a certain age (typically 17 or 18). Juveniles could now be held in violation of the law for offenses such as truancy, curfew, drinking alcohol, and running away from home as well as for vague transgressions such as immoral behavior, incorrigibility, and habitual disobedience.

Platt's interpretation of the developing juvenile justice system utilizes a **conflict theory** of society. According to conflict theory, society is divided into conflicting groups, and the group that holds the most economic power exerts disproportionate influence over the political and legal system (Chambliss and Seidman 1971; Quinney 1977; Turk 1969). Moreover, the "law is differentially administered to favor the rich and powerful and control the have-not members of society" (Siegel and Senna 1988:198). Thus, according to Platt and other conflict theorists, the new juvenile justice system was directed primarily against the less privileged youths of society, that is, those from the lower and working classes. Moreover, Platt believes that the juvenile justice reforms were, in part, a means of "preparing youth as a disciplined and devoted work force" that would promote the expansion of corporate capitalism in the United States.

In Chapter 2, "Best-Laid Plans: The Ideal Juvenile Court," Ellen Ryerson offers a different take on the emergence of the juvenile justice system. Although acknowledging the limitations of the early juvenile justice reforms, Ryerson is more positive than Platt about the genuineness of the child-savers' humanitarian desire to help children and to prevent crime through a program of individualized treatment, family revitalization, and probation rather than incarceration.[2] In her view, a more balanced and nuanced interpretation of the rise of the juvenile justice system recognizes its "inherently double nature." Although some aspects "appear 'conservative' because they emphasized social control, . . . other aspects appear 'reformist' because they emphasized the rehabilitative ideal and found new ways to pursue it."

Finally, Chapter 3 supplements Ryerson's account by tracing the history of the juvenile justice system up to contemporary times. In "History Overtakes the Juvenile Justice System," Theodore Ferdinand argues that many of the system's problems "can be understood in terms of how the [juvenile] court adjusted over the years to the custodial institutions, clientele, and treatment facilities it served," particularly to the "system of juvenile institutions already dominated by a custodial if not a punitive viewpoint." He considers the apparent failure of rehabilitative treatment and the growing demand for reform and offers his views of how the system might live up to its initial promises. Although some criminologists and legal scholars advocate abolition of a separate system of juvenile justice (Feld 1990, 1993), Ferdinand believes that "historical analysis can pinpoint the sources of the court's difficulties and thereby suggest appropriate lines of reform."

Notes

1. The doctrine goes back to the Middle Ages when the king invoked his power to protect the inheritance rights of children and when the state asserted the right to assume wardship of children when "the natural parents or testamentary guardians were adjudged unfit to perform their duties" (Binder, Geis, and Bruce 1988:213).

2. See Schlossman (1977) for a similar assessment and Hagan and Leon (1977) for a critique of Platt's interpretation based on their analysis of the Canadian juvenile justice system. See Shelden and Osborne (1989) for research supporting Platt's position.

References

Aries, Philippe. 1962. *Centuries of Childhood.* New York: Knopf.

Binder, Arnold, Gilbert Geis, and Dickson D. Bruce. 1988. *Juvenile Delinquency: Historical, Cultural, and Legal Perspectives.* New York: Macmillan.

Bremner, Robert H. (ed.). 1970. *Children and Youth in America: A Documentary History.* Cambridge, MA: Harvard University Press.

Chambliss, William J., and Robert B. Seidman. 1971. *Law, Order, and Power.* Reading, MA: Addison-Wesley.

DeMause, Lloyd (ed.). 1974. *The History of Childhood.* New York: Psychohistory Press.

Empey, Lamar T. 1982. *American Delinquency: Its Meaning and Construction.* Homewood, IL: Dorsey Press.

Feld, Barry C. 1990. "The Punitive Juvenile Court and the Quality of Procedural Justice: Disjunctions Between Rhetoric and Reality." *Crime and Delinquency* 36: 433–466.

———. 1993. "Juvenile (In)Justice and the Criminal Court Alternative." *Crime and Delinquency* 39:403–424.

Gillis, John R. 1974. *Youth and History.* New York: Academic Press.

Hagan, John, and Jeffrey Leon. 1977. "Rediscovering Delinquency: Social History, Political Ideology, and the Sociology of Law." *American Sociological Review* 42: 587–598.

Hall, G. Stanley. 1905. *Adolescence: Its Psychology and Its Relationship to Physiology, Anthropology, Sociology, Sex, Crime, Religion, and Education.* New York: Appleton.

Quinney, Richard. 1977. *Class, State, and Crime.* New York: McKay.

Rothman, David. 1980. *Conscience and Convenience.* Boston: Little, Brown.

Schlossman, Steven L. 1977. *Love and the American Delinquent: The Theory and Practice of "Progressive" Juvenile Justice: 1825–1920.* Chicago: University of Chicago Press.

Shelden, Randall, and Lynn T. Osborne. 1989. "'For Their Own Good': Class Interests and the Child Saving Movement in Memphis, Tennessee, 1900–1917." *Criminology* 27:747–767.

Siegel, Larry J., and Joseph J. Senna. 1988. *Juvenile Delinquency: Theory, Practice, and Law.* St. Paul, MN: West.

Thornton, William E., Lydia Voigt, and William G. Doerner. 1987. *Delinquency and Justice.* New York: Random House.

Turk, Austin T. 1969. *Criminality and the Legal Order.* Chicago: Rand McNally.

The Child-Saving Movement and the Origins of the Juvenile Justice System

Anthony Platt

This chapter discusses the emergence of the child-saving movement that was ostensibly designed to ameliorate the plight of underprivileged children. In the area of juvenile justice reform, Anthony Platt argues, the child-saving movement tried to "achieve order, stability and control while preserving the existing class system and [unequal] distribution of wealth." According to Platt, the new juvenile justice system, and the informality associated with it, was a means by which the state expanded its jurisdiction over an increasing number of youths without providing them with constitutional due process protections against unwarranted governmental intrusion in their lives.

The Child-Saving Movement

. . . Although the modern juvenile justice system can be traced in part to the development of various charitable and institutional programs in the early nineteenth century,[1] it was not until the close of the century that the modern system was systematically organized to include juvenile courts, probation, child guidance clinics, truant officers, and reformatories. The child-saving movement—an amalgam of philanthropists, middle-class reformers and professionals—was responsible for the consolidation of these reforms.[2]

The 1890s represented for many middle-class intellectuals and professionals a period of discovery of "dim attics and damp cellars in poverty-stricken sections of populous towns" and "innumerable haunts of misery throughout the land."[3] The city was suddenly discovered to be a place of scarcity, disease, neglect, ignorance, and "dangerous influences." Its slums were the "last resorts of the penniless and the criminal"; here humanity reached the lowest level of

Excerpt from "The Triumph of Benevolence: The Origins of the Juvenile Justice System in the United States," in Richard Quinney (ed.), *Criminal Justice in America* (Little, Brown, 1974), pp. 362–383. Reprinted by permission of the author.

degradation and despair.[4] These conditions were not new to American urban life and the working class had been suffering such hardships for many years. Since the Haymarket Riot of 1886, the centers of industrial activity had been continually plagued by strikes, violent disruptions, and widespread business failures.

What distinguished the late 1890s from earlier periods was the recognition by some sectors of the privileged classes that far-reaching economic, political and social reforms were desperately needed to restore order and stability. In the economy, these reforms were achieved through the corporation, which extended its influence into all aspects of domestic and foreign policies so that by the 1940s some 139 corporations owned 45 percent of all the manufacturing assets in the country. It was the aim of corporate capitalists to limit traditional laissez-faire business competition and to transform the economy into a rational and interrelated system, characterized by extensive long-range planning and bureaucratic routine.[5] In politics, these reforms were achieved nationally by extending the regulatory powers of the federal government and locally by the development of commission and city manager forms of government as an antidote to corrupt machine politics. In social life, economic and political reforms were paralleled by the construction of new social service bureaucracies which regulated crime, education, health, labor and welfare.

The child-saving movement tried to do for the criminal justice system what industrialists and corporate leaders were trying to do for the economy— that is, achieve order, stability and control while preserving the existing class system and distribution of wealth. While the child-saving movement, like most Progressive [era] reforms, drew its most active and visible supporters from the middle class and professions, it would not have been capable of achieving significant reforms without the financial and political support of the wealthy and powerful. Such support was not without precedent in various philanthropic movements preceding the child-savers. New York's Society for the Reformation of Juvenile Delinquents benefited in the 1820s from the contributions of Stephen Allen, whose many influential positions included Mayor of New York and president of the New York Life Insurance and Trust Company.[6] The first large gift to the New York Children's Aid Society, founded in 1853, was donated by Mrs. William Astor.[7] According to Charles Loring Brace, who helped to found the Children's Aid Society, "a very superior class of young men consented to serve on our Board of Trustees; men who, in their high principles of duty, and in the obligations which they feel are imposed by wealth and position, bid fair hereafter to make the name of New York merchants respected as it was never before throughout the country."[8] Elsewhere, welfare charities similarly benefited from the donations and wills of the upper class.[9] Girard College, one of the first large orphanages in the United States, was built and furnished with funds from the banking fortune of Stephen Girard,[10] and the Catholic bankers and financiers of New York helped to mobilize support and money for various Catholic charities.[11]

The child-saving movement similarly enjoyed the support of propertied and powerful individuals. In Chicago, for example, where the movement had some of its most notable successes, the child-savers included Louise Bowen and Ellen Henrotin, who were both married to bankers.[12] Mrs. Potter Palmer, whose husband owned vast amounts of land and property, was an ardent child-saver when not involved in the exclusive Fortnightly Club, the elite Chicago Woman's Club or the Board of Lady Managers of the World's Fair;[13] another child-saver in Chicago, Mrs. Perry Smith, was married to the vice-president of the Chicago and Northwestern Railroad. Even the more radically-minded child-savers came from upper-class backgrounds. The fathers of Jane Addams and Julia Lathrop, for example, were both lawyers and Republican senators in the Illinois legislature. Jane Addams' father was one of the richest men in northern Illinois, and her stepbrother, Harry Haldeman, was a socialite from Baltimore who later amassed a large fortune in Kansas City.[14]

The child-saving movement was not simply a humanistic enterprise on behalf of the lower classes against the established order. On the contrary, its impetus came primarily from the middle and upper classes who were instrumental in devising new forms of social control to protect their privileged positions in American society. The child-saving movement was not an isolated phenomenon but rather reflected massive changes in productive relationships, from laissez-faire to monopoly capitalism, and in strategies of social control, from inefficient repression to welfare state benevolence.[15] This reconstruction of economic and social institutions, which was not achieved without conflict within the ruling class, represented a victory for the more "enlightened" wing of corporate leaders who advocated strategic alliances with urban reformers and support of liberal reforms.[16]

Many large corporations and business leaders, for example, supported federal regulation of the economy in order to protect their own investments and stabilize the marketplace. Business leaders and political spokesmen were often in basic agreement about fundamental economic issues. . . . "Few reforms were enacted without the tacit approval, if not the guidance, of the large corporate interests." For the corporation executives, liberalism meant "the responsibility of all classes to maintain and increase the efficiency of the existing social order."[17]

Progressivism was in part a businessmen's movement and big business played a central role in the Progressive coalition's support of welfare reforms. Child labor legislation in New York, for example, was supported by several groups, including upper-class industrialists who did not depend on cheap child labor. According to Jeremy Felt's history of that movement, "the abolition of child labor could be viewed as a means of driving out marginal manufacturers and tenement operators, hence increasing the consolidation and efficiency of business."[18] The rise of compulsory education, another welfare state reform, was also closely tied to the changing forms of industrial production and social control. Charles Loring Brace, writing in the mid-nineteenth century, antici- pated the use of education as preparation for industrial discipline when, "in the interests of public order, of liberty, of property, for the sake of our own safety and the endurance of free institutions here," he advocated "a strict and careful law, which shall compel every minor to learn and read and write, under severe penalties in case of disobedience."[19] By the end of the century, the working class had imposed upon them a sterile and authoritarian educational system which mirrored the ethos of the corporate workplace and was designed to pro- vide "an increasingly refined training and selection mechanism for the labor force."[20]

While the child-saving movement was supported and financed by corpo- rate liberals, the day-to-day work of lobbying, public education and organiz- ing was undertaken by middle-class urban reformers, professionals and special interest groups. The more moderate and conservative sectors of the feminist movement were especially active in anti-delinquency reforms.[21] Their success- ful participation derived in part from public stereotypes of women as the "nat- ural caretakers" of "wayward children." Women's claim to the public care of children had precedent during the nineteenth century and their role in child rearing was paramount. Women, generally regarded as better teachers than men, were more influential in child-training and discipline at home. The fact that public education also came more under the direction of women teachers in the schools served to legitimize the predominance of women in other areas of "child-saving."[22]

The child-saving movement attracted women from a variety of political and class backgrounds, though it was dominated by the daughters of the old landed gentry and wives of the upper-class nouveau riche. Career women and society philanthropists, elite women's clubs and settlement houses, and polit- ical and civic organizations worked together on the problems of child care, ed- ucation and juvenile delinquency. Professional and political women's groups regarded child-saving as a problem of women's rights, whereas their oppo- nents seized upon it as an opportunity to keep women in their "proper place." Child-saving became a reputable task for any woman who wanted to extend her "housekeeping" functions into the community without denying anti-femi- nist stereotypes of woman's nature and place.[23]

For traditionally educated women and daughters of the landed and indus- trial gentry, the child-saving movement presented an opportunity for pursuing socially acceptable public roles and for restoring some of the authority and spiritual influence which many women felt they had lost through the urbaniza- tion of family life. . . .[24] The child-savers were aware that their championship of social outsiders such as immigrants, the poor and children, was not wholly motivated by disinterested ideals of justice and equality. Philanthropic work filled a void in their own lives, a void which was created in part by the decline of traditional religion, increased leisure and boredom, the rise of public education, and the breakdown of communal life in large, crowded cities. "By simplifying dress and amusements, by cutting off a little here and there from our luxuries," wrote one child-saver, "we may change the whole current of many human lives."[25] Women were exhorted to make their lives useful by participating in welfare programs, by volunteering their time and services, and by getting acquainted with less privileged groups. They were also encouraged to seek work in institutions which were "like family-life with its many-sided developments and varied interests and occupations, and where the woman-element shall pervade the house and soften its social atmosphere with motherly tenderness."[26]

While the child-saving movement can be partly understood as a "symbolic crusade,"[27] which served ceremonial and status functions for many women, it was by no means a reactionary and romantic movement, nor was it supported only by women and members of the old gentry. Child-saving also had considerable instrumental significance for legitimizing new career openings for women. The new role of social worker combined elements of an old and partly fictitious role—defender of family life—and elements of a new role—social servant. Social work and professional child-saving provided new opportunities for career-minded women who found the traditional professions dominated and controlled by men.[28] These child-savers were members of the emerging [middle class] created by the new industrial order.

It is not surprising that the professions also supported the child-saving movement, for they were capable of reaping enormous economic and status rewards from the changes taking place. The clergy had nothing to lose (but more of their rapidly declining constituency) and everything to gain by incorporating social services into traditional religion. Lawyers were needed for their technical expertise and to administer new institutions. And academics discovered a new market which paid them as consultants, elevated them to positions of national prestige and furnished endless materials for books, articles and conferences. . . .

While the rank and file reformers in the child-saving movement worked closely with corporate liberals, it would be inaccurate to simply characterize them as lackeys of big business. Many were principled and genuinely concerned about alleviating human misery and improving the lives of the poor. Moreover, many women who participated in the movement were able to free themselves from male domination and participate more fully in society. But for the most part, the child-savers and other Progressive reformers defended capitalism and rejected socialist alternatives. Most reformers accepted the structure of the new industrial order and sought to moderate its cruder inequities and reduce inharmonies in the existing system.[29] Though many child-savers were "socialists of the heart" and ardent critics of society, their programs were typically reformist and did not alter basic economic inequalities.[30] Rhetoric and righteous indignation were more prevalent than programs of radical action.

◼ Images of Crime and Delinquency

. . . The child-savers viewed the "criminal classes" with a mixture of contempt and benevolence. Crime was portrayed as rising from the "lowest orders" and threatening to engulf "respectable" society like a virulent disease. Charles Loring Brace, a leading child-saver, typified popular and professional views about crime and delinquency:

> As Christian men, we cannot look upon this great multitude of unhappy, deserted, and degraded boys and girls without feeling our responsibility to God for them. The class increases: immigration is pouring in its multitudes of poor foreigners who leave these young outcasts everywhere in our midst. These boys and girls . . . will soon form the great lower class of our city. They will influence elections; they may shape the policy of the city; they will assuredly, if unreclaimed, poison society all around them. They will help to form the great multitude of robbers, thieves, and vagrants, who are now such a burden upon the law-respecting community. . . .[31]

This attitude of contempt derived from a view of criminals as less-than-human, a perspective which was strongly influenced and aggravated by nativist and racist ideologies.[32] The "criminal class" was variously described as "creatures" living in "burrows," "dens," and "slime"; as "little Arabs" and "foreign childhood that floats along the streets and docks of the city—vagabondish, thievish, familiar with the vicious ways and places of the town";[33] and as "ignorant," "shiftless," "indolent," and "dissipated."[34]

The child-savers were alarmed and frightened by the "dangerous classes" whose "very number makes one stand aghast," noted the urban reformer Jacob Riis.[35] Law and order were widely demanded:

> The "dangerous classes" of New York are mainly American-born, but the children of Irish and German immigrants. They are . . . ignorant [and] . . . far more brutal than the peasantry from whom they descend, and they are much banded together . . . ready for any offense or crime, however degraded or bloody. . . . Let but Law lift its hand from them for a season, or let the civilizing influences of American life fail to reach them, and, if the opportunity offered, we should see an explosion from this class which might leave this city in ashes and blood.[36]

These views derived considerable legitimacy from prevailing theories of social and reform Darwinism which . . . proposed that criminals were a dangerous and atavistic class, standing outside the boundaries of morally regulated relationships. Herbert Spencer's writings had a major impact on American intellectuals and

Cesare Lombroso, perhaps the most significant figure in nineteenth-century criminology, looked for recognition in the United States when he felt that his experiments on the "criminal type" had been neglected in Europe.[37]

Although Lombroso's theoretical and experimental studies were not translated into English until 1911, his findings were known by American academics in the early 1890s, and their popularity, like that of Spencer's works, was based on the fact that they confirmed widely-held stereotypes about the biological basis and inferior character of a "criminal class." A typical view was expressed by Nathan Allen in 1878 at the National Conference of Charities and Correction: "If our object is to prevent crime in a large scale, we must direct attention to its main sources—to the materials that make criminals; the springs must be dried up; the supplies must be cut off."[38] This was to be achieved, if necessary, by birth control and eugenics. Similar views were expressed by Hamilton Wey, an influential physician at Elmira Reformatory, who argued before the National Prison Association in 1881 that criminals had to be treated as a "distinct type of human species."[39]

Literature on "social degradation" was extremely popular during the 1870s and 1880s, though most such "studies" were little more than crude and racist polemics, padded with moralistic epithets and preconceived value judgments. Richard Dugdale's series of papers on the Jukes family, which became a model for the case-study approach to social problems, was distorted almost beyond recognition by anti-intellectual supporters of hereditary theories of crime.[40] Confronted by the . . . disciples of the biological image of behavior, many child-savers were compelled to admit that "a large proportion of the unfortunate children that go to make up the great army of criminals are not born right."[41] Reformers adopted and modified the rhetoric of social Darwinism in order to emphasize the urgent need for confronting the "crime problem" before it got completely out of hand. A popular proposal, for example, was the "methodized registration and training" of potential criminals, "or these failing, their early and entire withdrawal from the community."[42]

Although some child-savers advocated drastic methods of crime control—including birth control through sterilization, cruel punishments, and lifelong incarceration—more moderate views prevailed. This victory for moderation was related to the recognition by many Progressive reformers that short-range repression was counter-productive as well as cruel and that long-range planning and amelioration were required to achieve economic and political stability. The rise of more benevolent strategies of social control occurred at about the same time that influential capitalists were realizing that existing economic arrangements could not be successfully maintained only through the use of private police and government troops.[43] While the child-savers justified their reforms as humanitarian, it is clear that this humanitarianism reflected their class background and elitist conceptions of human potentiality. The child-savers shared the view of more conservative professionals that "criminals" were a distinct and dangerous class, indigenous to working-class culture, and a threat to "civilized" society. They differed mainly in the procedures by which the "criminal class" should be controlled or neutralized.

Gradually, a more "enlightened" view about strategies of control prevailed among the leading representatives of professional associations. Correctional workers, for example, did not want to think of themselves merely as the custodians of a pariah class. The self-image of penal reformers as "doctors" rather than "guards," and the medical domination of criminological research in the United States at that time facilitated the acceptance of "therapeutic" strategies in prisons and reformatories.[44] Physicians gradually provided the official rhetoric of penal reform, replacing cruder concepts of social Darwinism with a new optimism. Admittedly, the criminal was "pathological" and "diseased," but medical science offered the possibility of miraculous cures. Although there was a popular belief in the existence of a "criminal class" separated from the rest of humanity by a "vague boundary line," there was no good reason why this class could not be identified, diagnosed, segregated, changed and incorporated back into society.[45]

By the late 1890s, most child-savers agreed that hereditary theories of crime were [overly] fatalistic. The superintendent of the Kentucky Industrial School of Reform, for example, told delegates to a national conference on corrections that heredity is "unjustifiably made a bugaboo to discourage efforts at rescue. We know that physical heredity tendencies can be neutralized and often nullified by proper counteracting precautions."[46] E. R. L. Gould, a sociologist at the University of Chicago, similarly criticized biological theories of crime as unconvincing and sentimental. "Is it not better," he said, "to postulate freedom of choice than to preach the doctrine of the unfettered will, and so elevate criminality into a proprietary sacrifice?"[47]

Charles Cooley, writing in 1896, was one of the first American sociologists to observe that criminal behavior depended as much upon social and economic circumstances as it did upon the inheritance of biological traits. "The criminal class," he observed, "is largely the result of society's bad workmanship upon fairly good material." In support of this argument, he noted that there was a "large and fairly trustworthy body of evidence" to suggest that many, "degenerates" could be converted into "useful citizens by rational treatment."[48]

Although there was a wide difference of opinion among experts as to the precipitating causes of crime, it was generally agreed that criminals were abnormally conditioned by a multitude of biological and environmental forces, some of which were permanent and irreversible. Strictly biological theories of crime were modified to incorporate a developmental view of human behavior. If, as it was believed, criminals are conditioned by biological heritage and brutish living conditions, then prophylactic measures must be taken early in life. "We must get hold of the little waifs that grow up to form the criminal element just as early in life as possible," exhorted an influential child-saver. "Hunt up the children of poverty, of crime, and of brutality, just as soon as they can be reached."[49]

Efforts were needed to reach the criminals of future generations. "They are born to crime," wrote the penologist Enoch Wines, "brought up for it. They must be saved."[50] New institutions and new programs were required to meet this challenge.

Juvenile Court and the Reformatory System

The essential preoccupation of the child-saving movement was the recognition and control of youthful deviance. It brought attention to, and thus "invented" new categories of youthful misbehavior which had been hitherto unappreciated. The efforts of the child-savers were institutionally expressed in the juvenile court which, despite recent legislative and constitutional reforms, is generally acknowledged as their most significant contribution to progressive penology. There is some dispute about which state first created a special tribunal for children. Massachusetts and New York passed laws, in 1874 and 1892 respectively, providing for the trials of minors apart from adults charged with crimes. Ben Lindsey, a renowned judge and reformer, also claimed this distinction for Colorado where a juvenile court was, in effect, established through an educational law of 1899. However, most authorities agree that the Juvenile Court Act, passed by the Illinois legislature in the same year, was the first official enactment to be recognized as a model statute by other states and countries.[51] By 1917, juvenile court legislation had been passed in all but three states and by 1932 there were over 600 independent juvenile courts throughout the United States.[52]

The juvenile court system was part of a general movement directed towards developing a specialized labor market and industrial discipline under corporate capitalism by creating new programs of adjudication and control for "delinquent," "dependent" and "neglected" youth. This in turn was related to augmenting the family and enforcing compulsory education in order to guarantee the proper reproduction of the labor force. For example, underlying the juvenile court system was the concept of *parens patriae* by which the courts were authorized to handle with wide discretion the problems of "its least fortunate junior citizens."[53] The administration of juvenile justice, which differed in many important respects from the criminal court system, was delegated extensive powers of control over youth. A child was not accused of a crime but offered assistance and guidance; intervention in the lives of "delinquents" was not supposed to carry the stigma of criminal guilt. Judicial records were not generally available to the press or public, and juvenile hearings were typically conducted in private. Court procedures were informal and inquisitorial, not requiring the presence of a defense attorney. Specific criminal safeguards of due process were not applicable because juvenile proceedings were defined by statute as civil in character.[54]

The judges of the new court were empowered to investigate the character and social background of "predelinquent" as well as delinquent children; they concerned themselves with motivation rather than intent, seeking to identify the moral reputation of problematic children. The requirements of preventive penology and child-saving further justified the court's intervention in cases where no offense had actually been committed, but where, for example, a child was posing problems for some person in authority, such as a parent or teacher or social worker.

The role model for juvenile court judges was doctor-counselor rather than lawyer. "Judicial therapists" were expected to establish a one-to-one relationship with "delinquents" in the same way that a country doctor might give his time and attention to a favorite patient. Juvenile courtrooms were often arranged like a clinic and the vocabulary of its participants was largely composed of medical metaphors. "We do not know the child without a thorough examination," wrote Judge Julian Mack. "We must reach into the soul-life of the child."[55] Another judge from Los Angeles suggested that the juvenile court should be a "laboratory of human behavior" and its judges trained as "specialists in the art of human relations." It was the judge's task to "get the whole truth about a child" in the same way that a "physician searches for every detail that bears on the condition of the patient."[56] Similarly, the judges of the Boston juvenile court liked to think of themselves as "physicians in a dispensary."[57]

The unique character of the child-saving movement was its concerns for predelinquent offenders—"children who occupy the debatable ground between criminality and innocence"—and its claim that it could transform potential criminals into respectable citizens by training them in "habits of industry, self-control and obedience to law."[58] This policy justified the diminishing of traditional procedures and allowed police, judges, probation officers and truant officers to work together without legal hindrance. If children were to be rescued, it was important that the rescuers be free to pursue their mission without the interference of defense lawyers and due process. Delinquents had to be saved, transformed and reconstituted. "There is no essential difference," noted a prominent child-saver, "between a criminal and any other sinner. The means and methods of restoration are the same for both."[59]

The juvenile court legislation enabled the state to investigate and control a wide variety of behaviors. As Joel Handler has observed, "the critical philosophical position of the reform movement was that no formal, legal distinctions should be made between the delinquent and the dependent or neglected."[60] Statutory definitions of "delinquency" encompassed (1) acts that would be criminal if committed by adults; (2) acts that violated county, town, or municipal ordinances; and (3) violations of vaguely worded catch-alls—such as "vicious or immoral behavior," "incorrigibility," and "truancy"—which "seem to express the notion that the adolescent, if allowed to continue, will engage in more serious conduct."[61]

The juvenile court movement went far beyond a concern for special treatment of adolescent offenders. It brought within the ambit of government control a set of youthful activities that had been previously ignored or dealt with on an informal basis. It was not by accident that the behavior subject to penalties—drinking, sexual "license," roaming the streets, begging, frequenting dance halls and movies, fighting, and being seen in public late at night—was especially characteristic of the children of working-class and immigrant families. Once arrested and adjudicated, these "delinquents" became wards of the court and eligible for salvation.

It was through the reformatory system that the child-savers hoped to demonstrate that delinquents were capable of being converted into law-abiding citizens. Though the reformatory was initially developed in the United States during the middle of the nineteenth century as a special form of prison discipline for adolescents and young adults, its underlying principles were formulated in Britain by Matthew Davenport Hill, Alexander Maconochie, Walter Crofton and Mary Carpenter. If the United States did not have any great penal theorists, it at least had energetic administrators—like Enoch Wines, Zebulon Brockway and Frank Sanborn—who were prepared to experiment with new programs.

The reformatory was distinguished from the traditional penitentiary in several ways: it adopted a policy of indeterminate sentencing [an unspecified period of incarceration, with release dependent on the juvenile's successful rehabilitation]; it emphasized the importance of a countryside location; and it typically was organized on the "cottage" plan as opposed to the traditional congregate housing found in penitentiaries. The ultimate aim of the reformatory was reformation of the criminal, which could only be achieved "by placing the prisoner's fate, as far as possible, in his own hand, by enabling him, through industry and good conduct to raise himself, step by step, to a position of less restraint. . . ."[62]

Based on a crude theory of rewards and punishments, the "new penology" set itself the task of resocializing the "dangerous classes." The typical resident of a reformatory, according to one child-saver, had been "cradled in infamy, imbibing with its earliest natural nourishment the germs of a depraved appetite, and reared in the midst of people whose lives are an atrocious crime against natural and divine law and the rights of society." In order to correct and reform such a person, the reformatory plan was designed to teach the value of adjustment, private enterprise, thrift and self-reliance. "To make a good boy out of this bundle of perversities, his entire being must be revolutionized. He must be taught self-control, industry, respect for himself and the rights of others."[63] The real test of reformation in a delinquent, as William Letchworth told the National Conference of Charities and Correction in 1886, was his uncomplaining adjustment to his former environment. "If he is truly reformed in the midst of adverse influences," said Letchworth, "he gains that moral strength which makes his reform permanent."[64] Moreover, reformed delinquents were given every opportunity to rise "far above the class from which they sprang," especially if they were "patient" and "self-denying."[65]

Reformation of delinquents was to be achieved in a number of different ways. The trend from congregate housing to group living represented a significant change in the organization of penal institutions. The "cottage" plan was designed to provide more intensive supervision and to reproduce, symbolically at least, an atmosphere of family life conducive to the resocialization of youth. The "new penology" also urged the benefits of a rural location, partly in order to teach agricultural skills, but mainly in order to guarantee a totally controlled environment. This was justified by appealing to the romantic theory that corrupt delinquents would be spiritually regenerated by their contact with unspoiled nature.[66]

Education was stressed as the main form of industrial and moral training in reformatories. According to Michael Katz, in his study on nineteenth-century education, the reformatory provided "the first form of compulsory schooling in the United States."[67] The prominence of education as a technique of reform reflected the widespread emphasis on socialization and assimilation instead of cruder methods of social control. But as Georg Rusche and Otto Kirchheimer observed in their study of the relationship between economic and penal policies, the rise of "rehabilitative" and educational programs was "largely the result of opposition on the part of free workers," for "wherever working-class organizations were powerful enough to influence state politics, they succeeded in obtaining complete abolition of all forms of prison labor . . . or at least in obtaining very considerable limitations, such as work without modern machinery, conventional rather than modern types of prison industry, or work for the government instead of for the free market."[68]

Although the reformatory system, as envisioned by urban reformers, suffered in practice from overcrowding, mismanagement, inadequate financing and staff hiring problems, its basic ideology was still tough-minded and uncompromising. As the American Friends Service Committee noted, "if the reformers were naive, the managers of the correctional establishment were not. Under the leadership of Zebulon R. Brockway of the Elmira Reformatory, by the latter part of the nineteenth century they had co-opted the reformers and consolidated their leadership and control of indeterminate sentence reform."[69] The child-savers were not averse to using corporal punishment and other severe disciplinary measures when inmates were recalcitrant. Brockway, for example, regarded his task as "socialization of the antisocial by scientific training while under completest governmental control."[70] To achieve his goal, Brockway's reformatory became "like a garrison of a thousand prisoner soldiers" and "every incipient disintegration was promptly checked and disinclination of individual prisoners to conform was overcome."[71] Child-saving was a job for resolute professionals who realized that "sickly sentimentalism" had no place in their work.[72]

"Criminals shall either be cured," Brockway told the National Prison Congress in 1870, "or kept under such continued restraint as gives guarantee of safety from further depredations."[73] Restraint and discipline were an integral part of the "treatment" program and not merely expediencies of administration. Military drill, "training of the will," and long hours of tedious labor were the essence of the reformatory system and the indeterminate sentencing policy guaranteed its smooth operation. "Nothing can tend more certainly to secure the most hardened and desperate criminals than the present system of short sentences," wrote the reformer Bradford Kinney Peirce in 1869.[74] Several years later, Enoch Wines was able to report that "the sentences of young offenders are wisely regulated for their amendment; they are not absurdly shortened as if they signified only so much endurance of vindictive suffering."[75]

Since the child-savers professed to be seeking the "best interests" of their "wards" on the basis of corporate liberal values, there was no need to formulate legal regulation of the right and duty to "treat" in the same way that the right and duty to punish had been previously regulated.[76] . . . The myth of the child-saving movement as a humanitarian enterprise is based partly on a superficial interpretation of the child-savers' rhetoric of rehabilitation and partly on a misconception of how the child-savers viewed punishment. While it is true that the child-savers advocated minimal use of corporal punishment, considerable evidence suggests that this recommendation was based on managerial rather than moral considerations. William Letchworth reported that "corporal punishment is rarely inflicted" at the State Industrial School in Rochester because "most of the boys consider the lowering of their standing the severest punishment that is inflicted."[77] Mrs. Glendower Evans, commenting on the decline of whippings at a reform school in Massachusetts, concluded that "when boys do not feel themselves imprisoned and are treated as responsible moral agents, they can be trusted with their freedom to a surprising degree."[78] Officials at another state industrial school for girls also reported that "hysterics and fits of screaming and of noisy disobedience, have of late years become unknown. . . ."[79]

The decline in the use of corporal punishment was due to the fact that indeterminate sentencing, the "mark" or "stage" system of rewards and punishments, and other techniques of "organized persuasion" were far more effective in maintaining order and compliance than cruder methods of control. The chief virtue of the "stage" system, a graduated system of punishments and privileges, was its capacity to keep prisoners disciplined and submissive.[80] The child-savers had learned from industrialists that persuasive benevolence backed up by force was a far more effective device of social control than arbitrary displays of terrorism. Like an earlier generation of penal reformers in France and Italy, the child-savers stressed the efficacy of new and indirect forms of social control as a "practical measure of defense against social revolution as well as against individual acts."[81]

Although the child-saving movement had far-reaching consequences for the organization and administration of the juvenile justice system, its overall impact was conservative in both spirit and achievement. The child-savers' reforms were generally aimed at imposing sanctions on conduct unbecoming "youth" and disqualifying youth from the benefit of adult privileges. The child-savers were prohibitionists, in a general sense, who believed that social progress depended on efficient law enforcement, strict supervision of children's leisure and recreation, and enforced education. They were primarily concerned with regulating social behavior, eliminating "foreign" and radical ideologies, and preparing youth as a disciplined and devoted work force. The austerity of the criminal law and penal institutions was only of incidental concern; their central interest was in the normative outlook of youth and they were most successful in their efforts to extend governmental control over a whole range of youthful activities which had previously been handled locally and informally. In this sense, their reforms were aimed at defining, rationalizing and regulating the dependent status of youth.[82] Although the child-savers' attitudes to youth were often paternalistic and romantic, their commands were backed up by force and an abiding faith in the benevolence of government.

The child-saving movement had its most direct impact on the children of the urban poor. The fact that "troublesome" adolescents were depicted as "sick" or "pathological," imprisoned "for their own good," addressed in paternalistic vocabulary, and exempted from criminal law processes, did not alter the subjective experiences of control, restraint and punishment. It is ironic, as Philippe Aries observed in his historical study of European family life, that the obsessive solicitude of family, church, moralists and administrators for child welfare served to deprive children of the freedoms which they had previously shared with adults and to deny their capacity for initiative, responsibility and autonomy. . . .[83]

◼ Notes

1. For discussions of earlier reform movements, see Robert S. Pickett, *House of Refuge: Origins of Juvenile Reform in New York State, 1815–1857* (Syracuse, NY: Syracuse University Press, 1969), and Sanford J. Fox, "Juvenile Justice Reform: An Historical Perspective," 22 *Stanford Law Review,* (1970), pp. 1187–1239.

2. The child-saving movement was broad and diverse, including reformers interested in child welfare, education, reformatories, labor and other related issues. This paper is limited primarily to child-savers involved in anti-delinquency reforms and should not be interpreted as characterizing the child-saving movement in general.

3. William P. Letchworth, "Children of the State," National Conference of Charities and Correction, *Proceedings* (St. Paul, Minnesota, 1886), p. 138.

4. R. W. Hill, "The Children of Shinbone Alley," National Conference of Charities and Correction, *Proceedings* (Omaha, 1887), p. 231.

5. William Appleman Williams, *The Contours of American History* (Chicago: Quadrangle Books, 1966), especially pp. 345–412.

6. Pickett, op. cit., pp. 50–55.

7. Committee on the History of Child-Saving Work, *History of Child-Saving in the United States* (National Conference of Charities and Correction, 1893), p. 5.

8. Charles Loring Brace, *The Dangerous Classes of New York and Twenty Years' Work Among Them* (New York: Wynkoop & Hallenbeck, 1880), pp. 282–83.

9. Committee on the History of Child-Saving Work, op. cit., pp. 70–73.

10. Ibid., pp. 80–81.

11. Ibid., p. 270.

12. For more about these child-savers, see Anthony Platt, *The Child-Savers: The Invention of Delinquency* (Chicago: University of Chicago Press, 1969), pp. 75–100.

13. Louise C. Wade, *Graham Taylor: Pioneer for Social Justice, 1851–1938* (Chicago: University of Chicago Press, 1964), p. 59.

14. G. William Domhoff, *The Higher Circles: The Governing Class in America* (New York: Random House, 1970), p. 48, and Platt, op. cit., pp. 92–98.

15. "The transformation in penal systems cannot be explained only from changing needs of the war against crime, although this struggle does play a part. Every system of production tends to discover punishments which correspond to its productive relationships. It is thus necessary to investigate the origin and fate of penal systems, the use or avoidance of specific punishments, and the intensity of penal practices as they are determined by social forces, above all by economic and then fiscal forces." Georg Rusche and Otto Kirchheimer, *Punishment and Social Structure* (New York: Russell & Russell, 1968), p. 5.

16. See, for example, Gabriel Kolko, *The Triumph of Conservatism: A Reinterpretation of American History, 1900–1916* (Chicago: Quadrangle Books, 1967); James Weinstein, *The Corporate Ideal in the Liberal State, 1900–1918* (Boston: Beacon Press, 1969); Samuel Haber, *Efficiency and Uplift: Scientific Management in the Progressive Era, 1890–1920* (Chicago: University of Chicago Press, 1964); and Robert H. Wiebe, *Businessmen and Reform: A Study of the Progressive Movement* (Cambridge: Harvard University Press, 1962).

17. Weinstein, op. cit., pp. ix, xi.

18. Jeremy P. Felt, *Hostages of Fortune: Child Labor Reform in New York State* (Syracuse: Syracuse University Press, 1965), p. 45.

19. Brace, op. cit., p. 352.

20. David K. Cohen and Marvin Lazerson, "Education and the Corporate Order," 8 *Socialist Revolution* (1972), p. 50. See also Michael B. Katz, *The Irony of Early School Reform: Educational Innovation in Mid-Nineteenth Century Massachusetts* (Cambridge: Harvard University Press, 1968), and Lawrence A. Cremin, *The Transformation of the School: Progressivism in American Education, 1876–1957* (New York: Vintage, 1961).

21. It should be emphasized that child-saving reforms were predominantly supported by more privileged sectors of the feminist movement, especially those who had an interest in developing professional careers in education, social work and probation. In recent years, radical feminists have emphasized that "we must include the oppression of children in any program for feminist revolution or we will be subject to the same failing of which we have so often accused men: of not having gone deep enough in our analysis, of having missed an important substratum of oppression merely because it didn't directly concern us." Shulamith Firestone, *The Dialectic of Sex: The Case for Feminist Revolution* (New York: Bantam, 1971), p. 104.

22. Robert Sunley, "Early Nineteenth Century American Literature on Child-Rearing," in Margaret Mead and Martha Wolfenstein (Eds.), *Childhood in Contemporary Cultures* (Chicago: University of Chicago Press, 1955), p. 152; see also Orville G. Brim, *Education for Child-Rearing* (New York: Free Press, 1965), pp. 321–49.

23. For an extended discussion of this issue, see Platt, op. cit. and Christopher Lasch, *The New Radicalism in America, 1889–1963: The Intellectual as a Social Type* (New York: Alfred Knopf, 1965), pp. 3–68.

24. Talcott Parsons and Robert F. Bales, *Family, Socialization and Interaction Process* (Glencoe, IL: Free Press, 1955), pp. 3–33.

25. Clara T. Leonard, "Family Homes for Pauper and Dependent Children," Annual Conference of Charities, *Proceedings* (Chicago: 1879), p. 175.

26. W. P. Lynde, "Prevention in Some of its Aspects," Ibid., pp. 165–66.

27. Joseph R. Gusfield, *Symbolic Crusade: Status Politics and the American Temperance Movement* (Urbana: University of Illinois Press, 1963).

28. See, generally, Roy Lubove, *The Professional Altruist: The Emergence of Social Work as a Career, 1880–1930* (Cambridge: Harvard University Press, 1965).

29. Williams, op. cit., p. 373, and Weinstein, op. cit., p. 254.

30. Williams, op. cit., pp. 374, 395–402.

31. Committee on the History of Child-Saving Work, op. cit., p. 3.

32. See, generally, John Higham, *Strangers in the Land: Patterns of American Nativism, 1860–1925* (New York: Atheneum, 1965).

33. Brace, op. cit., pp. 30, 49; Bradford Kinney Peirce, *A Half Century with Juvenile Delinquents* (Montclair, New Jersey: Patterson Smith, 1969, originally published 1869), p. 253.

34. Nathan Allen, "Prevention of Crime and Pauperism," Annual Conference of Charities, *Proceedings* (Cincinnati, 1878), pp. 111–24.

35. Jacob A. Riis, *How the Other Half Lives* (New York: Hill & Wang, 1957, originally published in 1890), p. 134.

36. Brace, op. cit., pp. 27, 29.

37. See, for example, Lombroso's comments in the Introduction to Arthur MacDonald, *Criminology* (New York: Funk & Wagnalls, 1893).

38. Allen, op. cit.

39. Hamilton D. Wey, "A Plea for Physical Training of Youthful Criminals," *National Prison Association, Proceedings* (Boston, 1888), pp. 181–93. For further discussion of this issue, see Platt, op. cit., pp. 18–28 and Arthur E. Fink, *Causes of Crime: Biological Theories in the United States, 1800–1915* (New York: A. S. Barnes, 1962).

40. Richard L. Dugdale, *The Jukes: A Study in Crime, Pauperism, Disease, and Heredity* (New York: G.P. Putnam's Sons, 1877).

41. Sarah B. Cooper, "The Kindergarten as Child-Saving Work," *National Conference of Charities and Correction, Proceedings* (Madison, 1883), pp. 130–38.

42. I. N. Kerlin, "The Moral Imbecile," National Conference of Charities and Correction, *Proceedings* (Baltimore, 1890), pp. 244–50.

43. Williams, op. cit., p. 354.

44. Fink, op. cit., p. 247.

45. See, for example, Illinois Board of State Commissioners of Public Charities, *Second Biennial Report* (Springfield: State Journal Steam Print, 1873), pp. 195–96.

46. Peter Caldwell, "The Duty of the State to Delinquent Children," National Conference of Charities and Correction, *Proceedings* (New York, 1898), pp. 404–10.

47. E. R. L. Gould, "The Statistical Study of Hereditary Criminality," National Conference of Charities and Correction, *Proceedings* (New Haven, 1895), pp. 134–43.

48. Charles H. Cooley, "'Nature' in the Making of Social Careers," National Conference of Charities and Correction, *Proceedings* (Grand Rapids, 1896), pp. 399–405.

49. Committee on the History of Child-Saving Work, op. cit., p. 90.

50. Enoch C. Wines, *The State of Prisons and of Child-Saving Institutions in the Civilized World* (Cambridge: Harvard University Press, 1880).

51. Helen Page Bates, "Digest of Statutes Relating to Juvenile Courts and Probation Systems," 13 *Charities* (1905), pp. 329–36.

52. Joel F. Handler, "The Juvenile Court and the Adversary System: Problems of Function and Form," 1965 *Wisconsin Law Review* (1965), pp. 7–51.

53. Gustav L. Schramm, "The Juvenile Court Idea," 13 *Federal Probation* (September, 1949), p. 21.

54. Monrad G. Paulsen, "Fairness to the Juvenile Offender," 41 *Minnesota Law Review* (1957), pp. 547–67.

55. Julian W. Mack, "The Chancery Procedure in the Juvenile Court," in Jane Addams (Ed.), *The Child, the Clinic and the Court* (New York: New Republic, 1925), p. 315.

56. Miriam Van Waters, "The Socialization of Juvenile Court Procedure," 21 *Journal of Criminal Law & Criminology* (1922), pp. 61, 69.

57. Harvey H. Baker, "Procedure of the Boston Juvenile Court," 23 *Survey* (1910), p. 646.

58. Illinois Board of State Commissioners of Public Charities, *Sixth Biennial Report* (Springfield: H. W. Rokker, 1880), p. 104.

59. Frederick H. Wines, "Reformation as an End in Prison Discipline," National Conference of Charities and Correction, *Proceedings* (Buffalo, 1888), p. 198.

60. Joel F. Handler, op. cit., p. 9.

61. Joel F. Handler and Margaret K. Rosenheim, "Privacy and Welfare: Public Assistance and Juvenile Justice," 31 *Law & Contemporary Problems* (1966), pp. 377–412.

62. From a report by Enoch Wines and Theodore Dwight to the New York legislature in 1867, quoted by Max Grünhut, *Penal Reform* (Oxford: Clarendon Press, 1948), p. 90.

63. Peter Caldwell, "The Reform School Problem," National Conference of Charities and Correction, *Proceedings* (St. Paul, 1886), pp. 71–76.

64. Letchworth, op. cit., p. 152.

65. Committee on the History of Child-Saving Work, op. cit., p. 20.

66. See Platt, op. cit., pp. 55–66.

67. Katz, op. cit., p. 187.

68. Rusche and Kirchheimer, op. cit., pp. 131–32.

69. American Friends Service Committee, op. cit., p. 28.

70. Zebulon R. Brockway, *Fifty Years of Prison Service* (New York: Charities Publication Committee, 1912), p. 393.

71. Ibid., pp. 310, 421.

72. Ibid., pp. 389–408.

73. Ibid.

74. Peirce, op. cit., p. 312.

75. Wines, op. cit., p. 81.

76. On informal cooperation in the criminal courts, see Jerome H. Skolnick, "Social Control in the Adversary System," 11 *Journal of Conflict Resolution* (1967), pp. 52–70.

77. Committee on the History of Child Saving Work, op. cit., p. 20.

78. Ibid., p. 237.

79. Ibid., p. 251.

80. Rusche and Kirchheimer, op. cit., pp. 155–56.

81. Ibid., p. 76. For a similar point, see American Friends Service Committee, op. cit., p. 33.

82. See, generally, Frank Musgrove, *Youth and the Social Order* (London: Routledge & Kegan Paul, 1964).

83. Philippe Aries, *Centuries of Childhood: A Social History of Family Life* (New York: Vintage Books, 1965).

2

Best-Laid Plans:
The Ideal Juvenile Court

Ellen Ryerson

*Ellen Ryerson argues that a balanced and nuanced interpretation of the
historical emergence of the juvenile justice system should acknowledge its
"inherently double nature." Although some aspects "appear 'conservative'
because they emphasized social control, . . . other aspects appear 'reformist'
because they emphasized the rehabilitative ideal and found new ways to
pursue it." Thus Ryerson is more positive than Platt (see Chapter 1) about
the genuineness of child-savers' humanitarian desire to help children and
prevent crime through a program of individualized treatment, family
revitalization, and probation rather than incarceration.*

THE JUVENILE COURT MOVEMENT EMERGED FROM FRUSTRATION WITH
the dominant modes of dealing with child offenders. But the willingness to
dispense with the old did not itself give form to the new. Those who condemned the old system as harsh and ill conceived had still to define a specific
program, both more humane and more effective than the criminal law and the
penal system. . . . As the nearest approximation of a concrete model, . . . they
had the example of the state of Massachusetts.

Beginning in 1869, Massachusetts law had provided for the participation of
visiting agents or officers of the State Board of Charities in juvenile cases: these
agents investigated juvenile cases and made recommendations to the judges for
disposition. Between 1870 and 1877, a series of measures established separate
hearings, dockets, and records for children under sixteen, and a program of visitation by probation officers to homes in which delinquent children had been
"placed out." With separate hearings for children and a rudimentary probation

Excerpt from *The Best-Laid Plans: America's Juvenile Court Experiment,* by Ellen Ryerson (Hill
and Wang, 1978). Reprinted by permission of Farrar, Straus & Giroux, Inc.

system, Massachusetts had gone further than any other state in modifying criminal procedure and criminal sanctions in children's cases. It had not gone far enough, but it provided an example on which to build a system which would relieve child offenders of the undeserved burden of criminal responsibility and yet prevent them from going astray again.

Perhaps the most influential idea in shaping the juvenile court system was the thesis that the defect which produced juvenile crime lay not so much in the child as in the environment from which he had come and, therefore, that no child should be treated as a criminal. The child, naturally or at least potentially innocent and moral, learned antisocial behavior from contact with corrupt adults. Accordingly, the first principle of the new court apparatus and its ancillary institutions was to separate the child from adult offenders at all times. The notion that child saving depended on separation of children from adults was not new to the progressive period: the house of refuge had been organized on the same principle in the early nineteenth century. But the persisting incarceration of juveniles with adults in detention and correctional facilities and their commingling in the courtroom led progressive reformers to carry to its logical conclusion the effort to disentangle juvenile justice from adult justice. In this cause, juvenile court legislation usually prohibited the confinement of children with adults, and occasionally made nonsegregated confinement itself punishable as a misdemeanor. In the literature and the laws, founders of the juvenile court demanded not only separate reformatories but separate detention centers, and separate sessions or courtrooms as well.

Mandatory age segregation made implicitly the accusation that adult criminals were one cause of childhood corruption. Noncriminal adults also had to share the responsibility. In 1903, the Colorado legislature passed the first state law holding parents and guardians legally responsible for contributing to the delinquencies of their children.[1] Judge Ben Lindsey, pioneer of the Denver juvenile court and leader among reformers and defenders of wayward youth, claimed that the contributing-to-delinquency law "has done more than anything else to solve the problems of delinquency with us."[2] He considered the fining and jailing of citizens who encouraged or permitted delinquency in children under their charge his state's greatest contribution to the movement. Many localities followed Denver in coupling their juvenile court laws with provisions giving the court jurisdiction over contributing adults. These provisions gave institutional expression to the theory that the child was not ultimately responsible for his acts.

The reformers sought further expression of that theory and further detachment from the criminal law by trying to dispel from juvenile court proceedings the atmosphere of blame and recrimination which they detected in criminal proceedings. They hoped to remove entirely from the juvenile court process the implication that the child was capable of criminal intent or subject to criminal sanctions. In this they began at the beginning with the mode of initiating cases. Ideally, initiation by petition was to replace initiation by complaint. By this process any reputable person might bring to the attention of the court a child he had reason to believe delinquent within the meaning of the law or in need of the court's supervision. Unlike the complainant, the petitioner need have had no direct connection with the case, and was presumably engaged in securing help for the child rather than seeking revenge. The reformers hoped that this change would bring more needy and troublesome children into court, and make apparent to such children that the court took action out of interest in their welfare and not out of anger. Behind this change in procedure one senses an image of community involvement with the welfare of children that bears greater resemblance to disappearing village life than to the urban disorder with which the juvenile court was supposed to cope. But whether the right of petition was placed in the public at large or only in a probation staff which would screen referrals, the process was in contrast to criminal procedure in its emphasis on sympathetic rather than accusatory initiations. A similar purpose animated the recommended shift from a warrant for arrest to a summons as the court's means of compelling the appearance of a child who had been brought to its attention.

To realize the constructive potential of court control, the founders recommended that at some time between petition and hearing an officer of the court conduct a preliminary investigation into the background of the child. The officer's mission was to unearth information which might point to the source of the child's misbehavior and suggest the proper remedy. While in a criminal case the preparation for trial would focus upon evidence concerning the commission of a specific prohibited act, here the preparation for a hearing was to give full scope to a systematic and sympathetic inquiry which could form the basis for a disposition based on the circumstances of the child's life rather than on the question of guilt or innocence. The reformers hoped to effectuate as well as to symbolize the fusion of the interests of the child with those of society by placing responsibility for this investigation in the hands of the probation officer, who was by law required to represent the child, and at the same time to serve the court. The functions of defense counsel and prosecuting attorney, so far as they remained, now fell to a single individual.

That person also assumed responsibility for the accused during the detention period. In contrast to criminal proceedings, where the right to bail might postpone the impact of the state upon the accused until guilt had been proven beyond a reasonable doubt, juvenile court proceedings included the option of a constructive detention period that could serve as the opening stage of a reformation process for children whose hearings had not even commenced. Before the child appeared in court he might be separated from his parents and placed in the charge of a probation officer or in a detention home, not because he was otherwise unlikely to appear at his hearing, but because the reformers presumed that he would benefit by state supervision whether he proved to be delinquent or not, and because the detention period would allow the gathering of important data for the hearing.

In order that every stage of the child's experience with the court contribute to the reformation of his character, the founders set to work to modify courtroom procedure as well. They intended to sweep away all elements of criminal trials "so that an intimate, friendly relationship [might] be established at once between the judge and the child."[3] The reformers so favored procedural informality that they made it a crucial test of the adequacy of a juvenile court system. They insisted that the true juvenile court could not be criminal at all, that its proceedings had to be civil in fact as well as in form. While a few reformers in some states thought it wise to allow for jury trials and defense counsel on demand, they did so "in order to avoid constitutional difficulties or attacks upon the law" and not because they believed that "any such provisions are necessary."[4] Generally, juvenile court reformers regarded juries and lawyers as unnecessary restraints upon the flexible pursuit of the best interests of the child.

The elimination of procedural formality in the courtroom presumably freed the judge to employ all available resources in gaining the child's confidence and thereby beginning the resocialization process. In this context, the kind of person who served as juvenile court judge became extremely important. Participants in the movement frequently stated their conviction that the success of the juvenile court turned upon the capability of the judge.

Juvenile court literature exhibited relatively little concern with the qualities usually associated with a judge—a thorough knowledge of the law, an independent and even-handed sense of justice. Rather, it asserted the desirability of a judge who would appeal personally to the youngsters brought before him. Judge Ben Lindsey believed that "more is accomplished through love than by any other method,"[5] and most of the court's supporters agreed that the emphasis belonged on sympathy rather than on legal learning. In the juvenile court movement, Lindsey's own brand of friendly and fatherly involvement in the lives of delinquent children served as a model for the approach which Stephen Schlossman has called "affectional discipline."[6] The emphasis on personal qualities of wisdom and kindness did not, however, imply that the juvenile court judge might be an amateur at his duties: the reformers conceived of the juvenile court judgeship as a full-time specialty demanding the exclusive and long-term attention of the person who filled it.

The judge's task was, of course, to weigh all available evidence of the child's circumstances and to prescribe a treatment if treatment were in order. In collecting data about the child, the judge could and should allow testimony of any sort, irrespective of such constraints from criminal procedure as the rule against hearsay evidence. No scruples about the legal appropriateness of testimony in a criminal court could have outweighed in the founders' minds the potential value of knowing everything there was to know about the child and his environment.

The reformers overhauled court procedure in an effort, they said, to minimize future negative repercussions in the life of the offender. In order to prevent society from unjustly stigmatizing children who had appeared in court the reformers recommended the exclusion of all persons from juvenile court hearings except those directly involved in the case. The constitutional guarantee of a public trial seemed to them to carry more danger than protection. As a further precaution, the architects of the court suggested that only officials have access to the records of juvenile court proceedings and that evidence gathered in connection with such cases be inadmissible in any other court. Finally, the reformers recommended that juvenile courts make general adjudications of delinquency rather than of specific offenses, also in the hope that such general adjudications would be less stigmatizing.

Once having found the child delinquent, the court still had before it the most important part of its job—the formulation of an intelligent course of treatment, which meant by definition a course that took its direction from the specific needs of the child in question. Punishment to fit the crime might be uniform, but treatment to fit the child had to be individualized, and treatment rather than punishment was the business of the juvenile court. In 1884, John Peter Altgeld made a classic statement of the medical analogy which persuaded so many reformers of the appropriateness of individualized justice: "If the state were to enforce a system of medical practice and were to provide that but one prescription should be given for all the ills that afflict the flesh, it would not be more absurd than is the present system of treating offenders."[7] In 1926, the director of the Psychopathic Clinic in Detroit expressed the continuing scorn of juvenile court supporters for the notion that a "uniform system of treating all crime is going to be any more successful than a uniform system of treating all fevers would be."[8]

In pursuit of the ideal of individualized treatment, the reformers seemed to imagine an infinite range of choice in tailoring the disposition to fit the child. Nevertheless, both practical considerations and the premises of the movement itself circumscribed the judge's choice.

One of the distinctive features of the juvenile court movement was its primary, if not exclusive, commitment to probation as the most desirable disposition for child offenders. Where other generations had channeled their dissatisfaction with correctional institutions into redesigning such institutions, the progressives concentrated on developing an alternative which could occupy the foreground of juvenile corrections while the last resort (or threat) of institutionalization remained in the background. With the exception of a diagnostic detention period, a cardinal rule of the juvenile court movement and of child-welfare work in general in this period was that whenever possible the child should receive what care he needed in a home either his own or some other—rather than in an institution.

The preference for home rehabilitation still left the judge the choice of returning the child to his own home under the supervision of a probation officer or of having him placed in a new one. In this choice the reformers, and frequently the laws, guided the judge to make the first effort with the parents and to place a child in a foster home only if necessary. If the child was to be placed with another family, it was desirable that the relationship as closely as possible approximate a natural family setting. But except for the differences inherent in institutional and home living, the location and duration of the child's treatment were the only variables with which the courts could work directly. Whatever manipulation of the child's environment was actually to take place was likely to fall to the judgment and skill of the probation officer.

Regardless of the disposition of particular cases, the reformers intended that the child's experience with the court be free of accusation and full of constructive and friendly discipline. In all its dealings with delinquent children, the court was to take as its model the protective attitude of the state toward children who were abandoned or neglected or abused by their parents or guardians. A finding of delinquency might focus on the behavior of the child, while a finding of dependency or neglect focused on the behavior of his parents, but the former was only a symptom of the latter. The distinctions between dependent, neglected, and delinquent children were less important than their common need for state supervision in the manner of a wise and devoted parent. To each other and to the public the reformers pictured the court as a clinic for moral ills, an agent of moral and intellectual improvement, a school for the offending child and for the community. They proudly agreed that the juvenile court embodied a new understanding of the problem of delinquency and a new ideal of the relationship between society and its lawbreakers. Looking back over the first twenty years of the juvenile court movement, the executive secretary of the Ohio Humane Society wrote in 1922: "Against the old herd instinct we have a newer and more altruistic impulse in which all society gets together in an effort of reclamation."[9]

The reformers continually made these aims explicit and constantly put them in the foreground of their literature. But the tone of juvenile court propaganda and the implications of juvenile court techniques suggest that the goals of the reformers and the significance of the movement did not fit solely under the heading of more humane and effective treatments for child offenders. Or rather, the heading is too vague to convey fully the assumptions of the juvenile court movement or to reveal how its assumptions have made it vulnerable to criticism in spite of the general appeal of its stated goals.

The juvenile court promised the community that it would purge delinquents of their antisocial tendencies by giving them specialized treatment. The reformers pursued the ideal of such treatment by collecting data on the child's home life, school record, physical health, economic status, and so on. This aspect of the evidence, which reformers called "social" testimony, became so important to court supporters that they allowed and even encouraged it to overshadow evidence bearing upon questions of "guilt" or "innocence"—words which they rarely permitted to pass their lips. This studied disinterest in the facts of the alleged act of delinquency was often explicit. Julian Mack, the second judge of the Chicago juvenile court and an active participant in the movement, addressed an American Bar Association audience in 1909: "The problem for determination by the [juvenile court] judge is not, has this boy or girl committed a specific wrong, but what is he, how has he become what he is."[10] A survey of juvenile courts published in 1920 found: "the fundamental purpose of juvenile court proceedings is not to determine whether or not a child has committed a specific offense, but to discover whether he is in a condition requiring the special care of the State."[11]

While the literature customarily justified disinterest in specific offenses by a higher interest in providing children with needed guidance, and while this disinterest was in a way consistent with the movement's stated aim of benefiting the child, it suggested another aim as well. It suggested that the founders and supporters of the juvenile court were not exclusively or perhaps even primarily interested in juvenile offenders as that term had been understood before the passage of juvenile court laws but in a far broader area of jurisdiction, both over the child and over his family.

For the most part, before 1899, a child offender was a person who had broken a law or ordinance and who also happened to be a minor: his age, not his act, differentiated him from the adult offender. However, by minimizing questions of guilt and innocence of specific criminal acts, the founders changed the focus of correctional efforts. Far from simply trying to secure better treatment for children who had been convicted of illegal acts, they were directing their efforts to a newly defined and greatly enlarged class of children—those who seemed to need the state's care whether or not they had in a strict sense committed an offense, and who might never have otherwise come within the reach of the law. While undertaking to extend to child criminals the protection which had previously been afforded neglected or dependent children, the juvenile court reformers were also casting a net that could catch children who might hitherto have eluded legal sanction: children who were neither dependent nor neglected nor guilty of a criminal offense. A manual for probation officers in New York State explained the virtues of unofficial probation for children who had not so much as appeared in court by pointing out: "In many cases the delinquency is so incipient or the family circumstances are such that unless the cases could be dealt with unofficially they would never come to the attention of the court, or if they should, not until it was too late to secure the results possible through early unofficial treatment."[12] The ideal juvenile court and probation system was to be available for rehabilitative work with children even where official court action was unwarranted.

The definition of delinquency which eventually prevailed in juvenile court laws illustrated more graphically the reformers' desire to reach beyond juvenile criminals to influence the lives of other "unfortunate" children. Only a few juvenile court statutes stopped at the boundaries of old definitions—with children who had violated laws or ordinances. Reformers criticized such statutes, including the original Illinois law, and sought to amend them. They much preferred laws that included such offenses as smoking cigarettes, fighting, using profane language, habitually walking along railroad tracks, frequenting houses of prostitution, associating with thieves, running away from home, growing up in idleness, idly wandering the streets at night, or being "incorrigible." Grace Abbott's 1910 abstract of juvenile court laws declared: "Better laws make the definition much more inclusive so that the court will not be unable, because of any technical lack of jurisdiction, to place a child under the care of the court . . . if that seems to be for the best interest of the child."[13]

It is true that before the passage of juvenile court laws techniques were available to reach children who did some of the things which were now named as noncriminal conduct warranting a finding of delinquency. In some states "incorrigibility" had been grounds for commitment to a house of refuge, and disorderly-conduct laws undoubtedly brought to the criminal courts children who committed no independently criminal offense. Julia Lathrop described the juvenile clientele of the Chicago police courts just before the Illinois juvenile court act came into effect:

> [Three hundred and thirty-two] boys between the ages of nine and sixteen years were sent to the city prison. Three hundred and twenty of them were sent up on the blanket charge of disorderly conduct, which covered offenses from burglary and assault with a deadly weapon to picking up coal on the railway tracks, building bonfires, playing ball in the street, or "flipping trains," that is, jumping on and off moving cars. . . . Out of the 332 cases sent to the Bridewell during the first half of the year 1899, nearly one-third were pardoned by the mayor.[14]

This was the dilemma which provoked juvenile court reformers: the criminal law gave the alternatives of commitment to correctional institutions which had proven cruel failures, or of pardon (or acquittal) to avoid commitment. While the reformers undoubtedly wished through probation to avoid incarceration, they also wished to avoid the alternative of nonintervention. The lengthening list of noncriminal acts which warranted a finding of delinquency was intended to bring within the purview of the juvenile court the many children who were "'left off' by the justice or pardoned by the mayor" and on whose behalf, consequently, "no constructive work was done."[15]

By blurring the distinctions between dependent, neglected, and delinquent children, by minimizing questions of guilt or innocence of specific acts, and by including in the definition of delinquency noncriminal conduct, the juvenile court reformers were intentionally advocating a jurisdiction for the court which would augment the power of the state to intervene in the lives of children and in the relationships between the children and their parents.

Some scholars, Anthony Platt most notable among them, have implied that this expansiveness in the definition of delinquency gives the lie to the humanitarian claims of the juvenile court movement.[16] There is much to learn from this and other signs of the reformers' desire to expand state intervention into the lives of children and their families, but it is not direct evidence on the question of how "humane" were the intentions of juvenile court reformers. The usefulness of the question is mitigated by the danger that we are using more than one meaning of "humanitarian." First, the expansive definition of delinquency may have been largely intended to bring within the jurisdiction of the juvenile court acts which otherwise would have been gathered into the criminal courts under the label of disorderly conduct, as they were in Chicago just before the juvenile court law took effect. It is worth noting that the same behavior in juvenile court might bring years of probation until the age of majority was reached, while they might be followed by no action at all in criminal court or by sentences quite limited in time. But unless the definition of "humane" is irrevocably linked to nonintervention, even this observation does not give the lie to the reformers. Their definition of humanitarian treatment of children certainly was not mere leniency or nonintervention: it was constructive discipline, and this is not or was not an altogether implausible definition, even if it has little appeal in the present.

If the reformers had been accused of overextending juvenile court jurisdiction, they might have countered that such expansion of state intervention would prevent crime by bringing children within the scope of the law before their delinquent tendencies became criminal. And, indeed, prevention of crime counted among the founders' avowed intentions. Stephen Schlossman finds this aspect one of the few that really distinguish the ideas of the juvenile court movement from reform efforts on behalf of child offenders in the early nineteenth century.[17]

The defense of extended jurisdiction as a preventive measure against crime would have constituted an interesting though somewhat elliptical claim, since it omitted the vital demonstration of what represented a symptom of future criminality. The literature lacked any tightly reasoned argument to the effect that the commission of one of the new offenses indicated a propensity for the commission of genuine crimes later in life or to the effect that, in specific terms, boys who wandered around railroad tracks or used profane language were more likely than most eventually to rob banks. Nor was there any serious effort in the literature to make the more indirect connection between such behavior and laxness of parental control, which was in turn regarded as the breeding ground of more serious offenses. The issue of what constituted proto-criminal behavior was either too complicated or too self-evident to discuss. Or perhaps the relative silence on the subject reveals that the reformers were as dedicated to controlling these acts as an end in itself as they were to using them to detect potential criminals. While ostensibly legislating on matters of crime and punishment, they also legislated their preferences in the realm of manners and morals. By allowing noncriminal behavior on the part of children to trigger the intervention of a probation officer into family life, the juvenile court reformers were placing their movement among a number of others which were, in the progressive period, sending numerous missionaries from the dominant culture to the lower classes to acculturate immigrants, to teach mothers household management, and to supervise the recipients of charity.

Occasionally, the notions of individualized justice and positivist [scientific] criminology were frankly linked by their advocates to the aim of stricter social control. But on a less explicit and philosophical plane, there were many indications that juvenile court supporters intended more than the mere control of criminal behavior in children and more even than the prevention of criminal behavior in future adults. Judge Lindsey wanted not only "to teach children how and why they should obey the law" but also to make the children "really patriotic in spirit, protectors of the state and upholders of its laws."[18] Others hoped to direct the delinquent's thoughts into "pure channels and higher ideals for virtue and pure manhood," and to teach an "appreciation of the true, the beautiful, and the good," "neatness, cleanliness and correctness, and . . . a love and respect for other people's property and opinions."[19] Such statements elevated the mores of the middle class to the level of universal values, but even if these mores had been universally shared, they were not the usual business of a court of law, and went well beyond the stated aim of discouraging crime. Although the scholarship of the twentieth century has accustomed us to consider definitions of deviance in a sociological framework, the lengths to which these middle-class reformers were willing to go in reproducing an image of themselves in "unfortunate" children is indeed striking. One did not have to be clean and neat, correct and patient to stay within the law; one did not have to protect the state in order to stay out of its jails. The Reverend Malcolm Dana saw the rehabilitation of wayward youth as an occasion for a probation officer to become "practically a member of the family, and by lessons in cleanliness, and decency, of truth and integrity . . . he can transform the entire family into something the State need not be ashamed to own as its citizens."[20] In such declarations of purpose, the reformers exhibited a desire not simply to improve upon the criminal justice system but to retrain the child offender and his family in life patterns that were more acceptable to the middle class.

The dual role of the juvenile court system—a humanitarian gesture toward the downtrodden and a means of consolidating and protecting the safety and status of the more fortunate—is characteristic of reform as opposed to revolutionary movements, and many of the reform activities that occupied progressives exhibited the same duality. As Roy Lubove points out in his work on tenement-house reform, the miserable conditions of slum life prodded reformers into action not only because slums represented objective violations of universal standards of decency but also because they made the values of the middle class impossible to achieve.[21] The temperance movement aimed to rescue mankind from hideous dependence on alcohol as well as to ensure the reliability and productiveness of the work force. The public-health reformers exhibited solicitude for the physical condition of the poor and reflected the desire to protect the native population from contamination by unhealthy alien peoples.[22] The work of people interested in the process by which immigrants entered American life vacillated between the celebration of "immigrant gifts," of pluralism, and the anxious desire to remake foreigners in the safe and familiar image of Americans. The birth-control movement tried to provide individual families with the means of controlling their own destinies, but also sometimes seemed to provide the means by which the dominant middle class might preserve itself from the rampant fecundity of the lower orders, native and foreign.[23]

It is not mere conjecture to see similarly in the juvenile court movement elements of class and ethnic antagonism or of an effort to avoid them. According to the movement's own analysis, parental attitudes and home environment constituted the prime forces in molding a child's character. Also, according to that formula, "most of the children who come before the court are, naturally, the children of the poor."[24]

Responsibility for delinquency lay with the social and economic conditions of the lower class—conditions from which the reformers could easily sense their separateness. The men in the movement were usually lawyers, often judges, sometimes doctors and clergymen; the women, often well but less well educated and married to members of the same social status, were sufficiently free of domestic duties to devote much of their time to philanthropic causes. An awareness of their own good fortune was a virtual precondition of their efforts on behalf of others. Many saw that their mission involved crossing "that yawning chasm . . . dividing into hostile classes the rich and poor."[25] And they proposed to cross that chasm by offering delinquents and their families "those higher gifts that we are able to bestow."[26]

The reformers' sense of class differences between themselves and the objects of their philanthropy produced on occasion unconcealed disdain. Some court workers seemed convinced that no home deficient enough to produce a delinquent could command a child's—even a delinquent child's—affection. Henry Thurston, the chief probation officer of the Chicago juvenile court from 1906 to 1908, wrote about his reactions to the children and their families:

> Looking into their little faces, and watching them as they are taken away from their old unwholesome surroundings to be placed among environments that will lift them up and make them noble men and women instead of burdens upon society, one wonders how much these little ones really feel, and how deep their suffering really is when they are snatched away from home and parents.[27]

It did not seem at all likely that a delinquent would have parents worthy of love.

The theory that the cause of delinquency lay in lower-class environments, physical and cultural, translated into the practice of probation as uplifting contact between the delinquent and his social betters. Such contact was the very essence of probation at the beginning of the juvenile court movement, and probation lay at the heart of the ideal juvenile court.

What is novel about progressive attitudes toward child offenders is not the concern to mitigate class differences. Early nineteenth-century managers of the houses of refuge, as Stephen Schlossman points out, had seen their role in the lives of child offenders as inducing conformation to middle-class standards.[28] Rather, what is distinctive about the awareness of class differences in the progressive period is that the juvenile court movement contemplated not so much lifting the child out of his lower-class milieu as entering and transforming that milieu, not only for the child, but for his family, too.

The reformers' preference for returning the delinquent to his home did not jibe, at least superficially, with their conviction that the home had produced the delinquency in the first place. Nevertheless, for several reasons the reformers could live with this apparent contradiction. First, on the negative side, was their experience with institutional care as too rigid for individualized treatment and, more serious, as an environment more likely to teach the skills of criminality than good citizenship. Second, removing the child from his home in order to place him in another raised serious if not insurmountable legal, moral, and practical questions.

But the enthusiasm with which juvenile court reformers contemplated the probation system and its focus upon environmental as well as individual uplift cannot be accounted for by negative concerns about the alternatives alone. Schlossman believes that the juvenile court reformers' interest in a family setting for rehabilitative efforts was "one manifestation of a newly heightened sensitivity in the progressive period to the emotional bonds and educational possibilities in all families, even those in fairly dismal straits."[29] The faith in these possibilities is difficult to explain, since it seems to have emerged not from a belief in the growing strength and stability of family life but, on the contrary, from a concern that the family could not survive the effects of industrialization and the competition of other institutions—mainly educational and recreational—in socializing children.

It would appear that somehow progressive faith in the potential of family life outstripped the fear that the reality of family life was in decline. Juvenile delinquency was to provide an occasion to rejuvenate the family, and the rejuvenated family was to be an "ally"[30] in the reformation of the delinquent. Such optimism characterized to a remarkable degree the attitude of juvenile court reformers to the task of rehabilitation. The literature of the juvenile court movement contained many brief statements or summaries of the regeneration process, often presenting the task as one of impressive and even inspiring simplicity: "There is such a thing as an instantaneous awakening of the soul to the realization of higher and better things by the magnetic influence of one soul reacting upon another."[31] Thus, the process might have been as elementary as placing the delinquent in touch with a law-abiding citizen, or as simple as reasoning with him. Judge Lindsey wrote:

> We never release a boy on probation until he is impressed with the idea that he must obey. It is explained what the consequences will be if he does not obey and keep his word. It is kindly, but firmly, impressed why all this is so, and why after all it is for him we are working and not against him. We arouse his sense of responsibility.[32]

Lindsey seemed to suggest that hostility to society and its laws was just an error of judgment, a mistake that the child would recognize and correct if only someone took the trouble to point it out to him. This typical statement resembles an argument about madness made by a character in Dostoevsky's *Crime and Punishment:*

> In Paris they have been conducting serious experiments as to the possibility of curing the insane, simply by logical argument. . . . The idea is that there's really nothing wrong with the physical organism of the insane, and that insanity is, so to say, a logical mistake, an error of judgment, an incorrect view of things.[33]

This view of insanity implied that there existed a standard of reason not only universal in meaning but universally powerful in its appeal. The child-study movement took a similar position when it suggested that an appreciation of accepted morality inhered universally in human beings. The assumption that such standards of behavior had a natural hold on all human beings appeared subtly in many juvenile court articles. The superintendent of the Indiana Reform School for Boys told the National Conference of Charities and Correction in 1902: "We must place our boy under the guidance of an affable, firm, prudent master who will help by his own example. The courteous replies and gentlemanly ways of an officer have a tendency to draw as a magnet the respect and admiration of a boy."[34] The reformers assumed that the child offender had a "smoldering ambition" to be like the good men and women who worked for the court,[35] that he had within him all the while the potential and the desire to be an upstanding citizen, and that he needed only the example of "discreet persons of good moral character" to transform that potential into reality.

Only the assumption that accepted behavioral codes were inherent in the child could have explained the confidence with which the reformers contemplated the probation system. As originally conceived, probation treatment consisted of visits from a probation officer to the child and reports to the court by the child himself or by the probation officer. The visits and reports constituted the entire probation system, "the keystone which supports the arch of the juvenile law,"[36] the "cord upon which all the pearls of the juvenile court are strung."[37] The reformers expected the probation officer to show tact and patience and common sense, but they did not expect him to have professional skill or training. As with the judge, personal qualities mattered most: "The probation process is a process of education by constructive friendship.[38] The friendly side of the probation officers' work is the important side.[39] There is no more potent influence over a boy than a good man or woman. . . . The way to make a good boy is to rub him against a good man."[40] By expecting a casual, friendly relationship between a delinquent and a more fortunate adult to solve the child's behavioral problems, the reformers revealed a singular faith in the powers of spontaneous moral regeneration.

Thus, for all their concern about delinquency, the reformers' picture of the problem was rather rosy: whereas the child offender was clearly atypical in that he did not abide by the moral code natural to man, he was readily returned to normality; whereas for the moment he presented society with a problem, he would soon count as one of society's assets. Whatever his impulses toward crime and destruction, they were not basic, for as a normal human being his basic impulses by definition led him to preserve the social order.

The invention of the juvenile court was largely the work of the old middle class responding to one of the urban problems which troubled people in the 1890's, particularly after the panic of 1893. In a sense their response resembles what Wiebe would have considered an effort to imitate in the impersonal, urban world the informal patterns of social control which belonged to disappearing village life. The reformers' hope that disinterested observers in the community would petition the juvenile court on behalf of children is one point of resemblance. The importance of a fatherly judge in face-to-face contact with the children and their families is another. The initial commitment to volunteer probation service by people whose main qualification for the work was their social status is a third. As Geoffrey C. Hazard, Jr., has . . . written, "It often seems that juvenile law is operating on an unarticulated wish that young people would behave as though they were members of an integrated and static society living in untroubled times."[41]

On the other hand, the institution that this old middle class invented embodied much of what is characteristic of progressivism. It invited the kind of administration by the kind of people—the new middle class— . . . [associated] with progressivism and . . . modernization. While the emphasis on a judge with personal involvement in his work seems to have been genuine and to have endured, it also demanded specialization in juvenile court work. The emphasis on a personal approach in probation was clearly less enduring and probably made a virtue of necessity—the political necessity to avoid burdening juvenile court proposals with expensive probation systems, and the more mundane necessity to get along with amateurs, since social work itself had not yet become a profession and the social sciences were only just emerging. When social work did become professional and the social sciences became better developed, there was already a place for them in the juvenile court system.

The emphasis of the earliest reformers on the importance of "social" testimony in juvenile cases made that place. The vagueness of definitions of delinquency had moved the decision as to what a delinquent was out of the legislature, which made the criminal law, and into the court. The lack of a time limit, except the achievement of majority, on dispositions in juvenile court gave full scope to the discretion of specialists who from the moment of petition (and even without one) had flexible, continuous control. This scope was augmented by the disinclination to institutionalize children: children who went to reform schools passed out of the control of the juvenile court; children who went home on probation did not. Juvenile courts, unfettered by the rules of criminal procedure, took delinquency out of the adversary process much as other progressive reforms took issues out of the contentious, unpredictable world of electoral politics. . . .

That some aspects of the movement appear "conservative" because they emphasized social control and drew upon experiments already made, and that other aspects appear "reformist" because they emphasized the rehabilitative ideal and found new ways to pursue it, ought not to mystify us. As F. A. Allen has said, "No institution as complex as the juvenile court emerges suddenly and fully formed."[42] And the juvenile court reformers like most reformers were anxious to prove both that they had discovered something new which should be tried and that the trial would not be overly risky because it was related in spirit or form to tradition. It is also characteristic of the reformer, almost by definition, that he seeks to eliminate abuses in the system while preserving the system in its fundamentals. No one should be surprised to find in a reform program, particularly in the realm of penology, signs of such conservatism. Given the inherently double nature of reform movements, it makes little sense to seize excitedly upon one aspect or the other as its essence. This is as true of progressivism in general as it is of the juvenile court movement in particular.

That the juvenile court movement made an easy fit with progressivism is clear from its reception. The juvenile court idea was received as the height of social justice and "was one of the most popular innovations in an era renowned for its solicitous attention to children."[43] Optimism for the fulfillment of its promise pervaded the movement as it pervaded all the progressive era.

·

Notes

1. Laws of Colorado (1903), chap. 94.

2. From a discussion reported in *Procs. of NCCC*, XXXI (1904), p. 632.

3. Grace Abbott, "Topical Abstract of Juvenile Court Laws," in *Juvenile Court Laws in the United States Summarized*, ed. Hastings H. Hart (New York, 1910), p. 129.

4. Benjamin Lindsey, *The Problem of the Child and How Colorado Cares for Him* (Denver, 1904), pp. 47–48.

5. "The Reformation of Juvenile Delinquents through the Juvenile Court," *Pros. of NCCC*, XXX (1903), p. 213.

6. Stephen Schlossman, *Love and the American Delinquent* (Chicago, 1972).

7. *Our Penal Machinery and Its Victims* (Chicago, 1884), p. 47.

8. A. L. Jacoby, M.D., "The New Approach to the Problem of Delinquency: Punishment vs. Treatment," *Procs. of NCSW,* LIII (1926), p. 179.

9. Ruth Workum, "The Relation Between Functions of the Juvenile Court and Those of General Child-Rearing Agencies," *Procs. of NCSW,* XLIX (1922), p. 144.

10. Julian Mack, "The Juvenile Court," *Report of the American Bar Association,* XXXIV (1909), p. 470.

11. Evelina Belden, *Courts in the United States Hearing Children's Cases,* U.S. Children's Bureau Publication #65 (Washington, D.C., 1920), p. 8.

12. *Manual for Probation Officers in New York* (Albany, 1918), p. 58.

13. Abbott, op. cit., p. 126.

14. Introduction to Sophonsiba Breckenridge, *The Delinquent Child and the Home* (New York, 1912), pp. 2–4.

15. Ibid.

16. Anthony Platt, *The Child Savers* (Chicago, 1969), pp. 135, 139.

17. Schlossman, op. cit., pp. 57, 62.

18. From a discussion reported in *Procs of NCCC,* XXIX (1902), p. 425.

19. Arthur MacDonald, *Abnormal Man* (Washington, D.C., 1893), p. 53.

20. "Remedial Work on Behalf of our Youth," *Procs. of NCCC,* XXII (1895), p. 237.

21. *Progressivism and the Slums: Tenement House Reform in New York City 1890–1917* (Pittsburgh, 1962), pp. 2, 7.

22. David M. Kennedy, *Birth Control in America: The Career of Margaret Sanger* (New Haven, 1970), p. 15.

23. Ibid.

24. Mack, op. cit., p. 465.

25. Reverend Malcolm Dana, op. cit., p. 237.

26. Mary E. McDowell, "Friendly Visiting," *Procs. of NCCC,* XXIII (1896), p. 253.

27. "One Day in Juvenile Court," *Juvenile Court Record,* II, NO.1 (1900), quoted in his *Concerning Delinquency: Progressive Changes in Our Perspectives* (New York, 1942), p. 95.

28. Schlossman, op. cit., p. 24.

29. Ibid., p. 69.

30. Ibid., pp. 69–78.

31. J. J. Kelso, "Reforming Delinquent Children," *Procs. of NCCC,* XXX (1903), p. 231.

32. *The Problem of the Child,* p. 35.

33. From the speech of Lebeziatnikov to Rodya, p. 365 of the Bantam paperback edition of Feodor Dostoevsky's *Crime and Punishment.*

34. E. E. York, "The Cultivation of Individuality," *Procs. of NCCC,* XXIX (1902), p. 262.

35. MacDonald, op. cit., p. 53.

36. Timothy D. Hurley, "Juvenile Probation," *Procs. of NCCC,* XXXIV (1907), p. 225.

37. Henry Thurston, "Third Day in Juvenile Court" (1900), in *Concerning Delinquency,* p. 99.

38. Robert Baldwin, quoted in Hastings H. Hart, *Preventive Treatment of Neglected Children* (New York, 1910). p. 272.

39. Homer Folks, "Juvenile Probation," *Procs. of NCCC,* XXXII (1906), p. 118.

40. Waiter Wheeler in discussion, *Procs. of NCCC,* XXXI (1904), p. 570.

41. "The Jurisprudence of Juvenile Deviance," in Margaret Rosenheim, ed., *Pursuing Justice for the Child* (Chicago, 1976), p. 8.

42. *The Borderland of Criminal Justice: Essays in Law and Criminology* (Chicago, 1964), p. 46.

43. Schlossman, op. cit., p. 66.

3

History Overtakes the
Juvenile Justice System

Theodore N. Ferdinand

Theodore Ferdinand argues that many of the juvenile justice system's problems "can be understood in terms of how the [juvenile] court adjusted over the years to the custodial institutions, clientele, and treatment facilities it served," particularly to the "system of juvenile institutions already dominated by a custodial if not a punitive viewpoint." He considers the apparent failure of rehabilitative treatment and the growing demand for reform and offers his view of how the system might live up to its initial promises.

JUSTICE SYSTEMS HAVE A WAY OF SHAPING THEIR PARTS TO THE NEEDS of the whole, and the juvenile justice system is no exception. Many of the juvenile court's problems can be understood in terms of how the court adjusted over the years to the custodial institutions, clientele, and treatment facilities it served. Its deficiencies today stem largely from its roots in the civil courts and the difficulties it encountered in fulfilling *parens patriae* in a system of juvenile institutions already dominated by a custodial if not a punitive viewpoint. The juvenile justice system has acted very much as a loose but dynamic system over the . . . years, and to understand its difficulties we need to look to the historical contradictions that were built into the juvenile justice system. . . .

Of particular interest are several questions that have been raised repeatedly. . . . First, what purposes did the juvenile justice system serve when it was introduced in eastern cities during the early nineteenth century, and what role did the juvenile court play in that system when it was introduced in the early part of the twentieth century? Second, why has treatment been such an uneven enterprise in juvenile justice? Is the process of treating delinquents fraught with such obstacles that consistent success is impossible, or are less formidable

"History Overtakes the Juvenile Justice System," *Crime and Delinquency* 37, no. 2 (1991): 204–224. Reprinted by permission of Sage Publications, Inc.

reasons responsible for this inconsistency? Finally, why has juvenile justice been unable to maintain a *parens patriae* focus within its custodial institutions? Is there an inherent flaw in such institutions that ultimately vetoes any long term effort to improve juveniles in institutions?

. . . My approach . . . locate[s] the failures of juvenile justice not simply in compromise with routine, nor in the fallabilities of its pioneers, but in the conflicts that different approaches have built into juvenile justice over the years. We must probe the sources of juvenile justice's ailments in the nineteenth century, if we ever hope to understand their essential nature and correct them.

The Nineteenth Century Origins of Juvenile Justice

During the Jacksonian era [of the 1820s and 1830s] industrialization took firm root in several American cities. As trade with Europe, the Caribbean and other American cities flourished, as new factories for spinning yarn and weaving cloth were built, and as new schools opened, employment grew more plentiful. The slow drift of population to centers of commerce and industry grew very quickly to sizable proportions in the northeast, and several American cities began to encounter adolescent misbehavior and waywardness in a variety of forms (e.g., see Ferdinand 1989). Not only were wayward children nuisances on the city's streets, but when convicted of crimes in the criminal courts, they were sometimes sent to adult prisons where they mixed with hardened convicts and became career criminals.

But unless wayward children were criminals, the criminal courts had no jurisdiction over them. A convenient doctrine—*parens patriae*—however, enabled the civil courts to step in and take custody of these wayward or dependent children. The criminal law served for those children who had violated the criminal code, but for those who were merely beyond control, or whose parents were negligent, *parens patriae* sufficed. The child's first responsibility was to obey his or her parents, and the nascent juvenile justice system awaited those few who steadfastly rejected parental authority.

Furthermore, in many eastern cities bold plans for compulsory education were underway (see Schultz 1973). On the eve of the industrial revolution in 1789, Boston authorities established a system of free grammar schools, and in 1821 the city opened its first public high school, Boston English High. By 1826 Boston's school system enrolled a majority of its school-aged children (Kaestle & Vinovskis 1980).

These new schools represented a second arena wherein many children were held accountable. Just as children who were beyond parental control and roamed the city at night could not be ignored, so too children who disrupted school or truanted needed to be held in check. *Parens patriae* was applicable here as well, because the children were in school for their own well being. The schools' problem children became a second concern for the nascent juvenile justice system.

In short as compulsory education and industrialization swept America's cities in the nineteenth century, they produced a growing troop of wayward, incorrigible children who resisted in one fashion or another the efforts of society to shape them for adulthood. Something like a juvenile justice system was needed to bolster the authority of the family and the school in industrializing America so that both could be more effective in socializing young people. The juvenile justice system, as it emerged, represented the community's attempt to come to grips with a new social status: the juvenile.

At first the effort was limited to the major cities where education and economic development were centered, but soon it spread to entire states as whole regions were developed. The juvenile was expected to be obedient to both parents and teachers, and if he refused, he was held liable by the courts. The juvenile justice system was basically a sociological institution for holding juveniles accountable and for strengthening both the family and the school as they adapted to the changing social order.[1]

. . . John Sutton (1988) uncovered evidence that strongly confirms this view of the relationship between emerging school systems and juvenile justice. He investigated the impact of growing school enrollments on the introduction of juvenile reformatories in the latter half of the nineteenth century and found it more powerful than either industrialization or the growth of government. According to Sutton, "from 1850 to 1880, a 1 percent increase in school attendance is associated with a 13 percent increase in adoption rates" of juvenile reformatories (1988:114).

As a concept of the juvenile emerged, the juveniles' parents and teachers were responsible for them, and they were expected to obey both. *Parens patriae* was the relevant legal doctrine, because it allowed the state to intervene when either the family or the school was deficient. Because *parens patriae* was available only in the civil courts, juvenile delinquency was lodged in that jurisdiction. It covered all but the major criminal offenses by juveniles, which were still handled in the criminal courts.

Under *parens patriae* the civil courts acted in behalf of the child against ineffective parents or the child himself and provided dispositions that a responsible parent would. If the parents could control the child, the courts accepted them as the proper guardian. For the most part, state appellate courts endorsed this mission for the court (e.g., see *Ex parte Crouse* 1838; *In re Ferrier* 1882; *Commonwealth v. Fisher* 1905; Garlock 1979).

The civil courts still could not deal with juveniles who violated the criminal law, and many communities continued to send serious juvenile offenders to the criminal courts. Although most were sent to juvenile facilities upon conviction, some were still sent to adult institutions (see Garlock 1979).

Several facts stand out regarding the juvenile justice system up to 1899. First, it consisted of a very diverse collection of private and public institutions and community programs including probation for minor delinquents and status offenders, all served by the civil court and its doctrine of *parens patriae*. A survey of 30 juvenile reform schools conducted in 1880, for example, found an extraordinary heterogeneity (see Mennel 1973). Six accepted children convicted of crimes punishable by imprisonment, and fourteen took children who had committed minor offenses. Thirteen schools specialized in children rebelling against parental authority; seven accepted mainly neglected or deserted children; and five dealt with children committed by their parents for various reasons.[2] Coordination among such a diverse group of custodial institutions and the civil courts must have been difficult, indeed.

Second, the civil court with its doctrine of *parens patriae* provided moral leadership within the system. But its authority was at best exhortatory and informal. It had little control over the staffing, budgets, practices, or objectives of the far flung juvenile programs it served.

Third, this system was kept largely separate from the criminal justice system. Juvenile miscreants who warranted a criminal court hearing by virtue of serious offending were handled as adults. The rest were handled by the civil court and sent to juvenile facilities. In the nineteenth century a bifurcated justice system handled a bifurcated population of juvenile offenders. The early juvenile justice system neatly avoided today's complexity in which serious offenders are handled along with minor offenders in a single, *parens patriae* system.

This system was the result of separate initiatives at several different levels of government over the better part of a century. Even though most juvenile facilities were guided at first by a *parens patriae* philosophy, the system had no central authority that could impose a focus or common mission on the whole. Without a central organizing authority, however, the system was left to respond as local conditions dictated. And it continues today to embrace a growing variety of public and private facilities (Sutton 1990).

Moreover, as the nineteenth century drew to a close, it was becoming clear that the civil courts could not handle the sheer volume of juvenile cases coming into the system. As early as the Civil War, for example, the mass of juveniles arrested in Boston was already large, and the same was true of other eastern cities as well.

During the 1820s and early 1830s, very few juveniles were charged with serious offenses in Boston's felony court—the municipal court. But by 1850 indictments had grown in the municipal court to 220 per 10,000 juveniles and were the fastest growing component in Boston's crime problem. Furthermore, between 1849 to 1850 and 1861 to 1862 the arrest rate for juveniles rose 479 percent from 506 to 2,932 per 10,000 juveniles.[3] After the Civil War, juvenile arrests in Boston receded somewhat from the high rates of the Civil War period. Still, from 1870 to 1900 they ranged between 7,900 and 11,200 arrests annually (Ferdinand 1989).

This sizable flow of juvenile cases no doubt strengthened the argument that juveniles needed a specialized court—a court that was attuned to their special needs. First, they needed a judge who was familiar with the social psychological nuances of family conflict as well as the legal complexities of family/child problems. They needed a legal doctrine that took into account their social deficits as well as their misbehavior. Juveniles also needed a court whose officers were closely familiar with the range of facilities available for troubled children and could assign each to a program that was geared to his or her own needs.

The older civil court served the legal needs of juveniles, but it was devoted foremost to other issues. It dealt with divorces, torts, contracts, and wills—all adult issues. The civil law was narrow and intricate, and few probate judges or lawyers had a strong interest in the psychology of juveniles or their facilities and potential. They were largely amateurs in those areas most relevant to juveniles and their problems.

Frederick Wines, a noted criminologist, commented in Chicago in 1898 that "an entirely separate system of courts [was needed] for children . . . who commit offenses which would be criminal in adults. We ought to have a 'children's court' in Chicago, and we ought to have a 'children's judge,' who should attend to no other business" (quoted in Mennel 1973:131).

The New Juvenile Court

In 1899 the Illinois legislature enacted the first juvenile code and established, in Chicago, the first juvenile court. Its jurisdiction extended to virtually all juveniles—serious criminal offenders, status offenders, and neglected and dependent children. It embraced a much wider jurisdiction than the nineteenth century juvenile justice system ever had. Nevertheless, its mandate was to deal with all of them by means of *parens patriae*.

Several contemporary observers commented on the new court's usefulness. The new court gave custodial institutions "the legal status and powers that they have most stood in need of . . . [and] in large cities juvenile courts are little more than clearing houses to get together the boy or girl that needs help and the agencies that will do the most good" (Sutton 1988:143). It gave authority to social services, it provided intelligent assessments of juveniles, and it assigned them to programs that were closely related to their needs. It offered a specialized knowledge of and commitment to juveniles and their needs that the old civil courts could never provide.

In their enthusiasm, however, the reformers failed to ask whether serious offenders with criminal intent were appropriate subjects for a *parens patriae* court.[4] Furthermore, the new court did little to unify the juvenile justice system. It was still a very loose collection of programs and facilities with no central direction.

Despite these defects the remaining states quickly followed Illinois' example, and 30 states had established juvenile courts by 1920. By 1945 all had. The juvenile justice system was separate from the adult system. *Parens patriae* was the philosophic foundation of the court, and many if not most of its facilities and programs subscribed to that perspective.

These programs, as we have seen, had emerged in haphazard fashion during the preceding 80 years and most were organized by state or city governments. Because the juvenile court was generally lodged at the county level, juvenile programs both public and private were still largely free to follow their own mandate.

The new court was hailed as a visionary institution that would bring clarity, order, and humanity to the emerging juvenile justice system. In addition, the new court provided a podium for the *parens patriae* approach in the justice system, and its early judges were outspoken in advocating treatment and humane care for offenders.

judges

Judge Benjamin Lindsey of Denver, for example, was one of the first to argue in behalf of juveniles, and in 1904 he wrote, "The Juvenile Court rests upon the principle of love. Of course there is firmness and justice, for without this [*sic*] there would be danger in leniency. But there is no justice without love" (quoted in Mennel 1973:138). Many of the early judges felt the same way, although many were critical of Lindsey's flamboyance.

deep sympathy for deling-

The juvenile court maintained an informal atmosphere and gave the judges ample room to carry out their rehabilitative philosophy. The early courts were fortunate in that many judges showed a deep sympathy for young delinquents. Judge Richard Tuthill, the first judge of Chicago's juvenile court, proclaimed, "I talk with the boy, give him a good talk, just as I would my own boy, and find myself as much interested in these boys as I would if they were my own" (quoted in Mennel 1973:135). Judge George W. Stubbs of Indianapolis said, "It is the personal touch that does it. I have often observed that if . . . I could get close enough to [the boy] to put my hand on his head or shoulder, or my arm around him, in nearly every such case I could get his confidence" (quoted in Mennel 1973:135). With the appearance of the juvenile court in many communities, vigorous and often eloquent spokesmen for a *parens patriae* handling of juveniles got, and kept, the public's attention.

As the juvenile court spread through the states during the first two decades of the twentieth century, however, commitments to juvenile institutions went down (Sutton 1990). A growing number of judges were becoming uncomfortable with custodial institutions for children.

Parens Patriae *and Fairness*

Shortly after World War II the critique of the juvenile court got underway with Paul Tappan's (1946) keen analysis of the court's due process failures. Tappan, a legally trained criminologist, pointed out that many constitutional rights of juveniles were ignored in the *parens patriae* juvenile court.

Others took up the same complaint (see Allen 1964; Caldwell 1961). They noted that the court's therapeutic measures, even when sincerely applied, often turned out to be worse than routine punishments. It was not unusual in the

1960s to find that status offenders were punished more severely than all but the most serious delinquents (see Cohn 1963; Creekmore 1976; Terry 1967), and racial discrimination in the juvenile court, though not found in some courts, was all too common (see Fagan et al. 1987; Thornberry 1973; but see also Cohen 1976; Dungworth 1977; Rubin 1985).[5] Such flagrant violations of equal protection under the law were intolerable especially in the [socially tumultuous] atmosphere of the 1960s and 1970s.

racial discrimination common

A Growing Demand for Reform

In addition to Tappan's early criticism of the court's due process lapses and the discovery of racial and gender biases [see Chapter 21 for further discussion of race and gender biases in the juvenile justice system], steady reports of scandalous conditions in state training schools began to surface (see Deutsch 1950; Rothman 1980). The need for reform in juvenile justice was inescapable, and the response took several forms.

First, the states attempted to cope with difficulties inherent in combining serious and minor offenders in the same system by separating status offenders from delinquents in confinement and later, by removing most of them (status offenders) from the juvenile court's jurisdiction. California differentiated delinquents and status offenders in its original juvenile statute, and in 1962 New York passed a Family Court Act, which among other things distinguished status offenders (renamed PINS [Persons in Need of Supervision]) from delinquents. In 1973 the New York Court of Appeals ruled in *In re Ellery* that the policy of confining PINS with delinquents in an institution was unconstitutional, although in 1974 in *In re Lavette* the same court ruled that PINS could be confined in facilities organized for PINS.

(combining serious/ minor offenses)

In the decades that followed many states enacted similar statutes, separating status offenders and delinquents both in definition and treatment, and by the late 1970s many had gone even further by making court-ordered treatment plans for status offenders voluntary. Such children had committed no criminal offense and legally did not deserve custodial confinement.

Juvenile justice in the United States seemed to be following a path charted in Scandinavia in which problem juveniles under 22 years of age are treated voluntarily in social agencies, and serious offenders after 15 years of age are handled in the criminal courts (see Sarnecki 1988). Such a plan often fails, however, in that it permits status offenders to respond with either a "political" compliance to treatment suggestions or an impulsive rejection of them.

The Failures of Treatment

At the same time, ambiguities surrounding the rehabilitative approach spurred the federal government to sponsor a host of delinquency prevention projects.

In the mid-1960s under the impetus of President Lyndon Johnson's War on Poverty, a major effort to prevent delinquency and rehabilitate delinquents was undertaken by the Office of Economic Opportunity. As a centerpiece the War on Poverty mounted a massive preventive program on the Lower East Side of Manhattan—Mobilization for Youth. It was modeled after the Chicago Area Projects and addressed the problems of preschool children, juveniles, gangs, schools, and community adults. [See Chapter 14 for further discussion of the Chicago Area Project and Mobilization for Youth.] But it was too broad and complex to evaluate, and we will never know as with the Chicago Area Projects whether this community approach to delinquency prevention was effective.[6]

More specialized programs dealing with distinctive facets of delinquency were also fielded in Boston, Chicago, and elsewhere. Studies of innovative juvenile programs were funded in Michigan, Massachusetts, and Utah, and community-based treatment programs in California were generously supported. The federal government in conjunction with the Ford Foundation and other private groups sought to determine whether juvenile justice could remedy its ills. Sentiment for reform of the juvenile justice system was strong, but the direction of reform was still hotly debated. Should it focus on predelinquents with the idea of keeping them out of the juvenile justice system, should it reform the court itself, or should it concentrate on juvenile institutions? Much hinged on the outcome of the War on Poverty programs, and millions of dollars were spent to insure that sound methods and skilled researchers were used. But to nearly everyone's dismay, few if any initiatives were effective . . . [see Miller (1962); Klein (1971); Robin (1969)].

In Provo, Utah, Empey and Erickson (1972) designed a community program for delinquents in which they participated in group therapy sessions for five or six months. Empey and Erickson compared the delinquents with a comparison group of boys who had simply been placed on community probation and a second comparison group that had been sent to the state training school. Although the boys in the community treatment program averaged about half as many arrests as the boys who were sent to a training school, the difference between them and the boys placed on probation was small. Moreover, when a similar program was repeated at Silverlake in Los Angeles, boys in the community treatment program showed only slightly lower delinquency rates than boys who were sent to an open institution for delinquents (Empey & Lubeck, 1971). In effect the failure of these several delinquency treatment programs discredited treatment as a method for reforming delinquents or predelinquents.

To be sure, successes were also found among the treatment projects. Probation, for example, has been thoroughly studied in terms of the degree of supervision afforded juveniles and its success rate (see Diana 1955; Scarpitti & Stephenson 1968). The results indicate that despite haphazard supervisory practices a large majority of juveniles complete probation without further incident and go on to crime-free adult lives as well.

Further, Warren (1976) and Palmer (1974) reported strong results in treating specific types of delinquents in the community when compared with similar youngsters sent to custodial institutions in California. In addition, the studies of Street, Vinter, and Perrow (1966) in Michigan discovered that benign institutions with supportive staffs were much more effective in molding positive attitudes in children than custodial institutions and punitive staff. The former were especially successful in instilling a prosocial climate among the bulk of their children. Finally, Kobrin and Klein (1983) found that the level of coordination of [community] programs with established juvenile justice agencies strongly influenced their success. Where [community] programs were implemented in close cooperation with existing agencies, they were usually effective, but where the two worked at cross-purposes, [they were] ineffective.

Nearly all of these studies have been rigorously scrutinized, and serious reservations have been lodged against several (e.g., see Lerman 1975). However, the critics have not been able to defeat the obvious conclusion that significant numbers of juveniles respond to sound treatment programs, especially when these juveniles are assigned to program and treatment staff according to their need (see Lipsey 1991; Andres et al. 1990). Despite these results, the view took hold that treatment, whether in an institution or in the community, is ineffective in reducing delinquency (Martinson 1974).

The Crisis in Juvenile Justice

The conclusion that treatment does not work seemed to strike a chord in the nation at large, and the advantage swung quickly to those who favored a retributive approach to delinquency. Criminologists had been arguing for decades as to the causes of delinquency and the best methods of treatment. This quarrel was more basic and more serious.

The evidence was by no means unequivocal, but the fact that a [punitive] retributive response was so widely endorsed suggests that something much deeper was responsible. No doubt a general disillusionment with professionalism and government was a factor as well as the conservative views of the Nixon and Reagan administrations.

If the juvenile court could not provide wholesome treatment for juveniles under its care, it seemed to imply that the *parens patriae* court was discredited. *Parens patriae* was a noble idea, but if the juvenile court could not act effectively as a parent, the least it could do was act effectively as a court by finding guilt justly and by administering punishments fairly. In effect the juvenile court and *parens patriae* were held hostage to the ineffectiveness of community and institutional treatment programs in rehabilitating delinquents.

■ Why Do Treatment Programs Fail?

As we have seen, the juvenile court has never had much influence over treatment programs, whether in custodial institutions or in the community, because both were almost always organized by independent agencies. The one program the court did control, probation, has been effective in helping delinquents regain their social composure. In effect the juvenile court and *parens patriae* have been evaluated not only in terms of their relevance to the needs of juveniles, but also in terms of their ability to guide the rest of the juvenile justice system along the path of treatment.

The critics of the *parens patriae* court expected it to impose its rehabilitative mission on the rest of juvenile justice despite its very limited ability to shape therapeutic programs whether in the community or in custodial institutions. It was doomed from the start by the contradiction between its mission and its limited authority.

The *parens patriae* court did not fail. The state failed, because it enacted a *parens patriae* court without providing solid support for community and institutional treatment programs. True, state programs, first as individual juvenile institutions and then more recently as systems of state juvenile facilities, have been established, some even predating the juvenile court. But these programs had as their first objective the confinement of juveniles in large institutions where custodial policies and attitudes soon dominated (see Schlossman 1977; Brenzel 1983; Pisciotta 1985). Rehabilitation, though used effectively as a public relations device, was almost always a secondary consideration with these state-based programs. Rarely has a state agency had any responsibility for funding and directing treatment programs in the community for delinquents.

Many treatment institutions and community programs were established over the years with the help of private philanthropy, religious groups, social welfare agencies, and even the federal government. But these were either underfunded or short term, or both. These nonstate programs were hobbled by uncertainty. Because state correctional agencies were committed basically to providing secure facilities and nonstate rehabilitative programs were uncertain both as to funding and to endurance, inevitably the *parens patriae* effort fell short.

No state agency had primary responsibility for the treatment of delinquents, and no state agency developed the necessary skills in creating and administering programs for delinquents. However, without cumulative experience in staffing and administering treatment programs, no one gained the necessary skills to guide such programs. Ironically, in most states the only state agency serving delinquent youth was the department handling juvenile corrections. States became skilled in developing custodial facilities for juveniles, but no state agency had lengthy experience in providing effective treatment programs for juvenile delinquents.

A Proposal

It would seem that the solution to the problem of effective treatment programs is straightforward. A continuing public authority is needed with responsibility for treatment programs both in the community and in juvenile institutions.[7] Where it should be situated in the hierarchy of state services to juveniles, or the scope and details of its responsibilities to delinquents, need not concern us here. Whether it should be an independent department, part of the Department of Social Services, or the Department of Juvenile Corrections and Parole is not at issue at this point. Its mission should be treatment, and it should be in effect the court's rehabilitative arm, just as juvenile corrections is the court's custodial arm.[8]

Treatment programs for juveniles with psychological or social needs are as essential in civil society as unemployment insurance is for adults. Many juveniles need wise, skilled help in making a sound adjustment in adolescence, but unfortunately many cannot get such help from their families or anyone else, and to deny them by abandoning treatment programs is in effect cruel and socially destructive.

Treatment has worked only haphazardly because it has not been championed consistently by experienced agencies with roots in local communities. Where such agencies have emerged, as in Massachusetts during 1972 in the Department of Youth Services and in Utah during 1981 in the Division of Youth Corrections, the results have been generally humane and effective.[9]

Massachusetts under the Department of Youth Services has been using a system of community-based treatment programs for its delinquents since 1972 with solid results (see Loughran 1987). On any given day its youthful clients number about 1,700. Some 1,000 youths live at home and participate in a wide variety of treatment and educational community programs. The remaining children, 700, are divided between foster homes (30), nonsecure residential programs (500), and secure facilities (170). Serious offenders are dealt with via careful screening for violent tendencies, emotional stability, threat to the community, and social needs and are given programming specially designed for their situation.

The results in Massachusetts have been noteworthy (Krisberg et al. 1989; Miller & Ohlin 1985). In the beginning budgetary costs of caring for children via a system of community-based treatment programs were slightly more than for the old network of custodial institutions (Coates et al. 1976). However, the two systems were compared as of 1974, after only two years experience under the new system. More recently the system has become more effective, and today the annual cost per child in the Department of Youth Services (DYS) is about $23,000 compared with $35,000–40,000 reported by many other states (Krisberg et al. 1989).

Since 1974 DYS has strengthened its program, and by 1986 delinquency arraignments in Massachusetts had dropped by 24 percent from their 1980 level (Massachusetts Department of Youth Services 1987).[10] Further, delinquency arraignments for all released offenders compared with their level before admission to DYS is about one half, and arraignments for chronic or violent offenders decreased by slightly more than half (Krisberg et al. 1989). In addition, the number of adult inmates in Massachusetts who had also been clients of the juvenile justice system in that state dropped from 35 percent in 1972 to 15 percent in 1985 (Loughran 1987). Since 1974 recidivism rates measured in terms of delinquency arraignments among DYS youth have dropped sharply, from 74 percent in 1974 (see Coates et al. 1976) to about 51 percent in 1985 (Krisberg et al. 1989). In comparison with other states where recidivism has been measured comparably, DYS discharges have equaled or bettered the recidivism rates of all other state systems (Krisberg et al. 1989). These results suggest that many serious juvenile offenders within the Department of Youth Services have been helped by their experiences in the system.

In Utah, a new Division of Youth Corrections modeled after the Massachusetts Department of Youth Services was inaugurated in 1981 with full responsibility for secure and community-based treatment programs for delinquents in the state. Although the system is still too new to offer firm evidence of its effectiveness, its architects are delighted with results so far.

First, the shift to community-based programming required a budget $250,000 less than the old custodial-oriented system (Simon & Fagan 1987). The number of beds in secure facilities in Utah dropped from 450 in 1976 to 70 in 1986, while beds in community facilities increased from under 50 to 157 during the same period. Children in jails dropped from more than 700 in 1976 to 26 in 1986, and status offenders in detention declined from 3,324 to only 162 between 1976 and 1986. The shift was on to nonsecure facilities in Utah under the new treatment-oriented system.

Proof of its results is in the system's effects on delinquents. Preliminary data indicate that, as in Massachusetts, the community-based system is probably less criminogenic than the custodial system it replaced. A study by the Utah Division of Youth Corrections (1986) found that 73 percent of the youths who had received community placements remained free of criminal convictions for 12 months following their release, although fully 76 percent of the youths confined in secure facilities were reconvicted during their first year after release. Even here their offenses were much less serious. Before commitment these youths had averaged 24 convictions, including many serious violent and property offenses. After their term in Youth Corrections they were convicted primarily of minor offenses.

The twin goals of rehabilitation and justice can be blended effectively in the juvenile justice system. If dependable diagnostic and treatment programs can be made available to juvenile judges via a state treatment authority, justice in adjudication can be balanced with humane, effective treatment in dispositions.

Bifurcation: A Stumbling Block?

A difficult problem still remains. The history of juvenile justice confirms that secure facilities tend to become more punitive with age. Since the time of the houses of refuge, custodial institutions have shown a clear custodial drift with time (Ferdinand 1989).

According to Cohen (1985), institutions tend to differentiate themselves into custodial, punitive, *exclusionary* programs and rehabilitative, community-based, *inclusionary* programs. Cohen saw this bifurcation as paralleling a bifurcation of the system's clientele. On one hand, we have a small stream of stigmatized, antisocial offenders committed to a criminal way of life. On the other, we have a large stream of tractable but problem-bound offenders who want to become contributing citizens. Punitive, exclusionary programs serve the former and transform them into hardened, predatory criminals who are feared and shunned by the community. Inclusionary programs serve constructive offenders who are still looking for a rewarding life in mainstream society. Many of them, however, become agency-dependent and socially peripheral (see Ferdinand 1989).

According to Cohen (1985), inclusionary programs themselves become punitive and stigmatizing and are transformed thereby into exclusionary programs by virtue of the fact that newly established programs draw off the best clientele from older programs, leaving them to deal mainly with intractable inmates. As older programs adapt to a deteriorating population mix, they change slowly into punitive centers. Inclusionary programs gradually become exclusionary programs, and a long term pattern of institutional decay is established as the system repeatedly attempts to reform itself by reaching out to more responsive populations and relegating the rest to older, established programs.

Although Cohen was interested primarily in the adult system, he describes almost exactly the century-long development of juvenile justice in the United States (Ferdinand 1989). The houses of refuge were greeted enthusiastically by reform-minded progressives, only to see them transformed into punitive, stigmatizing institutions over the years (Brenzel 1983; Pisciotta 1982). The same was true of the state juvenile reformatories established in the last half of the nineteenth century (Rothman 1980; Schlossman 1977).

Ultimately, the juvenile correctional system in many states came to resemble a hierarchical system (see Steele & Jacobs 1975, 1977) of punitive, exclusionary institutions at the deep end (the maximum-security level) serving predatory, antisocial inmates, coupled with inclusionary, community-based programs at the shallow end serving a social tractable clientele with more focused problems. As each new program came on stream, it attracted the most promising clientele and the most progressive staff, and the rest were forced to adapt as best they could in the ensuing realignment.

An answer to this repetitive pattern of reform and decay, however, is not difficult to imagine. New programs need not focus on just the more tractable, responsive clientele. They could focus also on the other end—on the more serious, predatory offenders. After all, these are the offenders that spell the most trouble for society in the long run, and any advances in dealing with their problems would certainly be helpful. In this case the older programs would be asked to give up some of their least responsive inmates; their inmate mix would improve with each reform at the deep end; and one source of custodial drift, at least, would be arrested.

Such a policy would avoid drawing off the more promising clientele from the older, more experienced centers, but it would also foster small, specialized treatment settings—exactly the kind of centers that foster personal relationships among staff and children and thereby offer a chance for the staff to influence youth in positive ways (Street et al. 1966). Such centers are also easier to manage and supervise, with the result that treatment policies can be implemented more consistently over the long term.

This policy has been followed by Massachusetts since 1977—small, treatment oriented centers for virtually all juveniles in the Department of Youth Services (the largest is only 36 beds)—and no doubt some of the success of the DYS can be attributed to the positive attitudinal climate that small centers usually generate (see Krisberg et al. 1989). But if this analysis is correct, this policy will also help to inhibit the souring of the custodial centers as their programs become routine.

A system of small treatment facilities must still be closely monitored lest some of them stray from their assigned mission. There is always the possibility that a center will develop punitive policies for other reasons. To avoid such missteps it is essential that each center be held closely accountable to clear standards of performance. Each center should be required to justify its policies with verifiable research.

Conclusion

Few maintain that juvenile justice has lived up to its promise in the United States, and many assert that its future lies basically with [an adversarial/retributive] orientation. If treatment and rehabilitation are abandoned, however, in favor of a [retributive] policy whereby serious delinquents are punished in large, custodial institutions, several untoward consequences would probably result.

First, delinquency would deepen in seriousness and expand its sway, laying the foundation for a worsening problem among adult predatory criminals in the years ahead. Second, an important voice for humane programs in the justice system would be stilled with the result that a monolithic retributive system and its programs would prevail not only in delinquency but in criminal justice as a whole.

The difficulties of treating juveniles in residential centers are, however, soluble. Differentiated systems of small, community-based treatment facilities in both Massachusetts and Utah have shown themselves as more humane, comparable in cost, and more effective than the traditional network of juvenile custodial institutions. A permanent state agency committed to delinquency treatment programs would be a more responsible manager over the long term than the haphazard collection of private philanthropy, correctional departments, and federal agencies that have spearheaded most treatment reforms in the states up to now.

State departments of treatment services for delinquents also need research arms that can evaluate their programs with an eye to weeding out those programs that are ineffective. They need detailed information on their programs to represent the rehabilitation philosophy to state government and the mass media. The people of a state must ultimately choose the direction that is best for them, but they must be fully informed of the alternatives.

If such departments were available at the state level, it would give an immense lift to the juvenile court. This court has long pursued *parens patriae* in the community but with uncertain success and lately with waning confidence. A department of treatment services could provide both the variety in community programming and political support that the court needs to carry out its mission effectively.

The juvenile court cannot be both classification agent and programs agent for the rehabilitative process. It was never given a mandate to sponsor community-based treatment programs. The court is reasonably effective as a juvenile classification and assignment agency, but it needs an effective right arm to create and evaluate treatment programs throughout the state geared to local needs. Local juvenile courts working hand in glove with a state department of treatment services could finally realize the full potential of *parens patriae*.

To improve the juvenile court it is important to strengthen its links with the rest of the system, especially with those agencies that sponsor treatment programs. Up to now responsibility for these programs has been left mainly to custodial or private initiatives. Without a concept of the system as a whole, reform of the court inevitably focuses on inappropriate remedies, and the situation of delinquents only deteriorates. If the failure to rehabilitate juveniles lies with juvenile custodial facilities, reform should focus there and not solely on the *parens patriae* mandate of the court. Historical analysis can pinpoint the sources of the court's difficulties and thereby suggest appropriate lines of reform. Without such analyses our efforts will remain limited by ideological blinders and our reforms will decay as usual into tomorrow's problems.

Notes

1. It is interesting that as the juvenile court's jurisdiction over status offending has eroded in the last 30 years, runaways and school misbehavior have grown dramatically (see Gough 1977; Shane 1989). Although other factors have been active in this arena,

the court's abandonment of status offenders may have contributed to the reemergence of these problems in the modern era.

2. Overlap among these schools accounts for the fact that their sum is much more than 30.

3. These figures were computed from statistics issued by the Boston Police Department and the US Bureau of the Census. The population data for 1860 were gathered during an especially turbulent period, and may have missed a substantial portion of the transient population including juveniles. Thus delinquency arrest rates for that period may be overestimated.

4. In this sense the new court was a step back from the old civil court, because it handled the most hardened, serious offenders in the same way as minor status offenders.

5. There is no room in juvenile justice for racial or gender bias, but most studies of bias have ignored an important fact that throws new light on the problem. Because the community (parents, school officials, and neighbors) enjoys wide discretion in defining juvenile offending, an office's decision to make an arrest, or a court's decision to detain a juvenile depends heavily on the biases of the complainant (see Hazard 1976; Black & Reiss 1970). Where a biased victim demands action against a minority juvenile, chances are good that the police or the court will comply. A dismissal is difficult, if a complainant seeking punishment is close at hand. Thomas and Cage (1977) found in a study of more than 1,500 juveniles that their sanctioning in court was more severe if someone close to the case was pushing it.

6. Earlier the renowned Chicago Area Projects initiated by Henry Shaw and Clifford McKay in the 1930s probably had been successful, even though a failure to use an experimental design rendered a definitive statement as to their success impossible (see also Schlossman & Sedlak 1983).

7. We might call this authority the Department of Youth Services. Many states have a Department of Family Services that serves nondelinquent children, and the Department of Youth Services would offer many of the same programs for delinquents and children at risk of delinquency. It would coordinate its efforts with the juvenile courts, just as juvenile corrections does. Three state agencies, therefore, would provide social services to adolescents: Juvenile Corrections, which manages custodial institutions for juveniles; the Department of Youth Services, which manages the treatment effort for juvenile delinquents; and the Department of Family Services, which manages the treatment function for nondelinquent youth. Further consolidation of these three agencies need not be ruled out.

8. Some will say, "The state has already proven its ineptness in programs for youth. It does not deserve a second chance." My response is, if that is true, then the only alternative is the status quo, that is, a due process court and punitive juvenile institutions. Rehabilitating delinquents is too important to abandon simply because the state has stumbled in its efforts to fulfill *parens patriae*. If we can understand some of the reasons behind the state's ineptness, for example, a primary commitment to security in facilities, we can correct them.

9. Youth Services Bureaus, an offspring of Lyndon Johnson's 1960s campaign against delinquency, represented a similar effort to bring treatment programs together under a single community agency. They were locally financed and suffered budget problems in many small cities, and they often differed with judges as to what delinquents needed.

10. Certainly, other factors, for example, the downside of the baby boom and the cooling of the drugs epidemic among high schoolers, have contributed to this decline. But the size of the decline—24 percent—is consistent with a positive effect from juvenile justice.

References

Allen, Francis A. 1964. *The Borderland of Criminal Justice*. Chicago: University of Chicago Press.

Andres, D. A., et al. 1990. "Does Correctional Treatment Work? A Clinically Relevant and Psychologically Informed Meta-Analysis." *Criminology* 28:369–404.

Black, Donald J. & Albert J. Reiss, Jr. 1970. "Police Control of Juveniles." *American Sociological Review* 15:63–77.

Brenzel, Barbara M. 1983. *Daughters of the State*. Cambridge: MIT Press.

Caldwell, R. G. 1961. "The Juvenile Court: Its Development and Some Major Problems." *Journal of Criminal Law, Criminology & Police Science* 51:493–511.

Coates, Robert B., Alden D. Miller & Lloyd E. Ohlin. 1976. *Diversity in a Youth Correctional System*. Cambridge: Ballinger.

Cohen, Lawrence E. 1976. *Delinquency Dispositions: An Empirical Analysis of Processing Decisions in Three Juvenile Courts*. National Criminal Justice Information and Statistics Service, Law Enforcement Assistance Administration. Washington, DC: US Government Printing Office.

Cohen, Stanley. 1985. *Visions of Social Control*. Cambridge: Polity Press.

Cohn, Yona. 1963. "Criteria for Probation Officers' Recommendations to the Juvenile Court." *Crime & Delinquency* 1:267–75.

Commonwealth v. Fisher, 213 Pa. 48, 1905.

Creekmore, Mark. 1976. "Case Processing: Intake, Adjudication, and Disposition." Pp. 119–51 in *Brought to Justice? Juveniles, the Courts, and the Law*, edited by R. Sarri & Y. Hasenfeld. Ann Arbor: University of Michigan.

Deutsch, Albert. 1950. *Our Rejected Children*. Boston: Little, Brown.

Diana, Lewis. 1955. "Is Casework in Probation Necessary?" *Focus* 34:1–8.

Dungworth, Terrence. 1977. "Discretion in the Juvenile Justice System: The Impact of Case Characteristics on Prehearing Detention." Pp. 19–43 in *Little Brother Grows Up*, edited by T. Ferdinand. Beverly Hills, CA: Sage.

Empey, Lamar & Maynard Erickson. 1972. *The Provo Experiment: Evaluating Community Control of Delinquency*. Lexington, MA: Lexington Books.

Empey, Lamar & Steven G. Lubeck. 1971. *Silverlake Experiment: Testing Delinquency Theory and Community Intervention*. Chicago: Aldine Press.

Ex parte Crouse, 4 Whart. 9, Pa. 1838.

Fagan, Jeffery, Ellen Slaughter & Elliot Hartstone. 1987. "Blind Justice? The Impact of Race on the Juvenile Justice Process." *Crime & Delinquency* 33:224–58.

Ferdinand, Theodore N. 1989. "Juvenile Delinquency or Juvenile Justice: Which Came First?" *Criminology* 27:79–106.

Garlock, Peter D. 1979. "'Wayward' Children and the Law, 1820–1900: The Genesis of the Status Offense Jurisdiction of the Juvenile Court." *Georgia Law Review* 13:341–448.

Gough, Aidan R. 1977. "Beyond Control Youth in the Juvenile Court—the Climate for Change." Pp. 271–96 in *Beyond Control: Status Offenders in the Juvenile Court*, edited by L. Teitelbaum & A. Gough, Cambridge, MA: Ballinger.

Hazard, Geoffrey C., Jr. 1976. "The Jurisprudence of Juvenile Deviance." Pp. 3–19 in *Pursuing Justice for the Child*, edited by M. Rosenheim. Chicago: University of Chicago Press.

In re Ellery C., 347 N.Y. 2d 51, 1973.

In re Ferrier, 103 Ill. 367, 1882.

In re Lavette M., 359 N.Y. 2d 201, 1974.

Kaestle, Carl F. & Maris A. Vinovskis. 1980. *Education and Change.* London: Cambridge University Press.

Klein, Malcolm. 1971. *Street Gangs and Street Workers.* Englewood Cliffs, NJ: Prentice-Hall.

Kobrin, Solomon & Malcolm Klein. 1983. *Community Treatment of Juvenile Offenders.* Beverly Hills, CA: Sage.

Krisberg, Barry, James Austin & Patricia A. Steele. 1989. *Unlocking Juvenile Corrections: Evaluating the Massachusetts Department of Youth Services.* San Francisco: National Council on Crime and Delinquency.

Lerman, Paul. 1975. *Community Treatment and Control.* Chicago: University of Chicago Press.

Lipsey, Mark W. 1991. "Juvenile Delinquency Treatment: A Meta-Analytic Inquiry into the Variability of Effects." *Meta-Analysis for Explanation: A Casebook.* New York: Russell Sage Foundation.

Loughran, Edward J. 1987. "Juvenile Corrections: The Massachusetts Experience." Pp. 7–18 in *Reinvesting in Youth Corrections Resources: A Tale of Three States,* edited by L. Eddison. Ann Arbor: School of Social Work, University of Michigan.

Martinson, Robert. 1974. "What Works—Questions and Answers about Prison Reform." *Public Interest* 32:22–54.

Massachusetts Department of Youth Services. 1987. "Annual Report 1986." Pp. 1–16. Boston: Author.

Mennel, Robert M. 1973. *Thorns & Thistles.* Hanover, NH: University Press of New England.

Miller, Alden D. & Lloyd E. Ohlin. 1985. *Delinquency and Community.* Beverly Hills, CA: Sage.

Miller, Walter. 1962. "The Impact of a 'Total-Community' Delinquency Control Project." *Social Problems* 10:68–91.

Palmer, Ted. 1974. "The Youth Authority Community Treatment Project." *Federal Probation* 38:3–14.

Pisciotta, Alexander W. 1982. "Saving the Children: The Promise and Practice of *Parens Patriae,* 1838–1898." *Crime & Delinquency* 28:410–25.

———. 1985. "Treatment on Trial: The Rhetoric and Reality of the New York House of Refuge, 1857–1935." *American Journal of Legal History* 29:151–81.

Robin, Gerald N. 1969. "Anti-Poverty Programs and Delinquency." *Journal of Criminal Law, Criminology & Police Science* 60:327.

Rothman, David J. 1980. *Conscience and Convenience.* Boston: Little, Brown.

Rubin, H. Ted. 1985. *Juvenile Justice,* 2nd ed. New York: Random House.

Sarnecki, Jerzy. 1988. *Juvenile Delinquency in Sweden.* Stockholm: National Council for Crime Prevention, Information Division.

Scarpitti, Frank R. & Richard M. Stephenson. 1968. "A Study of Probation Effectiveness." *Journal of Criminal Law, Criminology & Police Science* 3:361–69.

Schlossman, Steven L. 1977. *Love and the American Delinquent.* Chicago: University of Chicago Press.

Schlossman, Steven L. & Michael Sedlak. 1983. "The Chicago Area Project Revisited." *Crime & Delinquency* 29:398–462.

Schultz, Stanley K. 1973. *The Culture Factory: Boston Public Schools, 1789–1860.* New York: Oxford University Press.

Shane, Paul G. 1989. "Changing Patterns of Homelessness and Runaway Youth." *American Journal of Orthopsychiatry* 59:208–14.

Simon, Cindy & Julie Fagan. 1987. "Youth Corrections in Utah: Remaking a System." *National Conference of State Legislatures* 12:1–12.

Steele, Eric H. & James B. Jacobs. 1975. "A Theory of Prison Systems." *Crime & Delinquency* 21:149–62.

———. 1977. "Untangling Minimum Security: Concepts, Realities, and Implications for Correctional Systems." *Journal of Research in Crime & Delinquency* 14:68–83.

Street, David, Robert D. Vinter & Charles Perrow. 1966. *Organization for Treatment.* New York: Free Press.

Sutton, John R. 1988. *Stubborn Children.* Berkeley: University of California Press.

———. 1990. "Bureaucrats and Entrepreneurs: Institutional Responses to Deviant Children, 1890–1920s." *American Journal of Sociology* 95:1367–1400.

Tappan, Paul. 1946. "Treatment Without Trial?" *Social Problems* 24:306–11.

Terry, Robert. 1967. "Discrimination in the Police Handling of Juvenile Offenders by Social Control Agencies." *Journal of Research in Crime & Delinquency* 4:212–20.

Thomas, Charles W. & Robin J. Cage. 1977. "The Effects of Social Characteristics on Juvenile Court Dispositions." *Sociological Quarterly* 18:237–52.

Thornberry, Terence P. 1973. "Race, Socioeconomic Status and Sentencing in the Juvenile Justice System." *Journal of Criminal Law & Criminology* 64:90–98.

Utah State Division of Youth Corrections. 1986. "Planning Task Force Final Report." Salt Lake City, December.

Warren, Marguerite. 1976. "Intervention with Juvenile Delinquents." Pp. 176–204 in *Pursuing Justice for the Child,* edited by M. Rosenheim. Chicago: University of Chicago Press.

PART 2

The Measurement and Social Distribution of Delinquency

THIS SECTION OF THE BOOK EXAMINES ISSUES RELATED TO THE MEAS-urement and social distribution of delinquency as it pertains to age, class, race/ethnicity, and gender. Whereas subsequent sections will expose you to *qualitative* delinquency research, this section offers a *quantitative* look. The most widely used data on crime in the United States come from the official government statistics published in the *Uniform Crime Reports (UCR)* of the Federal Bureau of Investigation (FBI). Since the 1930s, the FBI has compiled annual data from police departments across the country on crimes *reported* to the police (or known to the police) and *arrests*. The *UCR* makes a distinction between **Index crimes, or Part I offenses,** and **non-Index crimes, or Part II offenses.** Part I offenses include four **crimes against persons,** or violent crimes: homicide, forcible rape, robbery, and aggravated assault; and four **crimes against property:** burglary, larceny-theft, motor vehicle theft, and arson.[1] Although data on reports and arrests are published for Part I offenses, only data on arrests are published for Part II offenses. These latter offenses include 21 additional categories of (mostly nonviolent) violations such as embezzlement and fraud, drug and liquor violations, vandalism, disorderly conduct, and running away.[2] Data from the *UCR* have been used to measure trends in criminal behavior for the country as a whole, various regions and localities, and particular demographic subgroups (Berger, Free, and Searles 2009).

The data on crimes reported to the police are more appropriate than arrests for measuring the actual level of crime in any given year, since not all crimes that are committed result in arrest. Arrest data must be used to learn about the rate variations for different subgroups, however, since the characteristics of the offender(s) can only be made known after an arrest is made. The FBI publishes arrest data by age, race/ethnicity, and gender. Unfortunately, arrest data for class are not collected, although estimates of the class distribution of arrests are often inferred from the race/ethnicity statistics, since nonwhite groups are disproportionately represented in the lower-income stratum of US society and economic disadvantage is often postulated as a major cause of crime (see Chapters 14, 18, and 20).[3]

The accuracy of the *UCR* as a basis for making generalizations about crime has been questioned by many criminologists. These data are influenced not only by the actual behavior of law violators but also by police department classification systems and policies regarding enforcement of particular laws, by officers' discretionary decisionmaking in the field, and by citizens' crime-reporting practices. Thus variations in these factors can produce changes in crime statistics independent of law-violating behavior (Berger, Free, and Searles 2009). Consequently, criminologists have supplemented *UCR* data with alternative sources when studying criminal and delinquent behavior. One alternative source comes from **victimization surveys,** where respondents are asked to report on their personal experiences as victims of crime. A second alternative has been **self-report surveys,** where respondents are asked to self-report on the crimes they have committed. In delinquency research, the self-report survey method has become the primary means by which criminologists measure law-violating behavior of youths. The two chapters in this section, as well as several in subsequent sections, use this measure.

▨ Age and Crime

UCR arrest data show that rates of arrests increase through adolescence and early adulthood and then decline fairly steadily after the mid-twenties (Berger, Free, and Searles 2009; Siegel, Welsh, and Senna 2003; Steffensmeier et al. 1989). Property crimes tend to peak at about age 16 and violent crimes at about age 18. Steffensmeier and colleagues explain this pattern in terms of

> the increased criminogenic reinforcement experienced by young people . . . [and] the powerful institutional pressures for conformity that accompany adulthood. Juveniles have not yet developed either a well-defined sense of self or strong stakes in conformity. . . . They are barred from many legitimate avenues for achieving socially valued goals; their dependent status insulates them from many of the social and legal costs of illegitimate activities; and their stage of cognitive development limits prudence concerning the consequences of their behavior. (1989:806)

Self-report and victimization data show a similar pattern, although the self-report studies indicate that the peak age for some crimes may actually be lower than suggested by the *UCR* (Ageton and Elliott 1978; Loeber 1987). Perhaps police use their discretionary authority to be more lenient with young children, or perhaps they concentrate their enforcement efforts against older youths. Self-report studies also find that older adolescents commit more serious crimes than younger ones, but the earlier one becomes involved in crime, the longer is the duration of one's criminal career (Farrington 1986; Hirschi 1969; Williams and Gold 1972). Victimization surveys indicate that the victims in these crimes are often of similar age as the offenders and that "adolescent involvement in delinquent life-styles strongly increases the risk of both personal and property victimizations" (Lauritesen, Sampson, and Laub 1991:265; see also Berger, Free, and Searles 2009).

Because young people appear to account for a disproportionate amount of the *types of crime* measured in the *UCR,* self-report, and victimization surveys,[4] some criminologists have attributed the rise in crime rates that occurred nationally in the 1960s and early 1970s to dramatic increases in the youthful population associated with the post–World War II "baby boom." As the baby boom generation aged, however, and the size of the youthful population began to decline, property crime rates stabilized (Cohen and Land 1987; Steffensmeier, Allen, and Harer 1987). The violent crime rate, on the other hand, has been more resilient to such demographic shifts, perhaps because of the increased presence of urban street gangs and the availability of guns among youths (Conklin 2003; Fagan and Wilkinson 1998). In the 1990s the crime rate noticeably declined, and law enforcement, politicians, and the media orchestrated a good deal of fanfare over the apparent success of various crime control policies.

The reasons for these trends are complex and involve much more than the changing age composition of society. LaFree (1998), for example, attributes the earlier rises to a general decline in the legitimacy of social institutions (economic, political, and familial) that occurred during that era, a situation that weakened societal control over individuals and lowered their commitment to the conventional social order. As for the 1990s, Conklin (2003) estimates that age composition alone explains from 8 percent (for motor vehicle theft) to 20 percent (for homicide) of the declining crime rate of the 1990s, depending on the particular Index crime that he assessed. Levitt (1999) also concluded that changing age structure accounts for only a small proportion of variations in crime rates in comparison to other social and economic factors.[5] Blumstein (2002) believes that stabilization of the crack cocaine market, passage of gun control laws, and a vibrant economy were the most significant factors in the decline. Although Conklin (2003) thinks that increasing incarceration rates may have been even more important, Avanites and DeFina (2006) confirmed Blumstein's hypothesis about the economy, finding that measures of economic growth were more closely associated with declining *UCR* rates of property crime and robbery than were rates of incarceration. Zimring concludes that the crime decline of the 1990s "was a classic example of multiple causation, with none of the many contributing causes playing a dominant role" (2007:197).[6] In recent years, the decline has tapered off somewhat, perhaps owing to a reversal of these factors (Berger, Free, and Searles 2009).

Class, Race/Ethnicity, and Delinquency

In addition to concern with the age distribution of crime, one of the most controversial debates has occurred over the question of whether juveniles from lower-class backgrounds and minority racial and ethnic groups have higher rates of offending than other youths.

As noted earlier, *UCR* data on class are not collected for the nation as a whole, although some studies from particular localities have found an inverse relationship between class status and arrests, that is, lower-status people had higher rates of arrest than higher-status people (Shaw and McKay 1942; Tracy, Wolfgang, and Figlio 1990). One classic study of this nature, conducted by Marvin Wolfgang and colleagues (Wolfgang, Figlio, and Sellin 1972), followed the delinquent careers of a Philadelphia birth cohort—nearly 10,000 boys who were born in the city of Philadelphia in 1945. Although more than one-third of these boys had some police record by the age of 18, boys from lower-class census tracts were more likely to be delinquent than boys from higher-class tracts (45 percent of lower-class boys versus 27 percent of higher-class boys). Wolfgang, Figlio, and Sellin also reported that more than half of the delinquent boys had more than one police contact, more than one-third had two to four contacts, and nearly one-fifth had five or more contacts. This latter group of high frequency, or **chronic offenders,** constituted about 6 percent of the total youths in the cohort. Moreover, lower-class boys were more likely than higher-class boys to be in the chronic offender group.

Minority racial/ethnic status, as suggested earlier, has also been viewed as a proxy indicator of class. Here *UCR* data are reported for four groupings: white, black, American Indian/Alaskan Native (AI/AN), and Asian/Pacific Islander (A/PI). US census data indicate that about 66 percent of the US population is white, followed by Hispanics (14 percent), blacks (13 percent), Asians (4 percent), AI/AN (1 percent), and A/PI (less than 1 percent) (US Census Bureau 2007). Unfortunately, *UCR* data are notoriously deficient in reflecting this racial/ethnic diversity, especially as Hispanics are usually included as white. Moreover, "the criminal justice officials responsible for classifying persons may be poorly trained and may rely on their own stereotypes" about the appearance of different groups (Walker, Spohn, and DeLone 2004:14). Since AI/ANs and A/PIs comprise a relatively small percentage of the population, most assessments using *UCR* data typically compare blacks and whites, although some studies collapse AI/ANs and A/PIs with blacks into a general "nonwhite" category (Berger, Free, and Searles 2009).

UCR arrest data consistently show that in comparison to their numbers in the population, African American youths are disproportionately arrested for crimes. This fact is not in dispute. What is in dispute, however, is whether this pattern reflects an actual disparity in law violation or, rather, a greater chance of arrest due to class bias, racial/ethnic discrimination, or other factors (see Chapter 21). Self-report research can be especially useful in shedding light on this question.

The first known self-report survey was conducted by Porterfield (1943) with a sample of adolescents and young adults in Fort Worth, Texas. Porterfield was interested in comparing the law-violation rates of youths who had juvenile court records with college students who did not. His survey results revealed comparable rates among these two groups. Porterfield explained his findings in terms consistent with what later became known as **labeling theory,** suggesting that the higher class status of college youths had insulated them from arrest. According to labeling theory, official crime data are as much a product of the differential selection practices of law enforcement as they are of the differential involvement in crime by offenders. The labeling approach assumes that many (if not most) of us have violated the law at one time or another. If we were never caught, however, we were never officially designated or stigmatized "criminal." What matters most then is the societal reaction to our behavior (Becker 1963; Lemert 1951; Schur 1971).[7]

In addition to Porterfield's work, other self-report research also failed to confirm the class and racial/ethnic disparities found in official crime statistics, leading some to claim that the purported relationship between social disadvantage and delinquency was a "myth" (Title, Villemez, and Smith 1978). The implications of this discrepancy are far reaching, for if delinquency is viewed primarily as a lower-class or minority-group problem, then the root causes of crime will be sought in the social conditions associated with economic disadvantage. If, on the other hand, there is little relationship among class, race/ethnicity, and delinquency, then the causes can be attributed to other factors that affect all social groups (Berger, Free, and Searles 2009).

Two important attempts at reconciling the discrepant findings of official and self-report measures of delinquency first appeared in the *American Sociological Review,* the premier general sociology journal. Hindelang and colleagues were the first to argue that the discrepancy between official (*UCR* arrests) and self-report measures of delinquency was "largely illusory," because the two sources of data did not "tap the same domain of behavior" (Hindelang, Hirschi, and Weis 1978:995–996). Self-report surveys, they observed, generally ask about a wider range of behaviors than are reported in the *UCR* and are skewed toward less serious items that remain largely "outside the domain of behavior that elicits official attention." Thus Hindelang and colleagues argued that there is no relationship among class, race/ethnicity, and *less serious* delinquency but that official data provide a valid measure of the *more serious* youthful offenses that are of primary concern to law enforcement authorities.

In another important study, Elliott and Ageton (1980) examined race and class differences for different categories of self-reported offenses based on the

National Youth Survey (NYS) conducted by the Behavioral Research Institute at the University of Colorado: *predatory crimes against persons* (e.g., assault, robbery), *predatory crimes against property* (e.g., burglary, auto theft), *illegal service crimes* (e.g., prostitution, selling drugs), *public disorder crimes* (e.g., carrying a weapon, disorderly conduct, marijuana use), *status offenses* (e.g., running away, truancy), and *hard drug use* (e.g., heroin, cocaine). Elliott and Ageton found statistically significant race differences for property crimes and class differences for violent crimes (i.e., higher rates for African American and lower-class youths) but not for the other offense categories. They also found that most of the race and class differences, to the extent they existed, stemmed from a small number of high-frequency offenders who inflated the overall rates of their respective groups. Elliott and Ageton concluded that the differences between their findings and those of earlier self-report studies were "the result of differences in the specific [self-report] measures used" (p. 95).

In analyses of subsequent NYS samples, Delbert Elliott and David Huizinga confirmed the results for class variations but not race variations, which suggests that racial influences (to the extent they exist) may best be explained by class influences (Elliott and Huizinga 1983; Huizinga and Elliott 1987). Regardless, Elliott and colleagues' self-report research points to an important distinction between the **prevalence of offending** and the **incidence of offending.** Prevalence refers to the proportion of a particular group that has engaged in law violation, whereas incidence refers to the frequency of offending within the subgroup of offenders (Paternoster and Triplett 1988). The theoretical significance of this distinction has been noted by Blumstein and Grady: "It is reasonable to expect . . . that one set of factors distinguishes between those persons who become involved in crimes the first time and those who do not, and that a different set of factors distinguishes those who persist in crime once involved, from those who discontinue criminality at an early age" (1982:265).

We will explore the influence of these various factors through the remainder of this book. In this section, however, we offer a couple of illustrations of how the self-report method is used in delinquency research. In Chapter 4, "Gangs, Drugs, and Delinquency in a Survey of Urban Youth," Finn-Aage Esbensen and David Huizinga studied delinquent youths in the city of Denver, which at the time of their research they described as an "emerging" gang city. Their focus is on gangs in "high-risk" neighborhoods that are marked by economic disadvantage and social disorganization and where large numbers of minorities reside. Esbensen and Huizinga examine issues that are central to the measurement and social distribution of delinquency, including demographic patterns (i.e., race/ethnicity, age, and gender), the prevalence and incidence of offending (they refer to incidence as the "individual offending rate"), and the temporal relationship between gang membership and subsequent delinquent behavior. Among their many findings is the fact that gang membership, even in these "high-risk" neighborhoods, was of a relatively short duration: during the four-year period examined in this study, 67 percent of gang members were involved for one year, 24 percent for two years, 6 percent for three years, and 3 percent for four years.

▓ Gender and Delinquency

Another of Esbensen and Huizinga's findings was the surprising number of females who were involved in delinquent gangs. At the time of their research, this was not expected, for unlike the controversy over the race/ethnicity and class question, the relatively low rate of female involvement in delinquency had been one of the most consistent findings in the delinquency literature (Harris 1977). Indeed, prior to the mid-1970s, most researchers treated girls and women as marginal to the study of delinquency and crime. Albert Cohen (1955), for instance, well known for his research on male gang delinquency, paid only token attention to females, proposing that boys' delinquency was versatile, whereas girls' was sexual in nature, having to do with their preoccupation with establishing sexual relationships with boys. As he wrote: "For the adolescent girl as well as for the adult woman, relationships with the opposite sex and those personal qualities which affect the ability to establish such relationships are central in importance. . . . 'Boys collect stamps, girls collect boys.' . . . Dating, popularity with boys, pulchritude, 'charm,' clothes and dancing are preoccupations so central and so obvious that it would be useless pedantry to attempt to document them" (pp. 142, 147). Similarly, in his influential book, *Causes of Delinquency,* Travis Hirschi relegated females to a footnote that said: "In the analysis that follows, the 'non-Negro' becomes 'white,' and the girls disappear" (1969:35). When female offenders were discussed in criminology, they were described in various disparaging ways—for example, as childish, ugly, masculine, manipulative, sexually unsatisfied, plagued by penis envy, or inherently deceitful (because they could conceal lack of sexual arousal and fake orgasm) (see Balkan, Berger, and Schmidt 1980; Klein 1973 for reviews).

With these characterizations, criminologists were reflecting the attitudes and stereotypes of their day. Times, thankfully, have changed, and the analysis of gender is now a vibrant area of criminological inquiry. The concept of **gender** (as opposed to biological sex) refers to the "social statuses and meanings assigned to women and men" in society (Richardson, Taylor, and Whittier 1997:31). According to this perspective, societal notions of masculinity and femininity are socially constructed and historically linked to institutional arrangements of power that have entailed men's dominance and social privilege vis-à-vis women.[8]

Traditionally, gender socialization has encouraged females to be more supportive, nurturing, and expressive of feelings than males. Girls have been more closely supervised by their families and given less freedom to "sow their wild oats." Boys, on the other hand, have been encouraged to be more aggressive and competitive and to take risks, both with each other and with females. These gendered norms and expectations have been reflected in patterns of delinquent and criminal behavior. Males commit the overwhelming majority of crimes, particularly crimes of violence. Prostitution, shoplifting, and adolescent running away from home are the only crimes for which females have ever constituted a majority of arrests (Berger 1989; Berger, Free, and Searles 2009).

Beginning in the mid-1970s, however, studies began to indicate that female lawbreaking was on the rise and that a new type of female offender had emerged who was more violent and aggressive than her predecessors (Adler 1975). Although such claims were exaggerated, and males' rates of law violation continue to exceed those of girls and women, there have been some moderate increases in female rates over the last three decades (Berger 1989; Berger, Free, and Searles 2009).

In the 1970s, researchers offered various explanations for this phenomenon. One interpretation advanced by Freda Adler in her book, *Sisters in Crime: The Rise of the New Female Offender,* has been called the **masculinity-liberation theory** of female criminality. According to Adler: "The phenomenon of female criminality is but one wave in . . . [the] rising tide of female assertiveness—a wave which has not yet crested and may even be seeking its level uncomfortably close to the high-water mark set by male[s]. . . . [Females are now] robbing banks single-handedly, committing assorted armed robberies, muggings, loan-sharking operations, extortions, murders, and a wide variety of other aggressive violence-oriented crimes" (pp. 1, 14). Adler purported to explain this trend in terms of medical and technological advances that had freed women from unwanted pregnancies and lightened the burden of housework, and of the women's rights movement (feminism or women's liberation), which she believed had promoted an "imitative male machismo competitiveness," or the masculinization of female behavior (p. 98).

Research has not generally supported the proposition that female offenders have become masculinized or proponents of feminist ideology, however. Survey studies that examined the relationship between self-reported delinquency and several stereotypical masculine gender traits (e.g., aggressiveness, competitiveness, leadership, ambition) have yielded mixed or inconsistent results, and males have been found to be more delinquent than females regardless of gender orientation (Belknap 2007; Berger 1989; Chesney-Lind and Shelden 2004). Giordano and Cernkovich (1979) found no relationship between self-reported female delinquency and "liberated" attitudes toward family and occupational roles (e.g., whether women should have to do all the housework or stay at home and take care of the family; whether women should receive equal pay as men for equal work or be able to work in nontraditional occupations). Figueria-McDonough (1984) similarly reported that pro-feminist attitudes were unrelated to delinquency among female high school youths, although they were positively associated with higher grades and more ambitious career goals. Giordano and Cernkovich (1979) even found that traditional beliefs about male-female personality traits and interpersonal relationships (e.g., men are more logical than women; a guy likes a girl to look up to him; girls can't trust other girls with their boyfriends) were associated with higher rates of female delinquency. These studies are consistent with research on adult female offenders who have been found to hold traditional beliefs about motherhood and women's dependency on men and to reject or be indifferent to the women's movement (Glick and Neto 1977; Miller 1986; Ogle, Maier-Katkin, and Bernard 1995).

At the same time, Giordano and Cernkovich (1979) did find that delinquent girls expressed nontraditional attitudes about what actions they considered appropriate, acceptable, or possible for girls. For instance, delinquent girls were more likely than nondelinquents to agree with the statements: *"I just want to get in on a piece of the action—Gotta do what I gotta do to get ahead in this world"* and *"I think sometimes, if a guy can do it, why can't I?"* They also were more likely to think they had as much right as a guy to swear and to go into a bar alone.

Although delinquent girls in Giordano and Cernkovich's study said they were most likely to get into trouble when they were with a mixed group of boys and girls, they were not involved in these groups in passive ways, as mere accomplices to males. Most girls disagreed with the statement: *"It's usually the guys' idea and I just go along for the ride."* One girl even remarked, "While dudes are generally in on it some way, the girls are as much or more into it as they are" (1979:475). In fact, many girls indicated that they were most likely to get into trouble when they were alone or with a group of other girls. Giordano and Cernkovich concluded that contemporary females face a complex, multidimensional, and often contradictory set of behavioral scripts that specify what is "likely, possible, unlikely and impossible" for them to do, and that they are capable of simultaneously identifying with both traditional and nontraditional gender norms and expectations (p. 469).

Researchers now emphasize that the female population is not an undifferentiated group and the question of the relationship between gender and delinquency is much more complex, as that relationship is conditioned by other factors such as race/ethnicity and class (Berger, Free, and Searles 2009). For instance, in a study of gender-specific arrest data from the state of Pennsylvania, Steffensmeier and Allen (1988) found that within the same racial group, female crime rates were consistently lower than male rates, but that female rates were often higher than male rates for different subgroups of the population: the black female rate was higher than the white male rate for crimes against persons, the urban female rate approximated or exceeded the rural male rate for minor property offenses, and the younger female rate was higher than the older male rate for both serious and minor property crimes.

In Chapter 5, "The Impact of Sex Composition on Gangs and Gang Member Delinquency," Dana Peterson, Jody Miller, and Finn-Aage Esbensen also complicate the study of gender and delinquency by looking not only at the question of male and female involvement in gangs but also at the question of how and why the sex composition of gangs affects gang members' rates of delinquency. Using self-report data from a sample of eighth-grade students in 11 cities who participated in the national Gang Resistance Education and Training program, Peterson, Miller, and Esbensen found significant differences between "gang members' characterizations of their gangs' organization and activities, as well as . . . their individual participation in delinquency," depending on whether they were members of *all male* gangs, *majority male* gangs, *all female* gangs, *majority female* gangs, or *sex balanced* gangs.[9] The authors explore competing hypotheses to interpret these findings and conclude that the sex *composition* of gangs "plays an important part in shaping the norms and activities of gangs and their members" independent of the influence of gender per se.

Notes

1. Arson was not initially included but was added in 1979. Arson is only included in the data on arrests, however, and not in the data on reports.

2. Simple or nonviolent assault is the only nonviolent crime included in the Part II category.

3. In their classic research in the city of Chicago, Shaw and McKay (1942) found support for an economic or class-based interpretation of racial variations in delinquency. They documented the association between high-crime areas (as measured by official crime rates) and the conditions of urban slums: concentrated poverty and unemployment, physical dilapidation of buildings, residential overcrowding, absence of home ownership, high residential mobility, and the absence of "constructive agencies intended to promote well-being and prevent maladjustment" (quoted in Sykes and Cullen 1992:292).

4. It is important to note that a whole host of "white-collar crimes" committed by adults working in corporations and government is not measured. Also, adult criminal organizations are better able to insulate their members from arrest than juvenile gangs and other law-violating youth groups. In other words, one should be cautious about assuming that young people in general are more criminally inclined than adults (see Berger, Free, and Searles 2009).

5. More important than age, Donahue and Levitt (2001) argue, was the effect of the 1973 landmark US Supreme Court *Roe v. Wade* decision that legalized abortion in the United States. The resultant reduction in the number of unwanted births to low-income women, Donahue and Levitt believe, thus reduced the number of "at risk" disadvantaged youths who might have been prone to criminality. The statistical methods used by Donahue and Levitt to make their case are complex and provoked an equally complex empirical literature that attempted to rebuff their claims. Zimring, for example, noted "the extraordinary difficulty of using trends in crime to test the delayed effects of legal change that happened decades earlier" (2007:85). He also examined data that showed no association between legalized abortion and the percentage of "at risk" births, hence undermining one of Donahue and Levitt's key assumptions. Rosenfeld, another skeptic, argued that the theory of abortion, "though not implausible," should have predicted a crime-rate decline that began earlier than the 1990s (2004:87).

6. Nevin (2000) even found that environmental policies leading to reduction in lead from motor-vehicle exhaust and paint were associated with lower crime rates. (Exposure to lead is associated with cognitive problems that put parents and children at risk of low impulse control and behavioral aggression; see the introduction to Part 3).

Another factor postulated as accounting for crime reduction includes aggressive law enforcement against "quality of life" offenses such as jumping subway turnstiles, public drunkenness and underage drinking, truancy, prostitution, panhandling, graffiti writing, and playing loud music in public (Bratton 1998). This approach is based on the "broken windows strategy" initially developed by Wilson and Kelling (1982)—the idea being that broken windows left unrepaired send a message that no one cares about the community, leaving untended property available for vandals and setting in motion a downward spiral of increasing disorder that emboldens more serious criminals. Thus proponents of this view hope that a "zero tolerance" toward minor transgressions will have a trickle-down effect on reducing serious crime as well.

7. Labeling theory is not concerned with explaining "primary deviation," the initial impulse for law violation, but with "secondary deviation," how labeling transforms the initial behavior into a stable pattern.

8. Gender theory and research in criminology are closely associated with feminist scholarship that examines gender as a central dimension of social stratification (Daly and Chesney-Lind 1988; Simpson 1989).

9. *Majority male* and *majority female* gangs were defined as those having at least two-thirds of the members as male or female, respectively. All told, 10 percent of gang members were involved in *all male* gangs, and 37 percent of gang members were involved in *majority male* gangs, whereas only 3 percent of gang members were involved in *all female* gangs, and 2 percent of gang members were involved in *majority female* gangs. Nearly half of gang members were involved in *gender-balanced* gangs (see also Chapter 18).

▨ References

Adler, Freda. 1975. *Sisters in Crime: The Rise of the New Female Offender.* New York: McGraw-Hill.

Ageton, Suzanne S., and Delbert S. Elliott. 1978. *The Incidence of Delinquent Behavior in a National Probability Sample of Adolescence.* Boulder, CO: Behavioral Research Institute.

Arvanites, Thomas M., and Robert H. DeFina. 2006. "Business Cycles and Crime." *Criminology* 44:139–164.

Balkan, Sheila, Ronald J. Berger, and Janet Schmidt. 1980. *Crime and Deviance in America: A Critical Approach.* Belmont, CA: Wadsworth.

Becker, Howard S. 1963. *Outsiders: Studies in the Sociology of Deviance.* New York: Free Press.

Belknap, Joanne. 2007. *The Invisible Woman: Gender, Crime, and Justice.* Belmont, CA: Wadsworth.

Berger, Ronald J. 1989. "Female Delinquency in the Emancipation Era: A Review of the Literature." *Sex Roles: A Journal of Research* 21:375–399.

Berger, Ronald J., Marvin D. Free, and Patricia Searles. 2009. *Crime, Justice, and Society: An Introduction to Criminology.* 3rd ed. Boulder, CO: Lynne Rienner.

Blumstein, Albert. 1993. "Making Rationality Relevant." *Criminology* 31:1–16.

———. 2002. "Why Is Crime Falling—Or Is It?" In A. Blumstein et al. (eds.), *Perspectives on Crime and Justice.* Rockville, MD: National Institute of Justice.

Blumstein, Albert, and Elizabeth Grady. 1982. "Prevalence and Recidivism in Index Arrests: A Feedback Model." *Law and Society Review* 16:265–290.

Bratton, William. 1998. *Turnaround: How America's Top Cop Reversed the Crime Epidemic.* New York: Random House.

Chesney-Lind, Meda, and Randall G. Shelden. 2004. *Girls, Delinquency, and Juvenile Justice.* Belmont, CA: Wadsworth.

Cohen, Albert K. 1955. *Delinquent Boys: The Culture of the Gang.* Glencoe, IL: Free Press.

Cohen, Lawrence E., and Kenneth C. Land. 1987. "Age Structure and Crime: Symmetry Versus Asymmetry and the Projection of Crime Rates Through the 1990s." *American Sociological Review* 52:170–183.

Conklin, John E. 2003. *Why Crime Rates Fell.* Boston: Allyn and Bacon.

Daly, Kathleen, and Meda Chesney-Lind. 1988. "Feminism and Criminology." *Justice Quarterly* 5:497–538.

Donahue, John J., and Steven D. Levitt. 2001. "The Impact of Legalized Abortion on Crime." *Quarterly Journal of Economics* 116:379–420.

Elliott, Delbert S., and Suzanne S. Ageton. 1980. "Reconciling Race and Class Differences in Self-Reported and Official Estimates of Delinquency." *American Sociological Review* 45:95–110.

Elliott, Delbert S., and David Huizinga. 1983. "Social Class and Delinquent Behavior in a National Youth Panel." *Criminology* 21:149–177.

Fagan, Jeffrey, and Deanna L. Wilkinson. 1998. "Guns, Youth Violence, and Social Identity in Inner Cities." In M. Tonry and M. Moore (eds.), *Crime and Justice: A Review of Research,* vol. 24. Chicago: University of Chicago Press.

Farrington, David P. 1986. "Age and Crime." In M. Tonry and N. Morris (eds.), *Crime and Justice: An Annual Review of Research,* vol. 7. Chicago: University of Chicago Press.

Figueria-McDonough, Josefina. 1984. "Feminism and Delinquency: In Search of an Elusive Link." *British Journal of Criminology* 24:325–342.

Giordano, Peggy C., and Stephen A. Cernkovich. 1979. "On Complicating the Relationship Between Liberation and Delinquency." *Social Problems* 26:467–481.

Glick, Ruth M., and Virginia V. Neto. 1977. *National Survey of Women's Correctional Programs.* Washington, DC: US Government Printing Office.

Harris, Anthony R. 1977. "Sex and Theories of Deviance: Toward a Functional Theory of Deviant Type-Scripts." *American Sociological Review* 42:3–16.

Hindelang, Michael J., Travis Hirschi, and Joseph G. Weis. 1978. "Correlates of Delinquency: The Illusion of Discrepancy Between Self-Report and Official Measures." *American Sociological Review* 44:995–1014.

Hirschi, Travis. 1969. *Causes of Delinquency.* Berkeley: University of California Press.

Huizinga, David, and Delbert S. Elliott. 1987. "Juvenile Offenders: Prevalence, Offender Incidence, and Arrest Rates by Race." *Crime and Delinquency* 33:206–233.

Klein, Dorie. 1973. "The Etiology of Female Crime: A Review of the Literature." *Issues in Criminology* 8:3–30.

LaFree, Gary. 1998. *Losing Legitimacy: Street Crime and the Decline of Social Institutions in America.* Boulder, CO: Westview.

Lauritesen, Janet L., Robert J. Sampson, and John H. Laub. 1991. "The Link Between Offending and Victimization Among Adolescents." *Criminology* 29:265–292.

Lemert, Edwin M. 1951. *Social Pathology.* New York: McGraw-Hill.

Levitt, Steven D. 1999. "The Limited Role of Changing Age Structure in Explaining Aggregate Crime Rates." *Criminology* 37:581–597.

Loeber, R. 1987. "The Prevalence, Correlates, and Continuity of Serious Conduct Problems in Elementary School Children." *Criminology* 25:615–642.

Miller, Eleanor. 1986. *Street Woman: The Illegal Work of Underclass Women.* Philadelphia: Temple University Press.

Nevin, Rick. 2000. "How Lead Exposure Relates to Temporal Changes in IQ, Violent Crime, and Unwed Pregnancy." *Environmental Research* 83:1–22.

Ogle, Robin S., Daniel Maier-Katkin, and Thomas J. Bernard. 1995. "A Theory of Homicidal Behavior Among Women." *Criminology* 33:173–193.

Paternoster, Raymond, and Ruth A. Triplett. 1988. "Disaggregating Self-Reported Delinquency and Its Implications for Theory." *Criminology* 26:591–625.

Porterfield, Austin L. 1943. "Delinquency and Its Outcome in Court and College." *American Journal of Sociology* 49:199–208.

Richardson, Laurel, Verta Taylor, and Nancy Whittier (eds.). 1997. *Feminist Frontiers.* New York: McGraw-Hill.

Rosenfeld, Richard. 2004. "The Case of the Unsolved Crime Decline." *Scientific American,* February, 82–89.

Schur, Edwin M. 1971. *Labeling Deviant Behavior.* New York: Harper and Row.

Shaw, Clifford. R., and Henry D. McKay. 1942. *Juvenile Delinquency and Urban Areas.* Chicago: University of Chicago Press.

Siegel, Larry J., Brandon C. Welsh, and Joseph L. Senna. 2003. *Juvenile Delinquency: Theory, Practice, and Law.* Belmont, CA: Wadsworth.

Simpson, Sally S. 1989. "Feminist Theory, Crime, and Justice." *Criminology* 27:605–631.

Steffensmeier, Darrell J., and Emile Anderson Allen. 1988. "Sex Disparities in Arrests by Residence, Race, and Age: An Assessment of the Gender Convergence/Crime Hypothesis." *Justice Quarterly* 5:53–80.

Steffensmeier, Darrell J., Emile Anderson Allen, and Miles D. Harer. 1987. "Relative Cohort Size and Youth Crime in the United States, 1953–1984." *American Sociological Review* 52:702–710.

Steffensmeier, Darrell J., Emile Anderson Allen, Miles D. Harer, and Cathy Streifel. 1989. "Age and the Distribution of Crime." *American Journal of Sociology* 94: 803–831.

Sykes, Gresham, and Frances T. Cullen. 1992. *Criminology.* Fort Worth, TX: Harcourt Brace Jovanovich.

Title, Charles R., Wayne J. Villemez, and Douglas A. Smith. 1978. "The Myth of Social Class and Criminality: An Empirical Assessment of the Empirical Evidence." *American Sociological Review* 43:643–656.

Tracy, Paul J., Marvin E. Wolfgang, and Robert M. Figlio. 1990. *Delinquency Careers in Two Birth Cohorts.* New York: Plenum.

US Census Bureau. 2007. *The 2007 Statistical Abstract;* available at www.census.gov.

Walker, Samuel, Cassia Spohn, and Miriam DeLone. 2004. *The Color of Justice: Race, Ethnicity, and Crime in America.* Belmont, CA: Wadsworth.

Williams, Jay R., and Martin Gold. 1972. "From Delinquent Behavior to Official Delinquency." *Social Problems* 20:209–229.

Wilson, James Q., and George L. Kelling. 1982. "The Police and Neighborhood Safety: Broken Windows." *Atlantic Monthly,* March, 29–38.

Wolfgang, Marvin E., Robert M. Figlio, and Thorsten Sellin. 1972. *Delinquency in a Birth Cohort.* Chicago: University of Chicago Press.

Zimring, Franklin. 2007. *The Great American Crime Decline.* New York: Oxford University Press.

4

Gangs, Drugs, and Delinquency in a Survey of Urban Youth

Finn-Aage Esbensen and David Huizinga

In this self-report study of delinquent youths in the city of Denver, Finn-Aage Esbensen and David Huizinga focus on gangs in "high-risk" neighborhoods that are marked by economic disadvantage and social disorganization and where large numbers of minorities reside. Esbensen and Huizinga examine issues that are central to the measurement and social distribution of delinquency, including demographic patterns (i.e., race/ethnicity, age, and gender), the prevalence and incidence of offending (they refer to incidence as the "individual offending rate"), and the temporal relationship between gang membership and subsequent delinquent behavior.

GANG-RELATED RESEARCH CAN BE TRACED BACK TO THE EARLY PART of [the twentieth] century (e.g., Asbury 1927; Puffer 1912; Thrasher 1927) and has been closely associated with the development of criminological theory. During the 1950s, coinciding with [increased] media coverage of gangs, social science researchers and theorists such as Cohen (1955), Miller (1958), and Cloward and Ohlin (1960) paved the way for subsequent researchers in the scientific study of gangs (e.g., Klein 1971; Moore 1978; Short & Strodbeck 1965; Spergel 1966). These research efforts were either generally grounded in prior theory or interested in testing new theoretical explanations of gang delinquency. By the 1970s, however, interest in gangs had become passé and some wondered if gangs had met their demise (Bookin-Weiner & Horowitz 1983).

It was not until the urban gang violence of the early and mid-1980s that academic and media attention once again focused on the gang problem. As with most of the early gang studies, the majority of recent gang research has relied on observational methods and has produced a wealth of information

"Gangs, Drugs, and Delinquency in a Survey of Urban Youth," *Criminology* 31, no. 4 (1993): 565–587. Reprinted by permission of the American Society of Criminology.

79

about specific gangs and their members (e.g., Campbell 1991; Hagedorn 1988; MacLeod 1987; Sullivan 1989; Vigil 1988). Relatively few gang research projects have used survey methods, however. Notable examples of survey research on gangs include Bowker and Klein (1983), Esbensen et al. (1993), Fagan (1989), Klein (1971), Morash (1983), Thornberry et al. (1993), and Winfree et al. (1991). . . . In addition to observational and survey methods, other gang researchers have relied on law enforcement records to examine gang offenses and to describe gang members. Klein and Maxson (1989) and Spergel (1990) discussed the extent to which official data provide rather subjective assessments of gang behavior.[1]

While research design and methods of data collection have been varied and the generalizability of results has been questioned, concern has also been raised with regard to the applicability of the old gang knowledge to the new gang situation. . . . A number of other gang commentators have echoed the need for further theoretical and empirical examination of gang formation and behavior. Interestingly, one point of consensus in the voluminous gang literature is the high rate of criminal activity among gang members. Regardless of methodology and design, the consensus is that gang members commit all kinds of crimes at a greater rate than do nongang members.

The call for more empirical analysis of gangs in conjunction with the consistent finding of high rates of offending by gang members provided the impetus for conducting the analyses reported here. Despite almost a century of gang research, an important question (and the one guiding this research) remains: Are gang members more delinquent because of their gang affiliation or were they predisposed to delinquent activity prior to their gang initiation? That is, is the gang unit a criminogenic peer group, do delinquent youths seek out gangs, or do both processes occur? Using longitudinal data from the first four years (1988–1991) of the ongoing Denver Youth Survey (DYS)[2] we examine the temporal ordering of gang membership and involvement in delinquent activity.

Study Description

Sample and Ecological Areas

In order to ensure sufficient numbers of serious or chronic juvenile offenders in a household sample of Denver, we identified "high-risk" neighborhoods from which to select prospective respondents.[3] Based on the results of earlier studies, we selected 35 variables from the 1980 census data representing seven conceptual areas: family structure, ethnicity, socioeconomic status (SES), housing, mobility, marital status, and age composition. Using a factor analysis of variables within each of these seven conceptual domains, we identified 11 distinct factors. [See the book appendix for a brief explanation of the statistical techniques used in this chapter, e.g., factor analysis and cluster analysis.] Four of the theoretically derived concepts identified above produced two distinct factors. The socioeconomic domain, for example, resulted in the identification of an upper SES (e.g., high education, household income over $40,000, and professional and managerial occupations) and a lower SES factor (e.g., families in poverty, incomes under $10,000, and laborer occupations).

We subsequently ran a cluster analysis to identify and combine similar block groups of the city. Seven distinct clusters emerged, three of which we very loosely identified as being "socially disorganized." The first cluster or grouping of block groups was economically disadvantaged; it had high rates of poverty and unemployment and high numbers of unemployed school-dropout youths. It also had a high racial mix (white, African American, and Hispanic), and high rates of single-parent households and persons per room (density). The second cluster was also economically disadvantaged, although not as severely as the first: it had a highly mobile population, many unmarried persons and few intact families, and many multiple-unit dwellings. The third cluster was a predominantly minority cluster (African American) with higher than average rates of single-parent and unmarried-person households and a high rate of persons per room.

The geographic areas covered by these clusters include areas identified by arrest data from the Denver Police Department as having high crime rates. Using arrest data, we identified those neighborhoods within the socially disorganized areas that were in the upper one-third of the crime distribution.[4] These socially disorganized, high-crime areas became the neighborhoods for inclusion in the study sample. Although this sample selection precludes generalizations to the total disorganized areas, it ensures that youths living in these areas are likely to be in highly criminogenic environments as well, and it is to these disorganized, high-crime areas that findings apply. A more detailed description of the sampling design and the social ecology analysis is provided in Esbensen and Huizinga (1990).

Selection of Respondents

The overall design of the ongoing research project is based on a prospective, sequential longitudinal survey. The longitudinal survey involves a sequence of annual personal interviews with a probability sample of five birth cohorts. At the point of the first annual survey, the birth cohorts were 7, 9, 11, 13, and 15 years of age. Assuming the period effects between adjacent cohorts are not too large, the use of these birth cohorts (samples) results in overlapping age ranges during the first four years of the study, which allows examination of developmental sequences across the full span from age 7 to 18.

To identify study participants, a stratified probability sample of 20,300 households was selected from the 48,000 in the targeted households. Then a screening questionnaire was used to identify those households that contained an appropriately aged respondent (i.e., 7, 9, 11, 13, or 15 years old). This sampling procedure resulted in 1,527 completed interviews in the first year (a completion rate of 85 percent among identified eligible youths); the youths were distributed across the five cohorts. Fifty-two percent of the sample are male, 48 percent female; 33 percent are African American, 45 percent Hispanic, 10 percent Anglo, and 12 percent "other" (primarily Asian and Native American).

Annual retention rates for the first four annual in-person interviews have been high by prevailing standards, 91 percent to 93 percent,[5] and complete data covering all four years are available for 85 percent of the original sample (some youths not interviewed in a given year are located and interviewed in later years). In this paper, only data from the three oldest cohorts are used for the full analyses because of the distinctly different developmental stages represented by the two youngest cohorts (aged 7 and 9 during the first annual data collection) for whom gang involvement was not a major factor. Data for the 9-year-old cohort, however, were included in the specific analyses for years three and four, when these youths were aged 11 and 12.[6]

Methods

Definition of Gangs and Gang Membership

Arriving at a definition of the term *gang* is no simple task; considerable debate exists regarding an appropriate definition (see Covey et al. 1992). We have adopted the position espoused by Miller (1974) and Klein and Maxson (1989), that is, in order to be considered a gang, the group must be involved in illegal activity.

Considerable data about gang membership were collected during the survey's 90-minute, in-person interviews. One early finding from this line of questioning was that approximately 5 percent of youths in the DYS indicated that they were gang members in any given year (39 in wave 1, 37 in wave 2, 41 in wave 3, and 76 in wave 4). Respondents were asked early in the interview if they were "members of a street or youth gang." All those responding affirmatively were later asked a series of questions about their gangs. Examination of this follow-up information indicated that what some of the youths described as gangs could best be defined as informal youth groups, or in some instances, church groups, that did not necessarily include involvement in delinquent behavior. As mentioned above, to be considered a gang member, the youth had to indicate that the gang was involved in illegal activity. An affirmative response to either of two follow-up questions (i.e., perceived gang involvement in fights with other gangs and participation in illegal activities) was used to exclude nondelinquent gangs from the analysis. While the exclusion of respondents who indicated their gang was not involved in these activities reduced the number of potential gang members to 27 in wave 1, 33 in wave 2, 32 in wave 3, and 68 in wave 4, this process permits a more stringent and, arguably, more accurate description of juvenile *delinquent* gang membership and activity. The 32 gang members in wave 3 represent 2.7 percent of the general sample of youths aged 11 to 17, and the 68 gang members in wave 4 represent 6.7 percent of the youths when they were 12 to 18 years of age. From this, one might conclude that gang membership is a relatively infrequent phenomenon in Denver, even among this "high-risk" sample of urban youths.

What are these gangs like? Descriptive data provided by respondents paint a picture of what Yablonsky (1959:109) referred to as "near groups"—groups characterized by limited cohesion, impermanence, shifting membership, and diffuse role definition, but at the same time that had some level of identification as a gang, as evidenced by having a gang name and use of gang colors and initiation rites. Year 4 data are representative of the descriptive information provided across the four years of data collection: 97 percent of the members indicated their gangs had a formal name (37 gangs were identified by the 68 gang members); 86 percent indicated their gang had initiation rites; and 97 percent reported that their gang had symbols or colors. With regard to shifting membership and impermanence, when asked what role they would like to have or what role they expect to have in the gang someday, over 60 percent of year 4 gang members indicated that they would like to not be a member and expected not to be a member sometime in the future.

Self-reported delinquency data were also collected from all respondents. The measures are improved versions of our earlier work (e.g., Huizinga & Elliott 1986) and avoid some of the problems of even earlier self-report inventories. The measures exclude traditional trivial offenses, such as defying parental authority, and include serious offenses often excluded from early self-report inventories (e.g., rape, robbery, and aggravated assault). Additionally, follow-up questions were included as integral parts of the measures. These follow-up questions allow for determination of the seriousness and appropriateness of initial responses. If, for example, a respondent indicated that he or she had committed an aggravated assault during the prior year but follow-up information revealed that it was accidental and that the victim truly was not injured, the original response would be changed to zero.

For analysis purposes, our delinquency and drug use measures focus on those behaviors often considered to be of greatest concern. To this end, we developed four levels of delinquency: (1) street offending, (2) other serious offending, (3) minor offending, and (4) nonoffending. We used a subset of the street offenses to create a measure of drug sales[7] in order to address the concern that gangs are disproportionately involved in drug distribution (e.g., Fagan 1989). One gang expert has even suggested that youth gangs of the 1990s have established a national network of drug distribution similar to the "mafia's" alcohol distribution network during prohibition (Taylor 1990).

Street offenses focus on serious crimes that occur on the street and are often of concern to citizens and policymakers, alike. *Other serious offenses* include behaviors that, while not in the street crime category, are nevertheless considered as serious delinquency. *Minor offenses* refer primarily to status offenses and other public nuisance type behaviors. These categories of delinquent behavior generally reflect the seriousness weighting used by Wolfgang et al. (1985). We dichotomized *drug use* into alcohol use and "other drug use," including marijuana and other illicit drugs. For the analyses reported below, all youths were categorized based on their most serious level of involvement in delinquency and drug use. Thus, if an individual reported committing a minor, a serious, and a street offense in a given year, that individual was classified as a street offender. Appendix 4.1 provides a listing of the items included in the self-reported delinquency and drug use classifications.

Results

Gang Member Demographics

Gangs have traditionally been thought of as being a predominantly male phenomenon, and relatively few studies have concentrated on female gang members (exceptions include Bowker & Klein 1983; Campbell 1990, 1991; Giordano 1978; Harris 1988; Morash 1983; Quicker 1983). This has resulted in considerable ignorance concerning not only the role of female gang members, but also the number of females involved in gang activity. Campbell (1991) reports a long and rich history of female gangs and female members in male gangs; she suggests that at one point approximately 10 percent of New York City gang members were female, and that female membership might have been as high as 33 percent in one gang. Fagan (1990) reported female gang membership to be approximately 33 percent in his survey.

The demographic characteristics of both gang and nongang members are presented in Table 4.1. As seen there, the DYS data confirm that a significant proportion of all gang members are female—a fact not generally acknowledged in media presentations of gangs. Cross-sectional analysis of DYS gang data reveals that females constituted from 20 percent to 46 percent of gang members during the four-year study period. Thus, while there is evidence that gang members are primarily males, there is reason to believe that females are more involved in gangs than is generally acknowledged. One caveat, however, is that while female gang membership may well be greater than that presented in the popular press, female gang members are less likely to report high levels of involvement in delinquent activity. In wave 3, for example, female gang members reported an average individual offending rate of 14.0 on the general delinquency scale, and male gang members reported an average offending rate of 36.9 offenses on that scale.

As with gender, it is often assumed that gang members are youths from ethnic-racial minority backgrounds (e.g., Fagan 1989; Spergel 1990). A 1989 survey of law enforcement officials in 45 cities across the nation found that

Table 4.1 Demographic Characteristics of the Denver Youth Survey Sample

	Year 1		Year 2		Year 3		Year 4	
	Gang	Nongang	Gang	Nongang	Gang	Nongang	Gang	Nongang
Sex								
Male N	15	441	27	397	24	555	53	511
Column %	54%	52%	80%	52%	74%	52%	80%	50%
Female N	12	400	7	390	8	514	13	516
Column %	46%	48%	20%	48%	25%	48%	20%	50%
Total N	**27**	**841**	**33**	**801**	**32**	**1,102**	**68**	**1,027**
Race								
Af. Am. N	7	320	14	283	15	385	28	371
Column %	26%	38%	42%	37%	48%	36%	42%	36%
Hisp. N	16	374	14	352	14	470	35	443
Column %	60%	45%	43%	46%	42%	44%	52%	43%
White N	0	71	2	65	0	104	2	103
Column %		9%	7%	8%		10%	3%	10%
Other N	4	75	1	67	2	110	2	110
Column %	14%	9%	8%	9%	7%	10%	3%	11%
Total N	**27**	**830**	**33**	**801**	**32**	**1,102**	**68**	**1,026**
Age, Birthyear								
1972 N	14	256	11	226	11	228	18	227
Column %	52%	30%	33%	30%	35%	22%	27%	22%
1974 N	10	291	17	268	11	275	20	257
Column %	38%	35%	52%	35%	33%	26%	31%	25%
1976 N	3	294	5	273	10	276	24	257
Column %	10%	35%	16%	36%	32%	26%	36%	25%
1978 N	—	—	—	—	0	291	5	285
Column %						27%	7%	28%
Total N	**27**	**830**	**33**	**801**	**32**	**1,102**	**68**	**1,027**

Note: The data are weighed to represent the stratified sample. As a result, the integral values are approximates and do not always provide the exact percentage.

African Americans and Hispanics made up 87 percent of gang membership (cited in Gurule 1991). Due to the nature of the DYS sample (78 percent of the sample is African American or Hispanic), it is not possible to address the ethnic distribution of gang membership, although it does appear that African American and Hispanic youths tend to be overrepresented in the DYS gang subsample (ranging from 85 percent to 94 percent of gang members in the various years). Given the disproportionate number of minority youths in the sample, however, it should be expected that the majority of gang members would also be African American or Hispanic.

Gang membership does appear to be somewhat associated with age. In year 4, for example, 27 percent of gang members were 18 years old, 31 percent were 16, 36 percent were 14, and 7 percent were 12. Given this age distribution, at what age do youths join gangs? Gang members were asked when they joined their gang. Analysis of these responses for year 4 revealed that most did not join until their teenaged years, although a few respondents did indicate that they joined the gang before the age of 12.

Gang Delinquency

Are gang members more involved in delinquency than nongang members? Examination of Table 4.2 results in a firm yes for males and a qualified yes for female gang members.[8] Both prevalence and individual offending rates [*prevalence* refers to the proportion of a particular group that has engaged in law violation, while *individual offending rates* refers to the frequency of offending within a subgroup of offenders] for gang members and nongang members are reported for four types of delinquent behavior and two types of drug use during year 4. It is important to examine prevalence rates first in that this identifies the number of active offenders involved in each specific behavior.

The prevalence rates for male and female gang members are significantly greater than those for their nongang counterparts. Gang membership is almost synonymous with involvement in all types of delinquency. Male gang members, for example, reported a prevalence rate of .85 for street offenses and .83 for other serious offenses. This is substantially higher than the prevalence rates of .18 and .32, respectively, for nongang males. The difference in prevalence rates is even more pronounced for females; .76 of female gang members reported involvement in street offending compared with .07 for nongang females. For each type of behavior, the prevalence rate for female gang members is consistently greater than that for male nongang members. Gang members during year 4 report being involved in a variety of delinquent activities; with male prevalence rates ranging between .29 for drug sales and .87 for minor offending,

Table 4.2 Year 4 Prevalence and Individual Offending Rates (IOR) of Gang and Nongang Members Controlling for Sex

| | Males | | | | | | Females | | | | | |
| | Gang | | | Nongang | | | Gang | | | Nongang | | |
Offense Type	N	Prev.	IOR	N	Prev.	IOR	N	Prev.	IOR	N	Prev.	IOR
Street	53	.85*	22.3**	511	.18	8.3	13	.76*	5.9	515	.07	2.7
Drug Sales	53	.29*	22.8**	511	.03	30.5	13	.18*	10.5	515	.01	6.8
Serious	53	.83*	31.8**	510	.32	10.0	13	.61*	5.1	516	.18	10.0
Minor	49	.87*	29.0**	500	.56	11.6	13	.93*	18.7	499	.54	10.1
Alcohol Use	53	.71*	48.4**	510	.35	24.1	13	.85*	36.9	516	.32	16.7
Other Drug Use	52	.52*	46.8**	491	.13	20.0	13	.69*	11.9	516	.13	23.6

*p < .05 (chi-square)
**p < .05 (t-test, separate variance estimate of t)

these youths clearly do not specialize in any one type of activity. Nongang members had much lower rates of involvement in all types of delinquent activities and drug use than did the gang members, as evidenced by prevalence rates of .01 and .03 for females and males, respectively, involved in drug sales, and nongang prevalence rates of .07 and .18 for female and male involvement, respectively, in street-level offending (compared with .76 and .85 for female and male gang members).

With respect to the individual offending rates, however, there are no statistically significant differences between female gang and nongang members. Nongang females who were involved in delinquent activity, whether assault, theft, or drug use, reported nearly the same level of activity. Male gang members, however, had individual offending rates that were two to three times greater than those of nongang males involved in each specific activity, with the exception of drug sales. To illustrate the value of examining both prevalence and individual offending rates, we interpret the street-level offending data for males. While there were only 53 male gang members, 85 percent of them (45 members) reported involvement in street offenses. Those 45 gang members reported committing an average of 22.3 offenses per person. This translates into 1,003 (45 x 22.3 = 1,003.5) offenses.[9] For the nongang members, only 18 percent of the 511, or 92 males, reported committing street crimes. And, they reported committing only 8.3 offenses per person, for a total of 764 offenses. Thus, while male gang members accounted for only 33 percent of street offenders in year 4, they reported committing 57 percent of street offenses.

Additional analyses were conducted to determine if the level of gang involvement was associated with levels of offending. Gang members were categorized as core or peripheral members based on their responses to the question: How would you describe your position in the gang? All those indicating that they were leaders or one of the top persons were classified as core members. All others were considered as peripheral members. No age or sex differences were found between the core and peripheral members. More important, and perhaps somewhat surprising, introduction of this control did not result in any statistically significant differences between the two levels of gang involvement and self-reported delinquency. That is, the peripheral members reported the same level of delinquent activity as did the core members.

With respect to gang activity, gang members were asked a series of questions about the kinds of activities in which the gang was involved. Given our definition of gangs and desire to describe *delinquent* gangs, the responses listed below confirm that in addition to being delinquent gangs, the *perception* of gang members is that members of their gangs are involved in a wide range of illegal activity. While fights with other gangs is the most frequently mentioned form of illegal activity, approximately three-fourths of the gang members reported that their gang was involved in the following: robberies, joyriding, assaults of other people, thefts of more than $50, and drug sales. Clearly, illegal activities are a prominent part of the *perceived* gang experience, and these descriptions coincide with the self-reported levels of delinquency discussed above. It is interesting, however, that only 30 percent of male and 18 percent of female gang members indicated in the self-report inventory that they themselves were involved in drug sales during the preceding year.

Longitudinal Analyses

With four years of longitudinal data available for 85 percent of the original sample, it becomes possible to examine the stability of gang membership. Consistent with the research literature (e.g., Hagedorn 1988; Klein 1971; Short & Strodbeck 1965; Thornberry et al. 1993; Vigil 1988; Yablonsky 1959, 1963), we found gang membership to lack stability.[10] Of the 90 gang youths for whom we have complete data for all four years, 67 percent were members in only one year, 24 percent belonged for two years, 6 percent belonged for three years, and only 3 percent belonged for all four years.

A major purpose of this paper is to address the temporal ordering of delinquency and gang membership. That is, are gang members more delinquent prior to becoming gang members or is the heightened level of delinquent activity contemporaneous with gang membership? And, perhaps equally important, what is the delinquency level of gang members in years following their departure from the gang? Answers to these questions help identify gang influences on behavior and address the often debated theoretical issue of "feathering versus flocking." [The issue here is whether "birds of a feather flock together" or whether the flocking itself produces homogeneity (and increased delinquency) among otherwise heterogeneous youths.] Table 4.3 summarizes the relationship between gang membership and street-level offending during the four years examined. This particular analysis is restricted to those youths in the three oldest cohorts for whom complete longitudinal data were available (N = 730).

Annual prevalence data illustrate that, overall, gang members were particularly likely to be involved in street offenses during the year in which they were gang members, with lower levels of involvement both before and after their time in the gang. However, the indication is that regardless of their year of membership, youths who have been gang members at some point in time have higher prevalence rates for street offending than do youths who have never belonged to a gang. Among year 1 gang members, 72 percent were classified as street offenders. By years 2, 3, and 4, when these youth were no longer in a gang, the percentage of those youths who were street offenders had decreased substantially and was only slightly higher than the prevalence rate for nongang youths. For year 2 gang members, 23 percent were classified as street offenders in year 1, 65 percent in year 2 (when they were gang members), and then 32 percent and 35 percent, respectively, in the two subsequent years when they were no longer in the gang. For youths who were gang members during year 3 or year 4, a gradual increase in the number of street offenders

Table 4.3 Prevalence of Street Offending Among Gang and Nongang Members Controlling for Year of Membership (N = 730)

Year of Gang Membership[a]	N[b]	Prevalence of Street Offending			
		Year 1	Year 2	Year 3	Year 4
Nongang	640	70	72	94	80
		.11	.11	.15	.13
Year 1 Only	10	7	1	2	3
		.72	.09	.20	.28
Year 2 Only	9	2	6	3	3
		.23	.65	.32	.35
Year 3 Only	10	1	2	8	5
		.09	.21	.77	.53
Year 4 Only	31	3	8	12	23
		.10	.25	.39	.74
Years 3 and 4	10	4	7	9	9
		.44	.73	.91	.88
Years 2, 3, and 4[c]	5	3	3	5	5
Years 1, 2, 3, and 4[c]	3	2	3	3	2

Notes: These data are weighted to represent the stratified sample. As a result, the integral values are approximates and do not always provide the exact percentage.

a. These refer to consecutive years of membership. An additional 12 youths reported gang membership during 2 nonconsecutive years.

b. The N reflects those cases for which four years of complete data are available. For gang members, complete four-year data are available for 90 of 112 (80%) youths. For nongang youths, complete four-year data are available for 640 of 729 (88%) youths.

c. Samples are too small to allow calculation of reliable prevalence estimates.

can be seen prior to their joining the gang, and then a sharp increase in the prevalence rate over the year immediately preceding gang membership (from 21 percent to 77 percent for year 3 gang members and from 39 percent to 74 percent for year 4 members). The prevalence rates of street offending for stable gang members, that is, those reporting gang membership for two or more consecutive years, exceed those of the transient, one-year-only members.

In Table 4.3 we controlled for the actual years of gang membership and the prevalence of street offending, which permitted examination of stable and transient members. Due to the low number of stable gang members and interest in other delinquency measures, in Table 4.4 we report differences in the prevalence rate between gang members and nongang youths for two types of delinquency (street-level offending and other serious offenses) and illicit drug use. In this table, the behavior of gang members in a specific year is tracked for the four-year study period. This means that the stable gang members are included in multiple years, which inflates the overall pattern. However, we thought it inappropriate to exclude stable members from the analysis.

In Table 4.4, *year of gang membership* refers to all those individuals who reported belonging to a gang that year. *Prevalence of offending* refers to whether these individuals reported engaging in any of the specified behaviors in each year. Consistent with the detailed findings for street offending reported in Table 4.3, prevalence rates for each type of behavior are highest during the gang member's year of actual gang membership. For example, among the year 3 gang members, 43 percent committed street offenses in year 1, 55 percent in year 2, 90 percent in year 3, and 77 percent in year 4. Each of these prevalence rates is substantially greater than the comparable annual rate for those youths who were not gang members in year 3, all of which were between [13 percent and 15 percent]. In separate analyses controlling for gang membership status (i.e., transient and stable), similar differences between gang and nongang youths were found, although the differences between transient members and nongang youth were less pronounced.

Examination of these prevalence rates across years permits an assessment of the temporal relationship between gang membership and delinquency. . . . In Table 4.4 there is some evidence to support the selection or "birds of a feather" explanation. Gang members have higher prevalence rates of involvement in delinquency in years preceding their gang membership. Year 3 gang members,

Table 4.4 Prevalence of Street Offending, Serious Offending, and Illegal Drug Use Among Gang and Nongang Members

| Year of Gang Membership | Sample Size | | Prevalence of Offending | | | | | |
| | | | Street Offenses | | Serious Offenses | | Illicit Drug Use | |
	Gang	Nongang	Gang	Nongang	Gang	Nongang	Gang	Nongang
Year 1 Membership								
Year 1 Behavior	25	835	.85*	.15	.93*	.36	.42*	.13
Year 2 Behavior	25	766	.41*	.15	.61*	.32	.52*	.15
Year 3 Behavior	21	782	.39*	.20	.51	.36	.36*	.14
Year 4 Behavior	22	779	.40*	.19	.48	.30	.27	.19
Year 2 Membership								
Year 1 Behavior	32	757	.50*	.13	.66*	.37	.29*	.13
Year 2 Behavior	33	764	.69*	.13	.89*	.30	.47*	.13
Year 3 Behavior	30	737	.59*	.18	.68*	.35	.44*	.14
Year 4 Behavior	30	729	.63*	.18	.70*	.28	.39*	.18
Year 3 Membership								
Year 1 Behavior	31	768	.43*	.13	.53	.37	.23	.13
Year 2 Behavior	29	736	.55*	.14	.67*	.32	.42*	.13
Year 3 Behavior	32	1,059	.90*	.15	.75*	.32	.60*	.10
Year 4 Behavior	30	1,026	.77*	.15	.66*	.27	.42	.15
Year 4 Membership								
Year 1 Behavior	61	733	.33*	.13	.54*	.35	.13	.13
Year 2 Behavior	60	695	.51*	.12	.73*	.29	.34*	.14
Year 3 Behavior	65	983	.58*	.14	.65*	.31	.37*	.10
Year 4 Behavior	67	1,026	.83*	.12	.79*	.25	.56*	.13

*p < .05 (chi-square)

for example, have a higher rate of participation in street offending [43 percent compared with 13 percent], but not other serious offenses or illicit drug use, in year 1 than do nongang members. By year 2, the prevalence rates for year 3 gang members are higher than those of the nongang members for all three behaviors, and in year 3, the largest discrepancy is noted.

While rates of participation are, in fact, higher in years preceding and during gang membership, Table 4.4 also reveals that these rates of delinquent activity decline in years subsequent to gang membership.[11] By year 4, the year 1 gang members are more similar to those youths who reported never having belonged to a gang, although they still report statistically significant higher rates of participation in street offending (40 percent compared with 19 percent).

The preceding discussion focused on the prevalence of street offending and other types of delinquency among gang and nongang members. Of equal importance, and essential to the understanding of the level of delinquent behavior, is examination of individual offending rates, or lambda (i.e., average number of offenses per active offender) for these two groups (Table 4.5). As

Table 4.5 Individual Offending Rates of Street Offending, Serious Offending, and Illegal Drug Use Among Gang and Nongang Members

| | Individual Offending Rates | | | | | |
| | Street Offenses | | Serious Offenses | | Illicit Drug Use | |
Year of Gang Membership	Gang	Nongang	Gang	Nongang	Gang	Nongang
Year 1 Membership						
Year 1 Behavior	29.2*	6.8	31.4*	8.8	47.4*	15.8
Year 2 Behavior	12.9	6.8	15.0	7.9	34.1	14.9
Year 3 Behavior	7.2	5.9	9.7	5.9	13.1	14.8
Year 4 Behavior	10.7	5.2	17.6*	5.6	26.4	10.9
Year 2 Membership						
Year 1 Behavior	19.7*	4.5	17.3*	7.1	13.0	12.2
Year 2 Behavior	31.2*	7.6	32.2*	11.1	38.2*	17.4
Year 3 Behavior	9.2	8.5	15.3*	6.3	21.0	17.3
Year 4 Behavior	10.8	9.2	11.4	8.1	19.6	14.9
Year 3 Membership						
Year 1 Behavior	13.9*	2.0	12.7*	5.1	10.6	7.1
Year 2 Behavior	20.9*	2.0	24.8*	7.2	22.3*	8.0
Year 3 Behavior	34.5*	5.7	29.8*	8.3	56.8*	23.3
Year 4 Behavior	22.9*	4.2	29.4*	6.6	38.8	20.1
Year 4 Membership						
Year 1 Behavior	8.8*	1.8	9.1*	3.8	3.6	6.2
Year 2 Behavior	13.4*	1.7	22.1*	4.0	11.2	9.2
Year 3 Behavior	14.4*	2.8	13.3*	5.6	27.0*	11.6
Year 4 Behavior	19.7*	6.7	28.1*	10.0	39.5*	21.7

*$p < .05$ (t-test, separate variance estimate of t)

with prevalence rates, the individual offending rates of gang members are substantially greater than those of nongang members.[12] As with prevalence rates, gang members clearly have higher offending rates than do nongang members, but this is especially pronounced during the year in which the youths reported being a gang member (e.g., in year 2, gang members categorized as street offenders committed an average of 31.2 street offenses each, compared with 7.6 such offenses for nongang members).

Table 4.5 also reveals that the mean number of street offenses committed by gang members in years preceding their joining the gang is significantly higher than that of nongang members, but that in the years following their departure, there is a dramatic reduction, although they remain more delinquent than their nongang counterparts. By year 2, for example, there were no statistically significant differences between the year 1 gang members and those who were not gang members in year 1. Similarly, by year 3, there were no statistically significant differences for street offending and illicit drug use between the year 2 gang and nongang members.

A popular perception is that gang members are frequent drug users. During their year of membership, gang members reported significantly higher rates of marijuana and other illegal drug use. However, unlike the delinquency measures, drug use prior to and subsequent to gang membership, generally, was not found to be statistically different from the drug use of nongang youths.

In sum, while gang members had higher rates of involvement than nongang members in street offending and other serious offending not only during the year in which they were gang members but also in the years preceding membership, the rate is particularly high and pronounced during the gang years. These higher rates of individual offending, however, decrease substantially once the youths leave the gang. In analyses not presented, this trend is especially pronounced for males in the sample. Illegal drug use fits the same pattern—it is highest during the gang year. However, drug use by gang members is not significantly different from that of nongang members in years when they're not affiliated with a gang.

■   **Summary and Discussion**

In the preceding analyses, we addressed three issues: (1) the prevalence and demographic characteristics of gang members in a general survey of urban youths; (2) the relationship between delinquency and drug use among gang youths; and (3) the temporal relationship between offending and gang membership. With regard to the number of urban youths who belong to gangs, two observations should be made. First, even in a sample of high-risk urban youths, gang membership is a statistically infrequent phenomenon. Second, depending on the definition of gang used, different estimates of gang membership are obtained. Prior to controlling for the criminal conduct of gangs, estimates of gang membership were in excess of 5 percent during each study year. However, when the analysis was restricted to youths who belonged to delinquent gangs, slightly less than 3 percent of the total sample during years 1 through 3 could then be classified as gang members. By year 4, when the cohorts were aged 12 to 18 years, the number of youths reporting to be members of delinquent gangs had increased to almost 7 percent. Such definitionally induced discrepancies in prevalence of gang membership highlight the need to establish consensus on an operational definition of gangs.

As has been repeatedly argued by Klein and Maxson (1989) and more recently by Spergel and Chance (1991), there is considerable need for a uniform definition of gang and gang behavior. Whether from a research or policy perspective, it is important that a common consensus be reached. While the earlier calls for a uniform definition emphasizing jurisdictional differences among law enforcement agencies, our research suggests that a common definition should be employed by survey researchers. A uniform definition of gangs and gang behavior would be a point of departure for a better understanding of a phenomenon that may well be substantially distorted because of a lack of a common means for studying, describing, and regulating gang behavior.

The importance of general surveys is highlighted by examination of the demographic characteristics of gang members. Contrary to much prior research on gangs, females were found to be quite active in gangs (approximately 25 percent of gang members during the four-year study period were female). While this is higher than the prevailing stereotype, it is consistent with Fagan's (1990) and Campbell's (1991) estimates. Why is it that so many studies fail to report any substantial involvement of females in gangs? It may be, as Campbell (1991:vii) suggests, that writings about gangs, as well as other social science topics, historically have been written by men about men. Thus, female gang membership may well have been systematically underreported in prior research endeavors. A casual examination of early gang research provides some evidence for this argument. Cohen (1955) and Cloward and Ohlin (1960), for example, excluded females from their research and conceptualizations.

A second possibility is that the reliance on official data or purposive samples of gang members has resulted in a biased representation of not only gang membership, but gang behavior as well. Yet another possible explanation may be associated with the sampling or site selection in the DYS and other general surveys. In any localized survey project, it is possible that a particular site or sample is atypical and nonrepresentative of other populations or sites. However, given the similarity of findings between Fagan's (1990) three-city study and the DYS, the high percentage of male gang members may be an accurate accounting of gang membership in the late 1980s. A fourth possibility is that there has been a historical change in female delinquency or in the role of females in gangs. With respect to this issue, Huizinga and Esbensen (1991) reported no change in self-reported levels of offending among two samples of urban females, one from 1978 and the other from 1989.

Another characteristic of gang membership found to be contrary to widely held, media-promoted stereotypes is the notion that youths become gang members for life. While media accounts generally portray gangs as surrogate families for disenfranchised youths, this view is not supported by our research nor by the majority of gang research of the past three decades (e.g., Fagan 1989; Hagedorn 1988; Klein 1971; Short & Strodbeck 1965; Thornberry et al. 1993; Vigil 1988; Yablonsky 1959, 1963). Very few of the youths in the DYS survey reported being in a gang for more than one year. And many of those youths in a gang indicated that they would like *not* to be a gang member and expected to leave the gang in the future. It appears that the majority of gang members are peripheral or transitory members who drift in and out of the gang.

With regard to involvement in delinquent activity, gang members were found to be considerably more active in all types of delinquency, including drug sales and drug use, than were nongang members. It is important, however, to provide a caveat concerning gang involvement in drug sales. As concluded by Klein et al. (1991), while drug sales/distribution is an activity engaged in by individual gang members, we did not find evidence that drug sales was an organized gang activity involving all gang members. That is, although 80 percent of the year 4 gang members indicated that the gang was involved in drug sales, only 28 percent of these very gang members reported that they sold drugs. Further, drug sales is only one of a variety of illegal activities in which the gang is involved. As reported by Fagan (1989), we found that all of the gangs were involved in what Klein (1984) has called "cafeteria-style" delinquency.

The temporal relationship between offending and gang membership is important, and one that can best be examined with longitudinal data of a general population. Participant observation of existing gang members relies on selective retrospective information and generally excludes comparison groups. Cross-sectional surveys cannot examine the developmental sequences that we believe are necessary to explain the process of gang recruitment.

The longitudinal analyses reported here indicate that involvement of gang members in delinquency and drug use is rather strongly patterned. While gang members had higher rates of involvement than nongang members in street crime and other serious forms of offending even before joining the gang, their prevalence and individual offending rates were substantially higher during the actual year of membership. Similar results were also reported in a study of high-risk youths in Rochester, New York (Thornberry et al. 1993). Their findings for "stable" gang members mirrored those reported here. Their "transient" gang members, however, did not appear to have significantly higher rates of offending than nongang members in years prior to or following gang membership. Our findings, in conjunction with those from the Rochester study, lead us to conclude that it is not solely individual characteristics that are associated with higher levels of involvement in street crime. Rather, there may well be factors within the gang milieu that contribute to the criminal behavior of gang members.

Thus, while the high prevalence and individual offending rates prior to gang membership may lead one to espouse the view that they are supportive of a social control perspective, which maintains that people select others of similar values as friends (e.g., Hirschi 1969), that may be premature. [Social control postulates that youths with weak ties to conventional others, institutions, and beliefs will be attracted to each other. This theory will be discussed in more detail later in the book; see especially Chapter 11.] Given that the highest rates of offending occurred during gang years, these data may be more supportive of a [social] learning perspective, which maintains [that] behavior is learned within particular groups and settings [that reinforce delinquency] (e.g., Burgess & Akers 1966; Elliott and Menard 1996; Sutherland & Cressey 1970). [Social learning theory will be discussed in more detail later in the book; see especially Chapter 7.] A third possibility is what Thornberry et al. (1993:59) have referred to as an "enhancement" model, in which both processes are operative. Without a test of theoretically relevant variables, such conclusions are mere projection. The temporal ordering of such key factors as peer group norms and values and respondent behavior must be examined prior to going beyond the mere speculation stage. Elliott and Menard (1996) have documented with National Youth Survey data that the acquisition of delinquent friends generally precedes the onset of delinquency. The data we have presented suggest that delinquent involvement precedes gang membership. It is here that we do not want to make the tempting juxtaposition and equate gang membership with delinquent friends, for it may well be that gang membership is but a more formalized form of co-offending that was initiated within a delinquent peer group in prior years. Answers to such theoretically important issues should be tested fully, and we hope that our research provides a basis for subsequent work on this issue.

From a policy standpoint, our findings suggest, at least tentatively, that gang intervention strategies should focus not only on decreasing the influence of gangs on individual gang member behavior, but also on the conditions that foster gang development. Although gang members are more highly delinquent than their nongang peers, the trend toward increasing delinquency is prevalent at least two years prior to gang initiation. An important aim should thus be to retard this initial escalation of delinquent activity and disrupt gang effects before peer group behavior becomes formalized within the gang environment.

Appendix 4.1 Self-Report Delinquency and Drug Use Scales

Street Delinquency
1. Stole or tried to steal money or things worth more than $50 but less than $100.
2. Stole or tried to steal money or things worth more than $100.
3. Stole or tried to steal a motor vehicle.
4. Went into or tried to go into a building to steal something.
5. Attacked someone with a weapon or with the idea of seriously hurting or killing him.
6. Used weapons, force, or strongarm methods to get money or things from people.
7. Physically hurt or threatened to hurt someone to get that person to have sex.
8. Been involved in gang fights.
9. Snatched someone's purse or wallet or picked someone's pocket.
10. Stole something from a car.
11. Sold marijuana.
12. Sold hard drugs.
13. Knowingly bought, sold, or held stolen goods or tried to do these things.

Other Serious Delinquency
1. Stole or tried to steal money or things worth more than $5 but less than $50.
2. Stole or tried to steal money or things worth less than $5.
3. Went joyriding.
4. Hit someone with the idea of hurting him.
5. Threw objects such as rocks or bottles at people.
6. Had or tried to have sexual relations with someone against the person's will.
7. Carried a hidden weapon.
8. Purposely damaged or destroyed property belonging to someone else.
9. Purposely set fire to a house, building, car, or other property or tried to do so.
10. Used checks illegally or used a slug or fake money to pay for something.
11. Used or tried to use credit or bank cards without the owner's permission.

Minor Delinquency
1. Avoided paying for things such as movies, bus or subway rides, food, or computer services.
2. Lied about your age to get into someplace or to buy something.
3. Ran away from home.
4. Skipped classes without an excuse.
5. Hitchhiked where it was illegal to do so.
6. Been loud, rowdy, or unruly in public place.
7. Begged for money or things from strangers.
8. Been drunk in a public place.
9. Been paid for having sexual relations with someone.

Alcohol Use
1. Drank beer.
2. Drank wine.
3. Drank hard liquor.

Marijuana Use
1. Used marijuana or hashish.

Other Drugs
1. Used tranquilizers such as valium, librium, thorazine, miltown, equanil, or meprobamate.
2. Used barbiturates, downers, reds, yellows, or blues.
3. Used amphetamines, uppers, ups, speed, pep pills, or bennies.
4. Used hallucinogens, LSD, acid, peyote, mescaline, or psilocybin.
5. Used cocaine, or coke other than crack.
6. Used crack.
7. Used heroin.
8. Used angel dust or PCP.

▦ Notes

1. One common problem, for example, is whether any crime committed by a gang member should be labeled a gang crime regardless of the circumstances surrounding the offense. Using law enforcement data from Chicago and Los Angeles, Maxson and Klein (1990) examined gang homicide rates by applying the different definitions of "gang-related" criminal activity used in those two cities. Using the more narrow definition of gang-related homicides employed by the Chicago police (i.e., "a killing is considered gang-related only if it occurs in the course of an explicitly defined collective encounter between two or more gangs," Maxson and Klein [1990:77]) would reduce the gang homicide rate in Los Angeles by about half. The fact that such discrepancies in prevalence rates can be derived simply by different definitional criteria should cause researchers, theorists, and policymakers substantial discomfort.

2. This research is part of the Program of Research on the Causes and Correlates of Delinquency, with companion projects at the University at Albany-SUNY and the University of Pittsburgh.

3. An apparently recent development in American gang structure or organization is that gangs are no longer confined to "chronic" gang cities but are making an appearance in "emerging" gang cities, often small and medium-sized cities with no history of gang activity (Spergel 1990:182). According to Lou Lopez, former commander of the Denver Police Department Gang Intervention Program, "the gang influence can be traced back to the late 1970s when Denver Police officers started to notice young Hispanic youth dressed in 'chollo' attire" (Lopez 1989:i).

4. A number of block groups defined as socially disorganized did not have high crime rates, and, therefore, were excluded from the sample. Conversely, block groups that had high crime rates but were not socially disorganized according to our analysis also were excluded from the high-risk sample.

5. Given that the survey was conducted in "high-risk" neighborhoods with high rates of mobility, these high retention rates are a testament to the diligence and expertise of the field staff involved in tracking respondents throughout the survey.

6. Some concern may be raised by the relatively young age range included in this sample (i.e., ages 11 through 18). We acknowledge that others have documented the recent trend of youths remaining in gangs well into their twenties and even thirties. Clearly, the DYS sample is an adolescent sample and may not be representative of gangs in general. As a result of the sampling frame, this sample may contain more "transient" members than would an older sample. Analyses of transient and stable members, however, did not produce different results. . . .

7. The drug sale measure consists of two items from the street offending scale. We ran specific analyses to verify that these drug sale items were not "driving" the street offender results.

8. Throughout the analyses reported in this paper, we truncated the self-reported frequency of offending at 99 in order to minimize the effect of "outliers." We also limited the frequency analysis to active offenders and thus use the terms individual offending rates and lambda interchangeably throughout the text to refer to the average offending rate among active offenders. For a discussion of lambda, consult Blumstein et al. (1988).

9. Given what is known about the extent of co-offending among juveniles, it is exceedingly difficult, if not impossible, to make a reasonable transition from offender-specific data to offense data. For example, the fact that 20 youths reported committing an aggravated assault does not necessarily mean that 20 assaults were committed. For discussion of this co-offending issue, consult, for example, Elliott et al. (1985), Fagan (1990), Johnson (1979), and Krohn (1986).

10. In their study of high-risk youth in Rochester, for example, Thornberry et al. (1993) found that 55 percent of gang members were members for only one year.

11. Analyses in which the sample was disaggregated by gender produced similar results for males. Female gang members, however, only had higher prevalence rates than female nonmembers during the actual year of membership.

12. Once again, analyses disaggregated by gender reveal that these differences are more pronounced for male gang members than female gang members. While males seem to be on a trajectory of increasingly higher rates of offending in years prior to gang initiation, as with prevalence rates, females appear to have higher rates of offending primarily only during their actual year of gang membership.

▧ References

Asbury, Herbert. 1927. *The Gangs of New York.* New York: Capricorn.

Blumstein, Alfred, Jacqueline Cohen & David Farrington. 1988. "Criminal Career Research: Its Value for Criminology." *Criminology* 26:1–35.

Bookin-Weiner, Hedy & Ruth Horowitz. 1983. "The End of the Gang: Fact or Fad?" *Criminology* 21:585–602.

Bowker, Lee H. & Malcolm W. Klein. 1983. "The Etiology of Female Juvenile Delinquency and Gang Membership: A Test of Psychological and Social Structural Explanations." *Adolescence* 18:740–51.

Burgess, Robert L. & Ronald L. Akers. 1966. "A Differential Association-Reinforcement Theory of Criminal Behavior." *Social Problems* 14:128–47.

Campbell, Anne. 1990. "Female Participation in Gangs." In C. R. Huff (ed.), *Gangs in America.* Newbury Park, CA: Sage.

———. 1991. *The Girls in the Gang.* 2d ed. Cambridge, MA: Basil Blackwell.

Cloward, Richard A. & Lloyd E. Ohlin. 1960. *Delinquency and Opportunity: A Theory of Delinquent Gangs.* New York: Free Press.

Cohen, Albert. 1955. *Delinquent Boys: The Culture of the Gang.* Glencoe, IL: Free Press.

Covey, Herbert C., Scott Menard & Robert J. Franzese. 1992. *Juvenile Gangs.* Springfield, IL: Charles C. Thomas.

Elliott, Delbert S., David Huizinga & Suzanne S. Ageton. 1985. *Explaining Delinquency and Drug Use.* Beverly Hills, CA: Sage.

Elliott, Delbert S. & Scott Menard. 1996. "Delinquent Friends and Delinquent Behavior: Temporal and Developmental Patterns." In J. D. Hawkins (ed.), *Current Theories of Crime and Deviance.* Cambridge: Cambridge University Press.

Esbensen, Finn-Aage & David Huizinga. 1990. "Community Structure and Drug Use: From a Social Disorganization Perspective." *Justice Quarterly* 7:691–709.

Esbensen, Finn-Aage, David Huizinga & Anne W. Weiher. 1993. "Gang and Non-gang Youth: Differences in Explanatory Variables." *Journal of Contemporary Criminal Justice* 9:94–116.

Fagan, Jeffrey. 1989. "The Social Organization of Drug Use and Drug Dealing among Urban Gangs." *Criminology* 27:633–99.

———. 1990. "Social Processes of Delinquency and Drug Use among Urban Gangs." In C. R. Huff (ed.), *Gangs in America.* Newbury Park, CA: Sage.

Giordano, Peggy C. 1978. "Girls, Guys, and Gangs: The Changing Social Context of Female Delinquency." *Journal of Criminal Law & Criminology* 69:126–32.

Gurule, Jimmy. 1991. "The OJP Initiative on Gangs: Drugs and Violence in America." *NIJ Reports* 224:4–5.

Hagedorn, John M. 1988. *People and Folks: Gangs, Crime and the Underclass in a Rustbelt City.* Chicago: Lakeview Press.

Harris, Mary G. 1988. *Cholas: Latino Girls and Gangs.* New York: AMS.

Hirschi, Travis. 1969. *Causes of Delinquency.* Berkeley: University of California Press.

Huizinga, David & Delbert S. Elliott. 1986. "Reassessing the Reliability and Validity of Self-report Delinquency Measures." *Journal of Quantitative Criminology* 2: 293–327.

Huizinga, David & Finn-Aage Esbensen. 1991. "Are There Changes in Female Delinquency and Are There Changes in Underlying Explanatory Factors?" Paper presented at the annual meeting of the American Society of Criminology, San Francisco.

Johnson, Richard E. 1979. *Juvenile Delinquency and Its Origins.* Cambridge: Cambridge University Press.

Klein, Malcolm W. 1971. *Street Gangs and Street Workers.* Englewood Cliffs, NJ: Prentice- Hall.

———. 1984. "Offense Specialization and Versatility among Juveniles." *British Journal of Criminology* 24:185–94.

Klein, Malcolm W. & Cheryl L. Maxson. 1989. "Street Gang Violence." In N. Weiner & M. Wolfgang (eds.), *Violent Crime, Violent Criminals.* Newbury Park, CA: Sage.

Klein, Malcolm W., Cheryl L. Maxson & Lea C. Cunningham. 1991. "'Crack,' Street Gangs, and Violence." *Criminology* 29:623–50.

Krohn, Marvin D. 1986. "The Web of Conformity: A Network Approach to the Explanation of Delinquent Behavior." *Social Problems* 33:581–593.

Lopez, Lou. 1989. *Gangs in Denver.* Denver, CO: Denver Public Schools.

MacLeod, Jay. 1987. *Ain't No Makin' It: Leveled Aspirations in a Low-Income Neighborhood.* Boulder, CO: Westview Press.

Maxson, Cheryl L. & Malcolm W. Klein. 1990. "Street Gang Violence: Twice as Great or Half as Great?" In C. R. Huff (ed.), *Gangs in America.* Newbury Park, CA: Sage.

Miller, Walter B. 1958. "Lower Class Culture as a Generating Milieu for Gang Delinquency." *Journal of Social Issues* 14:5–19.

———. 1974. "American Youth Gangs: Past and Present." In A. Blumberg (ed.), *Current Perspectives on Criminal Behavior.* New York: Knopf.

Moore, Joan W. 1978. *Homeboys: Gangs, Drugs, and Prison in the Barrios of Los Angeles.* Philadelphia: Temple University Press.

Morash, Merry. 1983. "Gangs, Groups, and Delinquency." *British Journal of Criminology* 23:309–31.

Puffer, J. Adams. 1912. *The Boy and His Gang.* Boston: Houghton Mifflin.

Quicker, John C. 1983. *Homegirls: Characterizing Chicana Gangs.* San Pedro, CA: International University Press.

Short, James F. & Fred L. Strodbeck. 1965. *Group Processes and Gang Delinquency.* Chicago: University of Chicago Press.

Spergel, Irving A. 1966. *Street Gang Work: Theory and Practice.* Reading, MA: Addison-Wesley.

———. 1990. "Youth Gangs: Continuity and Change." In N. Morris & M. Tonry (eds.), *Crime and Justice: An Annual Review of Research.* Chicago: University of Chicago Press.

Spergel, Irving A. & Ronald L. Chance. 1991. "National Youth Gang Suppression and Intervention program." *NIJ Reports* 224:21–24.

Sullivan, Mercer L. 1989. *Getting Paid: Youth Crime and Work in the Inner City.* Ithaca, NY: Cornell University Press.

Sutherland, Edwin H. & Donald R. Cressey. 1970. *Criminology.* New York: Lippincott.

Taylor, Carl S. 1990. "Gang Imperialism." In C. R. Huff (ed.), *Gangs in America*. New-
    bury Park, CA: Sage.
Thornberry, Terence, Marvin D. Krohn, Alan J. Lizotte & Deborah Chard-Wierschem.
    1993. "The Role of Juvenile Gangs in Facilitating Delinquent Behavior." *Journal
    of Research in Crime & Delinquency* 30:55–87.
Thrasher, Frederick M. 1927. *The Gang: A Study of One Thousand Three Hundred
    Thirteen Gangs in Chicago*. Chicago: University of Chicago Press.
Vigil, James D. 1988. *Barrio Gangs: Street Life and Identity in Southern California*.
    Austin: University of Texas Press.
Winfree, L. Thomas, Teresa Vigil & G. Larry Mays. 1991. "Social Learning Theory
    and Youth Gangs: A Comparison of High School Students and Adjudicated Delin-
    quents." Paper presented at the annual meeting of the American Society of Crim-
    inology, San Francisco.
Wolfgang, Marvin, Robert M. Figlio, Paul E. Tracy & Simon L. Singer. 1985. *The Na-
    tional Survey of Crime Severity*. Washington, DC: US Government Printing Office.
Yablonsky, Lewis. 1959. "The Delinquent Gang as a Near Group." *Social Problems*
    7:108–17.
———. 1963. *The Violent Gang*. New York: Macmillan.

5

The Impact of Sex Composition on Gangs and Gang Member Delinquency

Dana Peterson, Jody Miller, and Finn-Aage Esbensen

Using self-report data from a sample of eighth-grade students in eleven cities who participated in the national Gang Resistance Education and Training program, Dana Peterson, Jody Miller, and Finn-Aage Esbensen examine the question of how and why the sex composition of gangs affects gang members' rates of delinquency. They found significant differences between "gang members' characterizations of their gangs' organizations and activities, as well as . . . their individual participation in delinquency," depending on whether they were members of all male gangs, majority male gangs, all female gangs, majority female gangs, or sex balanced gangs. The authors explore competing hypotheses about the sex composition of gangs to interpret their findings.

THE ORGANIZATIONAL STRUCTURE OF AMERICAN YOUTH GANGS IS A topic of considerable interest to researchers and policymakers. Although gangs are often discussed as though they were a monolithic phenomenon, researchers have paid increasing attention to variations across gangs, using a variety of frameworks to classify gangs according to their organization, duration, and activities [see Fagan 1989; Spergel & Curry 1993; Taylor 1990]. . . . In perhaps the most comprehensive study to date, Klein and Maxson (1996) distinguish among [different] types of gangs . . . according to a series of dimensions: size, age range, duration, subgroupings, territoriality, and crime patterns.

Despite this attention to organizational structure, few studies have considered the impact of sex composition on gangs and their members, and only recently have researchers moved beyond Miller's (1975) now decades-old

"The Impact of Sex Composition on Gangs and Gang Member Delinquency," *Criminology* 39, no. 2 (2001): 411–439. Reprinted by permission of the American Society of Criminology.

typification of female gang involvement as occurring within auxiliary, mixed, or independent groups. However, there are reasons to consider the issue an important one, not just for female gang members, but also for males. Scholars in the sociology of organizations have long recognized sex composition as a key feature shaping interactional dynamics within groups (e.g., see Blalock 1967; Blau 1977; Gutek 1985; Kanter 1977a, 1977b). Moreover, several recent qualitative studies of female gang involvement suggest that the sex composition of gangs, as well as other organizational factors, have an impact on girls' experiences and activities within these groups (Joe-Laidler & Hunt 1997; Miller 2001; Nurge 1998). Another recent study also points to the importance of sex composition for understanding some facets of male gang involvement (Miller & Brunson 2000).

Using a quantitative approach, this paper adds to the small body of literature on the topic. Drawing from a sample of male and female gang youths from 11 cities, we examine whether sex composition within gangs has an impact on gang members' characterizations of their gangs' organization and activities, as well as on their individual participation in delinquency. By focusing specifically on sex as a structural feature of gangs, our goal is to contribute to a more complex picture of its impact on gangs and their male and female members.

■ Sex Composition and Its Impact within Groups

A central research question in organizational sociology is the impact of demographic composition on the normative features of groups as well as majority and minority group members' experiences and behaviors. Earlier theoretical approaches were *generic,* in that they suggest that any group in the numeric minority will face similar experiences based on their proportion within a given group (see Blau 1977; Kanter 1977a, 1977b). More recently, minority group members' social position is also recognized as an important consideration. These *institutional* approaches suggest that members of numeric minorities will have different experiences within groups, "depending upon the social significance of particular demographic characteristics in society at large and in the particular organization" (Konrad et al. 1992:115; see also Gutek 1985). Thus, theorists adopting an institutional approach argue that females in majority male groups will have different experiences than will males in majority female groups, largely because of asymmetrical social definitions of masculinity and femininity and their links with sexual inequality.

Several competing theoretical approaches have been brought to bear on the impact of sex ratios within groups, each of which has received some empirical support. Blau's (1977) examination of the quantitative properties of social structure is a purely generic theory of the impact of group proportion on intergroup interaction. He suggests that the amount of intergroup association between two groups, and thus the nature of majority-minority group interactions, can be predicted based on the statistical probabilities associated with group proportion. Specifically, Blau states that "the rate of intergroup associations between two groups is higher for the smaller of the two" (1977:250). That is, when females are a smaller proportion of the total group, for purely numeric reasons, they will have more interactions with male group members, although male members will have few interactions with females. When females are a larger proportion of the total group, they will have fewer opportunities to interact with male members and will have more interactions with other females. In these more heterogeneous groups—where males are not a clear majority— male group members will have increased interactions with females and intergroup interactions overall will be increased. Further, Blau suggests that intergroup contact improves minority/majority relations:

> When group differences are conspicuous and intergroup relations are rare, group pressures [on dominant group members] are likely to arise that further discourage the deviant practice of associating with members of the out-group. . . . [I]ncreases in heterogeneity, by making intergroup relations less rare, weaken in-group pressures that inhibit sociable interaction with members of out-groups and thus lessen discrimination against out-groups. (1977:80–81)

Consequently, Blau's theory would suggest that heterogeneous groups should be those with the most cooperative between-gender relations (see also South et al. 1983).

One of Blau's predictions is that males in primarily male groups will have fewer interactions with female members than will males in groups with more females. Likewise, in her seminal work on sex ratios and organizations, Kanter distinguishes between skewed groups, in which "there is a large preponderance of one type over another" such that individuals in the numerically smaller type are tokens, versus tilted or balanced groups, in which the numeric minority has a larger and sizeable representation within the group (1977a:966; 1977b). She suggests that when groups "begin to move toward less extreme distributions, dominants are just a majority and tokens a minority. Minority members are potentially allies, can form coalitions, and can affect the culture of the group" (Kanter 1977a:966). Kanter extends Blau's theory through an examination of the effects—in addition to the ratio of contacts—of token membership in skewed groups. She argues that the most extreme effects of minority membership will be experienced among tokens, and she reports that female tokens in primarily male groups are subject to three perceptual phenomena: "visibility (tokens capture a disproportionate awareness share), polarization (differences between tokens and dominants are exaggerated), and assimilation (tokens' attributes are distorted to fit preexisting generalizations about their social type)" (Kanter 1977a:965). Thus, she argues that female tokens in primarily male groups will be more marginalized and less accepted within the group than will women in either tilted or balanced groups.

Kanter's theory has received some empirical support when the minority group under examination is female (e.g., see Spangler et al. 1978; Yoder et al. 1983), whereas studies of males as token minorities fail to support Kanter's hypotheses (e.g., see Fairhurst & Snavely 1983b; Heikes 1991). Much of the research testing Kanter's approach offers credence to the *institutional* rather than the *generic* character of the impact of demographic composition: It is not necessarily pure numbers that affect the experiences of group members, but a combination of the number of males and females and other factors, such as the status of group members, gender stereotyping, and the activities and goals of the group (e.g., see Fairhurst & Snavely 1983a, 1983b; Gutek 1985; Konrad et al. 1992; Williams 1992; Yoder 1991). Particularly in groups that are male-dominated and associated with stereotypically masculine traits, females may have an especially difficult time integrating in the group (Gutek 1985).

An alternative set of hypotheses emerges from Blalock's (1967) majority group power theory. Researchers who have applied Blalock's theory to sex and gender suggest a backlash effect. That is, when women's numbers increase within a group setting, their presence is experienced as a greater threat than when they remain a token minority. Consequently, majority group members (in this case, males) are more likely to take action against members of the minority group (females) in what Kanter calls tilted or balanced groups. Thus, although Kanter argues that women in tilted or balanced groups are less marginalized because they are better able to shape the culture of the group, and Blau would suggest increased and improved relations between women and men in such groups, Blalock's theory instead would suggest greater social and behavioral distance between males and females as they approach more equal numbers in groups.

Majority group power theory is predicated on the assumption of competition between majority (male) and minority (female) group members, such that an encroaching number of minority members will be perceived as a threat to the higher status group. This threat will be dealt with by increased negative action and control in an effort to maintain the dominant group's position. By contrast, the theory would also predict that when females remain tokens in primarily male groups, they must rely on males for access to the group's resources and, thus, do not pose a competitive threat. Majority group power theory has been particularly well supported in the literature on race (e.g., Baker et al. 1989; Chiricos et al. 1997; Covington & Taylor 1991; Wordes & Bynum 1995), but has also received some empirical support with regard to sex (see South et al. 1982).

The theories reviewed thus far have been tested in settings such as organizations, work groups, and ecological communities. They provide consistent evidence, despite conflicting findings, that "purely numeric factors can and do exert fundamental influences on patterns of social interaction" (South et al. 1982:598). Whether these factors operate in the ways predicted by Blau (1977), Kanter (1977a, 1977b), Blalock (1967), or others is a focal point of debate.

Some scholars suggest the issue should be examined in the specific context of the particular groups in question, particularly given evidence against the utility of a generic approach (Konrad et al. 1992; South et al. 1983). Although this body of research demonstrates the importance of groups' sex composition as a line of inquiry, how sex composition affects gang members' activities, and whether it is associated with other organizational features of gangs, is an issue that has received little empirical examination. In the next section, we further document the utility of such an approach.

■ Sex, Gender, and Gang Involvement

Research consistently indicates that both males and females are involved in gangs in fairly large numbers (see Bjerregaard & Smith 1993; Esbensen & Deschenes 1998). Estimates suggest that males account for approximately 54 percent to 80 percent of gang members, and females 20 percent to 46 percent (Esbensen & Huizinga 1993; Esbensen & Winfree 1998; Winfree et al. 1992). There is also evidence of variation in sex composition across gangs. Although standard approaches for categorizing (presumably or implicitly) male gangs continue to focus on a broad range of issues exclusive of sex (e.g., see Jankowski 1991; Klein & Maxson 1996; Spergel & Curry 1993; Taylor 1990), studies of female gang types focus specifically on sex organization, most often drawing from Miller's (1975) tripartite classification: (1) mixed-sex gangs with both female and male members, (2) female gangs that are affiliated with male gangs, which he refers to as "auxiliary" gangs, and (3) independent female gangs (but see Hagedorn & Devitt 1999; Nurge 1998).

There are several case studies of these various gang types (see Fleisher 1998; Lauderback et al. 1992; Quicker 1983), but less evidence of their prevalence. Curry's (1997) study of female gang members in three cities found that only 6.4 percent of girls described being in autonomous female gangs, whereas 57.3 percent described their gangs as mixed-sex, and another 36.4 percent said they were in female gangs affiliated with male gangs. Miller (2001) and Nurge (1998) report that the majority of girls in their studies were in groups that were mixed-sex rather than "auxiliary" or female-only, but with varying sex compositions. For example, of the 42 members of mixed-sex gangs in Miller's (2001) sample, 74 percent were in groups that were majority-male, with just under a third (31%) in gangs in which 80 percent or more of the members were males. Likewise, Miller and Brunson (2000) note that 61 percent of the male gang members they interviewed reported being in mixed-sex rather than male-only gangs, with two-thirds of those in mixed-sex gangs reporting that their groups were 80 percent or more male.

Given the import of sex composition in shaping group dynamics, the variation reported within gangs would appear to be a significant issue. Kanter (1977a) notes that often conclusions drawn about differences between males and females, and attributed to "gender roles" or cultural differences between women and men, are in fact more appropriately attributable to situational or structural factors, such as the sex composition of groups. Indeed, the fact that sex composition has been shown to influence group members' experiences could help explain the sometimes disparate findings scholars report about young women in gangs (see Curry 1998 for an overview).

Several debates and incongruous findings exist within the literature on female gang involvement. Curry (1998), for example, notes the tension between perspectives that focus on gangs as "liberating" for their female members, as evidenced by solidarity and support among female members (e.g., see Campbell 1990; Lauderback et al. 1992; Taylor 1993), and those perspectives that focus on the "social injury" young women experience in and as a consequence of their participation in gangs, resulting in part from sexual inequality and exploitation within these groups (see, for example, Fleisher 1998; Miller 1998; Moore 1991).

In addition, several scholars report greater variation in young women's participation in delinquent activities than in young men's. Although it is evident that young women in gangs have higher rates of delinquency than do their nongang peers, both male and female (Bjerregaard & Smith 1993; Esbensen & Winfree 1998; Thornberry et al. 1993), several studies have noted "a bimodal distribution [for girls], with nearly as many multiple index offenders as petty delinquents" (Fagan 1990:201; see also Miller 2001). Moreover, there is debate concerning whether participation in delinquency, particularly of a violent nature, is a normative feature of gang involvement for females. Although scholars have long argued that delinquency is a predominant normative feature of youth gangs (see Decker 1996; Klein 1995), some scholars have argued that this is not the case for young women (see Campbell 1993; Joe & Chesney-Lind 1995). For example, Joe and Chesney-Lind report that "for boys, fighting—even looking for fights—is a major activity within the gang. . . . For girls, violence (gang and otherwise) is not celebrated and normative" (1995: 224, 228). Other scholars suggest that female gang members' lesser involvement in serious gang crime is not a function of differences in the norms adopted by males and females, but instead results from "the structural exclusion of women from male delinquent activities" (Bowker et al. 1980:516). That is, male gang members block young women's participation in central activities within the gang.

As Curry suggests, some of these disparate findings may result from different perspectives, whereas from the dialectical perspective he proposes, "there is really no theoretical problem in the same social activity being simultaneously rewarding and destructive" (1998:109). It may also be that the discrepancies found in various studies of female gang involvement result in part from variations in the sex composition of those gangs under investigation—a feature that most research on female gang involvement has overlooked. Miller's (2001) qualitative

study provides some preliminary evidence of the importance of sex composition within gangs by examining how the sex composition of girls' gangs shapes
their experiences and perceptions. She reports that girls in primarily female
gangs (whether independent or affiliated with male gangs), as well as girls in
mixed-sex gangs with a substantial proportion of female members, are more
likely to emphasize the social and relational aspects of their gangs, particularly
their friendships with other girls. As noted, this is in keeping with a number of
studies that highlight these features of young women's gang involvement (Campbell 1990; Joe & Chesney-Lind 1995; Lauderback et al. 1992).

On the other hand, Miller (2001) reports that girls in gangs that Kanter
(1977a) would classify as skewed or tilted in favor of males were more likely
to emphasize the delinquent aspects of gang life and to describe themselves
as "one of the guys." Likewise, Miller and Brunson's (2000) study of male
gang members suggests that young men in "balanced" groups highlighted the
social aspects of their interactions with female gang members, but differentiate[s] males' and females' participation in delinquent activities. Young men in
"skewed" gangs, with a majority of male members, embraced the few young
women in their gangs as "one of the guys" and described these girls as essentially equal partners in many of their delinquent endeavors.

These findings, as noted earlier, suggest that taking sex composition into
account could help explain some of the incongruent findings with regard to
sex that arise in studies of gangs. Our goal in the present study is to address
these issues. Specifically, we pose two general research questions, as follows:

(1) Are there differences in gang characteristics, activities, and members'
experiences depending on the sex composition of the gang? Stated differently, can gangs of differing sex compositions be distinguished by
their organizational characteristics, activities, and their members' participation in delinquency?
(2) Do descriptions of gang activities and individual delinquency differ
for males and females in varying gang types? For example, do females
in one gang type differ from females in other gang types (i.e., within-
sex, across-gang type comparisons), and do males and females within
gang types differ from each other (i.e., between-sex, within-gang type
comparisons)?

The first of these questions will allow us to explore how the sex composition
of the gang is related to the gang's characteristics and the activities—both prosocial and delinquent—in which the gang is involved. The second question will provide insight into how the sex composition of the gang operates for both male and
female members of these gangs. Comparing both within and across sex will help
to disentangle whether effects, if any, are associated with sex differences or the
sex composition of the gang. Given the significance of delinquency as both a

key normative feature and activity of gang members, our examination of delinquency also provides the opportunity to test the relative import of the theoretical perspectives reviewed above.

For example, Kanter's work would lead us to predict that due to their marginalization, female members of majority-male gangs will have lower rates of delinquency than will their male counterparts in these gangs. By contrast, Kanter and Blau's theories both would predict that females' delinquency in mixed-sex (what we will call "sex-balanced" in our study) gangs will more closely match that of the males in their gangs than in other groups. Moreover, assuming (as Kanter suggests) that a larger proportion of female members affects the culture of the group, if delinquency is of less normative significance for females than males, we would also expect lower rates of delinquency among males in sex-balanced than in majority-male or all-male gangs, and the lowest rates of delinquency in majority-female and all-female gangs. Blalock's majority group power theory would suggest opposite predictions: Not only will girls in sex-balanced groups be less delinquent than will their female counterparts in primarily male gangs, but there will also be greater differences between male and female delinquency in sex-balanced groups, resulting from Blalock's prediction of greater social and behavioral distance between males and females as they approach more equal numbers in groups.

■ Research Design

This investigation of gang youth is part of a larger study, the National Evaluation of the Gang Resistance Education and Training (G.R.E.A.T.) program. Site selection and sampling procedures were dictated by that evaluation's design. Because the G.R.E.A.T. program is a seventh-grade curriculum, eighth-grade students were surveyed to allow for a one-year follow-up while guaranteeing that none of the sample was currently enrolled in the program. This multisite, multistate cross-sectional survey was completed during the Spring of 1995. Site selection was limited to cities in which the G.R.E.A.T. program had been delivered in school year 1993–1994 (when the targeted students were seventh graders).[1]

Site Selection

Records provided by the Bureau of Alcohol, Tobacco, and Firearms, the federal agency with oversight of the G.R.E.A.T. program, were used to identify prospective sites meeting two criteria. First, only those agencies with two or more officers trained prior to January 1994 to teach G.R.E.A.T. were considered eligible. Second, in order to enhance the geographic and demographic diversity of the sample, some potential cities were excluded from consideration.[2] The 11 sites (Las Cruces, N. Mex.; Omaha, Nebr.; Phoenix, Ariz.; Philadelphia,

Pa.; Kansas City, Mo.; Milwaukee, Wis.; Orlando, Fla.; Will County, Ill.; Providence, R.I.; Pocatello, Idaho; and Torrance, Calif.) selected for this phase of the evaluation provide a diverse sample.

Within the selected sites, schools that offered G.R.E.A.T. during the previous two years were selected, and questionnaires were administered in group settings to all eighth graders in attendance on the specified day. School attendance rates varied from a low of 75 percent at one Kansas City middle school to a high of 93 percent at several schools in Will County and Pocatello. This resulted in a final sample of 5,935 eighth-grade students representing 315 classrooms in 42 different schools.[3]

This public school–based sample has the standard limitations associated with school-based surveys (i.e., exclusion of private school students; exclusion of truants, sick, or tardy students; and potential underrepresentation of "high-risk" youths). With this caveat in mind, the current sample comprises all eighth-grade students in attendance on the days questionnaires were administered in these 11 jurisdictions. The sample includes primarily 13- to 15-year-old students[4] attending public schools in a cross section of communities within the continental United States. This is not a random sample, and generalizations cannot be made to the adolescent population as a whole. However, students from these 11 jurisdictions represent the following types of communities: large urban areas with a majority of students belonging to a racial or ethnic minority (Philadelphia, Phoenix, Milwaukee, and Kansas City); medium-sized cities (population ranging between 100,000 and 500,000) with considerable racial or ethnic heterogeneity (Providence and Orlando) and medium-sized cities with a majority of white students but a substantial minority enrollment (Omaha and Torrance); a small city (less than 100,000 inhabitants) with an ethnically diverse student population (Las Cruces) and a small racially homogenous (i.e., white) city (Pocatello); and a rural community in which more than 80 percent of the student population is white (Will County). This diversity in locations and in sample characteristics allows for a unique exploration of the impact of sex composition of gangs in an age group generally excluded from gang research.

Measures

The student questionnaire consisted of demographic, attitudinal, and behavioral measures. We report first on the demographic composition of the sample (sex, age, race/ethnicity), and then focus on gang characteristics and behaviors associated with gang membership for both males and females. Although there is lack of consensus about what constitutes gang membership, we chose to use a self-nomination procedure.[5] This self-definition method has become the standard not only in survey research, but also is widely accepted in law enforcement practice. In the present study, two filter questions introduce the gang-specific section of the questionnaire: "Have you ever been a gang member?" and "Are you now in a gang?" Given the current sample, with almost all respondents under the age of 15, even affirmative responses to the first question followed by a negative response to the second may still indicate a recent gang affiliation. To limit our sample to members of delinquent gangs, we employed a restrictive definition of gang status. Thus, only those youths who reported ever having been in a gang and who reported that their gangs engaged in at least one type of delinquent behavior (fighting other gangs, stealing cars, stealing in general, or robbing people) were classified as gang members.[6]

The next step was to categorize gang youth according to their reports of the sex composition of their gangs. In an open-ended question, respondents were asked to record the number of males and number of females in their gangs. Although a substantial number of gang members failed to provide complete data on the number of males and females in their gangs, we did receive enough valid responses to enable us to make our intended comparisons. Of the 623 gang members in the full sample, 369 (59%) provided sufficient information. Analyses were conducted to compare those who gave insufficient information—and who were thus excluded from the present study—to those who provided the necessary information. No statistically significant differences between the two groups were found for the demographic or behavioral variables under examination in this study. [See the book appendix for a brief explanation of the statistical techniques used in this chapter, i.e., chi-square tests and t-tests.]

If the respondents indicated a positive number of one sex and no members of the other sex, they were classified as being in "all-male" or "all-female" gangs. Gang members were classified as being members of "majority-male" or "majority-female" gangs if the majority sex comprised at least two-thirds of the gang. Those who reported that neither sex exceeded two-thirds of the gang membership were classified as being in "sex-balanced" gangs.[7] We also examined youths' self-defined place in their gang. Five concentric circles were drawn on a chalkboard, with the center circle labeled "1" and representing the center of the gang, and the outer circle labeled "5," representing the periphery of the gang. Respondents were asked to circle the number that best described their place in their gang. Those circling 1 or 2 were considered "core" gang members and those circling 3, 4, or 5 were considered "noncore."

Youths were then asked to describe their gangs in terms of structural and organizational characteristics and behaviors. In response to the question, "Do the following describe your gang?", gang members were asked to circle as many answers as applied, including such possibilities as "There are initiation rites" and "The gang has established leaders." In terms of their gangs' activities, particularly the group's involvement in delinquency, gang members responded to the question, "Does your gang do the following things?", by circling as many answers (e.g., "Get in fights with other gangs" and "Steal things") as applied. With respect to delinquency comparisons among males

and females in gangs of differing sex compositions, we examined annual frequency[8] (i.e., "How many times in the past 12 months have you . . . ?") of self-
reported participation in a range of delinquent acts, including property crimes,
crimes against persons, and drug sales.

Results

Consistent with the findings of Curry (1997), Miller (2001), and Nurge (1998),
our sample of 369 gang members includes youths in gangs with varied sex
compositions. Approximately 45 percent of male gang members described
their gangs as having a majority of male members; 38 percent said their gangs
were sex-balanced; 16 percent were in all-male gangs; and just under 1 percent (two cases) reported being in gangs that were majority-female. Young
women were more likely than were young men to describe belonging to sex-
balanced, rather than majority-male, gangs. Fully, 64 percent of girls described
their gangs as sex-balanced, followed by 30 percent in majority-male gangs,
and 13 percent in majority-female (eight cases) or all-female (10 cases) gangs.
In keeping with reports that gangs are primarily masculine enterprises, the
least prevalent gang types in our study were female-only and majority-female
gangs. Nonetheless, gangs with both male and female membership were by far
the most common. Of the total sample of 369 gang members, only 10 percent
reported membership in male-only gangs. Our goal here is to explore whether
and how sex composition is related to other gang characteristics and activities
and to gang member behaviors.

Table 5.1 reports demographic characteristics of male and female gang
members, as well as their self-defined place in their gangs. The dispersion of
ages among males was consistent across gang types—under one-fifth were 13
or younger, the majority were age 14, and approximately 25 percent were 15 or
older. This pattern was similar for girls in sex-balanced gangs, but not for girls
in majority-male or all/majority-female gangs. In majority-male gangs, approximately one-quarter were 13 or younger, and fully 44 percent of girls in major-
ity- or all-female gangs were 13 or younger. Half of the girls in all/majority-
female gangs were age 14, along with 70 percent of girls in majority-male
gangs. These differences among females were statistically significant, as were
the differences between males in all-male gangs and females in primarily female gangs. Evidence from longitudinal research suggests that girls' gang involvement tends to be of a shorter duration than is boys', with girls' peak gang
involvement around eighth and ninth grades (Thornberry 1999). Our data suggest that this is most likely to be the case in primarily female and primarily
male gangs.

There was no significant variation by race among gangs of different sex
compositions.[9] African-American males were the largest proportion of boys in
all-male gangs, but they were much more likely to be in gangs with female

Table 5.1 Gang Member Characteristics by Sex and Gang Type[a]

	All Male	All/Majority Female	Majority Male		Sex Balanced	
	M N=37	F N=18	M N=105	F N=31	M N=87	F N=86
Age:[b,c]						
13 and under	14%	44%	16%	23%	11%	17%
14	60%	50%	58%	70%	62%	59%
15 and over	26%	6%	26%	7%	27%	25%
Race:						
White	22%	33%	29%	29%	29%	23%
African American	44%	33%	29%	26%	35%	26%
Hispanic	11%	17%	26%	23%	19%	24%
Other	22%	17%	16%	23%	18%	27%
Place in Gang:						
Core	50%	64%	52%	39%	22%	57%
Noncore	50%	36%	48%	61%	56%	43%

Notes: a. For all analyses, both within-sex, across-gang type and between-sex, within-gang comparisons were conducted. Only statistically significant results from these comparisons are reported in the table.

b. Chi-square test, p <. 05, comparison between females.

c. Chi-square test, p <. 05, comparison of males in all-male gangs to females in all/majority-female gangs.

membership, as was the case for all males, regardless of race. Likewise, several studies indicate that African-American girls are more likely to be in independent female gangs than are other girls (Lauderback et al. 1992; Taylor 1993). Although four of the 10 girls in our sample reporting membership in all-female gangs were African American, this represents only 11 percent of the African-American female gang members.[10]

With regard to self-defined place in the gang, the membership appears to be fairly evenly split between those claiming core and noncore positions within their gangs. However, fewer females in majority-male gangs reported holding central positions in their gangs than did girls in other gang types. In addition, the proportion of females in majority-male gangs who were core members was lower compared with males in those gangs, and a greater proportion of females than males in sex-balanced gangs reported holding core positions. The former of these findings appears to offer support for Kanter's (1977a, 1977b) and Blau's (1977) predictions of greater marginalization for minorities in unbalanced groups compared with groups with relatively equal numbers. However, because male participation in majority-female groups is rare, we are unable to ascertain whether this is a generic phenomenon or if it applies primarily to minorities who are not just in the numeric minority, but who also hold less power within American society at large (e.g., females; see Gutek 1985; Konrad et al. 1992).[11]

Gang Characteristics and Activities

Table 5.2 reports youths' descriptions of key characteristics of their gangs. Here, we examine whether boys and girls across gang types, as well as boys and girls in the same gang types, characterized their gangs differently. We did not find differences between males and females within the same gang types with regard to their descriptions of gang characteristics. However, there were some differences within-sex, across-gang types. Specifically, males in all-male gangs reported the lowest levels of gang organization and males in sex-balanced gangs the highest. Statistically significant differences were reported by boys for the following organizational characteristics of their gangs: specific rules, regular meetings, and the adoption of symbols or colors. Nonetheless, with the exception of having regular meetings, the majority of males and females in all gang types reported these characteristics.

The results for girls were less straightforward. Girls in all- or majority-female gangs were less likely to report regular meetings or specific rules than were girls in the other gang types, but otherwise girls' descriptions of gang characteristics were consistent across gang types. The only finding of statistically significant differences for girls was for the gangs' regular meetings. No significant differences were found between girls and boys in the same gang types. Given the extent that these features of gang organization vary across cities (Klein & Maxson 1996), the overall lack of striking differences may be a result of our multicity sampling. Moreover, whether these characteristics are actual measures of gang organization, or are more aptly a reflection of gang characteristics as they are influenced by the cultural diffusion of gangs, remains an open question (see Klein 1995; Miller 2001). Nonetheless, our findings suggest that on the whole the sex composition of youths' gangs does not appear to be significantly related to other organizational characteristics of

Table 5.2 Gang Characteristics by Sex and Gang Type[a]

	All Male	All/Majority Female	Majority Male		Sex Balanced	
	M N=37	F N=18	M N=105	F N=31	M N=87	F N=86
Initiation Rites	65%	78%	74%	76%	77%	78%
Established Leaders	79%	83%	76%	79%	83%	89%
Regular Meetings[b,c]	33%	39%	58%	52%	66%	67%
Specific Rules	60%	67%	71%	87%	84%	87%
Symbols for Colors	78%	83%	90%	100%	94%	88%

Notes: a. For all analyses, both within-sex, across-gang type and between-sex, within-gang type comparison were conducted. Only statistically significant results from these comparisons are reported in the table.

b. Chi-square test, p < .05, comparison between males.

c. Chi-square test, p < .05, comparison between females.

these girls' groups, although three of five significant differences for characteristics of boys' gangs suggest some relationship.

In terms of gang activities, however, the differences are somewhat more dramatic for females. Table 5.3 reports the results of gang members' descriptions of the activities of their gangs, inducing both prosocial and delinquent behaviors. Although these differences are not statistically significant, boys in all-male gangs, and particularly girls in all- or majority-female gangs, were the most likely to report that their gangs were involved in prosocial activities, as measured by helping out in the community. Moreover, girls in all- or majority-female gangs described their groups as substantially and, in some cases, significantly less involved in delinquency than did their female counterparts in sex-balanced and majority-male gangs. A much smaller proportion of girls in majority/all-female gangs reported the gang's involvement in all measures of delinquency, and they were significantly less likely to report that the gang fought with other gangs, stole cars, sold marijuana, or sold illegal drugs other than marijuana.

Likewise, boys in sex-balanced and majority-male gangs reported comparable rates of delinquency for their gangs, whereas boys in all-male gangs reported lower rates of gang delinquency. However, none of the differences among males' descriptions of their gangs' activities was statistically significant. Males and females within gang types were fairly similar in their descriptions of gang activities, with one exception. Females in majority-male gangs were significantly more likely than were males in those gangs to report that their gangs sold marijuana (97% compared with 80%). Overall, based on member reports, it appears that majority/all-female gangs were the least delinquent groups, followed by all-male gangs, whereas sex-balanced and majority-male

Table 5.3 Gang Activities by Sex and Gang Type[a]

	All Male	All/Majority Female	Majority Male		Sex Balanced	
	M N=37	F N=18	M N=105	F N=31	M N=87	F N=86
Help in Community	38%	41%	30%	15%	25%	26%
Fight Other Gangs[b]	87%	78%	93%	94%	90%	95%
Steal Things	60%	71%	78%	90%	70%	77%
Rob Others	51%	41%	61%	73%	68%	62%
Steal Cars[b]	60%	47%	73%	87%	73%	69%
Sell Marijuana[b,c]	69%	69%	80%	97%	85%	84%
Sell Other Drugs[b]	49%	24%	64%	72%	64%	67%
Damage or Destroy	66%	77%	82%	90%	81%	79%

Notes: a. For all analyses both within-sex, across-gang type and between-sex, within-gang type comparisons were conducted. Only statistically significant results from these comparisons are reported in the table.

b. Chi-square test, $p < .05$, comparison between females.

c. Chi-square test, $p < .05$, comparison of males to females in majority-male gangs.

gangs were more delinquent and were similar with regard to the gangs' involvement in delinquent activities.

If gang members' reports of their gangs' activities are a reflection of the goals and norms of these groups, these differences between single-sex and majority-female gangs versus sex-balanced and majority-male gangs are noteworthy. In keeping with the findings of other scholars (Campbell 1993; Joe & Chesney-Lind 1995), our findings suggest that delinquency, particularly of a serious nature, is a less normative feature of primarily female gangs than of other gangs. To interpret this as a function of differences between male and female values, however, is problematic, given the comparably low rates of reported delinquency among all-male gangs. Instead, sex composition appears to be the salient issue: Gangs with both male and female membership (with the exception of primarily female gangs) are those most likely to be oriented toward delinquent activities.

Gang Member Delinquency

Finally, we turn to gang members' reports of their participation in delinquency. Comparing groups with both male and female membership based on their sex composition (e.g., sex-balanced versus majority-male gangs), recall that Kanter's and Blau's theories would lead us to predict the greatest differences in rates of delinquency would occur when comparing males and females in majority-male gangs. Both theorists suggest females' marginalization in majority-male groups will result in exclusion from the primary status-enhancing activities of the group (e.g., delinquency; see Decker 1996; Klein 1995). Moreover, if delinquency is less normative for females than for males, Kanter and Blau would also predict that both males and females in sex-balanced gangs would have lower rates of delinquency than would males in majority-male gangs, given females' increased influence on the groups' norms and activities. In contrast, Blalock's majority group power theory predicts the opposite: The greatest difference in rates of delinquency will be found in sex-balanced, rather than in majority-male groups. As females' numbers increase within the group, male members are more likely to exclude them from the gangs' primary activities to reduce the threat of territorial encroachment on normatively "masculine" endeavors. Blalock's theory would also predict that female members of majority-male gangs must rely on males for access to group rewards and acceptance and, thus, pose less of a threat to male group members. Consequently, they are less likely to be systematically blocked from the gangs' activities than are girls in sex-balanced groups.

Tables 5.4 and 5.5 report gang members' self-reported frequency of participation in a variety of delinquent acts by sex and gang type. In line with the predictions of Blalock (1967), t-tests comparing males and females within gang types (Table 5.4) reveal significant differences between males and females in sex-balanced gangs on nearly every measure, but few differences between males

Table 5.4 Male to Female t-Test Comparisons of Delinquency Frequency Within Gang Types

	All Male	All/Majority Female	Majority Male		Sex Balanced	
	M N=37	F N=18	M N=105	F N=31	M N=87	F N=86
Damage Property	4.32 (4.48)	3.33 (4.72)	5.76 (4.62)	4.67 (4.74)	5.51* (5.01)	3.54 (4.42)
Illegally Spray Paint	4.03* (4.93)	1.00 (2.50)	5.51* (5.41)	3.80 (4.96)	4.52* (5.07)	2.68 (4.19)
Steal Less than $50	3.66 (4.54)	3.00 (4.75)	5.71 (5.02)	4.93 (4.83)	4.28 (5.03)	3.77 (4.47)
Steal More than $50	1.56* (2.51)	.12 (.49)	3.67 (4.34)	2.27 (3.89)	3.56* (4.81)	1.50 (2.94)
Go into Building to Steal Something	2.19 (4.13)	1.44 (3.76)	3.59 (4.84)	2.93 (4.39)	2.37 (3.99)	2.17 (3.91)
Steal Motor Vehicle	1.51* (3.37)	.17 (.38)	2.05 (3.51)	1.71 (3.23)	3.37* (4.62)	1.17 (2.61)
Sell Marijuana	2.21 (3.91)	2.24 (4.24)	5.47* (5.48)	3.86 (4.99)	3.97* (5.04)	2.83 (4.36)
Sell Other Drugs	1.50* (3.68)	.29 (1.21)	3.03 (4.96)	3.10 (5.15)	2.90* (4.80)	1.50 (3.61)
Carry Hidden Weapon	5.29* (4.94)	2.44 (4.16)	6.98 (5.13)	6.63 (4.95)	6.92* (5.29)	3.48 (4.59)
Rob Someone	.97* (2.04)	.00 (.00)	2.33 (4.17)	1.87 (4.06)	1.84* (3.76)	.86 (2.66)
Hit Someone with the Idea to Hurt Him or Her	4.82 (4.59)	5.44 (4.69)	6.25 (4.82)	5.86 (4.67)	5.70* (5.13)	5.00 (4.61)
Participate in Gang Fights	3.97 (4.08)	2.50 (4.31)	5.63 (4.69)	4.93 (4.91)	5.46* (4.89)	4.35 (4.25)
Attack Someone with a Weapon	2.24* (3.34)	.17 (.71)	3.09 (4.29)	3.03 (4.57)	2.61* (4.30)	1.58 (3.00)
Shoot at Someone	.62* (1.38)	.00 (.00)	1.57 (3.43)	1.47 (3.25)	1.85* (3.82)	.78 (2.33)

*$p < .05$, comparison of males to females within gang types.

and females in majority-male gangs. Among youths in sex-balanced gangs, female members were significantly less involved than were male members in 12 of the 14 measures of delinquency. Only for two property offenses—stealing less than $50 and going into a building to steal something—were females' rates comparable to those of young men. They were significantly less involved in serious property offending (stealing more than $50, stealing cars), drug sales, carrying hidden weapons, as well as all violent offenses recorded.

In contrast, there were only two significant differences between males and females in majority-male gangs: Female members were significantly less involved in illegal spray painting and selling marijuana. However, their frequencies of involvement in the other 12 illegal activities—including violent offenses—were not

Table 5.5 T-Test Comparisons of Property and Person Delinquency Frequencies by Sex and Gang Type[a]

	All Male	All/Majority Female	Majority Male		Sex Balanced	
	M N=37	F N=18	M N=105	F N=31	M N=87	F N=86
Property Offense	2.16	1.16	3.77	2.98	3.52	2.14
Index[b,c,f]	(2.40)	(1.97)	(3.58)	(3.24)	(3.69)	(2.72)
Person Offense	2.15	1.36	3.30	3.03	3.16	2.10
Index[b,c,d,e,f]	(2.17)	(1.17)	(3.26)	(3.42)	(3.39)	(2.40)

Notes: a. For all analyses, both within-sex, across-gang type and between-sex, within-gang type comparisons were conducted. Only statistically significant results from these comparisons are reported in the table.

b. $p < .05$, comparison between males in all-male and majority-male gangs.

c. $p < .05$, comparison between all-male and sex-balanced gangs.

d. $p < .05$, comparison between females in all/majority-female gangs and majority-male gangs.

e. $p < .05$, comparison of males in all-male gangs to females in all/majority-female gangs.

f. $p < .05$, comparison of males to females in sex-balanced gangs.

significantly lower than were the frequencies of involvement of their male counterparts in majority-male gangs. The final between-sex comparison reveals that girls in majority/all-female gangs were less frequently involved in delinquency than were males in all-male gangs, with significant differences reported for 8 of the 14 offenses measured, particularly more serious offenses (stealing more than $50, stealing cars, selling drugs other than marijuana, carrying hidden weapons, committing robberies, attacking others, and shooting at someone).

In order to facilitate within-sex comparisons across gang types, we examined two indices of delinquent behavior: property offenses (stealing less than $50, stealing more than $50, going into a building to steal something, and stealing motor vehicles) and person offenses (hitting someone with the idea of hurting him/her, attacking someone with a weapon, robbing someone, and shooting at someone). As Table 5.5 reveals, males in all-male gangs were significantly less involved in property offenses and offenses against persons than were males in either majority-male or sex-balanced gangs. No significant differences emerged between males in majority-male and sex-balanced gangs, as would be expected if increased female membership shifted the norms and activities of gangs toward more prosocial activities. Females in majority- or all-female gangs had lower frequencies of delinquency than did their counterparts in sex-balanced and majority-male gangs, and they were significantly less involved in person offending than were females in majority-male gangs.

Again, as predicted by Blalock's majority group power theory, between-sex differences were found for those youths in sex-balanced gangs. Males in this gang type reported greater rates than did females of both property and person offending. Females in primarily female gangs also differed significantly from males in all-male gangs in rates of offending against persons.

Overall, girls in all- and majority-female gangs had the lowest rates of delinquency, followed by girls in sex-balanced gangs, boys in all-male gangs, girls in majority-male gangs, boys in sex-balanced gangs, and finally, boys in gangs with a majority of male members. Thus, membership in a gang with a minority of female members and a majority of males was correlated with higher rates of delinquency for both males and females. In fact, it is notable that girls in majority-male gangs were more delinquent than were boys in all-male gangs.

Discussion

Prior to discussing the relevance of our findings, we would like to acknowledge three methodological limitations of our work: the cross-sectional research design, the relative young age of our gang members, and missing data for a number of respondents on the sex composition measure. First, at the suggestion of one reviewer, analyses were conducted to compare current and former gang members on delinquency. As expected, these analyses revealed several significant differences; however, there was no differential attrition across gang types, so these differences should not affect the overall pattern of our results, except in underestimation of these behaviors. Second, even though our sample is young and sex composition of groups may have different effects at different ages, we can have confidence in our results based on the fact that qualitative studies with older samples have found similar patterns regarding the impact of sex structure on males' and females' experiences within the gang (see Miller 2001; Miller & Brunson 2000). Finally, no statistically significant differences were found on any of the key variables between gang members who provided the required information about their gangs' sex composition and gang members who failed to provide this information. Thus, we have no reason to believe that the findings reported here cannot generalize to our entire gang member sample.

With these limitations in mind, the goal of this study was to explore the relationship of gang sex composition to both gang characteristics and activities and individual gang members' delinquent behavior. We examined within-sex differences across gang types to investigate whether males and females within gangs of one particular sex composition provided similar or different descriptions from their same-sex peers in other gang types. In addition, we examined whether males and females within gangs of the same sex composition characterized their gangs and activities in the same or differing ways. These analyses allowed us to examine (1) whether gangs of differing sex compositions can be distinguished by their characteristics and activities, as well as by the delinquency of their members; and (2) whether differences in gang members' descriptions appear to result from sex differences or from the sex structure of their gangs.

As highlighted above, literature from the field of organizational sociology strongly suggests the latter (i.e., the impact of sex structure) more so than the former (normative sex differences, for instance, resulting from "gender role" differences). Our findings are consistent with this literature. With regard to descriptions of gang characteristics and activities, for example, youths in all-male and all/majority-female gangs reported fewer of the organizational features typically associated with youth gangs (e.g., leadership, meetings, the adoption of symbols or colors), although these differences were not marked. Likewise, youths in all-male and all/majority-female gangs reported their gangs' greater participation in prosocial activities and lesser participation in delinquency than did youths in other gang types.[12] We also found significant differences in individual delinquency across gang type and (in the case of sex-balanced gangs) across sex.

In testing the demographic composition theories proffered by organizational sociology, our findings support the significant influence of sex composition on male and female group members' behavior. Specifically, we find much stronger support for Blalock's (1967) majority-group power theory than for the theories of Kanter (1977a, 1977b) or Blau (1977). Both of the latter theories would lead us to predict the greatest sex differences among youths in majority-male gangs, resulting from the marginalization of female tokens. They would also predict that a larger proportion of female members may influence the normative features of the group, such that (assuming delinquency is a "masculine" norm) males in sex-balanced gangs would have considerably lower rates of delinquency than would males in majority-male gangs.

In contrast, Blalock's (1967) minority-group threat hypothesis suggests that as the proportion of the lower status group (i.e., females) increases, the higher status group (i.e., males) increases negative action and control in an effort to maintain a dominant position. Thus, it would be in sex-balanced gangs—those with a sizeable proportion of female members—that the greater sex differences would emerge with regard to participation in delinquency. Our findings are in line with this prediction. Males and females in majority-male gangs did not report significantly different rates of offending, whereas males and females in sex-balanced gangs did. Thus, it may be that males in sex-balanced gangs, in which the percentage of females is nearly equal that of males, feel a gendered status threat and respond by narrowing girls' opportunities for involvement in "masculine" activities such as delinquency[13] (see also Bowker et al. 1980; Miller 2001). By contrast, males in majority-male gangs feel little status threat from the small number of females in their gangs, and thus, these females are granted greater freedom (see also Miller & Brunson 2000).

Our findings are also somewhat consistent with prior research indicating that groups consisting of both males and females are more prone to delinquency than are other group types (Giordano 1978; Warr 1996). In our study, youths in majority-male and sex-balanced gangs described both their gangs and themselves as involved in the greatest amounts of delinquent behavior. This was true for both males and females in these gang types, despite the differences reported for individual delinquency by girls and boys in sex-balanced gangs. Giordano (1978) and Warr (1996) have suggested that females learn their delinquent behavior from males in these groups, as their results show that females in groups with both male and female membership exhibit far greater delinquency than do those in exclusively female groups.

Such an interpretation would follow the argument that girls are less oriented toward delinquency than are boys, as a result of gender or cultural differences between males and females. Increased rates of female delinquency, thus, result from girls learning and adapting to the masculine behavioral norms of the group. In fact, Kanter (1977a) explicitly makes this suggestion when she analyzes tokens' responses to their marginalized position. She suggests that female tokens typically adopt two strategies: overachievement according to the "masculine" standards of the group and attempting to become "socially invisible"—to "minimize their sexual attributes so as to blend unnoticeably into the predominant male culture" (Kanter 1977a:974; see also Konrad et al. 1992). Although this could be an explanation for the high rates of delinquency reported by females in majority-male gangs, we did not find evidence to suggest that these girls' opportunities for participation in delinquency were blocked in the first place, as evidenced by our data's support of Blalock's (1967) majority group power theory. Miller and Brunson's (2000) work likewise suggests that males in majority-male gangs accept female members as "one of the guys" and describe girls' participation in many of the gang's delinquent activities, whereas males in mixed-sex gangs note stronger differences in male and female gang members' delinquent activities. Thus, it does not appear that tokenism has a marginalizing effect on girls in majority-male gangs.[14]

Moreover, in contrast to perspectives that assume cultural differences between males and females at the outset, our research also indicates that males in all-male gangs are far less delinquent than are males in other gang types, and even less delinquent than girls in majority-male gangs. This calls into question Giordano's (1978) and Warr's (1996) gendered social learning approach. In fact, at first glance, this finding seemed puzzling, even to us. Some sex-composition theories would lead us to believe that all-male groups would tend to be the most aggressive and competitive in their orientation. Gutek (1985), for example, argues that sex-role spillover in male-dominated groups results in the adoption of stereotypical masculine traits that come to define the group.

Our findings offer challenge to this perspective, as well as to those of Giordano and Warr. We appear to be witnessing a phenomenon associated with the gendered organization of groups, not simply the interplay of differences between males and females. If gang delinquency is both a normative feature of gangs and a decidedly "masculine" one, it is enacted most strongly by males in gangs with female membership, as witnessed by their significantly higher rates of delinquency, than by their counterparts in all-male gangs. These findings attest to the fluidity of masculinity and femininity—they are *situationally* defined and enacted, rather than resulting from deeply entrenched gender differences (see Connell 1987, 1995; West & Fenstermaker 1995). In the case of gangs, it appears that the participation of females in these groups results in increased levels of male delinquency, regardless of the activities of female members.[15]

Finally, we suggested at the outset that a number of discrepant reports regarding female gang involvement might be accounted for by considering the import of gangs' sex compositions, particularly as these may impact the norms and activities of these groups. As we have just discussed, the examination of sex composition can help address the question of whether delinquency is a normative feature of girls' gang activities, as well as differences in reported rates of girls' participation in delinquency. Another series of debates concerns whether gangs offer their female members the solidarity, support, and "sisterhood" of other girls (see, e.g., Campbell 1990; Joe & Chesney-Lind 1995; Lauderback et al. 1992; Taylor 1993) versus reports that some female gang members tend to be male-identified and critical rather than supportive of other girls (see Miller 2001). Again, our findings suggest that attention to gangs' sex structures may help account for these differences.[16] Studies of girls in sex-balanced and especially all- or majority-female gangs would most likely sustain the former explanation, and studies of girls in majority-male gangs the latter.

In sum, our findings support organizational sociologists' assertion that some differences often attributed to gender or cultural differences between males and females are more appropriately attributable to group structure. They also are consistent with the observations of qualitative studies that the sex composition of gangs, independent of sex, plays an important part in shaping the norms and activities of gangs and their members (Joe-Laidler & Hunt 1997; Miller 2001; Miller & Brunson 2000; Nurge 1998). Just as other gang research indicates the importance of considering such factors as geographic location, organizational structure, and age (see Esbensen et al. 1999; Klein & Maxson 1996), our findings highlight the significance of the gang's sex structure. Attention to this issue is an important line of inquiry for future research on gang and group delinquency.

Notes

1. In another paper, Esbensen and Osgood (1999) examined program effects. As part of those analyses, preexisting differences between the G.R.E.A.T. program students and the comparison group were examined. No systematic differences on demographic characteristics were found between the two groups.

2. With the program's origin in Phoenix, cities in Arizona and New Mexico were overrepresented in the early stages of the G.R.E.A.T. program. Thus, cities such as

Albuquerque, Tucson, Scottsdale, and other smaller cities in the southwest were excluded from the eligible pool of potential sites.

3. Passive consent procedures, which require parents to respond only if they do not want their child to participate in a research project, were approved in all but the Torrance site. The number of parental refusals at each school ranged from 0 percent to 2 percent at one school. Thus, participation rates (the percent of students in attendance on the day of administration actually completing questionnaires) varied between 98 percent and 100 percent at the passive consent sites. Participation rates in Torrance, where active consent procedures were required, ranged from 53 percent to 75 percent of all eighth-grade students in each of the four schools. Five weeks of intensive efforts to obtain active parental consent in Torrance produced an overall return rate of 90 percent (72% affirmative and 18% refusals). Despite repeated mailings, telephone calls, and incentives, 10 percent of parents failed to return the consent form. Ninety percent of those students with parental permission completed the questionnaires. For a discussion of active parental consent procedures and their effect on response rates, see Esbensen et al. 1996.

4. Our sample, at an average age of 14, is relatively young. Although it is true that sex composition may have different effects at 14 than at older ages, it is encouraging that similar patterns of sex structure and experiences within the gang are also reported in qualitative studies with older youths (see Miller 1998; Miller & Brunson 2000).

5. For further discussion of this definitional issue, see Decker and Kempf-Leonard (1991), Winfree et al. (1992), or Maxson and Klein (1990). We concur with Klein (1995) that it is the illegal activity of gangs that is of research and policy interest. For that reason, we restrict our definition of gangs to include only those youths who report their gangs are involved in illegal activities.

6. The cross-sectional portion of the National Evaluation showed that youths who participated in the G.R.E.A.T. program were subsequently less delinquent and more prosocial in their behaviors than were youths in the control group (Esbensen & Osgood 1999). Because our sample includes gang members who participated in the G.R.E.A.T. program, as well as those who did not, analyses were conducted to compare these two groups on all demographic and behavioral characteristics under examination in the present study. No significant differences were found; thus, inclusion of gang members who received G.R.E.A.T. will not affect our findings. For a discussion of differences between gang and nongang youths in the G.R.E.A.T. sample, see Esbensen and Deschenes (1998) and Esbensen and Winfree (1998).

7. Because only two young men reported membership in majority-female gangs, they were not included in the analyses that follow. Females in majority-female and all-female gangs were combined for the analysis (N = 18).

8. The skewness of self-report frequency data presents analysis problems. Various approaches can be used in attempts to remedy this problem, including transforming the data using the natural log, truncating at the ninetieth percentile (Nagin & Smith 1990), or truncating the high-frequency responses according to some conceptual reasoning. We chose to truncate items at 12. Our premise is that commission by eighth graders of most of these acts on a monthly basis constitutes high-frequency offending. In support of this, frequency data indicated that few respondents committed more than 12 of each offense during the designated time period. We are thus able to examine these high-frequency offenders without sacrificing the detail of open-ended self-report techniques.

9. The "other" category includes a small number of Asian and American Indian youths, but is primarily composed of youths who describe themselves as biracial, multiracial, or members of "white" ethnic groups (e.g., Italian, Irish).

10. Other research suggests that Hispanic girls are more likely to be found in "auxiliary" branches of male gangs (Curry 1997; Lauderback et al. 1992; Quicker 1983). Given the nature of our measure of sex composition, this is not an issue we are able to address.

11. Of the two young men in our study reporting membership in majority-female gangs, one described himself as a core member, the other as noncore.

12. Our restricted definition of gang membership may have excluded some groups that were more prosocial in nature. It is telling that even among these delinquent gangs, all-male and primarily female gangs appear to be more prosocial and less delinquent than do other gang types.

13. Nonetheless, there is also evidence that some young women choose to exclude themselves from delinquent activities they find dangerous or morally troubling—exclusionary practices by young men are but one factor in a larger set of gendered processes (see Miller 1998, 2001; Miller & Decker 2001).

14. An operating factor that may be involved is that males dictate who is allowed to join the gang (see Miller & Brunson 2000), so that only those females who demonstrate "male" qualities such as "toughness" succeed in gaining access to male-dominated gangs. Control of entry may also serve to lessen the status threat girls pose—a situation that would be different in the workplace, where male coworkers have little input into the hiring practices of the organization.

15. Another possibility that may be considered is that the interaction of boys and girls may somehow stimulate delinquency; for example, as one reviewer suggested, it may be that boys in mixed-sex gangs feel the need to "show off" more so than do boys in all-male gangs, and this may account for some of the differences in delinquency involvement.

16. Likewise, although we did not examine victimization in this study, some preliminary evidence suggests that girls' social injury within gangs (see Curry 1998) may also be shaped by the sex composition of these groups (see Joe-Laidler & Hunt 1997; Miller & Brunson 2000).

References

Baker, Robert L., Birgitte R. Mednick & Linn Carothers. 1989. "Association of Age, Gender, and Ethnicity with Victimization In and Out of School." *Youth & Society* 20:320–341.

Bjerregaard, Beth & Carolyn Smith. 1993. "Gender Differences in Gang Participation, Delinquency, and Substance Use." *Journal of Quantitative Criminology* 4:329–355.

Blalock, Hubert M. 1967. *Toward a Theory of Minority-Group Relations.* New York: Wiley.

Blau, Peter M. 1977. *Inequality and Heterogeneity: A Primitive Theory of Social Structure.* New York: Free Press.

Bowker, Lee H., Helen Shimota Gross & Malcolm W. Klein. 1980. "Female Participation in Delinquent Gang Activities." *Adolescence* 15:509–519.

Campbell, Anne. 1990. "On the Invisibility of the Female Delinquent Peer Group." *Women & Criminal Justice* 2:41–62.

———. 1993. *Men, Women, and Aggression.* New York: Basic Books.

Chiricos, Ted, Michael Hogan & Marc Gertz. 1997. "Racial Composition of Neighborhood and Fear of Crime." *Criminology* 35:107–132.

Connell, R. W. 1987. *Gender and Power.* Stanford, CA: Stanford University Press.

———. 1995. *Masculinities.* Berkeley: University of California Press.

Covington, Jeanette & Ralph B. Taylor. 1991. "Fear of Crime in Urban Residential Neighborhoods: Implications of Between- and Within-Neighborhood Sources for Current Models." *Sociological Quarterly* 32:231–49.

Curry, G. David. 1997. "Selected Statistics on Female Gang Involvement." Paper presented at the Fifth Joint National Conference on Gangs, Schools, and Communities, Orlando, FL.

———. 1998. "Female Gang Involvement." *Journal of Research in Crime & Delinquency* 35:100–18.

Decker, Scott H. 1996. "Collective and Normative Features of Gang Violence." *Justice Quarterly* 3:243–64.

Decker, Scott H. & Kimberly Kempf-Leonard. 1991. "Constructing Gangs: The Social Definition of Youth Activities." *Criminal Justice Policy Review* 5:271–91.

Esbensen, Finn-Aage & Elizabeth Piper Deschenes. 1998. "A Multi-site Examination of Youth Gang Membership: Does Gender Matter?" *Criminology* 36:799–827.

Esbensen, Finn-Aage, Elizabeth Piper Deschenes & L. Thomas Winfree, Jr. 1999. "Differences between Gang Girls and Gang Boys: Results from a Multi-site Survey." *Youth & Society* 31:27–53.

Esbensen, Finn-Aage et al. 1996. "Active Parental Consent in School-based Research: An Examination of Ethical and Methodological Issues." *Evaluation Review* 20:737–53.

Esbensen, Finn-Aage & David Huizinga. 1993. "Gangs, Drugs and Delinquency in a Survey of Urban Youth." *Criminology* 31:565–90.

Esbensen, Finn-Aage & D. Wayne Osgood. 1999. "Gang Resistance Education and Training (GREAT): Results from the National Evaluation." *Journal of Research in Crime & Delinquency* 36:194–255.

Esbensen, Finn-Aage & L. Thomas Winfree, Jr. 1998. "Race and Gender Differences between Gang and Non-gang Youths: Results from a Multi-site Survey." *Justice Quarterly* 15:505–26.

Fagan, Jeffrey. 1989. "The Social Organization of Drug Use and Drug Dealing among Urban Gangs." *Criminology* 27:633–67.

———. 1990. "Social Processes of Delinquency and Drug Use among Urban Gangs." In C. R. Huff (ed.), *Gangs in America*. Newbury Park, CA: Sage.

Fairhurst, Gail Theus & B. Kay Snavely. 1983a. "Majority and Token Minority Group Relationships: Power Acquisition and Communication." *Academy of Management Review* 8:292–300.

———. 1983b. "A Test of the Social Isolation of Male Tokens." *Academy of Management Journal* 26:353–61.

Fleisher, Mark S. 1998. *Dead End Kids: Gang Girls and the Boys They Know.* Madison: Wisconsin University Press.

Giordano, Peggy. 1978. "Girls, Guys, and Gangs: The Changing Social Context of Female Delinquency." *Journal of Criminal Law & Criminology* 69:126–32.

Gutek, Barbara A. 1985. *Sex and the Workplace.* San Francisco, CA: Jossey-Bass.

Hagedorn, John M. & Mary Devitt. 1999. "Fighting Female: The Social Construction of Female Gangs." In M. Chesney-Lind & J. Hagedorn (eds.), *Female Gangs in America*. Chicago, IL: Lakeview Press.

Heikes, Joel E. 1991. "When Men are the Minority: The Case of Men in Nursing." *Sociological Quarterly* 32:389–401.

Jankowski, Martin Sanchez. 1991. *Islands in the Streets: Gangs and American Urban Society.* Berkeley: University of California Press.

Joe, Karen A. & Meda Chesney-Lind. 1995. "'Just Every Mother's Angel': An Analysis of Gender and Ethnic Variations in Youth Gang Membership." *Gender & Society* 9:408–30.

Joe-Laidler, Karen A. & Geoffrey Hunt. 1997. "Violence and Social Organization in Female Gangs." *Social Justice* 24:148–69.

Kanter, Rosabeth Moss. 1977a. "Some Effects of Proportions on Group Life: Skewed Sex Ratios and Responses to Token Women." *American Journal of Sociology* 82:965–90.

———. 1977b. *Men and Women of the Corporation.* New York: Basic Books.

Klein, Malcolm W. 1995. *The American Street Gang.* New York: Oxford University Press.

Klein, Malcolm W. & Cheryl L. Maxson. 1996. "Gang Structures, Crime Patterns, and Police Responses." Final Report to the National Institute of Justice.

Konrad, Alison M., Susan Winter & Barbara A. Gutek. 1992. "Diversity in Work Group Sex Composition: Implications for Majority and Minority Members." *Research in the Sociology of Organizations* 10:115–40.

Lauderback, David, Joy Hansen & Dan Waldorf. 1992. "'Sisters are Doin' It for Themselves': A Black Female Gang in San Francisco." *Gang Journal* 1:57–70.

Maxson, Cheryl L. & Malcolm W. Klein. 1990. "Street Gang Violence: Twice as Great or Half as Great?" In C. R. Huff (ed.), *Gangs in America.* Newbury Park, CA: Sage.

Miller, Jody. 1998. "Gender and Victimization Risk among Young Women in Gangs." *Journal of Research in Crime & Delinquency* 35:429–53.

———. 2001. *One of the Guys: Girls, Gangs and Gender.* New York: Oxford University Press.

Miller, Jody & Rod K. Brunson. 2000. "Gender Dynamics in Youth Gangs: A Comparison of Males' and Females' Accounts." *Justice Quarterly* 17:419–48.

Miller, Jody & Scott H. Decker. 2001. "Young Women and Gang Violence: An Examination of Gender, Street Offending and Violent Victimization in Gangs." *Justice Quarterly* 18:115–40.

Miller, Walter. 1975. *Violence by Youth Gangs and Youth Groups as a Crime Problem in Major American Cities.* Washington, DC: US Government Printing Office.

Moore, Joan. 1991. *Going Down to the Barrio: Homeboys and Homegirls in Change.* Philadelphia: Temple University Press.

Nagin, Daniel S. & Douglas A. Smith. 1990 "Participation In and Frequency of Delinquent Behavior: A Test for Structural Differences." *Journal of Quantitative Criminology* 6:335–65.

Nurge, Dana. 1998. "Female Gangs and Cliques in Boston: What's the Difference?" Paper presented at the annual meeting of the American Society of Criminology, Washington, DC.

Quicker, John C. 1983. *Homegirls: Characterizing Chicana Gangs.* San Pedro, CA.: International University Press.

South, Scott J., Charles M. Bonjean, William T. Markham & Judy Corder. 1982. "Social Structure and Intergroup Interaction: Men and Women of the Federal Bureaucracy." *American Sociological Review* 47:587–99.

———. 1983. "Female Labor Force Participation and the Organizational Experiences of Male Workers." *Sociological Quarterly* 24:367–80.

Spangler, Eve, Marsha A. Gordon & Ronald M. Pipkin. 1978. "Token Women: An Empirical Test of Kanter's Hypothesis." *American Journal of Sociology* 84:160–70.

Spergel, Irving A. & G. David Curry. 1993. "The National Youth Gang Survey: A Research and Developmental Process." In A. Goldstein & C. R. Huff (eds.), *The Gang Intervention Handbook.* Champaign, IL: Research Press.

Taylor, Carl S. 1990. "Gang Imperialism." In C. R. Huff (ed.), *Gangs in America.* Newbury Park, CA: Sage.

———. 1993. *Girls, Gangs, Women and Drugs.* East Lansing: Michigan State University Press.

Thornberry, Terence P. 1999. Personal correspondence, April 2.

Thornberry, Terence P., Marvin D. Krohn, Alan J. Lizotte & Deborah Chard-Wierschem. 1993. "The Role of Juvenile Gangs in Facilitating Delinquent Behavior." *Journal of Research in Crime & Delinquency* 30:75–85.

Warr, Mark. 1996. "Organization and Instigation in Delinquent Groups." *Criminology* 34:11–37.

West, Candace & Sarah Fenstermaker. 1995 "Doing Difference." *Gender & Society* 9:8–37.

Williams, Christin L. 1992. "The Glass Escalator: Hidden Advantages for Men in the 'Female Professions.'" *Social Problems* 39:253–67.

Winfree, L. Thomas, Jr., Kathy Fuller, Teresa Vigil & G. Larry Mays. 1992. "The Definition and Measurement of 'Gang Status': Policy Implications for Juvenile Justice." *Juvenile & Family Court Journal* 43:29–37.

Wordes, Madeline & Timothy S. Bynum. 1995. "Policing Juveniles: Is There a Bias against Youths of Color?" In K. Kempf-Leonard, C. Pope & W. Feyerherm (eds.), *Minorities in Juvenile Justice.* Thousand Oaks, CA: Sage.

Yoder, Janice D. 1991. "Rethinking Tokenism: Looking Beyond the Numbers." *Gender & Society* 5:178–92.

Yoder, Janice D., Jerome Adams & Howard T. Prince. 1983. "The Price of a Token." *Journal of Political & Military Sociology* 11:325–37.

PART 3

The Social Psychology of Delinquency

IN PART 2 OF THIS BOOK, WE BRIEFLY INTRODUCED SOME ISSUES PER-taining to the causes of delinquency. In Parts 3 and 4, we focus more directly on causal explanations and various sociological theories that attempt to account for why delinquent behavior is more common among some individuals and groups and not others. Before pursing this line of inquiry, however, a few cautionary remarks are in order. Delinquency is a diverse and complex problem that undoubtedly requires multiple theories or explanations because no single one can hope to explain all types of delinquent behavior; and different factors may be involved in accounting for why different individuals may engage in similar behavior. Moreover, as noted in Part 2, one set of factors may distinguish "between those persons who become involved in crimes the first time and those who do not, and . . . a different set of factors" may distinguish between "those who persist in crime once involved [and] those who discontinue criminality at an early age" (Blumstein and Grady 1982:265).

Casual explanations in the social and behavioral sciences rely on both theoretical formulations and empirical research. Although **theory** is sometimes perceived as "a tangled maze of jargon . . . that [is] irrelevant to the real world," we all use theory—a set of "interconnected abstractions or ideas that condense and organize knowledge"—to help explain our lives and the world around us (Neuman 2003:41–42). If, for example, you believe that youths commit crime because they do not face any credible punishment for their actions, you are invoking a particular theory about criminal motivation and the societal reaction (or lack thereof) to it. Moreover, theory has practical implications, because

127

proposals to address the crime and delinquency problem explicitly or implicitly assume a particular explanation or set of underlying causes. If the theory associated with a particular prevention or other intervention program is inaccurate, then the program is likely to fail.

Theory is, of course, also intertwined with empirical research: theory guides research, which in turn confirms or disconfirms theory. Unfortunately, it sometimes seems as if researchers all too often become mired in competing theories and endless empirical tests that only produce mixed or inconsistent results. Nevertheless, sound and carefully tested theory offers a better guide to social policy than a hit-or-miss or purely ideological approach.

In this section of the book we focus on **social psychological theories** that deal with the ways in which delinquents interpret or account for the meaning of their actions and learn to favor or disfavor criminal courses of conduct; and in Part 4 we examine social structural influences on delinquency related to families, schools, community organization, and work. Before turning to these issues, however, we first briefly review some nonsociological explanations of delinquency that have been the province of other disciplines that locate the central causes within the individual rather than within the social environment. These **individualistic theories** typically characterize delinquents as particular "kinds of persons" who possess some flawed or defective trait that makes the "normal prohibitions against crime relatively ineffective" (Herrnstein 1995:40). More specifically, we consider biological and psychological approaches.

■ Biological Approaches

Charles Darwin's (1809–1882) work on evolution was historically a major factor in the rise of biological thinking about crime. Darwin postulated that life had evolved through a process of natural selection or "survival of the fittest" among diverse species, including humans. Herbert Spencer (1820–1903) applied this notion to the social realm, asserting that some people had natural qualities that made them more fit, more adaptable members of society, whereas others lacked such redeeming traits.

Theories following in this tradition assumed that criminals were essentially "born" not "made" and that genetics or heredity were more important than environment. Italian physician Cesare Lombroso (1835–1909), for example, postulated that many criminals were born **atavists,** throwbacks to an earlier stage of human evolution. He believed that these criminals were less highly evolved than law-abiding citizens and that they could be recognized by distinctive physical traits that he considered common among "savages and apes" and "the coloured races" (e.g., hairy bodies, curly hair, receding foreheads, long arms, and large skulls, nostrils, jaws, and ears) (cited in Beirne and Messerschmidt 1995:350). According to Lombroso, these individuals were low in intelligence, excessively idle, and insensitive to pain; and they were lovers of orgies who had an "irresistible craving for evil for its own sake" (p. 350).[1]

Rafter (1992) notes that in the United States **criminal anthropology,** as she calls it, even predated Lombroso and continued to have adherents into the twentieth century. Criminal anthropology refers to the practice of studying the criminal "as a physically anomalous human type" (p. 525). Sheldon (1949), for instance, advanced a theory that body type was associated with personality and behavioral traits. He compared a group of official delinquent and nondelinquent boys according to three body types: the thin and introverted *ectomorph,* the rotund and easygoing *endomorph,* and the muscular and aggressive *mesomorph,* who, as you might suspect, was the criminal type in Sheldon's scheme. This theory occupied the attention of mainstream criminologists through the 1950s and is even taken seriously by some today (Glueck and Glueck 1950; Wilson and Herrnstein 1985).

In the 1960s, biological explanations of crime and delinquency turned inward, toward internal attributes of individuals rather than observable physical traits. One approach that has received a good deal of attention is the **XYY chromosome syndrome.** Whereas the normal male has one X and one Y chromosome, about one in 1,000 has an extra Y chromosome. XYY males appear to be taller, to have longer arms, more severe acne, more mental retardation, and, on average, lower intelligence than XY males. In the 1960s researchers began to postulate that they also exhibited more criminal violence (Binder, Geis, and Dickson 2001; Katz and Chambliss 1995).

On closer examination, however, researchers discovered that the criminal histories of XYY males consisted primarily of property offenses, not violence. Their overrepresentation in prisons may have been related to their tendency to have lower intelligence and greater impulsivity and perhaps to legal biases against individuals with this physical appearance. In any event, the trait is so rare that it could at best account for only a small fraction of criminal behavior. Theilgaard concluded that "there is no ground for anticipating that a person with a certain [chromosomal] status will demonstrate a preordained, inflexible and irremediable personality or pathology" (1984:108).

A more promising line of biological investigation has focused on the **autonomic nervous system** (ANS), which regulates bodily processes such as breathing and perspiring. Eysenck (1977) postulated that some ANS disorders make individuals less responsive to external stimulation, thus impeding their ability to be socially conditioned. Mednick and colleagues (Mednick, Pollock, and Volavka 1982) argued that chronic delinquents suffer from a sluggish ANS that interferes with the way in which fear (toward a punishing adult, for instance) inhibits aggressive impulses. They found that delinquents displayed significantly slower electrodermal responses (usually measured through sweat gland activity) than those in a nondelinquent control group. More recent research with other measures of ANS activity (e.g., low resting heart rate) supports the finding for serious but not minor juvenile offenders (Cauffman, Steinberg, and Piquero 2005).

Other studies have found that "abnormalities" or "deficits" in the **prefrontal lobe cortex** of the brain—perhaps caused by an injury, poor nutrition, or substance abuse—are associated with serious juvenile offending (Cauffman, Steinberg, and Piquero 2005). This trait is found in individuals who exhibit disruptive behavior disorders as well as short-sightedness and low impulse control. Additionally, studies have linked low levels of **serotonin,** a neurochemical transmitter that carries messages between the brain and the body, to violence. Low-serotonin individuals appear to respond more slowly to emotional stimuli and are less inhibited in their aggressive or impulsive behaviors (Ellis and Walsh 2000; Fishbein 1990; Moffitt et al. 1998).

It is important to point out, however, that the sources of such biological maladies—whether they are genetic or environmentally induced—are not always clear. Take nutritional deficiencies and lead exposure, for instance, which have been linked to a variety of cognitive problems that put one at risk for low intelligence quotient (IQ), memory loss, depression, and behavioral aggression (Dietrich et al. 2001; Needleman et al. 1996; Nevin 2000). Poor nutrition and children's exposure to lead from paint chips in dilapidated buildings, for instance, are not genetic but are inversely related to socioeconomic life situations. Inadequate diet and alcohol or drug use during pregnancy similarly can seriously impair fetal development and have deleterious long-term consequences. Such effects are caused by parental behavior, not genetics. But one should not simply write these off as "lifestyle choices," since a mother's ability to eat a balanced diet during pregnancy or to obtain access to an alcohol or drug treatment program is clearly related to social class. Moreover, unhealthy prenatal and ineffective postnatal child-rearing practices are so intertwined that it is often difficult to distinguish the effect of one from the other (Barkan 2006; Fishbein 1990).[2]

Consideration of such nuances are often absent as well from one of the more fascinating areas of biological inquiry: twin and adoption studies. Several studies of twins have found greater similarity in behavior (whether criminal or noncriminal) among identical or monozygotic twins (one ovum that divided after fertilization by one sperm) than among fraternal or dizygotic twins (two ova fertilized by two separate sperm). These findings suggest a genetic influence on criminality, since identical twins have the same biological makeup whereas fraternal twins do not. Critics of these studies have long noted, however, that identical twins are more likely than fraternal twins to be treated similarly by others, and thus their common behavior patterns "could just as easily be due to environmental influences" (Bartol and Bartol 1989:144). Dalgard and Kringlen (1976), for example, found that any genetic influence on the criminality of twins was negligible when they controlled for such factors. Yet it is difficult to disentangle genetic characteristics from early childhood and family influences. Family experiences that are common to parents and children include diet, exposure to toxins, neighborhood conditions, and television-viewing habits (Ellis and Walsh 2000; Fishbein 1990; Katz and Chambliss 1995; Walters and White 1989).

Some adoption studies also have found greater similarity in criminal behavior between adoptees and their biological parents than would be expected by chance, especially for chronic or repeat offenders. When the biological parent is both criminal and alcoholic, the adoptee's behavior tends to be disproportionately violent. But since adoption agencies often match the class and racial background of adopted and natural parents, it is unclear whether the adoptee's behavior is attributable to genetics rather than environmental factors. In addition, the age at which an individual was adopted needs to be considered, for increased criminality among adoptees has been associated with the amount of time spent with biological parents or in orphanages (Barkan 2006; Berger, Free, and Searles 2009).

Both the twin and the adoption studies often beg the question of what precisely is being inherited that supposedly causes crime. Clearly no one today seriously believes there is a "bad seed" or crime gene that is inherited. And most contemporary biocriminologists have accepted the proposition that there is an interaction between biology and social environment. What they do propose is that there are genetic predispositions for alcoholism, intelligence, mental disorders, or temperamental traits such as impulsivity, extroversion, hyperemotionality, anger, and deceitfulness that make one more vulnerable to environmental strains that trigger criminality (Ellis and Walsh 2000; Fishbein 1990; Rowe 1986).

Intelligence and Delinquency

Claims regarding the role of intelligence, or lack thereof, in delinquent conduct require particular scrutiny. The idea that intelligence is hereditary is often linked to the work of the French psychologist Alfred Binet. In 1904 Binet was commissioned by the French Ministry of Public Education to develop a test to measure children's cognitive (linguistic and mathematical) abilities at various age levels. From this was born the IQ test. Contrary to what is sometimes assumed, Binet did not consider one's score on this test to be genetic or impervious to accumulated experience. When the IQ test was introduced in the United States, however, a different attitude prevailed, even though tests administered to army recruits during World War I indicated that about half scored below the cognitive level expected of a 13-year-old (Katz and Chambliss 1995).

A number of studies have found that low IQ is correlated with higher rates of official and self-reported juvenile delinquency (Felson and Staff 2006; Hirschi and Hindelang 1977; Wilson and Herrnstein 1985), though obviously not with those crimes that require a good deal of intelligence (e.g., computer and financial crimes). How should we interpret the apparent IQ-delinquency association? Is intelligence genetic, environmental, or a combination of the two? How much are we limited by our genes? How much does an enriching environment matter? Who would deny the significance of social influences such as parents and teachers who encourage children to read and enjoy learning? Regardless, criminologists often argue that since IQ is associated with the cognitive abilities that lead to academic success, youths with low IQs may be more likely to feel alienated from or dissatisfied with school, which in turn may weaken their stake in conformity and increase their attraction to delinquency.

Perhaps the greatest point of contention regarding the IQ test has been its alleged class and race bias. In their well-publicized book, *The Bell Curve,* Richard Herrnstein and Charles Murray (1994) compiled data that indicated that African Americans, on average, scored lower on IQ tests than European Americans and that Asian Americans scored the highest. (The bell curve refers to the shape of the distribution of IQ scores in a population from low to middle to high.) Herrnstein and Murray also argued that low IQ or cognitive disadvantage was causally related to a variety of social ills, including out-of-wedlock births, welfare dependency, and crime. Moreover, they claimed that IQ is in large part genetic and that it is *immutable,* impervious to change. Hence government programs (e.g., early childhood education) designed to improve the lives of the cognitively disadvantaged are bound to fail.

The Bell Curve has been subjected to numerous criticisms, many of which were previously advanced against earlier works. For example, critics contend that the content of IQ test questions advantages individuals who are familiar with the white, middle-class cultural experience. Moreover, the property tax–based system of school funding means that low-income communities will have fewer educational resources for students, who consequently perform more poorly in school. Schools also use test scores to track students into vertical (high to low) tracks, which in turn become self-fulfilling prophecies of educational attainment, denying some youths access to desirable social roles (Katz and Chambliss 1995; Cullen et al. 1997; Menard and Morse 1984).

In a compelling empirical critique of *The Bell Curve,* Francis Cullen and colleagues (Cullen et al. 1997) examined data from nearly 500 studies containing more than 42,800 offenders. These studies contain measures not only of intelligence and crime but also of respondents' social background (e.g., socioeconomic status, urban versus rural residence, religious participation, living with mother and father). Cullen and colleagues concluded that the association between IQ and crime was at best small, if not insignificant, after taking into account other social influences. Moreover, these social influences are often *amenable to change* (unlike Herrnstein and Murray's claims about IQ).

Cullen and colleagues believe that having "knowledge of an offender's intellectual capacity and aptitude is advantageous in designing" rehabilitative treatment programs. They also advocate a broadened conception of IQ that includes not just the standard linguistic and mathematical criteria but practical intelligence as well, that is, "a person's ability to learn and profit from experience, to monitor effectively one's own and others' feelings and needs, and to solve everyday problems" (pp. 403–404). Nevertheless, they believe that Herrnstein and Murray's thesis and policy conclusions are based more on ideology than on empirical science.

Applications of Biological Approaches

We would be naive to deny that "biological conditions have a profound impact on the adaptive, cognitive, and emotional abilities" of individuals (Fishbein 1990:56). But we must be wary of premature and injudicious applications of biological thinking about crime. At its extreme we have the association of biological approaches with **eugenics**—a philosophy of social intervention to regulate the genetic composition of the population through methods such as compulsory sterilization and restrictions on marriages and immigration of allegedly biologically inferior groups, even extermination as in the case of Nazi Germany (Berger, Free, and Searles 2009; Katz and Chambliss 1995). But even when used with the best intentions, to prevent crime by diagnosing and delivering needed services to at-risk children, for example, biological interventions are fraught with ethical problems. Notice that here we are talking about *potential* offenders, children who might commit crimes some day. How will we avoid mistakenly diagnosing children or adversely stigmatizing them with a potentially harmful label or setting in motion a self-fulfilling prophecy? What type of treatment will we employ? Will it be physiological (e.g., drugs), psychological, or social? Or will we simply isolate or quarantine suspect populations?

With convicted offenders as well, the imposition of rehabilitative biological treatments is problematic. Diane Fishbein notes that "the appropriate administration of a medication or other treatment may . . . be warranted for some individuals with [an] identifiable pathology . . . [that] played a role in . . . [their] antisocial behavior" (1990:54, 56). She adds, however, that biological variables cannot be manipulated without attention to interacting factors. By the time individuals have entered the juvenile or criminal justice system, their behavior problems have been so substantially compounded that treating only one facet of their condition will be unlikely to yield the desired therapeutic results.

■ Psychological Approaches

Like biological theories, psychological explanations assume that criminals are different kinds of persons. They postulate an assortment of defective mental, emotional, or personality traits that either cause criminal behavior or predispose one to the environmental factors that trigger the onset of criminal behavior. (Behaviorism, which we will discuss later in this section, is an exception.) To a large extent, many of the biological theories we have reviewed identify such traits as intervening between biology and crime, and individual traits such as intelligence are sometimes elements of psychological (as well as biological) theories of crime.

Freudian Psychology

One of the earliest psychological formulations was advanced by Austrian physician Sigmund Freud (1856–1939), whose **psychoanalytic theory** was quite influential in early explanations of delinquency (Aichhorn 1935; Friedlander 1947; Healy and Bronner 1936). Freud and his followers believed that the human personality consists of three interdependent yet often conflicting elements: the **id, ego,** and **superego.**

> The *id* is the unrestrained, primitive, pleasure-seeking component with which each child is born. The *ego* develops through the reality of living in the world and helps manage and restrain the id's need for immediate gratification. The *superego* develops through interactions with parents and other significant people and represents the development of conscience and the moral rules that are shared by most adults. . . . All three segments of the personality operate simultaneously. The id dictates needs and desires, the superego counteracts the id by fostering feelings of morality and righteousness, and the ego evaluates the reality of a position between the two extremes. (Siegel, Welsh, and Senna 2003:84; emphasis in original)

According to Freudian theory, basic personality formation is completed in early childhood, and thus early parent-child interaction is of paramount importance. If parents are neglectful or abusive or exert too little or too much discipline, imbalances may develop among the id, ego, and superego, creating unconscious psychological conflicts within individuals. Later-life delinquency and adult criminality may represent a symbolic expression or acting out of such conflicts. If parental socialization is weak or inadequate, for instance, the child's superego will be underdeveloped and the id will dominate the personality. Later in life this may lead the person to insist on the immediate gratification of selfish needs, to lack compassion or sensitivity to others, or to behave impulsively and aggressively. If, on the other hand, parental discipline is overbearing and punitive, the individual may become overly rebellious and defiant of authority.

Critics of Freudian psychology contend that it is too speculative. The postulated personality components are neither observable nor measurable, requiring one to rely on a psychoanalyst's retrospective "interpretation of a patient's interpretation of what is occurring in the [un]conscious" (Sheley 1985:202). Moreover, the influence of early-life events can be significantly altered by later experiences. Several criminological studies, for example, have found that earlier involvement in crime is substantially reduced with the acquisition of adult commitments conducive to law-abiding behavior, particularly marriage and stable employment (Sampson and Laub 1993; Simons et al. 2002; Warr 1998).

Nevertheless, Freud was one of the first to draw attention to the important influence of family socialization, which we will consider more fully in Part 4 of the book (see especially Chapter 11).

Personality Factors

There are other psychological perspectives that reject Freudian theory (in whole or in part) but that still postulate the existence of developmental personality types or ways of thinking that distinguish criminals from noncriminals. Delinquents have been variously described as emotionally unstable, mentally disordered, paranoid, schizophrenic, neurotic, egocentric, narcissistic, hedonistic, extroverted, aggressive, impulsive, hostile, defiant, attention-deficit disordered, learning disabled, insecure, low in self-esteem, shortsighted, and so forth—the list goes on and on (Berger, Free, and Searles 2009).

Sociological critics of personality theory point to the ambiguity of psychological labeling and to the multiple definitions of the personality concept, which "render it so vague that it could mean almost anything" (Sanders 1983: 21). The majority of personality inventories (studies utilizing questions or true-false statements that attempt to ascertain personality types) examined in an early review failed to confirm the hypothesis that criminals have different personalities than noncriminals (Schuessler and Cressey 1950). Although subsequent assessments suggested a more positive reading of the post-1950s research, with the Minnesota Multiphasic Personality Inventory, an instrument developed by Hathaway and Monachesi (1963), given the most favorable review, methodological problems have led many criminologists to downplay the significance of this line of research (Tennenbaum 1977; Waldo and Dinitz 1967).

Some personality inventories have been faulted for containing similar items in both the personality and the criminality sections of the questionnaire, thereby biasing findings in favor of an association between the two (Caspi et al. 1994). For example, one section might include an item such as "Sometimes when I was young I stole things," whereas the other section includes "I have never been in trouble with the law." Sometimes the criminal behavior itself is used as a criterion for the classification of the aberrant personality type. And like the biological research on crime, personality studies tend to rely on relatively small samples and focus on officially labeled criminals and delinquents. Moreover, the research finds that personality differences *between law violators* is at times greater than the differences *between offenders and nonoffenders*. The research also finds that the amount of mental disorder among offenders or the amount of crime among the disordered is no more than is found among the general population (Akers and Sellers 2009; Monahan and Steadman 1983).

Psychologists have argued that much sociological criticism of personality theory reflects a disciplinary bias against individualistic explanations and unfairly represents the evidence (Andrews and Wormith 1989). Indeed, there are reputable studies that have found personality differences between offenders and nonoffenders (Caspi et al. 1994; Miller and Lynam 2001). Gottfredson and Hirschi (1990) argue that the myriad traits identified in this research tradition can best be characterized as a matter of **low self-control,** which is indicative of individuals who have difficulty delaying gratification and tolerating frustration, who are unable to solve problems through verbal rather than physical means, and who are self-centered and indifferent to the needs and feelings of others. They argue that self-control is "for all intents and purposes, *the* individual-level cause of crime" (p. 232). The association between low self-control and criminality is well documented in the research literature, although not to the exclusion of (or to a greater extent than) other social variables (Baron 2003; Longshore et al. 2004; Morris, Wood, and Dunaway 2006; Pratt and Cullen 2000). Moreover, a critical task of sociological theory and research is to explain why such personality differences exist in the first place. Does the cause of crime and delinquency reside within the individual, in the developmental years of childhood, or in broader social factors that we have yet to explore?

Behaviorism

Psychological **behaviorism,** also called "operant conditioning" or "learning-reinforcement" theory, offers another way of understanding individual behavior. Behaviorism, which is associated with the work of B. F. Skinner (1953), differs from Freudian and personality theories in that it focuses on observable behavior rather than on unconscious or personality factors. It postulates that "behavior is acquired or conditioned by the effects, outcomes, or *consequences* it has on a person's environment" (Akers 1985:43; emphasis in original). Behavior that is reinforced by a reward or positive consequence will persist, whereas behavior that is unrewarded or punished will be discontinued. Individuals learn to favor particular courses of action, including the criminal variety, depending on the particular mix of rewards and punishments that is attached to their behavior. Rewards and punishments may be *social* or *nonsocial* in nature. The social include favorable or unfavorable reactions from other individuals (e.g., you receive approval or disapproval from parents or friends); the nonsocial include the pleasurable or unpleasurable physical sensations associated with behavior (e.g., you feel euphoric or ill after consuming alcohol or drugs). Learning also takes place through the imitation or modeling of other people's behavior (Akers and Sellers 2009; Wood et al. 1997).

Since behaviorist explanations necessarily implicate social relationships, we will defer discussion of the behaviorist approach called "social learning" theory until later in this section. For now it suffices to say that behaviorism postulates that the psychological mechanisms underlying delinquent behavior are essentially the same as those underlying law-abiding behavior. Psychologically speaking, most delinquents are actually *not so different* from the rest of us.

Applications of Psychological Approaches

Psychological theories have been very influential in establishing the rehabilitative approach to crime control. These theories suggest therapeutic interventions designed to transform the offender from an individual with an abnormal or maladaptive personality to an individual with a normal personality. Such interventions typically employ professional therapists (e.g., psychiatrists, psychologists, social workers) who attempt to (1) help offenders uncover the childhood root causes of their behavior or gain insight more generally into why they behave as they do, and (2) train individuals to monitor and control their actions more effectively (Einstadter and Henry 1995). These strategies also have been applied to at-risk youths with the goal of *prevention,* and as such pose some of the same ethical dilemmas that biological treatments pose—issues regarding accurate diagnosis, stigmatizing labels, and unwarranted intrusion into the lives of youths who have not yet committed crimes. On the other hand, failure to intervene to help individuals in need has potential costs as well.

Yochelson and Samenow (1976, 1977) reject the "couch therapy" approach to psychology and focus instead on the delinquent's current way of thinking. They are not interested in past environmental influences or the emotional burdens of childhood. Rather, they want to confront the individual's calculating, narcissistic personality. Offenders must acknowledge they are responsible and accountable for their own behavior, and they must reject "errors-in-thinking" that rationalize or blame others for their actions. According to Yochelson and Samenow, only through the development of such "internal deterrents" will the likelihood of future criminality be reduced.

Overall, the rehabilitative record of conventional psychotherapies is weak (Lundman 2001; Whitehead and Lab 1989). Behaviorist interventions that manipulate the distribution of rewards and punishments (e.g., a token economy or point system that grants or denies privileges based on the person's behavior) appear somewhat effective in inducing conformity within correctional settings, but they have negligible impact upon release (Trojanowicz, Morash, and Schram 2001). Successful programs generally require a more comprehensive approach than is typically available. Andrews and colleagues (1990) believe that the most effective correctional interventions utilize behaviorist and social learning principles, are carefully matched to offenders' particular learning styles and psychological needs, enhance aggression management and stress management as well as academic and vocational skills, change antisocial attitudes and ways of thinking, reduce chemical dependencies, foster familial bonds, modify peer associations and role models, and help access appropriate service agencies (Cullen and Applegate 1997; Gibbons 1999; Pearson et al. 2002).

Social Psychological Approaches

The readings in this section present various social psychological approaches, which, as noted earlier, consider the ways in which delinquents interpret or account for the meaning of their actions and learn to favor or disfavor criminal courses of conduct. Rather than characterizing delinquents as particular "kinds of persons" who possess some flawed or defective trait, these approaches emphasize the common ways in which "normal" people respond to varying social environments (Orcutt 1983).

The Rational Criminal

One of the oldest theories of criminal behavior has its roots in the eighteenth- and nineteenth-century thinking of European social theorists Cesare Beccaria (1738–1794) and Jeremy Bentham (1748–1842), who believed in the doctrine of **free will.** In their view, individuals who violate the law *rationally choose* to commit crime because they believe that the pleasures or benefits of such actions outweigh the pains or costs. The role of government is to manipulate this rational calculation of benefits and costs by maintaining a level of punishment that exceeds the potential rewards of crime. In contemporary parlance this is known as the principle of **deterrence,** and in contemporary criminological theory it is known as **rational-choice theory** (Beirne and Messerchmidt 1995; Berger, Free, and Searles 2009).

In Chapter 6, "Scared Straight: A Question of Deterrence," Richard Lundman considers rational-choice theory and deterrence as it applies to prison-based efforts designed to scare youths into believing that "crime does not pay." The "scared straight" strategy brings youths to a prison where they are confronted by convicts who graphically describe the harsh realities of prison life. Lundman reviews evaluation studies of various programs of this nature and concludes that they are generally ineffective and not the panacea to the delinquency problem that proponents initially claimed them to be.

The less than impressive results of scared straight strategies are not really surprising in light of other deterrence research. Deterrence researchers, as Lundman notes, distinguish between the **certainty of punishment** (the likelihood of apprehension), the **swiftness of punishment** (the immediacy of punishment following an offense), and the **severity of punishment** (the harshness of sanctions), with studies finding that certainty of punishment generally has the greatest deterrent, because if certainty is low, swiftness and severity are irrelevant to the cost-benefit calculus of offenders. These studies found that even the effect of certainty of punishment is weak, however (Krohn 2000; Paternoster 1987; Webster, Doob, and Zimring 2006).

There are several factors that appear to mitigate the deterrent effect of punishment. Research indicates that individuals' *perceptions* of punishment may be more significant than the actual punishment itself (Krohn 2000; Paternoster 1987; Williams and Hawkins 1986). And this is the premise of the scared straight approach, which attempts to alter youths' perceptions of what they can expect if they continue to violate the law. At the same time, as the ineffectiveness of scared straight programs suggests, a youth's decision to violate is affected by an array of other factors, for example, a youth's perception of his or her stake in the status quo and the relative availability of legal and illegal opportunities for economic success (Piliavan et al. 1986; Williams and Kornblum 1985).

Research also suggests that a youth's internalized or normative evaluation of right and wrong may be more central to the decision to violate the law than perceptions of punishment and that informal sanctions or extralegal threats such as shame, embarrassment, and disapproval from family and peers may deter law violation more than formal punishment (Erickson, Gibbs, and Jensen 1977; Paternoster 1987; Williams and Hawkins 1986). Moreover, Matza (1964) observed that as juveniles grew older, many underwent **maturational reform** and desisted from delinquency as they took on the responsibilities of work and family life. And Carpenter and colleagues (1988) found that by age 16, some juveniles reported being deterred by the fact that they would face greater consequences than they had so far if they continued to offend. These youths recognized that as they grew older they would end up not just in the juvenile justice system but in the more punitive adult criminal justice system.

Social Learning and Symbolic Interaction

Edwin Sutherland's (1947) classic theory of **differential association** is the appropriate place to begin our consideration of social learning and symbolic interaction theories of delinquency, as it has been characterized as both behaviorist and interactionist in orientation (Einstadter and Henry 1995; Empey and Stafford 1991). The behaviorist orientation, as we noted earlier, focuses on delinquent behavior as learned or conditioned through the particular mix of rewards and punishments that are attached to a person's behavior. Symbolic interaction, on the other hand, is concerned with the symbolic meaning of social action for the individual and on how the individual defines or interprets his or her social world and acquires a sense of self or personal identity through interaction with others (Sandstrom, Martin, and Fine 2006).

According to differential association theory, criminal and delinquent "behavior is learned in interaction with other persons in a process of communication . . . within intimate personal groups" (cited in Akers and Sellers 2009:86). The learning of crime and delinquency includes not only "the techniques of committing the crime, which are sometimes very complicated and sometimes very simple" but also "the specific direction of motives, drives, rationalizations, and attitudes" underlying the illegal behavior. A person becomes criminal or delinquent when he or she is exposed to "an excess of definitions favorable to violation of law over definitions unfavorable to violation of law." Since individuals are typically exposed to both crime-inducing and crime-inhibiting associations, what matters is the relative *frequency* (how often one spends time with particular others), *duration* (how much time one spends with them on each occasion), *priority* (how early in life one began associating with them), and *intensity* (how much importance one attaches to them) of each.

In a large body of theory and research, Akers and colleagues advanced a **social learning theory** that merges principles of differential association theory with those of behaviorist psychology in order to examine processes that both "motivate and control criminal behavior" and "promote and undermine conformity" (Akers and Sellers 2009:89). From Sutherland, Akers takes the concepts of *differential association* and *definitions* and adds the behaviorist concepts of *imitation* and *differential reinforcement.* Imitation refers to one's observation and replication of role models' behavior in both actual and simulated environments (i.e., the media). Akers and colleagues' research indicates that imitation is "more important in the initial acquisition and performance of novel behavior than in the maintenance or cessation of behavioral patterns once established" (p. 93). Differential reinforcement "refers to the *balance* of anticipated or actual rewards and punishments that follow or are consequences of behavior" (pp. 91–92; emphasis added). As noted earlier, rewards and punishments can be both social and nonsocial, and they can range from approval or disapproval of parents and friends to the euphoric or unpleasant physical effects of drugs. The earlier discussion also showed that studies find anticipation of informal sanctions from others to be a more salient deterrent to crime than anticipation of formal sanctions from the law.

Both social learning and differential association theories make use of the concept of **definitions** when describing the process by which individuals come to define or interpret law-violating behavior as acceptable or unacceptable. In some studies, definitions have been operationalized according to Sykes and Matza's concept (1957) of **techniques of neutralization.** Sykes and Matza argued that most law violators have some appreciation or respect for conventional values and must therefore neutralize the hold these values have on them through various self-rationalizations or justifications.

In their research on delinquent youths, Sykes and Matza identified five general techniques of neutralization. *Denial of responsibility* involves the delinquent's assertion that his or her behavior is due to external forces such as "unloving parents, bad companions, or a slum neighborhood." Youths often view themselves "as helplessly propelled into" unlawful behavior, as "more acted upon than acting" (p. 667). For example, a youth may explain that "the alcohol made me do it" or "the other guy started the fight." *Denial of injury* describes the offender's view that no harm has been caused by his or her actions—for instance, by drinking alcohol, smoking marijuana, or "borrowing" someone's car for a joyride. *Denial of the victim* is used as a way to distinguish people who are deserving targets of crime, such as a black person who's gotten "out of his place," a teacher who's been unfair, or a store owner who's ripped off customers. *Condemnation of the condemners* shifts attention away from the youth and toward the disapproving others, who are viewed as "hypocrites, deviants in disguise, or impelled by personal spite" (p. 688). For example, a youth may resent police officers who are corrupt, teachers who show favoritism, or parents who abuse their children. Finally, *appeal to higher loyalties* involves the imperative to sacrifice the rules of the larger society for the demands of the smaller group, such as the friendship clique or gang.[3]

In terms of practical applications, the learning-interactionist approach suggests rehabilitative interventions that utilize group dynamics to reinforce conventional behavior. Such applications are referred to variously as guided group interaction, peer-group counseling, positive peer culture, and therapeutic communities (Gottfredson 1987). In juvenile correctional settings these approaches offer advantages over individual-oriented treatments. Insofar as offenders often manifest their law-violating behavior as part of a group, the group therapy situation is the natural vehicle for personal change or growth: "The [beginning] stages of the group are used to vent hostility and aggression. Initially, the groups' members are self-centered and unable to realistically or meaningfully involve themselves or their peers in the problem-solving process. Later, as the group progresses and the . . . members see that their . . . peers have similar problems and backgrounds, empathy and group identification are facilitated, . . . ultimately produc[ing] insight and new patterns of adaptation" (Trojanowicz, Morash, and Schram 2001:363–364). These groups are often staffed by ex-offenders and ex-addicts and "show remarkably consistent reductions" in criminal behavior for those who complete the programs (Lipton 1996:12).

Be that as it may, in Chapter 7, "Social Learning Theory, Drug Use, and American Indian Youths: A Cross-Cultural Test," Thomas Winfree, Curt Griffiths, and Christine Sellers offer one example from a larger body of research that supports this learning-interactionist proposition about the causes of delinquency, particularly the elements that are related to differential association with peer groups and definitions that encourage law violation.[4] An important point is that Winfree, Griffiths, and Sellers provide a multicultural test of social learning, comparing American Indian and Caucasian youths, demonstrating that the basic propositions of the theory are valid for diverse cultural groups. Although they did find some group differences, the authors argue that "constructs and variables derived from social learning [theory] . . . performed . . . largely as anticipated" and that the theory has the "conceptual flexibility to accommodate different sources and processes of learning."

In Chapter 8, "Delinquents' Perspectives on the Role of the Victim," Cheryl Carpenter, Barry Glassner, Bruce Johnson, Julia Loughlin, and Margret Ksander employ Sykes and Matza's concept of techniques of neutralization— mainly denial of the victim and denial of injury—to uncover ways in which youths distinguish between appropriate and inappropriate targets of particular types of crimes. Their interviews with delinquent youths highlight the need to understand "how youths *themselves* define the illegal activities in which they become involved" (emphasis added).

In Chapter 9, "Self-Definition by Rejection: The Case of Gang Girls," Anne Campbell uses observations and interviews with low-income Puerto Rican gang girls in New York City to show how youths construct their identity or sense of self through social talk, particularly through gossip and "put downs" that vilify others' action and character. Campbell argues that delinquency research would profit greatly by taking "disparaging social talk as a legitimate focus of inquiry."

General Strain and Gender Theory

In Chapter 10, "Explaining School Shooters: The View from General Strain and Gender Theory," Ronald Berger illuminates the problems of bullying and suburban and school shooters through the perspectives of two relatively recent social psychological perspectives, **general strain theory** and **gender theory.** General strain theory, according to Berger, posits that delinquency is the outcome of an "array of stressful or negative life experiences that strain one's relationship with society." Gender theory posits that "societal notions of masculinity and femininity are socially constructed" and that "the dominant form of masculinity in society" sanctions displays of aggression and a "might makes right" ethos as a means of asserting and preserving one's social standing among peers. Berger notes that school shooters have often been victims of persistent bullying and other public degradations to their masculine status that results in what he calls **masculine gender strain,** which eventually erupts into public displays of retaliation. His analysis suggests that the phenomenon of school shootings cannot be addressed without understanding the more general problem of bullying as a source of strain and gender status degradation in our society.

▓ Notes

1. Readers may be surprised that someone who advanced such ideas could have become a central figure in criminology. Lombroso was a man of his time, when such racial prejudice was not uncommon. (Variants of such views continue to persist even today.) But it was Lombroso's attempt to prove his theory with the methods of science that brought him his fame. He measured and recorded in great detail the physical attributes of living and deceased Italian prisoners, compared these findings with data from nonprisoners, and claimed his hypothesis proven.

Nevertheless, Lombroso's research was methodologically flawed (Barkan 2006; Berger, Free, and Searles 2009). The prisoner and nonprisoner samples were not pure types. The former may have included people who were innocent of the crimes they had been convicted of, and the latter likely included offenders who had not been caught and convicted. Moreover, the alleged physical differences found by Lombroso were rather trivial. And even if the alleged differences were noticeable, the fact that the prisoners were disproportionately Sicilian made the research problematic. For although Sicilians may have tended to have some of the physical traits Lombroso attributed to criminals, their low status in Italian society would have increased their chances of imprisonment. The earliest scientific refutation of Lombroso's work was published by Goring (1913), who compared the physical attributes of some 3,000 English prisoners with those of a large control group and found no differences along the lines postulated by Lombroso.

2. It also is important to note that fathers as well as mothers can contribute to birth defects in children. Exposure to environmental toxins can damage ova and sperm and be transmitted to fetuses, even during intercourse *after* conception has occurred (Narayan 1995).

3. Critics have faulted Sykes and Matza for failing to establish that techniques of neutralization actually *precede* rather than *follow* delinquent acts, arguing that techniques of neutralization are mechanisms that facilitate the "hardening" of youths already involved in crime (Hamlin 1988; Minor 1984). Others have observed that rationalizations are used not so much to neutralize moral commitments as to minimize "risks or other tactical considerations" (Schwendinger and Schwendinger 1985:139). For instance, delinquents may rationalize stealing from people they perceive as "careless victims," that is, as people whose "inefficiency in protecting their possessions makes them 'responsible' in part for their own victimization" (e.g., people who leave their keys in their car, who don't lock up their bicycles, or who leave their houses unlocked) (Carpenter et al. 1988:104; see Chapter 8).

4. Akers and Sellers summarize the results of empirical research on social learning theory: "There is abundant evidence to show the significant impact . . . of differential association in primary groups such as family and peers. . . . Delinquency may be . . . directly affected by deviant parental models, ineffective and erratic supervision and discipline . . . and the endorsement of values and attitudes favorable to deviance. . . . In general, parental . . . criminality is predictive of . . . children's future criminality. . . . The role of the family, however, is usually as a conventional socializer against delinquency. . . . It provides anticriminal definitions, conforming models, and the reinforcement of conformity through parental discipline. . . . Other than one's own prior . . . behavior, the best single predictor of the onset, continuance, or desistance of . . . delinquency is differential association with conforming or law-violating peers. . . . It is in peer groups that the first availability and opportunity for delinquent acts are typically provided. Virtually every study that includes a peer association variable finds it to be significantly and usually most strongly related to delinquency . . . and other forms of deviant behavior" (2009:99–101).

References

Aichhorn, August. 1935. *Wayward Youth*. New York: Viking.

Akers, Ronald L. 1985. *Deviant Behavior: A Social Learning Approach*. Belmont, CA: Wadsworth.

Akers, Ronald L., and Christine S. Sellers. 2009. *Criminological Theories: Introduction, Evaluation, Application*. New York: Oxford University Press.

Andrews, D. A., and J. S. Wormith. 1989. "Personality and Crime: Knowledge Destruction and Construction in Criminology." *Justice Quarterly* 6:289–309.

Andrews, D. A., et al. 1990. "Does Correctional Treatment Work? A Clinically Relevant and Psychologically Informed Meta-analysis." *Criminology* 28:369–404.

Barkan, Steven E. 2006. *Criminology*. Upper Saddle River, NJ: Prentice-Hall.

Baron, Stephen W. 2003. "Self-Control, Social Consequences, and Criminal Behavior: Street Youth and the General Theory of Crime." *Journal of Research in Crime and Delinquency* 40:403–425.

Bartol, Curt R., and Anne Bartol. 1989. *Juvenile Delinquency.* Englewood Cliffs, NJ: Prentice-Hall.

Beirne, Piers, and James W. Messerschmidt. 1995. *Criminology.* Fort Worth, TX: Harcourt Brace.

Berger, Ronald J., Marvin D. Free, and Patricia Searles. 2009. *Crime, Justice, and Society: An Introduction to Criminology.* 3rd ed. Boulder, CO: Lynne Rienner.

Binder, Arnold, Gilbert Geis, and Dickson D. Bruce. 2001. *Juvenile Delinquency: Historical, Cultural, and Legal Perspectives.* New York: Macmillan.

Blumstein, Albert, and Elizabeth Grady. 1982. "Prevalence and Recidivism in Index Arrests: A Feedback Model." *Law and Society Review* 16:265–290.

Carpenter, Cheryl, Barry Glassner, Bruce D. Johnson, and Julia Loughlin. 1988. *Kids, Drugs, and Crime.* Lexington, MA: Lexington.

Caspi, Avshalom, et al. 1994. "Are Some People Crime-Prone? Replications of the Personality-Crime Relationship Across Countries, Genders, Races, and Methods." *Criminology* 32:163–195.

Cauffman, Elizabeth, Lawrence Steinberg, and Alex R. Piquero. 2005. "Psychological, Neuropsychological, and Physiological Correlates of Serious Antisocial Behavior in Adolescence: The Role of Self-Control." *Criminology* 43:133–175.

Cullen, Francis T., and Brandon K. Applegate (eds.). 1997. *Offender Rehabilitation: Effective Treatment Intervention.* Aldershot, UK: Ashgate.

Cullen, Francis T., Paul Gendreau, G. Roger Jarjoura, and John Paul Wright. 1997. "Crime and the Bell Curve: Lessons from Intelligent Criminology." *Crime and Delinquency* 43:387–411.

Dalgard, Odd Steffen, and Einar Kringlen. 1976. "A Norwegian Twin Study of Criminality." *British Journal of Criminology* 23:711–741.

Dietrich, Kim, et al. 2001. "Early Exposure to Lead and Juvenile Delinquency." *Neurotoxicology and Teratology* 23:511–518.

Einstadter, Werner J., and Stuart Henry. 1995. *Criminological Theory.* Fort Worth, TX: Harcourt Brace.

Ellis, Lee, and Anthony Walsh. 1997. "Gene-Based Evolutionary Theories in Criminology." *Criminology* 35:229–276.

———. 2000. *Criminology: A Global Perspective.* Boston: Allyn and Bacon.

Empey, Lamar T., and Mark C. Stafford. 1991. *American Delinquency: Its Meaning and Construction.* Homewood, IL: Dorsey.

Erickson, Maynard L., Jack P. Gibbs, and Gary F. Jensen. 1977. "The Deterrence Doctrine and the Perceived Certainty of Legal Punishment." *American Sociological Review* 42:305–317.

Eysenck, Hans Jurgen. 1977. *Crime and Personality.* London: Routledge and Kegan Paul.

Felson, Richard B., and Jeremy Staff. 2006. "Explaining the Academic Performance–Delinquency Relationship." *Criminology* 44:299–319.

Fishbein, Diana H. 1990. "Biological Perspectives in Criminology." *Criminology* 28:27–72.

Friedlander, Kate. 1947. *The Psychoanalytic Approach to Juvenile Delinquency.* London: Routledge and Kegan Paul.

Gibbons, Don. 1999. "Review Essay: Changing Lawbreakers—What Have We Learned Since the 1960s?" *Crime and Delinquency* 45:272–293.

Glueck, Sheldon, and Eleanor T. Glueck. 1950. *Unraveling Juvenile Delinquency.* New York: Commonwealth Fund.

Goring, Charles. 1913. *The English Convict.* London: H.M.S.O.

Gottfredson, Gary. 1987. "Peer Group Interventions to Reduce the Risk of Delinquent Behavior: A Selective Review and a New Evaluation." *Criminology* 25:671–714.

Gottfredson, Michael R., and Travis Hirschi. 1990. *A General Theory of Crime.* Stanford, CA: Stanford University Press.

Hamlin, John E. 1988. "The Misplaced Role of Rational Choice in Neutralization Theory." *Criminology* 26:425–438.

Hathaway, Starker R., and Elio Monachesi. 1963. *Adolescent Personality and Behavior.* Minneapolis: University of Minnesota Press.

Healy, William, and Augusta F. Bronner. 1936. *New Light on Delinquency and Its Treatment.* New Haven, CT: Yale University Press.

Herrnstein, Richard J. 1995. "Criminogenic Traits." In J. Wilson and J. Petersilia (eds.), *Crime.* San Francisco: Institute for Contemporary Studies.

Herrnstein, Richard J., and Charles Murray. 1994. *The Bell Curve: Intelligence and Class Structure in American Life.* New York: Free Press.

Hirschi, Travis, and Michael J. Hindelang. 1977. "Intelligence and Delinquency: A Revisionist Critique." *American Sociological Review* 43:571–587.

Katz, Janet, and William J. Chambliss. 1995. "Biology and Crime." In J. Sheley (ed.), *Criminology: A Contemporary Handbook,* rev. ed. Belmont, CA: Wadsworth.

Krohn, Marvin. 2000. "Sources of Criminality: Control and Deterrence Theories." In J. Sheley (ed.), *Criminology: A Contemporary Handbook.* 3rd ed. Belmont, CA: Wadsworth.

Lipton, Douglas S. 1996. "Prison-Based Therapeutic Communities: Their Success with Drug-Abusing Offenders." *National Institute of Justice Journal* (February): 12–30.

Longshore, Douglas, Eunice Chang, Shi-chao Hsieh, and Nena Messina. 2004. "Self-control and Social Bonds: A Combined Control Perspective on Deviance." *Crime and Delinquency* 50:542–564.

Lundman, Richard J. 2001. *Prevention and Control of Juvenile Delinquency.* New York: Oxford University Press.

Matza, David. 1964. *Delinquency and Drift.* New York: Wiley.

Mednick, S., V. Pollock, and J. Volavka. 1982. "Biology and Violence." In M. Wolfgang and N. Weiner (eds.), *Criminal Violence.* Beverly Hills: Sage.

Menard, Scott, and Barbara J. Morse. 1984. "A Structuralist Critique of the IQ-Delinquency Hypothesis: Theory and Evidence." *American Journal of Sociology* 89: 1347–1378.

Miller, Joshua D., and Donald Lynam. 2001. "Structural Models of Personality and Their Relation to Antisocial Behavior: A Meta-Analytic Review." *Criminology* 39:765–795.

Minor, W. William. 1984. "Neutralization as a Hardening Process: Considerations in the Modeling of Change." *Social Forces* 62:995–1019.

Moffitt, Terrie E., et al. 1998. "Whole Blood Serotonin Relates to Violence in an Epidemiological Study." *Biological Psychiatry* 43:446–457.

Monahan, John, and Henry J. Steadman. 1983. "Crime and Mental Disorder: An Epidemiological Approach." In M. Tonry and N. Morris (eds.), *Crime and Justice: An Annual Review of Research,* vol. 4. Chicago: University of Chicago Press.

Morris, Gregory D. , Peter R. Wood, and R. Gregory Dunaway. 2006. "Self-control, Native Traditionalism, and Native American Substance Use: Testing the Cultural Invariance of a General Theory of Crime." *Crime and Delinquency* 52:572–598.

Narayan, Uma. 1995. "The Discriminating Nature of Industrial Health-Hazard Policies and Some Implications for Third World Women Workers." In J. Callahan (ed.), *Reproduction, Ethics, and the Law.* Bloomington: Indiana University Press.

Needleman, H. L., J. A. Riess, M. J. Biesecker, and J. B. Greenhouse. 1996. "Bone Lead Levels and Delinquent Behavior." *Journal of the American Medical Association* 275:363–369.

Neuman, W. Lawrence. 2003. *Social Research Methods.* Boston: Allyn and Bacon.

Nevin, Rick. 2000. "How Lead Exposure Relates to Temporal Changes in IQ, Violent Crime, and Unwed Pregnancy." *Environmental Research* 83:1–22.

Orcutt, James P. (ed.). 1983. *Analyzing Deviance.* Homewood, IL: Dorsey.

Paternoster, Raymond. 1987. "The Deterrent Effect of the Perceived Certainty and Severity of Punishment: A Review of the Evidence and Issues." *Justice Quarterly* 4:173–217.

Pearson, Frank S., Douglas S. Lipton, Charles M. Cleland, and Dorline S. Yee. 2002. "The Effects of Behavioral/Cognitive Programs on Recidivism." *Crime and De- linquency* 48:476–496.

Piliavan, Irving, Rosemary Gartner, Charles Thornton, and Ross L. Matsueda. 1986. "Crime, Deterrence, and Rational Choice." *American Sociological Review* 51: 101–119.

Pratt, Travis C., and Francis T. Cullen. 2000. "The Empirical Status of Gottfredson and Hirchi's General Theory of Crime: A Meta-analysis." *Criminology* 38:931–964.

Rafter, Nicole Hahn. 1992. "Criminal Anthropology in the United States." *Criminology* 30:525–545.

Rowe, David C. 1986. "Genetic and Environmental Components of Antisocial Behav- ior: A Study of 265 Twins." *Criminology* 24:513–532.

Sampson, Robert J., and John H. Laub. 1993. *Crime in the Making: Pathways and Turning Points Through Life.* Cambridge, MA: Harvard University Press.

Sanders, William B. 1983. *Criminology.* Reading, MA: Addison-Wesley.

Sandstrom, Kent L., Daniel D. Martin, and Gary Alan Fine. 2006. *Symbols, Selves, and Social Reality: A Symbolic Interactionist Approach to Social Psychology and So- ciology.* Los Angeles: Roxbury.

Schuessler, Karl F., and Donald R. Cressey. 1950. "Personality Characteristics of Crim- inals." *American Journal of Sociology* 43:476–484.

Schwendinger, Herman, and Julia Siegel Schwendinger. 1985. *Adolescent Subcultures and Delinquency.* New York: Praeger.

Sheldon, William H. 1949. *Varieties of Delinquent Youth.* New York: Harper and Row.

Sheley, Joseph F. 1985. *America's "Crime Problem."* Belmont, CA: Wadsworth.

Siegel, Larry J., Brandon C. Welsh, and Joseph J. Senna. 2003. *Juvenile Delinquency: Theory, Practice, and Law.* Belmont, CA: Wadsworth.

Simons, Ronald L., et al. 2002. "A Test of Life-Course Explanations for Stability and Change in Antisocial Behavior from Adolescence to Young Adulthood." *Crimi- nology* 40:401–434.

Skinner, B. F. 1953. *Science and Human Behavior.* New York: Macmillan.

Sutherland, Edwin H. 1947. *Principles of Criminology,* 6th ed. Philadelphia, PA: Lippincott.

Sykes, Gresham, and David Matza. 1957. "Techniques of Neutralization: A Theory of Delinquency." *American Sociological Review* 22:664–670.

Tennenbaum, David J. 1977. "Personality and Criminality: A Summary and Implica- tions of the Literature." *Journal of Criminal Justice* 5:225–235.

Theilgaard, Alice. 1984. "A Psychological Study of the Personalities of XYY- and XY- Men." *Acta Psychiatrica Scandinavia* 69:1–133.

Trojanowicz, Robert C., Merry Morash, and Pamela J. Schram. 2001. *Juvenile Delin- quency: Concepts and Controls.* Englewood Cliffs, NJ: Prentice-Hall.

Waldo, Gordon P., and Simon Dinitz. 1967. "Personality Attributes of the Criminal: An Analysis of Research Studies." *Journal of Research on Crime and Delinquency* 4:185–201.

Walters, Glen D., and Thomas W. White. 1989. "Heredity and Crime: Bad Genes or Bad Research?" *Criminology* 27:455–485.

Warr, Mark. 1998. "Life-Course Transitions and Desistance from Crime." *Criminology* 36:183–216.
Webster, Cheryl Marie, Anthony N. Doob, and Franklin E. Zimring. 2006. "Proposition 8 and Crime Rates in California: The Case of the Disappearing Deterrent." *Criminology and Public Policy* 5:417–448.
Whitehead, John T., and Steven P. Lab. 1989. "A Meta-Analysis of Juvenile Correctional Treatment." *Journal of Research in Crime and Delinquency* 26:276–295.
Williams, Kirk R., and Richard Hawkins. 1986. "Perceptual Research on General Deterrence: A Critical Review." *Law and Society Review* 20:211–236.
Williams, Terry, and William Kornblum. 1985. *Growing Up Poor.* Lexington, MA: Lexington.
Wilson, James Q., and Richard J. Herrnstein. 1985. *Crime and Human Nature.* New York: Simon and Schuster.
Wood, Peter B., Walter P. Gove, James A. Wilson, and John K. Cochran. 1997. "Nonsocial Reinforcement and Habitual Criminal Conduct: An Extension of Learning Theory." *Criminology* 35:335–366.
Yochelson, Samuel, and Stanton E. Samenow. 1976, 1977. *The Criminal Personality,* vols. 1–2. New York: Jason Aronson.

6

Scared Straight:
A Question of Deterrence

Richard J. Lundman

This chapter considers the question of deterrence as it applies to prison-based efforts designed to scare youths into believing that "crime does not pay." The "scared straight" strategy brings youths to a prison where they are confronted by convicts who graphically describe the harsh realities of prison life. Richard Lundman reviews evaluation studies of various programs of this nature and concludes that they are generally ineffective and not the panacea to the delinquency problem that proponents initially claimed them to be.

ON NOVEMBER 2, 1978, AN INDEPENDENT TELEVISION STATION IN LOS Angeles presented a film documentary entitled *Scared Straight.*[1] This documentary was a partial record of an intensive confrontation session between adult inmates serving long or life sentences at New Jersey's Rahway State Prison and juveniles brought to the prison in an effort to control their involvement in delinquency. On March 5, 1979, *Scared Straight* was shown on national television, although some local stations initially refused to air it because of its frank language and graphic scenes.[2] In April 1979, *Scared Straight* won an Academy Award for best film documentary.

State legislators and prison administrators were quick to take notice of *Scared Straight.* California legislators introduced a bill requiring the busing of 15,000 juveniles to state prisons for Rahway-type confrontation sessions. Alabama juveniles attended confrontation sessions where one inmate told of being gang raped while in prison.[3] In New York City, children of 11 and 12 years of age were taken on tours of city jails.[4]

What attracted the attention of legislators and prison administrators were the phenomenal claims of success advanced in *Scared Straight.* All 17 of the

---

Excerpt from *Prevention and Control of Juvenile Delinquency,* 3rd ed., by Richard J. Lundman (Oxford University Press, 2001). Reprinted by permission of Oxford University Press.

juveniles appearing in the documentary were described as frequently and seriously delinquent. Three months later, according to the film, 16 had become law-abiding. This was said to be common. Of the nearly 8,000 juveniles attending intensive confrontation sessions at Rahway State Prison through 1978, *Scared Straight* reported that approximately 90 percent had not experienced further trouble with the law, a success rate "unequalled by traditional rehabilitation methods."

This chapter examines prison-based efforts to scare juveniles straight. It begins by briefly demonstrating that Rahway-type programs are grounded in the deterrence approach to the control of delinquency. Attention is then directed to Professor James O. Finckenauer's assessment of Rahway's Juvenile Awareness Project. Next, review of two replicative efforts to scare juveniles straight is undertaken. Last, an overview of the current state of efforts to scare juveniles straight is provided, with a special focus on the creation and abrupt suspension of a scared straight program at Norway's Ullersmo Prison in the mid-1990s.

▪ Scared Straight and Deterrence

Efforts to scare juveniles straight are firmly grounded in the deterrence approach to juvenile delinquency,[5] especially the idea that fear of severe punishment suppresses involvement in delinquency. During scared-straight intensive confrontation sessions, adult inmates appear to work very hard to alter juveniles' perceptions of the pains of imprisonment.[6] They tell vivid tales of sad men living dangerous lives inside the walls of shabby and overcrowded prisons. Their message is that deprivation, assault, rape, and murder are routine parts of the prison experience. They tell juveniles that if they continue their delinquent ways, they too will end up behind bars and on the receiving end of the pains of imprisonment. [Figures and tables that appeared in the original article have been omitted from this chapter.]

▪ The Rahway State Prison Juvenile Awareness Project

The Juvenile Awareness Project at New Jersey's Rahway State Prison (now called East Jersey State Prison) is easily the best known and most controversial of prison-based efforts to scare juveniles straight. In addition to the award-winning documentary, Rahway's program has been the subject of debate in the popular and social science literature[7] and the topic of several books,[8] including two by Rutgers University criminologist James O. Finckenauer. . . .

Description of the Project

The Juvenile Awareness Project[9] began at Rahway State Prison in September 1976. It continues to operate, although controversy over its methods and effectiveness has decreased the number of juveniles attending and, at least through the early 1990s, dramatically changed the nature of their experiences at Rahway. As early as 1980, for instance, Professor Finckenauer reported "that sessions declined from ten a week to about two per week; participation from two-hundred juveniles a week to about twenty-five."[10] In addition, sessions were less intensive and involved "forum . . . [and] . . . discussion" rather than angry-appearing and threatening inmates. By the late 1990s, the number of juveniles attending sessions remained down, but the sessions apparently have reverted back to the intensity characteristic of the start of the Juvenile Awareness Project.[11] This section of the chapter, however, focuses on the Juvenile Awareness Project as it was conducted during the late 1970s.

Through May 1979 over 13,000 juveniles had attended intensive confrontation sessions run by adult inmates serving long or life sentences. According to the documentary *Scared Straight,* juveniles attending these sessions were "chronic . . . young offenders already desensitized and willing to continue their petty careers as muggers, rip-off artists, pickpockets, and so forth."[12] Actually, very little is known about the over 13,000 juveniles who attended intensive confrontation sessions at Rahway. Moreover, what little is known suggests that many were straight even before they were scared.

In June 1979, Jerome Miller, President of the National Center on Institutions and Alternatives, appeared before a United States House of Representatives subcommittee holding hearings on Rahway's Juvenile Awareness Project.[13] Dr. Miller testified that the young people who appeared in *Scared Straight* lived in a small, middle-class New Jersey suburb, one without a serious delinquency problem. The juveniles congregated in a local park and had agreed to participate when asked to do so by a local police sergeant. Dr. Miller also testified that he had visited the high school attended by the juveniles appearing in the documentary. He learned that of the 1,200 middle-class students, 450 had already attended sessions at Rahway and that the typical method of recruitment was to make an announcement over the school's loudspeaker. The apparent goal was to have all 1,200 students eventually attend sessions at Rahway.

Professor Finckenauer's data also challenge the image that juveniles attending Rahway sessions were seriously and frequently delinquent. As part of his assessment of the Juvenile Awareness Project, Professor Finckenauer found that 49 agencies had sent juveniles to Rahway in the three months ending in November 1977. He reported that most were counseling, educational, employment, and recreational organizations rather than agencies dealing exclusively with delinquent juveniles.[14] In addition, of the juveniles directly involved in his assessment of the project, 41.3 percent had no prior record of delinquency. Of those with a prior record, most had committed minor offenses.[15]

Type of Treatment

The Juvenile Awareness Project was designed to control delinquency by altering juveniles' perceptions of the severity of punishment for criminal acts.[16] It was hypothesized that attending intensive confrontation sessions would cause juveniles to stay within the law out of fear that if they strayed they too could end up in a place like Rahway State Prison.

The effort to alter juveniles' perceptions of the severity of punishment began with a brief tour of Rahway State Prison. The juveniles saw the crowded cells, heard the almost constant metal on metal sound of a maximum security institution, and listened to the verbal taunts of hardened prisoners. If the juveniles were attractive, inmates undoubtedly indicated what would happen to them in prison.

At the end of the brief tour, juveniles in groups of about 15 were taken to a room for an intensive confrontation session with about 20 adult inmates serving long or life sentences. During these sessions inmates attempted to "cover the full spectrum of crime and its nonrewards, [explain] about prison, crime and its ramifications, [show] young people that the stories about the big house . . . being the place of bad men is in all reality the place of sad men, [and] prove the fact of what crime and its involvement is really all about."[17]

Explaining about crime and the reality of prison life involved shouting, swearing, and threats of physical abuse. What follows are some of the statements directed at the juveniles by the adult inmates:

> I'm gonna hurt you.
> You take something from me and I'll kill you.
> You see them pretty blue eyes of yours? I'll take one out of your face and squish it in front of you.
> Do you know what we see when we look at you—we see ourselves.
> If someone had done this to me I wouldn't be here.
> Who do you think we get? Young, tough motherfuckers like you. Get a pretty fat buck like you and stick a prick in your ass.[18]

Confrontation sessions sometimes even went beyond taunts and threats. Jerome Miller testified that:

> An earlier study of the program sponsored by the New Jersey Department of Corrections indicated that the Juvenile Awareness Program had two primary techniques: (1) "exaggeration" and (2) "manhandling." This latter technique has probably led to certain incidents which have generally not been publicly known. We received allegations of certain youngsters being culled about, lifted by the head and shaken, "goosed" or pinched on their behind. We are also aware of more serious allegations which we would prefer to corroborate more completely before specifying.[19]

Professor Finckenauer reports much the same thing, noting that some of the adolescent males attending sessions were "kissed and fondled" by inmates.[20]

Evaluative Design

Professor Finckenauer's goal was to evaluate the Juvenile Awareness Project experimentally.[21] He secured the names of the 49 community agencies that had sent juveniles to Rahway in the fall of 1977. He then selected a random sample of these agencies (N = 28) and contacted them to determine whether they would be willing to permit random assignment of juveniles to an experimental and a control group. Of the agencies contacted, 11 promised cooperation. However, only five of these agencies actually abided by the random assignment procedures. Of the other six agencies, "two . . . took both experimental and controls to Rahway, . . . [t]wo other sponsors failed to take the experimentals . . . as scheduled, . . . [o]ne agency . . . twice failed to show up at Rahway, [and] one other agency . . . backed out."[22]

These problems resulted in two important changes in Professor Finckenauer's evaluation procedures. The projected sizes of the comparison groups were reduced from 50 each to 46 in the Rahway-visit group and 35 in the control group. More important, initial refusals by agencies to cooperate along with mistakes by cooperating agencies in sending or failing to send experimental juveniles to Rahway resulted in a quasi-experimental evaluative design.

Measure of Results

The extent to which attending intensive confrontation sessions altered juveniles' perceptions of the severity of punishment was assessed by Professor Finckenauer using questionnaires. These instruments were designed to probe attitudes toward prisons and punishment. Professor Finckenauer found that attending intensive confrontation sessions did not alter juveniles' perceptions of the severity of punishment.[23]

Attending intensive confrontation sessions also did not lead to control of juvenile delinquency. Among juveniles visiting Rahway, 41.3 percent committed a new offense during the six months following their visit. By comparison, only 11.4 percent of the juveniles in the control group committed a new offense during that same time period. The Juvenile Awareness Project not only failed to control delinquency, but it apparently made things worse.

Replication: Michigan Reformatory Visitation Program

Although the Juvenile Awareness Project at Rahway State Prison is easily the best-known effort to scare juveniles straight, it was not the first such attempt. Some 15 years earlier a nearly identical project took place at the Michigan Reformatory with results strikingly similar to those reported by Professor Finckenauer. This section therefore stretches the meaning of replication by examining the Michigan Reformatory Visitation Program.[24] Attention is then directed to a true replication of the Juvenile Awareness Project. . . .

When the program began in the early 1960s at the Michigan Reformatory in Ionia, Michigan, the institution was already 100 years old and showing its age. Surrounded by walls over 18 feet high, the Michigan Reformatory was overcrowded and barely able to meet the needs of young male inmates who were serving "unusually long sentences, who [were] an escape risk or . . . who [had] been unresponsive to treatment programs in other facilities."[25]

Very little is known about the juveniles who met with inmates at the Michigan Reformatory, other than the fact that they lived in Ingham County some 40 miles southeast of the reformatory, that they were male, and that they had been adjudicated delinquent. The age, race, and social class of the juveniles as well as the types of offenses they had committed are all unknown.

However, it is possible to infer two of these characteristics: their age and the severity of their offenses. The juveniles involved almost certainly were on probation because one purpose of the program was to act as a "catalyst to later counseling." Probationary status also seems likely because it would have made little sense to take youths out of one correctional facility and make them visit another. Given the fact that they apparently were on probation, it seems reasonable to infer that they were young offenders adjudicated delinquent for status or minor criminal offenses.

Little also is known about the nature of the treatment juveniles received at the Michigan Reformatory. The brief report describing the project indicates that they visited the reformatory and met with the young inmates serving long or life sentences. It is unlikely, however, that they were shouted at or physically threatened by the inmates. The report describing the program calls the trip to the reformatory a "visit," not an intensive confrontation session. Additionally, adults were not as worried about the delinquent actions of juveniles in the mid-1960s[26] and thus not as likely to permit inmates to verbally and physically threaten young offenders.

What does seem likely is that the juveniles toured the facility, talked with administrators and perhaps custodial personnel, and then met with the young adult inmates. They certainly saw the aged and imposing reformatory grounds, witnessed the regimentation of life in an overcrowded institution, and listened to inmates' descriptions of the "pains of imprisonment."[27] It appears most accurate to view the juveniles' visit as similar to an unusual school field trip.

Other aspects of the Michigan Reformatory Visitation Program are certain, with two of prime importance. First, the visitation program was one of the first-known attempts to scare juveniles straight by showing young offenders "the ultimate consequences of delinquency."[28] Second, the project was experimentally evaluated. Members of the Ingham County juvenile court staff furnished Michigan Department of Corrections research personnel with the names of juveniles about to visit the Michigan Reformatory. Using a table of random numbers, research personnel assigned juveniles to the experimental visitation group or to a control group that did not visit the reformatory.

The results of the visitation program were assessed using juvenile court records obtained six months after the experimental group visited the reformatory. Among juveniles who participated in the visitation program, 43 percent had a court petition or probation violation entered on their records as compared to only 17 percent of the juveniles in the control group. Clearly, visiting a reformatory did not control delinquency. On the contrary, visits to the Michigan Reformatory, as was true of intensive confrontation sessions at Rahway State Prison some 15 years later, apparently increased involvement in delinquency.

▦   Replication: The Insiders Crime Prevention Program

. . . [T]he Insiders Juvenile Crime Prevention Program [is] a project that was inspired by the early reports of success at Rahway.[29] It began in November 1978 at the Virginia State Penitentiary, also known as "The Walls," then one of the nation's oldest continuously operating penitentiaries. Through June 1979, approximately 600 juvenile and young adult offenders had attended "shock-confrontation lectures" at the penitentiary. All of those attending were between the ages of 13 and 20 and had been convicted of at least two criminal offenses. The Insiders Program continued to operate until late 1984.

The purpose of the Insiders Program was to "demonstrate the realities of prison life to hard-core youthful offenders in an effort to deter them from a life of crime and incarceration."[30] The young offenders visiting the penitentiary were searched, stripped of their personal possessions, and then briefly locked in one of the small cells. The major part of the three-hour visit was devoted to a shock-confrontation lecture "full of very explicit, descriptive, and loud street language. . . . Inmates tell juveniles of murder, drugs, prison gangs, and [rape] inside the prison, and are threatened that this will be part of their experience if they continue their life of crime."[31]

The Insiders Program was experimentally evaluated and complete court appearance measures were collected after 6 months for both experimental and control subjects. Follow-up measures of recidivism were collected for some of the subjects 9 and 12 months following the shock-confrontation session at the penitentiary. After 6 months, a point when the data were complete for all subjects, there was no difference between the two groups. After 9 and 12 months, points where data were complete for only some of the subjects, those attending shock-confrontation sessions were less criminal than their control counterparts.

However, there are two good reasons to question results based on the 9- and 12-month follow-up data. The data are seriously incomplete. After 12 months, the court records of less than half of the experimental (17 of 39, or 43.6 percent) and control (19 of 41, or 46.3 percent) subjects are part of the

analysis. Further, the data are from the summer of 1981. If there was an enduring positive story to be told, then we would have heard it by now.

In the end, any conclusions with respect to the Insiders Program must be
based on the complete six-month data. Using only those data, it is clear that
the Insiders Program failed to deter additional trouble with the law.

■   The Current State of Efforts to Scare Juveniles Straight

Despite clear evidence that this approach simply does not work, efforts to control delinquency by scaring juveniles continue to operate in our nation's prisons. According to Professor Finckenauer and colleagues, the Juvenile Awareness Project at the East Jersey State Prison in Rahway continues to operate and
it has returned to near the same level of intensity and intimidation characteristic of its earliest days.[32] Professor Finckenauer also reports that similar projects operate in other states, including "Georgia, South Carolina, Wisconsin,
New York, Virginia, Alaska, Ohio, and Michigan."[33]

Norway's Ullersmo Prison Project

Scaring kids straight is not limited to the United States, however. Norwegian
social scientists Arild Hovland and Elisabet Storvall provide a riveting account
of a scared straight program at Norway's Ullersmo Prison.[34] It began in 1992
following a visit by an Ullersmo Prison official to Rahway to observe and
learn from Juvenile Awareness Project confrontation sessions. Between 1992
and 1997, approximately 144 young men and young women visited Ullersmo
Prison and attended sessions.

Their experiences at Ullersmo are entirely familiar in the wake of our review of scared straight programs in the United States. The Norwegian young
people first saw the prison's yard or open area in the middle of the institution and
were next taken to the prison's dining room for an intensive confrontation session. Approximately four inmates then entered the dining room and took turns
telling and yelling stories about the nature of life inside Ullersmo. Each session
also involved a theatrical and what the inmates believed to be a convincing display of anger involving the sudden pushing of salt and pepper shakers to the
floor. Following the intensive confrontation session, the young people were
shown security cells and had the opportunity to talk quietly with the inmates.
Some two hours after the young people entered Ullersmo Prison, their visit
was concluded. One young man described some of his experiences this way:

> They started throwing us around, you know, up against the wall, holding us
> by the collar. At least this is what they did to me. I can't quite remember what
> they said but they did try to scare me. They said: "Do you really want to end
> up here?" And then they said: "If ever you come here again we're gonna beat
> you every day." Such stuff. There was more of that for a while. They were
> really mean, threw me against the wall.[35]

The Ullersmo Prison Project was halted by the Norwegian government in 1997 in the wake of description and assessment prepared by social scientists Arild Hovland and Elisabet Storvoll.[36] From a distance, it appears that the decision to end efforts to scare juveniles straight in Norway was grounded in deep concern over the ethics of exposing children, who at worst were in minor trouble with the law, to the nature of life inside a Norwegian prison.

■ Summary and Conclusions

This chapter examined prison-based efforts to scare juveniles straight. . . . The projects examined and assessment of other prison-based programs[37] clearly indicate that intensive confrontation sessions do not deter. At best, taking juveniles to prisons for intensive confrontation sessions has no effect. At worst, intensive confrontation sessions make children more rather than less delinquent. . . .

■ Notes

1. Description of the film *Scared Straight* is based on notes I took when it was shown in Columbus, Ohio, on May 16, 1979. Other sources consulted include Aric Press and Donna Foote, "Does 'Scaring' Work?" *Newsweek,* May 14, 1979, p. 131; James O. Finckenauer, *Scared Straight! and the Panacea Phenomenon* (Englewood Cliffs, NJ: Prentice Hall, 1982), pp. 91–110; National Center on Institutions and Alternatives, *Scared Straight: A Second Look* (1337 22nd Street. N.W. Washington, DC 20037, undated); James O. Finckenauer, "Juvenile Awareness Project: Evaluation Report No. 2," unpublished paper, Rutgers University School of Criminal Justice, April 18, 1979; and Testimony Before the Subcommittee on Human Resources, United States House of Representatives, by Jerome G. Miller and Herbert H. Hoelter. Hearings on Rahway State Prison "Juvenile Awareness Project" and the *Scared Straight* film, June 4, 1979. The last source will hereafter be identified as Subcommittee, *Rahway State Prison.*

2. For example. *Scared Straight* was not shown in Columbus, Ohio, until May 16, 1979.

3. Press and Foote, "Does 'Scaring' Work?"

4. Subcommittee, *Rahway State Prison,* p. 3.

5. A classic analysis of deterrence theory can be found in Jack P. Gibbs, *Crime, Punishment, and Deterrence* (New York: Elsevier, 1975). A second analysis is Anne L. Schneider, *Deterrence and Juvenile Crime* (New York: Springer-Verlag, 1990).

6. Finckenauer, *Scared Straight,* pp. 29–63.

7. Press and Foote, "Does 'Scaring' Work?"; Eileen Keerdoja et al., "Prison Program Gets a New Boost," *Newsweek,* November 3, 1980. p. 16; Finckenauer, *Scared Straight,* pp. 190–208.

8. Finckenauer, *Scared Straight;* Sidney Langer, *Scared Straight: Fear in the Deterrence of Delinquency* (Washington, DC: University Press of America, 1982); James O. Finckenauer and Patricia Gavin, with Arnold Hovland and Elisabeth Storvoll, *Scared Straight: The Panacea Phenomenon Revisited* (Prospect Heights, IL: Waveland Press, 1999). The last source will hereafter be referred to as Finckenauer and Gavin, *Scared Straight . . . Revisited.*

9. Description of Professor Finckenauer's evaluation of the Juvenile Awareness Project is based on Finckenauer, "Juvenile Awareness Project"; Finckenauer, *Scared Straight;* and Finckenauer and Gavin, *Scared Straight . . . Revisited.*

10. Finckenauer, *Scared Straight,* p. 196.

11. Finckenauer and Gavin, *Scared Straight . . . Revisited,* p. 124.

12. Notes taken during showing of *Scared Straight* in Columbus, Ohio, on May 16, 1979.

13. Subcommittee, *Rahway State Prison.*

14. Finckenauer, *Scared Straight,* p. 118. See also National Center, *Scared Straight,* p. 7, where it is asserted that "40 to 60% of the juveniles who were visiting Rahway had never been inside an institution, gone to court, or even had a police record."

15. Finckenauer, "Juvenile Awareness Project," p. 7. See also Finckenauer, *Scared Straight,* pp. 111–12.

16. Finckenauer, *Scared Straight,* pp. 29–44.

17. Cited in National Center, *Scared Straight,* p. 6.

18. From notes I took when *Scared Straight* was shown in Columbus, Ohio, on May 16, 1979.

19. Subcommittee, *Rahway State Prison,* pp. 14–15.

20. Finckenauer, *Scared Straight,* p. 85.

21. Ibid., pp. 111–31.

22. Ibid., p. 121.

23. Ibid., pp. 156–70.

24. This section is based on Research Report #4, Michigan Department of Corrections, "Six-Month Follow-up of Juvenile Delinquents Visiting the Ionia Reformatory," May 22, 1967. I thank James C. Yarborough, who in 1980 was chief of research, Program Bureau, Michigan Department of Corrections, Stevens T. Mason Building, Lansing, MI 48913, for having the report retyped and sent to me. The report was reprinted in Finckenauer, *Scared Straight,* pp. 59–61. In 1992 Yarborough was warden at the Richard A. Handlon Michigan Training Unit, P.O. Box 492, Ionia, MI 48846 (telephone conversation December 24, 1991).

25. Michigan Department of Corrections, *Dimensions: A Report of the Michigan Department of Corrections.* Lansing, MI: Michigan Department of Corrections, Fall 1976, p. 44, I again thank James C. Yarborough for providing me with a copy of this report and for assuring me in a letter dated October 20, 1980, that "there has been little if any change" in the Michigan Reformatory since the mid-1960s, the time of the Michigan Reformatory Visitation Program.

26. Writing in 1973, Edwin M. Schur argued that the deterrence approach "does not at present exert a significant influence on delinquency policies." See Edwin M. Schur, *Radical Non-Intervention: Rethinking the Delinquency Problem* (Englewood Cliffs, NJ: Prentice Hall, 1973), p. 19.

27. The classic statement on the "pains of imprisonment" is Gresham M. Sykes, *The Society of Captives: A Study of a Maximum Security Prison* (Princeton, NJ: Princeton University Press, 1958).

28. Research Report, "A Six-Month Follow-up," p. 1.

29. Description of the Insiders Program is based on Stan Orchowsky and Keith Taylor, "The Insiders Juvenile Crime Prevention Program: An Assessment of a Juvenile Awareness Program," Research and Reporting Unit, Division of Program Development and Evaluation, Virginia Department of Corrections, August 1981, report no. 79111. I thank Stan Orchowsky for sending me a copy of this report.

30. Orchowsky and Taylor, "The Insiders," p. 11.

31. Ibid.

32, Finckenauer and Gavin, *Scared Straight . . . Revisited,* pp. 126–27.

33. Ibid., p, 127.

34. Ibid., pp. 143–214.

35. Ibid., p. 173.

36. Ibid., pp. 143–214. See also http://wl.2223.telia.com/-u222300437/.

37. James C. Yarborough, "Evaluation of JOLT as a Deterrence Program," Program Bureau, Michigan Department of Corrections, Stevens T. Mason Building, Lansing, MI 48912, July 18, 1979; David Dykes Cook and Charles L. Spirrison, "Effects of a Prisoner-operated Delinquency Deterrence Program," *Journal of Offender Rehabilitation* 17 (1992):89–99; Finckenauer and Gavin, *Scared Straight . . . Revisited,* pp. 129–39; and Anthony J. Petrosino, Carolyn Turpin-Petrosino, and James O. Finckenauer, "Well-Meaning Programs Can Have Harmful Effects! Lessons from Experiments of Programs Such As Scared Straight," *Crime and Delinquency* 46 (2000):354–79.

7

Social Learning Theory, Drug Use, and American Indian Youths: A Cross-Cultural Test

L. Thomas Winfree, Jr.,
Curt T. Griffiths, and Christine S. Sellers

This chapter offers one example from a larger body of research that supports a social learning theory of delinquency, particularly the elements of the theory that are related to differential association with peer groups and definitions that encourage law violation. It is important to note that L. Thomas Winfree, Curt Griffiths, and Christine Sellers provide a multicultural test of social learning, comparing American Indian and Caucasian youths, demonstrating that the basic propositions of the theory are valid for diverse cultural groups.

SINCE THE 1970S CRIMINOLOGISTS HAVE EVIDENCED A GROWING SEN-sitivity to the failure of earlier scholars to include women and other social, political, and cultural minorities in their research and theorizing agenda (Adler 1975; Leonard 1982; Reasons & Kuykendall 1972; Simon 1975). In this context, one critical issue that has surfaced is the extent to which theories that were developed without specific regard for these minority groups have relevance for understanding their troublesome behavior (Downs 1985; Matsueda & Heimer 1987; Smith & Davidson 1986). . . . Theories that are able to predict and to explain events outside a single cultural context are generally preferred over theories that are culture-bound (Gibbs 1972).

The present study provides a multicultural test of selected constructs drawn from a single contemporary theory of delinquency, namely social learning theory.

"Social Learning Theory, Drug Use, and American Indian Youths: A Cross-Cultural Test," *Justice Quarterly* 6, no. 3 (1989): 395–417. Reprinted by permission of the Academy of Criminal Justice Sciences.

We make no attempt to provide a detailed explanation of this theory or a complete test of its implications. Instead we explore the predictive utility of selected aspects of social learning theory, using two ethnically unique groups of youths living close to one another. Such a test should provide insight into the extent to which ethnic and cultural variability is accommodated within the conceptual framework of this view of youthful misbehavior.[1] The basic question that the current study addresses is "How universal are contemporary theories of crime and delinquency?" Because one of the subgroups in the present study consists of members of a single American Indian tribe and the other subgroup is composed of indigenous Caucasians, it is appropriate to begin with a brief discussion of contemporary views of Indian delinquency as unique and distinct from delinquency by other ethnic groups.

▨ Contemporary Views of Native American Indian Delinquency and Drug Use

The social ills that plague many American Indian tribes, including alcohol and drug use and abuse, suicide, and even crime and delinquency, have been characterized by contemporary sociologists and anthropologists as structural, cultural, and biological in origin (see Bennion & Li 1976; Jilek-Aall 1981; May 1977, 1982a, 1982b, 1986; Schaefer 1981; Van Winkle & May 1986; Weibel-Orlando 1984). Collectively, the macro-level concepts of acculturation and integration are thought to provide a strong base from which to view problems that are apparently endemic and diffuse among American Indians, regardless of tribal affiliation. Gordon (1964) suggests that acculturation, or cultural assimilation, has occurred when a group changes its cultural patterns to resemble those of the host society; further, social integration, or structural assimilation, is reflected by the group's entrance into the institutions of the host society. Acculturation can be slowed by spatial isolation and segregation, voluntary or involuntary, such as occurs in the rural areas where most American Indian reservations are located.

Indeed, acculturation has been the focus of much research into patterns of American Indian drug use. Jilek-Aall (1981) suggests that the alcohol-related problems of contemporary American Indians are the direct result of alcohol use as a means of facilitating the acculturation of Indians to western lifestyles. Levy and Kunitz (1974) also note that acculturation is correlated highly with frequency and volume of drinking: being like a white man means drinking like a white man.

There is some disagreement, however, as to the purported linear nature of the relationship between acculturation and drug use. For instance, May (1982a, 1982b) notes that American Indian tribes are affected differentially by modernization and acculturation stresses, depending on tribal and even intratribal characteristics.[2] It has been reported that drug use [was] lowest for Indian youths reporting the highest levels of acculturation; Indian youths with middle-level acculturation were highest in stress and drug use (Longclaws et al. 1980; May 1982b). Indians adhering principally to traditional beliefs and ways of life had the lowest level of alcohol-related problems.

May (1981) proposes further that social integration, as measured by the individual's role in the community, is a significant factor in determining drug use susceptibility among American Indians. Indians with well-defined social roles in both traditional and modern society have the lowest susceptibility, followed by Indian traditionalists and western modernists; Indians who fall into the cracks between western modern and traditional Indian social roles have the highest susceptibility (May 1982a). In a discussion of Indian suicide rates, Van Winkle and May (1986) observe that lack of social integration may account for suicide among the Apache, but it did not account for the fact that Pueblo Indians had higher rates than the Navajo. Rather, in the estimation of Van Winkle and May, the uneven acculturation of Pueblo Indians and the relative isolation of the Navajo accounted for their somewhat paradoxical finding.

A crucial question remains unanswered: How might these macro-level concepts translate into the social psychology of an individual Indian youth? At any level of study, researchers interested in the problems of American Indians tend to report difficulties simply in gaining access to the appropriate samples and in translating non-Indian constructs into what is called the "Indian experience" (May 1982a, 1982b; Oetting & Goldstein 1979; Robbins 1984, 1985). The various Indian cultures in America, although rather diverse (see Jensen et al. 1977; Levy & Kunitz 1974), all tend to share patterns of secrecy, aloofness, and distrust (May 1982a, 1982b). . . . As a consequence, there have been few direct tests of traditional delinquency theories involving Indian samples.

In spite of these problems and biases, much is known about the impact of such micro-level factors as family and peer ties on Indian delinquency; references to contemporary delinquency theories, however, are conspicuous by their absence. For instance, although Longclaws et al. (1980) refer to no single theoretical framework, nonetheless they provide support for Hirschi's (1969) bonding components [derived from his social control theory] of *involvement* (participation in hobbies), *attachment* (strength of family ties), and *belief* (the influence of traditional Indian normative structures). [Hirschi's social control theory, also known as social bonding theory, postulates that youths who are weakly bonded to conventional others, institutions, and beliefs will have higher rates of delinquency. In Hirschi's initial formulation, he measured four components of the social bond—attachment, commitment, involvement, and belief—with different variables; for further discussion, see Chapter 11.] Wax (1967) and others (see also Longclaws et al. 1980; Swanson et al. 1971; Weibel-Orlando 1984) report that permissive and even laissez-faire child-rearing patterns, coupled with culturally determined parental tolerance, have led to diffuse patterns of socially accepted drinking (see also Heidenreich 1976; May 1975;

Meriam 1928; Weibel-Orlando 1984). Thus they suggest that drinking patterns, like other aspects of one's culture, are learned from one's parents. The social and even forced nature of some groups of Indians' drinking habits provides further theoretical evidence of peer impact (Bach & Bornstein 1981; Cockerham 1977; Longclaws et al. 1980; May 1975; Weibel-Orlando 1984). According to Albaugh and Albaugh (1979), moderation is not an option in the drinking group. Rather, conformity to excessive social drinking is a mandate.

Additional problems, however, are reported by those few researchers who attempt theory-based studies on such problems as drug use or delinquency among American Indians. Robbins (1984, 1985) provides perhaps the most complete Indian-based test of any current delinquency theory, in her case Hirschi's (1969) [social control] theory. Robbins obtained her data from three groups of Seminole Indians. With respect to attachment, she (1984) reports an apparent differential attachment to Indian and to non-Indian significant other adults.[3] Robbins's attempt to measure attachment to Indian persons was unsuccessful; she suggests that her attachment items, as well as those which measure peer delinquency and peer attachment, have no direct translation into the Seminole Indian experience. She concludes that any attempt to measure Indian expressions of attachment based on norms of interaction that are nonexistent in American Indian culture is doomed to failure. Robbins suggests further that the level of attachment to non-Indian institutions is related to Indian misbehavior. Without citing chapter and verse, she has articulated both the acculturation and the social integration theses.

In another article based on the same Indian surveys, Robbins (1985) reports considerable support for the link between commitment and belief and self-reported delinquency.[4] On the other hand, her survey data seem to support the cross-cultural utility of belief, commitment, and (to a lesser extent) attachment. At the same time she states that "the data presented here provide no conclusive statements about commitment of Seminole youth to either Anglo or Indian culture" (Robbins 1985:61). Ultimately she retreats to a popular theme in Indian studies: non-Indian researchers may not be able to develop appropriate measures of commitment and belief; because Indian youths must function in two cultures, researchers must show them to be free of controls in both Anglo and Indian society. The culture-bound quality of social control theory thus limits its utility in explaining Indian delinquency. The extent to which bonding theory is able to explain Indian delinquency may simply reflect its use as an alternative measure of the level of acculturation and social integration.

One delinquency theory that does not seem to be delimited by cultural considerations is social learning theory (Matsueda & Heimer 1987; Vold & Bernard 1986; Williams & McShane 1988). Although Akers (1985) recognizes possible differences in the cultural content of the learning environment (see also Akers et al. 1988), he holds that the processes underlying the learning of either conforming or deviant behavior are largely unaffected by variations in endemic culture, social structure, or sociodemographic characteristics. In other words, culture may affect *what* is learned, but not *how* it is learned (Akers 1985). Thus one possible solution to the problems associated with Robbins's results is to examine juvenile misbehavior in geographically similar groups of American Indian and Caucasian youths and to compare the explanations provided by the constructs of this more generic theory. We employ this strategy in the present study.

The Present Study

As a general observation, social learning theory attempts to identify the process by which deviant behavior is learned. Its original formulation by Burgess and Akers (1966) borrows heavily from behaviorism (Bandura 1977) and from [Sutherland's] differential association (Sutherland & Cressey 1966); this orientation is maintained in later explications of the theory (Akers 1985). Four main constructs are identified in social learning theory. *Imitation* involves the extent to which one's behavior reflects the modeling of others' behavior. This variable, however, often has been dropped from empirical evaluations of the theory; indeed, little empirical support for imitation has been generated (Akers et al. 1979). The concept of *differential reinforcements* includes basic principles of behavioral learning. Behavior is strengthened through positive or negative reinforcement and weakened through positive or negative punishments. To the extent that deviant behavior is reinforced through rewards or the avoidance of punishment while alternative behavior is discouraged by aversive stimuli or the loss of rewards, deviant behavior is more likely to occur. *Differential definitions* is a concept borrowed directly from differential association theory, whereby the individual, through interactions with others, learns evaluations of behavior as good or bad. Deviant behavior is more likely to result when individuals develop definitions that are favorable rather than unfavorable to that behavior. Finally, *differential associations* . . . focuses on the extent to which one interacts with individuals or groups that provide alternative role models, reinforcements, and definitions. The most important of these groups are one's family and friends.

On balance, tests of the full social learning model demonstrate considerable support for the theory, regardless of the type of deviant behavior being examined (Akers et al. 1979; Akers et al. 1985; Akers et al. 1986). Numerous studies testing key social learning variables also have provided strong support, especially in comparison with other theories of deviance (Akers & Cochran 1985; Conger 1976; Elliott et al. 1985; Goe et al. 1985; Weis & Sederstrom 1981). Many of these tests of social learning theory focus particularly on the explanation of drug use among adolescents (Akers & Cochran 1985; Akers et al. 1979; Sellers & Winfree 1990; Winfree & Griffiths 1983). In general, these tests have demonstrated similarly the predictive utility of social learning in explaining these specific forms of adolescent misbehavior. Studies of drug use that employ variables derived from social learning theory rarely deviate far from mainstream American culture (see Ginsberg & Greenley 1978; Winfree & Griffiths 1983; Winfree et al. 1981).

The intent of this paper, therefore, is to examine the adequacy of social learning, purportedly a culture-free theory, as an explanatory model of adolescent misbehavior, in this case alcohol and marijuana use. We include selected indicators of two major constructs of social learning: differential definitions and differential associations. Further, we evaluate the accuracy of these indicators in predicting the level of self-reported involvement with alcohol and marijuana in two groups, one Caucasian and the other American Indian. Similarity in the explanatory power of the variables derived from these constructs would support the notion that social learning is indeed culture-free. Yet to the extent that there are differences in the ability of social learning to explain drug use in these two groups, we would suggest that behavior is learned through processes that depend heavily on one's cultural heritage.

Methods and Measures

The Census: Personal Biographical Characteristics and Drug Use Patterns

We surveyed a single rural school district to obtain a census of all middle and high school students. The school district was located in a Rocky Mountain town of approximately 2,500 residents. The students in Grades 6 through 12 were informed as to the purpose of the study and its voluntary nature, and were guaranteed confidentiality. Of the 578 questionnaires that were administered in homeroom classes by a member of the research team, 549 were returned by the end of the class. This figure represents more than 95 percent of the available students in the middle school (Grades 6 through 8) and the high school (Grades 9 through 12). We had to eliminate 41 questionnaires, however, because of missing data for key variables (i.e., sex or ethnicity was not indicated). Another 23 were completed by youths who were not Caucasian or American Indian; thus we eliminated them from further consideration. In spite of this shortcoming, the 485 usable questionnaires represented more than 73 percent of the registered students and nearly 84 percent of the students attending school on the day the questionnaires were administered.

Table 7.1 contains summaries of key biographical and self-reported use data for the 113 American Indian and 372 Caucasian youths examined here. The youths in both subgroups ranged in age from 12 to 20 years. Few, however, were over 18 years of age. The mean age for the Indian youths was 15.1; . . . the Caucasian subgroup was slightly older, with a mean of 15.2 years. . . . Most of the Indians were males (52.2%); females were in the majority in the Caucasian subgroup (51.9%).

Table 7.1 Socio-Demographic Characteristics and Level of Self-Reported Drug Use by Ethnicity (N = 485)

Characteristics				Ethnicity	
				American Indians	Caucasians
Age:	(1)	12 years		12.4	8.6
	(2)	13 years		15.9	15.6
	(3)	14 years		15.9	14.0
	(4)	15 years		16.8	19.9
	(5)	16 years		9.7	12.9
	(6)	17 years		11.5	12.9
	(7)	18 years		13.3	11.8
	(8)	19 years		2.7	4.3
	(9)	20 years		1.8	0.5
Sex:	(1)	Male		52.2	48.1
	(2)	Female		47.8	51.9
Alcohol Use:*			(1) no use	43.4	46.2
			(2) 1–2 times	10.6	12.9
			(3) 3–5 times	9.7	7.8
			(4) 6–9 times	8.8	7.0
			(5) 10 or more times	27.4	26.1
Marijuana Use:**			(1) no use	69.9	83.1
			(2) 1–2 times	10.6	5.6
			(3) 3–5 times	6.2	2.7
			(4) 6–9 times	0.0	1.1
			(5) 10 or more times	13.3	7.5
Totals				100.0	100.0
				(113)	(372)

*Number of times alcohol was used in past year.
**Number of times marijuana was used in past year.

The two dependent variables employed in this study were self-reported alcohol and marijuana consumption for the past 12 months. These two measures are particularly useful for the present study for several reasons. First, they represent the classic distinctions between status offenses and true acts of delinquency. That is, the possession or use of alcohol by all but a handful of the youths in the present study was "illegal" because the respondents were less than 18 years of age: underage alcohol imbibers were committing a status offense. Marijuana possession, however, not to mention sale and distribution, was at the time of the study a violation of state law for either a juvenile or an adult. In the case of juveniles, adjudication by a court of law carried the status of delinquent, as opposed to the status of misdemeanant or felon for a convicted adult.

The second reason why these two drugs are particularly well suited for the present study is that alcohol use and abuse, as discussed previously, constitutes a major social problem for American Indians and has roots deep in the social fabric of the Indian community. Marijuana use, on the other hand, has no such cultural roots for the members of the Rocky Mountain American Indian tribe which we examined in the present study. As a consequence, employing these two drugs as dependent variables should provide a thorough cross-cultural test of social learning constructs.

The levels of alcohol and marijuana use reported by the youths under study are the final two variables reported in Table 7.1. The proportions of each subgroup that consumed no alcohol were roughly equal. Roughly the same percentage of each group fell into the highest consumption category. A slightly different picture emerged for marijuana use. More of the American Indian youths reported some use of marijuana than did the Caucasians (30.1% versus 16.9%), and more Indians were in the highest use category (10 or more times in the past year) than were Caucasians (13.3% versus 7.5%). Although the "average" youth in both subgroups had had some experience with alcohol in the past year, marijuana smoking was far less common for either group, but especially the Caucasian youth.

Social Learning Variables

Differential associations. The current study employed a single indicator of differential associations: the perceived level of peer involvement with drugs. Akers et al. (1979) refer to this construct as "differential peer associations." Because the study focused on the use of alcohol and marijuana, we constructed two drug-specific measures of differential associations. Each respondent was asked to indicate which of the following categories best described the proportion of his or her "best" friends that (1) used marijuana and (2) drank alcohol: (1) I don't know, (2) none, (3) less than half, (4) about one-half, (5) more than half.

Differential definitions. We employed three different measures of differential definitions. All three measures address the direction of the definitions to which the adolescent was exposed. That is, each measure focuses on whether the definitions were disposed favorably or unfavorably towards law violations. The first measure, *personal definitions,* assesses the respondent's own approval or disapproval of drug use. Three separate questions were asked of each respondent. Each question followed the basic format for three groups of substances: alcohol, marijuana, and other drugs: "How do you feel about the use of _____?" Responses formed a five-point scale ranging from "strongly disapprove" to "strongly approve," with a midpoint response of "don't know." Guttman scaling showed that the approval-disapproval of the use of these three classes of substances formed a fairly unidimensional scale.[5] [See the book appendix for a brief explanation of the statistical techniques used in the chapter, i.e., Guttman scaling and regression analysis.] The higher the scale score, the greater the variety of drugs receiving the respondent's approval.

The two remaining measures of differential definitions are modeled after a technique reported by Johnson, Marcos, and Bahr (1987). Specifically, they state that both friends and parents are possible sources of pro- and antidrug use definitions (Johnson et al. 1987:331). Regardless of the source, *antidrug defini-tions* are stimuli that are designed principally to extinguish a behavior. On the other hand, positive or *prodrug definitions* are regarded as stimuli whose pri-mary purpose is to continue or increase the behavior in question. Rather than conceiving of peers simplistically as sources of *prodrug definitions* and parents as sources of antidrug definitions, however, these measures were designed to address both the frequency and the content of discussions with either group.

In the present study, we employed an initial screen question to indicate the frequency of drug-related discussions between each youth and his or her close friends and parents. Possible answers included the following: (1) never, (2) rarely, (3) occasionally, (4) often. After it was ascertained that such discus-sions indeed had occurred, the specific content of these discussions was broached. Two of the possible subject matter choices were (1) the dangers of drug use (antidrug) and (2) the enjoyments that drugs bring (prodrug).[6]

In the third step in creating the final definitional measures, we divided the frequency of prodrug discussions with either parents or friends by the fre-quency of antidrug discussions with the respective sources. This procedure created a total of seven different ratios. A value of 1 showed that both prodrug and antidrug topics were discussed, regardless of their frequency, or that re-spondents never discussed drugs with their parents. If they never discussed an-tidrug topics but discussed prodrug topics with either their peers or their par-ents, they could receive a peer or parental differential definitions ratio ranging from 2 (rarely) to 4 (often), signifying a condition conducive to the learning of prodrug definitions. If they never discussed prodrug topics but discussed an-tidrug topics, they could receive a parental or peer differential definitions ratio ranging from .5 (rarely) to .25 (often), signifying a condition not conducive to the learning of prodrug definitions.[7]

Design of the Analysis

This study explores the extent to which theoretical constructs that evolved as explanations of delinquency in largely white, middle-class America yield in-sights into the misbehavior of a culturally diverse subpopulation. Thus we offer no major modifications of the conceptual and operational definitions com-monly employed with these constructs. In fact, the analytical model examined in this study is derived essentially from social learning theory (Akers 1985; Akers et al. 1979).

The data analysis consists of four regression equations (OLS). In each equation we regressed the self-reported alcohol and marijuana use first of the American Indian and then of the Caucasian youths, on variables drawn from two social learning constructs, differential definitions and associations, along with variables based on selected personal-biographical information about the subjects. In the present instance, the tactic of providing race-specific analyses has a key advantage over treatment of race as an independent variable. As Smith and Davidson (1986) observed, analyses based on "pooled" responses may obscure unique social processes that affect various racial and ethnic groups differentially. The problems of pooled effects are even greater when the minorities in question are "rare" or token minorities such as American Indians; these minorities are so small relative to the local population that frequently they are overlooked entirely by researchers or perhaps even by nonminority-group members in the same community (Cockerham et al. 1978). In the present case, then, the race-specific analyses should reveal the direct effects of the variables derived from the key constructs on the explained variance for self-reported marijuana use by each subgroup, and subsequently should identify any key differences in the operation of these variables. [The appendix at the end of the chapter] contains the intercorrelation matrix and measures of central tendency and dispersion for all variables by ethnic group.

Findings

Predicting Alcohol Use

Table 7.2 contains a summary of two multiple regression equations. The equation for the American Indian students revealed that among the social learning variables, only the personal definitions and the differential associations measured had a significant impact on alcohol use. The direct contribution of personal approval (beta = .41) was twice that reported for differential associations (beta = .20). Two additional personal biographical features had significant effects. Female Indian school children reported significantly higher levels of involvement with alcohol than did their male counterparts (beta = .17), and older Indian youths reported significantly higher involvement (beta = .22). The total explained variance for this equation was 37 percent.

The pattern for Caucasian youths was somewhat different from that observed for the Indians. Most noteworthy is the significant contribution of three of the four social learning variables. Only parental definitions failed to make a significant impact in this equation. Differential associations, in a fashion consistent with the literature (Johnson et al. 1987; Marcos et al. 1986; Sellers & Winfree 1990), made the largest direct contribution (beta = .38), followed by personal definitions (beta = .20) and peer discussions (beta = .16). Age, not unexpectedly, also made a statistically significant contribution; the older a youth was, the greater the reported involvement with alcohol over the past year (beta = .18). The six independent variables explained 42 percent of the variance in Caucasian alcohol use.

These findings seem to support the position that the pattern of Caucasian alcohol use is far more consistent with the principles of social learning than is alcohol use by Indians. This statement does not mean, however, that social learning theory fails to reveal any insights into Indian patterns of alcohol use. Consider

Table 7.2 Social Learning and Drugs: Alcohol Use

	Ethnicity							
	American Indians				Caucasians			
Independent Variables	r	B	Beta	t-test	r	B	Beta	t-test
Social Learning Variables:								
Personal definitions	.49	.23	.41	4.06***	.43	.12	.20	4.05***
Differential definitions: peers	.19	-.05	-.03	-.35	.35	.30	.16	3.53***
Differential definitions: parents	.19	-.09	-.04	-.43	.12	.02	.00	.08
Differential associations: best friends	.49	.21	.20	2.04*	.56	.41	.38	7.86***
Controls:								
Age	.47	.17	.22	2.35*	.45	.15	.18	3.78**
Sex	-.11	-.58	-.17	-1.96*	.00	-.04	-.01	-.29
Multiple R			.61				.65	
Multiple R²			.37				.42	

*Probability equal to or greater than .05 but less than .01.
**Probability equal to or greater than .01 but less than .001.
***Probability equal to or greater than .001.

the following observations. First, the zero-order correlation coefficients for the Indian subpopulation between alcohol use and three of the learning variables— differential associations and peer and parental differential definitions—although generally less than that observed for the Caucasian youth, were more than negligible (.49 and .19, respectively). Second, the simultaneous examination of the six endogenous variables results in direct, standardized effects. These effects, when compared to those reported in the equation for Caucasians, were very similar for both groups, with the exception of peer differential definitions. It appears that for the American Indians the total effects of these variables are largely indirect and occur through personal definitions.

These two observations make sense when one reexamines the literature that employs macro-level constructs to explain American Indian alcohol use. Whether as a result of history, biological variations, or cultural diversity, Indian students as a group are exposed to differential associations and other peer influences at a far younger age and to a far more pervasive extent than are the Caucasians (Bach & Bornstein 1981; Longclaws et al. 1980; Weibel-Orlando 1984). In keeping with both differential association theory and social learning theory, once one's personal definitions are prodrug or more generally supportive of the behavior in question, there is less reliance on or even less need for differential association or peer definitions (Sellers & Winfree 1990). Employing marijuana as a dependent variable, a drug with no real cultural roots for the Indian youths involved in this study, should provide a test of this interpretation.

Predicting Marijuana Use

Marijuana can be differentiated from alcohol in that its possession and use are both nonnormative and illegal for both ethnic groups. Table 7.3 contains the regression equations for the use of marijuana by both American Indians and Caucasians. Fully 52 percent of the Indian involvement with marijuana is predicted by the six independent variables. More important, all four social learning variables made similar and statistically significant contributions: the standardized regression coefficients ranged from a low of .19 for personal disapproval to a high of .29 for differential associations. The remaining two coefficients, those for peer and parental differential definitions, were nearly identical to that for personal approval (beta = .22 and beta = .20, respectively). Neither of the control variables exhibited more than a negligible, nonsignificant direct impact on marijuana use.

All four social learning variables also made significant contributions in the equation for Caucasians. The major difference between the two subgroups was that parental differential definitions made a significant contribution, but the standardized coefficient for that variable was one-half of that observed for any of the other social learning variables. In addition, the differential associations variable, in keeping with previous research, made the greatest single contribution to the

Table 7.3 Social Learning and Drugs: Marijuana Use

	Ethnicity							
	American Indians				Caucasians			
Independent Variables	r	B	Beta	t-test	r	B	Beta	t-test
Social Learning Variables:								
Personal definitions	.58	.09	.19	2.10*	.57	.10	.24	5.34***
Differential definitions: peers	.53	.26	.22	2.76**	.57	.35	.28	6.40***
Differential definitions: parents	.51	.38	.20	2.56**	.29	.28	.10	2.45*
Differential associations: best friends	.63	.29	.29	3.28**	.58	.35	.32	7.29***
Controls:								
Age	.40	.08	.12	1.63	.26	.02	.04	1.11
Sex	.08	-.22	-.08	-1.14	-.02	-.10	-.05	-1.27
Multiple R			.72				.71	
Multiple R²			.52				.51	

*Probability equal to or greater than .05 but less than .01.
**Probability equal to or greater than .01 but less than .001.
***Probability equal to or greater than .001.

equation for Caucasian students. Once again, the control variables contributed few insights into marijuana use. The total explained variance for the Caucasians was virtually identical to that for Indians (51% versus 52%).

As predicted, social learning theory was a far stronger predictor of the level of Indian involvement with marijuana than with alcohol; the key social learning variables performed similarly for both ethnic groups. The single major exception to this generalization involved parental definitions, a variable that was less significant in the equation for Caucasians than for Indians. One solution to this anomaly is provided by the observations of social anthropologists, particularly their insights into Indian child-rearing patterns. The adjectives applied consistently to American Indian child-rearing patterns include "permissive" (Longclaws et al. 1980), "laissez-faire" (Wax 1967), and "excessively tolerant" (Weibel-Orlando 1984). Wax (1967) reports that among the Oglala Sioux, parental tolerance is so strong a cultural imperative that parents must not intervene in their children's actions.

Cross-tabulating the parental differential definitions variable with ethnicity (data not shown) revealed that a higher percentage of American Indian students reported receiving prodrug statements or balanced treatment of drugs from their parents than did Caucasian youths in the study (55.8% versus 37.8%). Far more Indians than Caucasians, however, also stated that they had had no discussions with their parents about drugs (47.8% versus 32.8%). The former difference was statistically significant, . . . as was the latter. . . . In keeping with the literature, then, the parents of American Indians were less inclined to make known their views on drugs. Yet when such discussions did occur— and when the parents favored the use of drugs—these views had a greater impact on the Indian children than was the case for Caucasians.

■ Summary and Conclusions

It has been suggested that theories of crime and delinquency are largely a reflection of contemporary white middle-class society. Furthermore, such theories—and the current operationalizations of the major constructs associated with these theories—may not reflect accurately the life experiences of some ethnic groups, including American Indians. The universality of theories developed to explain delinquency in the dominant culture among members of a minority group provided the central focus of the current study.

The subjects for the present study all lived close to each other in a single relatively isolated county of a Rocky Mountain state and represented two distinct subgroups, one members of a single American Indian tribe and the other Caucasians. In the case of alcohol use, we found ethnic-specific differences for the performance of the variables drawn from social learning theory. The use of alcohol was not only a status offense for virtually all of the subjects, but also evoked strong subcultural norms for the American Indians. In the case of marijuana use, which was a crime or true act of delinquency with no associated subcultural prohibitions, the social learning variables performed similarly for both groups. Finally, the social learning variables performed in virtually identical fashion for the use of both alcohol and marijuana by Caucasians; differential associations provided the strongest direct ties in each case.

The variable performance of certain social learning measures does not necessarily mean that learning mechanisms are not at work. Rather, some adolescents, particularly those with different subcultural heritages and living under a different set of cultural imperatives, may learn the appropriateness or inappropriateness of certain behaviors at a much younger age; alternatively, definitional sources and differential associations other than peers and parents may be at work. Involvement in disapproved behavior that lacks cultural imperatives, in this case marijuana smoking, may occur largely in concert with the principles established by social learning theory.

The current study confirms and extends social learning theory. It confirms the theory in that the constructs and variables derived from social learning performed (with the aforementioned exceptions) largely as anticipated. In addition, the explained variance was robust, with a range from 37 percent to 52 percent depending on the drug and the group examined; this finding is consistent with prior research (Akers et al. 1979; Akers et al. 1985). In fact, the differences observed in the explained variance by drug type were a repetition of those reported in previous tests of social learning theory (Akers et al. 1979; Krohn et al. 1982).

We also extended our understanding of the relative importance of different social learning constructs. In particular, among subcultural or ethnic groups that do not entirely share the same "norm qualities"—definitions favorable or unfavorable to the behavior in question (Krohn et al. 1982)—some factors, such as peer associations, may be less important than others, including differential definitions or personal definitions. It seems highly likely that these differences may be subcultural in origin, as in the case of cultural imperatives forbidding or condoning a particular behavior or variations in culturally endorsed child-rearing patterns. In addition, similar processes may be at work regarding peer and parental differential definitions. We found that the impact of these variables is also differential, depending either on the drug used or on the ethnic group examined. For example, peer and parental differential definitions contributed to our understanding of marijuana use by both groups, whereas only peer differential definitions contributed significantly to alcohol use by Caucasian students. The fact that differential and variable sources of learning are accommodated within the general constructs of social learning theory is not insignificant; it speaks to the power of the theory.

Future cross-cultural examinations of social learning theory might focus on subcultures with variable levels of social integration and acculturation, or might provide comparisons of samples across national boundaries.[8] As for the prospect that additional cross-cultural and even cross-national research will provide additional support for social learning theory, one need only consider the fact that the theory has repeatedly demonstrated its predictive viability; further, it has the required conceptual flexibility to accommodate differing sources and processes of learning. Even so, a simple caveat seems in order. Perhaps no theory of crime or delinquency is completely free of inherent cultural content, which delimits its applicability.

Appendix Intercorrelation Matrix and Measures of Central Tendency and Dispersion for All Variables (Caucasians above the diagonal; American Indians below the diagonal)

	(A)	(B)	(C)	(D)	(E)	(F)	(G)	(H)	(I)	(J)*	(K)*
(A) Personal Approval	1.00	.49	.34	.30	.47	.25	.01	.43	.57	6.4	2.7
(B) Differential Definitions: Peers	.45	1.00	.29	.19	.43	.16	.07	.35	.57	1.1	.9
(C) Differential Definitions: Parents	.48	.41	1.00	.04	.14	.07	.13	.12	.29	.6	.4
(D) Differential Associations: Best Friends Drink Alcohol	.36	.24	.15	1.00	.53	.53	.00	.56	.27	3.2	1.5
(E) Differential Associations: Best Friends Smoke Marijuana	.58	.45	.40	.67	1.00	.32	−.04	.38	.58	2.3	1.0
(F) Age	.40	.16	.21	.53	.42	1.00	−.04	.45	.26	15.2	2.0
(G) Sex	.29	.19	.23	−.25	.03	.01	1.00	.00	−.02	.5	.5
(H) Alcohol Use	.49	.19	.19	.49	.58	.47	−.11	1.00	.49	2.5	1.7
(I) Marijuana Use	.58	.53	.51	.39	.63	.40	.08	.58	1.00	1.4	1.1
(J) Mean**	7.6	1.3	.9	3.2	2.8	15.1	.5	2.7	1.8		
(K) Standard Deviation**	3.0	1.2	.7	1.6	1.4	2.1	.5	1.7	1.4		

*Central tendency and dispersion measures for Caucasian youths.
**Central tendency and dispersion measures for American Indian youths.

Notes

1. In fact, general critics of the cultural bias inherent in most contemporary theories of crime and juvenile delinquency point to two global weaknesses. First, most noncritical/nonracial theories, including differential association theory, social control/bonding theory, and social learning theory, imply that youths exhibit an almost blind adherence to middle-class value systems (Chambliss 1976; see also Carey 1978; Larson 1984; Reid 1985; Taylor et al. 1973). Second, virtually all minority groups except blacks and Hispanics have been represented poorly in tests of these theories; in addition, as suggested by Reasons (1972), the unique problems of culture conflict and acculturation experienced by these groups are addressed rarely, if ever (Reasons 1972; see also Lex 1987; May 1982a,b; McBride & Page 1980; Tucker 1985).

2. Jensen et al. (1977:255) state that to examine only tribal variations may have "no bearing on explanations of Indian/non-Indian differences, nor can we be certain that the tribal differences . . . reflect cultural traditions of the various tribes."

3. At times it is not clear whether Robbins (1984) refers to the exact text of the questions or to an abbreviated form. The issue of Indian versus non-Indian significant others is a case in point. She lists among non-Indian conventional "institutions" the following items, without reference to their possible "Indianness": teachers, school, and police. Similarly, Indian conventional "institutions" include (again with no reference to the possibility of a non-Indian state) such contacts as relatives, friends, and other family adults. In short, the mutual exclusivity of items such as friends and non-Indians or such as "teachers liking you" and Indians is questionable.

4. Basing the entire analysis on individual items when an entire construct is the focus of attention seems a dangerous practice, especially in view of the resulting occurrence of several perfect (1.00) gamma coefficients. Beyond this relatively minor objection, we question the validity of the selected items. Commitment is a sense of adherence to conventional goals, usually long-term, and bears some conceptual similarity to deferred gratification. The measures used by Robbins (1985) allegedly ask about "long-term plans and the risk associated with getting caught." In using this definition, Robbins merges bonding theory with deterrence's certainty of punishment (see also Gibbs 1975; Meier 1982; Meier et al. 1984; Minor & Harry 1982). In fact, one of the items she employs is linked to the severity of punishment ("How much trouble do you think you would get into?"). Finally, included in the list of examples of commitment, but apparently excluded from the analysis, is the following classic commitment item: "How much schooling do you actually expect to get eventually?" In light of the items included (and omitted), Robbins's external control/commitment measures bear little face validity in relation to Hirschi's concept of commitment.

5. The biserial coefficients for the three items ranged from .424 for alcohol to .686 for drugs other than alcohol and marijuana. The average Yule's Q coefficient was .773. The coefficient of reproducibility for personal definitions was .949; the coefficient of scalability was .821.

6. The present scale differs from that employed by Johnson et al. (1987) in two significant ways. First, the drug discussions reported by Johnson et al. were drug-specific (e.g., that occasional use of a specific drug was harmless fun or that too many people use a specific drug). The items in the current study are more general and lack a specific drug referent. Second, in the study by Johnson et al. the respective ratios were obtained by dividing the sum of prodrug topics by the sum of antidrug items. This step was not taken in the present study because it was the frequency of such discussions, not their variety, which provided the basis of the ratio scale.

7. It is important to observe that we employed a single screen question for both types of discussions, prodrug and antidrug. Thus in the case of youths who had both types of discussions with their parents, it is impossible to determine whether prodrug topics outnumbered antidrug topics in frequency, or vice versa. Grouping all youths who either had no such discussions or who had both types of discussions together in the middle group, designated as unity or 1, seemed a prudent if somewhat conservative approach to this shortcoming in the data. In this manner, only those youths who clearly had either prodrug or antidrug discussions with their parents or peers were accorded a value other than unity.

8. Note, for instance, the observation by Cockerham et al. (1978) that a "token" minority is one which is numerically small in a particular community, even though elsewhere it may be on equal footing with the "majority." By this definition, blacks in the Rocky Mountain states may be a token minority, while Caucasian youths in the inner city would qualify similarly as a minority.

■ References

Adler, Freda. 1975. *Sisters in Crime: The Rise of the New Female Criminal.* New York: McGraw-Hill.

Akers, Ronald L. 1985. *Deviant Behavior: A Social Learning Approach.* 3rd ed. Belmont, CA: Wadsworth.

Akers, Ronald L. & John K. Cochran. 1985. "Adolescent Marijuana Use: A Test of Three Theories of Deviant Behavior." *Deviant Behavior* 6:323–46.

Akers, Ronald L., Marvin D. Krohn, Lonn Lanza-Kaduce & Marcia Radosevich. 1979. "Social Learning and Deviant Behavior. A Specific Test of a General Theory." *American Sociological Review* 44:635–55.

Akers, Ronald L., Anthony J. LaGreca, John K. Cochran & Christine S. Sellers. 1986. "Alcohol Behavior among the Elderly: A Test of Social Learning Theory." Unpublished manuscript.

Akers, Ronald L., Anthony J. LaGreca & Christine L. Sellers. 1988. "Theoretical Perspectives on Deviant Behavior among the Elderly." In B. McCarthy & R. Langworthy (eds.), *Older Offenders.* New York: Praeger.

Akers, Ronald L., William F. Skinner & Marvin D. Krohn. 1985. "Social Learning Theory and Adolescent Cigarette Use." Unpublished manuscript.

Albaugh, Bernard & Patricia Albaugh. 1979. "Alcoholism and Substance Sniffing among the Cheyenne and Arapaho Indians of Oklahoma." *International Journal of the Addictions* 14:1001–7.

Bach, Paul J. & Philip H. Bornstein. 1981. "A Social Learning Rationale and Suggestions for Behavioral Treatment of American Indian Alcohol Abusers." *Addictive Behavior* 6:75–81.

Bandura, Albert. 1977. *Social Learning Theory.* Englewood Cliffs, NJ: Prentice-Hall.

Bennion, L. & T. K. Li. 1976. "Alcohol Metabolism in American Indians and Whites." *New England Journal of Medicine* 294:9–13.

Burgess, Robert L. & Ronald L. Akers. 1966. "A Differential Association-Reinforcement Theory of Criminal Behavior." *Social Problems* 14:1128–47.

Carey, James T. 1978. *Introduction to Criminology.* Englewood Cliffs, NJ: Prentice-Hall.

Chambliss, William J. 1976. "Functional and Conflict Theories of Crime." In W. Chambliss & M. Mankoff (eds.), *Whose Law, What Order?* New York: Wiley.

Cockerham, William C. 1977. "Patterns of Alcohol and Marijuana Drug Use among Rural White and American Indian Adolescents." *International Journal of the Addictions* 12:271–85.

Cockerham, William C., Peter B. Imprey & Sidney J. Kronus. 1978. "The 'Token' Minority: An Attitudinal Comparison of Black, Oriental and Anglo Rural Youth Utilizing a Matched Set Analysis." *Sociological Methods & Research* 6:493–513.

Conger, Rand D. 1976. "Social Control and Social Learning Models of Delinquent Behavior—A Synthesis." *Criminology* 14:17–40.

Curtis, Lynn A. 1975. *Violence, Race, and Culture.* Lexington, MA: Lexington.

Downs, William R. 1985. "Using Panel Data to Examine Sex Differences in Causal Relationships among Adolescent Alcohol, Norms, and Peer Alcohol Use." *Journal of Youth & Adolescence* 14:469–85.

Elliott, Delbert S., David Huizinga & Susan S. Ageton. 1985. *Explaining Delinquency and Drug Use.* Beverly Hills: Sage.

Gibbs, Jack B. 1972. *Sociological Theory Construction.* Hinsdale, IL: Dryden Press.

———. 1975. *Crime, Punishment and Deterrence.* New York: Elsevier.

Ginsberg, Irving J. & James R. Greenley. 1978. "Competing Theories of Marijuana Use: A Longitudinal Study." *Journal of Health & Social Behavior* 19:22–34.

Goe, W. Richard, Ted L. Napier & Douglas C. Bachtel. 1985. "Use of Marijuana among Rural High School Students: A Test of a Facilitative Constraint Model." *Rural Sociology* 50:409–26.

Gordon, Milton M. 1964. *Assimilation in American Life.* New York: Oxford University Press.

Heidenreich, C. Adraian. 1976. "Alcohol and Drug Use and Abuse among Indian Americans: A Review of Issues and Sources." *Journal of Drug Issues* 6:256–72.

Hirschi, Travis. 1969. *Causes of Delinquency.* Berkeley: University of California Press.

Jensen, Gary F., Jay H. Stauss & V. William Harris. 1977. "Crime, Delinquency and the American Indian." *Human Organization* 36:252–57.

Jilek-Aall, Louise. 1981. "Acculturation, Alcoholism and Indian-Style Alcoholics Anonymous." *Journal of Studies of Alcoholism,* Supplement 9:143–58.

Johnson, Richard E., Anastasios Marcos & Stephen Bahr. 1987. "The Role of Peers in the Complex Etiology of Adolescent Drug Use." *Criminology* 25:323–29.

Krohn, Marvin D., Ronald L. Akers, Marcia J. Radosevich & Lonn Lanza-Kaduce. 1982. "Norm Qualities and Adolescent Drinking and Drug Behavior: The Effect of Norm Quality and Reference Group on Using and Abusing Alcohol and Marijuana." *Journal of Drug Issues* 12:343–57.

Larson, Calvin J. 1984. *Crime, Justice and Society.* Bayside, NY: General Hall.

Leonard, Eileen B. 1982. *Women, Crime, and Society: A Critique of Criminology Theory.* New York: Longman.

Levy, Jerrold E. & Stephen J. Kunitz. 1974. *Indian Drinking.* New York: Wiley Interscience.

Lex, Barbara W. 1987. "Review of Alcohol Problems in Ethnic Minority Groups." *Journal of Counseling & Clinical Psychology* 55:293–300.

Longclaws, Lyle, Gordon E. Barnes, Linda Grieve & Ron Duhoff. 1980. "Alcohol and Drug Use among the Brokenhead Ojibwa." *Journal of Studies on Alcohol* 41:21–36.

Marcos, Anastasios M., Stephen J. Bahr & Richard E. Johnson. 1986. "Test of Bonding/Association Theory of Adolescent Drug Use." *Social Forces* 65:135–61.

Matsueda, Ross L. & Karen Heimer. 1987. "Race, Family Structure, and Delinquency: A Test of Differential Association and Social Control Theories." *American Sociological Review* 52:826–40.

May, Philip A. 1975. "Arrests, Alcohol, and Alcohol Legalization among an American Indian Tribe." *Plains Anthropologist* 20:129–34.

———. 1977. "Explanations of Native American Drinking: Alternative Views." *Plains Anthropologist* 22:223–32.

———. 1982a. "Susceptibility to Substance Abuse among American Indians: Variations across Sociocultural Settings." In *Problems of Drug Dependence, 1981,* NIDA Research Monograph No. 41. Washington, DC: Department of Health and Human Services.

———. 1982b. "Substance Abuse and American Indians: Prevalence and Susceptibility." *International Journal of the Addictions* 17:1185–1209.

———. 1986. "Alcohol and Drug Misuse Prevention Programs for American Indians: Needs and Opportunities." *Journal of Studies on Alcohol* 47:187–95.

May, Philip A., Karen J. Hymbaugh, Jon M. Aase & Jonathan M. Samet. 1985. "Epidemiology of Fetal Alcohol Syndrome among American Indians of the Southwest." *Social Biology* 30:374–87.

McBride, Duane C. & J. B. Page. 1980. "Adolescent Indian Substance Abuse: Ecological and Sociological Factors." *Youth & Society* 11:475–92.

Meier, Robert E. 1982. "Perspectives on the Concept of Social Control." *Annual Review of Sociology* 8:35–55.

Meier, Robert E., Steven R. Burkett & Carol A. Hickman. 1984. "Sanctions, Peers, and Deviance: Preliminary Models of a Social Control Process." *Sociological Quarterly* 25:67–82.

Meriam, Lewis. 1928. *The Problems of Indian Administration.* Baltimore: Johns Hopkins.

Minor, William & Joseph Harry. 1982. "Deterrent and Experiential Effects of Perceptual Deterrence Research: A Replication and Extension." *Journal of Research in Crime & Delinquency* 19:190–203.

Napier, Ted L., Richard Goe & Douglas C. Bachtel. 1984. "An Assessment of Influence of Peer Association and Identification on Drug Use among Rural High School Students." *Journal of Drug Education* 14:227–48.

Oetting, E. R. & G. S. Goldstein. 1979. "Drug Use Among Native American Adolescents." In G. Beschner & A. Freidman (eds.), *Youth Drug Abuse.* Lexington, MA: Lexington.

Reasons, Charles E. 1972. "Crime and the Native American." In C. Reasons & J. Kuykendall (eds.), *Race, Crime, and Justice.* Pacific Palisades: Goodyear.

Reasons, Charles E. & Jack L. Kuykendall (eds.). 1972. *Race, Crime, and Justice.* Pacific Palisades: Goodyear.

Reid, Sue Titus. 1985. *Crime and Criminology.* New York: Holt, Rinehart & Winston.

Robbins, Susan P. 1984. "Anglo Concepts and Indian Reality: A Study of Juvenile Delinquency." *Journal of Contemporary Social Work* 65:235–41.

———. 1985. "Commitment, Belief and Native American Delinquency." *Human Organization* 44:57–62.

Schaefer, James M. 1981. "Firewater Myths Revisited." *Journal of Studies of Alcohol,* Supplement 9:99–117.

Sellers, Christine S. & L. Thomas Winfree, Jr. 1990. "Differential Associations and Definitions: A Panel Study of Youthful Drinking Behavior." *International Journal of the Addictions* 7:755–71.

Sheu, Chuen-Jim. 1986. *Delinquency and Identity: Juvenile Delinquency in an American Chinatown.* Albany: Harrow & Heston.

Simon, Rita James. 1975. *Women and Crime.* Lexington, MA: Heath.

Smith, Douglas A. & Laura A. Davidson. 1986. "Interfacing Indicators and Constructs in Criminological Research: A Note on the Comparability of Self-Report Violence Data for Race and Sex Groups." *Criminology* 24:473–88.

Sutherland, Edwin H. & Donald Cressey. 1966. *Criminology.* Philadelphia: Lippincott.

Swanson, David W., Amos P. Bratrude & Edward M. Brown. 1971. "Alcohol Abuse in a Population of Indian Children." *Diseases of the Nervous System* 31:835–42.

Taylor, Ian P. Walton & Jock Young. 1973. *The New Criminology.* Boston: Routledge & Kegan Paul.

Townsley, H. C. & G. S. Goldstein. 1973. "One View of Etiology of Depression in American Indians." *Public Health Reports* 92:458–61.

Tucker, M. Belinda. 1985. "U.S. Ethnic Minorities and Drug Abuse: An Assessment of the Science and Practice." *International Journal of the Addictions* 20:1021–47.

Van Winkle, Nancy Westlake & Philip A. May. 1986. "Native American Suicide in New Mexico, 1957–1979: A Comparative Study." *Human Organization* 45:296–309.

Vold, George B. & Thomas J. Bernard. 1986. *Theoretical Criminology.* New York: Oxford University Press.

Wax, Rosalie H. 1967. "The Warrior Dropouts." *Transactions* 4:40–46.

Weibel-Orlando, Joan. 1984. "Substance Abuse among American Indian Youth: A Continuing Crisis." *Journal of Drug Issues* 14:313–35.

Weis, Joseph G. & J. Sederstrom. 1981. *The Prevention of Serious Delinquency: What To Do?* Washington, DC: US Department of Justice, National Institute of Justice.

Williams, Frank P., III & Marilyn D. McShane. 1987. *Criminological Theory*. Engle-wood Cliffs, NJ: Prentice-Hall.

Winfree, L. Thomas, Jr. & Curt T. Griffiths. 1983. "Social Learning and Adolescent Marijuana Use: A Trend Study of Deviant Behavior in a Rural Middle School." *Rural Sociology* 48:219–39.

Winfree, L. Thomas, Jr., Harold E. Theis & Curt T. Griffiths. 1981. "Drug Use in Rural America: A Cross-Cultural Examination of Complimentary Social Deviance Theories." *Youth & Society* 12:465–89.

8

Delinquents' Perspectives on the Role of the Victim

Cheryl Carpenter, Barry Glassner, Bruce D. Johnson,
Julia Loughlin, and Margret Ksander

This chapter, based on interviews with delinquent youths, utilizes Sykes and Matza's concept of techniques and neutralization—mainly denial of the victim and denial of injury—to uncover ways in which youths distinguish between appropriate and inappropriate targets of particular types of crime. Cheryl Carpenter and colleagues' research highlights the need to understand "how youths themselves *define the illegal activities in which they become involved" (emphasis added).*

AN IMPORTANT LINE OF INQUIRY IN RESEARCH ON JUVENILE DELIN-
quency addresses how youths themselves define the illegal activities in which they become involved. This chapter analyzes one aspect of that topic—the perceptions that underlie delinquents' selection of victims for their illegal behavior.

Sykes and Matza have delineated several "techniques of neutralization" invoked by delinquents; these take the "form of justifications for deviance that are seen as valid by the delinquent but not by the legal system or society at large" (1957:666). One of these techniques, "denial of the victim," holds that the crime "is not really an injury; rather, it is a form of rightful retaliation or punishment" of a victim who is perceived as a wrongdoer (p. 668). The victim may be physically absent, unknown, or a vague abstraction (such as a public building). Similarly, "denial of injury" permits the delinquent to feel that "his behavior does not really cause great harm despite the fact that it runs contrary to the law" (p. 688). Property destruction is "having fun," creating "mischief," or doing "pranks"; autos are "borrowed"; fights are "private disputes" (Harlan & McDowell 1980; Jensen & Rojek 1980; Sykes & Matza 1957). These two

Excerpt from *Kids, Drugs, and Crime,* by Cheryl Carpenter et al. (Lexington Books, 1988). Reprinted by permission of Rowman & Littlefield Publishing Group.

183

themes, denial of the victim and denial of injury, are apparent in the extracts from the interviews quoted herein. In addition, however, the extracts demonstrate how a positive intention to avoid harming individuals limits some youths' delinquent behavior. This, in turn, suggests the potential effectiveness of simple precautions against theft.

The data for this analysis come from interviews with 42 youths who reported involvement in criminal activities. . . . Twelve had been involved only in episodic, minor crimes, such as vandalism and shoplifting, and 30 had been involved in serious juvenile crime. . . . [T]he criteria for defining crimes as serious were: (1) crimes that caused bodily harm to victims; (2) crimes of theft regardless of whether accompanied by property damage; (3) crimes involving property damage (including vandalism) or destruction alone; and (4) crimes involving systematic drug sales and otherwise minor offenses (such as petty theft or minor vandalism) that were reported as being common activities for a given youth.

Each respondent's interview transcript was read carefully, and every account of an actual crime, a planned crime, or an illegal event that the subject reported but was not involved in was noted. Answers to questions about hypothetical situations involving honesty or trust (or avoidance of crime) were also reviewed. As the following findings indicate, victims were not defined in the abstract, but in relation to different kinds of criminal events. Youths also shared some of their understandings about the role of the victim in a criminal event. Several themes emerged from the analysis of the transcripts: (1) the careless person is an appropriate victim of theft; (2) an individual who offends the juvenile or who victimizes others is also an appropriate victim; (3) family members, friends, and individuals who are "innocent" or who are particularly vulnerable are inappropriate victims; and (4) crimes are legitimated if there is no perceived individual victim.

■ Careless Victims

The most common crime reported by sample members was property theft. A dominant theme in the reports of such thefts was the ease with which victims whom they defined as "careless" could be located. Not only is it easy to steal from the careless, whether they are individuals or business establishments, but their inefficiency in protecting their possessions makes them "responsible" in part for their own victimization. This view, that the careless victim has "asked for it," was articulated dramatically in a 16-year-old's report of the theft of his own bike stolen from the driveway of his home:

> A: Well, I was out riding my bike and I heard the phone ring and I rode in, put my bike in the driveway, was talking to you, and when I hung back up I went outside and my bicycle was gone. And I admire that person whoever did that.

Q: Why?

A: They deserve the bike. They were, they had nerve, they were fast, for sure. I mean, it was broad daylight, it was like maybe six o'clock, not even, and it was, how long were we on the phone, you know, that takes . . . I admire them!

Q: So you're not concerned or upset about having lost the bike?

A: They deserve it, I think, and they deserve it more than I did.

Q: How much was the bike worth?

A: $180 that I paid for it with the money I earned myself.

This same youth, although he was involved in chronic drug use and sales, vandalism, car theft, and burglary, had never been apprehended. He elaborated on the theme of the careless victim in a discussion of business establishments that fail to apprehend shoplifters:

Q: Have you ever told somebody in authority that somebody else was stealing something?

A: No.

Q: Have you ever been in that kind of situation where you could have? I mean where you saw someone?

A: Yeah.

Q: How come you didn't tell?

A: Because if someone stole, and they allow people to steal from their store, and a store should either safeguard against people stealing or you know, if they can't catch them . . . like I felt about my bike. If they don't get caught, they deserve it. . . . I don't feel that way to the deepest of my heart, but, you know, that's a general rule. No sucker deserves to keep his money, you know.

Of the 42 youths in this . . . sample, 25 reported frequent incidents of taking cars either for joyriding or for extended use or sale. The ease with which they located vehicles vulnerable to theft because of the owner's carelessness dominates reports of such criminal activity.

A 17-year-old involved in, though not arrested for, repeated episodes of auto theft, theft from autos (including stealing a police revolver from a patrol car), and drug selling provided an account of a typical incident.

A: [T]his guy was up on Lowell Street, down toward Underwood more, and we were walkin' by, and he . . . parked his car and left it runnin' and went in this house; we just jumped in that sucker, and we were gone.

Q: How long did you have it altogether, then?

A: Three days. We just, I would just park it, couple blocks away, and then go get it when it got dark out. And that was it.

A 13-year-old, who was in the group detained by the juvenile authorities when interviewed, talked about taking a car in similar fashion. . . .

Q: What happened with the car?

A: I don't know. I was walking down, I skipped school, I was walking down Eve Street and I saw a key . . . a car with the keys in it. I looked around, I jumped in it, I started driving away.

A 19-year-old who admitted drug selling, auto theft, and gambling described the theft of a moped from a careless owner. In his recollection of the event, the carelessness of the owner not only made him a likely victim but, in the subject's view, negated the criminality of the act altogether:

> Q: How old were you?
> A: I think I was 10. Stole it, and I didn't really steal it, it was at the store, and somebody must have planned on keeping it running, running right in and running right back out. I just jumped it and went off. Then I gave it to this older kid, and he took it from me. And I didn't never see it again.

Although the subjects depended on carelessness on the part of victims, they also conceived of victims as careless even when the victim may, in fact, have taken routine steps to prevent theft. This conception facilitates the neutralization of theft as "borrowing." Subjects spoke of taking vehicles in such terms:

> Q: What do you mean "we borrowed a car"?
> A: Well, the keys were in it, underneath the car, you know, one of those hide-a-key things? They're great. A lot of people have those. And it was late, about one o'clock in the morning. We borrowed the car and I don't know what we did. We brought the car back about five o'clock in the morning.
> Q: Put it back where you found it?
> A: Yup, didn't damage it or anything. We might of even put a couple bucks worth of gas in, I'm not sure though.

In many interviews subjects also reported searching for careless victims. An 18-year-old respondent, . . . well known from field work for "rowdy" delinquency, described both searching and borrowing:

> Q: Have you ever stolen anything like a car or motorcycle and stuff?
> A: Uh-huh.
> Q: When was that?
> A: We would . . . take the car, see we just looked for cars with keys in them, and we'd drive it around, let it run out of gas, and then bring it back to where we took it from . . . leave the keys in, leave it. Exactly where it was that means. . . .

Another 18-year-old . . . (involved in auto theft, burglarizing automobiles and houses, property destruction, and drug sales and distribution) described a search for a careless owner in the following account of stealing a van in order to burglarize a rival drug dealer:

> Q: So tell me how you managed, how did you get the van and everything?
> A: I stole that from the airport. In the airport they leave the keys underneath the floor mat.
> Q: Well, the people out at the airport must have known the van was missing and come after you or something.

> A: Nope, 'cause people go on weekend trips, you know, or, you know, sometimes they'll come back early and they take the car without anybody knowing.
> Q: Oh, you mean it was just parked in the parking lot out there?
> A: Yeah, I just hopped in.
> Q: It was unlocked?
> A: No. I busted the vent window. I busted that, reached in and unlocked the door, and that's how I lift up the floor mat and there was the key . . . and all that.

Despite the owner's precaution of leaving the van locked and in a paid (presumably controlled) lot, the delinquent viewed the owner as having left himself vulnerable to victimization.

▨ Deserving Victims: What Goes Around, Comes Around

Whereas careless victims are typically viewed as having "asked for it," "deserving" victims are viewed as "having it coming." The delinquents used the adage "What goes around, comes around." That is, those who injure others will eventually be injured themselves.

One 16-year-old boy who sold drugs explained, for example, how he refrained from becoming a deserving victim:

> Q: You ever . . . been tempted to do that to somebody [cheat his customers on the quality or amount of drugs]?
> A: Oh, many times, I could do it with speed in a second.
> Q: Why don't you?
> A: Because, what goes around comes around. . . . [Y]ou know, I sell them the speed, . . . they'd know something was up, they'd come back to me you know. . . .

Schools and their personnel are common targets of vindictive vandalism for wrongs inflicted on delinquent youth (see also Gold 1977; Harlan & McDowell 1980; Toby 1983a, 1983b). In a representative account from a 16-year-old boy who had been detained, breaking and entering and destruction of school property are revealed as retribution against the principal:

> A: Okay, coming back from a party, and I'm . . . on the way home, I dropped Ivy off and I was with Irwin. And we got out to take a short cut, we got to go across the field at Ashdale. So I, you know, he said, well man, want to break in? Yeah, let's do it!
> Q: Well, how'd you get the idea, how did that come into your head?
> A: 'Cause its principal, remember I told you about the principal?

The subject goes on to detail the vandalism and destruction perpetrated in the school, including the following symbolic victimization of the principal:

A: . . . I found a set of handcuffs in his [the principal's] desk. We drew a picture of . . . Mr. Sutton with the . . . the handcuffs hanging off the wall right by the thing. "It's going to be you when I get done with you" . . . .

This retribution was because the principal had earlier suspended the boys from school for behavior they defined as a minor infraction of the rules.

Another very clear theme in the interviews was the youths' sensitivity to being treated without respect by adults, especially those in authority. Retribution for such perceived insults was sometimes immediate and direct. For example, a 16-year-old detained youth involved in burglary and chronic shoplifting described a physical altercation with a teacher:

A: Yeah, and I hit the teacher, man, 'cause she be talkin' smart about that math, man, and if I can't get an answer from her, throw a pencil on the floor, ya know, she came over, ah, "The poor little baby," ya know, and I cuss her out for callin' me a baby, and threaten her, man.

On the other hand, retribution may also involve considerable planning. An 18-year-old youth . . . for example, described an elaborate burglary of a neighbor's home. In discussing the incident, he implied that the neighbor, a drug dealer, had been an appropriate victim because he failed to "respect" the youth's maturity and skill. The burglary had netted an expensive stereo and a large sum of money, but the primary goal was 50 pounds of marijuana, which provided the youth with a two-year supply for personal use and sales. The victim had refused to sell the youth marijuana and had treated him like "just another kid down the street."

Another type of "deserving" victim is a commercial establishment that "rips off" the delinquent, peers, or the general public. One youth who stole an expensive stereo noted that stealing from individuals was not a routine crime for him. He only did that when he got "rowdy" and had the support of others. He was, however, a skillful and persistent shoplifter and was unabashed about it:

A: I only do that when I get real rowdy. I don't like doing that, that's mean, you know, that to a person, I mean if you did it, to a store, it's all right if you do it to a store, I think, that's the least I do. Store robs you anyways. So you can steal from them, who the hell cares. But if you take from a person, man, they, they got to work for their money. It's not right.

One youth had worked out a sophisticated scheme with his friends for going to the movies without paying:

Q: Have you done that since?
A: No, that was justifiable by the way.
Q: Why?
A: Well, I may be 15, but how come I can't get into an R-rated movie alone? But I have to pay adult prices, so I figured I pay one out of two movies I see is fair.

Q: You thought it was fair then?
A: I know it's fair.

The subjects' discussions of retributive crime suggest that these acts help restore injured self-esteem and respect among peers.

Still another category of "deserving" victim includes those who engage in some illegal activity themselves. This may involve other delinquent peers, such as those who shoplift or steal and those who prostitute or fence goods. Take, for example, the following account given by Kevin, a 20-year-old self-reported drug addict with a long history of delinquent involvement and detention. . . . When asked about types of persons against whom he might use force in order to take money, he ruled out his mother, brothers, and fellow students, but reported that one category whom he and his associates routinely victimized were fellow delinquents:

> Q: Tell me about that one.
> A: We used to rob the robbers—other people that robbed—when they hit something, you know: "Hey, give me some money." They would give it to us, I can remember a couple of times we went out and checked his pockets.
> Q: Did you do that by yourself or who did you usually do that with?
> A: Ivan.
> Q: How old were you then?
> A: Fifteen.
> Q: So that was the same period in here with stealing and robbing?
> A: Yeah.
> Q: Okay, you ever get caught?
> A: Doing something like that!
> Q: Yeah . . . you say you "robbed the robbers," you make it sound like there was this whole huge network of people who were robbing and stuff. Was that a pretty common type of thing among the people you hung with and stuff?
> A: Hmm-mmm.

Persons involved in drug sales, either as dealers or as buyers, were particularly vulnerable to being victimized. Expectations of dealer/buyer victimization routinely characterized subjects' accounts of drug dealing. Often, knowledge of drug networks and supplies led to a fellow user-dealer being marked for victimization. A 16-year-old delinquent . . . for example, described how he and three close friends acquired their "head stash" by cooperating in the theft of a large marijuana plant from the garden of a known dealer.

In our study, respondents who sold drugs were almost in a class by themselves as persons who "deserved" to be victimized—because they were expected to "rip off" the customer in some way. Dealers were well aware of their dual role of victimizer and potential victim, as the following account shows (see also Goldstein 1985; Johnson et al. 1983; Johnson et al. 1985). A detained boy justified his practice of holding out "three or four joints" when selling marijuana to someone he did not know well. Friends to whom he sold would, he said, get him high as part of the transaction. Strangers to whom he sold might not acknowledge this convention, so he took care of himself. This practice, he argued, was expected.

> A: . . . [A] person I don't know buys it from me, I don't know if he's gonna get me high, if he does, he does, if he doesn't, he doesn't. But if I always got four joints, I always know I'll get high after. You know, see you make a little profit out of it.
> Q: What would you think if somebody did that to you?
> A: It's always bein' done. I don't mind. . . . But I always get mine. . . . I never buy from strangers anyways.

Inappropriate Victims

The respondents were asked to discuss not only actual criminal behavior but also hypothetical situations. In these discussions, many explicitly rejected the possibility of assaulting or stealing from people they knew. They also expressed an unwillingness to harm "innocent" or helpless persons. The subjects reported several strategies for avoiding harm to other individuals. In the case of theft, they often selected victims they thought could bear the loss, avoided friends and relatives, and chose impersonal victims such as corporations.[1]

Among these seriously delinquent youths, very clear norms define empathy for and identification of one's family or friends of one's family as inappropriate victims. A 16-year-old girl commented about stealing:

> A: I mean from my mom's friends. I would never steal from them.
> Q: How come?
> A: I don't know. I just wouldn't. I have no respect for that.

An 18-year-old . . . emphasized both the self-protective and empathetic content of this behavior:

> A: I don't steal from people that I know.
> Q: The burglaries and all, were you usually in some white neighborhoods, or black neighborhoods, or did it matter?
> A: Usually, white neighborhoods, upper class. But . . . I wouldn't steal anything unless I knew it wouldn't hurt anyone.

It was important to a substantial number of these delinquent youths that no undeserving person suffer. An 18-year-old . . . explained his reasons for refraining from crime in some situations:

> Q: Could you tell me about times you could easily have taken things and gotten away without punishment, but did not do so?
> A: Well, I could take all kinds of stuff from the labs at school. And the only way of anybody knowing it is me.

Q: Why don't you?
A: It's mean. Someone else is going to suffer from it.

The subject goes on to explain the distinctions made in deciding whether or not a crime is "mean," decisions informed largely by norms regarding empathy:

Q: I'm a little confused, then. How about when you took the . . . hub-caps? How come that wasn't mean?
A: 'Cause the insurance will pay for that.
Q: But is that mean to the insurance company?
A: I don't give a shit about big insurance companies. It's multimillion dollars.

A 16-year-old boy was explicit about not wanting to hurt those who are innocent:

Q: Okay, . . . how about, ever throw stones or snowballs or rocks at win-dows of cars or buses?
A: Yeah, in the winter I always chuck 'em at buses. Raptram buses; I don't do it to school buses or cars 'cause I might scare them and make them lose control. I always hit the bus from the rear.
Q: How come you do that?
A: 'Cause I just. . . . I don't want to be responsible for anyone getting hurt if the bus driver swerves and runs into a tree or somethin'.

This theme of not being "mean," not "hurting" others, and protecting younger or helpless persons frequently includes specific references to empa-thy: "I wouldn't want anyone to do that to me," "I know how I'd feel." These youths may define breaking the law as only *formally* wrong if they have an ac-ceptable motive. But they define violations of norms protecting certain classes of people from victimization as *morally* wrong.

When the crime involves personal contact, it is more difficult for youths to avoid not only injury but also an awareness of the victims' definition of the situation as unfair and frightening. No subject reported indifference to this problem; one solution was to select victims who were not "helpless."

A 17-year-old boy . . . who also had been involved in burglary talked about purse snatching with an accomplice. He specifically rejected helpless victims:

A: Would run by. One would knock the person down, one would grab the purse and take off. But, you know, that's a real nasty thing, now that I think about it, you know.
Q: Who, what kind of people would you do it to?
A: Um, ladies, you know, they're the only ones carrying their purses.
Q: Like old ladies, or . . . ?
A: No, not . . . young, young ladies that would have a chance to fight back or would chase us or something.

This youth was asked if he had ever been given too much change by a cashier.

> Q: What do you do?
> A: I've—that's only happened to me once, and I had to bring it back, 'cause I felt guilty, stomach was churning, I was about to throw up. Because . . . I was at, going to the dentist and it was this blind lady, at one of those concession things. And, she gave me, one of those Susan B. Anthony dollars back instead, for a quarter. I said Otto man, shit, you know, Otto's always been with me when some of this shit's been going down and said, no, I got to take it back, took it back. And . . . she told me to keep it anyway. She said keep it, keep it.

▥ Negation or Escalation of Harm to Victim

When, despite care in selecting victims, harm (from the victim's perspective) does occur, the victim's actions in the scene are seen as contributing to the nature of the victimization:

> Q: Did you ever hurt the people when you did it?
> A: Well, one lady, would not let go of the purse. Did not want to let go of the purse, and like, my brother like dragged her a few houses down and she, you know, it was on grass, though, you know. We, she was walking like, and we went by, knocked her over and dragged her onto the grass, you know; it didn't hurt her or nothing. . . . But, no, we never really hurt anybody.

If the woman had let go of "the purse" (notice it is depersonalized in the subject's account, not "her purse"), she would not have been dragged or physically harmed. In this and similar accounts, subjects expressed their perception that they did not "hurt" the victim(s) and that whatever harm occurred was the victim's own doing. The victim here was viewed as causing the incident to become atypical or problematic in the sense of converting a simple purse snatching into something not intended by the perpetrators.

In other instances, however, the victim's "overreaction," in the delinquents' terms, may lead to the youths' discontinuing their behavior. That is, interaction within the setting of the criminal event may make clear that, in fact, the target is an inappropriate victim and may lead the delinquents to cancel the criminal encounter rather than violate their own norms regarding victims. A clear and colorful example of such a foiled encounter is detailed in the following account wherein the subject was discussing the choice of victims for robbery. The account shows how an individual deemed appropriate by usual standards can come to be seen as inappropriate.

> Q: What kind of people would you usually do that to?
> A: Suckers.
> Q: How can you tell?
> A: You can, I can tell a sucker a mile away.
> Q: White, black, old, young?

A: Any—there's always suckers; any race, any color, any age; there's always a sucker, "a sucker born every minute." . . . But . . . one guy, this was pretty funny, it's not funny, but it is funny. Because we're sitting there, right? And we jumped him. He gave us this watch, his wedding ring, and his wallet, and he said, "Just don't beat me, man, come to my house, take my TV, my stereo, my wife," you know? We were dying, we were laughing. The guy, we said, "Here, take your stuff, we don't want it."

Q: How old was he?

A: He was, uh, about 35. Hispanic guy. . . .

Q: You knew him?

A: No. We just looked at his watch and . . . you know. I was getting pretty, I said, "Man," I said, "You want us to take your wife? Take your stuff back." We gave him all his stuff back.

Here, an apparently appropriate victim (a stranger, not too young, not too old, in possession of watch, rings, and so forth) was found by the subject and his companions to be, in fact, inappropriate because he behaved contrary to their expectations. As the subject and his friends viewed the interaction, the victim was never in danger of being beaten. The victim's humorous and inappropriate response in offering his wife and his general overcompliance conflicted so sharply with the youths' expectations about the event as to lead them to abandon the intended act.

A victim's refusal to behave positively, however, may lead to an escalation of the criminal event. A . . . subject reported on such an incident, the one that had resulted in his arrest:

A: I was going for his tape player man, it was all really nice shit. The dude wouldn't give it up, I told him to just give it up, man, and we could forget about it, you know . . . forget about it man. . . . [T]he dude wouldn't give it up, man. I was hitting him and he was still holdin' it there.

Q: You have to start over; we've got half the story here, from the beginning, who was with you, when did it happen, what time of day?

A: I was by myself. . . . I [got old friends] there, . . . jes kicked the door in, ya know. . . . I didn't figure nobody was there, it's a little small apartment. I went inside, [saw] a tape player . . . [and] started pullin' it, ya know, [and] it was dark and he'd pull it back again . . . and I'd pull it, and pull it back again. . . . And all of a sudden, the lights came on, and [he] say, "No, you can't have my tape" and I say, "[Jes give me] the tape . . . [and] we can forget about this, . . . we ain't got to go through [this]. . . . I pull it, pull it back, man, and he wouldn't let go, man, and I was hittin' him . . . damn! man, I got caught at it too. White guy damn! Dude wouldn't turn it loose, damn! I mean, that the least he could've did, man; turn it loose. . . . And I got mad, I was kickin' him, man, hittin' him.

Within this encounter, the delinquent lost control of the situation. Lack of cooperation—in the form of physical resistance by the victim—led the youth to redefine the situation as calling for more serious harm to the victim than he had intended. Moreover, the subject saw himself as having been placed at greater risk in terms of the seriousness of the crime committed, the possibility of being physically harmed himself, and the possibility of being caught. In either type of event (escalation or negation), being an inappropriate victim amounts in practice to displaying behavior that does not comply with the delinquents' own expectations and that causes the delinquent thereby to lose control of the criminal event.

■ Victimless Crime

Some of the criminal activity reported by the respondents did not involve a victim from their perspective. Rather, objects in their environment were used in ways they found appropriate. Many of these events involved financial loss or discomfort for others, but such losses were not part of the youths' definition of the situation. From their perspective, they found impersonal targets, not personal victims, for their activity—what Sykes and Matza (1957) call "denial of the victim."

A 17-year-old girl . . . herself involved in routine shoplifting from stores and school, vandalism, and occasional theft from houses in which she babysat, characterized her own family's victimization by vandalism in just such terms:

> A: Yeah, and they wrote terrible rude and crude words on my house.
> Q: Same kids?
> A: Yep, as far as I know,
> Q: What did they write it with?
> A: Crayon. Says "come fuck" or something fuck.
> Q: When was that?
> A: I don't know, I just noticed that the other day because I was pulling out of the driveway . . . and . . . our little garage thing on the side of our house, they kept going in there. Breaking stuff that was in there, playing around with it, and that's about it.
> Q: Why do you think your house has become a target?
> A: I don't know.
> Q: No idea?
> A: Just it's available I guess, I don't know.

Of interest is the subject's matter-of-fact assessment that the victimization had no direct relationship to her or her family but, rather, was more or less incidental to the act of vandalism—any "available" garage would have been equally appropriate.

Objects incidental to settings similarly become targets of criminal or delinquent acts precisely because they are characterized as "nonvictims." In his description of deliberate property destruction, a 17-year-old male . . . was clear about recognizing when a circumstantial object is appropriate to delinquent activities:

> A: Oh yeah, I've done that a couple of times, that was fun, though. But you know there's this—they were going to tear it down, you know, condemned

to be torn down, I just—I had my pellet gun, I just put out a couple windows. But I'm not into damaging other people's things, you know. . . . I'm on that "do unto others" kick!

In this incident, the subject already had his gun with him, so it was not a question of intentionally securing the gun in order to inflect the damage on the building. Rather his encounter with the target object was incidental and, because the building was "condemned to be torn down" (which, in fact, was not true) and not perceived as belonging to another person, circumstances—in the youth's view—provided the target of the delinquent activity. The important point is that in this and each of the other incidents reported in this subsection, the precise object targeted for criminal activity was, in and of itself, of little or no significance to the delinquent. The object's impersonal or public character constituted its appropriateness for the particular act. By such reasoning, subjects may clearly "deny the victim."

An additional theme that is evident in subjects' accounts about circumstantial targets is that the acts [perpetrated] served no purpose other than "fun" or expressivity. Consider the following account from a 16-year-old regarding an incident of arson that resulted in his expulsion from elementary school:

A: I set the bathroom . . . at St. Mark's . . . on fire. . . . Took a lighter to school and just wanted to play around with it, and I lit the paper towel roll on fire, the gas line, and the toilet paper, and the garbage can. And anything that would burn, I'd burn it. And then when I opened the door and all the smoke just poured out and I went down to the room, some kid asked to go to the bathroom and came back up and said, "Ah. . . ." The teacher said, "What's wrong?" He says "There's a fire in the bathroom."
Q: How did they catch you—how did they know it was you?
A: They found the lighter on me. I kept the lighter.
Q: What—did you do that on purpose? I mean did you want to set the bathroom on fire?
A: No, I just wanted to watch it burn!

This subject was subsequently suspended from junior high school for another incident involving playing with fire.

Note that shooting out the windows, as described in the earlier excerpt, was similarly characterized as "fun." Subjects routinely reported the "thrills" involved in being what they call "rowdy"—a residual category of behavior used by all types of subjects in referring to any boisterous, usually spontaneous behavior that might be conventional or unconventional, but was definitely not, from their perspective, "good."

■ Summary and Conclusions
The respondents . . . who engaged in illegal activities were in substantial agreement about their expectations regarding persons they victimized and how they

expected victims to behave during a crime. In some respects, their expectations appear to represent an extension of generally held social norms. They expressed an empathy for family and friends that ordinarily protected them from being selected as victims. In addition, children, the elderly, and the handicapped were not perceived as appropriate victims. Even among "appropriate" victims, there was a clear rule against imposing gratuitous physical harm.

Delinquents defined strangers as being appropriate victims, especially if they were perceived to be "careless." Such persons were believed to participate in their own victimization. ("There's a sucker born every minute.") Victims were perceived to be careless if they did not protect their property or took only routine precautions (locking a car but leaving a key hidden somewhere in the car, or leaving valuable possessions in a coat pocket or a locked car). Persons who took effective precautions (leaving cars locked with no key available) were generally not victimized. Similarly, stores that used effective security measures and prosecuted shoplifters were not victimized by youths who routinely shoplifted; they generally went elsewhere.

Also perceived as appropriate or "deserving" victims were persons considered to "have it coming" because they had injured or insulted the perpetrator in some important respect. The delinquents . . . mentioned a maxim, "What goes around, comes around," which emphasizes reciprocal expectations. The delinquent perceived that he was being victimized or insulted by someone and in turn retaliated against such "deserving" persons. Delinquents also frequently victimized and expected to be victimized by others who engaged in illegal activity. When they were the victims, they were likely to engage in retribution against the perceived offender. Moreover, they also expected retribution from others. Sometimes this expectation of retribution prevented them from victimizing others, but at other times they accepted the fact that they would be victimized in a similar fashion.

"What goes around, comes around" is especially important to delinquents who sell drugs; dealers seem to be particularly likely to cheat or otherwise victimize their customers or to have their customers perceive that they are doing so. Thus, drug dealers are likely to suffer retribution from customers who may steal or burglarize their supply of drugs, inflict personal injury, or steer potential customers to other dealers.

Most of the crimes committed by our respondents were generally designed to avoid personal interaction with the victims. When an offense did require personal interaction between the delinquent and the victim, the delinquent expected the person to be a "good" victim—that is, to allow the delinquent to control the situation, to turn over money and possessions, and to offer no physical resistance. When the victim did not abide by these expectations, the criminal event might escalate in terms of seriousness (a purse snatch might become a robbery) and the potential for physical injury (the victim might be assaulted).

The tone of these delinquents' discussions of their criminal activities and interactions with victims was neither hostile nor aggressive. Rather, it was one of controlled risk taking; generally accepted norms defined which classes of persons were "appropriate victims" and how all parties should behave during the criminal event. The delinquents recognized, however, that society might impose sanctions if they were apprehended, and it was ultimately in reference to societal norms that delinquents evaluated their responsibility for involvement in criminal events.

Note

1. . . . [S]ome youths reported stealing small amounts of money or items from their parents and/or neighbors. Even in these cases, however, they were clear about not stealing from persons they viewed as unable to afford such a loss.

References

Gold, Martin. 1977. "Scholastic Experiences, Self-Esteem, and Delinquent Behavior: A Theory for Alternative Schools." *Crime & Delinquency* 24:290–308.

Goldstein, Paul J. 1985. "The Drugs/Violence Nexus: A Tripartite Conceptual Framework." *Journal of Drug Issues* 15:493–506.

Harlan, John P. & Charles P. McDowell. 1980. "Vindictive Vandalism and the School: Some Theoretical Considerations." *Journal of Police Science & Administration* 8: 399–405.

Jensen, Gary & Dean G. Rojek. 1980. *Delinquent: A Sociological View.* Lexington, MA: D. C. Heath.

Johnson, Bruce D. et al. 1983. "Violence among Heroin Abusers." Paper presented at the annual meeting of the American Sociological Association, Detroit.

Johnson, Bruce D. et al. 1985. *Taking Care of Business: The Economics of Crime by Heroin Abusers.* Lexington, MA: Lexington Books.

Sykes, Gresham M. & David Matza. 1957. "Techniques of Neutralization: A Theory of Delinquency." *American Sociological Review* 22:664–70.

Toby, Jackson. 1983a. "School Violence." In M. Tonry & N. Morris (eds.), *Crime and Justice—An Annual Review of Research.* Chicago: University of Chicago Press.

———. 1983b. *Violence in Schools.* NIJ Research in Brief. Washington, DC: National Institute of Justice.

9

Self-Definition by Rejection: The Case of Gang Girls

Anne Campbell

Anne Campbell uses observations and interviews with low-income Puerto Rican gang girls in New York City to show how youths construct their identity or sense of self through social talk, particularly through gossip and "put downs" that vilify others' actions and character. Campbell argues that delinquency research would profit greatly by taking "disparaging social talk as a legitimate focus of enquiry."

ALTHOUGH THERE IS EVIDENCE THAT YOUNG WOMEN HAVE PARTICI-pated in urban street gangs since the mid-nineteenth century (Asbury 1970; Salisbury 1958; Thrasher 1927), it is only recently that they have received attention as a topic of study in their own right. Prior to the 1970s, female gangs were usually treated as journalistic curiosities (Hanson 1964; Rice 1963) or as footnotes to the study of male gangs (Cohen 1955; Cohen & Short 1958; Short & Strodtbeck 1965; Thrasher 1927). Two themes are apparent in much of this early work: the psychological problems and inappropriate [gender] role behavior of female gang members.

Psychological studies portrayed female gang members as immature, anxious, and maladjusted (Thompson & Lozes 1976), as relatively low in intelligence (Rice 1963), and as socially inept and sexually promiscuous (Ackley & Fliegel 1960; Cohen 1955; Welfare Council of New York City 1950). Thus, this early research attributed many of the same characteristics to gang members which were used to describe female delinquents in general (Smart 1976). However, Bowker and Klein (1983) reanalyzed data from the 1960s and found only trivial differences between gang and nongang girls on a variety of psychological tests.

"Self Definition by Rejection: The Case of Gang Girls," *Social Problems* 34, no. 5 (1987): 451–466. Reprinted by permission of the author and the University of California Press.

Early studies by social workers and sociologists tended to decontextualize the behavior of ghetto girls and to compare it unfavorably with middle-class stereotypes of femininity. Social workers placed particular emphasis upon gang girls' slipshod appearance, their preference for pants over skirts, and their poor personal hygiene, posture, and manners (Ackley & Fliegel 1960; Hanson 1964). Girls' failures in these areas were taken as indications of low self-esteem, prompting remedial efforts to turn them into young ladies (Short & Strodtbeck 1965). These departures from appropriate feminine behavior were also seen as the surface manifestations of a more profound problem: their promiscuity. Although the evidence for this was drawn from a highly questionable source—reports of male gang members—the promiscuity of gang girls was highlighted in Cohen's (1955) theoretical analysis of working-class delinquency. He argued that because emotional and romantic conquests are the female counterpart of societal achievement among boys, these young women expressed their rejection of the "middle-class measuring rod" by freely dispensing sexual favors. Thus, while boys boast about delinquent acts in order to achieve masculine status within their own oppositional subculture, girls should logically flaunt their promiscuity as a badge of their oppositional female identity.

Examination of the slim quantity of ethnographic work on delinquent and gang girls in fact suggests that this is not the case. The social talk of delinquent girls generally shows that they not only reject sexual activity outside the context of a steady relationship but even reject friendships with "loose" girls whose reputation might contaminate them by association (Smith 1978; Wilson 1978). Horowitz (1983) reinforces this point in her examination of barrio lifestyles of teenage girls in Chicago. As part of the Chicano culture, they must maintain the appearance of virginity and restraint even though the broader US culture encourages and condones sexual experience. The girls manage this contradiction by ascribing pregnancy to momentary passion in the context of a love relationship (the use of contraception would imply a cold-blooded and more permanent commitment to sexual experience). They can maintain their "virgin" status even after motherhood if their public demeanor continues to emphasize their commitment to motherhood and rejection of casual sexual adventures.

Female members of New York street gangs described in this paper had club rules which explicitly required serial monogamy, and girls who spread their sexual attentions too far were disciplined by the gang's "godmother." The pejorative potency of terms such as "whore" and "slut" is clearly seen in the way these teenage girls used such terms to characterize their enemies and rivals, and epithets such as these are often the triggers which spark female fights (Campbell 1986). It was this observation that gave rise to the present study: The words and typifications we use to characterize our enemies are often an important guide to the ascriptions we most reject in ourselves. By extension, our self concept may evolve from our rejection of such negative personal attributes rather than from the active construction of a social identity.

Using data from Puerto Rican gang members, I show how the girls' sense of self as gang members is derived from their rejection of various aspects of membership of three interlocking societal identities: class, race, and gender. They arrive at a female gang identity by default rather than by affirmation. The fragmented and reactive nature of their self definition helps to make sense of many of the contradictions which are present in the social talk of the gang girl. By "backing away" from one aspect of an assigned role, she may run the risk of being cast in another unacceptable role from which she must also extricate herself. For example, in rejecting women's passivity toward men, a girl may endorse her support for abortion. However, in doing so, she risks being seen as cheap or as a bad mother. Her support for abortion in one context may be withdrawn in another. To achieve self-presentational consistency, the individual must have formed a coherent schema of her ideal self to which she refers. As long as her self presentation depends upon rejecting an interlocking set of actions or qualities, she is likely to find herself escaping from one rejected identity but risking entry into another. The point is that not all components of a given role are rejected; indeed, it is hard to imagine what the result of such a total rejection would be. The girls accept the desirability of some aspects of femininity, class, or ethnicity but reject others. Essentially they are saying, "I am not that kind of woman," which is very different from saying, "I am not a woman."

In focusing upon self presentation through the words of the social actors themselves, the present study has much in common with the study of accounts (Goffman 1959; Scott & Lyman 1968). Accounts are usually given by actors in anticipation of or in response to listeners' negative evaluation of the actors' behavior. They are the means by which actors excuse or justify instances of untoward behavior. Stokes and Hewitt (1976) go further to argue that accounts serve to reconcile prevailing norms with innovative or deviant behavior and, over time, can alter group norms. In the case of delinquency, Sykes and Matza (1957) describe various "techniques of neutralization" which deny the wrongfulness of crime or justify it with respect to some superordinate value. My analysis of gang girls' accounts differs in three major respects from this tradition. First, I focus on social identities rather than on discrete actions. Girls see actions as characteristic of certain types of persons and they vilify these behaviors not for their own sake but because they are the manifestations of a rejected identity. This idea is tacitly embodied in some of Sykes and Matza's justifications and excuses. For example, an "appeal to higher loyalties" often invokes reference to the overriding importance of group solidarity, which can be seen from the present perspective as colloquially indicating "I am not the kind of person who deserts my buddies." Second, the accounts I describe are not directed only at antisocial behaviors. The qualities which gang girls reject include passivity, submissiveness, and provincialism as well as drug addiction and prostitution. Tension exists not only between deviance and respectability but also between old-fashioned and modern values, between poverty and glamour.

Third, while accounts are usually efforts to justify the speaker's own behavior, I focus mainly on disparagement of others' behavior. That is, I am concerned with gossip and "put-downs." As Moore notes, "Gossip, heavily judgmental, is at the heart of much sociability at the frequent parties. Gossip is fun. It also means that everybody—adult and adolescent—has a 'reputation' that is continuously shifting and renewed" (1978:52).

This putting-down of others is a crucial component of the establishment of a self image. To accuse neighboring gang members of being "whores" or "glue sniffers" clearly announces that the speaker denies the applicability of such terms to herself. Analysis of the vilification of others is not only a useful methodological tool, but this process of symbolic rejection may be at the heart of how gang girls arrive at their own self definition. They do not actively work at constructing a coherent female group image but rather arrive at one by default as they reject components of the identities they attribute to others.

Method

Between 1979 and 1981 I attached myself to three New York City female gangs as a participant observer. During the first six months of research, I made initial contacts with a number of city gangs through site visits to gang outreach programs and introductions arranged by the New York Gang Crimes Unit. At the end of this period, I selected three gangs for in-depth observation and subsequently spent six months with each of them. In each case, I selected one girl as the focus of the research and spent approximately four days a week with her in day-to-day activities—during the course of which I came to meet her fellow gang members, family, and neighbors. Whenever possible I tape-recorded dialogues between individual girls and myself, as well as group interactions between the girls and between female and male members. I augment my analysis of these recordings with material from my field notes.

One of the three groups I studied was the Five Percenters, a black Islamic movement organized into gang-like structures in a number of East Coast cities. However, I restrict my focus here to the accounts of Puerto Rican gang members, the majority of whom belonged to the Sex Girls and the Sandman Ladies.[1] As with female gangs described in other major cities (Miller 1975; Quicker 1983), both gangs were affiliated with previously established male gangs and adopted a feminized version of the male gang's name. Female members constituted approximately 10 percent of gang membership in the city (Collins 1979). The girls had their own leader and made most of their decisions independently of the males, including the acceptance, initiation, and discipline of their members. Gang members ranged in age from 12 to 28.

The Sandman Ladies were located on the west side of Manhattan with headquarters in the apartment of the female and male leaders (a married couple) in a housing project. They referred to themselves as a club or a family rather than as a gang, and identified themselves as "bikers," although the 20 male and 11 female members possessed only one working motorcycle between them. Their primary source of income was from street sales of marijuana, augmented by burglary and by hiring themselves out to protect cocaine sellers in the midtown area.

The Sex Girls were located in the East New York section of Brooklyn and most of the members lived within a few blocks of their clubhouse—one of the many abandoned buildings in the neighborhood. Their male counterparts named themselves the Sex Boys in honor of one of the local streets (Essex Street) when they split from the Ghetto Brothers in 1972. The male and female gangs were in a state of decline by 1979. A number of members were dead or imprisoned, and the formal structure of the gangs was in disarray. Although the Sex Girls allegedly had 50 members in the mid-1970s, their numbers had declined to about 10 by the time of my research. The gangs' main source of revenue was drug dealing. During my field work, they were involved in a dispute with an Italian group of dealers over territorial rights to selling, which resulted in the deaths of three of the male members. Their income was augmented by petty criminality such as stripping cars and abandoned buildings.

A content analysis of the verbal "put downs" that appeared in the social talk of gang girls revealed 10 recurrent topics. In each of these, the girls expressed rejection of specific behaviors or qualities and clearly identified themselves as distinct from individuals who could be characterized by them. For ease of presentation, I have conceptualized them as shown in Figure 9.1 as locations in a matrix of three interlocking structural variables: poverty, ethnicity, and gender. It should be stressed that this conceptualization is mine and did not arise explicitly from the girls themselves. Rather these topics of social talk occurred sporadically throughout my field work and the girls themselves did not specifically relate any given "put-down" to these sociological categories. It should also be noted that the diagrammatic representation is not meant to imply that all three components contribute equally to self definition. For some girls, being female seemed superordinate to being poor or Puerto Rican while for others it was not.[2]

Ethnicity

Anachronistic Values and Social Monitoring

Many gang members were born in Puerto Rico or have visited the island frequently to stay with relatives. As with any immigrant group, their feelings for the homeland tend to be mixed. Often the gang members would talk nostalgically of the sunshine and the fruit growing wild on the trees. Such positive recollections were usually tempered with less pleasant memories of poverty: the lack of indoor plumbing, the perpetual diet of rice and beans, the lack of new

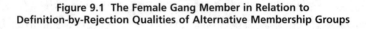

Figure 9.1 The Female Gang Member in Relation to Definition-by-Rejection Qualities of Alternative Membership Groups

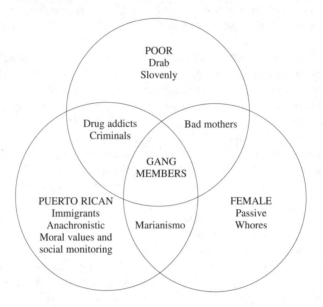

clothes or shoes. Aside from the material deprivation they associated with the island, gang members often expressed the views that Puerto Rico continued to adhere to anachronistic moral values and that islanders were old fashioned in comparison with New Yorkers. For example, many of the gang members who returned to the island for vacations were shocked at the great importance local police attached to marijuana possession. The girls saw the tough enforcement and stiff penalties as indicative of the old fashioned attitude of their homeland. In contrast, they viewed the ready availability of "herb" in corner stores in New York City as an indication of a more progressive and liberal attitude toward marijuana on the mainland. The rigid moral values in Puerto Rico prohibited many of the activities that the girls found most attractive in New York—hanging out in the street, dressing fashionably, flirting, drinking, getting "high," and attending parties. When they stayed with relatives on the island, they were required to come home early and to help with household chores. Some girls said their New York clothing caused consternation among their Puerto Rican kin. The girls' parents seemed to share such views, in that a frequent response to the girls' misbehavior was to send them to stay with relatives on the island. Girls who were associating with undesirable boys, who became pregnant, or who were beyond the control of their parents were often shipped back to Puerto Rico where they would be less tempted by the freedom of the mainland.

The girls also noted that these traditional conceptions of appropriate behavior were enforced by claustrophobic social monitoring which was conspicuously absent in their life in New York. The girls viewed the anonymity and mobility of city life as reflections of the progressive values of the United States. Gang members often complained about the confining tightness of social controls on the island. As one girl put it:

> Puerto Ricans are very simple minded and the atmosphere is very, very close—and that's ideal for whoever likes to be close to people. Not me. I personally like New York. It's very cold and people think twice about speaking to you. I don't like being watched. Over there, close communities everywhere you go. Everybody knows everything. I can't deal with that. This is the only place where you can come here and be yourself to an extreme but you can still be a faggot—that's an extreme. Or bitch. Dress that way, and I'm not saying it's going to be accepted by everybody, but you can still survive. Feel your identity—whether it be religion or whatever.

The tension between the sense of belonging associated with these extended networks and discomfort with their tight social monitoring has also been noted by Horowitz (1983) in her ethnographic research on Chicanas.

Immigrants

Gang members more than anything else see themselves as American and identify strongly with the special reputation of New York. They are not "hicks" but streetwise people who cannot be tricked, conned, or fooled. They know all the hustles and are not taken in by them. They strongly reject the old superstitions of the island which they see as evidence of its backward status. For example, many villagers in Puerto Rico continue to believe in "esperititas"—that curses can be placed upon individuals and only be removed through consultation with mediums who locate the source of the curse. The curse can then be lifted by the use of candles and herbs purchased from the local botanica. Although botanicas exist in New York City, they are supported by older Puerto Ricans who are unwilling to openly discount the supernatural. However, gang members saw these beliefs as anachronistic and provincial. In seeking revenge over a rival, they were far more likely to fight it out or "drop a dime" (inform on them) to the police.

In stressing their status as Americans and their superiority over other more recently arrived immigrants, gang members took particular pride in the commonwealth relationship between Puerto Rico and the United States. They viewed the fact that they could come and go from the island without visas as evidence that they were not "immigrants." They saw other newcomers to the city such as Haitians, Dominicans, and Cubans as naive, provincial, and backward in their outlook. As one girl observed:

America doesn't really want foreigners like me coming in, but right now Puerto Rico isn't foreign. Yeah. Dominican. Cuban. All those kinds of people. They came by boat. They can come on a boat from Santo Domingo or Puerto Rico. A lot of them get caught though, but a lot of them get in. And that's what fucks up the country. . . . Well, now the Blacks and Puerto Ricans don't have anything to worry about—it's the Cubans now. You know I saw a movie and it said if there were no niggers, we'd have to invent them. Do you know what? The Cubans are taking over the oppressed group now.

A source of particular irritation was the inability of some of these newly arrived groups to speak English. This was particularly striking because many of the gang members themselves spoke "Spanglish," switching from one language to another sometimes in mid-sentence. Nevertheless, their pride in their children's ability to speak and write standard English was evident, and they were often apologetic about their parents' inability to converse in anything but Spanish. For gang members, assimilation into mainstream American life was demonstrated by fluency in English which at the same time indicated the acquisition of "advanced" material values and skills.

Poverty

Drabness

The majority of gang members came from families that received welfare assistance and lived in communities where this was the norm. The families of many gang members were female-headed, and the mother often represented the only constant parent in the girl's life. Many of the girls themselves had their first child during their teenage years, after which they either lived at home, sharing child-rearing duties with their mother, or moved into a local apartment with the child's father. Gang girls with children were in the more secure position of receiving AFDC [Aid to Families with Dependent Children] checks, but they still relied on their wits (or those of their boyfriends) to provide for any unanticipated expenses. Consequently, males who had successful hustles were a prized commodity and addicted males were considered a liability since any income they might obtain was spent on heroin. The boys would hustle money on a day-to-day basis by stripping abandoned buildings, selling marijuana, or rolling drunks. Girls did not draw distinctions between legal and illegal income—provided the latter did not invite police attention. The frequent crises of poverty were managed by circles of relatives and neighbors who relied on one another to borrow and lend food or money until the arrival of the next check (Lewis 1965; Sheehan 1976). Life on a shoestring budget meant that there were frequent trips to corner stores to buy items of food, often at inflated prices.

After motherhood, the girls rarely considered taking up employment. They saw their duty as first and foremost to their children, and their role as mothers not only provided a measure of dignity but a legitimate reprieve from the alien world of work. Their low level of literacy and lack of high school diploma meant that they would be eligible only for manual work paying minimum wages. Such jobs would not add sufficiently to the quality of their life to justify leaving their children. Besides, the girls were clearly apprehensive about employment, since most of them had never held a job and doing so would mean leaving their immediate neighborhood. Gang members rarely ventured beyond a few blocks radius from their homes, and the principal source of influence from beyond the neighborhood was television. The girls avidly watched soap operas and game shows during the day. Their favorite shows were filled with images of glamour and conspicuous consumption in which women were either kept in limitless luxury by men or worked in highly attractive jobs. It is perhaps not surprising that, when queried about the kind of job they would like, gang members frequently cited dancing, singing, and modeling (see McRobbie 1978). The contrast between these aspirations and their actual job opportunities was striking and typified their rejection of any image of themselves as poor or drab. If work entailed menial labor, they would rather remain at home where their role as mothers engendered a measure of respect.

A good deal of their self presentation involved an image of devil-may-care casualness about the reckless spending of unanticipated income. They spent unexpected money immediately on drugs or alcohol and on trips to movies and steak houses. Many commentators on ghetto life have taken this as evidence of an inability to plan, save, or defer the gratification of immediate pleasure (see Meissner 1966). When viewed as part of the development of self image by rejection, the spending of money on glamourous leisure experiences represents the denial, albeit temporary, or the conception of themselves as poor.

Slovenliness

Gang members also place considerable emphasis upon the purchase of the "right" brand names in jeans, sneakers, alcohol, and stereo equipment. They considered it particularly important that their children dressed well, especially at Easter, and they spent large sums of money on clothes that children would outgrow within a few months. They refused second-hand clothes as indicative of the poverty which they made every effort to deny:

> Your kid might come home and say, "Mom, you got to buy me $30 sneakers, $2.99 sneakers ain't doing it for me. I just can't stand criticism any more. You have to buy me $30 sneakers." What do you do? You go out there and you try to get them for your kids—the best way you can, the best way you know how or something.

Their effort to distance themselves from poverty stereotypes was reflected in great concern about cleanliness in appearance. Although they sometimes referred to themselves as "outlaws," they never displayed the disregard for personal hygiene and appearance that has been described among biker groups like the Hell's Angels (Thompson 1967). Getting ready to "hang out" often took some time because the girls were so meticulous about their clothing and make-up. Jeans were dry cleaned rather than washed, and boots were oiled and sneakers whitened every day. Some gang girls rejected the wearing of "colors" because they felt it made them look cheap and dirty. They wore the full uniform of boots, jackets, and scarves only when they anticipated a run-in with a neighboring girl gang:

> We used to wear hankies over here, hankies over here. Pockets, on necks, pants, hats, all over. I used to think "Oh, that's bad. That's nice." But then I realized, "Look at me. I'm a girl. That doesn't look right." Like, "Look at that little tramp or whore." . . . You know—my jacket, . . . my clothes. I never like to wear them. Only when I'm going to fight or rumble, something like that.

Drug Addicts

The poverty-level Puerto Rican neighborhoods in which these gang members lived had high levels of crime and drug addiction. The fact that the girls belonged to highly visible gangs meant that they were viewed by the police and the community as being involved in both of these activities. The girls denied this. When they talked about drug abuse, they drew a clear line between recreational use and addiction. Marijuana was both used and sold by gang members and its place in their life was as uncontroversial as that of alcohol. They occasionally used LSD and amphetamines at parties. However, heroin use was strongly condemned. While some girls had experimented with "skin popping," they viewed intravenous injection of the drug as the index of real dependence. The girls took pains to distance themselves from any such involvement. Heroin users were seen as undependable, capricious, and irresponsible, and they were generally not welcome within the gang. They frequently stole from other members, failed to pay back loans, and were unavailable when needed for defense of the neighborhood. In spite of such vocal condemnation of heroin users, a number of the gang members were enrolled in methadone programs and had relapses into heroin use.

The gang placed firm demands for reform upon such members. As one female leader told an addict who wanted to rejoin the gang after leaving temporarily during a bout of heroin use:

> It's harder coming back the second time. I watch you more. You were fucking up a lot before, you were always nodding. Always told to shut up and you didn't listen. If you blend, you blend. If you don't, you don't. You've been to a different place. So just pretend you never left. Don't be talking about it. I don't want to hear nothing you've got to say.

A few days later, the girl stole three pairs of jeans and disappeared, confirming once again the gang's mistrust of an addict's commitment to anyone but herself. Significantly, a term of disparagement frequently leveled against rival gangs was that they were "dope fiends" or "glue sniffers."

Criminals

The girls did not consider many victimless offenses as criminal in spite of the fact that they might be against the law. These included drug selling, inter-gang warfare, organized crime, prostitution, domestic violence, stripping of abandoned buildings and automobiles, shoplifting, and burglary of businesses. Nevertheless, gang members assumed a condemnatory stance toward people they defined as "criminals." To affirm their own exclusion from this category, they employed a number of self-presentation devices. They symbolically distanced themselves from criminals by reserving the term for "crazy" people—[such as] Charles Manson or David Berkowitz. Criminals also included rapists and child molesters.[3] Nevertheless, gang members were still left with the problem of accounting for their residential burglaries and robberies which by their own definition were wrong. They achieved this through the use of two favored techniques of neutralization: appeal to necessity and denial of responsibility (see Sykes & Matza 1957). In the first case, they often justified property offenses with reference to a temporary financial crisis which left them no other option. In the second, they argued that they were "crazy" from drugs or alcohol while committing the act. However, neither of these justifications was accepted if the crime was committed on the gang's own turf:

> It was this old lady, she had a bunch of money in her pocket and we was on the corner, you know. We seen the money and I told Little Man, "Come on, Little Man, you want to do it? Let's take the money." So this old lady we know for a long time. She was a little bit crazy. I said "Come on Little Man, let's do it." Then she walked to the corner and we walked to the corner, right? And then we grab her and took the money but it was on the same block. The cops came and everything but we did it wrong because it was on the same block, so then Danny didn't like it. He started to scream at me, but he wasn't my [the girl gang's] leader, he can't do nothing.

Members accounted for their gang's existence by pointing out the jungle-like quality of city life. Similarly to male members of the Lions in Chicago (Horowitz 1983), they noted the high local crime rate and the need for some form of protection for themselves and their children. Frequently, the presence of rival gangs was given as their *raison d'etre*. They reasoned that since the other gang had "hardware" they had no option but to arm themselves also. As they saw it, they represented a vigilante force on behalf not only of themselves but of friends and neighbors too. In this regard, they felt a sense of cooperative rivalry with the police. The gang too was in the business of maintaining security, and the police frequently came to them to seek information on the perpetrators of neighborhood crime. As one member boasted:

> What the community cannot get to, I can get to. Sometimes the cops come in and nobody will tell them a goddamn thing. Nobody is going to tell nothing—even to save their hide, they won't tell them—but I will come along and they will tell me. They will open up to me because they know, having gone through that shit, everybody opens up willing. They let me know what's up and that way I bring up what happened [to the police].

Because of their cooperation—at least in instances where the crime in question was not committed by them and especially where it was perpetrated by another gang or by competing drug sellers—they saw themselves as undercover assistants. Accordingly, they were outraged when the police arrested one of them. They felt betrayed and pointed out that the local precinct house would be unable to keep order in the neighborhood without their help.

The Guardian Angels represented a major thorn in their side. The media portrayed the Angels as "good" kids, but the gang members believed that this group received disproportionate credit for its crime control efforts. They often accused the Angels of perpetrating as much crime as they prevented:

> The Guardian Angels got media recognition, they got everything now. They say they're this and they are that, that they're protecting the subway. That's bullshit, man. That's bullshit, right. They've already gotten busted for ripping somebody off on the subway, with their shit on, with their berets and their Magnificent Thirteen T-shirts and all their bullshit.

At the same time, gang members resented their own media image as "bad kids" and believed the press was conspiring to deny them appropriate publicity.

Femininity

Bad Mothers

Much has been written about motherhood as an important rite of passage among disadvantaged teenage girls (Rainwater 1960; Stack 1974; Staples 1971; Sullivan 1985). From an early age gang girls assisted in the raising of their younger siblings, although often with considerable ambivalence, and their own sexual experimentation began early. Many gang girls had their first intercourse at or before puberty and, consequently, pregnancy by the age of 15 was not uncommon. In New York City, about half of all teen pregnancies result in the birth of a child.[4] Although the girls' parents may initially react with anger, they usually come to accept the situation and provide practical, if not financial, support.

Motherhood means that the girl may now legitimately leave school and receive her own welfare check (although in the case of minors it may be paid through her mother). The young couple may marry but more often they do not; in Puerto Rico there is a long tradition of consensual unions (Fitzpatrick 1971). Although the teenage father takes pride in this public demonstration of his manhood, his commitment to the mother and child is often temporary. Consequently, many teenage mothers face a future on public assistance in which men come and go, offering varying degrees of support or exploitation. As Horowitz (1983) points out, the Hispanic girl is likely to be deeply concerned about her identity as a good mother. To avoid any imputation of irresponsibility as a mother, she must make every effort to demonstrate her dedication to the welfare of her child. A good deal of gossip among gang members centered on girls who failed to take adequate care of their children. Motherhood did not require abandonment of the gang, but it did entail making satisfactory arrangements for the child. Girls who brought their children with them to the corner to hang out were considered irresponsible (see also Horowitz 1983:128). The appropriate course of action was to leave the child with the grandmother for the night. After an all-night party, the girls would conscientiously return home in the early hours to get their children ready for school. Childcare revolved very heavily around physical appearance, and the children's clothes were washed and ironed carefully. Especially with daughters, considerable sums were spent on "cute" dresses and on straightening or perming their hair. Keeping their children in school and off the streets preoccupied the gang members, and much shame was attached to having a child in a "special class." Any failure on the child's part that might be traced back to inadequate motherhood was strongly condemned.

Passivity

Even as they extolled the importance of being a good mother, the girls opposed any view of themselves as being at the mercy of men. They took pride in their autonomy and rejected any suggestion that they could be duped or conned by males, especially in the area of having children. For many of the boys, parenthood symbolized the couple's commitment to one another, and the males would often express their desire to father a child as evidence of their warm regard for the girl. After their first or second child, the girls objected, realizing that ultimately they would be left "holding the baby":

> In Puerto Rico those ladies, boy, they have to suffer a lot. Those men, they play you dirty. All having a bunch of kids. All dirty and shit. And you see a man like that, why you going to keep having kids? For the same fucking man? Having four, six, seven kids like women do in Puerto Rico? I say "Uh-uh, that's not me." I do me an abortion. And like I tell you, I do four abortions already.

Abortion was a problematic issue for most of the girls. Wholehearted support might be construed as callous disregard for human life and place them in jeopardy of being seen as "bad mothers." On the other hand, too many children could lead to a male-dependent lifestyle and suggest that they were vulnerable to being "conned" by men. Consequently, abortion was accepted as legitimate after the first or second child but was generally condemned in a first pregnancy. Adding fuel to their justification for abortion was the strongly condemnatory stance taken toward it in Puerto Rico; having an abortion was also an acceptance of being a modern American woman.

Whores

Because of the local public perception of the "loose" sexual morality of female gang members, the girls were faced with particular problems of self presentation in this sphere. The cultural context of Hispanic life places considerable emphasis upon the purity of young women before marriage, although sex in the context of an exclusive love relationship is acceptable (Acosto-Belen & Christenson 1979; Pescatello 1973). In the gang, serial monogamy was the norm and sexual promiscuity was frowned upon. One of the most frequent disparagements of rival gang members was that they were "nothing but a bunch of ho's" (whores).[5] This epithet was one about which the girls were very sensitive:

> People say I'm a whore? They got to prove that. They can't say "You're a whore" just like that. They got to prove a lot of things. They ain't got no proof, so what's up? Right. So I say I don't live with the people no more. I live by myself. What the people say, I don't care. You know. Let it go.

Although it was in no way a requirement of membership, attachment to the gang often resulted in the girl becoming sexually involved with one of the male members. Once an exclusive romantic relationship had been established, the male would feel free to exert control over her public behavior and demeanor. At parties, for example, girls would sometimes get "high" and flirt mildly with other boys. This behavior usually provoked severe disapproval from their partners. During the summer, the boys would not allow their girlfriends to wear shorts or low cut T-shirts on the street. The girls chafed against these kinds of restrictions since they believed that flirting and fashion did not betoken promiscuity; however, they did accept the general premise that sexually suggestive behavior was inappropriate. Controls which males exerted in their role as boyfriends would certainly have been rejected by the girls had the males tried to impose them as a gang on the female affiliate.

The girls also exerted a good deal of social control over one another's sexual behavior. New girls in the group who, unaware of the prevailing norms, slept around with a variety of men were called to account for their behavior at meetings and instructed that serial monogamy was required. While this was in part motivated by the girls' own self interest in protecting their exclusive relationship with their boyfriends, members also referred to the danger of losing male respect by this kind of unselective sexuality:

> We think that she's a whore? She's a tramp? We just call her and we tell her "You got to get down with that one. But don't let everyone go to you. You're going to play with that one? Play with one, but the other ones, they're like friends." They [the boys] used to talk about her. We used to tell her, "Look, they talk about you—this and that. You think you're doing it right, but you doing it wrong. Because they're talking about you like a dog." She cool out in the end.

Marianismo

In their effort to avoid the stigma of cheapness through serial monogamy, the girls ran the risk of becoming overdependent on men. The term *marianismo* describes the qualities of femininity which are reciprocal to those of machismo in men. It refers to the cult of the Virgin Mary. A good woman accepts the dominance of men, values her own compliance and nurturance, and consistently places the needs of her family, especially her husband, above her own (Pescatello 1973). Gang girls, socialized in the United States, strongly rejected this subordinate view of female life. Most girls had seen their mother tolerate, for various periods of time, the blatant abuse and infidelity of their fathers. They frequently expressed disgust that their mothers had remained in the situation:

> Yeah—Puerto Rican women they hurt a lot. Some women they hurt a lot. They suffer a lot because of the man. Or because of their kids. I don't know. Like my mother—I say "Mommy, why don't you leave Poppy?" "Ah, because I love him at the time and I don't want you to have a stepfather." I used to tell her, "Oh, man, sometimes you're stupid."

The right of the Puerto Rican male to exercise physical control in his own house has been noted frequently, and the girls' history of physical abuse from their fathers and stepfathers made them unwilling to tolerate similar beatings from their own partners. After violent domestic confrontations, when they saw their boyfriend repeating the same cycle of abuse that their mothers had accepted, they often made exaggerated efforts to assert their own independence:

> I said, "Don't think because I have kids I'm going to put up. I'm not." Like some women will put up, I won't. I'll leave him. I don't have to put up with him. I'll find somebody else that will give me more. I try not to aggravate him so what I do is I worry him a lot. I'll leave him even if it takes killing myself to do it. If I have to escape and that's the only way because he's watching, because he doesn't want me to get away, I'll do it. I'll kill myself.

Infidelity on the part of the male represented an ever present threat to the stability of their social arrangements. Puerto Rican culture emphasizes male autonomy in many spheres including that of extramarital affairs (Acosto-Belen & Christenson 1979; Pescatello 1973). Although the males' traditional role as breadwinners and the exclusive rights it gave them have eroded, the double standard of sexual morality continues to exist in many New York communities. Puerto Rican women regard men with both fear and condescension as violent, sexual, free, and childish. Men's immaturity and irresponsibility are part of their nature for which they cannot be held fully accountable. Nongang girls in the neighborhood were often attracted by the boys' outlaw image. The boys felt that to refuse an offer of sex was tantamount to admitting homosexuality and argued that if a girl "put it in his face" they had no choice but to go along. The girls accepted this rogue male image and so had to exert their own control over rival girls. They did this vigorously as if to underline their unwillingness to repeat the *marianismo* of their mother:

> We'll still find out. We'll always find out. They'll swear on their mother, their father, their sister, their brother "I didn't do it. I didn't do it with that bitch. I wouldn't make good with that bitch." . . . But I already know the deal with them. "Alright, yeah, yeah, yeah." And that's when I go . . . up to the girl. And they don't even bother hitting us 'cos they know they're gonna get worse. I would just go up. "Hey, I hear you made it with my old man." This and that. And blat, that's it. The whole thing is over 'cos they don't even raise their hands. They put their head down and they cut out fast.

In this way many romantic disputes involving couples were actually resolved between the young women. The necessity of being attached to a male in order to have sexual relations, combined with a reluctance to challenge the boy directly over his infidelity, had a very divisive effect upon the girls' relationships with one another. As Horowitz (1983) also notes, disputes over men constituted a major source of aggression among the girls.

However, gang girls do take pride in their ability to fight. In rejecting passivity, they stress their aggressiveness and work hard at developing a reputation as a fighter.

> Girls around here they see a girl that's quiet, they think that she's a little dud. Yeah—let's put it that way. They think they don't know how to fight. . . . Round here you have to know how to fight. I'm glad I got a reputation. That way nobody will start with me—they *know*, you know. They're going to come out losing. Like all of us, we got a reputation. We're crazy. Nobody wants to fight us for that reason—you know. They say "No, man. That girl might stab me or cut my face or something like that."

Among the Chicana girls studied by Horowitz (1983), aggression was only acceptable when it was directed against other females. Even here, it was seen by the community as an untypical behavior flying in the face of the self control that was expected of young women. However, Quicker's (1983) description of Chicana gang members in Los Angeles reveals strong similarities with the girls in Puerto Rican gangs. Although aggression was most often directed at females, either "squares" or members of rival gangs, the girls I studied took particular pride in recounting episodes in which they had fought with male gang members from neighboring groups. Hispanic gang boys express considerable ambivalence about the girls' aggression. On one hand they are proud of the girls' "heart," while at the same time they will often intervene in a female fight to prevent injury to the girls (see also Horowitz 1983). Whatever the boys' attitude, the Puerto Rican girls clearly took pride in their willingness to fight and saw it as an indication of their commitment to the gang, to their relationships, and to their self-respect. More than winning a fight, it was important to be ready to enter one. Before a fight they prepared by tightly securing their hair with oil (so that opponents could not grab it) and donning boots and jeans. Rival gang members were disparaged as hanging out with their men only when times were good and failing to support them during gang wars:

> Tramps. All they think about is screwing. It's true. It's true, shit. They don't fight. They don't go to rumbles with their guys. Nothing. They're punks. They're a bunch of punks. . . . The Cheeseburgers are a bunch of punks? They're not tough. They're a bunch of dope fiends.

The importance of not "ranking out" or backing down from a fight was frequently stressed. It was seen as indicative of moral weakness. Fighting was sufficiently highly valued that the initiation of new "prospects" required them to demonstrate their fearlessness in the face of physical attack.

> Well when we started it was like initiating people—when you take them to the park, like, to see. Like there's some girls that join, like "I get in trouble, I got backup." Now for us this wasn't that. We used to take a new girl to the park. Now that girl had to pick one of our girls, and whoever she wanted, she had to fight that girl to see if she could take the punches. Now if she couldn't, she wouldn't fight. Then we wouldn't take her. Because then we know that someday—you know, somewhere in the streets—she's going to wind up getting hurt. So we knew that she could fight her battles and we used to let her join. She had to fight first. Without crying.

Discussion and Conclusions

Previous work on female gang members has placed considerable emphasis upon their sexuality either [as] an area for reform through social work, as a symptom of their rejection of middle-class values, or as the single most important impression management problem which they face. While any examination of self concept clearly must include attention to the management of appropriate

male or female identity, I believe it is a disservice to girls in gangs not to recognize other salient features of their self definition. These young women are
stigmatized by ethnicity and poverty as well as gender.

By virtue of their marginal position, both economically and socially, they
live their lives within a bounded geographical area where the major sources of
influence and support are likely to be families, friends, and neighbors. Without the opportunity to fulfill themselves in mainstream jobs beyond the ghetto,
their sense of self must be won from others in the immediate environment.
Within this context, gang girls see themselves as different from their peers.
Their association with the gang is a public proclamation of their rejection of
the lifestyle which the community expects from them. Sociological portraits
that deny the girls' sense of differentness from other neighborhood youth deny
the validity of the way the girls see themselves.

The sense of differentness experienced by the girls is fragmented and diffuse—as indeed it must be since they do not fully embrace an oppositional deviant identity. They do not buy into a countercultural role that is well-articulated
and wholly coherent. Rather they reject bits and pieces of the conventional lifestyle that is expected of them in the local community. Inevitably, the girl finds
herself in a contradictory and vulnerable position as she attempts to retain her integrity within her shifting self definition. She is Puerto Rican but neither provincial nor un-American. She may be poor but her life is neither drab nor criminal.
She enjoys her femininity but rejects passivity and suffering.

My evidence suggests that much can be learned from examining how we
vilify the traits and actions of others. Much of our social life is spent in talk,
and a significant portion of it is concerned not with our own behavior but with
that of others. The terms of condemnation in gossip reveal a good deal about
our own preoccupations and values. When we criticize others' behavior we assure the listener and ourselves that we are exempt from similar accusations—
we set ourselves apart from the object of our derision. Sometimes we level our
criticism at figures beyond our acquaintance such as media personalities or
politicians, but the most salient reference point[s] for our self definition are
those individuals or groups whose social niche we share. This is particularly
true for disadvantaged groups who are caught in a restricted social environment with little hope of mobility.

Important questions remain to be answered about the present approach, as
about other sociological analyses of accounts. The chronology of gang membership and self definition by rejection remains uncertain. Do gangs act as
clearing houses for those who have already felt their distance from "straight"
lifestyles, or does gang membership encourage and articulate this kind of self
definition? What changes occur in the evaluation of previously rejected qualities
when the girl falls away from the gang? Answers to these questions will only be
found if researchers continue to take disparaging social talk as a legitimate focus

of inquiry. Closer examination of the vilification of others may indicate that gossip is a strategic resource for the development of a sense of selfhood.

Notes

1. For a fuller account of these gangs, see Campbell (1984).

2. There is, of course, considerable scholarly debate as to the primacy of each of these factors, and researchers in women's studies, minority studies, and economics would certainly disagree as to the relative influence of gender, race, and class on lifestyles and self-conceptions.

3. It should be borne in mind that gang members themselves are not exempt from victimization. When one of the gang girls was the victim of an attempted rape, it was clear to gang members that the perpetrators were "criminals."

4. Personal Communication with Planned Parenthood of New York City, Inc., January 1984.

5. None of the girls I spoke with admitted to prostitution in their past. Where money was accepted from men after a date, it was treated as an unanticipated act of generosity. For example, one girl occasionally met men outside a Manhattan swingers club and went in with them. This lowered the men's admission price. The money they gave her at the end of the evening was considered a gift.

References

Ackley, Ethel & Beverly Fliegel. 1960. "A Social Work Approach to Street Corner Girls." *Social Work* 5:29–31.

Acosta-Belen, Edna & Elia H. Christenson. 1979. *The Puerto Rican Woman.* New York: Praeger.

Asbury, Herbert. 1970. *The Gangs of New York.* New York: Capricorn Books.

Bowker, Lee H. & Malcolm W. Klein. 1983. "The Etiology of Female Juvenile Delinquency and Gang Membership: A Test of Psychological and Social Structural Explanations." *Adolescence* 8:739–51.

Campbell, Anne. 1984. *The Girls in the Gang.* New York: Basil Blackwell.

———. 1986. "Self Report of Fighting by Females." *British Journal of Criminology* 26:28–46.

Cohen, Albert K. 1955. *Delinquent Boys: The Culture of the Gang.* New York: Free Press.

Cohen, Albert K. & James F. Short. 1958. "Research in Delinquent Subcultures." *Journal of Social Issues* 14:20–37.

Collins H. Craig. 1979. *Street Gangs: Profiles for Police.* New York: New York City Police Department.

Fitzpatrick, Joseph P. 1971. *Puerto Rican Americans: The Meaning of Migration to the Mainland.* Englewood Cliffs, NJ: Prentice Hall.

Goffman, Erving. 1959. *The Presentation of Self in Everyday Life.* New York: Doubleday Anchor.

Hanson, Kitty. 1964. *Rebels in the Streets: The Story of New York's Girl Gangs.* Englewood Cliffs, NJ: Prentice Hall.

Horowitz, Ruth. 1983. *Honor and the American Dream.* Chicago: University of Chicago Press.

Lewis, Oscar. 1965. *La Vida: A Puerto Rican Family in the Culture of Poverty: San Juan and New York.* New York: Vintage Books.

McRobbie, Angela. 1978. *Jackie: An Ideology of Adolescent Femininity.* Binningham, England: Centre for Contemporary Culture Studies.

Meissner, Hanna H. 1966. *Poverty and the Affluent Society.* New York: Harper & Row.

Miller, Walter B. 1975. *Violence by Youth Gangs and Youth Groups as a Crime Problem in Major American Cities.* Washington, DC: U.S. Government Printing Office.

Moore, Joan. 1978. *Homeboys: Gangs, Drugs, and Prison in the Barrios of Los Angeles.* Philadelphia, PA: Temple University Press.

Pescatello, Ann. 1973. *Female and Male in Latin America.* Pittsburgh, PA: University of Pittsburgh Press.

Quicker, John C. 1983. *Homegirls: Characterizing Chicana Gangs.* San Pedro, CA: International Universities Press.

Rainwater, Lee. 1960. *And the Poor Get Children: Sex, Contraception and Family Planning in the Working Class.* Chicago: Quadrangle.

Rice, Robert. 1963. "A Reporter at Large: The Persian Queens." *New Yorker* 39:153–87.

Salisbury, Harrison E. 1958. *The Shook-Up Generation.* New York: Harper & Bros.

Scott, Marvin & Stanford Lyman. 1968. "Accounts." *American Sociological Review* 33:46–62.

Sheehan, Susan. 1976. *A Welfare Mother.* Boston: Houghton Mifflin.

Short, James F. & Fred Strodtbeck. 1965. *Group Process and Gang Delinquency.* Chicago: University of Chicago Press.

Smart, Carol. 1976. *Women, Crime and Criminology.* London: Routledge & Kegan Paul.

Smith, Lesley S. 1978. "Sexist Assumptions and Female Delinquency: An Empirical Investigation." In C. Smart & B. Smart (eds.), *Women, Sexuality and Social Control.* London: Routledge & Kegan Paul.

Stack, Carol B. 1974. *All Our Kin: Strategies for Survival in a Black Community.* New York: Harper & Row.

Staples, Robert (ed.). 1971. *The Black Family: Essays and Studies.* Belmont, CA: Wadsworth.

Stokes, Randall & John P. Hewitt. 1976. "Aligning Actions." *American Sociological Review* 41:838–45.

Sullivan, Mercer L. 1985. *Teen Fathers in the Inner City: An Exploratory Ethnographic Study.* New York: Vera Institute of Justice.

Sykes, Gresham M., & David Matza. 1957. "Techniques of Neutralization: A Theory of Delinquency." *American Sociological Review* 22:664–70.

Thompson, Hunter. 1967. *Hell's Angels.* New York: Ballantine.

Thompson, Robert J. & Jewel Lozes. 1976. "Female Gang Delinquency." *Corrective & Social Psychiatry & Journal of Behavior Technology Methods & Therapy* 22:1–5.

Thrasher, Frederick. 1927. *The Gang.* Chicago: University of Chicago Press.

Welfare Council of New York City. 1950. *Working with Teenage Groups: A Report on the Central Harlem Project.* New York: Welfare Council of New York City.

Wilson, Deidre. 1978. "Sexual Codes and Conduct: A Study of Teenage Girls." In C. Smart & B. Smart (eds.), *Women, Sexuality and Social Control.* London: Routledge & Kegan Paul.

10

Explaining School Shooters: The View from General Strain and Gender Theory

Ronald J. Berger

Ronald Berger illuminates the problems of bullying and suburban school shooters through the perspectives of general strain and gender theory. He notes that school shooters have often been victims of persistent bullying and other public degradations to their masculine status that result in what he calls masculine gender strain, which eventually erupts into public displays of retaliation. Berger argues that the phenomenon of school shootings cannot be addressed without understanding the more general problem of bullying as a source of strain and gender status degradation in our society.

IN PEARL, MISSISSIPPI, IN OCTOBER 1997, 16-YEAR-OLD LUKE WOODHAM went to his high school and opened fire on his classmates, killing two and wounding seven others (Cowley 1998).[1] Between December of that year and May 1998, the news media reported on five other similar incidents that occurred in such unlikely places as West Paducah, Kentucky; Jonesboro, Arkansas; Edinboro, Pennsylvania; Fayetteville, Tennessee; and Springfield, Oregon. All told these five other shootings resulted in the deaths of nine students and two teachers and wounded 32 others (*Wisconsin State Journal* 1999a).[2]

These incidents were by no means the first or the last shootings of this nature that have occurred in suburban and rural communities in the United States in recent years (Kimmel and Mahler 2003; *Wisconsin State Journal* 1999b), but arguably the one that stands out most in people's minds—the paradigmatic case—is the one that occurred at Columbine High School in Littleton, Colorado in April 1999, when Eric Harris and Dylan Klebold went on a shooting rampage killing 12 students and a teacher and then taking their own lives (Larkin 2007).[3] It was the largest mass murder to occur in the United States between the time Timothy McVeigh bombed the Alfred Murrah Federal Building in Oklahoma City in 1996 and the attacks on the World Trade Center and the Pentagon on September 11, 2001.

Inner-city schools generally experience more overt violence than schools in suburban and rural areas (Irvine 2006; Lawrence 1998), but it is arguably the latter that attract the bulk of media attention. And with each new incident, similar claims of disbelief emerge from the residents: "How could it happen *here?*" "This isn't the inner city." "We're not that kind of people" (Smith 2006; Wahlberg 2006; Williams 1999). Indeed, at first glance, Columbine High School would seem to have been a particularly unlikely target insofar as it was known as "one of the best schools in the state. . . . Its sports teams . . . were perennial contenders for state championships. . . . Its students won academic honors . . . averag[ing] in the 71st percentile in reading and the 67th percentile in math nationwide; 82 percent of its seniors go on to college. . . . Few communities in America are as culturally homogenous" (p. 12). The seemingly pristine picture, as we shall see, is more complicated, however.

Many analysts attribute these suburban/rural school shootings to the psychopathology of the assailants, who have been variously called—depending on the particular individual and analyst—psychotic, psychopathic, schizophrenic, delusional, megalomaniacal, and depressive (Cullen 2004; *Frontline* 2000a; Kellerman 1999; Wooden and Blazak 2001). I do not wish to dispute these diagnoses, although there may be reasons to question them in some cases (Larkin 2007). Rather, I would like to make sociological sense of these tragedies, to see if any of the theories we have at our disposal can shed light on this phenomenon.

That these shooters have generally been white adolescent males with easy access to firearms, and that their particular tastes in rock-and-roll music and violent video games tended toward the extreme, is not in much dispute (Larkin 2007; Tsai and Sarche 2006; Wooden and Blazak 2001). Public policies that address the ready availability of guns and the media's glorification of violence are certainly worth pursuing (see Berger, Free, and Searles 2009; Grossman and Degaetano 1996). But this is not my focus in this chapter. Instead I want to apply concepts from *general strain theory* and *gender theory* to advance a *gendered-strain theory* of suburban/rural school shootings.

■ General Strain Theory

The theoretical roots of general strain theory run deep in the sociological tradition, reaching as far back as the work of European social theorist Émile Durkheim (1897/1952). In his classic study of suicide, Durkheim found that rates of suicide varied between groups and regions and fluctuated over time. He argued that these patterns could be explained not by psychological or individualistic factors but by factors related to the social organization of society.

Durkheim coined the term "anomie" to help explain social patterns of suicide. Anomie refers to the state of normlessness whereby individuals are isolated, cut adrift, and lacking in a common bond that brings them into sympathetic relationships with other people in society. Later, however, Robert Merton (1938) reformulated the concept of anomie to analyze the structural disjuncture between predominant *culturally approved goals* (i.e., financial success and bountiful material consumption) and the *available opportunities* to achieve these goals through legitimate means (i.e., education, employment). According to Merton, people who lacked access to the legitimate means to achieve these goals were structured into a relationship of strain with society and experienced frustration and a sense of injustice about their lot in life. Over time, this Americanized version of anomie theory also came to be known as "classic strain theory" (Agnew et al. 1996).[4] Survey research on classic strain theory and delinquency has focused on the disjuncture between individuals' aspirations and expectations regarding their goals in life (typically educational and economic/occupational) and their level of dissatisfaction, frustration, or sense of injustice about their plight (see Agnew et al. 1996; Empey and Stafford 1991; Messner and Rosenfeld 2001).

Cohen (1955) was one of the first to point out that for youths a great source of strain is not the lack of economic opportunity per se but an educational system that was ostensibly designed to prepare youths for economic success. Youths who experience the strain of school failure lose their stake in conformity and are more likely to engage in delinquency. Moreover, school failure is associated with delinquency among students of all social classes, not just the lower class (Agnew 2001; Frease 1973; Maguin and Loeber 1996; Polk, Frease, and Richmond 1974).[5]

Greenberg (1977) noted that much of youths' experience of school strain derives from the rules and regimentation of the school itself, the boredom and perception that education is a waste of time, and the denial of youths' autonomy at a point in life when they are trying to establish their independence. Some students view school as a hostile territory and express resentment directly through vandalism of school property and assaults against teachers. Indeed, much juvenile crime is committed on school grounds and sometimes involves crime against other students. Proximity to high schools is also related to higher crime rates in adjacent residential areas (Agnew 2000; Lawrence 1998; Roncek and Gaggiani 1985; Roncek and LoBosco 1983).

In an attempt to account for this cross-class relationship between strain and delinquency, but also going beyond the school or economy as casual factors, Robert Agnew (1992) advanced a social psychological or micro-level "general strain theory" in which he argued that delinquency was an outcome of a broader array of stressful or negative life experiences that strain one's relationship with society. In contrast to classic strain theory, general strain theory postulates that strain results not simply from the actual or perceived failure to achieve educational and economic/occupational goals. According to Agnew, strain may result from the actual or anticipated *removal* of any "positively valued stimuli" (e.g., death of a parent, end of a romantic relationship, moving from one's neighborhood) as well as the actual or anticipated *presentation* of any "negatively valued stimuli" (e.g., an abusive parent, an unfair teacher, hostile peers). Agnew also suggests that the relationship between strain and delinquency is mediated by a youth's *emotional reactions* (e.g., frustration, depression, anger) and *coping strategies* (e.g., talking to others, cathartic physical exercise, revision of goals) that affect the behavioral outcomes of structurally induced experiences (Agnew 2000, 2001). In recent work, Agnew has placed considerable emphasis on the role of "negative emotionality" (particularly anger) and "low constraint" (impulse control) as personality traits that condition the effect of strain on delinquency (Agnew et al. 2002). In general, a growing body of research lends support to the basic tenets of general strain theory (see Baron 2004 for a review).

Gender Theory

Gender theory in criminology is closely associated with feminist scholarship that examines gender as a central dimension of social stratification (Daly and Chesney-Lind 1988; Simpson 1989). The concept of gender (as opposed to biological sex) refers to the "social statuses and meanings assigned to women and men" in society (Richardson, Taylor, and Whittier 1997:31). According to gender theory, societal notions of masculinity and femininity are socially constructed and historically linked to institutional arrangements of power that have entailed men's dominance and social privilege vis-à-vis women. Although gender roles have undergone considerable change over the years, many of the traditional patterns persist (Berger, Free, and Searles 2009).

Masculinity theory is a particular branch of gender theorizing that focuses on the behavior of boys and men. According to Connell (1995), the hegemonic or dominant form of masculinity in society entails social patterns of conduct that encourage men to maintain power over women and other men (see also Berger, Free, and Searles 2009; Messerschmidt 2004). "Displays of aggression, independence, and a rejection of femininity are thought to be culturally honored ways of *being a man*" (Kreager 2007:709, emphasis added). Challenges or personal affronts to one's masculinity can erode one's social standing and eat away at one's self-esteem and thus need to be responded to in kind if the boy or man is to maintain his status and sense of self-worth. Criminological studies have documented this dynamic among lower-class (especially minority) youths who live in communities where "might makes right" and the maintenance of "respect"—being treated with proper deference—is of paramount importance. Humility or "turning the other cheek" is no virtue and can in fact be dangerous. Failure to respond to intimidation or "dissing" from another only encourages further victimization (Anderson 1999; see Chapters 19 and 20). As we shall see, this dynamic is also prevalent among suburban and rural youths.

I propose that insights from general strain and gender theory can be integrated to illuminate the phenomenon of suburban and rural school shootings.

Research indicates a common pattern whereby youths who perpetrated these crimes had often been the victims of persistent bullying and other public degradations to their social status and self-esteem. These degradations may be viewed as a form of *masculine gender strain,* which (in conjunction with other conditioning factors that predispose one to aggression) can erupt into public displays of retaliation.

Bullying and School Shooters

Bullying is now "recognized as one of the major problems facing United States' schools today," with about 30 percent of students involved as bully, victim, or both (Holt and Keys 2004:121). Olweus defines bullying as "repeated, negative ill-intentioned behavior" by one youth directed against another who has "difficulty defending himself or herself" and notes that "most bullying occurs without any apparent provocation on the part of the student who is exposed" (quoted in APA Online 2008:1). Leff and colleagues (2004) add that bullying entails an imbalance of power between bully and victim and can be both physically and emotionally harmful.

In a study of 28 school shootings since 1982, Kimmel and Mahler found that "most of the boys who opened fire were mercilessly and routinely teased and bullied and that their violence was retaliatory against threats to their manhood" (2003:1439; see also *Frontline* 2000b). Often the threats to manhood involve persistent taunts about being a "fag," "queer," "homo," or "sissy" (Kimmel and Mahler 2003; Larkin 2007; Stein et al. 2006; Wooden and Blazak 2001). While most victims simply sulk away in defeat or become depressed about their situation, and some contemplate, attempt, or commit suicide, a minority may suddenly explode in a fit of violent rage. Or others, as in the Columbine case, may contemplate and plan their retaliation over an extended period of time (Larkin 2007; Pollock 1998; Richmond 2006; Wooden and Blazak 2001).

In his study of the Columbine case, Larkin (2007) found that Eric Harris and Dylan Klebold were but two of a number of students who were constantly bullied by the so-called "good kids" in the school, primarily by some of the football players and wrestlers. (Football and wrestling are the two types of sports most known for athletes who are especially prone to violence [Kreager 2007].) This group of predatory students were known as "jocks," as opposed to other nonpredatory students involved in sports who were simply known as "athletes."

Adolescent groups in high school are stratified according to higher-status, middle-status, and lower-status youths. Those who participate in sports are typically among the elite students in the school. An assortment of other students may be considered "losers" who are disdained by the other students.[6] These students are often the victims of bullying. Brooks Brown, a friend of Harris, was by his own account one of the "loser" students (Larkin 2007). He described the routine harassment he experienced this way:

> At lunchtime jocks would kick our chairs, or push us down on the table or throw food as we were walking by. When we sat down, they would pelt us with candy from another table. In the hallways, they would push kids into lockers and call them names while their friends stood by and laughed at the show. In gym class, they would beat kids up in the locker room . . . [when] the teachers weren't around.
>
> Seniors at Columbine would do things like pour baby oil on the floor, then literally "go bowling" with freshmen; they would throw the kid across the floor, and since he couldn't stop, he crashed right into other kids while the jocks pointed and giggled. The administration finally put a stop to it after a freshman girl slipped and broke her arm. . . . One guy, a wrestler who everyone knew to avoid, liked to make kids get down on the ground and push pennies along the floor with their noses. (Brown and Merritt 2002:50)

The harassment wasn't restricted to school grounds either. One youth, identified by Larkin as SJ, said:

> Almost on a daily basis, finding death threats in my locker. . . . It was bad. . . . I always walked home. And everyday when they'd drive by, they'd throw trash out their windows at me, glass bottles. . . . [Y]ou get hit with a glass bottle that's going 40 miles an hour, that hurts pretty bad. . . . This is something that I had to put up with nearly every day for four years. (Larkin 2007:91)

School officials were aware of some of the harassing behavior, but thought it was minimal, something that they had under control. But Larkin believes that their dismissive attitude was part of the problem that sanctioned a normative climate of bullying at Columbine. As Brown observed, "Teachers would see it and look the other way. 'Boys will be boys,' they'd say, and laugh" (Brown and Merrit 2002:5). Larkin adds that the adults, "especially teachers who were also coaches, either inadvertently or openly encouraged or participated in the harassment and humiliation of students" (2007:98; see also Kurtz 1999). Moreover, the predatory students viewed themselves as "defending the moral order of the school, . . . as acting with the will of the majority of students. The mere presence of outcast students [like Brown, SJ, Harris, and Klebold] was judged to be a blot on the pristine nature of Columbine, . . . which gave them the right to harass and humiliate them" (2007:103). If anyone wants "to know what Columbine was like," Brown said:

> I'd tell them about the bullies who shoved the kids they didn't like into lockers, called them "faggots" every time they walked past. I'd tell them about the jocks who picked relentlessly on anyone they considered to be below them. The teachers turned a blind eye to the brutalization of their pupils, because those pupils weren't the favorites. . . . [I'd tell] them about the way those who were "different" were crushed. . . . [I'd tell] them what it was like to live in constant fear of other kids who'd gone out of control, knowing full well that teachers would turn a blind eye. (Brown and Merritt 2002:163)

Larkin believes that the "most serious and corrosive result of adult sanc-tioning of predatory behavior is a sense" of powerlessness and injustice it causes among the victimized students (2007:106). Most of the victims of Columbine's bullying just did the best they could to muddle through, but Har-ris and Klebold sought revenge. Since they could not expect any help from the authorities, they decided to take matters into their own hands and began plot-ting "to blow up the school and kill as many" people as possible (p. 121). Ar-guably the youths were emotionally disturbed, but they were responding to a social reality that was not a figment of their imaginations. Harris had had homicidal thoughts a year prior to the shootings and started compiling a "S-hit list" of all the "students who had slighted him in some way"—a list that num-bered 67 (p. 126). But the killing of specific individuals was not their goal; they wanted "to inflict pain on the entire community" (p. 5). Harris had actu-ally created his own website where he wrote:

> I will rig up explosives all over town and detonate each one of them after I mow down a whole fucking area full of you snotty ass rich motherfucking high strung godlike attitude worthless pieces of shit whores [sic]. I don't care if I live or die in the shoot out, all I want to do is to kill and injure as many of you pricks as I can, especially a few people. (Larkin 2007:127)
>   . . . [Y]ou all better fucking hide in your house because I'm comin for EVERYONE soon, and I WILL be armed to the fuckin teeth and I WILL shoot and kill and I WILL fucking KILL EVERYTHING! (Brown and Merrit 2002:86–87; emphasis in original)[7]

▓ Gendered Strain and the Righteous Slaughter

Whatever psychopathology suffered by Harris and Klebold and other school shooters of their ilk, general strain theory most certainly describes the *removal* of "positively valued stimuli," the *presentation* of "negatively valued stimuli," and the *emotional reactions* that constituted their social and psychological lives. But the particular nature of the strain experienced by youths who be-come school shooters is arguably a gendered phenomenon. As Wooden and Blazak suggest,

> This experience . . . led to the inevitable counterswing. The boys tapped into the dominant image of masculinity present in popular Arnold Schwartze-neger, Sylvester Stallone, and Bruce Willis films—gun violence. . . . [T]he dramatic killing sprees were the result of repeated experiences of emascula-tion that created a situation in which the boys needed . . . to reclaim their manhood. (2001:111)

In some sense, the masculine "code of honor" almost *requires* violence as a response to shame or humiliation—especially imputations to one's sexual-ity—if one is to remain a "man." For young men, nothing stimulates violence as much as the experience of shame and humiliation (Gibbs and Roche 1999). It is this dynamic that I describe as masculine gender strain. As Luke Wood-ham said, "Murder is not weak and slow-witted, murder is gutsy and daring. . . . I killed because people like me are mistreated every day" (quoted in Cowley 1998:25).[8]

Finally, I would add that there is an important performative element to the violence of school shootings as well, whereby shooters desire to act out their rage to a wider audience "on stage." There is a megalomaniacal element, too—Harris thought of himself as an "avenging angel" of sorts who was destined "not so much to right the wrongs of humanity but to terrorize lesser humans and demonstrate his own superiority" (Larkin 2007:135). In this sense, the shooting very much illustrates the type of homicide that Katz (1988) calls the "righteous slaughter," a concept he develops in his provocative book, *Seductions of Crime: Moral and Sensual Attractions of Doing Evil*. According to Katz, "When people sense that they have no resort but to confront a challenge to their ultimate personal worth, they need not respond with a violent attack. A common alternative is to turn the challenge against the self and endure humiliation" (p. 22). Would-be killers, however, undergo an emotional process whereby they transform what they initially experience as "an eternally humiliating situation" into a blind rage, "forging a momentary sense of eternal unity with the Good" (p. 19). Katz adds that the "would-be killer must successfully organize his behavior to maintain the required perspective and emotional posture while implementing [his] particular project" (p. 19; see also Perlmutter 1999).

Larkin notes that Harris and Klebold thought that their righteous slaughter would, in Harris's words, "kick-start a revolution" among the marginalized, despised, and dispossessed students of the world (2007:193). While they have not succeeded in their grandiose vision, in their deaths they have indeed achieved celebrity status. Indeed, there has been a copycat element to many of the subsequent shootings—Columbine is not only the paradigmatic case for sociologists theorizing about this phenomenon, but for potential shooters themselves. In 2006, 17-year-old Eric Stutz planned a Columbine-like massacre with two of his friends in Green Bay, Wisconsin, but the youths were caught before they could execute their plans. Stutz had told a friend (not one of the plotters) that he planned to "shoot the place up." His friend asked, "Well, do you mean like Columbine?" Stutz replied, "Well, yeah, exactly" (Richmond 2006:C3). There is even an Internet video game that some youths play that is modeled after Columbine called "Super Columbine Massacre" (Tsai and Sarche 2006). In 2006, 25-year-old Kimveer Gill killed one student and wounded 19 others on a college campus in Montreal, Quebec. Gill said that he liked to play the game. In an online profile he wrote, "Life is a video game you've got to die sometime" (Tsai and Sarche 2006:A9).[9] There are also Internet sites and chat rooms devoted to Harris and Klebold where people debate whether they are heroes or villains.

Clearly the Columbine killings struck a chord with some of Harris and Klebold's peers. The Columbine youths did not kick-start a revolution, but "they have provided outcast students with the possibility of an alternative to passive acceptance of abuse from their higher-status peers" (Larkin 2007:195). Their personal and collective angst is explicable sociologically. It should not be dismissed as entirely psychopathological. Sociological theory offers a way of understanding and talking about this phenomenon without resorting to psychological reductionism or dismissing it as "random violence," as if it were without social patterning (see Best 1999).[10] In this chapter I offered a theory of gender strain, based on insights from general stain theory and gender theory, to help make the shootings explicable. Further research employing this perspective may help illuminate these and other social processes that underlay this tragic dimension of contemporary American life.

Notes

1. Before his school rampage, Woodham also stabbed his mother to death.

2. Kip Kinkel of Springfield, Oregon, also killed his parents.

3. This chapter focuses on high school shootings and does not cover those that have occurred on college campuses such as Virginia Tech and Northern Illinois University in recent years.

4. In Chapter 14 I call this anomie-opportunity or macro-level strain theory. See that chapter for macro-level applications of this theory.

5. Cohen focused on lower-class youths and did not anticipate this cross-class relationship between school strain and delinquency.

6. See Chapter 17 for a more detailed discussion of adolescent social types.

7. Harris and Klebold also reviled the Christian students who were publicly assertive about their beliefs, were intolerant of other religions and nonbelievers, and who thought of themselves as a moral elite. Ironically, according to Larkin, some of "the worst predators on campus" were members of this group (2007:106)

8. Some youths, as noted earlier, may respond to this strain by committing suicide. Humiliation from girls who have rejected them has also been an element in some suicides and school shootings (Perlmutter 1999; Richmond 2006).

9. Danny Ledonne, creator of the game, estimates that it has been downloaded over 100,000 times. He refuses to take responsibility for shooters who play the game: "Yeah, there are violent video games, violent movies, but guess what? I can turn on the news and see violence in the real world. Violent video games are a reflection of our societal issues." The purpose of the game, he said, "was to give some insight into these two young men, to put you into their heads, so to speak, to perhaps understand why they may have done this" (Tsi and Sarche 2006:A9).

10. See Agnew (1995, 2000, 2001) for policy recommendations derived from general strain theory.

References

Agnew, Robert. 1992. "Foundation for a General Strain Theory of Crime and Delinquency." *Criminology* 30:47–87.

———. 1995. "Controlling Delinquency: Recommendations from General Strain Theory." In H. Barlow (ed.), *Crime and Public Policy.* Boulder, CO: Westview Press.

————. 2000. "Strain Theory and School Crime." In S. Simpson (ed.), *Of Crime and Criminality*. Thousand Oaks, CA: Sage.

————. 2001. *Juvenile Delinquency: Causes and Control*. Los Angeles: Roxbury.

Agnew, Robert, Timothy Brezina, John Paul Wright, and Francis T. Cullen. 2002. "Strain, Personality Traits, and Delinquency: Extending General Strain Theory." *Criminology* 40:43–71.

Agnew, Robert, Francis T. Cullen, Velmer S. Burton, and R. Gregory Dunaway. 1996. "A New Test of Classic Strain Theory." *Justice Quarterly* 13:681–704.

Anderson, Elijah. 1999. *Code of the Street*. New York: Norton.

APA Online. 2008. "School Bullying Is Nothing New, but Psychologists Identify New Ways to Prevent It," retrieved from www.psychologymatters.org.

Baron, Stephen W. 2004. "General Strain, Street Youth and Crime: A Test of Agnew's Revised Theory." *Criminology* 42:457–83.

Berger, Ronald J., Marvin D. Free, and Patricia Searles. 2009. *Crime, Justice, and Society: An Introduction to Criminology,* 3rd ed. Boulder, CO: Lynne Rienner.

Best, Joel. 1999. *Random Violence: How We Talk About New Crimes and New Victims*. Berkeley: University of California Press.

Brown, Brooks, and Rob Merritt. 2002. *No Easy Answers: The Truth Behind Death at Columbine*. New York: Lantern Books.

Cohen, Albert K. 1955. *Delinquent Boys: The Culture of the Gang*. New York: Free Press.

Connell, R. W. 1995. *Masculinities*. Berkeley: University of California Press.

Cowley, Geoffrey. 1998. "Why Children Turn Violent." *Newsweek*, April 6:25.

Cullen, Dave. 2004. "The Depressive and the Psychopath," retrieved from www.slate .msn.com.

Daly, Kathleen, and Meda Chesney-Lind. 1988. "Feminism and Criminology." *Justice Quarterly* 5:497–538.

Durkheim, Émile. 1897/1952. *Suicide*. New York: Free Press.

Empey, Lamar T., and Mark C. Stafford. 1991. *American Delinquency: Its Meaning and Construction*. Homewood, IL: Dorsey.

Frease, Dean E. 1973. "Delinquency, Social Class, and the Schools." *Sociology and Social Research* 57:443–59.

Frontline. 2000a. "The Killer at Thurston High: 111 Years Without Parole," available online at www.pbs.org.

————. 2000b. "The Killer at Thurston High: 'Profiling' School Shooters," available online at www.pbs.org.

Gibbs, Nancy, and Timothy Roche. 1999. "The Columbine Tapes." *Time*, Dec. 20:40–51.

Greenberg, David F. 1977. "Delinquency and the Age Structure of Society." *Contemporary Crises* 1:189–223.

Grossman, Dave, and Gloria Degaetano. 1996. *Stop Teaching Our Kids to Kill: A Call to Action Against TV, Movies and Video Game Violence*. New York: Crown.

Holt, Melissa K., and Melissa A. Keys. 2004. "Teachers' Attitudes Toward Bullying." In D. Espelage and S. Swearer (eds.), *Bullying in American Schools*. Mahwah, NJ: Lawrence Erlbaum.

Irvine, Martha. 2006. "School Killings Not the Worst Picture." *Wisconsin State Journal*, Oct. 15:A5.

Katz, Jack. 1998. *Seductions of Crime: Moral and Sensual Attractions of Doing Evil*. New York: Basic Books.

Kellerman, Jonathan. 1999. *Savage Spawn: Reflections on Violent Children*. New York: Random House.

Kimmel, Michael S., and Matthew Mahler. 2003. "Adolescent Masculinity, Homophobia, and Violence." *American Behavioral Scientist* 46:1439–58.

Kreager, Derek. A. 2007. "Unnecessary Roughness? School Sports, Peer Networks, and Male Adolescent Violence." *American Sociological Review* 72:705–24.

Kurtz, Holly. 1999. "Columbine Like a Hologram: Life at School Depends on Angle of One's View." *Denver Rocky Mountain News,* July 25:4A.

Larkin, Ralph W. 2007. *Comprehending Columbine.* Philadelphia: Temple University Press.

Lawrence, Richard. 1998. *School Crime and Juvenile Justice.* New York: Oxford University Press.

Leff, Stephen S., Thomas J. Power, and Amy B. Golstein. 2004. "Outcome Measures to Assess the Effectiveness of Bullying-prevention Programs in Schools." In D. Espelage and S. Swearer (eds.), *Bullying in American Schools.* Mahwah, NJ: Lawrence Erlbaum.

Maguin, Eugene, and Rolf Loeber. 1996. "Academic Performance and Delinquency." In M. Tonry (ed.), *Crime and Justice.* Chicago: University of Chicago Press.

Merton, Robert K. 1938. "Social Structure and Anomie." *American Sociological Review* 3:672–82.

Messner, Steven E., and Richard Rosenfeld. 2001. *Crime and the American Dream.* Belmont, CA: Wadsworth.

Messerschmidt, James W. 2004. *Flesh and Blood: Adolescent Gender Diversity and Violence.* Lanham, MD: Rowman & Littlefield.

Perlmutter, Dawn. 1999. "Postmodern Iconoclasm: Violence in the School Yard," available online at www.religion.emory.edu/affiliate.

Polk, Kenneth, Dean E. Frease, and F. Lynn Richmond. 1974. "Social Class, School Experience, and Delinquency." *Criminology* 12:84–96.

Pollack, William. 1998. *Real Boys: Rescuing Our Sons from the Myth of Masculinity.* New York: Henry Holt.

Richardson, Laurel, Verta Taylor, and Nancy Whittier (eds.). 1997. *Feminist Frontiers.* New York: McGraw-Hill.

Richmond, Todd. 2006. "'I Have Suffered Long Enough.'" *Wisconsin State Journal,* Sept. 23:C3.

Roncek, Dennis, and Donald Gaggiani. 1985. "High Schools and Crime: A Replication." *Sociological Quarterly* 26:491–505.

Roncek, Dennis, and Antoinette LoBosco. 1983. "The Effect of High Schools on Crime in Their Neighborhood." *Social Science Quarterly* 64:589–613.

Simpson, Sally S. 1989. "Feminist Theory, Crime, and Justice." *Criminology* 27:605–31.

Smith, Susan Lampert. 2006. "The Sting of Twin Tragedies Is Extra Sharp in Tiny District." *Wisconsin State Journal,* Sept. 30:A1, A5.

Stein, Jason, Phil Brinkman, Lisa Schuetz, and Ed Treleven. 2006. "'I'm Here to Kill Somebody.'" *Wisconsin State Journal,* Sept. 30:A1, A5.

Tsai, Catherine, and Jon Sarche. 2006. "Columbine Fascination Lingers." *Wisconsin State Journal,* Sept. 19:A1, A9.

Wahlberg, David. 2006. "Copycat Syndrome and More Violence Feared." *Wisconsin State Journal,* Sept. 30:A5.

Williams, Patricia. 1999. "The Auguries of Innocence." *Nation,* May 24:9.

Wisconsin State Journal. 1999a. "Assaults on US Schools." April 21:A3.

———. 1999b. "Shootings in US Schools." May 21:A3.

Wooden, Wayne S., and Randy Blazak. 2001. *Renegade Kids, Suburban Outlaws: From Youth Culture to Delinquency.* Belmont, CA: Wadsworth.

PART 4

Social Structure and Delinquency: Family, Schools, Community, and Work

THIS SECTION CONTINUES OUR CONSIDERATION OF CAUSAL EXPLANA-
tions of delinquency that attempt to account for why delinquent behavior is
more common among some individuals and groups and not others, focusing
on social structural influences related to families, schools, community, and
work. Sociologists use the term **social structure** to refer to patterns of social
interaction and institutional arrangements that endure over time and that enable or constrain people's choices and opportunities. Social structure is, in a
sense, external to individuals insofar as it is not of their own making and exists prior to their engagement in the world. Most often, people behave in ways
that reproduce or maintain social structures, but this does not mean they are
incapable of transforming them as well. If this were not possible, individual
and social change could not occur (Berger 2008; Emirbayer and Mische 1998;
Giddens 1984; Juette and Berger 2008).[1]

■ Family and Delinquency

We begin with the family, which is as good a place to start as any, since families are the most immediate structures in which most people are embedded. In
Chapter 11, "Family Relationships and Delinquency," Stephen Cernkovich and
Peggy Giordano review family studies of delinquency, emphasizing that it is
not the *number* of parents in a child's home that makes the most difference—

often characterized as "broken" or "unbroken" families, that is, one- or two-parent families—but rather the *quality* of the relationship or interaction between the child and parents. More specifically, the authors examine propositions derived from Travis Hirschi's **social control theory.**

In his landmark book, *Causes of Delinquency,* Hirschi (1969) argued that most delinquency theories ask the wrong question: Why *do* youths engage in delinquency? Hirschi thought the more appropriate question to ask is: Why *don't* youths engage in delinquency? Hirschi assumed that human self-interest provided sufficient motivation for crime, and hence what is in need of explanation—the key theoretical issue—is how these impulses are controlled.

Hirschi agreed with the European social theorist Émile Durkheim (see Chapter 10), who argued that "the more weakened the groups to which [a person] belongs, the less he depends on them, the more he consequently depends only on himself and recognizes no other rules of conduct than what are founded on his private interests" (Durkheim [1897] 1952:209; see Chapter 10). Thus, Hirschi postulated that conformity arises only if, through the socialization process, a person establishes a bond with the conventional society. When this bond is weak, one is freed from social constraint and is more at risk for delinquency.

Hirschi conceptualized the social bond in terms of four key elements. *Attachment* refers to the ties of mutual affection and respect between children and their parents, teachers, and friends. People with such positive ties (with their parents especially) are reluctant to place those ties in jeopardy by engaging in law-violating behavior. *Commitment* suggests an individual's stake in conformity, as indicated by a youth's willingness to conform to the ideal requisites of childhood (e.g., getting an education; postponing smoking, drinking, and sex) and his or her assessment of anticipated losses associated with nonconformity. *Involvement* refers to participation in conventional activities that minimize idle and unsupervised time (e.g., chores, homework, organized sports, Scouts). *Belief* indicates acceptance of the moral validity of laws.

During childhood and adolescence, parents are the key agents of social control, since "the family is the most salient arena for social interaction" at this stage of life (Thornberry 1987:873). In Cernkovich and Giordano's study, the element of parental attachment and its relationship to delinquency is explored through a self-report survey the authors conducted in a large metropolitan area in the north central part of the United States. Among the many interesting and nuanced findings are that the quality of family interaction had similar effects on delinquency regardless of the number of parents. At the same time, it is important to point out that although Hirschi's theory has received considerable empirical support through this and other self-report studies, the evidence has appeared most compelling as an explanation of (1) minor rather than serious delinquency, (2) the onset of delinquency rather than the continuation of delinquency, and (3) delinquency in early rather than late adolescence (Agnew 1985; Krohn and Massey 1980; Paternoster and Triplett 1988).

Chapter 12, "Players and Ho's," is an excerpt from Terry Williams and William Kornblum's compelling ethnography of inner-city youths, *Growing Up Poor* (1985), in which the authors embed an examination of family relationships, including intrafamilial sexual abuse, in broader community context. These are youths whose disempowering family backgrounds have made it even more difficult for them to surmount the obstacles of their disadvantaged class and racial status. They turn to prostitution and pimping as they attempt to negotiate their way through the "underground economy." These youths, write Williams and Kornblum, may be "street wise and cynical . . . [but they] are not 'lost' or 'fallen,' even though they may think of themselves in such terms. Timely intervention by caring adults could counteract the experiences that led them into prostitution and could guide them onto more constructive paths to maturity."

Although some social control theorists, Hirschi included, downplay the significance of socioeconomic factors, elsewhere in their book Williams and Kornblum ask a question that is consistent with Hirschi's perspective: How is it that some lower-class youths "manage not only to survive in a community devastated by crime, drug addiction, and violence, but to be recognized as achievers and encouraged to realize their potential as fully as possible"? (1985:16). The answer, for many youths, is family involvement:

> In every low-income community there are young people who work and go to school and fulfill family responsibilities. The largest proportion of these youths is from homes where parents have struggled for years to provide them with as many of the benefits of stability and education as possible, even at great sacrifice to themselves. The influence of family values . . . , the relative security of religious beliefs and practices,[2] fortunate experiences with teachers and school—all of these factors are important in shaping the life chances of young achievers. (p. 17)

▨ Schools and Delinquency

In Chapter 13, "Getting Rid of Troublemakers: High School Disciplinary Procedures and the Production of Dropouts," Christine Bowditch examines the school as a social institution that has the power to weaken the bond between youths and society. Bowditch appropriates insights from labeling theory and related interactionist approaches to illuminate the ways in which school officials interpret, negotiate, and administer rules and apply them to students who come to their attention as "troublemakers" (see Becker 1963; Lemert 1951; Schur 1971). Labeling theory addresses the processes by which an initial rule violation, **primary deviance,** is transformed into a stable pattern, **secondary deviance,** as a result of the application of official sanctions. Labeling theory also suggests that the labeling of an individual as "deviant" can become a self-fulfilling prophecy as the labeled person internalizes the negative stigma, suffers a decline in self-esteem, and is denied access to opportunities that might steer him or her away from crime.[3] Thus Bowditch argues that the social processes involved in schools' efforts to rid themselves of troubled youths by suspending or expelling students and putting them on the street with nothing to do "may be one important but largely unacknowledged mechanism through which schools" inadvertently increase crime and "perpetuate the racial and class stratification of the larger society."

On the other hand, there is evidence that constructive educational interventions can have positive benefits on school achievement and hence ameliorate the prospect of delinquency (Agnew 2000; Gottfredson 1990; Lawrence 1998; Wooden and Blazak 2001). According to Hawkins and Lishner, these include "individualized instruction, rewards that are attainable and clearly contingent on effort and proficiency, . . . small school population, lower student-adult ratio, caring and competent teachers, and strong, supportive administrators" (1987:206). In addition, greater coordination with the broader community, including guest speakers, field trips, and internship programs, can increase students' interest and decrease their "view that schools are socially set apart from the rest of the world" (Bynum and Thompson 1992:337).

■ Community and Delinquency

In Chapter 14, "Organizing the Community for Delinquency Prevention," Ronald Berger takes a look at the organization of communities and how residents in disadvantaged urban areas have been mobilized to collectively address the problems that exacerbate crime and delinquency. Berger discusses three general models of community organization practice—*locality development, social planning,* and *social action*—and how these models have been applied through delinquency prevention programs. More specifically, Berger discusses the 1930s Chicago Area Projects, the 1960s provision of opportunity programs, and the 1960s comprehensive community action projects such as Mobilization for Youth—programs that "spanned a range of local and federal efforts that emphasized the alteration of neighborhood, institutional, and socioeconomic conditions that were believed to cause delinquency" and that "established the parameters . . . of what all prevention programs of this nature entail." Berger argues that "there are valuable lessons to be learned . . . that have implications for contemporary [prevention] efforts."

Along the way, Berger also considers the theoretical basis of these programs, most notably **social disorganization**[4] and **anomie-opportunity theory.** The former focuses on the social correlates of socioeconomic disadvantage, such as the breakdown in informal adult social control, that increase the influence of neighborhood law-violating peer groups; the latter focuses on the socially structured strain that emerges when there is a "disjuncture between . . . *culturally approved goals* (i.e., financial success and bountiful material consumption) and the *available opportunities* to achieve these goals through legitimate means (i.e., education, employment)" (emphasis in original).

▨ Work and Occupational Delinquency

In Chapter 15, "Juvenile Involvement in Occupational Delinquency," John Paul Wright and Francis Cullen illuminate a neglected aspect of juvenile delinquency: crimes that occur in occupational settings. Wright and Cullen note that this neglect "is so extensive that typical self-report measures of delinquency do not include questions that would assess offenses committed in the workplace." Through a survey of high school youths in Tennessee, Wright and Cullen explore the ways in which youths' general predisposition to delinquency, experience in negative work environments, and association with delinquent co-workers affect their involvement in occupational delinquency and subsequent nonoccupational delinquency. Although it is often assumed that unemployment increases criminality among the unemployed, Wright and Cullen highlight the criminogenic effects of the workplace itself.

▨ Notes

1. Sociologists refer to this as a capacity for "personal agency" (Berger 2008; Emirbayer and Mische 1998), which social psychologists also describe as a matter of "self-efficacy"—the ability to experience oneself as a causal agent capable of *acting upon* rather than merely *reacting to* the external environment (Gecas 1989; Bandura 1997).

2. Another source of social bonding (or lack thereof) between youths and society that is often associated with family, so much so that it appears to have little independent effect on delinquency, is religion (Cochran, Wood, and Arneklev 1994; Elifson, Peterson, and Hadaway 1983; Giordano et al. 2008). In one of the first major studies of the religion-delinquency (RD) relationship, Hirschi and Stark (1969) discerned no association between delinquency and church attendance or belief in the supernatural. To explain their findings, they suggested that churches were unable to instill neighborly love in their members and that "belief in the possibility of pleasure and pain in another world cannot now, and perhaps never could, compete with the pleasures and pains of everyday life" (pp. 212–213).

Other research suggests that the RD relationship may vary by denomination and geographical context. Several early studies found the lowest rates of delinquency among Jews and persons from fundamentalist or highly ascetic Christian denominations (e.g., Baptist, Mormon, Church of Christ) and also found that religion appeared to inhibit delinquency more in rural and southern communities than in urban and nonsouthern areas (see Berger 1996). Still other research indicates that the RD relationship appears strongest for behaviors such as alcohol or drug use and teenage sex that are not universally condemned by secular society (Burkett and Ward 1993; Jang and Johnson 2001; Johnson et al. 2000, 2001) and that it is mediated by additional social factors such as association with peers. Burkett and Warren (1987), for example, found that youths with less religious commitment were more vulnerable to the influence of delinquent peers. Stark (1984), however, argues that the critical issue is not a youth's personal beliefs but the beliefs of most of his or her friends: "In communities where most young people do not attend church, religion will not inhibit the behavior even of those . . . who personally are religious. . . . In communities where most kids are religious, then those who are will be less delinquent than those who aren't" (pp. 274–275).

3. Some labeling studies have found that the self-esteem of youths was more likely to decline among those who were less involved in or committed to delinquency (e.g., first-time, middle-class offenders) than among more involved or committed youths (e.g., high-frequency, lower-class offenders) who already possessed "a negative social status, . . . [who were] not highly integrated into society . . . [and who were] less sensitive and less affected by the judgments of officialdom" (Waegel 1989:113). Labeling may be irrelevant for those already designated as social outsiders, as having delinquent peers and engaging in delinquency may (in the short term) actually increase their self esteem (Jang and Thornberry 1998; Kaplan, Martin, and Johnson 1986). Labeling theory, however, distinguishes between *relative* and *absolute* labeling effects. Relative labeling refers to the impact of varying degrees of sanctions (e.g., probation versus incarceration), whereas absolute labeling refers to "the difference between those who are labeled and those who are not" (Paternoster and Iovanni 1989:385). The research on absolute labeling, as compared to the research on relative labeling, has been more supportive of the theory's propositions regarding secondary deviation (Berger 1996; Shoemaker 1996).

4. In many respects, social disorganization theory is the macrosociological analog of social control theory (Bursik 1988).

References

Agnew, Robert. 1985. "Social Control Theory and Delinquency: A Longitudinal Test." *Criminology* 23:47–61.

———. 2000. "Strain Theory and School Crime." In S. Simpson (ed.), *Of Crime and Criminality.* Thousand Oaks, CA: Sage.

Bandura, Albert. 1997. *Self-Efficacy: The Exercise of Control.* New York: W. H. Freeman.

Becker, Howard S. 1963. *Outsiders: Studies in the Sociology of Deviance.* New York: Free Press.

Berger, Ronald J. (ed.). 1996. *The Sociology of Juvenile Delinquency.* Chicago: Nelson Hall.

———. 2008. "Agency, Structure, and the Transition to Disability: A Case Study with Implications for Life History Research." *Sociological Quarterly* 49:309–333.

Burkett, Steven R., and David A. Ward. 1993. "A Note on Perceptual Deterrence, Religiosity Based on Moral Condemnation, and Social Control." *Criminology* 31:119–134.

Burkett, Steven R., and Bruce O. Warren. 1987. "Religiosity, Peer Associations, and Adolescent Marijuana Use: A Panel Study of Underlying Causal Structures." *Criminology* 25:109–134.

Bursik, Robert J. 1988. "Social Disorganization and Theories of Crime and Delinquency: Problems and Prospects." *Criminology* 26:519–551.

Bynum, Jack E., and William E. Thompson. 1992. *Juvenile Delinquency: A Sociological Approach.* Boston: Allyn and Bacon.

Cochran, John K., Peter B. Wood, and Bruce J. Arneklev. 1994. "Is the Religiosity-Delinquency Relationship Spurious? A Test of Arousal and Social Control Theories." *Journal of Research in Crime and Delinquency* 31:92–123.

Durkheim, Émile. [1897] 1952. *Suicide.* New York: Free Press.

Elifson, Kirk W., David M. Peterson, and C. Kirk Hadaway. 1983. "Religiosity and Delinquency: A Contextual Analysis." *Criminology* 21:505–527.

Emirbayer, Mustafa, and Ann Mische. 1998. "What Is Agency?" *American Journal of Sociology* 103:962–1023.

Gecas, Viktor. 1989. "The Social Psychology of Self-Efficacy." *Annual Review of Sociology* 15:291–316.

Giddens, Anthony. 1984. *The Constitution of Society: Outline of the Theory of Structuration.* Berkeley: University of California Press.

Giordano, Peggy C., Monica A. Longmore, Ryan D. Schroeder, and Patrick M. Seffrin. 2008. "A Life-Course Perspective on Spirituality and Desistance from Crime." *Criminology* 46:99–131.

Gottfredson, Denise C. 1990. "Changing School Structures to Benefit High Risk Youth." In P. Leone (ed.), *Understanding Troubled and Troubling Youth.* Newbury Park, CA: Sage.

Hawkins, J. David, and Denise M. Lishner. 1987. "Schooling and Delinquency." In E. Johnson (ed.), *Handbook on Crime and Delinquency Prevention.* Westport, CT: Greenwood Press.

Hirschi, Travis. 1969. *Causes of Delinquency.* Berkeley: University of California Press.

Hirschi, Travis, and Rodney Stark. 1969. "Hellfire and Delinquency." *Social Problems* 17:202–213.

Jang, Sung Joon, and Byron B. Johnson. 2001. "Neighborhood Disorder, Individual Religiosity, and Adolescent Use of Illicit Drugs: A Test of Multilevel Hypotheses." *Criminology* 39:109–141.

Jang, Sung Joon, and Terence P. Thornberry. 1998. "Self-Esteem, Delinquent Peers, and Delinquency: A Test of the Self-Enhancement Thesis." *American Sociological Review* 63:586–598.

Johnson, Byron B., Sung Joon Jang, David B. Larson, and Spencer De Li. 2001. "Does Adolescent Religious Commitment Matter? A Reexamination of the Effects of Religiosity on Delinquency." *Journal of Research in Crime and Delinquency* 38:22–44.

Johnson, Byron B., David B. Larson, Spencer De Li, and Sung Joon Jang. 2000. "Escaping from the Crime of Inner Cities: Church Attendance and Religious Salience Among Disadvantaged Youth." *Justice Quarterly* 17:377–391.

Juette, Melvin, and Ronald J. Berger. 2008. *Wheelchair Warrior: Gangs, Disability, and Basketball.* Philadelphia: Temple University Press.

Kaplan, Howard B., Steven B. Martin, and Robert J. Johnson. 1986. "Self-Rejection and the Explanation of Deviance: Specification of the Structure Among Latent Constructs." *American Journal of Sociology* 92:384–411.

Krohn, Marvin D., and James L. Massey. 1980. "Social Control and Delinquent Behavior: An Examination of the Elements of the Social Bond." *Sociological Quarterly* 21:529–543.

Lawrence, Richard. 1998. *School Crime and Juvenile Justice.* New York: Oxford University Press.

Lemert, Edwin M. 1951. *Social Pathology.* New York: McGraw-Hill.

Paternoster, Raymond, and Lee Ann Iovanni. 1989. "The Labeling Perspective and Delinquency: An Elaboration of the Theory and an Assessment of the Evidence." *Justice Quarterly* 6:359–394.

Paternoster, Raymond, and Ruth A. Triplett. 1988. "Disaggregating Self-Reported Delinquency and Its Implications for Theory." *Criminology* 26:591–625.

Schur, Edwin M. 1971. *Labeling Deviant Behavior.* New York: Harper and Row.

Shoemaker, Donald J. 1996. *Theories of Delinquency: An Examination of Delinquent Behavior.* New York: Oxford University Press.

Stark, Rodney. 1984. "Religion and Conformity: Reaffirming a Sociology of Religion." *Sociological Analysis* 45:273–282.

Thornberry, Terence P. 1987. "Toward an Interactional Theory of Delinquency." *Criminology* 25:863–891.

Waegel, William B. 1989. *Delinquency and Juvenile Control.* Englewood Cliffs, NJ: Prentice-Hall.

Williams, Terry, and William Kornblum. 1985. *Growing Up Poor.* Lexington, MA: D. C. Heath.

Wooden, Wayne S., and Randy Blazak. 2001. *Renegade Kids, Suburban Outlaws: From Youth Culture to Delinquency.* Belmont, CA: Wadsworth.

Family Relationships and Delinquency

Stephen A. Cernkovich and Peggy C. Giordano

Stephen Cernkovich and Peggy Giordano review family studies of delinquency, emphasizing that it is not the number of parents in a child's home that makes the most difference but rather the quality of the relationship or interaction between the child and parents. More specifically, they examine propositions derived from Travis Hischi's social control theory to understand the relationship between the family and delinquency.

THE STUDY OF THE RELATIONSHIP BETWEEN THE FAMILY AND JUVENILE delinquency has had a curious history, ebbing and flowing with the times and with the dominance of alternative theoretical perspectives. This area is best characterized, however, by a relative lack of interest on the part of criminologists—by the belief that family variables are not nearly as important as peer, school, and various structural factors in understanding delinquent behavior patterns (compare Rodman & Grams 1967; Wilkinson 1974). While there are numerous examples of research on the link between the family and delinquency, . . . [and] the emergence of social control theory . . . has reintroduced the importance of family variables, . . . the status of the family in delinquency theory and research . . . lags . . . behind other areas. . . . [Nonetheless] there is considerable evidence that the family is (or should be) related to delinquency involvement. In fact, this is one of the most replicated findings in the literature.

> The literature consistently indicates that . . . one-parent homes, . . . poor marriages, . . . lack of parental control, . . . ineffectual parental behavior, . . . very poor parent-child relationships . . . [and] association with delinquents as opposed to nondelinquents . . . are associated with delinquency. . . . All of these factors influencing delinquency have in common that they are likely to be a consequence of parental behavior, with parental behavior being causally linked to a lack of effective role models, a . . . [deficient] home environment,

"Family Relationships and Delinquency," *Criminology* 25, no. 2 (1987): 295–321. Reprinted by permission of the American Society of Criminology.

and a lack of parental supervision (which could explain their childrens' propensity to associate with delinquent friends). (Gove & Crutchfield 1982:304)

Yet much of this evidence has been ignored or downplayed by criminologists. Bordua (1962) has attributed this to a desire to avoid "psychologizing." That is, while criminologists include in their analyses such structural or social variables as social class, blocked opportunities, and peer relations, such variables as personality characteristics and parent-child relationships are avoided because they are "too psychological." This is yet another example of the misguided loyalty to artificial disciplinary boundaries which is far too characteristic of the social sciences.

As significant as this relative neglect of family variables is the quality of the data itself, as well as the general theoretical approach taken in examining these data. Nye (1958) suggested some time ago that it is not the structure of the family per se which is causally related to delinquency, but rather the actual relationship and interaction patterns which are the key variables. Still, it is rather obvious that the primary sociological focus, with the important exception of some recent research from a [social] control theory perspective, either has been on structural variables (e.g., broken homes [number of parents], family size, birth order), or interactional variables treated in an almost [dichotomous] either-or way (e.g., poor marital relations, parental supervision and control, maternal employment). While theoretical lip service usually is paid to the notion that the important variables are probably social-psychological and interactional in nature, the analyses have . . . only touch[ed] the interactional surface.

Studies of the relationship between broken homes and delinquency offer a good illustration. Many of the articles examining this relationship begin by asserting that far more important than the effects of the actual parental separation and/or living in a broken home on the child are the familial problems and conflicts that led to the separation in the first place. It appears to be generally accepted that harmonious yet physically broken homes are far less detrimental to the development and mental health of the child than are physically intact but psychologically broken homes (compare Arnold & Brungardt 1983; Patterson & Dishion 1985; Rankin 1983; Rosen 1985; Rutter & Giller 1984; Shoemaker 1984; Wells & Rankin 1986). Once this is asserted, however, much of the research in this area turns to a dichotomous, structural variable—broken/unbroken home—as the major antecedent to delinquency. Post hoc interpretations are then offered as to why broken homes apparently are related to delinquency. These explanations usually center on patterns of family interaction, but little or no data have been collected on the nature and quality of these relationships. Most studies of the broken home and delinquency, for example, have divided families into two discrete categories—broken and unbroken—and give "absolutely no clue as to the quality of life within either of them" (Empey 1982:264).

Research on the effects of maternal employment on child development offers another example of the approach usually taken. Researchers appear to agree that maternal employment affects behavior indirectly, through such factors as lack of supervision, loss of direct control, and attenuation of close relationships. Similarly, most agree that its effects depend on a number of conditions, such as social class background, race, the attitudes of family members regarding maternal employment, whether the employment is full- or part-time, and so forth (see Etaugh [1980] and Hoffman [1974] for . . . reviews of this literature). . . . Nye (1958) considered the loss of direct control due to maternal employment (as the reason for the relationship between maternal employment and delinquency) as so obvious that he did not even bother to analyze the relationship in any detail. Yet, as Hoffman (1974) has suggested, working mothers might very well be stricter and impose even more rules than nonworking mothers—the demands of their dual role may require a higher degree of structure in order for the household to run smoothly. She expresses surprise that few studies have obtained data on such basic child-rearing behaviors as these.

> The typical study deals only with two levels—the mother's employment status and a child's characteristic. The many steps in between—family roles and interaction patterns, the child's perceptions, the mother's feelings about her employment, the child-rearing practices—are rarely measured. . . . The distance between an antecedent condition like maternal employment and a child characteristic is too great to be covered in a single leap. Several levels should be examined in a single study to obtain adequate insight into the processes involved. (Hoffman 1974:205)

While a few researchers stand out because of their attempts to measure the nature and quality of family relationships (e.g., see Agnew 1985; Canter 1982; Hirschi 1969; Johnson 1986; Krohn & Massey 1980; LaGrange & White 1985; Norland et al. 1979; Wiatrowski et al. 1981), the degree of conceptualization and/or the measurement strategies generally employed are arguably inadequate to capture the full range or the real dynamic quality of the relationships. For example, although Norland et al. (1979) were interested in intrafamily conflict and delinquency, apparently only one question was included to measure family conflict: "There is a lot of tension and conflict in my home." Similarly, Canter (1982) . . . conceptualized and measured family involvement as the amount of time the adolescent spends with his/her family, and parental influence by the single item, "How much have your parents influenced what you've thought and done?" While these kinds of questions are clearly on the right track, they are not comprehensive measures of the nature, quality, and dynamics of the interactions which characterize relationships among family members. Research in this area has rarely gone beyond the very basic, surface level measure of family attachment and involvement. . . .

▨ Conceptual Orientation

The purpose of this article is to specify more precisely those family interaction mechanisms which are associated with delinquency involvement. Along with the peer group, the family is a major arena for social interaction, personal growth, and social and emotional maturation. . . . This article will report on the relationship of several dimensions of internal family dynamics to delinquent behavior. Since previous delinquency theory and research has stressed the role of broken homes, race and sex, this article also will examine the impact of family factors within categories of these sociodemographic variables.

The authors' [social control] theoretical orientation builds directly upon the work of Hirschi (1969). In his discussion of the family and delinquency, Hirschi maintains that attachment to parents forms the basis of conformity. Eschewing the concept of internalization, he believes that it is the attachment itself that is important: "The more strongly a child is attached to his parents, the more strongly he is bound to their expectations, and therefore the more strongly he is bound to conformity with the legal norms of the larger system" (p. 94). [Hirschi wrote before the time scholars used gender-inclusive pronouns.]

But exactly what constitutes attachment? Hirschi suggests that it is the parents' "psychological presence" in the child's mind during tempting situations that is the key. In this sense, direct control, per se, is relatively unimportant:

> The child is less likely to commit delinquent acts not because his parents actually restrict his activities, but because he shares his activities with them; not because his parents actually know where he is, but because he perceives them as aware of his location. Following this line of reasoning, we can say that the more the child is accustomed to sharing his mental life with his parents, the more he is accustomed to seeking or getting their opinion about his activities, the more likely he is to perceive them as part of his social and psychological field, and the less likely he would be to neglect their opinion when considering an act contrary to law which is, after all, a potential source of embarrassment and/or inconvenience to them. (1969:89–90)

Accepting this, how does one know if a child is attached or not, or more accurately, how can one determine the degree of attachment? One strong indicator is communication between the child and his/her parents. Hirschi maintains (1969) that the extent and nature of communication are as important as feelings of affection in this regard—that the degree of psychological presence of the parent is dependent in part upon the extent to which the child communicates with the parent.

Hirschi's data and reasoning about the importance of family attachment are convincing. However, it is desirable to be more specific with regard to exactly what constitutes this important dimension of attachment. Hirschi is somewhat ambiguous in this regard. On the one hand, he often gives the impression that attachment is a unidimensional construct; indeed, this is usually the way in which the theory is interpreted by others—attachment is one of four ways in which individuals are bound to the social order (in his initial formulation, the four elements of the social bond include attachment, commitment, involvement, and belief). On the other hand, however, as when he concentrates on the communication origins of attachment or on the feelings of affection which characterize attachment, Hirschi gives the impression that attachment is more multidimensional in nature.

The authors of this article believe the multidimensional interpretation to be the more accurate of the two. However, neither Hirschi nor other social control theorists and researchers have systematically identified what these dimensions might be. The purpose of this research is to examine the impact on delinquency of several dimensions of family attachment and interaction. As will be discussed in detail below, the analysis leads to the specification of seven conceptually distinct dimensions of family interaction.

In addition to this elaboration of the Hirschi model, the authors are also interested in whether the effects of these variables are consistent across different types of family structure, or whether there are important differences in interactional dynamics by family type. For example, is parental attachment more important in inhibiting delinquency in single-parent homes than in those where two parents are present? Hirschi argues that attachment to *a* parent is the important variable; that is, attachment to two parents does not mean the child is doubly insulated. If he is correct (and his data do support this position), this would explain "the fact that the one-parent family is virtually as efficient a delinquency controlling institution as the two-parent family, contrary to expectations deriving from 'direct control' hypotheses" (1969:103). This general issue of the effect of family structure on delinquency will be explored using a multidimensional model of family interaction. It is quite conceivable that some dimensions of family interaction will operate similarly in different family structures while others may be unique to a particular kind of structure.

Finally, the article will examine whether there are sex or race differences in the influence of family interaction variables. Previous research leads one to believe that there are (compare Krohn & Massey 1980), but as noted previously, this research has typically been based on a unidimensional conceptualization of family attachment. The multidimensional model used here will shed some important light on these demographic differences.

▪ Research Design

The data for this study are based on a 1982 sample of adolescents living in private households in a large North Central Standard Metropolitan Statistical Area. In order to obtain a cross section of youth between 12 and 19 years of age geographically dispersed throughout the metropolitan area, a multistage modified probability sample design was used in which geographically defined area segments were selected with known probability. The segments were stratified, using the most up-to-date census data available (1980), on the basis of racial composition and average housing value. Within the segments, households and eligible respondents were selected for interviews to fill specified sex and race quotas; no specific age quotas were allocated, although the ages of respondents were tracked as the interviews were conducted to ensure adequate representation of teens of all ages.

A total of 942 interviews were successfully completed. Of these, 51 percent were with adolescent females, 49 percent with males; 45 percent of the respondents were white, the remaining nonwhites being predominantly black (50% of the total sample). The respondents ranged in age from 12 through 19: 21 percent were either 12 or 13, 32 percent 14 or 15, 32 percent 16 or 17, and 15 percent 18 or 19 years of age.[1]

Delinquency involvement was measured by a modified version of Elliott and Ageton's (1980) self-report delinquency scale. Twenty-seven individual delinquent behaviors were represented in the scale; subjects indicated how many times during the past year they had committed each act. The coding scheme was as follows: never = 0, once or twice a year = 2, once every 2–3 months = 5, once a month = 12, once every 2–3 weeks = 22, once a week = 52, and 2–3 times a week or more = 130. These numerical codes were derived by extrapolating the implied frequency over the period of one year.

In order to avoid some fairly serious limitations inherent in more typical measures of delinquency (compare Cernkovich et al. 1985; Hindelang et al. 1981), a frequency/seriousness-based offender typology will be used as the dependent variable in the following analysis. This typology defines five levels of increasingly serious and frequent delinquent involvement: nonoffenders are those youth who reported no major offenses and no minor offenses; low-frequency minor offenders are those who reported no major offenses and a low rate of minor offenses; high-frequency minor offenders reported no major offenses but a high rate of minor offenses; low-frequency major offenders reported a low rate of major offense involvement, while high-frequency major offenders reported a high rate of major offenses. The offender index is coded from 1 through 5, with high-frequency major offenders receiving the highest score.[2]

A number of family variables are included in this study. Home Status defines the youth's structural family living arrangement. Rather than follow the convention of defining as broken any home which is characterized by the absence of at least one biological parent, the authors discriminated among several types of family structures (see Wells & Rankin 1986). This is made possible by the representation of several family types in the sample: 49 percent of the subjects lived with both parents, 28 percent with mother only, 3 percent with father only, 11 percent with mother and stepfather, 3 percent with father and stepmother, and 6 percent with other relatives. However, because an analysis of variance revealed few significant differences in family factor characteristics by home status, and because of small sample sizes for three of the categories (that is, only 23 cases in father-stepmother homes, 26 in father-only homes, and

53 in other-relative homes), the analysis will be restricted to both-parent (N = 462), mother-only (N = 265), and mother-stepfather (N = 103) living arrangements [see the book appendix for a brief explanation of the statistical techniques used in this chapter (i.e., analysis of variance, Likert scaling, correlation and regression analysis, and the problem of multicollinearity)]. This decision combined with some minor missing data problems reduces the sample size to 824. While it would be preferable for the full range of living arrangements to be represented in the analysis, the use of these three has several advantages: they are clearly among the most typical in American society—the US Bureau of Census (1985:4) reports that 75 percent of all children under 18 live in two-parent homes (the Census Bureau does not, unfortunately, further break this category into natural parent and stepparent homes), 20 percent in mother-only homes, 2 percent each in father-only and other-relative homes, and the remainder in nonrelative homes; the categories used represent family living arrangements which long have been of interest to criminologists; and such a breakdown represents a significant improvement over the more crude broken-intact distinction usually made in criminological research.

The interview schedule included 28 family-related items, each coded in a 1–5 Likert format. A principle components factor analysis of the pooled items using oblique rotation resulted in seven distinct scales. A loading criterion of .500 was used for scale inclusion. The factor loadings of the individual items and the scale reliabilities are presented in [the appendix at the end of the chapter]. The seven scales are as follows:

Control and Supervision refers to the extent to which parents monitor the behavior of their children. This scale is represented by three items: "My parents want to know who I am going out with when I go out with other boys (girls)"; "In my free time away from home, my parents know who I'm with and where I am" (from Minor, no date); "My parents want me to tell them where I am if I don't come home right after school." High scores on this scale reflect high levels of control and supervision.

Identity Support during adolescence is particularly important because of the uncertainties and self-doubts which characterize this period of the life cycle. Positive identity support is characterized by the belief that parents respect, accept, and support the youth for what he/she is. This dimension is measured by the following negatively worded items: "My parents sometimes put me down in front of other people"; "Sometimes my parents won't listen to me or my opinions"; "My parents sometimes give me the feeling that I'm not living up to their expectations"; "My parents seem to wish I were a different type of person" (from Minor, no date). High scores on this scale indicate high levels of identity support.

Caring and Trust is an index of the degree of intimacy of a relationship. Probably the most critical area of support a family can provide to offspring is a basic sense of caring, trust, and affection. This dimension is measured by the following items: "My parents often ask about what I am doing in school" (from Hirschi 1969); "My parents give me the right amount of affection" (from Gold & Reimer 1972); "One of the worst things that could happen to me would be finding out that I let my parents down"; "My parents are usually proud of me when I've finished something I've worked hard at"; "My parents trust me" (from Minor, no date); "I'm closer to my parents than a lot of kids my age" (from Minor, no date). High scale scores reflect high levels of caring and trust.

Intimate Communication refers to the sharing of private thoughts and feelings. Hirschi (1969) recognized intimacy of communication between parent and child as an important dimension of attachment. The factor analysis isolated three items (all from West & Zingle 1969) as indicative of this dimension: "How often do you talk to your parents about the boy/girl whom you like very much?"; "How often do you talk to your parents about questions or problems about sex?"; "How often do you talk to your parents about things you have done about which you feel guilty?" High scores on this scale are indicative of high levels of intimate communication.

Hirschi's (1969) findings suggest that it is not just communication with parents per se that is important, but rather the *content* of that communication. Specifically, he found that the discussion of future plans was an important index of attachment. In the present research, *Instrumental Communication* is defined as a variable separate from intimate communication. It is measured by the following items (all from West & Zingle 1969): "How often do you talk to your parents about problems you have at school?"; "How often do you talk to your parents about your job plans for the future?"; "How often do you talk to your parents about problems with your friends?"; "How often do you talk to your parents about how well you get along with your teachers?" High levels of instrumental communication are indicated by high scale scores.

Parental Disapproval of Peers is, of course, all too descriptive of many parent-child relationships during adolescence. This variable is indexed by the following two items: "In general, what do your parents think of your friends?" (from Hirschi 1969); "In general, what do your parents think of your boyfriend/girlfriend?" High scale scores reflect high levels of parental disapproval.

Conflict is the extent to which parents and adolescents have arguments or disagreements with one another. Two items were flagged by the factor analysis as measuring this dimension: "How often do you have disagreements or arguments with your parents?"; "How often do you purposely not talk to your parents because you are mad at them?" High levels of parent-child conflict are indicated by high scale scores.

■ Analysis and Findings

Before examining the findings, it should be noted that the cross-sectional research design does not permit one to resolve completely the issue of causal order. It is quite conceivable, for example, that high degrees of control and supervision, conflict, and parental disapproval of peers *follow* delinquency rather than precede it. While [social] control theory does provide a theoretical rationale for assuming that family dynamics precede delinquency, there is also good reason to suspect that delinquency involvement affects family interaction as well. No doubt there is some truth to this reciprocal relationship. However, family attachments are formed long before youths begin to engage in delinquent behavior. Adolescents who are strongly attached to their families in the first place are unlikely to become involved in delinquency; as a result, there is no serious delinquency among these youths to threaten family attachment. Youths at the other end of the continuum, however, are more likely to become involved in delinquency (through association with delinquent peers or other intermediary processes) precisely because of their lack of family attachment. Their involvement in delinquency thus only reinforces already weak attachments. While there is considerable support for this position (compare Elliott et al. 1985; Hirschi 1969), the reader is cautioned that the cross-sectional design used here cannot firmly establish the causal order of the variables.

Table 11.1 presents the results of a four-way analysis of variance for each of the family dimensions by sex, race, home status, and level of delinquency. Age is controlled as a covariate. As expected, there are significant sex differences on most of the family dimensions: caring and trust, control and supervision, intimate communication, conflict, and instrumental communication. Surprisingly, males report a higher mean level of caring and trust, while females report more conflict with parents. As would be predicted from past research, however, females are subjected to greater control and supervision than are males, and they are more likely to engage in both intimate and instrumental communication with their parents. The only significant race differences in family characteristics occur for caring and trust and control and supervision, for which nonwhites report the highest rates, and conflict, for which whites report the highest levels. To the extent that the selected factors represent different dimensions of family attachment, it is clear from the outset that a simplistic attached-unattached dichotomy would have masked some important variation by sex and race.

Importantly, however, none of the seven family factors differ significantly by home status. This clearly weakens the traditional argument that broken homes, female-headed homes, or those with stepfathers are *necessarily* negative and/or disadvantageous socialization environments. At least for the family dimensions specified, all three family structures are characterized by similar levels of attachment and interaction. To the extent that such family dimensions are related to delinquency (and they are, as shall be seen shortly), one would expect to find essentially the same patterning of relationships within the three home status categories. This issue will be taken up in greater detail in the regression analysis.

With the exception of intimate communication, each of the family relationship dimensions is significantly related to delinquency involvement. The

Table 11.1 Mean Family Relationship Scores By Sex, Race, Home Status, and Level of Delinquency (Age Controlled)

	Caring and Trust		Control and Supervision[a]		Intimate Communication		Identity Support[b]		Parental Disapproval of Peers[c]		Conflict		Instrumental Communication	
	Mean	F	Mean	F	Mean	F	Mean	F	Mean	F	Mean	F	Mean	F
Sex														
Male (N = 401)	4.02	7.57**	3.78	80.33***	2.49	12.09***	3.29	.010	2.16	.069	2.23	11.07***	3.34	9.00**
Female (N = 423)	3.94		4.27		2.74		3.37		2.02		2.43		3.57	
Race														
White (N = 363)	3.88	17.01***	3.98	7.18**	2.68	2.36	3.32	.155	2.07	.638	2.51	12.40***	3.45	.263
Nonwhite (N = 461)	4.06		4.08		2.58		3.34		2.10	2.19	2.47		3.47	
Home Status														
Both Parents (N = 458)	4.00		4.04		2.60		3.37		2.05		2.27		3.46	
Mother Only (N = 264)	3.96	1.60	3.98	2.65	2.62	.563	3.31	.882	2.13	.351	2.34	2.17	3.45	.206
Mother/ Stepfather (N = 102)	3.95		4.14		2.73		3.24		2.14		2.57		3.49	
Delinquent Involvement														
Nonoffender (N = 71)	4.25		4.36		2.63		3.80		1.88		1.56		3.81	
Low-Frequency Minor (N = 305)	4.07		4.12		2.66		3.43		1.98		2.24		3.57	
High-Frequency Minor (N = 196)	3.95	10.02***	4.03	5.13***	2.65	.822	3.30	11.30***	2.11	6.52***	2.40	12.58***	3.48	8.46***
Low-Frequency Major (N = 153)	3.89		3.89		2.62		3.20		2.17		2.50		3.26	
High-Frequency Major (N = 99)	3.73		3.73		2.43		2.96		2.40		2.78		3.16	

Notes: a. Sex-by-race interaction (F = 4.11*); Sex-by-home status-by-delinquency interaction (F = 2.02*).
b. Delinquency-by-sex interaction (F = 2.90**); Sex-by-race interaction (F = 3.76 *).
c. Sex-by-home status interaction (F = 3.22*).
*p < .05   **p < .01   ***p < .001

differences are most apparent for identity support and conflict. Mean levels of identity support decrease in a linear fashion across the five offender categories, with nonoffenders reporting the highest and high-frequency major offenders the lowest levels. On the other hand, conflict means increase from the nonoffender to the high-frequency major offender category. These and the remaining patterns shown in Table 11.1 are consistent with preliminary expectations—delinquents have lower levels of caring and trust, control and supervision, identity support, and instrumental communication; on the other hand, the most delinquent youths are more likely to have conflicts with their parents, and the parents of delinquents are more likely than other parents to disapprove of their childrens' friends. When compared with the results of studies based on a single attached-unattached dimension, this analysis of seven distinct family interaction dimensions begins to give a more complete and precise sense of the kind of relationships which exist between parents and their relatively more or less delinquent children.

Before turning to this issue in more detail, the analysis of variance revealed several interaction terms which should be noted. First is that between sex and race for the control and supervision dimension. Nonwhite females report the greatest level of supervision (4.29), white males the least (3.68). The pattern of means (3.86 for nonwhite males, 4.25 for white females) clearly reveals that the sex difference is the more important of the two; that is, while there are large control and supervision differences by sex within race subgroups, the race differences within sex categories are unimpressive. Second, although there are no main race or sex effects for identity support, there is a significant sex-race interaction: among the four race-sex groupings, nonwhite females (3.43) report the greatest levels of identity support; the remaining three groups report significantly lower levels (white females = 3.29, white males = 3.35, and nonwhite males = 3.26).

Third, there is a significant sex-home status interaction for the parental disapproval of peers variable. Among males, respondents in mother-only (2.19) and both-parent (2.17) homes report higher levels of parental disapproval than those in mother/stepfather homes (2.00). Among females, however, those in mother/stepfather homes report the highest levels (2.25 versus 1.94 in both-parent and 2.07 in mother-only homes). Thus, it is only in mother/stepfather homes that females report greater disapproval rates than males. In fact, it is this category (females in mother/stepfather homes) which has the highest mean level of disapproval. This is contrary to what was expected, given the widespread assumption that stepfathers cause more difficulty for male than for female children. On the other hand, it is not altogether inconsistent with the female delinquency literature which assumes that broken homes have a more negative effect on females than upon males (compare Datesman & Scarpitti 1975).

Finally, there are also two interesting interaction terms involving family dimensions and delinquency. First is the delinquency-sex interaction for identity support. Female nonoffenders report the highest identity support levels by far.

In fact, it is only among nonoffenders that male-female differences in identity support are significantly different (3.31 versus 3.99). For the other four offender categories, the male-female means are virtually identical. As would be expected, high-frequency major offenders, both male (2.96) and female (2.97), report the lowest levels of identity support. The other interaction term involves delinquency, sex, and home status in the case of control and supervision. What is most apparent in the pattern of means is that females are subjected to more control than males in all three home status categories; and this is true for all levels of delinquency involvement as well. This is powerful evidence of the extent to which adolescent females are supervised as compared to their male counterparts. Overall, female nonoffenders in mother/stepfather homes report the greatest levels of control and supervision (although all females in the mother/stepfather category, regardless of level of delinquency, report almost equally high levels). On the other hand, male high-frequency major offenders from mother-only homes report the least amount of control and supervision.[3]

The analysis of variance results presented in Table 11.1 suggest some interesting patterns. However, these data are primarily descriptive in nature. The discussion turns now to the regression analyses in order to be more definitive about the relative effects of these variables on delinquency involvement. Table 11.2 presents the correlation matrix of delinquency, age, and the seven family interaction factors. With the exception of intimate communication, which is not significantly associated with delinquency . . . , all of the family dimensions are moderately associated with delinquency involvement in the expected direction. The matrix also indicates that while most of the family factors are associated with one another, the coefficients are not of sufficient magnitude to create problems of multicollinearity in the regression analyses.

The data in Table 11.3 summarize the results of a series of regression equations for the total sample and the three home status categories. The results of these analyses are presented separately for the various home status categories because the authors wanted to test the hypothesis that family interaction dynamics affect delinquency similarly for various types of family living arrangements. Sex and race are entered into the equations as dummy variables (coded 1 for males, 0 for females, and 1 for whites, 0 for nonwhites). Finally, age is included in each of the equations because of its association with both delinquency and control and supervision.

A general review of the data in Table 11.3 reveals that the family interaction variables explain relatively small portions of the variance in delinquency. This is disappointing, though not totally unexpected. The explained variance could have been boosted considerably had peer and school variables, for example, been included in the model. However, the goal of this inquiry is not to test a model of how, for example, family and peer associations combine to induce/ inhibit delinquency. Rather, the concern is more specifically with the impact of several dimensions of family interaction on delinquency across different

Table 11.2 Correlation Matrix

	Delinquency	Control and Supervision	Identity Support	Caring and Trust	Intimate Communication	Instrumental Communication	Disapproval of Peers	Conflict	Age
Delinquency	1.000								
Control and Supervision	-.221	1.000							
Identity Support	-.218	.052	1.000						
Caring and Trust	-.191	.393	.339	1.000					
Intimate Communication	-.051	.279	.172	.343	1.000				
Instrumental Communication	-.194	.317	.177	.400	.486	1.000			
Disapproval of Peers	.188	-.150	-.226	-.261	-.114	-.200	1.000		
Conflict	.192	-.062	-.338	-.321	-.058	-.117	.176	1.000	
Age	.105	-.147	.004	-.063	.055	-.077	.010	.012	1.000

Table 11.3 Regression Analysis by Home Status

	Total Sample			Both Natural Parents			Mother Only			Mother/Stepfather		
	Unstandardized b	s.e.	Beta	Unstandardized b	s.e.	Beta	Unstandardized b	s.e.	Beta	Unstandardized b	s.e.	Beta
Caring and Trust	-.054	.070	-.031	-.116	.103	-.062	-.066	.129	-.038	.128	.251	.085
Control and Supervision	-.181	.055	-.122	-.167	.083	-.102	-.229	.100	-.167	.021	.188	.042
Intimate Communication	.124	.045	.099	.113	.064	.089	.110	.085	.094	.128	.149	.110
Identity Support	-.181	.046	-.135	-.213	.068	-.153	-.126	.081	-.102	.003	.134	.002
Parental Disapproval of Peers	.138	.049	.090	.093	.072	.060	.131	.090	.089	.251	.151	.181
Conflict	.105	.031	.114	.102	.045	.107	.146	.057	.163	.089	.092	.109
Instrumental Communication	-.169	.055	-.115	-.187	.082	-.121	-.196	.093	-.150	-.404	.158	-.291
Age	.045	.019	.072	.052	.028	.083	.011	.038	.018	.044	.060	.075
Race Dummy	.011	.075	.005	.035	.105	.015	-.192	.153	-.076	.024	.236	.011
Sex Dummy	.302	.080	.127	.390	.114	.163	.092	.147	.041	.240	.259	.106
	F= 15, 874 (p < .001) Multiple R = .384 R^2 = .147			F = 8. 909 (p < .001) Multiple R = .408 R^2 = .166			F = 4.78 (p < .001) Multiple R = .400 R^2 = .160			F = 1.71 (p < NS) Multiple R = .400 R^2 = .160		

types of family structure. The aim is to investigate whether the multidimensional conceptualization of family interaction clarifies the relationship between the family and delinquency beyond that conveyed by more simplistic broken/intact and attached/unattached models.

Before proceeding, it should be noted that the equation for the mother/ stepfather home is not statistically significant, and that only one of the . . . coefficients (instrumental communication) is significant. This is in part a function of the small size of this category (N = 102), and the consequent larger standard errors of the estimates, which makes statistical significance more difficult to attain. Thus, while it would be misleading to make too much of these data, there are several noteworthy features about this subgroup. First, the single largest unstandardized . . . coefficient (–.404 for instrumental communication) in the table is found in the mother/stepfather family. Similarly, parental disapproval of peers is more strongly related to delinquency among youths in mother/stepfather homes than in any home status category. Last are several reversals in the sign of the coefficient (caring and trust, control and supervision, and identity support). Whether these coefficients are indicative of real and important differences in the dynamics of family interaction patterns in mother/stepfather homes as opposed to alternative living arrangements, or whether they are unstable products of insufficient sample size and large standard errors, is not known. A guess is that they reflect real differences. It is tempting to argue, for example, that control and supervision is not as effective in inhibiting delinquency in such homes and that disapproval of peers takes on greater importance because of the resentment that the youth has for the stepfather as an "outsider." The fact that the unstandardized coefficient for intimate communication is largest in this family structure seems to support this logic as well. There is certainly support for this general interpretation in the delinquency literature (compare Johnson 1986). Because of uncertainty about the statistical significance of the data, however, this group will be excluded from the discussion which follows. To echo Johnson's (1986) sentiment, there does seem to be something unique about mother/stepfather families, and future researchers are urged to include larger samples of mother/stepfather homes in order to examine these possibilities with greater certainty in the conclusions.

Turning to the other subgroups in Table 11.3, it is clear that the family interaction variables have similar effects on delinquency in varying family structures. All of the variables are associated with delinquency in the expected direction, with the exception of intimate communication. Intimate communication is actually *positively* associated with delinquency in the total sample and in both parent and mother-only homes. This is difficult to explain, especially since intimate communication is associated with all of the other variables in the expected direction (see Table 11.2).

Adolescents who are willing to discuss with their parents such sensitive matters as boyfriends, girlfriends, and sex apparently are not so attached to

254 SOCIAL STRUCTURE AND DELINQUENCY

their parents that delinquency is attenuated. This is ironic since communication between parent and child on such sensitive and private matters is presumably an index of a strong, intimate relationship which, in turn, is an important deterrent to delinquency (at least according to social control theory). It may be, however, that family discussions about girlfriends, boyfriends, and sex are not good indices of intimate communication. Perhaps these are topics of discussion between all adolescents and their parents; hence they do not discriminate between intimate and nonintimate relationships. There is, however, another possible interpretation.

Although detailed data on the nature and content of these conversations were not collected, it is conceivable that many of them are parent-initiated, often against the wishes of the child. One can envision the youth, cornered by the parents, being forced to discuss what are very personal and often embarrassing matters. Under these conditions, it is not difficult to see why this is not a valid index of the intimacy of a relationship and why it is not negatively associated with delinquency (as shown in Table 11.4, this relationship is strongest among males, especially white males; to the extent that males find it more difficult than females to discuss private and intimate matters with their parents, the post hoc explanation presented here makes some sense). The reader is cautioned, however, that this is pure speculation since the authors do not have any data which speak directly to the issue.

Comparison of the unstandardized regression coefficients across groups indicates that all of the family interaction variables are similarly related to delinquency involvement in the total sample, mother-only, and both-parent homes. While this does not necessarily mean that home status is an unimportant variable in delinquency involvement, it does suggest that similar family dynamics are operating within various types of family structure. If there are indeed family structure differences in delinquency involvement, then one must look elsewhere; such differences are not evident in the family dimensions the authors have examined. (They do appear in the mother/stepfather category but, as indicated above, the authors do not have confidence that the sample size is sufficient to pursue these differences.) This position is supported by separate analyses of the relationship between family structure and delinquency (not shown here) which found no significant relationship, either in the total sample or in any of the sex, race, or race-sex subgroups.

Within mother-only and both-parent homes, however, the *relative importance* of the family interaction variables does vary. In both-parent homes identity support, instrumental communication, conflict, and control and supervision are most important (as determined by the relative magnitude of their standardized Beta coefficients). In mother-only homes, however, control and supervision is most important, followed by conflict and instrumental communication. These differences in relative importance, however, are not large, and the authors are reluctant to conclude that differential family interaction patterns

Table 11.4 Unstandardized Regression Coefficients (Standard Error) and Variance in Delinquency Explained by Family Factors and Age

Sample group	Caring and Trust	Control and Supervision	Intimate Communication	Identity Support	Parental Disapproval of Peers	Conflict	Instrumental Communication	Age	RSQ	F of Equation
Males	-.083	-.257	.201	-.164	.151	.053	-.197	.064	.122	7.67*
(N = 405)	(.110)	(.079)	(.070)	(.068)	(.072)	(.046)	(.080)	(.028)		
Females	-.016	-.102	.065	-.177	.148	.160	-.154	.029	.142	9.76*
(N = 425)	(.091)	(.077)	(.059)	(.063)	(.068)	(.042)	(.074)	(.027)		
Whites	.034	-.211	.207	-.231	.206	.113	-.279	.056	.178	10.76*
(N = 364)	(.105)	(.076)	(.072)	(.071)	(.077)	(.045)	(.081)	(.028)		
Nonwhites	—	-.289	.059	-.175	.120	.091	-.114	.026	.112	8.03*
(N = 461)		(.071)	(.061)	(.062)	(.066)	(.044)	(.076)	(.027)		
White Males	-.139	-.219	.375	-.261	.206	.038	-.396	.064	.225	6.61*
(N = 174)	(.177)	(.120)	(.115)	(.110)	(.118)	(.065)	(.118)	(.043)		
Nonwhite Males	-.034	-.269	.087	-.104	.123	.058	-.060	.060	.075	2.52**
(N = 228)	(.148)	(.107)	(.092)	(.090)	(.093)	(.067)	(.112)	(.039)		
White Females	-.050	.070	.097	-.147	.165	.184	-.138	.075	.175	5.50*
(N = 190)	(.137)	(.110)	(.090)	(.090)	(.099)	(.060)	(.107)	(.036)		
Nonwhite Females	-.034	-.226	.052	-.195	.130	.135	-.149	-.004	.145	5.36*
(N = 233)	(.128)	(.109)	(.082)	(.089)	(.095)	(.060)	(.104)	(.039)		

*p < .001   **p < .01

are operating. Rather, the data continue to suggest that similar processes are involved in various family structures. Instrumental communication, identity support, control and supervision, and conflict appear to be significantly related to delinquency in all family contexts. The multidimensional conceptualization of family interaction thus permits one to be much more specific about the nature of these processes than do more unidimensional attached/unattached models.

In addition to the analyses represented by the data in Table 11.3, several potential interactions among the variables (for example, race-sex, sex–intimate communication, conflict–intimate communication) were also tested. With one exception, these did not add significantly to the variance accounted for by the main effects. This exception is the interaction between intimate communication and instrumental communication in both-parent homes (b = -.331). The most delinquent youths have the lowest score on the product of these two variables. This suggests that a combination of high instrumental communication and high intimate communication is indicative of strong attachment and has a delinquency inhibiting effect. An analysis of variance using a dichotomized version of this interaction term (the product of the two variables, each split at the median) shows that high-frequency major offenders have the lowest scores and low-frequency minor offenders the highest. The pattern of means is perfectly linear across the five offender categories, with the exception of non-offenders, who have a mean value below that of low-frequency minor and high-frequency minor offenders. The authors have speculated on the uniqueness of this nonoffender group elsewhere (Giordano et al. 1986).

Because the race and sex [variables] included in the analyses presented in Table 11.3 suggest that these variables affect delinquency involvement even after family interaction patterns have been controlled (that is, males are significantly more delinquent than females in all family contexts, while blacks are considerably more delinquent than whites in mother-only homes), and because the literature suggests important sex and race differences in the impact of family variables on delinquency (compare Gove & Crutchfield 1982; Rankin 1983), one last analysis was performed. The data in Table 11.4 present unstandardized regression coefficients for the family interaction dimensions by sex, race, and race-sex subgroups. While the authors would have liked to present breakdowns for race and sex groups by homes status (for example, intact white homes, mother-only black homes) the small samples which result when the data are combined in this way prohibited doing so.

As the data in Table 11.4 show, the amount of variance in delinquency explained by the model ranges from a high of 22.5 percent among white males to a low of 7.5 percent for nonwhite males.[4] While the explained variance is again disappointing, the data do reveal several interesting patterns. First, the model accounts for slightly more variance among females than among males (14.2% versus 12.2%). To the extent that the model specified here is a social control model, this is consistent with previous arguments that control theory does a better job of explaining female than male delinquency (compare Krohn & Massey 1980). Still, the variance explained for the two groups is quite similar, due in part to a more complete measurement of family interaction patterns in the model presented here. Previous research based on a unidimensional attachment variable may have masked differences in the *particular dimensions* of attachment which inhibit delinquency among males and females. For example, the data show that although the total explained variance is similar among males and females, the relative importance of the variables is not. Among males, control and supervision, intimate communication, and instrumental communication are most important (as determined by the relative magnitude of the coefficients). For females, however, identity support, conflict, instrumental communication, and parental disapproval of peers are the strongest predictors. This seems to suggest that while family attachment is important in inhibiting delinquency among all adolescents, the various dimensions of this bond operate somewhat differentially among males and females.

Second, the family variables also do considerably better in accounting for the delinquency of whites than for that of nonwhites (17.8% versus 11.2%). For both groups, control and supervision, identity support, disapproval of peers, and instrumental communication are important predictors. With the exception of the supervision variable, however, the coefficients are considerably larger among whites than among nonwhites. For whites, instrumental communication is clearly the best predictor, while among nonwhites, control and supervision heads the list.

Third, among the four race-sex subgroups, the model explains more variance in delinquency among whites, male (22.5%) and female (17.5%), than among nonwhites, male (7.5%) and female (14.5%). While identity support seems to be important in all four subgroups, there are important differences by group in the relative salience of the variables. Instrumental communication and intimate communication are the strongest predictors by far among white males, while control and supervision is most important among nonwhite males, conflict among white females, and control and supervision among nonwhite females. These differences offer further support for the contention that it is important to distinguish among various dimensions of family interaction and attachment so that one can specify which ones operate similarly and which operate differentially across particular subgroups.

Finally, a comparison of the unstandardized coefficients reveals, with few exceptions, that control and supervision, identity support, parental disapproval of peers, and instrumental communication are significantly related to delinquency involvement across all of the subgroups. On the other hand, intimate communication is more salient for whites, males, and especially white males than for any of the other subgroups (an examination of the instrumental communication–intimate communication interaction discussed earlier produced unstandardized coefficients of −.363 for whites, −.379 for males and −.460 for white males), while conflict is most predictive of delinquency among females generally, and white females in particular. In conjunction with the above data, these findings suggest that while there is a core of family attachment dimensions that appears important for all adolescents, there are several important subgroup differences which demand attention in subsequent research.

Discussion

Much of the literature dealing with the family and delinquency is characterized by a dichotomous attached/unattached conception of family relationships and a broken-intact model of family structure. The purpose of this article has been to show that a more detailed elaboration of the elements constituting family attachment provides a more rigorous test of exactly how family processes affect delinquency. Examining the effect of these relationships within different types of families also allows one to be more unambiguous about the relationship between family processes and family structure.

Although the explained variance in delinquency accounted for by the model is small, this does not mean that family variables are unimportant in understanding and predicting delinquency involvement. While there is no doubt that peer and school variables, for example, are more powerful predictors, the data (as well as considerable theory and previous research) indicate that family processes are too important to be excluded from criminological explanations. Family relationships assume a major role in one of the most powerful models of delinquency—social control theory. To the extent that more and more research is being conducted to test the propositions of this model, it is incumbent upon criminologists to attend to basic problems of conceptualization and measurement. Only when family interaction processes are properly conceptualized and operationalized can one begin to sort out the relative importance of family, peer, school, and other variables, and to specify how such factors might interact in their effect on delinquency. This research represents a modest step in this direction.

The findings indicate that while there are important sex and race differences in family interaction dynamics, there is no significant variation by family structure. Significant relationships between all but one of the family interaction dimensions and delinquency, coupled with the lack of any significant relationship between family structure and delinquency in the data, suggest that internal family dynamics are considerably more important than family structure in affecting delinquency. The family variables specified seem to have similar affects on delinquency in all types of family structures. The findings do not suggest that the effects of broken homes are mediated by family interaction dynamics, as is commonly assumed. Indeed, the findings indicate that there is no broken home effect (whether there might be a differential official reaction to delinquency on the basis of family structure [compare Johnson 1986] is an important, though separate issue; since the data are confined to self-reported delinquency, the authors cannot address this issue). However, the small number of cases in father-only, father/stepmother, and mother/stepfather homes forced a restriction of the analyses to both-parent and mother-only homes. As a result, research based on larger samples of these types of family structures, especially mother/stepfather homes, is required before any definitive conclusions can be drawn.

On the other hand, the regression analyses for the various sex, race, and race-sex subgroups suggest both important similarities and differences in the impact of family dynamics on delinquency. Subsequent research should pursue these in greater detail. All of these findings complicate the presumed relationship between the family and delinquency. The data make it clear that the traditional attached/unattached and broken/intact dichotomies mask many of the specific internal dynamics of family relationships. At the same time, these data point to the multidimensional nature of family attachment. While the family factors identified are associated with one another, they are clearly separate dimensions which have differential impacts on delinquency. It is equally obvious that there is considerable variation among sociodemographic subgroups in both the utility of the family variables, as measured by the explained variance, and in the specific combination of variables that are predictive of delinquency. It will be the task of future research to analyze these subtleties and to specify the causal ordering of their effects.

Appendix Family Scale Reliabilities and Factor Loadings

Caring and Trust (response format ranges along a five-point scale from "strongly agree" to "strongly disagree"). Alpha = .757[a]
   1. My parents often ask about what I am doing in school. .586
   2. My parents give me the right amount of affection. .731
   3. One of the worst things that could happen to me would be finding out I let my parents down. .636
   4. My parents are usually proud of me when I've finished something I've worked hard at. .698
   5. My parents trust me. .616
   6. I'm closer to my parents than a lot of kids my age are. .636

Identity Support (response format ranges along a five-point scale from "strongly agree" to "strongly disagree"). Alpha = .690
   1. My parents sometimes put me down in front of other people. −.699
   2. Sometimes my parents won't listen to me or my opinions. −.708
   3. My parents sometimes give me the feeling that I'm not living up to their expectation. −.761
   4. My parents seem to wish I were a different type of person. −.643

Intimate Communication (response format ranges along a five-point scale from "very often" to "never"). Alpha = .673
   1. How often do you talk to your parents about the boy/girl whom you like very much? .824
   2. How often do you talk to your parents about questions, or problems about sex? .798
   3. How often do you talk to your parents about things you have done about which you feel guilty? .589

Control and Supervision (response format ranges along a five-point scale from "strongly agree" to "strongly disagree"). Alpha = .691
   1. My parents want to know who I am going out with when I go out with other boys/girls. .774

2. In my free time away from home, my parents know who I'm with and where I am. .742
3. My parents want me to tell them where I am if I don't come home right after school. .815

Conflict (response format ranges along a five-point scale from "two or more times per week" to "hardly ever or never"). Alpha = .615
1. How often do you have disagreements or arguments with your parents? .822
2. How often do you purposely not talk to your parents because you are mad at them? .817

Instrumental Communication (response format ranges along a five-point scale from "very often" to "never"). Alpha = .654
1. How often do you talk with your parents about problems you have at school? −.680
2. How often do you talk with your parents about your job plans for the future? −.545
3. How often do you talk with your parents about problems with your friends? −.645
4. How often do you talk with your parents about how well you get along with your teachers? −.794

Parental Disapproval of Peers (response format ranges along a five-point scale from "strongly approve" to "strongly disapprove"). Alpha = .475
1. In general, what do your parents think of your friends? .756
2. In general, what do your parents think of your boyfriend/girlfriend? .730

[*Note:* a. Alpha is a measure of the internal consistency, or intercorrelation, of the items in a scale.]

Notes

1. The survey was managed by National Analysts, Inc. Interviews were conducted from late April through late June of 1982. Informed consent and written permission were obtained from each respondent and parent/guardian prior to the interview. The National Analysts staff validated 54 percent of the interviews to ensure that proper protocol was followed.

2. The typology is based on the distinction between major and minor offenses. Twenty-one of the 27 self-report items were used to construct major and minor offense subscales. The composition of the two scales is as follows:

Major: motor vehicle theft, grand theft, aggravated assault, selling hard drugs, rape, robbery, and breaking and entering.
Minor: throwing objects at cars or people, running away, lying about age, petty theft, prostitution, sexual intercourse, cheating on tests, simple assault, disorderly conduct, public drunkenness, theft $5–$50, truancy, drug use, and alcohol use.

For the minor offense subscale, 1–47 reported acts was defined as low frequency, 48 or more as high frequency. This is the median cutoff for those reporting any minor offense involvement. For the major offense subscale, 1–4 reported acts was defined as low frequency, 5 or more as high frequency. This is the median for those reporting any major offense involvement. For a more detailed description of the construction of the offender index, the reader is referred to the authors' earlier work (Cernkovich et al. 1985).

3. The reader is cautioned against interpreting this as a firm conclusion, as small cell sizes in a three-way interaction may produce unstable means.

4. While R^2 differences are compared across groups, the reader is reminded that R^2 is in part a function of a particular subgroup's variance. Because this can lead to potentially misleading conclusions, unstandardized regression coefficients will also be compared across groups, and the standard errors of these estimates will be presented.

■ References

Agnew, Robert. 1985. "Social Control Theory and Delinquency: A Longitudinal Test." *Criminology* 23:47–61.

Arnold, William R. & Terrance M. Brungardt. 1983. *Juvenile Misconduct and Delinquency.* Boston: Houghton Mifflin.

Bordua, David. 1962. "Some Comments on Theories of Group Delinquency." *Sociological Inquiry* 32:245–60.

Canter, Rachelle J. 1982. "Family Correlates of Male and Female Delinquency." *Criminology* 20:149–67.

Cernkovich, Stephen A., Peggy C. Giordano & M. D. Pugh. 1985. "Chronic Offenders: The Missing Cases in Self-report Delinquency Research." *Journal of Criminal Law & Criminology* 76:301–26.

Datesman, Susan K. & Frank R. Scarpitti. 1975. "Female Delinquency and Broken Homes: A Reassessment." *Criminology* 13:33–55.

Elliott, Delbert & Suzanne Ageton. 1980. "Reconciling Race and Class Differences in Self-reported and Official Estimates of Delinquency." *American Sociological Review* 45:95–110.

Elliott, Delbert, David Huizinga & Suzanne Ageton. 1985. *Explaining Delinquency and Drug Use.* The National Youth Survey, Project Report No. 21. Boulder, CO: Behavioral Research Institute.

Empey, LeMar T. 1982. *American Delinquency: Its Meaning and Construction.* Homewood, IL: Dorsey.

Etaugh, Claire. 1980. "Effects of Nonmaternal Care on Children: Research Evidence and Popular Views." *American Psychologist* 35:309–17.

Giordano, Peggy C., Stephen A. Cernkovich & M. D. Pugh. 1986. "Friendships and Delinquency." *American Journal of Sociology* 91:1170–1202.

Gold, Martin & David J. Reimer. 1974. *Changing Patterns of Delinquent Behavior Among Americans 13 to 16 Years Old, 1967–1972.* Report No. 1 of the National Survey of Youth. Ann Arbor: Institute for Social Research, University of Michigan (NIMH Grant No. MH 20575).

Gove, Walter R. & Robert D. Crutchfield. 1982. "The Family and Juvenile Delinquency." *Sociological Quarterly* 23:301–19.

Hindelang, Michael J., Travis Hirschi & Joseph G. Weis. 1981. *Measuring Delinquency.* Beverly Hills, CA: Sage.

Hirschi, Travis. 1969. *Causes of Delinquency.* Berkeley: University of California Press.

Hoffman, Lois Wladis. 1974. "Effects of Maternal Employment on the Child: A Review of the Research." *Developmental Psychology* 10:204–28.

Johnson, Richard E. 1986. "Family Structure and Delinquency: General Patterns and Gender Differences." *Criminology* 24:65–84.

Krohn, Marvin D. & James L. Massey. 1980. "Social Control and Delinquent Behavior: An Examination of the Elements of the Social Bond." *Sociological Quarterly* 529–43.

LaGrange, Randy L. & Helene Raskin White. 1985. "Age Differences in Delinquency: A Test of Theory." *Criminology* 23:19–45.

Minor, William. no date. *Maryland Youth Survey.* Institute of Criminal Justice and Criminology. College Park: University of Maryland.

Norland, Stephen, Neal Shover, William E. Thornton & Jennifer James. 1979. "Intrafamily Conflict and Delinquency." *Pacific Sociological Review* 2:223–40.

Nye, F. Ivan. 1958. *Family Relationships and Delinquent Behavior.* New York: Wiley.

Patterson, Gerald R. & Thomas J. Dishion. 1985. "Contributions of Families and Peers to Delinquency." *Criminology* 23:63–79.

Rankin, Joseph H. 1983. "The Family Context of Delinquency." *Social Problems* 30: 466–79.

Rodman, Hyman & Paul Grams. 1967. "Juvenile Delinquency and the Family: A Review and Discussion." President's Commission on Law Enforcement and the Administration of Justice, *Task Force Report: Juvenile Delinquency and Youth Crime.* Washington, DC: US Government Printing Office.

Rosen, Lawrence. 1985. "Family and Delinquency: Structure or Function?" *Criminology* 23:553–73.

Rutter, Michael & Henri Giller. 1984. *Delinquency: Trends and Perspectives.* New York: Guilford.

Shoemaker, Donald J. 1984. *Theories of Delinquency: An Examination of Explanations of Delinquent Behavior.* New York: Oxford University Press.

US Bureau of the Census. 1985. *Marital Status and Living Arrangements: March 1984.* Current Population Reports, Series P-20, No. 399. Washington, DC: US Government Printing Office.

Wells, L. Edward & Joseph H. Rankin. 1986 "The Broken Homes Model of Delinquency: Analytic Issues." *Journal of Research in Crime & Delinquency* 23:68–93.

West, Lloyd & Harvey W. Zingle. 1969. "A Self-disclosure Inventory for Adolescents." *Psychological Reports* 23:439–445.

Wiatrowski, Michael D., David B. Griswold & Mary K. Roberts. 1981. "Social Control Theory and Delinquency." *American Sociological Review* 46:525–41.

Wilkinson, Karen. 1974. "The Broken Family and Juvenile Delinquency: Scientific Explanation or Ideology?" *Social Problems* 21:726–39.

12

Players and Ho's

Terry Williams and William Kornblum

This excerpt from Terry Williams and William Kornblum's Growing Up Poor, *an ethnography of inner-city youths, embeds an examination of family relationships, including intrafamilial sexual abuse, in broader community context. Youths whose disempowering family backgrounds make it even more difficult for them to surmount the obstacles of their disadvantaged social status turn to prostitution and pimping as they attempt to negotiate their way through the "underground economy."*

> *I don't exactly fill out a W2 form after I turn a trick.* —Margo Sharp

Cooksey's, D's Inferno, Club 437, McDonald's, and the mall are familiar hangouts for teenagers in Louisville. The mall is located in downtown Louisville; although it is integrated, it is a meeting place for black youth from all over the city. Many of the teenagers hustle in the pool rooms and discos, peddling marijuana and sex.

For the young women, hustling is synonymous with prostitution. Indeed, in all the cities we studied, prostitution is the main occupation for girls in the underground economy—girls like Donna White, who hustles in Louisville's mall area.

> I am 19 years old. About two years ago my parents moved to a little town called Madisonville, Kentucky. I hated that place. But I stayed long enough to finish school at Norman Hopkins [High School]. I wanted to go places and see different things and not stay in that damn place. I wanted to make something out of myself so I left and came here to Louisville. I couldn't find no job for nine months here so I met up with some friends who told me I could hustle and make some money. They said they would show me how. All I had to do was learn.

Excerpt from *Growing Up Poor,* by Terry Williams and William Kornblum (Lexington Books, 1985). Reprinted by permission of Rowman & Littlefield Publishing Group.

So I first started hustling in the pool rooms and pushing a few petty drugs. My boyfriend and/or his friend would stand in the pool room or out in the hall and wait till they saw some men, soldiers, businessmen, or whatever, and ask them if they wanted to have some sex. If they said yes, he would steer them over to the pool room and then tell me where to go meet them.

In the Hough district of Cleveland, dilapidated, burned-out structures from the 1960s riots are still visible. The housing consists mainly of single-family units. It is odd to see so many old houses, many in the grand style, decaying, unpainted, and broken. Hough is the ghetto of Cleveland. Its citizens, black and white alike, seem helpless to change it. The community is bankrupt economically, politically, and socially. Many feel that Hough is being punished for the "sins" it committed in the 1960s.

Pearl Varnedoe has worked as a prostitute in the Hough area and downtown near the University of Cleveland since she was 14. Pearl left home in order to "make money and live free." She says hustling came easily to her because "my parents had a club that always had pimps, whores, and gamblers in it."

My mother was always beating me. My father tried to make her stop but he couldn't. My mother was always drunk and she couldn't stop that either. My father ran this after-hours club and when I left home I met up with some of them from his joint and they turned me out [set me up as a prostitute]. I always had real big titties and a nice body. As a matter of fact, the vice squad know me on sight and arrest me sometimes just to have something to do. I've been arrested about 21 times. They never knew I was a minor during all the time I spent there. When I went home to check on my father, I found out my mother had been beating my brothers and sisters too. Our neighbor had called in a child-abuse worker to talk to her. She told me she knew about my being on the street and filed a delinquency report with the juvenile authorities.

In Meridian, Mississippi, a large naval base on the outskirts of town has created a thriving market for drugs and sex. Thus the young people in Meridian perceive numerous opportunities in the illegal economy. The young men between the ages of 16 and 21 are the players or pimps, and the young women between the ages of 13 and 20 are the prostitutes making prostitution the main source of illegal income for youths. Teenagers like Curly and his girls make up the "supply side" of prostitution in Meridian.

Curly is 18 years old. His hustle is young women. He's a "player" and they are "ho's" or "tricks." (In Meridian "trick" refers to the prostitute or seller of sex; in New York the converse is true—"trick" refers to the buyer of sex.)

I have one or two girls on the street. I still got a couple of them doing things for me. You know I gotta have that paper [money]. The only rule I have is that my main lady don't go out there. The others I have them boosting, tricking, whatever, as long as they keep giving up the money. See, baby, you do what you have to do to survive in this world now. The more money they have, the more I have. They do what they want to get it. And when I ask them for it, I get it. Sometimes I'll help out if I get hip to someone who wants to make a buy. I'll let them know. But it depends on how much they get and how much I need. But I don't take all of their money. I usually leave them a little. And I don't feel I'm responsible for putting no ho on the street. Look, they are out there trying to be grown. They put themselves out there. If I didn't take their money, they would give it to someone else. Them tricks ain't gonna be nothing but whores. All I did was fuck them a couple of times and they started giving me money. See, a woman doesn't have to sell her body for a man to pimp her. There are plenty of women that are smart and pretty with good jobs and taking care of men. That's pimping.

Among Curly's "tricks" are Maylee Jones, Clara Thompson, and Dorothea Caddy, aged 16, 16, and 17, respectively. Here's what they have to say about "the life":

Maylee: There ain't no jobs around here. Besides I can make more money doing this. Sometimes I make one hundred or two, sometimes more, sometimes less. If I had a job, I wouldn't make that much. If I could make as much money in a job as I do hustling, I would work. The Navy boys they spend a lot of money. All these old white men do too. Anyway around here they give all the good jobs to the white people. . . . The most important thing in my life right now is surviving. That's all I believe in. Well, I believe in God but not preachers, 'cause all the preachers do is ride around in Cadillacs and wear silk suits.

Clara: I have four boyfriends who give me $15 a week to go to bed with them. I only go out with one of them. The money I get I just spend it on clothes and stuff to get high with. I don't like to do it too much. I think it might do something to me. All the men are young, in their twenties. I give them a bit here and there but they give me the money on time. I like to show my legs and breast. It fascinates me to watch men cream.

Dorothea: I started tricking because I didn't know what time it was. I was at a friend's house getting high and they said, hey, you want to turn a trick for someone? And I said, it depends on the cash, what time, and who. At that time, I needed the money, you know. My boyfriend was there and I didn't know he was no pimp. But he kept encouraging me to do it. Anyway, after that I set my own thing up with one of my girlfriends. I have them [johns] call her. I used to have them call my pimp till I got rid of him. He got mad, but he knew I could fight him if he tried some shit like hitting on me. I didn't need him anymore, you know. I only had him for protection and the first time I went to jail for fighting, the man was out of town. I would make $150 or so and put $75 back and show him the rest, and he would give me $25 of that plus what I had, you know. He didn't know what time it was.

Dorothea dropped out of school in the ninth grade. At 17 she organized a group of teenage prostitutes and set up a brothel in a fashionable black section of town.

Young women in each of these cities—and in New York as well—are shocked and depressed by the bleakness of their situation. Many do not believe they have a choice between getting a job and hustling. Hustling—meaning prostitution—is the only choice. (Theft and prostitution are often combined, but prostitution is by far the easiest, most convenient, and most profitable form of illegal activity for these teenagers.)

Most girls are recruited into prostitution, but some are tricked, coerced, or charmed into the life. The latter are talked into believing that it is an exciting life complete with fine cars and endless amounts of money. There is a note of self-delusion in some of their comments, like "A lot of the men are lonely and I feel I can help them" or "Most of the time the tricks don't know what time it is, so you can get their money."

While there are adult role models and community institutions that try to steer teenagers away from the life, many find the incentives too strong. Margo Sharp's life as a prostitute in Harlem illustrates the careers young women pursue in the underground economy.

Margo's parents separated when she was four years old. Her mother remarried, and during the ensuing years her father made sporadic appearances. When Margo was 12 or 13 her mother became embroiled in domestic problems with her stepfather. Arguments and fights were common. Margo's mother began to have relationships with other men, including some of her husband's friends. One of those men had a traumatic impact on Margo.

> My mother had an affair with this man who was later to become my stepfather. Well, he had this friend, best friend no less, who was this little horny Dominican motherfucker. I was 12 years old then and I knew about sex and all of that, although I had never had sex. He would come around the house all the time and even though my mother was seeing my stepfather, this guy would come over sometimes and they would laugh and drink and my stepfather would leave them alone sometimes because he trusted his friend so much. Well, my mother and this little Dominican started to have a thing behind my stepfather's back. And this little motherfucker was so horny, he wound up fucking my mother's best friend too.
>
> Anyhow, one day I was upstairs doing my homework and he comes into my room and tells me he wants to talk to me. I don't remember if anybody was home or not that day, but I assumed he was gonna talk about my mother and their little thing, you know. So he told me to sit on the bed next to him. And I did. Still not thinking anything about it. Well the next thing I know he's taking my blouse off. And all the time he's asking me if I feel anything. Well I don't know why I didn't scream or anything but I just sat there. After he had taken off my panties, the only thought I had in my mind was not to panic. Not to scream because I had read all about how men had killed women and kids molesting them or something, and I wasn't about to say a thing. So he took off my panties and the only thing that stood out in my mind was how big he was. It seemed like he was as big as a tree trunk, I swear to God, I was hurting so bad, I was so sore. I felt, my God, what did he do to me? Well, when it was over, he helped me put back on my clothes and I sat on the bed for a long time just thinking.
>
> I never told my mother anything for two years. And when I did her reaction was typical of women in love. She slapped me. She thought I was

lying for years after I told her this. She didn't believe nothing I told her. One day two years later this little bastard drove up to my house to see my mother. Well my mother told me to come out and say hello to him. But I was not too excited about seeing the little fucker ever again. So I refused. But she insisted so I went out to say hello. But when I saw his face I just got angry. The window of the car door was down. And he reached his face out to kiss me and I spat in it. My mother jerked me away and slapped me. But I grabbed her arm and told her I was no kid any more. I was 14 years old and that she had no reason to protect a man who had not only cheated on her by fucking her friend but had cheated on her by fucking her daughter. She didn't believe me. Like I said, she thought I was lying. She was so in love with this faggot that she didn't believe her own daughter. I hated him for that more than his act against me because it made my relationship with my mother a stormy one for years to come.

Margo was 14 then. Her mother was unwilling to assume responsibility for her wayward daughter, so she sent Margo to a social worker at the Children's Aid Society. After a series of bad experiences in a variety of schools, Margo finally dropped out. Considered gifted by her teachers, she could not make herself sit still long enough to complete her studies. Instead, she was habitually absent. Her lateness and absenteeism eventually resulted in expulsion.

Margo's attitudes about men were formed early. She was more game than most men could handle. Standing tall and shapely with big eyes and a warm, inquisitive intelligence, she was no child and knew it. After leaving school, she refused to work but always seemed to have money. Her mother occasionally asked her how she was able to get along without working, but Margo always had an explanation.

I would have $200, $300, $400 and my mother knew nothing about it. I wouldn't tell her where I had been. So half the time she didn't know. I didn't buy a lot of stuff or give her money because I was afraid she would ask me where I got it from. I tried to explain it to her one day. I told her a friend of hers, Mr. George, who was about 50 years old, had hinted he wanted to have sex with me. So I jokingly told my mom that if he wanted it, it would cost him a hundred bucks. Well, she laughed and said, "Yeah, that's better than giving it to him for free." So in a way, I guess, she didn't really object to what I was doing.

By the time Margo was 15 she was involved in casual prostitution, averaging $200 per customer. She was in the life as an "outlaw," that is, without benefit of a pimp. Her method was a bit unorthodox. When a man approached her, she would take the money from the transaction and give it to one of her male friends.

Sometimes my friend would look at me funny when I told him to hold the cash. It would be a few hundred dollars. And that I would be back later. I would go to a hotel and after it was over I'd go back to pick up my money. If a guy approached me and said I was beautiful and asked how much would it cost him to have me, I would tell him whatever came to my mind. If he looked well dressed and clean I would say $200, $300, $400. It depended on my mood. If I was real horny, I would react quicker but that didn't mean the price went down. I would just choose someone who I thought was good looking. Someone who I thought would be pleasant to fuck. Sometimes I would get off with these guys but most of the time I would pretend.

At least some liked it enough to pay high prices for it. It started out with offers of $100 or more for an hour or two. When they first started asking me I would decline, and then decided to stop being such a fool. I started accepting, not only money, but gifts, trips, etc. It was sort of like getting your cake and eating it too. I was not only compensated for time, but I was spent time with as well. The sexual acts were sexual acts. But if they brought on a smile, a kiss or hug the morning after, it was worthwhile. I felt not only wanted but needed. At the same time, a lot of lonely hearts were warmed. Call it what you will, I see my actions in a benevolent light. I enjoyed the money, spending highly, indulging in things I wouldn't normally have. The gifts were sweet. They showed a touch more of consideration. The men were usually much older than myself. I, in some cases, portrayed a prized china doll that they flaunted.

Yes, I did get tired of the life at times, but it was an experience, and I learned a lot. I met some very interesting people. I always tried to establish a good rapport with my friends. One never knows who one may need some day. But only as friends. My intimate relationships were always kept separate and never came about from a trick night. It was difficult at times having both a main man and my pastime, but I managed. In some cases, where I felt the person I was dealing with was due more respect, I would cool off my friendly encounters and devote myself to that one person.

For young women like Margo, prostitution becomes a distinctive lifestyle, known as "the life." But for the pimps or players, hustling sex isn't very different from any other kind of hustle. The young man usually has tried a variety of ways of earning money, finally settling on pimping as involving the least effort for the greatest reward. Ray-Ray Southern is typical.

I came to Meridian when I was 11 years old. I went to Oakland Heights Elementary School in the fifth grade. I got along very well with the teachers. We caught the city bus every day to school. I got out of school one day by playing sick and stole a bicycle. I had to go by the babysitter's house to pick up my little sister and brother. They were very happy to see me. My momma came home by the babysitter's house and found out about the bicycle. She asked me where it was and I told her somewhere else, but I didn't know where. Momma took me home and whipped me. The police came and talked to me and we got over that.

About three weeks later our house caught on fire. My sister was smoking a cigarette and threw the butt on the floor. After the fire, we changed schools and I met the wrong type of friends. I had a fight the first day of school. Later on, I stole another bicycle and I didn't get caught. I began to turn out with this girl I was running with. We would do things like stealing, smoking, drinking, and breaking out people's windows.

Everything was happening to me then. My girlfriend and I got caught in the act of love making. My mother was very upset. She wanted to whip me but my dad talked her out of it. She was upset because she didn't know I knew too much about sex. My mother talked to us about it but I wasn't listening. I liked what I was doing. After a few more incidents, we broke up because of her mother. So I met another girl. I was going over there every day. I was going to school but I would play hooky with her. We didn't stay together because all she wanted was sex. The first day of the next term I was kissing this girl and they said I had to go. This happened too many times. So I left because there was too many rules anyhow. You couldn't hold hands, you couldn't talk to white girls, etc.

I got into trouble again and this time they sent me to Columbia Training School. I was there for four months and two weeks. Three months later I was in more trouble—breaking and entering. I got some items out and sold them to the wrong person. I had to go back to the juvenile center. I was out one day and the next one I was in.

I got a job when I got out working at Morrison's [Restaurant] as a cook. But at $1.95 an hour, that's bullshit. At Morrison's they thought they had a real nigger working 'cause I really tried to keep that job. But that damn man [boss] was crazy. He started bitching with me. Now he knows a cook don't wash no damn dishes. I wouldn't do that shuffling routine, so I quit. I started stealing hams and making some money. I would take my girlfriend with me to the supermarket and I'd have a box underneath the cart. We'd walk around filling the box with steaks, pork chops, hams, chickens, all kinds of shit. I'd have tape in my pocket and some stamps with rope. This is so it would look like a package. That don't never fail to work. I'd steal about $1,500 worth of meat and sell it for $800. Sometimes I buy a little weed to sell. I pay $45 for an ounce or $150 for a pound and make more than $300 every three or four days. All I want is a Cadillac, two tons of weed, five pounds of crystal T, a nice house, and be financially well off. I would much rather work than hustle because working is steady. When you work you know where the money is coming from.

We did not find any consistent pattern in the backgrounds of young men who become pimps. Husbands, boyfriends, and transient players all play the role. Young boys sometimes identify with the player image—New York players set standards of dress and lifestyle that are widely imitated—but in most cases the motivation is economic necessity. Frances H., a close observer of the street scene in Meridian, described the situation of teenage pimps in this southern town as follows:

It's not that all these kids want to be players or hustlers. The first thing you think is they don't want to work. That's misleading. Most of them, and I mean the major portion of them, have tried at one time or another to get a job. They have beat down the doors of the unemployment offices. They have been in these stores, dealing with all these crackers who constantly make wisecracks and comments about how dumb they are and stuff like that. And they, rightly so, get tired of it. Then they come back out here on the street and say, "Fuck it. I'll make it any way I can. I'll be a player. I'll be a hustler. I'll be cool. I'll be clean." They want to have that paper. Just like everybody else does. You can't tell 'em they don't know what time it is because they think they do. So it ain't like they ain't tried. It's just that they got tired of all the bullshit. A lot of what this is about is discrimination. It's prejudice against these kids. Them young white boys can go to daddy and say, "I need a job" or "I need money" and get it. But these black kids have to kiss ass and then be told, "Ain't no jobs for you, nigger boy." So you know it ain't about not wanting to work.

The experiences of young people in other regions of the country reveal few differences in lifestyle and some basic similarities in values and outlook toward their immediate future. Most teenagers in the underground economy, regardless of region, maintain the traditional values of work, money, and success. Although these are limited commodities, the youths are as desperate in their search as anyone else.

One thing is clear—teenagers like Ray-Ray will more often than not find illegal opportunities more attractive than legal ones. Those who have had negative experiences in the work place, no matter how brief, will move on to the underground economy and try to forge an identity there. Ray-Ray, however, is the first to admit that he is not going to get rich stealing meat, selling marijuana, or even pimping.

Some teenage hustlers do manage to find jobs. But often they leave within a few months because the demands of the job appear to be too great, especially when hustling seems to offer an easier life. Here's what Margo has to say about her brief career in the nine-to-five world:

> If you're the type that can never be without a job, not having one may cause a problem. I'm not that type. I can live with or without one. I've never been one to worry about work. Occasionally I might find myself in a jam, but I believe things work themselves out and they usually do. Not working doesn't bother me so much as having to do that regular nine to five. I hate straight hours, time clocks and suspicious bosses. I enjoy not having to deal with the same environment and people within that structure on a daily basis. That type of contact, being constant, tires me. I love to freelance. I enjoy change in work situations. I'm trying other ways to make money, not necessarily legal ways, and I'm open to ideas.
>
> Not working steadily, I will admit, causes problems for me. Because the cash flow isn't there all the time. Naturally I will find other ways to make up for this lack of money, but the market isn't always open to me. When I say this, I'm speaking of the people I may be with at that particular time in my life, or my access to the street. Making illegal money is a whole different scene. It's part of what I categorized before as freelancing. Some examples of freelancing would be anything from hocking your personal property or someone else's, to dealing drugs or selling yourself, borrowing, mediating, touting, you know. If you can do any of these and hold down a tax-paying job, you're alright. But if you can keep this life up and survive from it alone, you're doing better.
>
> One thing about prostitution, it's a tax-free job. The risk is the thrill. I feel one has to be adventurous, daring, and mischievous to a point. The first thing one has to keep in mind is that you're going to get caught. Not by the authorities, no! That's the last thing in my mind. When I say get caught, I mean by the street. If you're dealing in anything against the law, you always have heavy competition. If your game is good, people want to tear it down.

It's a constant battle in the streets for survival. There is a lot of planning, scheming, lying, cheating, and a little bit of fear out there. The fear has to be natural or you're doomed. You have to love danger.

I hate what society considers normal. So I find other ways of living within this world, without letting it bother me. If it bothers others, that's their problem. Every man for himself. When it comes to money you will find very few are going to help you make it. And if you're the type that helps others, you'll find yourself taken for a sucker. So you resign to helping yourself. The advantages of this street business, hustling, it's on you. You wake up, eat, sleep, you don't punch no clocks, you don't conform to no rules and regulations or courtesy to coworkers, customers, bosses, clients, patients, staff, etc. Best of all, you don't pay taxes either.

Margo's work history includes both legitimate and illegitimate roles. Although she possesses the skills to work in a mainstream occupation, she has not developed the discipline to remain in a job very long. This is partly a result of immaturity. However, it is a well-known fact that few teenagers maintain jobs for more than a few months at a time. It is Margo's street and family values that have kept her at odds with the straight world. Her forays into the regular workaday routine are always of short duration because there is more money to be made on the streets. There is always an available market of older men who will buy her services, yet she sees the weakness of her own game. She knows that a prostitute's life—even a high-class call girl's life—is a short one. She knows she won't always have a youthful face and body. And when things get tough—for instance, after a brutal trick—she looks for work in a regular job. Margo sees no discernible difference between her straight out prostitution and what other women do as secretaries or as wives at home.

Margo's views are not shared by the parents and friends of most of the teenage prostitutes we met. There appears to be a double standard operating in this area: the pimps/players are seen as smooth, slick, and smart, the girls as stupid and dirty. Feelings of revulsion and pity were expressed by some of the parents, while others did not seem to know or care what their children were doing. Many of the girls turned to prostitution after becoming pregnant and being rejected by their boyfriends and parents.

Once a girl enters the life, ties with family and friends are usually broken. It is common practice for a pimp to insist that his girls sever all such relationships. Independent prostitutes like Margo may maintain contact with their friends but tend not to explain to them what they do for a living.

In addition to the availability of prostitution as an option and the perceived disadvantages of straight jobs, certain experiences during childhood and adolescence can lead to a career in prostitution. Rose M. of Hough is a case in point.

Things were okay at home until I turned 13. I moved out when I turned 13 and quit school. My stepfather and I couldn't get along any more. I kept moving in and out until I was 15. My mother didn't mind because I always let her know where I was and went by to see her when my stepfather was at work. I didn't have to worry about supporting myself then. When I was 14 I got put on probation for not going to school. At 15, when my mother died, my stepfather sent my sister and myself down south to stay with our real father. I didn't like my father so I came back to Cleveland to stay with a friend. I was getting a social security check from my father so I had money.

The girl I was staying with worked the streets. She was only 16. I didn't have to but I started working with her. It was scary but it was a living. I grew up very fast in the streets. I shot dope but I never got hooked. At 16 I got pregnant and left my man. I went to the Safe Space Station, a runaway shelter. The people were really nice. They tried to help, but I was used to being on my own. So I went back to my man and worked until I was seven months. I also shot dope while I was pregnant. The dope only made my baby small.

We moved from place to place after that. Then my stepfather had me put in D.H. and tried to take my baby. I stayed there for 10 days, then went to a childcare center for three weeks. I turned 17 in there. The court placed me in the custody of the county. My social worker took me down and got me on welfare. Before that I was still turning tricks. I still worked some even though I was on welfare and got social security because I wasn't used to getting money once a month. I still moved from place to place. My son has never had a stable home until now, and he'll be two next month.

Now I'm 18 and I'm three months pregnant. One thing I promised myself, with this baby I'm not going to go through the things I went through with the first. I feel I have an advantage over most people my age and older because I know and have experienced things they'll never know. The only disadvantage is I don't have as much interest in men like I had. My pimp beat me up and tried to make me have an abortion. But I ran away from him because I was tired of the streets and let myself get pregnant on purpose. I know I wasn't forced to get into the life. Because I used to do it a lot with my girlfriends after school to get money to buy extra clothes. When my mother would ask me where I got the clothes from I would tell her I exchanged them with friends. After my mom died and I wasn't going to my stepfather's anymore, I lived with the rest of the girls at my pimp's stable.

For some teenage girls, incestuous relationships with their fathers and encounters with pimps at school may have started them on the road to prostitution. Kate Strolls is a 17-year-old dropout who moved away from home after a series of incidents with her father.

I dropped out of school in the ninth grade. At this point I have no interest in going back. I used to live in the Woodland Projects apartments. It was ugly as hell. It had all these empty houses, old buildings, and winos everywhere. I first hooked up with this pimp at school. I started turning tricks in the afternoon and bringing some of the money home to my mother. She took the money and never asked me where I got it from. She just told me not to get myself killed.

My father moved away after we, my sister and me, got together and told my mother that he had been having sex with both of us and then threatening to kill us if we told anybody. I feel okay about the whole thing but my sister turned real mean and won't talk to nobody. She has no friends and stays at home with my brother even though she is old enough to be on her own. I don't feel that way about men. I just don't develop feelings for them when I'm working. And I prefer to be with women anyhow.

I had this woman stop me one night down on Prospect and give me $100 to go with her. I was scared but, shit, I figured I could outfight the broad if it got too crazy. She had this nice place to stay and all this nice furniture and a man. She turned me out that night.

For many young women, a crucial factor is the lifestyles of the adult women who are closest to them. This was the case for Margo. Her adult role models were her mother, her aunt, and a very close friend of her mother who was active in civil rights, all of whom were rebels and fought private battles at home or public battles against society. Unlike many of the other girls in our study, Margo had a relatively stable home and social environment. She had opportunities to travel, to attend school and do well. But the examples set by her family, her early experiences, and the complexities of her own personality led her to choose the fast life. There is no doubt that young women like Margo could lead successful lives in a professional career were it not for one or two incidents that shaped their life patterns. As she herself explains:

As a baby, not from what I recall, but only hearsay, I was alert, smart, too fast for my britches, and loved to party and drink. One might say that I haven't changed a bit. I was walking at the age of six months, but didn't let go of my bottle till around four years. I was a year old and one still couldn't tell whether I was a girl or a boy, since I still had not grown hair. There was no way to add ribbons, bows or clips to my scalp. So I spent my first year as a child with an undefined sexuality. At eight months my mom was fed up with me, so I say. She claims that it was in my best interest for her to have sent me to my grandparents in South America. This was for a period of three years. I've been told that as a toddler, I spoke too much, knew too much, ate too much, and never liked going to bed on time. I was spoiled, having been the first granddaughter, and yet was very charming and lovable.

At three-and-a-half, I was sent back home to my mother, who by this time I'd forgotten. This, of course, was after having traveled throughout South America and the Virgin Islands. I wish they would have saved those trips now. I arrived at Kennedy International Airport via Avianca Airlines, escorted by my aunt, and was received by everyone from a to z that was a member of my family or knew someone in it.

My room was filled with an accumulation of toys over the past three years. Most of them I still have. One that I loved in particular was a teddy bear named Moy-Moy. He used to be white and fluffy, nowadays he is skinned of all his hair, dyed and ripped. One of the dolls I used to have was four feet tall. Now I was a tiny three-and-a-half-year-old, so you can imagine in comparison to me this thing was a giant. Sometimes I honestly feel that parents are not practical. An example is that by the time I was five, my father, whom I rarely saw, had given me a collection of dolls from all different nations. By the time I was seven, the collection was destroyed. To this day, my mother still curses me out over it and calls me irresponsible.

I may sound ungrateful, but I'm really not. I really can't complain about my childhood. It's my teen years that I hated the most. I knew my real father as the man who came to give me money, or to take me shopping to buy things. He was very well off and he proved it to me. But I didn't want his fucking money. He deprived me of his presence. He deprived me of his love. What is money to try and replace that? I'll tell ya, it ain't shit. So I threw all of that in his face. I guess that's why he's been so reluctant to contact me now. He knows I hate what he did. All my life I've had negative feelings about my father due to the fact that in my eyes his time was too precious to spend with me. All these years I've denied ever having needed him, loved him, missed him, or wanting him. Now I wonder. I remember when I was real small. He would come in, pick me up, and put me on his shoulders. You see, my father was real tall and skinny and when he would lift me up, it seemed like—oh God—it was to the ceiling. It seemed so high to me. But I would hold my breath and close my eyes and in a few seconds I was on top of the world.

Teenage prostitutes, and the men who exploit them, have developed a negative self-image and considerable hostility toward members of the opposite sex. They are at risk of remaining in the criminal subculture as adults, and if they do not find better role models and opportunities that is the most likely prognosis. But these teenagers, street wise and cynical as they are, are not "lost" or "fallen," even though they may think of themselves in such terms. Timely intervention by caring adults could counteract the experiences that led them into prostitution and could guide them onto more constructive paths to maturity.

13

Getting Rid of Troublemakers: High School Disciplinary Procedures and the Production of Dropouts

Christine Bowditch

Christine Bowditch examines the school as a social institution that has the power to weaken the bond between youths and society. Bowditch appropriates insights from labeling theory and related interactionist perspectives to illuminate the ways in which school officials interpret, negotiate, and administer rules and apply them to students who come to their attention as "troublemakers." She argues that the social processes involved in schools' effort to rid themselves of troubled youths by suspending or expelling them may be an "important but largely unacknowledged mechanism through which schools" inadvertently increase crime and perpetuate social inequality in our society.

QUESTIONS ABOUT SCHOOLS AND STRATIFICATION HAVE BEEN AD-dressed at both the macro- and the micro-level and from the full spectrum of theoretical perspectives (Karabel & Halsey 1977). Although the dominant research tradition has looked to the characteristics of students or their families to explain patterns of school performance and subsequent occupational placement, a significant and growing body of scholarship has underscored the role played by the organization of schools and the practices of school personnel (e.g., Anderson 1982; Cicourel & Kitsuse 1977; Connell et al. 1982; Corcoran 1985; Fine 1991; Rutter et al. 1979; Weis et al. 1989). Both lines of research, until quite recently, have focused on differences between college-bound students and those who move into the work force after graduation. However, since the mid-1980s a resurgent interest in urban poverty has directed attention to high school dropouts and

"Getting Rid of Troublemakers: High School Disciplinary Procedures and the Production of Drop-outs," *Social Problems* 40, no. 4 (1993): 493–509. Reprinted by permission of the author and the University of California Press.

275

to the factors that distinguish them from graduates (Ekstrom et al. 1987; Fine 1986; Hahn & Danzberger 1987; Morrow 1986; Peng 1983; Rumberger 1983).

Dropout research has found that a disproportionate number of inner-city Hispanic and black students leave school before graduation and has identified a series of factors that place such students "at risk"[1] of dropping out: students are least likely to complete high school if they come from a low-income background, are frequently absent or truant, have a record of school disciplinary problems, are failing classes, and are overage in grade (Borus & Carpenter 1983; Ekstrom et al. 1987; Peng 1983; Rumberger 1983). Dropouts are also more likely to feel alienated from school and less likely to get along with their teachers (Wagenaar 1987). According to one conventional interpretation of these data, students become discouraged with multiple experiences of failure and walk away from school (see Finn 1989); hence a proposed solution to the dropout problem has been to convince "at risk" students to remain in school and to support them in their struggle to graduate.

Although this goal has become the publicly stated objective of many urban school districts, experience as well as research teaches that other pressures can subvert such ideals (see Fine 1991; Kozol 1991). This paper examines some of those countervailing forces. Specifically, this paper analyzes the routine disciplinary activities in an inner-city high school and shows that these policies and practices encouraged school workers to "get rid of" students deemed to be "troublemakers." Significantly, the indicators used to identify "troublemakers" were the very "risk factors" that emerge in the research on dropouts. The exclusion of "troublemakers," sometimes explicitly against their wishes, calls into question precisely why such students are "at risk." Are students at risk because they truly cannot or will not finish school? Or are they at risk because school personnel label their behaviors or attitudes as troublesome and, on that basis, encourage their departure from school? Answers to these questions can help us understand the role schools play in perpetuating social inequality.

▨ Discipline and Dropout

As previous scholarship has noted, the category "dropout," as employed by school districts and educational researchers, often includes "pushouts," "stop-outs,"[2] and those who fail academically, as well as disaffected students who decide to leave (Fine 1991; Hahn & Danzberger 1987; Morrow 1986). The number of students who leave via these routes is unknown since these paths to early school withdrawal are masked in the official statistics. Yet, in at least one study, as many as a quarter of the "dropouts" reported that they were discharged coercively (Fine 1991).

Recent scholarship has raised questions about how student characteristics interact with institutional practices in producing dropouts (Farrell 1988; Fine 1991; Miller 1988; Pittman 1986; Toles et al. 1986; Weis et al. 1989). Even though research has begun to examine how school environments produce truancy, academic failure, or disobedience, the relationship between these student be-haviors and dropping out is either ignored or treated as essentially unproblem-atic (Fine [1991] is a notable exception). Little has been done to examine how schools selectively label and respond to student actions.

The fact that African-American students experience a significantly higher rate of school suspension than do whites (Hahn & Danzberger 1987; Yudof 1975) as well as a higher dropout rate, underscores the importance of looking at disciplinary procedures. Recent findings seem to refute charges of racism in the use of suspension, but research in other institutional settings gives us rea-son to remain skeptical. When a student's past disciplinary record, grades, and demeanor are taken into account, neither race nor socioeconomic status ex-plains the type of disciplinary action taken by school officials (McCarthy & Hoge 1987). Parallel findings emerge from research on juvenile court disposi-tions (Cohen & Kleugel 1987; see also Empey 1982; Tittle 1980); however, the way certain youth come to police attention in the first place and the factors that influence police decisions to take official action—in other words, to con-struct a "prior" record—is connected to race and class (e.g., Morash 1984; Sampson 1986). We need to question, therefore, how school workers construct the records that "explain" suspensions. We need a much clearer understanding of how grades, demeanor, and prior record are linked in practice to suspen-sions, since a record of suspensions increases a student's "dropout" risk.

■ Theoretical Perspective

Following the research tradition established by Cicourel and Kitsuse (1977), this paper investigates how routine administrative decisions and actions affect a student's passage through high school. Whereas Cicourel and Kitsuse looked at the counselor's role in selecting students who will go on to college, this paper examines the disciplinarian's role in selecting students who will be "dropped."

The theoretical framework for this investigation borrows from both the la-beling perspective in criminology, which itself is informed by both conflict theory and symbolic interactionism (Paternoster & Iovanni 1989), and the "negotiated-order" approach to the study of organizations (Maines & Charlton 1985). According to the labeling perspective,[3] people in positions of formal authority—such as school board members or state legislators—define "de-viance" through a process of conflict and negotiation with other interested players. Practices at the organizational level—in this case, within schools—determine whose behavior fits those formal definitions of deviance. Analysis of school practices draws on the negotiated-order approach to the study of or-ganizations. That approach acknowledges that formal rules organize and define an agency's work, but calls attention to the fact that workers' informal, negotiated understandings determine the meaning and implementation of rules. Workers use and interpret the formal rules governing client interactions in ways that allow them to simplify their own work conditions; accommodate coworkers' expectations or routines; and pursue their own, unofficial understanding of the agency's proper goals (Lipsky 1980). Although research findings have been mixed, some labeling studies have concluded that the accused person's class or racial status makes him or her more vulnerable to being officially labeled (Paternoster & Iovanni 1989).

Labeling theory also addresses the source of "secondary deviance" (Becker 1963; Lemert 1967). In some instances, labeling produces additional deviance by strengthening identification with and commitment to deviance. However, since the accused individual's social, political, and economic resources shape the capacity to reject or mitigate the stigma of a deviant label, labeling may produce additional deviance merely by cutting off access to legitimate resources and opportunities. Alternatively, a social network which provides support and resources may allow an individual to renegotiate or disavow a deviant label (Paternoster & Iovanni 1989). Thus, the power and social resources attached to class and racial status may affect both the initial interpretation of a person's actions and the consequences following from that interpretation.

Methodological Approach

A labeling or interactionist perspective calls for an investigation of the tacit, unofficial rules employed by school workers as they engage in routine organizational activities, and thus favors an ethnographic approach to research (Cicourel & Kitsuse 1977; Mehan 1992). Accordingly, this paper draws on qualitative data collected as part of a case study of DuBois High School conducted between the spring of 1984 and the spring of 1987; the bulk of classroom observation was done during the 1985/86 school year. (All names, including the school's, have been changed.) Although I spoke regularly, throughout the study, to the school's disciplinary workers and security staff, most of the material considered in this paper comes from two 10-day periods of intensive observation in the boys' discipline office. The materials include written observations of daily disciplinary activities; notes on frequent *in situ* discussions with teachers, disciplinarians, nonteaching assistants (NTAs), students, and a small number of parents; tape-recorded *post hoc* interviews with key players in a particular case of a "troublemaker"; and publicly available disciplinary documents generated by the district and the school. I did not have access to confidential materials in student records except in cases where the materials were presented in a conference I attended or when a disciplinarian chose to show me a student file he or she thought I might find interesting.

The Field Setting

DuBois High was a troubled, inner-city school. Its all-black student body[4] came from an area of a highly segregated northern city where half of the adults never completed high school (Bureau of the Census 1983), almost half of the school's students lived in poverty, and more than 60 percent had only one parent or guardian at home (school figures 1984).[5] Many of the teenage girls had children of their own and most of the boys belonged to one of the area's five or six [street] corner groups or neighborhood gangs.

In the decade before my study, enrollment at DuBois had declined steadily as many students in its catchment area found their way to city magnet schools or private or parochial high schools. Of the more than 1,600 students still on the school's rolls, many came late, cut classes, or just did not attend. While I was there, as many as 400 missed school daily. Another 100 or more students arrived late. Two hundred or more students cut certain classes on a regular basis; perhaps as many or more skipped some of their classes on occasion.

Most of the students worked substantially below grade level. California Achievement Test scores for 1983 showed that while no student scored above the 85th percentile in reading, 53 percent scored below the 16th percentile and another 40 percent scored between the 16th and 49th percentiles. Records of school grades provided additional evidence of low achievement. Figures from the math department for the 1984/85 school year, for instance, showed that 74 percent of all tenth graders failed math. As a consequence of the widespread academic failure, each year the school retained in grade approximately a quarter of all its tenth graders.

Student disorder and disobedience figured prominently both in the public's perception of the school and in the school's self-assessment. DuBois frequently suspended a half dozen or more students each day; by the end of the year, more than a quarter of its students were suspended at least once, and many had multiple or serial suspensions.

Despite these facts, I did not encounter scenes of violence or chaos. Teachers did not complain of belligerence or open hostility; instead they talked about apathy, silliness, inattention, and poor attendance. During my months of fieldwork, I witnessed daily the essentially familiar scenes of high school life.

Students sent from class, picked up in the halls, or brought in by the police for truancy, misbehavior, or more serious misconduct all went to the discipline office, a crowded, first floor office divided into a small waiting area and four inner offices. Although they shared a physical space, girls' and boys' discipline was administered separately. Three disciplinarians handled cases involving boys and two disciplinarians dealt with girls.

The discipline office could go from complete quiet to the confusion of three or four cases without notice. In addition to the discipline staff, three or four nonteaching assistants, two district security officers assigned to the school, two city police officers assigned to the school, various teachers, one or two of the school's counselors, 20 or 30 students, and 5 to 10 parents moved in and out of the office in the course of a day. The design of the office ensured little privacy or protection from the noise and confusion of other cases. Just inside the

Table 13.1 California Achievement Test Schoolwide Distribution for Reading

Percentile	1980	1981	1982	1983
<16th	49	48	47	53
16th–49th	42	43	44	40
50th–84th	8	8	8	8
85th–100	0	1	1	0

door to the office, a half dozen mismatched classroom chairs placed between a couple of battered file cabinets and a table scattered with outdated school notices formed a waiting area. But since the partitions that separated the disciplinarians' offices from that area did not rise completely to the ceiling and were fitted with opaque glass, waiting parents and students could monitor much of the "private" conversation and activity; shouted comments or angry remarks in one conference often intruded upon other conferences.[6]

▪ Disciplinary Work

Within the school's bureaucratic organization, the discipline office staff's specialized tasks were to maintain files on the documented misbehavior of DuBois students, confer with students charged with rule violations, determine punitive actions to be taken against students, contact the parents of students who had violated school rules, and process the forms documenting disciplinary actions and protecting due process. Specific and extensive rules from the school district defined misconduct and outlined policies, procedures, and proper documentation for disciplinary actions.

The disciplinarian's responsibility, when a student entered the office, was to determine what the student had done, assess the seriousness of the offense, and take the appropriate disciplinary action. Most of the routine work involved either dealing with students who were late for class, caught cutting class, or accused of disrupting class, or meeting with students and their parents for the required conference following a suspension. Less routine, but still fairly common work involved determining punishments for students who were caught fighting; found in possession of marijuana; accused of theft, vandalism, or wall-writing; caught drinking alcohol; or charged with threatening a teacher. In rare instances, the disciplinary office handled cases involving a weapon, the sale of drugs, or violence directed against a teacher.[7]

Neither the formal description of disciplinary activities nor the rules and procedures governing the discipline office fully captured its operational practice. Disciplinary practice reflected the negotiated definitions, routines, and expectations developed among coworkers, and ongoing contests over work, authority, and responsibility within the school and between the school and parents.

Disciplinarians relied on informally developed understandings about the discipline office's goals, the typical forms of student misconduct the office should handle, the types of students who normally caused trouble, and the standard strategies for dealing with misconduct (see Sudnow 1965; Waegel 1981). Within this context, official rules became a resource for workers to regulate the conditions of their work and to pursue informally identified goals (see Lipsky 1980).

To complete its work, the discipline staff interacted with teachers, NTAs, security personnel, administrators, parents, and students. Although school workers' jobs were formally coordinated, they frequently contested the boundaries of their authority and responsibility. Teachers, for example, negotiated their own strategies of classroom control—some taking a "hard line" allowing no deviation from formal rules, some using rules selectively to "contain problems" rather than to enforce obedience—and therefore made different demands on the discipline office (see Bittner 1967; Rubinstein 1973). Each student a teacher sent to the discipline office was, in essence, a test case of that teacher's authority. The discipline office's handling of the student determined whether the school's coercive power endorsed the teacher's definition of the situation or refuted it.

The nature of the disciplinarians' work meant the student's behavior was not interpreted in terms of its threat to one teacher's struggle for authority and classroom control. Instead, a student's behavior was judged in relation to the other students processed through the office. The staff was concerned with regulating and controlling its work, protecting its authority, and, most important, maintaining the institution's authority.

Because disciplinarians judged student misconduct with reference to the concerns of the school as a whole, they sometimes disagreed with teachers over what types of problems required the intervention of their office, complaining "this is something the teacher should have handled." In those instances, they typically took no action or very limited action against a student. In other cases, where the disciplinarian agreed with the teacher's assessment, punitive actions, especially severe punitive actions, were occasionally blocked by the principal. The principal shared their concern for the school's interests, but nonetheless had to evaluate both student behavior and staff authority within the context of complaints or pressures from parents and the district, or with regard to the school's public image.

Disciplinary Penalties
The sanctions available to the disciplinary staff were few. Beyond talking to students, and short of transferring or expelling them, disciplinarians could hold students out of class, contact their parents, or enforce one to five day suspensions. Disciplinarians rarely, if ever, contacted parents outside the context of a suspension. Official responses to misbehavior were, thus, limited in practice to

Table 13.2 Reasons for the Suspension of Boys (N = 244)

	October 1986	February 1987	March 1987	Total	Percentage
Disruption of school	6	1	3	10	4.1
Damage/theft of school property	1	1	3	5	1.2
Damage/theft of private property	1	1	0	2	0.8
Assault on school property	0	0	1	1	0.4
Physical abuse of another student	5	5	11	21	8.6
Possession of weapon	0	0	2	2	0.8
Possession of drugs or alcohol	0	1	5	6	2.4
Repeated school violations	28	22	36	86	35.2
Disruptive/offensive language	14	19	12	45	18.4
No reason listed	27	6	35	68	27.8
Total	82	56	108	246	99.7

either a simple reprimand, holding the student in the office until the next class period, or a suspension.

The district's "Code Prohibiting Serious Student Misconduct" identified and defined the nine categories of misconduct that warranted suspension: (1) disruption of the school, (2) damage, destruction or theft of school property, (3) damage, destruction or theft of private property, (4) assault on a school employee, (5) physical abuse of a student or other person not employed by the school, (6) possession of weapons and dangerous instruments, (7) possession or use of narcotics, alcoholic beverages, and stimulant drugs, (8) repeated school violations, and (9) disruptive and/or offensive use of language (District Manual on Policies and Procedures 1984).[8]

At DuBois High, an estimated 35.2 percent of the boys' suspensions were for "repeated school violations."[9] That figure jumped to 63 percent with the inclusion of suspensions for which no specific reason was listed. Presumably, most unspecified cases were repeated school violations rather than some more specific and serious violation. A full 81.4 percent of the suspensions could be accounted for by adding the category "disruptive and offensive use of language." These figures demonstrate how heavily the discipline staff at DuBois, in accord with national patterns (see note 7), relied on suspensions to punish behaviors that threatened the school's authority rather than its safety. The figures also emphasize the amount of discretion called for in disciplinary work. The issue of "labeling" entered when we examine how disciplinarians determine the definition of "repeated" violations and the instances when profane or obscene language warrants punishment.

The procedural instructions in the district manual for "repeated school violations" explained that the rule "basically . . . is aimed at those students whose conduct is consistently at odds with normal school discipline"; these were the students disciplinarians defined as "troublemakers." The instructions went on to caution that a pupil should be suspended only when unaccepted behavior continued after all available school resources and services were tried or when an exceptionally serious act that warranted such action was committed.

Since the instructions did not define "available school resources and services," the discipline staff, in practice, operated as if any "legitimate" case entering their office came there either because it was "an exceptionally serious act," or because previous efforts by teachers, or perhaps counselors, had failed. Thus, beyond assessing whether "a teacher should have handled this," disciplinarians made little or no effort to consider other school services.[10]

■ The Social Construction of a Troublemaker

Conflicts over disciplinary practice arose because the definition of what constituted misconduct was itself problematic. Although the authors of the school's rules identified the categories of punishable student behavior, they realized judgments about the meaning and seriousness of any particular behavior depended upon its specific social setting, the student's intent, and the responses of others present. Understandably, some categories of misconduct, such as "disrupting class," were necessarily vague or ambiguous. The immediate context of a student's actions distinguished silliness or immaturity from insubordination or disruptiveness. Situational factors such as intent or provocation changed the meaning of an act. For that very reason, district regulations allowed disciplinarians considerable discretion.

In practice, disciplinarians rarely questioned students about the details of their misbehavior or the reasons behind them. Instead, after identifying the charge against the student, they moved on to a series of questions about grades, attendance, previous suspensions, and, in some instances, the student's year in school, age, or plans for employment. A student's answers, rather than the particular circumstances of his actions, identified the misconduct's meaning to the disciplinarians. Only when a student's academic profile seemed to violate the disciplinarians' expectations would he or she inquire further about the charges against the student. They sought to punish "types of students" more than "types of behavior."

Whereas most students occasionally violated school rules, the proper role of the discipline office, as its staff understood it, was to deal with troublemakers who persistently disregarded the institution's authority. Information on grades, attendance, and prior disciplinary problems created a profile of the student's relationship to the school used to interpret the meaning of misconduct and the appropriateness of disciplinary intervention.[11] Students who failed classes, played hookey, used drugs, or frequently troubled teachers with disruptive behavior were students who, in the minds of most school workers, did not belong in school.

The following example illustrates the use of questions to interpret the significance of a student's behavior:

> Mr. Leary picked up the next file on his desk and called out, "Is Kenneth Watson out there?" Kenneth stood up and walked over to Mr. Leary's doorway.
>
> Leary: "Kenneth?"
>
> Kenneth: "Yeah."
>
> Leary: "Sit down." Kenneth slumped into the chair in front of Mr. Leary's desk. In a combative voice: "I've got a pink slip here that says you were disrupting class. Talking. I thought we had this straightened out. Wasn't this straightened out?"
>
> Kenneth: Muttering. "Yeah, I guess so."
>
> Leary: "What do you mean, 'I guess so?' If it was straightened out, you wouldn't be here." He paused, looking down at the pink slip. "It says here you were talking in class. So what is this? *I've got three others here for the same thing.* Now what's the problem?"
>
> Kenneth: "I don't know."
>
> Leary: "Well, we already brought your mother in, didn't we?" Kenneth shook his head slightly, looking puzzled. "Yeah, you were present at the meeting." Mr. Leary looked again at the file. "What class is it?"
>
> Kenneth: "Math."
>
> Leary: "How are you doing in it?" Kenneth shrugged. "Well, *did you pass math in the last report?*"
>
> Kenneth nodded. "What grade did you get, then?" Mr. Leary shouted, clearly exasperated.
>
> Kenneth: After a slight hesitation, "Two A's and a B. I think I had an 89 for the last report and A's for the ones before."
>
> Leary: Visibly surprised. "You have A's and B's in math?" Slight pause, then, "You're in what, general math?"
>
> Kenneth: "Algebra."
>
> Leary: *"Are you passing all your classes?"*
>
> Kenneth: "Yeah."
>
> Leary: "Were you on the honor roll?"
>
> Kenneth: "I don't know," still mumbling, still sullen.
>
> Leary: "What do you mean you don't know! Were you in the lottery?"
>
> Kenneth: He gestured over his shoulder in the direction of the main hallway, "That attendance thing?"
>
> Leary: "No! We have one for grades, too. Didn't you go to the awards assembly?"
>
> Kenneth: "Oh, yeah. I went to that. I got a slip . . . said to report. . . I didn't know."
>
> Leary: Quite frustrated. "Yeah, well I was there. I gave out the certificate and prize." He paused and looked down at the file again. *"What does this mean, 'talking in class'?"*
>
> Kenneth: Still mumbling. "We have these preclass exercises on the board. When I got that done, I end up talking."
>
> Leary: "What, you have a problem to do when you get to class?"
>
> Kenneth: "Yeah."

Leary: In a reasoning tone, "Well, if you finish up early can't you help out someone who isn't as bright?"

Kenneth: "He wants us to do our own work."

Leary: "Yeah, well, ok. That doesn't mean you have to talk. You make it sound like you can't control yourself. Why don't you do some studying for another class? *A bright boy like you shouldn't have to go through all this.* So what's the solution to this problem?"

Kenneth: "I guess I shouldn't talk in class."

Leary: "Alright. *This is Mickey Mouse stuff.*" He paused. "You wait outside until the next period."

After Kenneth left the office, Mr. Leary turned to me and explained, "Clearly a classroom problem. *A kid like that can understand if you reason with him. It's not like some of the barely educable kids we see in here. The teacher—I don't know what the problem is—just wants to pass along the problem to us. We get a lot of that here. This teacher should just take him aside and talk to him, even if he has to do it every week.*" (April 1984; italics added)

During my observation, three pink slips for disrupting class, a prior interview with a parent, and a sullen and uncooperative demeanor normally led to a student's suspension, a significant act in the creation of an official record. Disciplinarians typically did not ask students, "What does this mean?" Instead, they took "talking in class" as a known and unproblematic form of disruption.

In the case above, Mr. Leary began with the assumption that Kenneth, a student repeatedly sent to the office for disrupting class, must be a troublemaker. In the course of their interaction, however, Kenneth became a kid you could reason with; the talking in class became "Mickey Mouse stuff"; the whole problem became something the teacher should have dealt with. Each of these reconstructions occurred because Kenneth's grades altered the meaning of this behavior.

In most school workers' minds, students who received high grades demonstrated that they accepted the school's requirements and, presumably, acknowledged the value of the school's work. According to this reasoning, Kenneth obviously posed no challenge to the school's aims or operation—and indeed was one of its few success stories. Therefore, his talking in class, even if it recurred weekly, represented not a "repeated violation of school rules" but a problem with the teacher's ability to control the class.

▨   Parental Involvement

A student's vulnerability to suspension, and to identification as a "troublemaker," may also depend upon his or her parents' ability to influence the actions of school personnel. As one NTA observed, "The only time you ever see a parent is when the kid is suspended and they have to come in." Indeed, according to district policy, "The primary purpose for the use of suspension is for the involvement of parents in the remediation of a problem."[12] In interviews, disciplinarians confirmed this objective. Ms. Gordon, an NTA working as a disciplinarian, told me: "Suspension is strictly for communication. Not to hurt the student or punish the student." Both she and the others did, however, qualify that objective with conditions such as "unless we can't keep the kid in school because it was something serious or he completely defies authority."

Although all agreed that suspensions served to bring parents into the school, the understanding among most school workers about what constituted "involvement of the parent in the remediation of a problem" challenged the claim that suspensions had no punitive intent. School workers expected parents to accept the school's authority and to support its goals and practices. They expected parents to force their children to comply with the school's rules. If parents suggested, through their words and demeanor, that they accepted the school's authority and shared its judgment of their child, then disciplinarians interpreted "involvement" as "notification." They informed the parents of the student's misbehavior and frequently suggested strategies for controlling the student's actions. However, if a parent either challenged the disciplinarian's version of events or argued that the student was responsible for him or herself, "involvement" became more punitive in intent. One teacher explained how a student's suspension would punish the parent and thereby encourage her to support the school's efforts:

> If you got to take a day off from work because of something your child has done, that's going to make you put more pressure on him. If you can't come up here, then you keep him home until you can come up here. He becomes your problem for four or five days. You got to worry about what he's doing in your apartment or your house while you're at work. Now you're a little more concerned about this. (Mr. Fisk, May 1987)

The relatively disadvantaged status of most parents vis-à-vis school workers meant that many parents received disrespectful and dismissive treatment.[13] Parents had few, if any, social or political resources with which to challenge a disciplinarian's actions. Freed from the constraints more powerful, higher status parents might have imposed, disciplinarians reverted to three tactics when they faced opposition from students and parents: (1) they denigrated the parenting skills of the mother or father; (2) they threatened the student with failure, arrest, or expulsion—frequently without the power or intent to make good their threat; and (3) they explicitly denied any personal responsibility or concern for resolving the problem.

In the course of a reinstatement conference, Carl told Mr. Weis, "She [the teacher] seen me, I was coming out of the bathroom, but she closed the door and wouldn't let me in." His mother characterized this as an "involuntary cut." Weis countered by repeating the rule, "If you're late to class, you're not allowed in class. It's a cut." The mother muttered something about knowing all about it since she'd gone to school, too.

> Weis: *"Perhaps if you talked to your son—"*
> Mother: "I talk to Carl every day. . . but I have to go to work, and sleep, I can't watch him every minute. And he is 16. . ."

Weis (to Carl): *"You want to go to disciplinary school? Or drop out?"*
(To mother): "Cuz that's where he's headed. *We won't take him for a third year in tenth grade. Not at 17.* (Mother mutters something.) You have a complaint that you're not gettin' serviced properly, there's a principal. . . . I really have a problem that you didn't insist on getting his second report [card]. *How important is education to you? I know if I had kids, I wouldn't let them get away with that . . .* unless you're going to support him for the rest of your life." (March 1987, italics added)

Mr. Weis told Carl's mother that he needed more responsibility and discipline at home. She claimed that her son acted responsibly at home, it was only when he came to school that he "acted like a fool." During the course of this discussion, someone delivered Carl's grades to Mr. Weis which showed he was failing all of his classes. After a few minutes of berating Carl for his grades, Mr. Weis said, "*I have no time for this. I am writing here, 'to be dropped from school at age 17 if there is no improvement in grades and attendance.'* So you'll receive a letter this summer, when we make our review." As they left the office, Mr. Weis turned to me and said, "All bluff." I asked, "You can't drop him?" Weis said, "Naw." "Will he get a letter?" I asked. He answered, "No."

Mr. Weis admitted to me that he was bluffing; but in such an example his threat's impact came less from his actual power to expel the student—which, informally, he could and had done—than from his presentation of the school as unforgiving and unconcerned. It was not, in fact, unusual to hear him say to a parent: "This is your problem. You'll have to deal with it. I'll readmit him, but—I don't mind, I'll keep suspending him. It's not my problem" (April 1984).

This posture by a school official seems likely to affect "secondary deviance," that is, the student's continued violation of the school's expectations. Mr. Weis has emphasized to Carl that the school has little stake in his success and a primarily negative vision of his social value and personal worth—the very conditions which may strengthen his hostility toward the school and to foster his commitment to the troublemaker role.[14] Even if Carl does not want to adopt the troublemaker identity, Mr. Weis has made it clear that he will be treated as one, in any case.[15] Moreover, as I have suggested above, it seems likely that Mr. Weis's easy rejection of Carl and his mother, and his willingness to push Carl out of school, is connected to their social position. A higher status mother might have been successful in her efforts to define Carl's behavior as an "involuntary cut" and to forestall his classification as a troublemaker.

▥ Getting Rid of Troublemakers

The discipline office had two strategies to get rid of students identified as troublemakers. One was to transfer the student; the other to drop the student from the roll. Transfers were of two types: "regular" transfers, arranged when students moved out of the school's catchment area; and "disciplinary transfers," known by their code as "21s." Dropping a student from the roll required that the student be 17 years old. At that age, schooling was no longer compulsory and the discipline office interpreted this to mean the school no longer had to keep the student.

Typically, if a disciplinarian sought a regular transfer for a troublesome student, arrangements were made for the student to shift his or her legal residence to the address of a relative in another part of the district. This procedure avoided the paperwork and legal proceedings of a disciplinary transfer. In the following incident, however, Mr. Weis discovered he could get rid of a troublemaker who already lived outside the normal bounds of the school. Mr. Weis began a conference with John, a boy I had seen in the office on two previous occasions, by asking, "What's your address?" After questioning, Weis discovered John's address put him in another school's catchment area. Weis called John's house:

> Hello, Mrs. Preston? . . . well you'll have to wake her up. This is DuBois High School calling. . . . Mrs. Preston, this is Carl Weis. John has been acting up again. He refused to take off his hat and has been disruptive. I have five pink slips on him. Look, I don't know why he's here and not at Northern Heights to start with. . . . Yeah, well, I'm going to write up a transfer for him and get all his records together. You'll have to come down tomorrow and take him over there and enroll him.

After John left the office, Weis turned to me and said: *"We didn't solve anything. "We just sent the problem along to Northern Heights. But we have to look out for ourselves. That's the way it is—crazy system"* (April 1984, italics added).

Although this case was unusual in that the student already lived in another school's catchment area, it was absolutely standard in intent. The goal of the discipline office, as Mr. Weis explained, was not to solve any problems a student might have, but to protect the school's operation. Thus, in the case of another transfer, Mr. Leary confirmed Mr. Weis's assessment of their goals. Mr. Leary escorted a boy and his mother out of the office and then sat down next to me. He explained:

> Now that mother came in here, her son was suspended weeks ago for having a weapon, marijuana. Now she wants him transferred to Washington High. You know, for us, that's fine. *We get rid of one.* I asked if 21 transfers helped. He said: *They help this school. They don't help the kid. But then, you can't do anything with those kids, anyway.* (March 1986, italics added)

Transfers were thus seen as an important resource for the discipline office. If they could build a sufficiently strong case, they could get rid of a troublemaker, even if he wanted to remain in the school, through the use of a disciplinary transfer. Because district rules prohibited the use of 21s on students whose only offenses were cutting class or missing school, the disciplinarians took pains to document all other forms of misconduct on potential or identified troublemakers. Since they would be used for a 21, Mr. Leary stressed the importance of being detailed and complete when making out "pink slips."

> You don't just write, "picked up for cutting class." You write, "cutting class, ran away from officer, used abusive language," all of which is true, but if you don't write it down—or if there's a disturbance in class, you write down, "shoved desks, said 'fuck you' to teacher"—you know, we're not squeamish. We write down just what they say, "fuck you" or "fuck you white mother."

Since the projected future or "career" of the forms influenced their form and content,[16] the pink slips represent an important point at which discretion or "bias" can enter into the construction of an official disciplinary record.

Once disciplinarians filed the paperwork on a 21, a parent had to come in for a conference. The parent has the right to a hearing in the district superintendent's office. If a parent does not want a hearing, he or she can sign a form during the conference transferring the child. The discipline staff and the principal work toward the goal, since all the paperwork goes to the district superintendent's office for review when the parent wants a hearing. As Mr. Leary complained: "Then they mostly do nothing. Send the kid back. Decide he needs another chance."

Student transfers were not the only means available to get rid of troublemakers. Another option used by the school was the informal expulsion of overage students. Although the state granted all students the right to attend public school until the age of 21, it did not require attendance past the age of 16. At DuBois, school workers understood that to mean that they were not required to keep a student in school once he or she turned 17.[17] It was not unusual, therefore, for disciplinarians to reason: "Look, he's already 18 and only in tenth grade. You know he can only stay in school 'til he's 21. I don't want him here. I'm going to talk to [the principal]." That logic also permitted the following scene. A police officer escorted four boys into the discipline office. The officer stopped at Weis's door. Weis sent the boys into Leary's office.

> The officer: Two with, two without IDs.
> Weis: This one I don't know. He might be an adult. I don't know if he's a juvenile. This one's a student. Doesn't come in very often.

Weis asked the boy he didn't recognize how old he was. The boy said he was 17, went to DuBois, and was in tenth grade.

> Weis: You don't go to DuBois. I just dropped you as of now. *I'm not suspending you. I'm dropping you from school.*

Weis said to the officer, in reference to the other boy who was younger:

> You're going to leave the building right now.
> Older boy: How many days suspension?

> Weis: I just told him. Two months, three months, 'til his mother comes in. (April 1986)

Although in this example the student demonstrated little interest in attending school,[18] other students who did want to attend but who ran into problems with the discipline office were also subject to the informal expulsion of an "over-age drop." In the following instance, Nicholas had missed most of his first period math classes because of familial responsibilities.

> Weis: What're you in for?
> Nicholas: Mr. Fisk suspended me cuz I missed his class.
> Weis: Let me get your folder.

He left the office and returned with the folder. To Nicholas's stepfather he said:

> As you are aware, sir, Nicholas was out of school and then let back in school. When he was readmitted, he signed a contract that he would attend school and behave himself. *Right now, he's overage, still in tenth grade, not passing [one class]. I recommend dropping him.*
> Nicholas: That's only one class!
> Weis: But that's enough. You are overage in tenth grade. You have to pass. . . .
> Nicholas: Don't you want to know why I missed—
> Weis: No reason is—you signed a contract.
> Nicholas: I had to do something for my mother.
> Weis: *You're 18 years old, third year in tenth grade, you have to set priorities. If that's to do something for your mother—you signed a contract that you would obey all the rules and attend all your classes.* You know, we wanted to transfer you before. Do you have a relative in another neighborhood? (March 1987, italics added)

The conference established that Nicholas was a classic troublemaker. He had previously been dropped from school, and was overage, behind in grade, and failing a class. Mr. Weis wanted him out of the school. Since he could not initiate a disciplinary transfer on the grounds of cutting class, Mr. Weis explored his two other options: an "overage" drop pressed on Nicholas because he had violated the terms of his readmission contract, and a regular transfer based on the pretense that Nicholas had changed residence.

It is important to note that because he did not conform to all of the school's demands, the school workers focused on how to exclude Nicholas rather than on how to solve his problems or to work around them. As I learned from lengthy interviews with both Nicholas and his stepfather, Nicholas had tried to work within the system. As he told me:

> I have this first period class and I'm supposed to be there at five minutes before eight. And I have to take my nieces to day care in the morning. . . . They

live with me, and there's no one else there, you know, that could take them. It's inconvenient for my mother cuz she leaves so early. And their mom is in Florida. So I was the only one that could take them. So I was taking them, and I wasn't making the class. But I was bringing notes and stuff in to show them. . . . Mr. Fisk wouldn't contact my mother or nothing. He just kept on telling me the notes aren't going to do no good. . . . I talked to my mother at one time. And that's when she told me she was going to try to work something out [about taking the girls to day care]. But at the moment to keep taking them. . . . You know, so that's when I went to see the counselor. She told me to see [someone else] . . . he was absent two days I brought in the note. . . . Probably if I went to see [the counselor] earlier, I would have probably got help. But I didn't know who to go to see. I thought he was the teacher, I was supposed to give the notes and all that to him. . . . [When I did see the counselor], she was saying there's not much you can do, and everything. I could have got a roster change if it was like the beginning.

The school workers blamed his mother for putting Nicholas in the position of having to care for his sister's daughters and blamed him for accepting that responsibility. Mr. Fisk explained:

Why should that responsibility become his? The parent has to take more active—why would you thrust that responsibility on your offspring if it's creating problems in the school? . . . If he's thrust into this situation and he knows it's threatening his possibilities for graduation, for promotion, for passing this class, if he's truly serious about passing, he has to lighten the load. And there's only one load he can lighten. And that's the supervision of this [niece]. So that means sitting down with whomever.

Mr. Fisk assumed that the solution to the problem involved "sitting down" with someone. Nicholas, therefore, was penalized for his mother's inability or unwillingness to make his education the family's priority.

Nicholas confronted a system which his parents had little skill in handling or power to influence, and which rejected his own efforts. Had he come from a middle-income family, it is likely he would have fared better. Not only would it have been less likely for such a family/school conflict to arise, but a middle-income parent would have had greater success in manipulating the bureaucratic requirements of the school system. As it was, Nicholas's family circumstances allowed—one might even argue, encouraged—both Mr. Fisk and Mr. Weis to dismiss him as another troublemaker who did not value education.

▩ Being "At Risk"

When I spoke to Ms. Riley, the vice principal of DuBois High, she was not "amazed" that 335 of her students had "dropped out" in the previous year. Instead, citing how many kids faced problems at home or on the streets, she was amazed that so many of them "made it." DuBois High students who face disruption, violence, substance abuse, or conflicting obligations to school and family were understandably distracted, uncooperative, or truant. Manifesting those symptoms of broader social ills, however, brought them into contact with the discipline office. There, troubled students were rather easily reconceptualized as troublemakers. And troublemakers were readily seen as undeserving of the school's services. This process is all the more disturbing when we consider that inner-city African Americans and Hispanics are disproportionately likely to suffer from such social ills. The activities of the discipline office, which routinely identified "troublemakers" and "got rid of" them through suspensions and involuntary drops, may be one important but largely unacknowledged mechanism through which schools perpetuate the racial and class stratification of the larger society.

Ironically, educational research has served to legitimate the actions of the disciplinarians. In a conference to reinstate a student following his suspension for poor attendance, Mr. Leary remarked:

> I'm talking to you like a man . . . *this is a turning point in your life. You can go either way: follow the rules and graduate, or drop out of the whole school system.* You signed this contract. I'm going to reinstate you. But I tell you quite frankly, you got to get up, whatever you got to do, and get to school. I know, there's no doubt in my mind, [the principal] *is going to want to drop you. Not because he wants to be mean, but statistics prove it out.* (March 1986, italics added)

Indeed, the statistics prove that students are most likely to "drop out" of high school if they come from a low-income background, are frequently absent or truant, have a record of school suspensions, are failing classes, and are over-age in grade (Hahn & Danzberger 1987; Natriello 1986). But what is proven? Those factors are the very indicators that disciplinarians used to define troublemakers and that led to suspensions, disciplinary transfers, and involuntary drops. Although it is unwise to generalize from the findings of one case study, we can nevertheless ask: are "risk factors" correlated with "dropping out" because they are used routinely by school workers to expel students? If that is the case, then disciplinarians' daily activities play an important role in regulating social mobility.

▪ Notes

1. For a critical discussion of "at risk" see Margonis (1992).

2. "Pushouts" refers to students who are forced to leave school. "Stopouts" refers to students who withdraw from school and then return.

3. See Rist (1977) for an explanation of labeling theory's utility in the study of schools.

4. Although all of the students were African Americans, the faculty's racial composition reflected the metropolitan area's labor pool and thus included many whites.

5. These figures come from a report prepared by the school for the visiting committee of the association charged with evaluating the school for accreditation. For reasons of

confidentiality, I cannot give the full name of this publication or of other reports issued by the school or the school district.

6. The irregular tempo of activity in the discipline office made it difficult to gather accurate, quantifiable data on the number, type, and disposition of cases. Although I solicited staff members' help at one point, asking each of them to mark on a chart the type and disposition of each case they handled, I found their recordkeeping unreliable. Moreover, such records masked the very assumptions and decisions I sought to investigate.

7. National studies report that most high school suspensions are for nonthreatening behavior—defying authority, chronic tardiness, chronic absence, and use of profanity and vulgarity. Black students are suspended three times as often as whites (Hahn & Danzberger 1987).

8. The physical education department also suspended students who were unprepared for gym class on three occasions. Those "one day" suspensions were not processed through the discipline office and are not a part of my report.

9. These figures come from the suspension reports compiled by one of the disciplinarians for the district. I selected three months, at random, from the 1986/87 school year and computed the percentages. These figures are compatible with my observations in the discipline office. The total number of boys suspended in those three months was 244.

10. Students had extremely limited access to any form of counseling. The few "guidance counselors" in the school each had responsibility for hundreds of students and seemed to limit their "guidance" to brief conferences on scheduling or attendance problems. The only other counselor I was aware of was a part-time drug counselor from a private agency.

11. McCarthy and Hoge (1987) found that school disciplinary sanctions were influenced by the student's past official record, grades, and "general demeanor in school." These findings suggest that the practices of the discipline staff at DuBois conform to those at other schools.

12. The other purposes of suspension noted in the district's guidelines were: removing the student from the scene of difficulty, diffusing a situation when the final outcome is not yet assured, and displaying the school's dissatisfaction with the student's behavior.

13. The relatively homogeneous background of DuBois students prohibited a comparative assessment of how a parent's race and class affected her or his treatment by disciplinarians.

14. Crespo (1974) found that a school's disciplinary responses to "skippers" (truants) did indeed lead to the amplification of deviance and, in many cases, encouraged students to drop out.

15. See Anderson's discussion of how "social selves" are constructed in social interaction: as he states, "a person is somebody because others allow him to be" (1976:38).

16. See Meehan (1986) for a discussion of how the projected use of police records shape their form and content as well as for a discussion of how police officers infer the meaning or accuracy of a record.

17. In the official statistics for the 1985/86 school year, all but six of the 335 dropouts were categorized as "overage."

18. Crespo noted, "students who do not find school rewarding are more prepared to consider missing it. In this sense, the tracking system provides the invitational edge to the activity of skipping" (1974:133). Students in lower tracks are offered less stimulating and less valuable educational experiences (Oakes 1985). We must remember, therefore, that the school bears some responsibility for its students' attitudes and behaviors.

References

Anderson, Carolyn. 1982. "The Search for School Climate: A Review of the Research." *Review of Educational Research* 52:368–420.

Anderson, Elijah. 1976. *A Place on the Corner.* Chicago: University of Chicago Press.

Becker, Howard. 1963. *Outsiders: Studies in the Sociology of Deviance.* New York: Free Press.

Bittner, Egon. 1967. "The Police on Skid-row: A Study of 'Peace Keeping.'" *American Sociological Review* 32:699–715.

Borus, Michael E. & Susan A. Carpenter. 1983. "A Note on the Return of Dropouts to High School." *Youth & Society* 14:501–07.

Cicourel, Aaron V. & John I. Kitsuse. 1977. "The School as a Mechanism of Social Differentiation." In J. Karabel & A. Halsey (eds.), *Power and Ideology in Education.* New York: Oxford University Press.

Cohen, Lawrence & James Kleugel. 1987. "Determinants of Juvenile Court Dispositions: Ascriptive and Achieved Factors in Two Metropolitan Courts." *American Sociological Review* 43:162–76.

Connell, R. W., Dean J. Ashenden, Sandra Kessler & Gary W. Dowsett. 1982. *Making the Difference: Schools, Families and Social Division.* Boston, MA: George Allen & Unwin.

Corcoran, Thomas. 1985. "Effective Secondary Schools." In *Reaching for Excellence: An Effective Schools Sourcebook.* Washington DC: US Department of Education.

Crespo, Manuel. 1974. "The Career of the School Skipper." In J. Hass (ed.), *Decency and Deviance: Studies in Deviant Behavior.* Toronto: McClelland & Stewart.

Ekstrom, Ruth B., Margaret E. Goertz, Judith M. Pollack & Donald A. Rock. 1987. "Who Drops Out of High School and Why? Findings from a National Study." In G. Natriello (ed.), *School Dropouts: Patterns and Policies.* New York: Teachers College Press.

Empey, Lamar. 1982. *American Delinquency: Its Meaning and Construction.* Homewood, IL: Dorsey.

Farrell, Edwin. 1988. "Giving Voice to High School Students: Pressure and Boredom, Ya Know What I' Sayin'?" *American Educational Research Journal* 25:489–502.

Fine, Michelle. 1986. "Why Urban Adolescents Drop Into and Out of Public High School." In G. Natriello (ed.), *School Dropouts: Patterns and Policies.* New York: Teachers College Press.

———. 1991. *Framing Dropouts: Notes on the Politics of an Urban Public High School.* Albany: SUNY Press.

Finn, Jeremy D. 1989. "Withdrawing from School." *Review of Educational Research* 59:117–42.

Hahn, Andrew & Jacqueline Danzberger. 1987. *Dropouts in America: Enough Is Known for Action.* Washington, DC: Institute for Educational Leadership.

Karabel, Jerome & A. H. Halsey (eds.). 1977. *Power and Ideology in Education.* New York: Oxford University Press.

Kozol, Jonathan. 1991. *Savage Inequalities: Children in American Schools.* New York: Crown.

Lemert, Edwin M. 1967. *Human Deviance.* Englewood Cliffs, NJ: Prentice-Hall.

Lipsky, Michael. 1980. *Street-Level Bureaucracy: Dilemmas of the Individual in Public Services.* New York: Russell Sage.

Maines, David R. & Joy C. Charlton. 1985. "Negotiated Order Approach to the Analysis of Social Organization." In H. Faberman & R. Perinbanayagam (eds.), *Foundations of Interpretive Sociology.* Greenwich, CT: JAI Press.

Margonis, Frank. 1992. "The Cooptation of 'At Risk': Paradoxes of Policy Criticism." *Teachers College Record* 94:343–64.

McCarthy, John & Dean Hoge. 1987. "The Social Construction of School Punishment: Racial Disadvantage Out of Universalistic Process." *Social Forces* 65:1101–20.

Meehan, Albert J. 1986. "Record-keeping Practices in the Policing of Juveniles." *Urban Life* 15:70–102.

Mehan, Hugh. 1992. "Understanding Inequality in Schools: The Contribution of Interpretive Studies." *Sociology of Education* 65:1–20.

Miller, Sandra E. 1988. "Influencing Engagement through Accommodation: An Ethnographic Study of At-risk Students." *American Education Research Journal* 25:465–87.

Morash, Merry. 1984. "Establishment of a Juvenile Police Record." *Criminology* 22:97–111.

Morrow, George. 1986. "Standardizing Practice in the Analysis of School Dropouts." In G. Natriello (ed.), *School Dropouts: Patterns and Policies.* New York: Teachers College Press.

Natriello, Gary (ed.). 1986. *School Dropouts: Patterns and Policies.* New York: Teachers College Press.

Oakes, Jeannie. 1985. *Keeping Track: How Schools Structure Inequality.* New Haven, CT: Yale University Press.

Paternoster, Raymond & Leeann Iovanni. 1989. "The Labeling Perspective and Delinquency: An Elaboration of the Theory and an Assessment of the Evidence." *Justice Quarterly* 6:359–394.

Peng, Samuel S. 1983. "High School Dropouts: Descriptive Information from High School and Beyond." *National Center for Education Statistics Bulletin.*

Pittman, Robert B. 1986. "Importance of Personal, Social Factors as Potential Means for Reducing High School Dropout Rate." *High School Journal* 70:7–13.

Rist, Ray C. 1977. "On Understanding the Processes of Schooling: The Contributions of Labeling Theory." In J. Karabel & A. Halsey (eds.), *Power and Ideology in Education.* New York: Oxford University Press.

Rubenstein, Jonathan. 1973. *City Police.* Farrar, Straus & Giroux.

Rumberger, Russell W. 1983. "Dropping Out of High School: The Influence of Race, Sex, and Family Background." *American Educational Research Journal* 20:199–220.

Rutter, Michael, Barbara Maughan, Peter Moritmore & Janet Ouston. 1979. *Fifteen Thousand Hours: Secondary Schools and Their Effects on Children.* Cambridge, MA: Harvard University Press.

Sampson, Robert J. 1986. "Effects of Socioeconomic Context on Official Reaction to Juvenile Delinquency." *American Sociological Review* 51:876–85.

Skolnick, Jerome H. 1975. *Justice Without Trial.* New York: Wiley.

Sudnow, David. 1965. "Normal Crimes: Sociological Features of the Penal Code in a Public Defender's Office." *Social Problems* 12:255–76.

Tittle, Charles. 1980. "Labeling and Crime: An Empirical Evaluation." In W. Gove (ed.), *The Labeling of Deviance.* Beverly Hills, CA: Sage.

Toles, T., E. M. Schulz & W. K. Rice. 1986. "A Study of Variation in Dropout Rates Attributable to Effects of High Schools." *Metropolitan Education* 2:30–38.

Waegel, William B. 1981. "Case Routinization in Investigative Police Work." *Social Problems* 28:263–75.

Wagenaar, Theodore C. 1987. "What Do We Know about Dropping Out of High School?" In R. Corwin (ed.), *Research in Sociology of Education and Socialization.* Greenwich, CT: JAI Press.

Weis, Lois, Eleanor Farrar & Hugh G. Petrie (eds.). 1989. *Dropouts from School: Issues, Dilemmas, and Solutions.* New York: SUNY Press.

Yudof, Mark G. 1975. "Suspension and Expulsion of Black Students from the Public Schools: Academic Capital Punishment and the Constitution." *Law & Contemporary Problems* 39:374–411.

14

Organizing the Community
for Delinquency Prevention

Ronald J. Berger

*Ronald Berger examines the organization of communities and how residents
in disadvantaged urban areas have been mobilized to collectively address
the problems that exacerbate crime and delinquency. He discusses three
general models of community organization practice — locality development,
social planning, and social action — and how these models have been
applied through exemplary delinquency prevention programs that offer
valuable lessons for contemporary prevention efforts.*

JUVENILE DELINQUENCY PREVENTION ENCOMPASSES A WIDE RANGE
of practices, and over the years researchers and practitioners have had different interpretations of what "prevention" actually means.[1] In general, three preventive orientations can be identified: *primary prevention, secondary prevention,* and *tertiary prevention* (Klein and Goldston 1977). Primary prevention
attempts to keep delinquent behavior from arising in the first place; it involves
strategies directed at the entire community and not just at individuals who are
"the casualties seeking treatment" (p. vii). Secondary prevention focuses on
early diagnoses and treatment of vulnerable or "at risk" children, and tertiary
prevention aims to avoid recidivist behavior after delinquent acts have already
occurred. Some observers think it is preferable to limit the concept of prevention to primary prevention, while rehabilitation is a more appropriate term for
secondary and tertiary strategies (Gilbert 1981; Klein and Goldston 1977).

In this chapter, I evaluate approaches to delinquency prevention that em-
body the notion of primary prevention. These efforts involve large-scale intervention and social change strategies in urban areas that attempt to provide opportunities to disadvantaged youths, develop community resources, implement
institutional reform, and organize and mobilize target-area residents for collective action.[2] I employ a typology of community organization practice developed by Jack Rothman (1979a) to analyze the assumptions, objectives, and
methods underlying programs of this nature (Cox, Erlich, and Rothman 1979;
Cox et al. 1984).[3]

Rothman identified three general models of community organization practice: *locality development, social planning,* and *social action.*[4] I use these models to evaluate three historically significant delinquency prevention programs: the 1930s Chicago Area Project, the 1960s provision of opportunity programs, and the 1960s comprehensive community action projects such as Mobilization for Youth. These programs spanned a range of local and federal efforts that emphasized alteration of neighborhood, institutional, and socioeconomic conditions that were believed to cause delinquency. To a large degree, these exemplary programs established the parameters—and illuminated the prospects and pitfalls—of what all prevention programs of this nature entail. Hence there are valuable lessons to be learned from an examination of these programs, lessons that have implications for contemporary efforts to prevent juvenile delinquency.

Models of Community Organization Practice

Community organizing may be defined as "intervention at the community level oriented towards improving or changing community institutions and solving community problems" (Cox, Erlich, and Rothman 1979:3). Each of Rothman's three models—locality development, social planning, and social action—has its own assumptions, utilities, and limitations. Locality development and social planning more readily lend themselves to a consensus view of society and the maintenance of social stability. Social action is oriented toward a conflict view of society and the promotion of institutional social change. However, these approaches need not be applied in a mutually exclusive manner and can be either mixed or phased as they are applied to specific community problems.

According to Rothman (1979a), the central assumption of locality development is that community change is best brought about by enlisting the broadest range of people at the local level to collectively identify needs, goals, and solutions to problems. The basic themes include "democratic procedures, voluntary cooperation, self-help, development of indigenous leadership, and educational objectives" (p. 27). Process goals are accorded the highest priority; that is, the primary goal is to establish cooperative working relationships and widespread interest and participation in community affairs. Consensus tactics are used by the community organizers to bring various interest groups, social classes, and racial/ethnic groups together to identify common concerns. It is assumed that these groups have interests that are basically reconcilable and amenable to rational problem-solving. However, it is the process of bringing the community together, rather than the accomplishment of particular tasks, that is often central to locality development.

In the social planning approach, emphasis is placed on the design and application of controlled rational change by "experts" who possess specialized skills and knowledge. The emphasis is on task goals, that is, the completion of a specified task related to the solution of a tangible problem. Community residents are viewed as customers or beneficiaries of services and are not involved in the planning or delivery process. Social change tends to be gradual, piecemeal, apolitical, and regulated and controlled by professionals who are not themselves members of the client population. Community organizers often act as mediators between conflicting interests and attempt to tone down more radical demands.

Finally, in the social action approach, organizers seek to mobilize the economically and politically disadvantaged members of the community to make effective demands for the redistribution of resources and alteration of institutional policies. This approach may involve both task and process goals. Conflict tactics are frequently engaged in as the organizers attempt to build a large constituency capable of obtaining and utilizing power to promote their interests. Dominant political and economic groups and institutions are often the targets of change and considered at least partly responsible for the community's problems. Community organizers act as partisans and advocates for the disenfranchised rather than as neutral arbitrators.

As ideal types, locality development, social planning, and social action identify the basic assumptions underlying various large-scale delinquency prevention programs. In the following sections, I use these models to evaluate the Chicago Area Project, provision of opportunity programs, and comprehensive community action projects. While these efforts were not pure applications of any single model of community organization practice, each contained different emphases that can be illuminated by applying community organization concepts.

■ The Chicago Area Project

The Chicago Area Project (CAP) is considered to be the classic illustration of locality development as applied to juvenile delinquency, as well as the foundation for most contemporary prevention efforts (Mech 1975; Reiss 1986). Originated by sociologist Clifford Shaw in 1934, it was "the first systematic challenge to the dominance of psychology and psychiatry in public and private programs for the prevention and treatment of . . . delinquency" (Schlossman et al. 1984:2). The CAP was rooted in a theory of *social disorganization* that was developed by Shaw and his colleagues while studying the ecological distribution of crime and delinquency in different areas of Chicago (Shaw et al. 1929; Shaw and McKay 1942). Their research documented the geographical association of crime and delinquency with the conditions of urban slums: concentrated poverty and unemployment, physical dilapidation of buildings, residential overcrowding, absence of home ownership, high residential mobility, and the absence of "constructive agencies intended to promote well-being and prevent maladjustment" (Shaw et al. 1929; Shaw and McKay 1942; quoted in Sykes and Cullen 1992:292).

However, unlike the macro-level anomie-opportunity or strain theory that formed the basis of later programs (to be explained shortly), Shaw and McKay did not consider economic deprivation per se to be the central problem.[5] Rather, the social disorganization of these communities was indicative of a breakdown in adults' ability to supervise and exert informal social control over youths and to socialize them (through familial, educational, and religious institutions) to law-abiding values and behaviors. In the absence of this control, youths' "most vital and intimate social contacts [were] often limited to the spontaneous and undirected neighborhood play groups and gangs whose activities and standards may vary widely from those of . . . parents and the larger social order" (Shaw and McKay 1942:293). Over time, the traditions of these delinquent groups became self-sustaining, transmitted through successive generations as youths "have contact not only with other delinquents who are their contemporaries but also with older offenders, who in turn had contact with delinquents preceding them, and so on back to the earlier history of the neighborhood" (p. 168; see also Bursik 1988; Simcha-Fagan and Schwartz 1986).

The underlying philosophy of the CAP was that only through the collective mobilization and active participation of the entire community was it possible to impact significantly upon the problem of delinquency. The CAP was overseen by a board of directors that raised and distributed money and assisted community groups in obtaining grants to match local government funds. Various committees that operated as independent, self-governing organizations with their own names and charters were formed (Dixon and Wright 1974; Krisberg 2005; Spergel 1969).

Thus, self-help and democratic procedures were major themes of the CAP. Project staff workers functioned in an advisory role, but decisions about policies and programs were made by community members, independent of the approval or disapproval of the staff. The task for community organizers was to convince local residents to assume responsibility for the prevention of delinquency, to help them exercise more influence over their children, and to facilitate cooperation and joint problem-solving among the residents, churches, schools, courts, police, and other community groups. The focus was on building community cohesion and pride and developing residents' confidence in their ability to change their lives (Empey and Stafford 1991; Schlossman and Sedlak 1983; Schlossman et al. 1984).

The CAP pioneered a number of activities that were later adopted by other prevention programs, including the development of recreation and camping activities, youth clubs, and hobby and rap (discussion) groups. The goal of these activities was to provide youths with structured, supervised alternatives to crime; and they also served as springboards for bringing people together, counseling delinquent youths, and providing minimal employment for youth leaders. In addition, the CAP sent "detached street workers" into the community to provide "curbstone counseling" for youths and identify indigenous gang leaders who might be encouraged to commit themselves to the project's goals. Such counseling was less social work per se and more an "aggressive, omnipresent caring and monitoring of 'youth at risk' in their natural, criminogenic habitats" (Schlossman et al. 1984:15).

Efforts to intercede in matters related to the schools and juvenile justice system foreshadowed more contemporary efforts at child advocacy and diversion. School interventions involved efforts to reform educational curricula to make school more relevant to students, to mainstream students who had been incorrectly placed in classes for deficient or incorrigible youth (or conversely, place students who required special treatment into appropriate programs), to transfer students to schools with more suitable programs or personnel, and to reinstate students who had been expelled for minor delinquencies (see Chapter 13). Similarly, juvenile justice interventions involved efforts to divert youths away from the justice system and toward other appropriate community agencies where they could receive the assistance they needed. The CAP also advocated reform of correctional institutions, and it assisted parolees in their adjustment to community life (Schlossman et al. 1984).

The CAP applied the model of locality development in a purist fashion and utilized consensus tactics. The accommodative spirit was illustrated by the community's willingness to accept responsibility for the city's dilapidated physical appearance and by its decision to not indict the city's service departments. On the other hand, the assumption of consensus and cooperative problem-solving that underlies locality development was often lacking. It was difficult to find common ground between local residents and representatives of the business community, schools, churches, and the juvenile justice system. For example, attempts to enlist the help of the business community in expanding the employment opportunities for delinquent youths were not always successful. The project was also criticized for its heavy reliance on the voluntary services of the Polish Catholic Church, which was accused of using the recreational programs to proselytize potential converts, even though the Church was effective in galvanizing community support. In addition, programs in some neighborhoods were criticized for interfering with those sponsored by other groups. Even the professional staff of organizers was sometimes annoyed and upset about its loss of control over the project, suggesting a preference for a social planning approach to community organizing (Schlossman and Sedlak 1983; Schlossman et al. 1984).

One of the strongest criticisms was leveled by Saul Alinsky, the CAP's most aggressive detached worker (see Alinsky 1946). Although the CAP attempted to increase community empowerment by training indigenous leadership and intervening in institutional affairs, Alinsky argued that it was inadequate to achieve significant economic change. He advocated confrontational tactics indicative of a social action approach to community organizing in order to force more fundamental political and economic concessions from the power structure. Alinsky's frustration undoubtedly derived from a basic dilemma of locality development strategies: how to sustain community interest following mobilization when process goals are given priority over task goals (Schlossman and Sedlak 1983). It is extremely difficult to modify community relationships through indigenous neighborhood processes when the resources necessary for change come from external institutional sources (see Bursik and Grasmick 1993; note 5).

In spite of some statistical evidence (particularly regarding the parolee assistance program) that delinquency was slightly reduced by the CAP in the first decade of its operation, Shaw himself was aware of the difficulty of demonstrating conclusively the effectiveness of the project (Krisberg 2005; Schlossman et al. 1984). As he observed, trends in rates of delinquency were influenced by variations in the official definition of delinquency, changes in population composition, and variations in the administrative procedures employed by law enforcement agencies. Nevertheless, Shaw was decidedly optimistic about the success of the CAP (Schlossman and Sedlak 1983), and perhaps, as Kobrin (1959) argued, the case for the CAP ultimately rests on logical and analytic grounds. Shaw was mainly interested in demonstrating the possibility of operationalizing his analysis of social problems through particular organizational mechanisms. He believed that: (1) delinquency was symptomatic of underlying social processes; (2) simply responding on a one-to-one basis with individual youths was ineffective; and (3) the entire community must and could be organized effectively to solve its own problems.

According to Krisberg, however, by the late 1950s the "vibrant and successful" CAP was co-opted and transformed into a rather staid bureaucratic organization as its staff positions were absorbed by the Illinois State Division of Youth Services (1978:33). Similarly, Schlossman and colleagues (1984) noted that external funding agencies began to exert greater influence over the goals and priorities of CAP community groups. In this way, the CAP lost some of the autonomy characteristic of a locality development approach to community organization. Nevertheless, in an evaluation of the "modern-day" CAP, published in 1984, Schlosmann and colleagues concluded that the evidence suggested that the CAP had been an effective delinquency prevention program. As they observed, "to rediscover the CAP is to be reminded" that disadvantaged communities "still retain a remarkable capacity for pride, civility, and the exercise of a modicum of self-governance" (p. 4). Indeed, criminologists increasingly recognize that collective efficacy, as Sampson and colleagues (1997) call it, is an important element of the informal social controls that are necessary to reduce crime. Collective efficacy may be defined as "the capacity of adults in a community to work together to achieve a sense of public order" (Press 2007:30). This was indeed the central insight of the CAP: individuals in a community can work together to bring about solutions to common problems.[6]

▨ Descendants of the CAP

Many observers view the delinquency prevention programs of the 1960s as direct descendants of the CAP (Empey and Stafford 1991; Freeman, Jones, and Zucker 1979; Ohlin 1983). However, there are significant differences that can be highlighted by applying Rothman's community organization typology. The various programs associated with the 1960s period and the "War on Poverty" that was declared by President Lyndon Johnson were predicated on the assumptions of *anomie-opportunity theory,* also known as macro-level *strain theory.* Whereas Shaw and McKay's social disorganization theory had viewed delinquency as a maladaptive response to a deficient local community milieu, anomie-opportunity advanced a broader critique of the problem as endemic to American society as a whole (Berger, Free, and Searles 2009).

Drawing on Durkheim's classic work on anomie,[7] Robert Merton (1938) was the first to argue that delinquent behavior (and other forms of criminality) develops because of a socially structured strain or disjuncture between the aspirations of disadvantaged youths for *culturally approved goals* (i.e., financial success and bountiful material consumption) and the *available opportunities* to achieve these goals through legitimate means (i.e., education, employment). People who lacked access to the legitimate means to achieve these goals were structured into a relationship of strain with society and experienced a sense of frustration and injustice about their lot in life (see also Cloward and Ohlin 1960; Cohen 1955; Messner and Rosenfeld 2001; Chapter 10).

Given the pervasive social inequality in the United States, anomie-opportunity theory postulates that the greatest strain or pressures for delinquent behavior reside in the lower classes and among disadvantaged racial and ethnic minority groups. Families from these backgrounds often lack the economic and social resources to prepare their children well for school, provide them with enriching cultural experiences, bail them out (literally and figuratively) if they get in trouble with the law, finance their college education (even after a mediocre pre-college career), and set them up in businesses or professions. Minorities face the additional problems of discrimination and lack of familiarity with the culture of white, middle-class institutional environments. Nevertheless, according to anomie-opportunity theory, those who turn to crime are not, at heart, so different from law-abiding folks. They are not predisposed to crime and would prefer to take a more conventional path to success if it were available to them. In general, the prescribed remedy for preventing delinquency, therefore, involved significant improvement in the economic and educational opportunities of low-income and minority youth (Cloward and Ohlin 1960; Cohen 1955; see also Hagan and McCarthy 1997; Newman 1999; Williams and Kornblum 1985).

The 1960s programs included two major orientations—the "provision of opportunity" programs and the "comprehensive community action" projects.

The former utilized a social planning model of community organization, while the latter employed a social action model mixed with locality development and social planning. Because the provision of opportunity programs relied on a single model, I will discuss them first and consider the comprehensive community action projects in the next section.

Provision of Opportunity Programs

The provision of opportunity programs attempted to increase low-income and minority youths' access to socially approved means of obtaining success. The Economic Opportunity Act (EOA) of 1964 authorized the Department of Labor to become involved in delinquency prevention through the Neighborhood Youth Corps and the Job Corps. The Neighborhood Youth Corps included both summer and year-round training and work programs for youths, some of whom were enrolled in school and some of whom were not. The Job Corps placed low-income urban youths in residential centers for job training and had both an urban and a rural component. The urban centers trained youths in skilled trades such as auto mechanics and carpentry. The rural centers often emphasized forest conservation skills, but also provided training for many others jobs as well (Griffen and Griffen 1978; Quadagno and Fobes 1995).

During the same decade, the Department of Health, Education and Welfare (HEW) and the Department of Housing and Urban Development (HUD) also developed a broad range of delinquency prevention initiatives. For instance, HEW's Upward Bound program was designed to facilitate educational achievement by increasing the motivation and skills of disadvantaged youths. Similarly, HUD's Model Cities program provided inner-city youths with college prep courses, college scholarships, and job placements, as well as direct social services such as counseling, drug abuse treatment, assistance for unwed mothers, recreation, and teen clubs.

The provision of opportunity programs were the outcome of a straightforward social planning approach. Professional planners with specialized skills and knowledge designed a program of controlled rational change to solve the delinquency problem. The planners, working for the government, created programs considered to be in the public interest, but the recipients of these services had a minimal or no role in the determination of program policies or goals. Community workers tended to operate as agents of the government, helping to regulate the poor and phase out social action–oriented projects and confrontational tactics (Piven and Cloward 1971).

Rooted in liberal ideology, the social planning approach to providing opportunities sought only to establish conditions of equal opportunity for individuals to compete for society's scarce economic rewards. While these programs did help to secure a fragile black middle class, equality of result has not been achieved for the intransigent underclass still living in squalor—the class that contributes disproportionately to the serious crime and delinquency problem in urban communities (see Anderson 1999; Wilson 1987; Chapters 18, 19). More-over, the success of some seems to have increased the sense of relative depri-vation and strain among those who have been left behind (see LaFree and Drass 1996).

While ignoring locality development strategies (e.g., community involve-ment, self-help, and use of indigenous community resources and leadership), the social planning model lent itself to an expensive, bureaucratic social welfare apparatus that administered "prevention" to clients but that created as much "opportunity" for social welfare professionals as it did for the target popula-tion. Moreover, the programs "undercut autonomous behavior by the poor, fostering dependency on institutions that were out of the poor's control" (Mc-Gahey 1986:255; Murray 1984; Piven and Cloward 1971). To some extent, the social planning programs were not community-focused per se, for their objec-tive was to serve high-risk youth rather than to mobilize all of the residents for collective action (see Rosenbaum 1988).

As was the case with the CAP, few of the provision of opportunity pro-grams were subjected to systematic program evaluation (Dixon and Wright 1974). Rather than reaching hard-core delinquent or delinquent-prone youth, the programs seemed to have primarily helped those who were more motivated and upwardly mobile to begin with (Grosser 1976; Spergel 1969). Though the Job Corps appeared to have some short-term success in reducing delinquency, because youths were "physically and socially removed from their high-crime neighborhoods and crime-prone peer groups" (McGahey 1986:257), one must question a social planning approach that emphasized rural-type employment training for urban youths returning to the city to search for jobs. Similarly, the Neighborhood Youth Corps merely offered job training without guaranteeing employment upon completion of training. And African-American trainees even experienced discrimination from some of the skilled trade unions (Quadagno and Fobes 1995).[8] Thus most of the training programs produced few demon-strable positive results on the long-term labor status or delinquent recidivism of participants (McGahey 1986).[9]

Conservative critics have pointed to the rise in crime rates that occurred during the 1960s, suggesting that the provision of opportunity programs were based on a naive liberal optimism and a blind "throwing money" approach to solving social problems (Wilson 1975). I will have more to say about the lim-itations of these programs after discussing the social action component of the 1960s efforts. It suffices here to say that anomie-opportunity or strain theory in its original form no longer guides delinquency prevention strategies in the United States today (Binder and Polan 1991).

Comprehensive Community Action Projects

Like the provision of opportunity programs, the comprehensive community action projects (CCAPs) of the 1960s attempted to prevent delinquency through alteration of social conditions that were believed to cause delinquency. However, promoters of CCAPs attempted to utilize and integrate all three models of community organization practice: locality development, social planning, and social action.

CCAPs began in the early 1960s through the auspices of the President's Committee on Juvenile Delinquency and Youth Crime and continued under the Office of Economic Opportunity. These large-scale, multidimensional social welfare programs were established under federal control and funded with government money, but were rooted in the local neighborhood. CCAPs placed a great deal of emphasis on locality development strategies of community organization. As in the CAP, residents were involved in autonomous, community-controlled organizations. The projects focused on increasing the ability of communities to develop the services and conditions necessary to enable both adults and youths to participate in and have influence upon community affairs (Freeman, Jones, and Zucker 1979; Grosser 1976). In 1964 a demonstration review panel summed up the basic assumption of CCAPs: "The panel is unanimous in its opinion that major involvement on the part of community residents to improve their own situation is the *sine qua non* of a successful comprehensive program to combat delinquency in disadvantaged and demoralized communities" (cited in Grosser 1976:24). One year later, Title II of the Economic Opportunity Act translated this recommendation into a mandate for "maximum feasible participation." This mandate generated much controversy and criticism when coupled with the social action components of these projects (Moynihan 1969).

Mobilization for Youth (MFY) is viewed as the blueprint for comprehensive community-based delinquency prevention strategies (Empey and Stafford 1991). Developed by Richard Cloward and Lloyd Ohlin working with the Henry Street Settlement on the Lower East Side in New York, MFY utilized a combination of all three community organization strategies to achieve a broad range of objectives (see Cloward and Ohlin 1960):

(1) the organization of the low-income community through the formation of neighborhood councils and the mobilization of residents for social action.
(2) the improvement of educational opportunities through teacher training, the development of relevant curricula and teaching methods, increased parent-school contacts, and preschool programs.
(3) the creation of job opportunities through work subsidies, vocational training, and career guidance.
(4) the provision of specialized services to youths through detached street workers, recreational programs, and rap groups.
(5) the establishment of specialized services to families through Neighborhood Service Centers offering childcare, counseling, and assistance in applying for public social services.

As such, MFY was conceived not merely as a social service program, but as a radical "social experiment" (Empey and Stafford 1991; Marris and Rein 1973; Moynihan 1969; Short 1975).

Inspired by MFY, the President's Committee sponsored additional legislation and invited other communities to submit proposals and demonstrate how they would set up a comprehensive, large-scale program aimed at achieving institutional and social change. The federal government offered funding and assistance in planning, but the communities had to utilize their own resources and involve local residents of the target area in the planning and implementation (Empey and Stafford 1991; Grosser 1976; Mech 1975). The central features shared by these diverse projects, which expanded to over 1,000 by the mid-1960s (McGahey 1986), were:

(1) the development and promotion of community involvement and self-help capabilities.
(2) the organization of formal structures for indigenous leadership and decisionmaking, such as neighborhood councils, policy boards, and committees.
(3) the maintenance of local autonomy.
(4) the involvement of both adults and youth in social action activities designed to increase the responsiveness of social institutions to the needs of the target population and redress specific grievances in areas such as housing, healthcare, and employment discrimination.

The social action component of CCAPs generated a great deal of criticism, debate, and withdrawal of support. In MFY, for example, the residents were encouraged to participate in strikes, protests, and confrontations with public institutions. The intended goal was to make political leaders aware that the community was an organized interest group that demanded their attention. Frequently, the community's grievances concerned the same institutions (e.g., schools, social services, juvenile justice system) that the prevention program attempted to bring together in a cooperative alliance. The consequence was that local, federal, and private sponsors became the targets of social action strategies (Gelfand 1981; Grosser 1976). It was a classic case of "biting the hand that feeds you," a dilemma created by attempting to mix the consensus tactics of locality development with the confrontational tactics of social action. This built-in contradiction pitted the goals of political leaders and funding agencies against community organizers and local residents. Whereas the politicians and funding agencies desired to achieve community stability by getting youths involved in legitimate activities, the community attempted to challenge the power structure and change the political process that distributed inequitable opportunities and resources in the first place. By the mid-1960s, MFY was derailed by accusations that it had communist sympathies and had misused government funds; and organizers who favored social action were eventually purged (Krisberg 2005; Moynihan 1969).[10]

Other CCAPs experienced similar difficulties. Local interest groups and institutions such as landlords, police, school officials, and the news media mounted a counteroffensive campaign that encouraged curtailment of funds.[11] The escalating Vietnam military budget also reduced funds, and remaining program resources had to be devoted to organizational survival rather than to the original social change objectives. Confrontational tactics and innovative programs were toned down or altered to conform to a social planning model of social service delivery that was more attractive to funding sponsors. Many were transformed into predominately counseling-treatment programs or ones that stressed vocational education or legal assistance (Krisberg 2005; McGahey 1986).

Some observers question whether there was ever full political support for the dramatic changes implied by anomie-opportunity/strain theory and CCAPs (Marris and Rein 1973). Many staff in community agencies did not believe that such large-scale changes could be justified merely to prevent delinquency (Ohlin 1983). Bureaucratic funding policies, administrative demands, and a preoccupation with accountability, efficiency, and cost-benefit analysis took precedence over innovation and experimentation. Many projects were only granted short-term funding with no commitment for continued, long-term support. Evaluation efforts assessing the impact of programs were unimpressive (see Braithwaite 1979; Grosser 1976; McGahey 1986; Rosenbaum 1988). It was difficult to demonstrate that the interventions of a specific program with particular methods brought about specific changes. It was not possible to designate control and experimental groups since services were not selectively provided, and it was difficult to isolate or disentangle the problem of delinquency from the wider range of community problems (see Fagan 1987). Finally, the explicit focus on delinquency tended to get lost in the escalation of the larger "War on Poverty."

The various approaches that were implemented in the 1960s appear to have failed to bring about the anticipated social changes and reductions in delinquency. Ohlin (1983) argued that programs proliferated too rapidly and exceeded the talent and knowledge available to achieve tangible results. Wilson believed "it was the failure to appreciate the importance of community and gravity of the threats to it that led to some mistaken views during the 1960s of the true nature of the 'urban crisis'" (1975:24). Ohlin's observations appear on target, but Wilson's critique depreciates the explicit focus on community that was at the heart of CCAPs. Thus, a more reasonable critique of CCAPs' ineffectiveness would emphasize:

(1) the lack of full political support and the counteroffensive efforts waged by vested interest groups.

(2) the limitations imposed by bureaucratic funding policies, administrative concerns, and competition for scarce resources.

(3) the provisions for job training without a concomitant effort to increase the supply of available jobs.

(4) the contradictions inherent in attempting to integrate different models of community organization practice, particularly, the conflict between social action strategies and those of locality development and social planning.

Publicly funded projects that organize residents for social action can expect to have great difficulties achieving consensus among diverse elements of the community, as well as establishing and perpetuating their autonomy and original objectives. Priority from funding agencies will inevitably be given to programs attempting to implement gradual, controlled reform through a social planning approach rather than through programs involving community action against established institutions.

■ From Offender Prevention to Victim Prevention

In the 1970s and 1980s community crime prevention strategies shifted away from strategies that attempt to reduce the propensity of potential *offenders* to commit crime and toward strategies that encourage potential *victims* to take measures, both individually and collectively, to prevent themselves from becoming victims of crime. This latter approach is known as "victim prevention," "target hardening," or "situational crime prevention" (Johnson 1987; Lewis and Salem 1981; Rosenbaum 1988).[12] For instance, individuals can install locks, alarms, window bars, and surveillance cameras in their homes; put identifying marks on their property; acquire large dogs, mace sprays, or guns for protection; take courses in karate or other forms of personal defense; and hire private security guards to patrol their neighborhoods. Homes, buildings, apartment complexes, and even entire communities can be architecturally or environmentally designed to ensure that walkways and other public areas are highly visible and well lighted. Access to particular areas can be reserved for particular purposes or users and prohibited for others (e.g., juveniles hanging out). Residents can organize themselves (often with assistance from police) into neighborhood or community-watch groups and even citizen patrols (Felson 1998; Newman 1972; Rosenbaum, Lurigio, and Davis 1998; Welsh and Farrington 2004).

Both the individual security and neighborhood measures that are part of this victim prevention approach entail efforts to increase the capacity of the community as a collectivity to respond to social problems (Lewis and Salem 1981). As such, they are also based on one or more of the community organization models I have been discussing in this chapter. Individual security strategies, for example, are indicative of a locality development approach to community organization insofar as they attempt to mobilize residents to take responsibility for crime control in their neighborhoods. At the same time, however, law enforcement officials (as well as political officials) have preferred a social planning orientation to these efforts. Although citizen involvement has been favored as a way to reduce reliance on expensive, bureaucratic methods of crime control, police desire to maintain their role as experts who possess the skills and knowledge necessary to "define the nature of the problem, gather the information necessary to implement the . . . preventative measures, and . . . oversee, supervise, and regulate" the community's activities (Boostrom and Henderson 1983:26). All too often the police view their involvement in victim prevention programs as a form of public relations or as an extension of their own outreach efforts, and they may not be particularly interested in responding to residents' suggestions regarding changes in police policies that they would like to see made (Fagan 1987). The conflict between locality development and social planning approaches is illustrated by police opposition to autonomous, citizen-initiated efforts such as the Guardian Angels (Michalowski 1983; Pennell et al. 1989). In addition, the social planning orientation favored by the police becomes especially problematic when their prevention activities favor middle-class communities and thus reinforce existing neighborhood patterns of victimization. Moreover, the relationship between residents and the police is generally more antagonistic in low-income communities (Skogan 1989).[13]

Boostrom and Henderson (1983) view architectural/environmental design as more conducive to the maintenance of the citizen autonomy that is characteristic of locality development. Because this approach requires the skills of urban planners and architects, not police officers, it contains no inherent mandate for expanded police resources or control. The themes of self-help and self-reliance are stressed over the surrender of "responsibilities to any formal authority" (Newman 1972:14). Residents are encouraged to develop a stake in protecting their neighborhood spaces and to define the norms of legitimate activity within these spaces.

Nevertheless, the locality development emphasis in victim prevention, as in offender-oriented prevention, is not without its inherent contradictions and dilemmas. On the one hand, locality development is predicated on a consensus approach to solving problems whereby different interest groups come together to identify common concerns and objectives. On the other hand, victim prevention may become a means by which residents attempt to defend the purity of their neighborhoods and prevent "undesirables" and "outsiders" from using their streets.[14] Thus it has the potential to create territorial conflicts between diverse classes and races that are attempting to establish their neighborhood boundaries and that may disagree about what behaviors should be tolerated by the community (Boostrom and Henderson 1983).

Moreover, evaluations of victim prevention programs indicate that such efforts have been "oversold as a stand-alone strategy" (Rosenbaum 1988:363),

with the best results obtained with measures of success that focus on "fear reduction" rather than on the reduction of crime per se (Police Foundation 1986;
Rosenbaum 1986). Curtis bemoans the fact that "the "institutionalization of
fear as an accepted measure of success" has been used by agencies operating
victim prevention programs as "a public relations vehicle" for the stand-alone
approach (1987b:76). Such an approach has obvious limitations for those residents who live in neighborhoods where fear of crime is a realistic assessment
of reality. Thus victim prevention strategies may be more appropriate for low-
crime neighborhoods than high-crime neighborhoods (Rosenbaum 1988; Skogan 1989). The primary problem in these latter communities is that they are
economically disadvantaged compared to other areas and are "consistently un-
derserved" by social service agencies (Bennett and Lavrakas 1989; Fagan
1987:68). Surveys indicate that residents, particularly in low-income communities, still view the offender-oriented approach as the most effective means of
crime prevention (Bennett and Lavrakas 1988; Podelefsky 1983; Podelefsky
and DuBow 1981).[15]

■ Back to Basics

Criticism of the stand-alone approach to victim prevention has led to renewed
interest in traditional offender-oriented approaches to delinquency prevention,
and evaluations of two demonstration projects in the 1980s reported in "Policies
to Prevent Crime: Neighborhood, Family, and Employment Strategies" have encouraged this interest and are worthy of our consideration here: the Violent Juvenile Offender Research and Development Program (VJORDP) and the Neighborhood Anti-Crime Self-Help Program (NASP) (Curtis 1987a, 1987b; Fagan
1987). VJORDP, NASP, and similar projects attempt to replicate "models of success" programs that utilize strategies reminiscent of the Chicago Area Project
and the 1960s comprehensive prevention programs. These strategies include:

(1) extended-family environments that address the emotional and self-
    esteem needs of youths.
(2) daycare, early childhood education, and parental training.
(3) foster-grandparent programs and neighborhood assistance for family
    problems.
(4) community health programs and drug treatment.
(5) educational and vocational training.
(6) neighborhood mediation of community conflicts.

In these various programs, one finds the themes of locality development: self-
help, volunteerism, and educating the community to become aware of and take
advantage of its own resources.

The VJORDP was a federally sponsored research and development project implemented between 1981 and 1986 through neighborhood organizations

in seven different communities around the country (Fagan 1987). Drawing upon social control and social learning theories (see Chapters 7, 11), the VJORDP attempted to increase youths' attachment or bonds to family and school, increase their commitment to conventional behavior and values, and reduce their attraction to peer group and neighborhood norms that encourage delinquency. Project staff assisted neighborhood volunteers in developing "resident mobilization councils" consisting of neighborhood leaders. Each council attempted to recruit other residents, including delinquent and nondelinquent youths. The councils in the different sites formulated intervention strategies in four areas: violent crime intervention, institutional mediation, family support networks, and youth skills development.

Recruiting neighborhood leadership was one of the most difficult problems experienced by the resident councils. Voluntary participation was difficult to sustain, in part, because residents felt that their neighborhood's real problems (e.g., economic disadvantage, underservice by social service agencies) could not be addressed (Fagan 1987; see also Skogan 1989). While youths who participated on the councils demonstrated improved decisionmaking, planning, and analytic skills, attempts to develop self-help businesses (e.g., automobile repair, housing rehabilitation) were unsuccessful.

The police and juvenile courts were generally cooperative, viewing the resident councils as complementary to their own efforts, and they were willing to provide assistance and grant access to data. However, several other institutions (i.e., schools, child protective services, juvenile probation, and district attorney offices) remained resistant to outside scrutiny. According to Fagan, the challenge for community organizations is to find ways to gain access to and open these "relatively closed institutions" to public scrutiny, although such efforts may require confrontational strategies more indicative of a social action approach than the locality development approach used by the VJORDP (1987:6).

As with earlier offender-oriented efforts, the overall impact of the VJORDP on reducing delinquency in the different project sites was unimpressive, although the short period of the projects "did not afford sufficient time to determine if the underlying crime-supporting conditions were altered" (Fagan 1987: 66). Nevertheless, Fagan believes that the VJORDP demonstrated "the natural strength of informal networks" of residents as a means of reweaving the social fabric of communities to control the delinquency problem (p. 70). Moreover, one resident council was able to attract additional outside funds to continue its drug program, and four of the councils were successful in getting the city or county to incorporate several of their intervention strategies into local government-sponsored efforts.

In 1982 the Eisenhower Foundation began another locality development demonstration project, the NASP, in 10 different communities around the country. Funds were provided by the government, private foundations, and businesses to help local community organizations carry out their programs and to provide them with technical assistance and consultants for an initial six months of planning and an additional two years of implementation. Community organizations applied for support if they could raise matching funds, "demonstrate that [they] had . . . a good management track record, a competent staff and board, and experience in organizing," and develop a prevention program that combined some form of victim prevention with initiatives that addressed offender prevention (Curtis 1987b:77–78). In addition to reducing crime, one of the key goals of the NASP was to help community organizations become financially self-sufficient.

Curtis (1987b) reviewed the initial results for eight of these locality development projects. Although the evidence was insufficient to convince skeptics (Rosenbaum 1988), Curtis reported positive outcomes for some areas of evaluation in six of the eight sites. For instance, five of the programs reported some reductions in crime and/or community fear. However, the "most successful single component" of the NASP was in the area of financial self-sufficiency (Curtis 1987b:87). All eight sites were able "to raise additional resources and carry on in one form or another after the original" funding period. Overall, the projects generated over one million dollars in additional revenues. One community developed several business enterprises, including a promising weatherization business that employed high-risk youths and ex-offenders. This community also reported improved math, budgeting, and tool use skills among project participants. Moreover, the NASP appeared to be less expensive and more effective in reducing crime than police-directed programs that did not integrate victim-oriented and offender-oriented approaches to prevention (see Police Foundation 1986). Curtis concluded:

> We have demonstrated that modestly funded initiatives (under two million dollars) that begin to address the causes of crime can be mixed with [victim prevention] reduction with considerable, if guarded, success in our most deteriorated inner cities. We have shown that such progress is possible with inner-city community organizations, rather than police, in the lead, even though police can and should play an important role. (1987b:88)

Bennett and Lavrakas (1989), on the other hand, reported on a more complete evaluation of all ten of the Eisenhower Foundation sites and noted that the victim prevention component of the programs yielded better results than the offender-oriented component, especially when measured by the degree of citizen involvement. Typically, however, the programs began with victim prevention and only later phased in offender-oriented strategies, which were underfunded and not well underway by the end of the evaluation period. Moreover, the offender-oriented component often focused on a small number of "high-risk" youths rather than on "community-wide activities that are more likely to involve numerous residents" (p. 356). These strategies were "more successful when the [community] organization assigned specific space to the youth program, when activities were held regularly and frequently (once a week or more), and when an experienced youth worker directed the program" (p. 359). Meeting residents' economic needs, particularly jobs, proved to be the most difficult problem to solve.

■ Conclusion

Large-scale approaches to the prevention of juvenile delinquency began with the 1930s Chicago Area Project and emerged full bloom in the 1960s provision of opportunity programs and comprehensive community action projects. All of these strategies shared a view of delinquency as symptomatic of underlying social conditions that could not be prevented or remedied by responding to individuals on a one-to-one basis. However, the programs applied the models of community organization practice in different ways. The Chicago Area Project pioneered the use of locality development in delinquency prevention, along with specific innovations such as use of recreation, detached street workers, and school interventions. The social planning model employed in the provision of opportunity programs has left its legacy on current efforts at economic and vocational training and equal opportunity programs; and the social action emphasis of the comprehensive community action projects has now been transmuted into increased citizen involvement in grass-roots, neighborhood organizations (see Beckwith 1996; Obama 2004; Rothman 1979b; Stoecker 1994).

Future efforts to implement primary delinquency prevention strategies will need to avoid replicating the problems encountered in earlier programs and avoid "merely trying to win back liberal ground lost to . . . conservative policy makers" (Michalowski 1983:13). However, in a period of budget deficits and declining state resources, it is not clear whether the constraints placed on community organization strategies can be overcome. The often praised emphasis on process goals in locality development has serious pitfalls. Expectations may be raised without providing concrete gains. This may lead to increased anger, frustration, apathy, and sense of relative deprivation. Local organizing efforts are ineffectual if they are not linked to legislation and policy at higher governmental levels. However, the experience of programs such as the Job Corps and Neighborhood Youth Corps demonstrates that social planning to equip youths with job skills is limited if the economy has no room for them. Similarly, social action strategies that confront public institutions with demands for better services are useless if legislators are endorsing significant cutbacks.

Many observers have long observed that prevention strategies that ignore the need for economic policies leading to full employment and mitigation of income inequality are likely to fail (Chester 1977; Conyers 1979; Phillips 1991). Colvin argued that "financial investments need to be publicly guided, not placed solely in the hands of a few wealthy people who may seek short-term profits at the expense of national growth and security" (1991:445). Michalowski (1983) suggested that publicly run nonprofit corporations might need to be established, along with increased taxation on corporate profits and restrictions on plant closures. Perhaps partnerships between the public sector and private businesses (such as in the Job Training Partnership Act), which include tax incentives for businesses, may provide a realistic means of financing job-creation efforts that provide youth employment and training (Kolberg 1987; Williams and Kornblum 1985). Jobs will also need to be sufficiently attractive, with opportunities for advancement, to motivate individuals to undertake adequate training (Colvin 1991).[16] These jobs should include a literacy component to help youths develop basic skills, as well as offer youths the opportunity to interact with positive adult role mentors (McGahey 1986; Williams and Kornblum 1985).[17] Otherwise, jobs and job training programs merely become "another temporary step in the dead-end urban labor market and . . . another erratic source of low income along with regular ill-paying jobs, transfer payments, and crime" (McGahey 1986:257).[18] Some of these economic policies would undoubtedly require community organization for social action to create pressure for change, but these actions in themselves could lead to short-term reductions in delinquency, as the experience of communities in protest has shown.[19]

In addition to social planning for economic reform, the principle of community control that is central to locality development should be maintained. Residents need to be involved in the planning and implementation process. Such involvement helps to minimize the sense of alienation that people can experience when services are "dispensed" to them by social welfare professionals. Residents must have a sense that the program "belongs" to them and that they are capable of succeeding on their own if given a fair chance (Walker 2001). Only in this way can programs begin to counter the loss of self-efficacy that is characteristic of residents in economically marginal communities (see Press 2007; Sampson et al. 1997; Wilson 1991).

More projects such as the Neighborhood Anti-Crime Self-Help Program that combine offender-oriented strategies with victim prevention would be beneficial. Community mobilization for victim prevention helps reduce the need for an expensive, bureaucratic law enforcement apparatus and thus makes funds available for neighborhood improvements and social services. In addition, youths' involvement in protective community patrols might reduce their alienation and divert interest from destructive community activities (Michalowski 1983; Pennell et al. 1989). Programs to assist juvenile victims of crime would also reinforce conventional standards of behavior (Alcabes and Jones 1980).

A major caveat of such a comprehensive approach to delinquency prevention is the difficulty of designing a method of quantitative program evaluation. Klein and Goldston argued that primary prevention strategies should not be expected "to prove that an individual who did not become the victim of a condition would without question have incurred the condition except for the preventive intervention" (1977:vii). Spergel (1969), on the other hand, suggested that primary prevention programs can be evaluated through the designation of experimental and control groups. However, such a design would offset the premise of a comprehensive community-based project—that the entire community be involved and that the provisions of the program be multifaceted. Moreover, the goal of primary prevention should not merely be decreased delinquency, but improvement in the quality of life for the entire community. Bureaucratic funding policies that require short-term demonstrations of delinquency reduction need to be reevaluated if primary prevention is to receive more long-term support. Primary prevention strategies cannot be expected to produce instantaneous results because the social, economic, and political patterns that underlie the delinquency problem are deeply ingrained.

Realistically, we must recognize that our society does not have a genuine commitment to the widespread social changes required for an effective primary prevention approach to delinquency (Curtis 1987b). Preference will inevitably be given to secondary and tertiary prevention strategies that are more limited in scope and more accurately characterized as rehabilitative rather than preventive in nature (Gilbert 1981; Klein and Goldston 1977). Even most professionals working within community-based agencies prefer a counseling and treatment approach to the delinquency problem (Selke 1982). Moreover, as Hagan observes, contemporary conservative political ideology argues that "social inequality encourages initiative, and therefore is necessary for economic progress" (1994:60; see also Davis and Moore 1945). Investments in reducing inequality are viewed as costly, wasteful, and even counterproductive. "This firmly rooted skepticism about efforts to reduce social inequality plays a central role in justifying social policies that divert investment from declining communities and disadvantaged individuals" (Hagan 1994:60).

In spite of the difficulties confronting future primary prevention efforts, the projects I have reviewed in this chapter indicate that it is possible to design and implement an effective strategy that mobilizes the entire community to address the delinquency problem. Typically, however, assessments of past successes and failures have been made in terms of the "scientific adequacy" of the particular theory underlying the program (Binder and Polan 1991; Empey and Stafford 1991), rather than the organizational mechanisms through which the theory was implemented. But while the popularity of various theories may change, the organizational principles underlying their application to large-scale prevention will continue to be predicated on the community organization models of locality development, social planning, and social action. Contemporary debates over the future direction of delinquency prevention should not be limited to considerations of theoretical adequacy. Greater attention needs to be given to the potentialities and limitations inherent in utilizing different models of community organization practice.

▨ Notes

1. See, for example, Curtis (1987a), Farrington and Welsh (2007), Johnson (1987), Lundman (2001), Rosenbaum, Lurigio, and Davis (1998), and Wright and Dixon (1977).

2. I will only address other forms of delinquency prevention (e.g., recreation, detached street workers, community-based treatment) insofar as they are related to or are included within large-scale programs.

3. It is rare to hear of a politician who came up through the ranks as a result of his or her work as a community organizer. Barack Obama is a notable exception. For an account of his experiences as a community organizer in Chicago, see Obama (2004).

4. Using a similar typology, Spergel (1969) identifies four community organization strategies: development, maintenance, contest, and conflict. Essentially, development is the same as Rothman's locality development, maintenance is similar to social planning, and contest and conflict are aspects of social action. Spergel also identifies four corresponding practitioner roles: developer, enabler, advocate, and organizer.

5. McGahey (1986) suggests that this was perhaps because Shaw and McKay believed that these problems were outside of the local community's control.

6. In their examination of 343 neighborhoods in the city of Chicago, Sampson, Raudenbush, and Earls (1997) found that, all other things being equal, more collective efficacy in a neighborhood was associated with lower rates of violent crime. At the same time, Sampson and colleagues found that collective efficacy is itself explained in large part by socioeconomic factors that are linked to the broader economic and political organization of society.

7. Durkheim (1897/1952) coined the term *anomie* to refer to a state of normlessness whereby individuals were isolated, cut adrift, and lacking in a common bond that bring them into sympathetic relationships with other people in society. Merton reformulated the concept to analyze the structural disjuncture between goals and means that constituted a state of anomie (see Berger, Free, and Searles 2009).

8. In a study of the Job Corps, Quadagno and Fobes (1995) document the initial political opposition to including females in the group of eligible trainees. Eventually the EOA required that one-third of the trainees be female. Still, it was the young men who received the training for the better-paying skilled jobs, while the young women received training in "home and family life and the development of values, attitudes, and skills that [would] contribute to stable family relationships and a good child-rearing environment" (p. 176). The idea was to prepare men to become primary breadwinners and to prepare women to become homemakers.

9. While initial evaluations of 1960s preschool programs such as Head Start were unimpressive, more recent studies found that such programs increase employment and lower delinquency among participants (Berrueta-Clement et al. 1984; Hawkins and Lishner 1987; McGahey 1986).

10. To be sure, there were gang members who misused federal grant monies they received, viewing these programs as just another "hustle" or cover for illegal activities (Klein 1971; Krisberg 1975).

11. See Dawley (1992) for an account of these experiences in Chicago during this period.

12. The theoretical underpinning of this approach is often referred to as the "routine activities" approach. First advanced by Cohen and Felson (1979), routine activities theory argues that it is possible, theoretically speaking, to bypass explanations of criminal motivation and simply assume there will always be a sufficient number of individuals willing to take advantage of the opportunity to commit crime. What criminologists needed to ascertain are the immediate situational circumstances that enable such individuals to translate their criminal inclinations into action. The probability of crime increases when there

is a convergence in space and time of three basic elements: motivated offenders (who are assumed but not explained), suitable targets, and the absence of capable guardians. The convergence of these three elements occurs as part of the routine activities of everyday life (see also Berger, Free, and Searles 2009; Felson 1998).

13. See Rosenbaum (1986, 1988) and Rosenbaum, Lurigio, and Davis (1998) for discussions of police-oriented programs.

14. This orientation can lead to incidents such as the one that occurred in the Howard Beach district of Queens, New York, in 1986, when three black men were chased onto a highway by a mob of white youths after the black men's car broke down; one of the men was killed when he was hit by the oncoming traffic (Curtis 1987b).

15. This might have been expected given studies that found social and demographic variables more related to crime than features of the physical environment (Byrne and Sampson 1986; Merry 1981; Taylor, Gottfredson, and Schumaker 1984).

16. Allen and Steffensmeier (1989) have shown that arrest rates of juveniles and young adults are associated with both the availability and the quality of employment (see also Uggen 1999).

17. Wilson (1987) and Anderson (1990) argue that the mass exodus of jobs, working families, and black professionals from the inner city have depleted these minority communities of positive role models.

18. Of course, youth should always be encouraged to remain in school, and part-time jobs linked to continued school attendance are preferable (McGahey 1986).

19. In a study of a Chicano community in Los Angeles during the 1970s, community members reported that gang activity subsided when the community was mobilized in protest actions (Erlanger 1979). Dawley (1992) also noted the reduction of gang activity among African-American youths in Chicago during that period.

▓ References

Alcabes, Abraham, and James A. Jones. 1980. "Juvenile Victim Assistance Programs: A Proposal." *Crime and Delinquency* 26:202–5.

Alinsky, Saul. 1946. *Reveille for Radicals.* Chicago: University of Chicago Press.

Allen, Emile Anderson, and Darrell J. Steffensmeier. 1989. "Youth, Underemployment, and Property Crime: Differential Effects of Job Availability and Job Quality on Juvenile and Young Adult Arrest Rates." *American Sociological Review* 54:107–23.

Anderson, Elijah. 1999. *Code of the Street.* New York: Norton.

Beckwith, David. 1996. "Ten Ways to Work Together: An Organizer's View." *Sociological Imagination* 33:164–72.

Bennett, Susan, and Paul J. Lavrakas. 1988. *Evaluation of the Planning and Implementation of the Neighborhood Program.* Final Process Report to the Eisenhower Foundation. Evanston, IL: Northwestern University, Center for Urban Affairs & Policy Research.

———. 1989. "Community-Based Crime Prevention: An Assessment of the Eisenhower Foundation's Neighborhood Program." *Crime and Delinquency* 35:345–64.

Berger, Ronald J., Marvin D. Free, and Patricia Searles. 2009. *Crime, Justice and Society: An Introduction to Criminology.* 3rd ed. Boulder, CO: Lynne Rienner.

Berrueta-Clement, John R., W. Steven Barnett, Ann S. Epstein, and David P. Weikart. 1984. *Changed Lives: The Effects of the Perry Preschool Program on Youth Through Age 19.* Ypsilanti, MI: High/Scope.

Binder, Arnold, and Susan L. Polan. 1991. "The Kennedy-Johnson Years, Social Theory, and Federal Policy in the Control of Juvenile Delinquency." *Crime and Delinquency* 37:242–61.

Boostrom, Ronald L., and Joel H. Henderson. 1983. "Community Action and Crime Prevention: Some Unresolved Issues." *Crime and Social Justice* 19:24–30.

Braithwaite, John. 1979. *Inequality, Crime, and Public Policy.* London: Routledge & Kegan Paul.

Bursik, Robert J. 1988. "Social Disorganization and Theories of Crime and Delinquency: Problems and Prospects." *Criminology* 26:519–51.

Bursik, Robert J., and Harold G. Grasmick. 1993. "Economic Deprivation and Neighborhood Crime Rates, 1960–1980." *Law and Society Review* 27:263–83.

Byrne, James, and Robert Sampson (eds.). 1986. *The Social Ecology of Crime.* New York: Springer-Verlag.

Chester, C. Ronald. 1977. "The Effects of a Redistribution of Wealth on Property Crime." *Crime and Delinquency* 23:272–89.

Cloward, Richard A., and Lloyd E. Ohlin, 1960. *Delinquency and Opportunity: A Theory of Delinquent Gangs.* Glencoe, IL: Free Press.

Cohen, Albert K. 1955. *Delinquent Boys: The Culture of the Gang.* Glencoe, IL: Free Press.

Cohen, Lawrence E., and Marcus Felson. 1979. "Social Change and Crime Rate Trends: A Routine Activities Approach." *American Sociological Review* 44:588–608.

Colvin, Mark. 1991. "Crime and Social Reproduction: A Response to the Call for 'Outrageous' Proposals." *Crime and Delinquency* 37:436–48.

Conyers, John. 1979. "Criminology, Economics, and Public Policy." *Crime and Delinquency* 25:137–44.

Cox, Fred M., John L. Erlich, and Jack Rothman (eds.). 1979. *Strategies of Community Organization.* Itasca, IL: Peacock.

Cox, Fred M., John L. Erlich, Jack Rothman, and John E. Tropman (eds.). 1984. *Tactics and Techniques of Community Practice.* Itasca, IL: Peacock.

Curtis, Lynn A. (ed.). 1987a. "Policies to Prevent Crime: Neighborhood, Family, and Employment Strategies." *Annals of the Academy of Political and Social Science* 494.

———. 1987b. "The Retreat of Folly: Some Modest Replications of Inner-City Success." *Annals of the Academy of Political and Social Science* 494:71–89.

Davis, Kingsley, and Wilbert Moore. 1945. "Some Principles of Stratification." *American Sociological Review* 10:242–47.

Dawley, David. 1992. *A Nation of Lords: The Autobiography of the Vice Lords.* Prospect Heights, IL: Waveland Press.

Dixon, Michael D., and William E. Wright. 1974. *Juvenile Delinquency Prevention Programs: An Evaluation of Policy Related Research on the Effectiveness of Prevention Programs.* Washington, DC: National Science Foundation.

Durkheim, Émile. 1897/1952. *Suicide.* New York: Free Press.

Empey, Lamar T., and Mark C. Stafford. 1991. *American Delinquency: Its Meaning and Construction.* Homewood, IL: Dorsey.

Erlanger, Howard S. 1979. "Machismo and Gang Violence." *Social Science Quarterly* 60:235–48.

Fagan, Jeffrey A. 1987. "Neighborhood Education, Mobilization, and Organization for Juvenile Crime Prevention." *Annals of the Academy of Political and Social Science* 494:54–70.

Farrington, David P., and Brandon C. Welsh. 2007. *Saving Children from a Life of Crime: Early Risk Factors and Effective Interventions.* New York: Oxford University Press.

Felson, Marcus. 1998. *Crime and Everyday Life.* Thousand Oaks, CA: Pine Forge Press.

Freeman, Howard E., Wyatt C. Jones, and Lynne G. Zucker. 1979. *Social Problems: A Policy Perspective.* Chicago: Rand McNally.

Gelfand, Mark I. 1981. "The War on Poverty." In R. Divine (ed.), *Exploring the Johnson Years.* Austin: University of Texas Press.

Gilbert, Neil. 1981. "Policy Issues in Primary Prevention." *Social Work* 27:293–97.

Griffen, Brenda S., and Charles T. Griffen. 1978. *Juvenile Delinquency in Perspective.* New York: Harper & Row.

Grosser, Charles F. 1976. *New Directions in Community Organization: From Enabling to Advocacy.* New York: Praeger.

Hagan, John. 1994. *Crime and Disrepute.* Thousand Oaks, CA: Pine Forge Press.

Hagan, John, and Bill McCarthy. 1997. *Mean Streets: Youth Crime and Homelessness.* Cambridge, UK: Cambridge University.

Hawkins, J. David, and Denise M. Lishner. 1987. "Schooling and Delinquency." In E. Johnson (ed.), *Handbook on Crime and Delinquency Prevention.* New York: Greenwood.

Johnson, Elmer H. (ed.). 1987. *Handbook on Crime and Delinquency Prevention.* New York: Greenwood.

Klein, Donald, and Stephen E. Goldston (eds.). 1977. *Primary Prevention: An Idea Whose Time Has Come.* Rockville, MD: National Institute of Mental Health.

Klein, Malcolm M. 1971. *Street Gangs and Street Workers.* Englewood Cliffs, NJ: Prentice-Hall.

Kobrin, Solomon. 1959. "The Chicago Area Project: A 25 Year Assessment." *Annals of the American Academy of Political and Social Science* 322:1–29.

Kolberg, William H. 1987. "Employment, the Private Sector, and At-Risk Youth." *Annals of the Academy of Political and Social Science* 494:94–100.

Krisberg, Barry A. 1975. *The Gang and the Community.* San Francisco: R & E Research Associates.

——— (ed.). 1978. *The Children of Ishmael: Critical Perspectives on Juvenile Justice.* Palo Alto, CA: Mayfield.

———. 2005. *Juvenile Justice: Redeeming Our Children.* Thousand Oaks, CA: Sage.

LaFree, Gary, and Kriss A. Drass. 1996. "The Effect of Changes in Intraracial Income Inequality and Educational Attainment on Changes in Arrest Rates for African Americans and Whites, 1957–1990." *American Sociological Review* 61:614–34.

Lewis, Dan A., and Michael G. Maxfield. 1980. "Fear in the Neighborhood: An Investigation of the Impact of Crime." *Journal of Research in Crime and Delinquency* 17:160–89.

Lewis, Dan A., and Greta Salem. 1981. "Community Crime Prevention: An Analysis of a Developing Strategy." *Crime and Delinquency* 27:405–21.

Lundman, Richard L. 2001. *Prevention and Control of Juvenile Delinquency.* New York: Oxford University Press.

Marris, Peter, and Martin Rein. 1973. *Dilemmas of Social Reform.* Chicago: Adline.

McGahey, Richard M. 1986. "Economic Conditions, Neighborhood Organization, and Urban Crime." In A. Reiss and M. Tonry (eds.), *Communities and Crime.* Chicago: University of Chicago Press.

Mech, Edmund V. 1975. *Delinquency Prevention: A Program of Intervention Approaches.* Portland: Regional Research Institute for Human Services, Portland State University.

Merry, Sally Engel. 1981. *Urban Danger: Life in a Neighborhood of Strangers.* Springfield, IL: Mombiosse.

Merton, Robert K. 1938. "Social Structure and Anomie." *American Sociological Review* 3:672–82.

Messner, Steven F., and Richard Rosenfeld. 2001. *Crime and the American Dream.* Belmont, CA: Wadsworth.

Michalowski, Raymond J. 1983. "Crime Control in the 1980's: A Progressive Agenda." *Crime and Social Justice* 19:13–23.

Moynihan, Daniel P. 1969. *Maximum Feasible Misunderstanding: Community Action in the War on Poverty.* New York: Free Press.

Murray, Charles A. 1984. *Losing Ground: American Social Policy, 1950–1980.* New York: Basic Books.

Newman, Katherine S. 1999. *No Shame in My Game: The Working Poor in the Inner City.* New York: Vintage Books.

Newman, Oscar. 1972. *Defensible Space: Crime Prevention Through Urban Design.* New York: Macmillan.

Obama, Barack. 2004. *Dreams from My Father.* New York: Three Rivers Press.

Ohlin, Lloyd E. 1983. "The Future of Juvenile Justice Policy and Research." *Crime and Delinquency* 29:463–72.

Pennell, Susan, Christine Curtis, Joel Henderson, and Jeff Tayman. 1989. "Guardian Angels: A Unique Approach to Crime Prevention." *Crime and Delinquency* 35: 378–400.

Phillips, Margaret B. 1991. "A Hedgehog Proposal." *Crime and Delinquency* 37:555–74.

Piven, Frances Fox, and Richard A. Cloward. 1971. *Regulating the Poor: The Functions of Public Welfare.* New York: Vintage.

Podelefsky, Aaron M. 1983. *Case Studies in Community Crime Prevention.* Springfield, IL: Thomas.

Podelefsky, Aaron M., and Fred DuBow. 1981. *Strategies for Community Crime Prevention: Collective Responses to Crime in Urban America.* Evanston, IL: Center for Urban Affairs.

Police Foundation. 1986. *Reducing Fear of Crime in Houston and Newark: A Summary Report.* Washington, DC: US Department of Justice.

Press, Eyal. 2007. "Can Block Clubs Block Despair?" *American Prospect,* May:29–33.

Quadagno, Jill, and Catherine Fobes. 1995. "The Welfare State and the Cultural Reproduction of Gender: Making Good Girls and Boys in the Job Corps." *Social Problems* 42:171–90.

Reiss, Albert J. 1986. "Why Are Communities Important in Understanding Crime?" In A. Reiss and M. Tonry (eds.), *Communities and Crime.* Chicago: University of Chicago Press.

Rosenbaum, Dennis P. 1986. *Community Crime Prevention: Does It Work?* Newbury Park, CA: Sage.

———. 1988. "Community Crime Prevention: A Review and Synthesis of the Literature." *Justice Quarterly* 5:323–95.

Rosenbaum, Dennis P., Arthur J. Lurigio, and Robert C. Davis. 1998. *The Prevention of Crime: Social and Situational Strategies.* Belmont, CA: Wadsworth.

Rothman, Jack. 1979a. "Three Models of Community Organization Practice: Their Mixing and Phasing." In F. Cox et al. (eds.), *Strategies in Community Organization.* Itasca, IL: Peacock.

———. 1979b. "Macro Social Work in a Tightening Economy." *Social Work* 24:274–81.

Sampson, Robert J., Stephen W. Raudenbush, and Felton Earls. 1997. "Neighborhoods and Violence Crime: A Multilevel Study of Collective Efficacy." *Science* 277: 918–24.

Schlossman, Steven L., and Michael W. Sedlak. 1983. "The Chicago Area Project Revisited." *Crime and Delinquency* 29:398–462.

Schlossman, Stephen L., Gail L. Zellman, Richard J. Shavelson, Michael W. Sedlak, and Jane Cobb. 1984. *Delinquency Prevention in South Chicago: A Fifty-Year Assessment of the Chicago Area Project.* Santa Monica, CA: Rand Corporation.

Selke, William L. 1982. "Diversion and Crime Prevention." *Criminology* 20:395–406.

Shaw, Clifford R., and Henry D. McKay. 1942. *Juvenile Delinquency and Urban Areas.* Chicago: University of Chicago Press.

Shaw, Clifford R., Frederick M. Zorbaugh, Henry D. McKay, and Leonard S. Cottrell. 1929. *Delinquency Areas.* Chicago: University of Chicago Press.

Short, James F. 1975. "The Natural History of an Applied Theory: Differential Opportunity and Mobilization for Youth." In N. Demarath et al. (eds.), *Social Policy and Sociology.* New York: Academic Press.

Simcha-Fagan, Ora, and Joseph E. Schwartz. 1986. "Neighborhood and Delinquency: An Assessment of Contextual Effects." *Criminology* 24:667–703.

Skogan, Wesley G. 1989. "Communities, Crime, and Neighborhood Organization." *Crime and Delinquency* 35:437–57.

Spergel, Irving A. 1969. *Community Problem Solving: The Delinquency Example.* Chicago: University of Chicago Press.

Stoecker, Randy. 1994. *Defending Community: The Struggle for Alternative Redevelopment in Cedar-Riverside.* Philadelphia: Temple University Press.

Sykes, Gresham, and Frances T. Cullen. 1992. *Criminology.* Fort Worth, TX: Harcourt Brace Jovanovich.

Taylor, Ralph B., Sally Ann Gottfredson, and Stephen A. Shumaker. 1984. *Neighborhood Responses to Disorder.* Baltimore: Johns Hopkins University, Center for Metropolitan Planning and Research.

Uggen, Christopher. 1999. "Ex-Offenders and the Conformist Alternative: A Job Quality Model of Work and Crime." *Social Problems* 46:127–51.

Walker, Samuel. 2001. *Sense and Nonsense About Crime: A Policy Guide.* Monterey, CA: Brooks/Cole.

Welsh, Brandon W., and David P. Farrington. 2004. "Surveillance for Crime Prevention in Public Space: Results and Policy Choices in Britain and America." *Criminology and Public Policy* 3:497-526.

Williams, Terry, and William Kornblum. 1985. *Growing Up Poor.* Lexington, MA: D.C. Heath.

Wilson, James Q. 1975. *Thinking About Crime.* New York: Random House.

Wilson, William J. 1987. *The Truly Disadvantaged: The Inner City, the Underclass, and Public Policy.* Chicago: University of Chicago Press.

———. 1991. "Studying Inner-City Social Dislocations: The Challenge of Public Agenda Research." *American Sociological Review* 56:1–14.

Wright, William E., and Michael C. Dixon. 1977. "Community Prevention and Treatment of Juvenile Delinquency." *Journal of Research in Crime and Delinquency* 14:35–67.

15

Juvenile Involvement in Occupational Delinquency

John Paul Wright and Francis T. Cullen

John Paul Wright and Francis Cullen illuminate a neglected aspect of the delinquency problem: crimes that occur in occupational settings. Through a survey of high school youths in Tennessee, they explore the ways in which youths' general predisposition to delinquency, experience in negative work environments, and association with delinquent coworkers affect their involvement in occupational delinquency and subsequent nonoccupational delinquency.

ALTHOUGH CONCERN WITH WHITE-COLLAR CRIME HAS GROWN CON-siderably in recent years, little research has been undertaken on the workplace misconduct of juveniles. This omission is noteworthy because of the extensive involvement of youths in the labor market. Accordingly, based on a sample of high school seniors, we explored the determinants of youths' occupational delinquency. The analysis revealed that work-related delinquency is affected both by underlying criminal propensities and by contact with delinquent coworkers on the job. It also appears that delinquent youths are selected into negative work environments in which they come into contact with fellow delin-quents—an interaction effect that amplifies their occupational delinquency. Fi-nally, the data suggest that associating with delinquent coworkers affects mis-behavior not only within, but also outside the workplace. . . .

In developing the concept of white-collar crime, Edwin Sutherland (1983) called attention to the way in which employment facilitated the commission of lucrative crimes. In seeking to revise the near-hegemonic view in his day of criminals as poor and pathological, he focused on the offenses "committed by a person of respectability and high social status in the course of his occupation"

"Juvenile Involvement in Occupational Delinquency," *Criminology* 38, no. 3 (2000): 863–896. Re-printed by permission of the American Society of Criminology.

(1983:7). In defining white-collar crime in this fashion, Sutherland succeeded in having an enduring effect on criminology: The mere mention of "white-collar" criminals conjures up images of those occupying high places committing "elite deviance" (Simon & Eitzen 1986) and "crimes of the powerful" (Pearce 1976).

The downside of Sutherland's intellectual legacy, however, is that less consideration has been given to occupational illegalities that, compared to the prototypical white-collar offender who masterminds a complex financial swindle, are relatively mundane, unskilled, easily accomplished, and modest in economic return. Yet, most occupationally related crimes including those committed by lower-level workers and middle-class workers in white-collar jobs have these very characteristics (e.g., see Daly 1989; Gottfredson & Hirschi 1990; Weisburd et al. 1991).

Relatedly, Sutherland wished criminologists and the public to see crime not merely as the province of young ruffians, but also of adults who had climbed their way up the occupational hierarchy. Indeed, his "respectable, high status" white-collar criminal—ostensibly the paragon of virtue in his (or her) community—stood in stark contrast to the shabbily dressed delinquent youth drawn from a disorganized inner-city neighborhood. Sutherland's claim that his theory of differential association could explain the criminality of both the adult white-collar criminal and the delinquent youth is a central reason that his theory was, and remains, provocative and powerful [see Chapter 7].

In short, Sutherland's development and application of the concept of white-collar crime substantially framed inquiry into the study of occupational crime. Most attention has been accorded high-profile cases involving corporate executives; less attention has been given to the more plentiful, but less glamorous, occupational misconduct of average employees. Most noteworthy—given our purposes here—criminologists have virtually ignored the occupational delinquencies committed by juveniles (for an exception, see Ruggiero et al. 1982).

The neglect of juveniles' occupationally related offending is so extensive that typical self-report measures of delinquency do not include questions that would assess offenses committed in the workplace—even though they often do measure crimes committed against family members and in the school (e.g., see Elliott et al. 1989; Hindelang et al. 1981). As noted below, this oversight occurs despite the fact that the workplace is now an integral part of most adolescents' development. . . .

■ The Workplace as a Domain of Delinquency

Most often, delinquency has been linked to youths' social experiences in the family, school, and peer group. Until recently, researchers only occasionally explored how going to work influences the delinquent involvement of school-aged youths (for exceptions, see Agnew 1986; Hirschi 1969; Sullivan 1989). When considered at all, it was largely assumed—not empirically demonstrated—that the absence of employment fosters delinquency (Agnew 1986; Williams et al. 1997). Again, even less attention has been given to the workplace as a setting in which delinquency could take place.

These oversights, however, are potentially consequential. Three factors have coalesced to make paid employment widespread among adolescents. First, the expansion of the service economy has created a continuing need for temporary, inexpensive labor in which businesses make little investment (Reubens et al. 1981; Steinberg 1996). Second, stimulated by intense marketing campaigns, youths have strong consumption desires (Bachman et al. 1984; Freedman & Thornton 1990; Steinberg 1996); indeed, youths spend [over $100] billion annually (St. John 1995). Participation in teenager social activities and acquiring status in peer groups requires a certain level of earning power (Greenberg 1993; Schneider & Schmidt 1996). Third, parents—including those of middle-class youths—believe that employment builds character and is beneficial for their offspring (Phillips & Sandstrom 1990). In short, there are ample opportunities, incentives, and support for youths going to work.

Statistics are clear in showing that the workplace is now a central social domain for teenagers. At any given time, about half of those aged 16 to 19 are employed (Bureau of Labor Statistics 1996). During the academic year, juniors work on average [nearly 20] hours a week, whereas seniors are on the job [over 20] hours a week (Ruhm 1995). At some point in their high school careers, as many as 9 in 10 students will hold a job (Schneider & Schmidt 1996; Steinberg 1996). Schneider and Schmidt observe that "work is perhaps the most common out of school activity among American teenagers" (1996:17). Echoing this view, Steinberg (1996:169) notes that by the time youths reach their senior year in high school, "many students spend more time on the job than they do in the classroom." Adolescent employment also appears to be a case of American exceptionalism: School-aged youths in the United States are far more likely to work than are their counterparts in other advanced industrial nations (Reubens et al. 1981; Steinberg 1996).

There is increasing evidence that extensive involvement in the labor market is deleterious to the social and psychological development of youths and fosters a range of deviant conduct (Steinberg 1996). Although the evidence is not uniform (Crowley 1984; Gottfredson 1985), research generally shows that for school-aged youths, working—especially working long hours—increases delinquent behavior (Agnew 1986; Cullen et al. 1997; Ploeger 1997; Wright et al. 1997). Whether working fosters delinquency on the job, however, is less clear.

Even so, Ruggiero et al. (1982) present at least preliminary evidence that similar to adults, the workplace is a context in which delinquency occurs. Based on a survey of 212 high school students in Orange County, California, who also held jobs, they found that 62 percent of the sample engaged in at least one act of "occupational deviance." In a multivariate analysis, they discovered that workplace misconduct was positively related to gender (being male) and materialistic attitudes. They also reported that occupational deviance was influenced by features of the workplace: It was increased by poor environmental conditions (e.g., noisy, hot) and opportunities for theft, and (unexpectedly) it was decreased by exposure to a negative social environment (e.g., unsupportive work relations).

To a degree, Ruggiero et al.'s research is suggestive that the quality of the workplace might influence the commission of occupationally related delinquencies. It is noteworthy that Agnew's (1992) general strain theory would predict that the presentation of noxious stimuli to workers would generate strain, negative emotions, and crime (see Agnew 1986; Chapter 10). Research does indicate that work dissatisfaction is related to occupational property offenses (Hollinger & Clark 1983). Conversely, it is plausible that positive work experiences might insulate against workplace illegalities. Adolescents typically work in minimum wage jobs concentrated in the secondary labor market. Most of the tasks they undertake are menial and monotonous, develop few cognitive skills, and offer limited opportunities for authority and responsibility (Steinberg 1996). Jobs that depart from this normative pattern and foster the development of skills might make work less stressful and more rewarding, and they might even foster social bonds to the employer (see Lasley 1988; Sampson & Laub 1993).

The work of Sutherland would suggest an alternative hypothesis: Social learning on the job encourages occupational delinquency. The new worker, noted Sutherland, is "inducted into white-collar crime. . . . He learns specific techniques of violating the law, together with definitions of situations in which those techniques may be used" (1983:245). Admittedly, Sutherland primarily focused on how employees were taught how to bilk customers, not how to steal from the company. Even so, it is conceivable that adolescent workers, who are surrounded by youths minimally supervised by adults (Steinberg 1996), will encounter peers that encourage wayward behavior on the job. Notably, theories that emphasize the criminogenic effects of being exposed to and learning an unethical organizational culture are common in analyses of adult white-collar crime (e.g., see Yeager 1986). In one study, Makkai and Braithwaite (1991) found little evidence that differential association was related to levels of regulatory compliance in a sample of nursing home chief executive officers. Moreover, in a study of advertisement professionals, Zey-Ferrell et al. (1982) found that measures of differential association produced mixed effects on engaging in "ethical and unethical" behavior. Their analysis, however, did point to the role differential associations play in influencing an individual's perception of opportunities to commit unethical behavior, such as "padding an expense account" and "divulging confidential information." Finally, qualitative accounts of corporate crime and misbehavior regularly depict certain work environments as criminogenic—that is, work environments where criminal values and motives flourish and are reinforced in small groups of workers. Notably, Geis's examination of the Heavy Electrical Equipment conspiracies (1967) and Vaughan's (1996) . . . analysis of the NASA space shuttle Challenger accident highlight the influence of normative structures of belief on individual action and conduct. Although instructive, these studies generally are focused on samples of professional, well-educated adults embedded in prestigious careers. It remains unclear, therefore, whether the learning environment found in the typical adolescent workplace would exert similar effects.

Other theorists would contend that workplace experiences have no impact on occupationally related crime. Thus, Gottfredson and Hirschi explicitly reject cultural explanations of white-collar crime and argue that, like other offenders, those committing occupational crimes are "people with low self-control, people inclined to follow momentary impulse without consideration of the long-term costs of such behavior" (1990:190–91). In essence, they contend that those with criminal propensities will manifest them in any social environment—in the family, in the school, in the streets, and in the workplace. Further, these enduring individual differences will account for any apparent effects of job-related social conditions. For example, if youths associate with delinquent peers at work and steal from the company, Gottfredson and Hirschi would assert that low self-control caused the youths both to "flock together" with other "bad kids" and to break the law (see Hirschi & Gottfredson 1995). In any event, other scholars have recognized that those predisposed to offending may acquire jobs and use the workplace as a source of illegal goods and income (e.g., see Horney et al. 1995; Sullivan 1989).

These considerations help to frame the analysis undertaken in the study. Thus, we explore how occupational delinquency is affected by the quality of the workplace—that is, whether youths are employed in a work environment that allows them to acquire positive job skills or that exposes them to negative job tasks and social relations. We also examine how coworkers' delinquency affects offending on the job. Alternatively, we weigh the influence of low self-control and past delinquency on workplace misconduct. Although limited by cross-sectional data, we then set forth a tentative causal model. We suggest that delinquent youths are more likely to work in negative environments, which in turn foster contact with coworkers who share delinquent orientations. We propose that delinquent predispositions affect workplace delinquency directly and by leading youths into occupational contexts where delinquent associates are acquired and affect social learning. If correct, this model would suggest that the workplace is a domain in which criminogenic peer associates are established—a possibility long understood by students of white-collar crime but heretofore ignored by delinquency theorists.

■ Methods

Sample

Data for this project come from the Tri-Cities Adolescent Employment Survey (TCAES), a cross-sectional survey conducted in eight high schools located in northeast Tennessee. The schools were selected because officials granted permission for their students to be interviewed during the school day. Within each school, a one-hour time period was allotted to complete the survey for all seniors present on the day the survey was administered. The surveys were administered in homeroom or in classes required of all seniors. Because of the restrictions placed on us by the local schools, only youths who had reached their senior year in high school could be surveyed (N = 436). Because our concern is with *workplace delinquency,* in the current study, we focus on those adolescents (N = 326) who were employed or who had reported working within the last year.

With the selection of schools and students within schools not accomplished through random methods, caution should be exercised in generalizing our findings to the population of adolescents at large. However, we do not believe that our results are the product of sampling for two reasons: First, the working seniors in our sample appear to compare favorably to working seniors across the United States. For example, in the nationally representative High School and Beyond Survey, 70 percent of the seniors reported working for pay. Seventy-three percent of the youths in the well-known Monitoring the Future Survey reported working for pay, and 70 percent of the adolescents in the National Survey of Families and Households worked for pay. Moreover, in a review of the literature, Steinberg and Cauffman (1995) note that most regional self-report studies also indicate that approximately 70 percent of youths are engaged in part-time employment (Mortimer & Finch 1996; Steinberg 1996). Specifically, Steinberg and Cauffman suggest that the available evidence shows that roughly 75 percent of all seniors are employed for pay. Data from the TCAES sample indicate that 75 percent of the high school seniors surveyed reported being employed at some point during high school, a very close approximation to the national estimates. Moreover, working students in our sample reported working 15 hours per week on average spread out over an average of three days per week, whereas working students reported starting to work at 15 years of age, working mostly after school, and having held two other jobs since beginning to work for pay.

Second, the pattern of findings lends a degree of predictive validity to these data. That is, variables typically found predictive of offending in previous studies, such as low self-control, are also associated in the expected direction with measures of delinquent behavior.

Measures

We included in the TCAES instrument previously published items and scales that measured a variety of work, family, school, and personal characteristics.

Moreover, because we were primarily interested in exploring how the quality of the work environment affects delinquent involvement, we also included several measures that assessed the work environment as well as the nature of social relationships within the work environment (see Appendix 15.1).

Occupational Delinquency. To measure work-related delinquent involvement, we employed a nine-item scale that was used previously by Ruggiero et al. (1982). The scale measures the extent to which working students engaged in acts such as theft at work, using alcohol and drugs while on the job, short-changing customers, placing more hours on a timecard than were actually worked, and calling in sick when they were not ill. The nine items in the occupational delinquency scale along with their frequencies are listed in Table 15.1.[1] The students were asked to state whether they engaged in each item "never," "sometimes," or "often." Cronbach's alpha for the scale was .83[2] [Cronbach's alpha is a measure of the internal consistency, or intercorrelation, of items in a scale. Also see the book appendix for a brief explanation of the other statistical techniques used in this chapter, e.g., OLS regression and the problem of multicollinearity in regression analysis.]

It is noteworthy that the level of involvement in the work-related delinquent acts closely matches the involvement found in the previous use of the scale by Ruggiero et al. (1982:436) in a sample drawn in Orange County, California. The only substantive differences are found in the items that measure calling in sick when not (12% higher in our study) and that measure stealing things from the employer or other coworkers (11% lower in our study). The remaining items correspond very closely with the distribution of offending generated in Ruggiero et al.'s data. The close correspondence of results between the two samples—drawn at different times and in widely disparate locations—suggests that the results reported here are unlikely to be idiosyncratic. The scale had a mean of 1.6. . . .

Table 15.1 Involvement of Youths in Occupational Delinquency, by Type of Item (N = 326)

Item	Percent Reporting		
	Never	Sometimes	Often
1. Put more hours on timecard than actually worked.	88	9	3
2. Purposely short-changed a customer.	95	4	1
3. Gave away goods or services for nothing without permission.	69	26	6
4. Took things from the employer or other coworkers.	93	5	2
5. Called in sick when not.	55	40	5
6. Drank alcohol or used drugs while on the job.	87	10	3
7. Purposely damaged employer's property.	96	2	2
8. Helped a coworker steal employer's property.	88	9	3
9. Lied to the employer to get or keep job.	95	4	1

Job Characteristics. Most adolescents work in minimum wage, service jobs that require few skills and limited training (Steinberg 1996). However, the quality of the adolescent workplace varies substantially. Therefore, we elected to measure directly characteristics of the workplace instead of relying on broad and ill-defined job titles, such as "fast-food" or "custodian."

We measure three separate aspects of the adolescent workplace. First, contact with delinquent peers is used frequently in studies as a measure of differential association (Akers 1998). Accordingly, we included a measure of *coworker delinquency.* For each of the nine items listed in Table 15.1, respondents were asked to state "how often your coworkers/supervisors" had engaged in certain acts. Again, the response options were "never," "sometimes," and "often." The alpha for the nine-item scale was .82.

Second, much of the stimulus to move adolescent students into the labor market has been predicated on the assumption that work benefits youths by teaching prosocial skills, such as discipline. We include a five-item scale, taken from Greenberger and Steinberg (1986a, 1986b), that assesses positive job skills, such as how well the jobs youths hold have taught them to manage their money, to take responsibility for their work, to be on time, to get along with others, and to follow directions (alpha = .82).

Third, several commentators have observed that adolescent work requires little training, is boring and mundane, and often involves working in unpleasant and dangerous conditions (Cullen et al. 1997; Steinberg 1996). Greenberger and Steinberg (1986a, 1986b) and Ruggiero et al. (1982) also note that autocratic supervision and general dissatisfaction with how much one is being paid accompany most adolescent work environments. Thus, using an 18-item scale, we measure *negative work environment* by summing scores along five dimensions that capture the quality of the workplace setting: poor work surroundings, dangerousness, job stress, autocratic supervision, and satisfaction with pay. The scale is standardized and has an alpha of .73 with a minimum of 2.67 and a maximum of 5.95.

Delinquent Propensity. We include measures that control for individual differences related to delinquency and adolescent employment for two reasons: First, delinquent youths may find the adolescent workplace a welcome alternative to family and school (Bachman & Schulenberg 1993; Cullen et al. 1997; Wright et al. 1997). Indeed, longitudinal evidence suggests that part of the correlation between adolescent employment and delinquent conduct, including drug use and educational failure, stems partly from preexisting individual differences that manifest temporally prior to entrance into the labor market (Bachman & Schulenberg 1993; Cullen et al. 1997; Mortimer et al. 1992). Thus, working, according to Bachman and Schulenberg, may "reflect one component of a syndrome of problem behavior or precocious development that is manifest before entry into part-time work" (1993:221; see also Newcomb & Bentler 1985).

Second, the importance of controlling for individual differences becomes all the more apparent when one considers that our primary purpose is to examine the effect of delinquent coworkers (peers) on levels of occupational delinquency. The criminological literature is replete with debate concerning the causal impact delinquent peers have on individual misconduct. In short, individual-level theorists argue that the association between delinquent peers and illegal behavior is spurious and accounted for by underlying delinquent propensities (Gottfredson & Hirschi 1990). However, social learning theory maintains that peers exert an independent, causal effect on behavior (Akers 1998). Without controls in place for self-selection, our results could be attributed to differences within individuals that predispose youths to work and to engage in delinquency.

Recognizing that we are constrained by cross-sectional data, we include two controls for *delinquent propensity*. Our measures have been used in longitudinal research and have been found predictive of future misconduct (Sampson & Laub 1993). First, we include a 12-item scale that measures the respondents' low self-control. Gottfredson and Hirschi (1990) argue that low self-control is a time-stable trait that is the cause of crime. The scale was a modified version of [the one] developed by Grasmick et al. (1993) . . . (see Appendix 15.1). Gottfredson and Hirschi argue that individuals with low self-control are likely to misbehave across settings, such as within schools or the workplace, and that because of their individual traits, youths with low self-control are also likely to select themselves into low-wage, low-skill jobs. Second, because much research points to delinquent involvement as beginning early in life and as relatively time stable, we also include a 13-item scale, taken from the National Youth Survey (Elliott et al. 1985), that captures whether a youth has ever engaged in certain delinquent behaviors, such as cheating on a test, being suspended from school, or having stolen something worth more than $50 (see Appendix 15.1). The alpha for the scale was .81. We note that we use a measure of the prevalence of delinquent involvement because we wish to capture prior participation in misbehavior.[3]

Social Characteristics. Aside from controlling for delinquent dispositions, we also include controls for the effects of school, beliefs, family, and background variables. *Grade point average* is a single-item measure that asked youths, on a five-point scale from 1 = Mostly F's to 5 = Mostly A's, what the average grade they received in their classes was. *School commitment* was measured through two items that ascertained how many hours, on average, the youth spent studying over the weekdays and weekends. . . . These measures are typically assumed to represent the bond of commitment and have been used frequently in prior studies (Hirschi 1969).

Materialism. Second, because Ruggiero et al. (1982) found that youths who strongly valued money committed more delinquency on the job (see also Agnew 1994), we included a three-item scale that measured *materialistic attitudes*. The scale assesses how important money is to respondents and whether their goals include "making a lot of money" (alpha = .79).

Family Background. Third, we also include three measures of the students' family background. The first, *parental attachment,* was measured through a 12-item scale that assessed the respondents' degree of emotional closeness to their parents. The scale was taken from the National Youth Survey (Elliott et al. 1985) and had a reliability of .90. The second, *family structure,* assessed whether the youth lived with both parents (0 = intact, 1 = nonintact). Finally, the third measure, *household size,* captured the number of people living within the household of the respondent.

We also included controls for gender (0 = male and 1 = female) and race (0 = white, 1 = minority). We note that we do not control for the effects of family income due to missing information, a problem typically found when youths are asked to report their parents' income. Previous research has generally not found family income to be a strong predictor of self-reported delinquency (Tittle & Meier 1990).[4] . . .

▨　Research Strategy

Our analyses proceeded in a sequential fashion. We first estimate an OLS [ordinary least-squares] regression equation that predicts levels of occupational delinquency. We include in the equation measures of job characteristics, delinquent propensity, the hazard term [controlling for selection bias], family and school background variables, and demographics. [The authors include a technical discussion of selection bias that we have omitted from this chapter. Selection bias in this case entails the question of whether some youths are more likely than others to work in the first place. The authors explain the statistical techniques they used to control for such bias, which they refer to as the "hazard term" in the subsequent analysis. Some additional statistical data not central to understanding the substantive results are omitted as well (see Berk 1983).] We hypothesize that the measure of coworker delinquency will exhibit substantial effects in predicting occupational delinquency, even with measures for delinquent propensity controlled.

Our attention then turns toward examining the predictors of coworker delinquency. If Gottfredson and Hirschi (1990) and Bachman and Schulenberg (1993) are correct, the delinquent predisposition variables should account for significant levels of variation in coworker delinquency, and they should account completely for the effects of other variables. Conversely, if Ploeger (1997) and Steinberg (1996) are correct in their assertion that the adolescent workplace acts to socialize youths into crime, the measure of negative work environment should demonstrate significant effects in predicting coworker delinquency.

As noted before, youths with a delinquent predisposition may find the adolescent workplace a welcome environment, because they may escape the restraints imposed by family and school and may receive earnings to be used for possibly illegal conduct (Cullen et al. 1997). However, if this logic is true and youths with delinquent propensities self-select themselves into adolescent workplace settings, they will also be more likely to interact with peers with similar criminal propensities. The interaction among youths high in delinquent potential associating with other delinquent youths may produce effects above and beyond the direct effects of being delinquent or of associating with delinquent coworkers. We test the possibility of an "amplification" effect by incorporating into a regression equation predicting occupational delinquency a multiplicative interaction between coworker delinquency and delinquent propensity.

What happens "under the roof" of the adolescent workplace also may have effects that "spill over" outside the workplace. Thus, the final OLS equation predicts delinquent involvement over the last year. We compute this equation to assess the extent to which the effects of adolescent employment "spill over" into out-of-work experiences. That is, we test to see if what transpires within the adolescent workplace predicts illegal behavior outside of the workplace.

Finally, we establish and test a path diagram that models the indirect effects of negative work environment on coworker delinquency and occupational delinquency.

◼ Results

Table 15.2 presents the results of the OLS regression equation predicting delinquency. As hypothesized, the measure of coworkers' delinquency exhibited substantive and statistically significant effects (beta = .446). No other job characteristic, however, predicted the job-related misbehavior of youths. These findings suggest that the effects of the adolescent work environment are shaped by the kinds of adolescents that are employed on the job—that is, by the content of social interactions that occur in the workplace.

Although the measure of coworker delinquency produced substantive effects on the occupational delinquency of youths, other variables also contributed to the explained variation in job-related misbehavior. Thus, higher levels of delinquent involvement predicted higher levels of occupational delinquency. Moreover, students with higher grade point averages had lower levels of job-related misbehavior, whereas youths who hold strong materialistic values reported significantly more involvement in occupational delinquency. . . . Taken together, these findings seemingly indicate that working students bring to the workplace certain character traits that predispose them to engage in delinquency while on the job. Although we are limited by cross-sectional data, these findings suggest that delinquent youths, who also do poorly in school and who place a strong value on money, import those characteristics into the workplace and, in turn, engage in job-related delinquency.

Table 15.2 The Effects of Job Characteristics on Occupational Delinquency (N = 299)

Independent Variables	b	Beta	S.E.	T-Value
Job Characteristics				
Delinquent Coworkers	.276	.446	.035	7.882
Positive Job Skills	−.011	−.016	.040	−.287
Negative Work Environment	.008	.058	.025	.421
Delinquent Propensity				
Low Self-Control	.011	.027	.027	.389
Delinquency	.157	.234	.057	2.737
School Background				
Grade Point Average	−.363	−.140	.147	−2.472
School Commitment	−.039	−.100	.027	−1.470
Materialism				
Materialistic Attitudes	.086	.103	.048	1.779
Family Background				
Parental Attachment	.007	.058	.008	.905
Household Size	.089	.054	.092	.965
Family Structure (0 = intact)	−.085	−.021	.245	−.345
Demographics				
Gender (1 = female)	−.286	−.074	.253	−1.129
Race (1 = minority)	.793	.114	.385	2.061
Selection Hazard				
Hazard Term	−2.181	−.112	1.777	−1.227
R^2	.385			

Finally, we also note that youths who were minority reported engaging in occupational delinquency at relatively higher levels and that the hazard term did not reach statistical significance.

Because evidence suggests that youths high in delinquent propensity self-select themselves into adolescent work roles and, consequentially, into work environments that contain other similarly predisposed youths (Bachman & Schulenberg 1983; Steinberg & Cauffman 1995), we calculated an OLS equation that predicts the presence of delinquent coworkers in a youth's work environment. The results are shown in Table 15.3. The strongest predictor of delinquent coworkers is the measure of negative work environment (beta = .268). To remind the reader, this measure captured certain negative dimensions of the adolescent workplace, such as job-related stress and autocratic supervision. Thus, the quality of the workplace does not appear to influence directly the occupational delinquency of working students (see Table 15.2); instead, it appears to influence their delinquency indirectly by structuring exposure to delinquent coworkers.

In further support of this interpretation, Table 15.3 also reveals that the hazard term [controlling for selection bias] reached statistical significance and exerted a substantial, positive, independent effect predicting delinquent coworkers.

Table 15.3 The Effects of Job Characteristics, Delinquent Disposition, Social Background, and Demographics on Delinquent Coworkers (N = 286)

Independent Variables	b	Beta	S.E.	T-Value
		Dependent Variable: Delinquent Coworkers		
Job Characteristics				
Positive Job Skills	.097	.083	.075	1.297
Negative Work Environment	.136	.268	.033	4.069
Delinquent Propensity				
Low Self-Control	.001	.016	.050	.198
Delinquency	.007	.006	.106	.061
School Background				
Grade Point Average	.279	.067	.276	1.011
School Commitment	.064	.103	.049	1.299
Materialism				
Materialistic Attitudes	.014	.010	.089	.155
Family Background				
Parental Attachment	−.013	−.063	.015	−.853
Household Size	.018	.007	.172	.103
Family Structure (0 = intact)	.200	.030	.461	.435
Demographics				
Gender (1 = female)	−.255	−.041	.473	−.539
Race (1 = minority)	1.222	.108	.723	1.689
Selection Hazard				
Hazard Term	7.505	.240	3.284	2.285
R^2	.150			

The direction of this effect indicates that youths at a higher risk for working while in school—that is, those who are delinquent, low in self-control, and who do poorly in school—are more likely to report the presence of delinquent coworkers. Again, these results suggest that contact with delinquent peers in the workplace is due both to self-selection (the importation of personal traits into the work environment) and to social causation (the effects of negative work environments structuring associations with delinquent coworkers).

These findings raise the issue of whether delinquent youths who come into contact with delinquent coworkers have more job-related misbehavior than is accounted for by the direct effects of delinquent involvement and coworker delinquency. We test this "amplification" thesis by constructing a multiplicative interaction between our measure of delinquency and the measure of coworker delinquency. We note that to combat multicollinearity, we centered the main terms prior to computing the interaction.

The results provide support for the amplification thesis and are shown in Table 15.4. The interaction term reached statistical significance and added 5 percent to the explained variance in occupational delinquency. Delinquent youths

Table 15.4 Ordinary Least-Squares Estimates of Interaction Between Delinquent Coworkers and Delinquency: A Test of the Amplification Thesis (N = 286)

	Occupational Delinquency			
Independent Variables	b	Beta	S.E.	T-Value
Job Characteristics				
Delinquent Coworkers	.264	.427	.034	7.843
Positive Job Skills	.002	.000	.038	.007
Negative Work Environment	.010	.039	.018	.695
Delinquent Propensity				
Low Self-Control	.039	.100	.027	1.468
Delinquency	.094	.140	.057	1.655
School Background				
Grade Point Average	−.296	−.115	.142	−2.091
School Commitment	−.024	−.062	.026	−.937
Materialism				
Materialistic Attitudes	.040	.048	.047	.848
Family Background				
Parental Attachment	.012	.099	.008	1.589
Household Size	.056	.052	.088	.969
Family Structure (0 = intact)	.020	.005	.237	.084
Demographics				
Gender (1 = female)	−.365	−.095	.244	−1.499
Race (1 = minority)	.757	.109	.369	2.052
Selection Hazard				
Hazard Term	−.585	−.030	1.740	−.336
Interaction Term	.049	.246	.011	4.452
R^2	.437			

interacting with delinquent coworkers increase their occupational delinquency above and beyond the direct effects of either engaging in delinquency or in associating with delinquent coworkers (beta = .246). Thus, it appears that when youths already high in delinquent potential enter the adolescent workplace and associate with similarly delinquent others, the joint effect is to produce substantively greater work-related misbehavior.

What transpires within the adolescent workplace likely carries over into other domains of behavior. That is, youths associating with delinquent coworkers while on the job are more likely to also engage in delinquent acts outside of the boundaries of the workplace. We test the possibility of a "spill-over" effect in the next regression equation by modeling delinquency "over the last year" as an outcome variable. The results are shown in Table 15.5.

Overall, the findings demonstrate that associating with delinquent coworkers predicts higher levels of delinquency conducted outside the workplace (beta = .190). The associations made within the workplace, thus, appear to carry with them behavioral consequences outside of the domain of work, implicating the

Table 15.5 The Effects of Job Characteristics on Delinquency in the Last Year (N = 286)

Independent Variables	b	Beta	S.E.	T-Value
		Dependent Variable: Delinquency Last Year		
Job Characteristics				
Delinquent Coworkers	.163	.190	.048	3.253
Positive Job Skills	−.009	−.009	.058	−.160
Negative Work Environment	−.006	−.015	.026	−.242
Delinquent Propensity				
Low Self-Control	.148	.279	.034	4.326
School Background				
Grade Point Average	−.236	−.071	.196	−1.207
School Commitment	−.053	−.102	.032	−1.665
Materialism				
Materialistic Attitudes	.061	.054	.067	.905
Family Background				
Parental Attachment	−.012	−.072	.011	−1.087
Household Size	−.077	−.035	.128	−.602
Family Structure (0 = intact)	−.137	−.025	.346	−.397
Demographics				
Gender (1 = female)	−.488	−.095	.305	−1.598
Race (1 = minority)	.528	.057	.535	.987
R^2	.230			

adolescent workplace as a source for delinquent peer associations. Moreover, the findings show that students low in self-control are also more likely to report higher levels of delinquent involvement.

Thus far, our findings suggest that self-selection and work-related socialization mechanisms contribute to occupational delinquency. In the final analysis, we present the results of a tentative causal model that locates low self-control as temporally prior to entrance into employment, an assumption strongly supported by individual-level theories (Gottfredson & Hirschi 1990; Wilson & Herrnstein 1985) and a substantial body of empirical research (Bachman & Schulenberg 1993). In turn, youths low in self-control are more likely to select themselves into greater on-the-job misconduct. We posit within the model, however, that low self-control will not fully account for the relationship between negative work environment and delinquent coworkers. Such a finding would demonstrate that the adolescent work environment structures exposure to delinquent coworkers and that such exposure increases the likelihood of associating with delinquent coworkers without regard to the characteristics of the working youth—that is, whether they are delinquent. We also note that we have controlled for the effects of the sample selection hazard term on each of the endogenous variables.[5]

The findings are shown in Figure 15.1. First, the proposed model fit the data well, . . . indicating that the proposed structure of relationships did not vary significantly from the covariance matrix. Second, as expected, low self-control appears to affect each of the other variables in the model, predicting selection into negative work environments, associations with delinquent co-workers, and increased occupational delinquency. However, even with correc-tions in place for self-selection, negative work environment still maintained effects on delinquent coworkers, which, in turn, predicted increased occupa-tional delinquency and increased involvement in delinquency over the last year. Thus, the pattern of results garnered from our path model suggests that work-ing in negative work settings acts to increase occupational delinquency indi-rectly by patterning the exposure to delinquent coworkers.

◼ Discussion

Criminologists have generally viewed adolescence as a time encompassed by families, schools, and peer groups. Although exceptions exist (e.g., see Cullen et al. 1997; Steinberg 1996; Sullivan 1989), they have not examined juveniles as economic actors who often spend substantial segments of their teenage years in the workplace; but for most youths, growing up in the United States means moving into the labor market during adolescence and while still of school age (Steinberg 1996). In short, the social world of juveniles includes going to work, and thus a full understanding of the factors affecting their de-velopment and potential misconduct will involve an assessment of their work-place experiences (Steinberg 1996).

In recent years, there has been a relatively small but growing body of re-search exploring the impact of work experiences on delinquency and on other

Figure 15.1 Modeling Effects of Self-Selection into Negative Work Environments, Delinquent Coworker Networks, and Occupational Delinquency

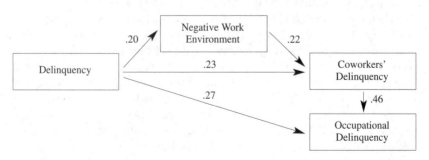

[*Note:* Some extraneous statistical information has been removed from the original figure.]

developmental outcomes (for summaries, see Steinberg 1996; Williams et al. 1997). With the exception of Ruggiero et al.'s (1982) study, however, virtually no quantitative research has investigated whether the workplace is a domain in which youths commit delinquent acts and, if so, what causal processes are operative. Again, the insights of Sutherland and other white-collar crime scholars suggest that employment may create the incentive and offer the opportunity for illegal behavior. A goal of our research is to call attention to and to explore empirically these possibilities.

The results support the conclusion that youths engage in occupationally related delinquency: In our study, two-thirds of the respondents reported committing at least one such delinquent act in the past year. Moreover, the frequency distributions across the nine items in the self-report scale were remarkably similar to those found in Ruggiero et al.'s (1982) study on Orange County, California, youths—a convergence that suggests the findings on our Tennessee sample are not idiosyncratic. More generally, future research seeking to measure self-reported delinquency would benefit from developing items that measure transgressions in the domain of work.

The analyses also have theoretical implications. First, we did not find that the quality of the workplace had a significant [direct] impact on occupational delinquency: Neither a negative work environment nor employment where positive jobs skills are acquired fostered or reduced misconduct. This finding was somewhat unexpected in light of research linking delinquency and other health outcomes to noxious work environments (Agnew 1986; Shanahan et al. 1991; Steinberg 1996). In any event, these results are not consistent with Agnew's (1992) general strain theory or with Sampson and Laub's (1993) informal social control theory, which would link crime to the presence of noxious stimuli and to the absence of positive bonds, respectively. Let us hasten to note that the results could well be revised if systematic measures of general strain and informal social bonds in the workplace were developed (see Lasley 1988; Makkai & Braithwaite 1991). The other possibility, however, is that the dominant influences on workplace delinquency reside elsewhere.

In this regard, our findings are favorable to the prominent view within white-collar crime scholarship—a view that extends to Sutherland (1983)—that the workplace is a social environment in which values and techniques supportive of wayward conduct are learned in interaction with coworkers. Admittedly, our analysis did not include measures of all components of social learning theory (see Akers et al. 1979). Even so, our measure of differential association—delinquent coworkers, who might be considered as "workplace peers"—was significantly and positively related to occupational delinquency. This relationship remained strong even with controls in the analysis for delinquent propensity, including past delinquency and self-control. Thus, it appears that workplace delinquency is not merely a reflection of individual differences imported into the job, and that the delinquent coworker–delinquency relationship is not spurious.

Two additional points regarding coworkers deserve comment. First, it appears that associating with delinquent peers on the job may increase delinquency outside of the workplace. Sutherland (1983) and white-collar crime scholars have largely assumed that workplace deviant learning experiences are domain specific: They cause employees to break the law at work but not necessarily in the community where they are "respectable" citizens (e.g., see Cressey 1953). In contrast, a broader social learning perspective would argue that delinquent peer associations—wherever they occur—may have criminogenic effects that are not restricted to a given social setting, such as the workplace (Akers 1998). The key issue may be whether a worker learns "definitions" or "neutralizations" whose content are specific to the situation (e.g., "it's okay to steal food at work because everyone does it") or learns general definitions that can affect behavior across social domains (see Akers 1998). Our results suggest that the social learning that occurs in the workplace has effects that are not domain specific but rather "spill over" into other areas of a youth's life.

Second and relatedly, the workplace might well be seen as a place in which peer relationships—whether criminogenic or not—are acquired. There is an implicit assumption in standard criminological discussions of delinquent peers that they are encountered in the immediate neighborhood or in schools. However true this may be, employment may expose youths to a more diverse social network. Further, when it is recalled that youths may spend upward of 20 hours a week working in close proximity with other youths—and often with minimal adult supervision (Steinberg 1996)—it seems likely that employment will be a source of peer relationships that potentially have substantial effects on a youth's orientations and behavior. Criminologists, thus, might profit from exploring how, similar to adults (Sampson & Laub 1993), the workplace offers opportunities for new social relationships that might foster or insulate against criminal behavior inside and outside the job.

Beyond the influence of delinquent coworkers, the data also revealed that delinquent propensities have direct effects on occupational delinquency. Again, the results are not consistent with Gottfredson and Hirschi's (1990) contention that occupational transgressions reflect exclusively underlying, enduring criminogenic propensities. Still, the analysis supports the view that youths who are delinquent outside the workplace are more likely to be delinquent on the job. Thus, it appears that there are individual differences in delinquent propensities between those who do and do not engage in occupational misconduct. This possibility is only infrequently considered by white-collar crime researchers (for an exception, see Collins & Schmidt 1993).

Perhaps more noteworthy, the analysis was suggestive that delinquent propensity may exert indirect effects on occupational delinquency. Consistent with other individual theorists (e.g., see Newcomb & Bentler 1985), Gottfredson and Hirschi (1990) contend that delinquent propensities—which they link to low self-control—will affect many choices and experiences in life, including success in employment. An alternative . . . view is that involvement in crime "knifes off" opportunities and depresses occupational attainment (e.g., see Sampson & Laub 1993). In either case, it appears that youths with delinquent propensities are selected (by themselves or by others) into jobs marked by negative work environments. It then appears that once in this workplace, they are likely to encounter youths similarly disposed to delinquency. These social interactions or "differential associations" in turn have an independent effect on occupational delinquency. This interpretation is consistent with the path model we presented as well as with the finding of the significant impact on occupational misconduct of the delinquency x delinquent coworkers interaction term.

More broadly, this line of reasoning indicates that individual differences, such as delinquent propensities, do not always operate independent of social context. In the case of occupational delinquencies, at least, they appear to be manifestations of propensities, coworker peer relations, and the interaction of the two. Although there may be theoretical utility in pitting individual difference positions versus social explanations (see Hirschi & Gottfredson 1995), it also appears that efforts should be made to discern how individual differences operate through social relationships and contexts (see Sampson & Laub 1993). For example, there may be particular benefit in exploring how the structure of opportunities for crime vary by work environment and interact with individual traits.

Although our results fit a pattern that suggests the importance of self-selection and social causation, we remind the reader that our data are cross-sectional and that our analyses are premised on some rather strong, but warranted, assumptions about the stability of delinquent propensity across time. Future research will have to verify our findings by employing a longitudinal design, preferably a design that measures the behavior of youths, their personality traits, and their social networks prior to their entrance into formal employment.

We should note, moreover, that the data set did not allow us to explore how employment may provide new opportunities to commit delinquent acts (e.g., access to money and goods to steal). Of course, the link of employment to criminal opportunity is frequently mentioned in scholarly works in white-collar crime (Coleman 1988). Future research should investigate how access to different types of jobs might furnish more or less opportunity to offend. . . . More broadly, Cloward (1959) argues that criminal opportunity involves more than the mere physical ability to perform an act (e.g., have access to goods to steal). Instead, he suggests that it also involves "learning structures" in which people learn the values and skills that make undertaking a criminal act possible. In this regard, delinquent peers in the workplace might help to foster access to opportunity by providing the learning structure for workplace illegalities.

Finally, we call attention to the impact of "materialistic attitudes" in increasing occupational delinquency. Two observations seem relevant. First, this finding suggests that future research should explore how work related or, more broadly, economically related attitudes influence delinquency. Previous research by Agnew is instructive in that it found divergent effects by types of attitudes. In one study, Agnew (1986) reported that a commitment to the "work ethic" insulated against delinquent involvement. In another study, and consistent with our results, he learned that "the desire for money" fostered misconduct (Agnew 1994).

Second, our finding on materialistic attitudes is open to two divergent, but potentially interrelated, explanations. On the one hand, the desire for money and for consumption—an orientation that might be seen as the opposite of belief in hard work and delayed gratification (Agnew 1994)—could be an element of or proxy for low self-control. That is, our measure of materialistic attitudes could be assessing an underlying orientation for immediate and easy gratification—the kind of propensity Gottfredson and Hirschi (1990) define as low self-control and link to criminal behavior.

On the other hand, Messner and Rosenfeld's macro-level [anomie-opportunity] theory illuminates the possibility that adolescence in the United States—much more than in other advanced industrial nations—has been "penetrated" by the dominance of economic institutions and its encouragement of the "fetishism of money" (1994:71; [see Chapter 14]). On the individual level, the overweening emphasis on money could increase crime by attenuating norms regulating goal attainment through legitimate means and by fostering a crass utilitarian individualism that justifies securing goals through the "technically most expedient means" (Messner & Rosenfeld 1994:85–87).

Perhaps more intriguing, however, is to consider how the penetration of economic influences into the life-course development of youths might help to create what Gottfredson and Hirschi call low self-control and that they attribute almost exclusively to parenting practices within the family. Critical criminologists, of course, have long alerted us to how capitalism can foster "egoism" (Bonger 1916) and strong materialistic needs (Greenberg 1993). On a more specific level, however, we can consider how the persistent, intense marketing of products, the creation of consumption desires, and the glorification of materialism—all of which occurs from early childhood onward—may attenuate internal restraints and solidify the desire for immediate, easy, and exciting gratifications (Gottfredson & Hirschi 1990:90). If so, individual differences in self-control may be, at least in part, a reflection not only of what parents do, but also of the cultural and structural contexts in which American youths are enmeshed.

Appendix 15.1

Variable

School Commitment: On average, how many hours per week do you spend on the weeknights studying? How many hours per week do you spend on the weekends studying?

Family Attachment: On a five point scale, from 1 = never to 5 = always

How often do you do things with your mother and/or your father?
How often do you do things with your parents that you enjoy?
How often do you talk to your parents about personal or private issues?
How often do you talk over important decisions with your parents?
How often do your parents miss important events?
How often do you feel like your parents are there for you when you need them?
How often do your parents listen to your side on an argument?
How often do your parents discuss important issues with you?
How often do you have a difficult time dealing with your parents?
How often do you argue or not get along with your parents?
How often do your parents know where you are at when you are away from home?
How often do your parents ask where you are going when you leave home to go someplace?
How often do your parents know who you are with when you are away from home?
(alpha = .90)

Materialistic Attitudes
My goal in life is to make a lot of money
Money is very important to have
My goal in life is to buy a lot of things
(alpha = .79)

Positive Job Skills
My job has taught me how to follow directions more closely
My job has taught me how to better get along with other people
My job has taught me how to be on time
My job has taught me how to take responsibility for my work
My job has taught me how to manage my money
(alpha = .82)

Negative Work Environment
My job duties are routine
I perform the same tasks daily
My job duties are boring
My job duties are repetitive
I do the same tasks over and over
My job requires little skill
My job offers little opportunity for learning
I am under a lot of pressure to get things done while at my job
I have too much work to do to get everything done at my job
I have to work very hard at my job
My job expects too much from me
Sometimes I am unclear about what I have to do on my job
I am often held responsible for things that happen on my job that I have no control over
I feel as if I cannot disagree with my supervisor
I am under close supervision while at work
I get along great with my supervisor
I rarely socialize with my supervisor or coworkers outside of work
I am satisfied with the rate of pay I receive
Have you ever been injured or hurt on any job badly enough that you needed to miss school or
     work for at least one day
In the past 12 months, how many times have you been hurt or injured on any job?
(alpha = .73)

Low Self-Control: On a four point scale, from 1 = strongly disagree to
4 = strongly agree
I often act on the spur of the moment without stopping to think
I often do whatever brings me pleasure here and now, even at the cost of
     some distant goal

I'm more concerned with what happens to me in the short run than in the long run
I frequently try to avoid projects that I know will be difficult
I dislike really hard tasks that stretch my abilities to the limit
Excitement and adventure are more important than security
I sometimes find it exciting to do things for which I might get into trouble
I try to look out for myself first, even if it means making things harder for other people
I will try to get the things I want even when I know it's causing problems for other people
I lose my temper easily
When I'm really angry other people better stay away from me
It doesn't take much for me to get really angry or to lose my temper
(alpha = .76)

Delinquency (ever and in the past year): Have you ever
Cheated on school tests?
Skipped school without your parents' permission?
Stole something worth less than $50.00?
Stole something worth more than $50.00?
Purposely damaged or destroyed school property?
Purposely damaged or destroyed someone else's property?
Been in a fist-fight?
Drank alcohol?
Smoked marijuana?
Been suspended from school?
Smoked cigarettes?
Been drunk in a public place?
Hit someone hard enough that they needed bandages or medical care?
(alpha = .81, ever; alpha = .83, in last year)

▓ Notes

1. The items that compose the occupational delinquency scale measure relatively minor forms of delinquent on-the-job behavior. However, commission of anyone of these specific acts can result in job termination and, if repeated across jobs, can result in an unstable job history—a hallmark of adult criminal histories. Moreover, methodological studies into the validity and reliability of measures of "common delinquency," or items that assess minor forms of delinquency and deviance, show that they often are more accurately reported than are more serious crimes because measures of serious crime "are typically more complex and ambiguous" (Hirschi et al. 1982:434; but see also Hindelang et al. 1981). Finally, we note that substantial covariance exists between the individual items that compose our occupational delinquency scale and the individual items that measure coworker delinquency and self-reported delinquent behaviors. Thus, although we cannot tell if the subjects in our sample are committing serious forms of crime at work, such as giving away valuable computers or inexpensive ice-cream cones, the pattern of correlations demonstrate substantial overlap between measures of nonserious occupational delinquency and more serious forms of misbehavior, including measures of theft, vandalism, assault, and drug use. Clearly, future research should measure a broader and more serious range of occupational misbehaviors.

2. Overall, the occupational delinquency scale contains limited, but sufficient, variation for analysis. We undertook several strategies to examine potential scale bias. First, to account for the skewness in our dependent measure, we conducted a series of transformations, including standardizing and logarithmic transformations. In no case did adjusting the distribution of the scale make a meaningful difference in the analy-

ses, which included OLS regression and logistic regression. Second, we estimated OLS models for each item that contained sufficient variation and logistic regression models for those individual items that contained only limited variation. For the logistic models, we collapsed certain items, such as "purposely damaged employer's property," into "yes" or "no" categories. Third, we also estimated a separate OLS model for the scale without item 5 included in the dependent variable (i.e., "called in sick when not"). This act is relatively nonserious and was committed by 40 percent of the sample. Regardless, in these analyses, the results were consistent with those reported for the scale as a whole.

3. Accounting for delinquent propensity with cross-sectional data is clearly problematic, because measures of propensity are made at the same time delinquency is measured. However, to provide a conservative test of our propositions, we chose to include measures that tap into individual differences in delinquent involvement and differences among youths in personality traits related to offending, such as low self-control. Although not perfect, the inclusion of these variables help to assure that our results cannot be attributed to self-selection factors. We also note that including a measure of the prevalence of delinquency in the equation predicting occupational delinquency should substantially reduce the likelihood of model misspecification, because the two scales share variance (r = .398) and measure different domains of misbehavior.

4. Adolescent estimates of parental income are notoriously unreliable and typically contain numerous missing data. Not surprisingly, our measure of parental income is also burdened by these problems. To ensure that the exclusion of parental income did not affect our results, we estimated various models with the income variable in place. Listwise, casewise, mean replacement and maximum-likelihood estimation techniques (using the EM algorithm) were used to estimate the effects of missing data. In no model did the parental income variable reach statistical significance.

5. Clearly, our path model is suggestive only, as we cannot definitively establish the causal ordering of all variables. However, the findings are theoretically consistent with our argument and with past studies (Steinberg 1996). We also note that in other models we included "delinquency over the last year" as an outcome variable. The results remained consistent with the conclusions already drawn about the potential for delinquency to "spill over" outside the work environment. To retain the focus of our study and to keep the model parsimonious, we present only the accompanying results.

References

Agnew, Robert. 1986. "Work and Delinquency among Juveniles Attending School." *Journal of Crime & Justice* 9:19–41.

———. 1990. "Adolescent Resources and Delinquency." *Criminology* 28:531–66.

———. 1992. "Foundation for a General Strain Theory of Crime and Delinquency." *Criminology* 30:47–86.

———. 1993. "Why Do They Do It? An Examination of the Intervening Mechanisms between Social Control Variables and Delinquency." *Journal of Research in Crime & Delinquency* 30:245–66.

———. 1994 "Delinquency and the Desire for Money." *Justice Quarterly* 11:411–27.

Akers, Ronald L. 1998. *Social Learning and Social Structure: A General Theory of Crime and Deviance.* Boston: Northeastern University Press.

Akers, Ronald L., Marvin D. Krohn, Lonn Lanza-Kaduce & Marcia Radosevich. 1979. "Social Learning and Deviant Behavior: A Specific Test of a General Theory."

American Sociological Review 44:635–55.

Bachman, Jerald G., Dawn E. Bare & Eric I. Frankie. 1986. *Correlates of Employment Among High School Seniors.* Ann Arbor: Institute for Social Research, University of Michigan.

Bachman, Jerald G., Lloyd D. Johnston & Patrick M. O'Malley. 1984. *Monitoring the Future: Questionnaire Responses from the Nation's High School Seniors, 1982.* Ann Arbor: Institute for Social Research, University of Michigan.

Bachman, Jerald G. & John Schulenberg. 1993. "How Part-time Work Intensity Relates to Drug Use, Problem Behavior, Time Use, and Satisfaction Among High School Seniors: Are These Consequences or Merely Correlates?" *Developmental Psychology* 29:220–35.

Berk, Richard A. 1983. "An Introduction to Sample Selection Bias in Sociological Data." *American Sociological Review* 48:386–98.

Bonger, William A. 1916. *Criminality and Economic Conditions.* Boston: Little, Brown.

Bureau of Labor Statistics. 1996. Internet Homepage (http://www.bls.gov/).

Chiricos, Theodore G. 1987. "Rates of Crime and Unemployment: An Analysis of Aggregate Research Evidence." *Social Problems* 34:187–212.

Cloward, Richard A. 1959. "Illegitimate Means, Anomie, and Deviant Behavior." *American Sociological Review* 24:164–76.

Coleman, James W. 1988. "Toward an Integrated Theory of White-collar Crime." *American Journal of Sociology* 93:406–39.

Collins, J. M. & F. L. Schmidt. 1993. "Personality, Integrity and White-collar Crime: A Construct Validity Study." *Personnel Psychology* 46:295–311.

Cressey, Donald R. 1953. *Other People's Money.* Glencoe, IL: Free Press.

Crowley, Joan E. 1984. "Delinquency and Employment: Substitutions or Spurious Associations." In M. Borus (ed.), *Youth and the Labor Market: An Analysis of the National Longitudinal Survey.* Kalamazoo, MI: W. E. Upjohn Institute for Employment Research.

Cullen, Francis T., Nicolas Williams & John Paul Wright. 1997. "Work Conditions and Juvenile Delinquency: Is Youth Employment Criminogenic?" *Criminal Justice Policy Review* 8:119–44.

Daly, Kathleen. 1989. "Gender and Varieties of White-collar Crime." *Criminology* 27: 769–94.

Elliott, Delbert S., David Huizinga & Suzanne S. Ageton. 1985. *Explaining Delinquency and Drug Use.* Beverly Hills, CA: Sage.

———. 1989. *Multiple Problem Youth: Delinquency, Substance Use and Mental Health Problems.* New York: Springer-Verlag.

Farrington, David. 1986. "Unemployment, School Leaving, and Crime." *British Journal of Criminology* 26:335–56.

Freedman, Deborah S. & Arland Thornton. 1990. "The Consumption Aspirations of Adolescents: Determinants and Implications." *Youth & Society* 21:259–81.

Geis, Gilbert. 1967. "White-collar Crime: The Heavy Electrical Equipment Antitrust Cases of 1961." In M. Clinard & R. Quinney (eds.), *Criminal Behavior Systems.* New York: Holt, Rinehart & Winston.

Good, David H., Maureen A. Pirog-Good & Robin C. Sickles. 1986. "An Analysis of Youth Crime and Employment Patterns." *Journal of Quantitative Criminology* 2:219–36.

Gottfredson, Denise C. 1985. "Youth Employment, Crime, and Schooling: A Longitudinal Study of a National Sample." *Developmental Psychology* 21:419–32.

Gottfredson, Michael R. & Travis Hirschi. 1990. *A General Theory of Crime.* Stanford,

CA: Stanford University Press.

Granovetter, Mark. 1985. "Economic Action and Social Structure: The Problem of Embeddedness." *American Journal of Sociology* 91:481–510.

———. 1992. "The Sociological and Economic Approaches to Labour Market Analysis: A Social Structural View." In M. Granovetter & R. Swedberg (eds.), *The Sociology of Economic Life.* Boulder, CO: Westview Press.

Grasmick, Harold G., Charles R. Tittle, Robert J. Bursik, Jr. & Bruce J. Arneklev. 1993. "Testing the Core Empirical Implications of Gottfredson and Hirschi's General Theory of Crime." *Journal of Research in Crime & Delinquency* 30:5–29.

Greenberg, David F. 1993. "Delinquency and the Age Structure of Society." In D. Greenberg, (ed.), *Crime and Capitalism.* Philadelphia: Temple University Press.

Greenberger, Ellen & Laurence Steinberg. 1986a. *When Teenagers Work: The Psychological and Social Costs of Adolescent Employment.* New York: Basic Books.

———. 1986b. "The Workplace as a Context for the Socialization of Youth." *Journal of Youth & Adolescence* 10:185–210.

Greenberger, Ellen, Laurence Steinberg & Mary Ruggiero. 1982. "A Job Is a Job Is a Job . . . or Is It?" *Work & Occupations* 9:79–96.

Heimer, Karen. 1995. "Gender, Race, and the Pathways to Delinquency: An Interactionist Explanation." In J. Hagan & R. Peterson (eds.), *Crime and Inequality.* Stanford, CA.: Stanford University Press.

Hindelang, Michael J., Travis Hirschi & Joseph Weis. 1981. *Measuring Delinquency.* Beverly Hills, CA: Sage.

Hirschi, Travis. 1969. *Causes of Delinquency.* Berkeley: University of California Press.

———. 1983. "Crime and the Family." In J. Wilson (ed.), *Crime and Public Policy.* San Francisco: ICS Press.

Hirschi, Travis & Michael R. Gottfredson. 1995. "Control Theory and the Life-course Perspective." *Studies on Crime & Crime Prevention* 4:131–42.

Hirschi, Travis, Michael J. Hindelang & Joseph G. Weis. 1982. *The Measurement of Delinquency by the Self-Report Method.* Cambridge, MA: Oelgeschlager, Gunn & Hain.

Hollinger, Richard D. & John P. Clark. 1983. *Theft by Employees.* Lexington, MA: Lexington.

Horney, Julie D., D. Wayne Osgood & Ineke Haen Marshall. 1995. "Criminal Careers in the Short-term: Intra-individual Variability in Crime and Its Relation to Local Life Circumstances." *American Sociological* Review 60:655–73.

Lasley, Jim. 1988. "Toward a Control Theory of White-collar Offending." *Journal of Quantitative Criminology* 44:347–62.

Makkai, Toni & John Braithwaite. 1991. "Criminological Theories and Regulatory Compliance." *Criminology* 29:191–220.

Messner, Steven F. & Richard Rosenfeld. 1994. *Crime and the American Dream.* Belmont, CA: Wadsworth.

Mortimer, Jeylan T. & Michael D. Finch. 1986. "The Development of Self-esteem in the Early Work Career." *Work & Occupations* 13:217–39.

Mortimer, Jeylan T., Michael Finch, Michael Shanahan & Seongryeol Ryu. 1992. "Adolescent Work History and Behavioral Adjustment." *Journal of Research on Adolescence* 21:59–80.

National Commission on Youth. 1980. *The Transition of Youth to Adulthood: A Bridge Too Long.* Boulder, CO: Westview Press.

Newcomb, Michael D. & Peter M. Bentler. 1985. "The Impact of High School Substance Use on Choice of Young Adult Living Environment and Career Direction." *Journal of Drug Education* 15:253–61.

Pearce, Frank. 1976. *Crimes of the Powerful.* London: Pluto Press.

Phillips, Sarah & Kent L. Sandstrom. 1990. "Parental Attitudes toward Youth Work." *Youth & Society* 22:160–83.

Ploeger, Matthew. 1997. "Youth Employment and Delinquency: Reconsidering a Problematic Relationship." *Criminology* 35:659–76.

Reubens, Beatrice G., John A. C. Harrison & Kalman Rupp. 1981. *The Youth Labor Force 1945–1995: A Cross National Analysis.* Totowa, NJ: Allenheld, Osmun.

Ruggiero, Mary, Ellen Greenberger & Laurence D. Steinberg. 1982. "Occupational Deviance among Adolescent Workers." *Youth & Society* 13:423–48.

Ruhm, Christopher J. 1995. "The Extent and Consequences of High School Employment." *Journal of Labor Research* 16:293–302.

Sampson, Robert J. & John H. Laub. 1993. *Crime in the Making: Pathways and Turning Points through Life.* Cambridge, MA: Harvard University Press.

Schneider, Barbara & Jennifer A. Schmidt. 1996. "Young Women at Work." In P. Dubeck & K. Borman (eds.), *Women and Work: A Handbook.* New York: Garland.

Shanahan, Michael J., Michael Finch, Jeylan T. Mortimer & Seongryeol Ruy. 1991. "Adolescent Work Experience and Depressive Affect." *Social Psychology Quarterly* 54:299–317.

Simon, David R. & Stanley Eitzen. 1986. *Elite Deviance.* Boston: Allyn & Bacon.

Steinberg, Laurence. 1996. *Beyond the Classroom: Why School Reform Has Failed and What Parents Can Do About It.* New York: Simon & Schuster.

Steinberg, Laurence & Elizabeth Cauffman. 1995. "The Impact of Employment on Adolescent Development." *Annals of Child Development* 11:131–66.

Steinberg, Laurence & Sanford M. Dornbusch. 1991. "Negative Correlates of Part-time Employment during Adolescence: Replication and Elaboration." *Developmental Psychology* 27:304–13.

Steinberg, Laurence & Ellen Greenberger. 1980. "The Part-time Employment of High-school Students: A Research Agenda." *Children & Youth Services Review* 2:161–85.

Steinberg, Laurence, Ellen Greenberger, Laurie Garduque, Mary Ruggiero & Alan Vaux. 1982. "Effects of Working on Adolescent Development." *Developmental Psychology* 18:385–95.

St. John, Warren. 1996. "They Blow Money." *George* (June–July):101–29.

Sullivan, Mercer L. 1989. *Getting Paid: Youth Crime and Work in the Inner City.* Ithaca, NY: Cornell University Press.

Sutherland, Edwin H. 1983 (1949). *White-Collar Crime: The Uncut Version.* New Haven, CT: Yale University Press.

Tittle, Charles R. & Robert F. Meier. 1990. "Specifying the SES/Delinquency Relationship." *Criminology* 28:271–99.

Vaughan, Dianna. 1996. *The Challenger Launch Decision: Risky Technology, Culture, and Deviance at NASA.* Chicago: University of Chicago Press.

Weisburd, David, Stanton Wheeler, Elin Waring & Nancy Bode. 1991. *Crimes of the Middle Classes.* New Haven, CT: Yale University Press.

Williams, Nicolas, Francis T. Cullen & John Paul Wright. 1997. "Labor Market Participation and Youth Crime: The Neglect of 'Working' in Delinquency Research." *Social Pathology* 2:195–217.

Wilson, James Q. & Richard J. Herrnstein. 1985. *Crime and Human Nature.* New York: Simon & Schuster.

Wright, John Paul, Francis T. Cullen & Nicolas Williams. 1997. "Working While in School and Delinquent Involvement: Implications for Social Policy." *Crime & Delinquency* 43:203–21.

Yamoor, C. & Jeylan T. Mortimer. 1990. "An Investigation of Age and Gender Differ-

ences in the Effects of Employment on Adolescent Achievement and Well Being."
    Youth & Society 22:225–40.
Yeager, Peter C. 1986. "Analyzing Illegal Corporate Behavior: Progress and Prospects."
    In J. Post (ed.), *Research in Corporate Social Performance and Policy,* vol. 8.
    Greenwich, CT: JAI Press.
Zey-Ferrell, Mary K., Mark Weaver & O. C. Ferrell. 1982. "Predicting Unethical Be-
    havior among Marketing Practitioners." *Human Relations* 32:557–69.

PART 5

Law-Violating Youth Groups and Gang Delinquency

FEW TYPES OF JUVENILE DELINQUENCY HAVE GENERATED MORE IN-
terest among criminologists than gang delinquency. Klein defined a **gang** as
consisting of youths who consider themselves to be a distinct group (usually
with a group name), who are perceived as a distinct group by others in the community, and who have "been involved in a sufficient number of delinquent incidents to call forth a consistent negative response from neighborhood residents
and/or law enforcement agencies" (1971:13). The third element in Klein's definition—a consistent negative response from the community—would exclude
as gangs many groups of adolescents who engage in delinquent acts but who
have avoided societal labeling. In Chapter 16, "The Saints and the Roughnecks," William Chambliss presents an ethnographic account in which he describes two groups of boys from different class backgrounds. The lower-class
Roughnecks—the "visible, poor, nonmobile, out-spoken, undiplomatic
'tough' kids"—were more likely to elicit a negative societal reaction from the
community. On the other hand, the more affluent Saints—the more "mobile
and monied" youths who had "established a reputation for being bright (even
though underachieving), disciplined and involved in respectable activities"—
remained essentially immune from condemnation even when they engaged in
law-violating behavior. Thus, Chambliss found that many delinquent youths
were not social outcasts but were well integrated into the "respectable" society both during and following adolescence.

Chambliss's study made clear that even though most delinquent acts are
committed in groups (see Erickson and Jensen 1977; Giordano, Cernkovich,
and Pugh 1986; Warr 2002), group delinquency is not synonymous with gangs

351

(Stafford 1984). Indeed, Miller (1980) found far more delinquent groups and delinquent group members than delinquent gangs or gang members in his study of several large urban cities; and he preferred the term **law-violating youth group** rather than *gang* to identify the most common peer groups that perpetuate delinquent acts. Miller defined a law-violating youth group as "an association of three or more youths whose members engage recurrently in illegal activities with the cooperation and/or moral support of their companions" (p. 118).

In Chapter 17, "Adolescent Subcultures, Social Type Metaphors, and Group Delinquency: Continuity and Change," Ronald Berger frames the phenomena of gangs and group delinquency in terms of a broader theory of adolescent subcultures. Berger reviews "research bearing on a general subcultural theory of adolescence and group delinquency" and examines "the social type names or metaphors used by youths to communicate with one another about the relative statuses of various youths," which delineate varying patterns of delinquency. Berger illuminates these processes through his own study of high school youths in Wisconsin during two periods of time, with an eye toward examining the "continuity and change" in adolescent subcultures over time. Then, in Chapter 18, Ronald Berger turns his attention to the phenomenon of "Urban Street Gangs: Class, Race/Ethnicity, and Gender" as he addresses "the basic features of urban street gangs in the United States, both historically and contemporarily, that are related to the social dimensions of class, race/ethnicity, and gender."

The subject of urban street gangs is also the focus of Chapter 19, Charis Kubrin's "Gangstas, Thugs, and Hustlas: Identity and the Code of the Street in Rap Music." Kubrin explains "how structural conditions in inner-city communities have given rise to cultural adaptations—embodied in a street code—that constitute an interpretive environment where violence" as a means of acquiring respect is accepted, if not encouraged. Through a content analysis of rap music lyrics, she shows how rappers "actively construct violent identities for themselves and for others," hence legitimatizing "certain aspects of the street code while ignoring other important and arguably more positive aspects of urban life."

Finally, in Chapter 20, "Community Tolerance of Gang Violence," Ruth Horowitz's ethnography illuminates a similar street code of personal honor that she found in a lower-class Chicano community in Chicago. It is important to note that Horowitz also shows how community tolerance of gang violence is a negotiated and tenuous phenomenon. On the one hand, gang youths are tolerated by adults in their communities because they are not social outsiders among residents; they are sons and daughters, grandchildren, nieces and nephews, the neighbors' kids. The majority of their time is not spent in law-violating activities, and their behavior is appropriate in most social situations. On the other hand, this tolerance of gangs breaks down when it disrupts community functions such as weddings or dances or directly implicates a family in violence. At such times, the negotiated sense of order is no longer tenable, and the incongruence between gangs and legitimate community norms becomes more salient.

References

Erickson, Maynard L., and Gary F. Jensen. 1977. "Delinquency Is Still Group Behavior: Toward Revitalizing the Group Premise in the Sociology of Deviance." *Journal of Criminal Law and Criminology* 68:388–395.

Giordano, Peggy C., Stephen A. Cernkovich, and M. D. Pugh. 1986. "Friendships and Delinquency." *American Journal of Sociology* 91:1170–1202.

Klein, Malcolm W. 1971. *Street Gangs and Street Workers.* Englewood Cliffs, NJ: Prentice-Hall.

Miller, Walter B. 1980. "Gangs, Groups, and Serious Youth Crime." In D. Shichor and D. Kelly (eds.), *Critical Issues in Juvenile Delinquency.* Lexington, MA: Lexington Books.

Stafford, Mark. 1984. "Gang Delinquency." In R. Meier (ed.), *Major Forms of Crime.* Beverly Hills, CA: Sage.

Warr, Mark. 2002. *Companions in Crime: The Social Aspects of Criminal Conduct.* Cambridge: Cambridge University Press.

16

The Saints and the Roughnecks

William J. Chambliss

*In this ethnographic account, William Chambliss describes two groups
of boys from different class backgrounds: the lower-class Roughnecks,
whose actions were more likely to elicit a negative societal reaction from
the community, and the more affluent Saints, who remained essentially
immune from condemnation even when they engaged in law-violating
behavior. Thus, Chambliss found that many delinquent youths were not
social outcasts but were well integrated into the "respectable" society
both during and after adolescence.*

EIGHT PROMISING YOUNG MEN—CHILDREN OF GOOD, STABLE, WHITE
upper-middle-class families, active in school affairs, good precollege students—
were some of the most delinquent boys at Hanibal High School. While community residents and parents knew that these boys occasionally sowed a few wild
oats, they were totally unaware that sowing wild oats completely occupied the
daily routine of these young men. The Saints were constantly occupied with truancy, drinking, wild driving, petty theft and vandalism. Yet not one was officially arrested for any misdeed during the two years I observed them.

This record was particularly surprising in light of my observations during
the same two years of another gang of Hanibal High School students, six
lower-class white boys known as the Roughnecks. The Roughnecks were constantly in trouble with police and community even though their rate of delinquency was about equal with that of the Saints. What was the cause of this disparity? the result? The following consideration of the activities, social class
and community perceptions of both gangs may provide some answers.

■ The Saints from Monday to Friday

The Saints' principal daily concern was with getting out of school as early as
possible. The boys managed to get out of school with minimum danger that

"The Saints and the Roughnecks," *Society* 11, no. 1 (1973): 341–355. Reprinted by permission of
Springer.

they would be accused of playing hookey through an elaborate procedure for obtaining "legitimate," release from class. The most common procedure was for one boy to obtain the release of another by fabricating a meeting of some committee, program or recognized club. Charles might raise his hand in his 9:00 chemistry class and ask to be excused—a euphemism for going to the bathroom. Charles would go to Ed's math class and inform the teacher that Ed was needed for a 9:30 rehearsal of the drama club play. The math teacher would recognize Ed and Charles as "good students" involved in numerous school activities and would permit Ed to leave at 9:30. Charles would return to his class, and Ed would go to Tom's English class to obtain his release. Tom would engineer Charles' escape. The strategy would continue until as many of the Saints as possible were freed. After a stealthy trip to the car (which had been parked in a strategic spot), the boys were off for a day of fun.

Over the two years I observed the Saints, this pattern was repeated nearly every day. There were variations on the theme, but in one form or another, the boys used this procedure for getting out of class and then off of the school grounds. Rarely did all eight of the Saints manage to leave school at the same time. The average number avoiding school on the days I observed them was five.

Having escaped from the concrete corridors the boys usually went either to a pool hall on the other (lower-class) side of town or to a cafe in the suburbs. Both places were out of the way of people the boys were likely to know (family or school officials), and both provided a source of entertainment. The pool hall entertainment was the generally rough atmosphere, the occasional hustler, the sometimes drunk proprietor and, of course, the game of pool. The cafe's entertainment was provided by the owner. The boys would "accidentally" knock a glass on the floor or spill cola on the counter—not all the time, but enough to be sporting. They would also bend spoons, put salt in sugar bowls and generally tease whoever was working in the cafe. The owner had opened the cafe recently and was dependent on the boys' business which was, in fact, substantial since between the horsing around and the teasing they bought food and drinks.

■ **The Saints on Weekends**

On weekends, the automobile was even more critical than during the week, for on weekends the Saints went to Big Town—a large city with a population of over a million 25 miles from Hanibal. Every Friday and Saturday night most of the Saints would meet between 8:00 and 8:30 and would go into Big Town. Big Town activities included drinking heavily in taverns or nightclubs, driving drunkenly through the streets, and committing acts of vandalism and playing pranks.

By midnight on Fridays and Saturdays the Saints were usually thoroughly high, and one or two of them were often so drunk they had to be carried to the cars. Then the boys drove around town, calling obscenities to women and girls; occasionally trying (unsuccessfully so far as I could tell) to pick girls up; and driving recklessly through red lights and at high speeds with their lights out. Occasionally they played "chicken." One boy would climb out the back window of the car and across the roof to the driver's side of the car while the car was moving at high speed (between 40 and 50 miles an hour); then the driver would move over and the boy who had just crawled across the car roof would take the driver's seat.

Searching for "fair game" for a prank was the boys' principal activity after they left the tavern. The boys would drive alongside a foot patrolman and ask directions to some street. If the policeman leaned on the car in the course of answering the question, the driver would speed away, causing him to lose his balance. The Saints were careful to play this prank only in an area where they were not going to spend much time and where they could quickly disappear around a corner to avoid having their license plate number taken.

Construction sites and road repair areas were the special province of the Saints' mischief. A soon-to-be-repaired hole in the road inevitably invited the Saints to remove lanterns and wooden barricades and put them in the car, leaving the hole unprotected. The boys would find a safe vantage point and wait for an unsuspecting motorist to drive into the hole. Often, though not always, the boys would go up to the motorist and commiserate with him about the dreadful way the city protected its citizenry.

Leaving the scene of the open hole and the motorist, the boys would then go searching for an appropriate place to erect the stolen barricade. An "appropriate place" was often a spot on a highway near a curve in the road where the barricade would not be seen by an oncoming motorist. The boys would wait to watch an unsuspecting motorist attempt to stop and (usually) crash into the wooden barricade. With saintly bearing the boys might offer help and understanding.

A stolen lantern might well find its way onto the back of a police car or hang from a street lamp. Once a lantern served as a prop for a reenactment of the "midnight ride of Paul Revere" until the "play," which was taking place at 2:00 A.M. in the center of a main street of Big Town, was interrupted by a police car several blocks away. The boys ran, leaving the lanterns on the street, and managed to avoid being apprehended.

Abandoned houses, especially if they were located in out-of-the-way places, were fair game for destruction and spontaneous vandalism. The boys would break windows, remove furniture to the yard and tear it apart, urinate on the walls and scrawl obscenities inside.

Through all the pranks, drinking and reckless driving the boys managed miraculously to avoid being stopped by police. Only twice in two years was I aware that they had been stopped by a Big City policeman. Once was for speeding (which they did every time they drove whether they were drunk or sober), and the driver managed to convince the policeman that it was simply an error. The second time they were stopped they had just left a nightclub and were walking through an alley. Aaron stopped to urinate and the boys began making obscene remarks. A foot patrolman came into the alley, lectured the boys and sent them home. Before the boys got to the car one began talking in a loud voice again. The policeman, who had followed them down the alley, arrested this boy for disturbing the peace and took him to the police station where the other Saints gathered. After paying a $5.00 fine, and with the assurance that there would be no permanent record of the arrest, the boy was released.

The boys had a spirit of frivolity and fun about their escapades. They did not view what they were engaged in as "delinquency," though it surely was by any reasonable definition of that word. They simply viewed themselves as having a little fun and who, they would ask, was really hurt by it? The answer had to be no one, although this fact remains one of the most difficult things to explain about the gang's behavior. Unlikely though it seems, in two years of drinking, driving, carousing and vandalism no one was seriously injured as a result of the Saints' activities.

The Saints in School

The Saints were highly successful in school. The average grade for the group was "B," with two of the boys having close to a straight "A" average. Almost all of the boys were popular and many of them held offices in the school. One of the boys was vice-president of the student body one year. Six of the boys played on athletic teams.

At the end of their senior year, the student body selected 10 seniors for special recognition as the "school wheels"; four of the 10 were Saints. Teachers and school officials saw no problem with any of these boys and anticipated that they would all "make something of themselves."

How the boys managed to maintain this impression is surprising in view of their actual behavior while in school. Their technique for covering truancy was so successful that teachers did not even realize that the boys were absent from school much of the time. Occasionally, of course, the system would backfire and then the boy was on his own. A boy who was caught would be most contrite, would plead guilty and ask for mercy. He inevitably got the mercy he sought.

Cheating on examinations was rampant, even to the point of orally communicating answers to exams as well as looking at one another's papers. Since none of the group studied, and since they were primarily dependent on one another for help, it is surprising that grades were so high. Teachers contributed to the deception in their admitted inclination to give these boys (and presumably others like them) the benefit of the doubt. When asked how the boys did in school, and when pressed on specific examinations, teachers might admit that they were disappointed in John's performance, but would quickly add that they "knew he was capable of doing better," so John was given a higher grade than he had actually earned. How often this happened is impossible to know. During the time that I observed the group, I never saw any of the boys take homework home. Teachers may have been "understanding" very regularly.

One exception to the gang's generally good performance was Jerry, who had a "C" average in his junior year, experienced disaster the next year and failed to graduate. Jerry had always been a little more nonchalant than the others about the liberties he took in school. Rather than wait for someone to come get him from class, he would offer his own excuse and leave. Although he probably did not miss any more classes than most of the others in the group, he did not take the requisite pains to cover his absences. Jerry was the only Saint whom I ever heard talk back to a teacher. Although teachers often called him a "cut up" or a "smart kid," they never referred to him as a troublemaker or as a kid headed for trouble. It seems likely, then, that Jerry's failure his senior year and his mediocre performance his junior year were consequences of his not playing the game the proper way (possibly because he was disturbed by his parents' divorce). His teachers regarded him as "immature" and not quite ready to get out of high school.

The Police and the Saints

The local police saw the Saints as good boys who were among the leaders of the youth in the community. Rarely, the boys might be stopped in town for speeding or for running a stop sign. When this happened the boys were always polite, contrite and pled for mercy. As in school, they received the mercy they asked for. None ever received a ticket or was taken into the precinct by the local police.

The situation in Big City, where the boys engaged in most of their delinquency, was only slightly different. The police there did not know the boys at all, although occasionally the boys were stopped by a patrolman. Once they were caught taking a lantern from a construction site. Another time they were stopped for running a stop sign, and on several occasions they were stopped for speeding. Their behavior was as before: contrite, polite and penitent. The urban police, like the local police, accepted their demeanor as sincere. More important, the urban police were convinced that these were good boys just out for a lark.

The Roughnecks

Hanibal townspeople never perceived the Saints' high level of delinquency. The Saints were good boys who just went in for an occasional prank. After all, they were well dressed, well mannered and had nice cars. The Roughnecks were a different story. Although the two gangs of boys were the same age, and both groups engaged in an equal amount of wild-oat sowing, everyone agreed that the not-so-well-dressed, not-so-well-mannered, not-so-rich boys were heading for trouble. Townspeople would say, "You can see the gang members at the drugstore night after night, leaning against the storefront (sometimes drunk) or slouching around inside buying cokes, reading magazines, and probably stealing old Mr. Wall blind. When they are outside and girls walk by, even respectable girls, these boys make suggestive remarks. Sometimes their remarks are downright lewd."

From the community's viewpoint, the real indication that these kids were in for trouble was that they were constantly involved with the police. Some of them had been picked up for stealing, mostly small stuff, of course, "but still it's stealing small stuff that leads to big time crimes. Too bad," people said. "Too bad that these boys couldn't behave like the other kids in town; stay out of trouble, be polite to adults, and look to their future."

The community's impression of the degree to which this group of six boys (ranging in age from 16 to 19) engaged in delinquency was somewhat distorted. In some ways the gang was more delinquent than the community thought; in other ways they were less.

The fighting activities of the group were fairly readily and accurately perceived by almost everyone. At least once a month, the boys would get into some sort of fight, although most fights were scraps between members of the group or involved only one member of the group and some peripheral hanger-on. Only three times in the period of observation did the group fight together: once against a gang from across town, once against two blacks and once against a group of boys from another school. For the first two fights the group went out "looking for trouble"—and they found it both times. The third fight followed a football game and began spontaneously with an argument on the football field between one of the Roughnecks and a member of the opposition's football team.

Jack had a particular propensity for fighting and was involved in most of the brawls. He was a prime mover of the escalation of arguments into fights.

More serious than fighting, had the community been aware of it, was theft. Although almost everyone was aware that the boys occasionally stole things, they did not realize the extent of the activity. Petty stealing was a frequent event for the Roughnecks. Sometimes they stole as a group and coordinated their efforts; other times they stole in pairs. Rarely did they steal alone.

The thefts ranged from very small things like paperback books, comics and ballpoint pens to expensive items like watches. The nature of the thefts varied from time to time. The gang would go through a period of systematically lifting items from automobiles or school lockers. Types of thievery varied with the whim of the gang. Some forms of thievery were more profitable than others, but all thefts were for profit, not just thrills.

Roughnecks siphoned gasoline from cars as often as they had access to an automobile, which was not very often. Unlike the Saints, who owned their own cars, the Roughnecks would have to borrow their parents' cars, an event which occurred only eight or nine times a year. The boys claimed to have stolen cars for joy rides from time to time.

Ron committed the most serious of the group's offenses. With an unidentified associate the boy attempted to burglarize a gasoline station. Although this station had been robbed twice previously in the same month, Ron denied any involvement in either of the other thefts. When Ron and his accomplice approached the station, the owner was hiding in the bushes beside the station. He fired both barrels of a double-barreled shotgun at the boys. Ron was severely injured; the other boy ran away and was never caught. Though he remained in critical condition for several months, Ron finally recovered and served six months of the following year in reform school. Upon release from reform school, Ron was put back a grade in school, and began running around with a different gang of boys. The Roughnecks considered the new gang less delinquent than themselves, and during the following year Ron had no more trouble with the police.

The Roughnecks, then, engaged mainly in three types of delinquency: theft, drinking and fighting. Although community members perceived that this gang of kids was delinquent, they mistakenly believed that their illegal activities were primarily drinking, fighting and being a nuisance to passersby. Drinking was limited among the gang members, although it did occur, and theft was much more prevalent than anyone realized.

Drinking would doubtless have been more prevalent had the boys had ready access to liquor. Since they rarely had automobiles at their disposal, they could not travel very far, and the bars in town would not serve them. Most of the boys had little money, and this, too, inhibited their purchase of alcohol. Their major source of liquor was a local drunk who would buy them a fifth if they would give him enough extra to buy himself a pint of whisky or a bottle of wine.

The community's perception of drinking as prevalent stemmed from the fact that it was the most obvious delinquency the boys engaged in. When one of the boys had been drinking, even a casual observer seeing him on the corner would suspect that he was high.

There was a high level of mutual distrust and dislike between the Roughnecks and the police. The boys felt very strongly that the police were unfair and corrupt. Some evidence existed that the boys were correct in their perception.

The main source of the boys' dislike for the police undoubtedly stemmed from the fact that the police would sporadically harass the group. From the standpoint of the boys, these acts of occasional enforcement of the law were whimsical and uncalled for. It made no sense to them, for example, that the police would come to the corner occasionally and threaten them with arrest for loitering when the night before the boys had been out siphoning gasoline from cars and the police had been nowhere in sight. To the boys, the police were stupid on the one hand, for not being where they should have been and catching the boys in a serious offense, and unfair on the other hand, for trumping up "loitering" charges against them.

From the viewpoint of the police, the situation was quite different. They knew, with all the confidence necessary to be a policeman, that these boys were engaged in criminal activities. They knew this partly from occasionally catching them, mostly from circumstantial evidence ("the boys were around when those tires were slashed"), and partly because the police shared the view of the community in general that this was a bad bunch of boys. The best the police could hope to do was to be sensitive to the fact that these boys were engaged in illegal acts and arrest them whenever there was some evidence that they had been involved. Whether or not the boys had in fact committed a particular act in a particular way was not especially important. The police had a broader view: their job was to stamp out these kids' crimes; the tactics were not as important as the end result.

Over the period that the group was under observation, each member was arrested at least once. Several of the boys were arrested a number of times and spent at least one night in jail. While most were never taken to court, two of the boys were sentenced to six months' incarceration in boys' schools.

■ The Roughnecks in School

The Roughnecks' behavior in school was not particularly disruptive. During school hours they did not all hang around together, but tended instead to spend most of their time with one or two other members of the gang who were their special buddies. Although every member of the gang attempted to avoid school as much as possible, they were not particularly successful and most of them attended school with surprising regularity. They considered school a burden— some thing to be gotten through with a minimum of conflict. If they were "bugged" by a particular teacher, it could lead to trouble. One of the boys, Al, once threatened to beat up a teacher and, according to the other boys, the teacher hid under a desk to escape him.

Teachers saw the boys the way the general community did, as heading for trouble, as being uninterested in making something of themselves. Some were also seen as being incapable of meeting the academic standards of the school. Most of the teachers expressed concern for this group of boys and were willing to pass them despite poor performance, in the belief that failing them would only aggravate the problem.

The group of boys had a grade point average just slightly above "C". No one in the group failed either grade, and no one had better than a "C" average. They were very consistent in their achievement or, at least, the teachers were consistent in their perception of the boys' achievement.

Two of the boys were good football players. Herb was acknowledged to be the best player in the school and Jack was almost as good. Both boys were criticized for their failure to abide by training rules, for refusing to come to practice as often as they should, and for not playing their best during practice. What they lacked in sportsmanship they made up for in skill, apparently, and played every game no matter how poorly they had performed in practice or how many practice sessions they had missed.

Two Questions

Why did the community, the school and the police react to the Saints as though they were good, upstanding, nondelinquent youths with bright futures but to the Roughnecks as though they were tough, young criminals who were headed for trouble? Why did the Roughnecks and the Saints in fact have quite different careers after high school—careers which, by and large, lived up to the expectations of the community?

The most obvious explanation for the differences in the community's and law enforcement agencies' reactions to the two gangs is that one group of boys was "more delinquent" than the other. Which group was more delinquent? The answer to this question will determine in part how we explain the differential responses to these groups by the members of the community and, particularly, by law enforcement and school officials.

In sheer number of illegal acts, the Saints were the more delinquent. They were truant from school for at least part of the day almost every day of the week. In addition, their drinking and vandalism occurred with surprising regularity. The Roughnecks, in contrast, engaged sporadically in delinquent episodes. While these episodes were frequent, they certainly did not occur on a daily or even a weekly basis.

The difference in frequency of offenses was probably caused by the Roughnecks' inability to obtain liquor and to manipulate legitimate excuses from school. Since the Roughnecks had less money than the Saints, and teachers carefully supervised their school activities, the Roughnecks' hearts may have been as black as the Saints' but their misdeeds were not nearly as frequent.

There are really no clear-cut criteria by which to measure qualitative differences in antisocial behavior. The most important dimension of the difference is generally referred to as the "seriousness" of the offenses.

If seriousness encompasses the relative economic costs of delinquent acts, then some assessment can be made. The Roughnecks probably stole an average of about $5.00 worth of goods a week. Some weeks the figure was considerably higher, but these times must be balanced against long periods when almost nothing was stolen.

The Saints were more continuously engaged in delinquency but their acts were not for the most part costly to property. Only their vandalism and occasional theft of gasoline would so qualify. Perhaps once or twice a month they would siphon a tankful of gas. The other costly items were street signs, construction lanterns and the like. All of these acts combined probably did not average $5.00 a week, partly because much of the stolen equipment was abandoned and presumably could be recovered. The difference in cost of stolen property between the two groups was trivial, but the Roughnecks probably had a slightly more expensive set of activities than did the Saints.

Another meaning of seriousness is the potential threat of physical harm to members of the community and to the boys themselves. The Roughnecks were more prone to physical violence; they not only welcomed an opportunity to fight, they went seeking it. In addition, they fought among themselves frequently. Although the fighting never included deadly weapons, it was still a menace, however minor, to the physical safety of those involved.

The Saints never fought. They avoided physical conflict both inside and outside the group. At the same time, though, the Saints frequently endangered their own and other people's lives. They did so almost every time they drove a car, especially if they had been drinking. Sober, their driving was risky; under the influence of alcohol it was horrendous. In addition, the Saints endangered the lives of others with their pranks. Street excavations left unmarked were a very serious hazard.

Evaluating the relative seriousness of the two gangs' activities is difficult. The community reacted as though the behavior of the Roughnecks was a problem, and they reacted as though the behavior of the Saints was not. But the members of the community were ignorant of the array of delinquent acts that characterized the Saints' behavior. Although concerned citizens were unaware of much of the Roughnecks' behavior as well, they were much better informed about the Roughnecks' involvement in delinquency than they were about the Saints'.

■ Visibility

Differential treatment of the two gangs resulted in part because one gang was infinitely more visible than the other. This differential visibility was a direct function of the economic standing of the families. The Saints had access to automobiles and were able to remove themselves from the sight of the community. In as routine a decision as to where to go to have a milkshake after school, the Saints stayed away from the mainstream of community life. Lacking transportation, the Roughnecks could not make it to the edge of town. The center of town was the only practical place for them to meet since their homes were scattered throughout the town and any noncentral meeting place put an undue hardship on some members. Through necessity the Roughnecks congregated in a crowded area where everyone in the community passed frequently, including teachers and law enforcement officers. They could easily see the Roughnecks hanging around the drugstore.

The Roughnecks, of course, made themselves even more visible by making remarks to passersby and by occasionally getting into fights on the corner.

Meanwhile, just as regularly, the Saints were either at the cafe on one edge of town or in the pool hall at the other edge of town. Without any particular realization that they were making themselves inconspicuous, the Saints were able to hide their time-wasting. Not only were they removed from the mainstream of traffic, but they were almost always inside a building.

On their escapades the Saints were also relatively invisible, since they left Hanibal and traveled to Big City. Here, too, they were mobile, roaming the city, rarely going to the same area twice.

Demeanor

To the notion of visibility must be added the difference in the responses of group members to outside intervention with their activities. If one of the Saints was confronted with an accusing policeman, even if he felt he was truly innocent of a wrongdoing, his demeanor was apologetic and penitent. A Roughneck's attitude was almost the polar opposite. When confronted with a threatening adult authority, even one who tried to be pleasant, the Roughneck's hostility and disdain were clearly observable. Sometimes he might attempt to put up a veneer of respect, but it was thin and was not accepted as sincere by the authority.

School was no different from the community at large. The Saints could manipulate the system by feigning compliance with the school norms. The availability of cars at school meant that once free from the immediate sight of the teacher, the boys could disappear rapidly. And this escape was well enough planned that no administrator or teacher was nearby when the boys left. A Roughneck who wished to escape for a few hours was in a bind. If it were possible to get free from class, downtown was still a mile away, and even if he arrived there, he was still very visible. Truancy for the Roughnecks meant almost certain detection, while the Saints enjoyed almost complete immunity from sanctions.

Bias

Community members were not aware of the transgressions of the Saints. Even if the Saints had been less discreet, their favorite delinquencies would have been perceived as less serious than those of the Roughnecks.

In the eyes of the police and school officials, a boy who drinks in an alley and stands intoxicated on the street corner is committing a more serious offense than is a boy who drinks to inebriation in a nightclub or a tavern and drives around afterwards in a car. Similarly, a boy who steals a wallet from a store will be viewed as having committed a more serious offense than a boy who steals a lantern from a construction site.

Perceptual bias also operates with respect to the demeanor of the boys in the two groups when they are confronted by adults. It is not simply that adults dislike the posture affected by boys of the Roughneck ilk; more important is the conviction that the posture adopted by the Roughnecks is an indication of their devotion and commitment to deviance as a way of life. The posture becomes a cue, just as the type of the offense is a cue, to the degree to which the known transgressions are indicators of the youths' potential for other problems.

Visibility, demeanor and bias are surface variables which explain the day-to-day operations of the police. Why do these surface variables operate as they do? Why did the police choose to disregard the Saints' delinquencies while breathing down the backs of the Roughnecks?

The answer lies in the class structure of American society and the control of legal institutions by those at the top of the class structure. Obviously, no representative of the upper class drew up the operational chart for the police which led them to look in the ghettoes and on streetcorners—which led them to see the demeanor of lower-class youth as troublesome and that of upper-middle-class youth as tolerable. Rather, the procedures simply developed from experience—experience with irate and influential upper-middle-class parents insisting that their son's vandalism was simply a prank and his drunkenness only a momentary "sowing of wild oats"—experience with cooperative or indifferent, powerless, lower-class parents who acquiesced to the law's definition of their son's behavior.

Adult Careers of the Saints and the Roughnecks

The community's confidence in the potential of the Saints and the Roughnecks apparently was justified. If anything, the community members underestimated the degree to which these youngsters would turn out "good" or "bad."

Seven of the eight members of the Saints went on to college immediately after high school. Five of the boys graduated from college in four years. The sixth one finished college after two years in the army, and the seventh spent four years in the air force before returning to college and receiving a B.A. degree. Of these seven college graduates, three went on for advanced degrees. One finished law school and is now active in state politics, one finished medical school and is practicing near Hanibal, and one boy is now working for a Ph.D. The other four college graduates entered submanagerial, managerial or executive training positions with larger firms.

The only Saint who did not complete college was Jerry. Jerry had failed to graduate from high school with the other Saints. During his second senior year, after the other Saints had gone on to college, Jerry began to hang around with what several teachers described as a "rough crowd"—the gang that was heir apparent to the Roughnecks. At the end of his second senior year, when he did graduate from high school, Jerry took a job as a used-car salesman, got married and quickly had a child. Although he made several abortive attempts to go to college by attending night school, when I last saw him (10 years after high school) Jerry was unemployed and had been living on unemployment for almost a year. His wife worked as a waitress.

Some of the Roughnecks have lived up to community expectations. A number of them were headed for trouble. A few were not.

Jack and Herb were the athletes among the Roughnecks and their athletic prowess paid off handsomely. Both boys received unsolicited athletic scholarships to college. After Herb received his scholarship (near the end of his senior year), he apparently did an about-face. His demeanor became very similar to that of the Saints. Although he remained a member in good standing of the Roughnecks, he stopped participating in most activities and did not hang around the corner as often.

Jack did not change. If anything, he became more prone to fighting. He even made excuses for accepting the scholarship. He told the other gang members that the school had guaranteed him a "C" average if he would come to play football—an idea that seems far-fetched, even in this day of highly competitive recruiting.

During the summer after graduation from high school, Jack attempted suicide by jumping from a tall building. The jump would certainly have killed most people trying it, but Jack survived. He entered college in the fall and played four years of football. He and Herb graduated in four years, and both are teaching and coaching in high schools. They are married and have stable families. If anything, Jack appears to have a more prestigious position in the community than does Herb, though both are well respected and secure in their positions.

Two of the boys never finished high school. Tommy left at the end of his junior year and went to another state. That summer he was arrested and placed on probation on a manslaughter charge. Three years later he was arrested for murder; he pleaded guilty to second degree murder and is serving a 30-year sentence in the state penitentiary.

Al, the other boy who did not finish high school, also left the state in his senior year. He is serving a life sentence in a state penitentiary for first degree murder.

Wes is a small-time gambler. He finished high school and "bummed around." After several years he made contact with a bookmaker who employed him as a runner. Later he acquired his own area and has been working it ever since. His position among the bookmakers is almost identical to the position he had in the gang; he is always around but no one is really aware of him. He makes no trouble and he does not get into any. Steady, reliable, capable of keeping his mouth closed, he plays the game by the rules, even though the game is an illegal one.

That leaves only Ron. Some of his former friends reported that they had heard he was "driving a truck up north," but no one could provide any concrete information.

▒ Reinforcement

The community responded to the Roughnecks as boys in trouble, and the boys agreed with that perception. Their pattern of deviancy was reinforced, and breaking away from it became increasingly unlikely. Once the boys acquired an image of themselves as deviants, they selected new friends who affirmed that self-image. As that self-conception became more firmly entrenched, they also became willing to try new and more extreme deviances. With their growing alienation came freer expression of disrespect and hostility for representatives of the legitimate society. This disrespect increased the community's negativism, perpetuating the entire process of commitment to deviance. Lack of a commitment to deviance works the same way. In either case, the process will perpetuate itself unless some event (like a scholarship to college or a sudden failure) external to the established relationship intervenes. For two of the Roughnecks (Herb and Jack), receiving college athletic scholarships created new relations and culminated in a break with the established pattern of deviance. In the case of one of the Saints (Jerry), his parents' divorce and his failing to graduate from high school changed some of his other relations. Being held back in school for a year and losing his place among the Saints had sufficient impact on Jerry to alter his self-image and virtually to assure that he would not go on to college as his peers did. Although the experiments of life can rarely be reversed, it seems likely in view of the behavior of the other boys who did not enjoy this special treatment by the school that Jerry, too, would have "become something" had he graduated as anticipated. For Herb and Jack outside intervention worked to their advantage; for Jerry it was his undoing.

Selective perception and labeling—finding, processing and punishing some kinds of criminality and not others—means that visible, poor, nonmobile, outspoken, undiplomatic "tough" kids will be noticed, whether their actions are seriously delinquent or not. Other kids, who have established a reputation for being bright (even though underachieving), disciplined and involved in respectable activities, who are mobile and monied, will be invisible when they deviate from sanctioned activities. They'll sow their wild oats—perhaps even wider and thicker than their lower-class cohorts—but they won't be noticed. When it's time to leave adolescence most will follow the expected path, settling into the ways of the middle class, remembering fondly the delinquent but unnoticed fling of their youth. The Roughnecks and others like them may turn around, too. It is more likely that their noticeable deviance will have been so reinforced by police and community that their lives will be effectively channeled into careers consistent with their adolescent background.

17

Adolescent Subcultures, Social Type Metaphors, and Group Delinquency: Continuity and Change

Ronald J. Berger

Ronald Berger situates the phenomenon of gangs, which is taken up more directly in subsequent chapters, in terms of a broader theory of adolescent subcultures. More specifically, he examines research on "the social type names or metaphors used by youths to communicate with one another about the relative statuses of various youths," which delineate varying patterns of delinquency. Berger illuminates these processes through his own study of high school youths in Wisconsin during two periods of time, with an eye toward examining the continuity and change in adolescent subcultures over time.

AS NOTED IN THE INTRODUCTION TO THIS SECTION OF THE BOOK, group delinquency should not be considered synonymous with gangs, and "law-violating youth" might be a preferable way to refer to the most common peer groups that perpetrate delinquent acts (Miller 1980). Others have suggested that the phenomenon of group delinquency might be addressed in terms of a broader theory of *adolescent subcultures* (Campbell and Muncer 1989; Schwendinger and Schwendinger 1985).[1] Bynum and Thompson (1992) define a subculture as consisting of members who adhere to many of the attitudes, values, beliefs, and normative expectations of the overall culture in which they live, but who also share particular characteristics that are unique to their particular group and that at times involve rejection of or conflict with the dominant culture. When the latter occurs, it may be called a counterculture or contraculture (Yinger 1960, 1982).

England (1967) traces the origins of a modern adolescent subculture to the rapid industrialization and urbanization experienced by capitalist societies in the late nineteenth century. After World War II, this subculture began to take on increasingly distinct characteristics. Campbell and Muncer note that in the age of mass media adolescent subcultures consist of "geographically diffuse social movement[s]" of youths who do not necessarily require face-to-face interaction to maintain a common set of argot, attitudes, beliefs, interests, and physical appearances (1989:272). However, the most essential elements of adolescent subcultural formation do occur in local interactional settings such as neighborhood hangouts, malls, and especially schools (Corsaro and Eder 1990; Wooden and Blazak 2001).

In advanced capitalist societies such as the United States, adolescents are differentiated from adults and are more or less segregated for years in educational institutions (Eisenstadt 1956; Greenberg 1981). Thus, the school rather than the neighborhood per se has become the physical site of much adolescent subcultural formation, and even youths who do not attend classes regularly generally go to school to meet their friends and hang out with others (Gottdiener and Malone 1985; Milner 2004; Wooden and Blazak 2001). The segregation of adolescents in schools increases the frequency and intensity of interaction among peers who turn to one another for social approval and personal validation. According to Schwartz and Merten, adolescent subcultures are "relatively self-contained" insofar as "peer-group interaction is guided by expectations which do not govern the behavior of other members of the community" (1967:453)

In this chapter, I review research bearing on a general subcultural theory of adolescence and group delinquency. In particular, I look at Herman Schwendinger and Julia Schwendinger's (1985) work on the social type names or metaphors used by youths to communicate with one another about the relative statuses of various youths. Examination of this "semantic domain" reveals an "internally consistent system" of values and norms that constructs and maintains the status hierarchy and establishes patterns of expected behavior within and between groups (Schwartz and Merten 1967:445). I also discuss my own research, based on data derived from student papers written for my courses on Juvenile Delinquency, on adolescent subcultures in Wisconsin during two periods (1983–1988 and 1997–2002) in order to examine the phenomenon of continuity and change in adolescent subcultures over time.

■ Adolescent Status and Social Type Metaphors

According to the Schwendingers (1985), adolescent subcultures reflect, yet are relatively independent of, social class background. Like social classes, networks of adolescent groups are stratified in terms of social status and prestige. The higher status groups invariably recruit from the middle and upper classes, and the lower status groups from the lower and working classes. As Schwartz and Merten note, the "dominant values institutionalized in the status system of the . . . high school are those held by the majority of the upper-middle-class segment of [the] youthful population" (1967:461). On the other hand, youths often disagree about the relative worth or status of different groups; and regardless of one's social class position, personal attributes such as athletic ability, physical attractiveness, personality, and interpersonal skills may allow movement up or down the status hierarchy of peer relations.

Research has shown that even children of preschool age "creatively appropriate information from the adult world to produce their own unique peer culture . . . [as they attempt] to challenge adult authority, . . . to gain control over their lives and to share that control with each other" (Corsaro and Eder 1990:200, 202). In elementary school, challenges to adult authority persist, but children become more concerned with asserting control and differentiating status among peers. Initial indications of this process become apparent when small cliques of boys and girls begin to set themselves apart from others by displaying inordinate attention to hair grooming and clothing styles. By the end of elementary school, children's preoccupation with impressing peers, rather than parents or teachers, becomes increasingly noticeable (Schwendinger and Schwendinger 1985).

The transition from childhood to adolescence that begins in junior high or middle school is accompanied by a consolidation of independent peer group formations consisting of youths who are rather self-centered, who compete intensively with one another for status recognition, and who are especially insensitive to lower-status youths (Milner 2004; Schwendinger and Schwendinger 1985). In urban areas in particular, where young people are confronted with large numbers of peers, the possibility exists for considerable expansion of cliques that occupy various positions in the status hierarchy (Corsaro and Eder 1990). However, the core of the elite group at this stage is likely to be based simply on "being known" by peers, a status typically achieved through positive visibility gained through participation in extracurricular activities, especially athletics, that draw large groups of spectators (Corsaro and Eder 1990; Eder 1985). In addition, gossip as well as teasing and insulting routines are key linguistic mechanisms that help establish status distinctions. The latter are especially important for boys, whose ability "to interpret insults as playful and responding with more clever or elaborate insults [is] essential for successful" peer group interaction (Corsaro and Eder 1990:212). Males who lack such skills become increasingly vulnerable as targets of ridicule and even physical attacks (Everhart 1983; Majors and Mancini 1992; McCall 1994).[2]

In their research, the Schwendingers found elementary school students already referring to peers who were distinguishable from others as "football and baseball types," the "gang of boys," the "crowd of sixth-grade girls," and the like (1985:68). By junior high, various linguistic categories or metaphors denoting social regularities in personal behavior, attitude, and appearance were used to identify particular crowds or cliques. For instance, members of the "in" crowd were perceived as "cool," while outsiders were "square." These metaphors "bestow either negative or positive esteem on those who manifest or exemplify [particular] personal characteristics" (Schwartz and Merten 1967:454).

While the adolescent subculture consists of a diversity of loosely knit, interlocking peer groups, crowds, or cliques, the Schwendingers (1985) identify three of the most persistent general social types that form the core of the subculture: *streetcorner, socialite,* and *intellectual* youths. Streetcorner groups recruit from the economically marginal sector of the adolescent population. These are the groups, like Chambliss's (1973) Roughnecks, that are more likely to be perceived and labeled as delinquent by authorities in the community (see Chapter 16). They are at a competitive disadvantage, economically and culturally, when they begin formal schooling, and their position relative to more privileged youths often deteriorates further as time goes on (see Chapter 13). Moreover, unlike more affluent youths with low school achievement, streetcorner adolescents do not have the family resources to provide them with the extra tutoring, counseling, cultural experiences (e.g., travel) and so forth that might help them recover from initial setbacks. Nor do they have the financial backing of their families, which would allow them a "second chance" in life by financing their way through college after a mediocre educational career (Jessor, Donovan, and Costa 1993; Schwendinger and Schwendinger 1985).

The socialite groups are akin to Chambliss's Saints. They are generally the elite group of adolescents who are, for the most part, college-bound regardless of academic achievement. These youths are better able to finance the material commodities necessary for full participation in adolescent subcultural activities—fashionable clothes, electronic devices, CDs/DVDs, cigarettes/alcohol/drugs, concert tickets, motor vehicles—that are the mark of an affluent society that has created a large leisure class of teenage consumers who are not yet fully employed (Greenberg 1981; Milner 2004; Wooden and Blazak 2001). While these youths "are less likely to be involved in the most serious violent and economic forms of delinquency, . . . the socialites are frequently equivalent to streetcorner youth, or not far behind, . . . with regard to vehicle violations, vandalism, drinking, gambling, petty theft, truancy, sexual promiscuity, and other garden varieties of delinquent behavior" (Schwendinger and Schwendinger 1985:56). When their delinquencies are discovered by the authorities, they are likely to be "treated as 'pranks,' lapses of judgment, or expressions of 'bad taste.'" and are typically ignored or covered up (p. 54). Hagan (1991) characterizes this group as a "party subculture" that is only "playing" at deviance. Though socialite youths are unlikely to get into trouble with the law, when they do they are better able than their streetcorner counterparts to finance fees for an attorney to help them avoid any serious consequences of their misconduct.

The third group of adolescents that the Schwendingers (1985) discuss is the intellectuals. These youth are high academic achievers who are sometimes "overspecialized" in their academic or technical interests (e.g., computers, electronics, mathematics, physics). They are the adolescents who spend "a greater amount of time after school doing homework, helping in household activities, or participating in adult-directed youth organizations" (p. 67). They are less interested in fashion and are the least delinquent (if at all) of the three adolescent groups. Ironically, the youths who are most committed to legitimate academic activities are often perceived negatively by other youths and have low status in the adolescent social hierarchy.[3]

The Schwendingers studied these three social types in various southern California communities between 1959 and 1967, interviewing youths about the different groups that constituted the adolescent subcultural system in their communities. The participants in their study referred to streetcorner groups variously as *Greasers, Hoods, Dudes, Rowdies, Jo-Bads,* and *Eses* (slang for "hey, man"). These youths shared particular stylistic characteristics. In the late 1950s, for example, both the Greasers (who were Anglo) and the Eses (who were Hispanic) wore "blue denims" or "khakis." Greaser boys typically wore "Sir Guy shirts," combed their hair straight back at the sides, and had pompadours in the front that flopped forward in a "jelly roll" and "ducktails" combed at the back. Greaser girls had high-combed "ratted" hair and wore short skin-tight skirts, tight sweaters over pointy brassieres, and long earrings. The socialite groups, most commonly known simply as *Socialites* or *Soc's* (pronounced soshes), dressed in an "ivy league" or "continental" style, with cashmere sweaters and white tennis shoes. Boys cut their hair short and often had "crew cuts." Girls had hairstyles known as "bubbles" and "guiches." The intellectual groups were known as *Brains, Bookworms, Egg Heads, or Pencil Necks.* They appeared conservative or undistinguished in their dress.

Along with these three most enduring general social types, the Schwendingers also found a variety of complementary, interrelated, or intermediary groups. For instance, the *Athletes* and *Surfers* (or *Gremmies*) often interpenetrated or overlapped with other groups such as the Soc's. These youths held relatively high status because of their athletic ability. While the Surfers were eventually absorbed by the more stable types, the Athletes (typically called *Jocks* today) have remained relatively distinct and one of the most clearly identifiable groups. Athletes or Jocks, particularly those in the aggressive, fast-paced spectator sports such as football and basketball, continue to symbolize the "ideal" male who is all-powerful and aggressive; and physically attractive athletes are especially desired by adolescent females (Larkin 1979; Milner 2004; Schwartz and Merten 1967; Wooden and Blazak 2001). In his study of a New Jersey suburban high school in the late 1970s, Larkin (1979) found that the leading crowd, the Jocks and *Rah-rahs,* consisted of male athletes and their friends, female cheerleaders, and other females who gained status through the achievements of their athlete boyfriends, their personal appearance, or their vivacious personality. The Jocks and Rah-rahs were known for being the core of "school spirit" and for their frequent dating, partying, and drinking. Larkin also noted the influence of the 1960s student protest movement on the *Politicos* (who were also considered intellectuals), the liberals in student government who expressed an affinity for the anarchist, anti-elitist ideologies of that period.

During the late 1960s to early 1970s, the *Hippies* (also known as *Freaks* or *Flower Children*) emerged as a relatively distinct social type. Drawing especially from the middle-class social stratum, the Hippies were known for their drug use and "free love" attitude toward sex. They also introduced more "feminized" hair and clothing styles for males (e.g., long hair, necklaces and earrings, colorful clothing) at a time when these styles were anathema to conventional masculinity norms. Although the Hippies were initially a countercultural movement, the Schwendingers suggest that they did not fundamentally alter the general characteristics of the socialite and streetcorner subcultures. During this era, drug use, which had already been firmly established among streetcorner groups, merely became more acceptable among socialite groups. Moreover, the "pseudo Hippies" studied by Weis (1973) in an upper-middle-class northern California community merely co-opted Hippie appearances— which had already been commercialized by the fashion industry as cultural innovations at the margins of society entered into the mainstream—without adopting the anti-competitive or anti-materialistic ideology associated with the Hippie counterculture. Similarly, the Freaks studied by Larkin (1979) expressed less interest in the Hippies' utopian idealism and more interest in achieving status through a masculinist competitiveness over sexual achievements and drug consumption.

In addition to the above-mentioned social types, the Schwendingers identified students who were referred to as *In-Betweens*. This neutral or nonderogatory term was used to identify adolescents who occupied an intermediary status position between socialite and streetcorner youths such as the Soc's and Greasers. These "in-between" youths were sometimes called *Neutralites* or *Regulars*. Some adolescents, however, preferred this group over the Soc's because they were "less snobbish, less exclusive, and more friendly" (Schwendinger and Schwendinger 1985:114). Larkin (1979) described this less distinguishable group as the "silent majority," which itself was subdivided into smaller groups according to particular interests.

Finally, the Schwendingers (1985) found a number of disparaging or derogatory metaphors used by youths who ridiculed peers as a means of establishing their own superior status. These metaphors included *Square, Spaz* or *Spastic, Clod, Misfit, Lame, Nerd, Weirdo,* and *Wimp*. Their common usage, particularly during the formative years of peer group development, typifies the bullying, insensitivity, and cruelty toward others that is often part of adolescent social interaction (see Espelage and Swearer 2004; note 2).

When the Schwendingers returned to southern California in the early 1980s, they noticed some changes, with new metaphors added to the mix. For example, *Preps* and *Preppies* had replaced Soc's and Socialites. *Punk Rockers* (or *Punkers*) and *Heavy Metalers* were now apparent among older, white, streetcorner youths. At teen clubs the Schwendingers observed a variety of fashion and grooming styles reflecting these latter groups (e.g,, black clothing with spikes, spiked or Mohawk hairstyles, black eye make-up, multiple ear-rings, nose rings). On the other hand, black and Hispanic streetcorner youths such as *Homeboys* and *Ese Vatos* ("hey, dude"), who lacked the buying power of white youths, appeared less affected by these changes (see also Wooden and Blazak 2001).

In another southern California high school of the early 1980s, Gottdiener and Malone (1985) observed five groups of white students—*Frats, Stoners, Surfers, Punks,* and *Good-Goodies.* They also found two groups of black students. One was not identified by a specific name, but was the black students' equivalent of the Frats, which the researchers dubbed the *Black Frats.* The other group, the *Thugs,* was perceived by the Black Frats as "low class," "dirty," and "stupid" (p. 34). The Hispanic or Chicano students were divided into three subgroups based on how well they spoke English and their degree of assimi-lation into American culture. Individuals who were the most assimilated and competent in English comprised the *Chicano Frats.* A second group that con-sisted of recent immigrants who spoke little English was not identified by a particular name. A third group, with members who were born in the United States and who spoke English and Spanish of varying degrees of proficiency, was analogous to the Thugs. They were called *Homeboys* (or *Cholos*) and *Homegirls.* However, they were not perceived by the other Chicanos as lower class, but rather as a group that rejected assimilation.[4]

In still another study of four southern California high schools from the late 1980s to the mid-1990s, Wooden and Blazak (2001) documented an elab-orate and varied adolescent subcultural system. The most common groups were called *Jocks, Preppies, Cheerleaders, Brains, Metalers* (or *Metal Heads*), and *Punks.* Other groups were called *Soc's, Partiers, Trendies, Surfers, Bandos* (or *Band members*), *Tweakies, Drama Freaks, Geeks, Nerds, Smacks, Dirt-bags, Burners, Death Rockers* (or *Dance Clubers*), *Sluts,* and *Loners.* Two His-panic groups were called *Cha-Chas* and *Cholos,* and one Asian group was sim-ply called *Asians.* In addition, Wooden and Blazak noted a number of derogatory metaphors used by students in the high schools: *Black Cockroaches* (kids who wore black), *Skanks* (girlfriends of heavy metalers), *Motorheads* (guys who drove Mustangs or Cameros), *Kickers* (cowboys), *BAs* (Native Amer-icans called "bows and arrows"), *Daddy's Girls* (spoiled rich girls) and *The Tuna Barge* (fast girls).

Finally, Milner (2004) studied a high school in Virginia in the late 1990s and found *Jocks, Preps, Yuppies, Brains, Whiz Kids, AP'ers* (students taking Advanced Placement courses), *Freaks, Hippies, Homies, Wiggers* (a contrac-tion of "white niggers"), *Skaters, Goths, Rednecks,* and *Drifters.* And in a study of Columbine High School in the aftermath of the infamous 1999 shoot-ings perpetrated by Eric Harris and Dylan Klebold (who were members of the

Trenchcoat Mafia), Larkin (2007) found *Soc's, Jocks, Cheers, Choir Kids* (which included many evangelicals), *Geeks, Nerds, Stoners, Skaters, Goths,* and *Skinheads.*

▣ Adolescent Subcultures in Wisconsin

The linguistic metaphors used by adolescents to identify status differences among various social types provide a "window" through which the characteristics of adolescent subcultures are illuminated. Importantly, the ways in which youths talk about each other is not simply a reflection of an underlying social reality, but is a way of "doing things with words" that helps bring that reality into being (Gubrium and Holstein 1997:49; see also Chapter 20). The research that has been conducted so far finds remarkable similarity in social type metaphors that have been prevalent in communities across the United States. At the same time, some metaphors appear to be unique to particular areas and may be virtually unknown by youths in other parts of the same city (Schwendinger and Schwendinger 1985).

In the remainder of this chapter, I identify and discuss a variety of adolescent subcultures that have been prevalent in various communities in Wisconsin. The data are derived from papers written by undergraduate students in my upper-division courses in Juvenile Delinquency in two time periods: 1983–1988 (N = 42) and 1997–2002 (N = 129). In these papers, I asked students to retrospectively reflect upon their adolescent years and write about the youth groups that congregated in and around their high school (see also Milner 2004). The papers were part of a broader assignment involving an autobiographical analysis of students' delinquent (or nondelinquent) histories and the impact of the larger community on their adolescent experiences (Berger 2001). While the data are limited by students' personal knowledge and recall ability and are by no means "scientific"—hence the particular percentages of each group identified in Table 17.1 should be interpreted with caution—they nonetheless indicate a fascinating array of adolescent groupings.

The data reflect the responses of students from cities and towns of different population sizes, from small, rural communities to the large metropolitan area of Milwaukee. In some cases, students who attended the same high school at different times identified different groups. The degree of social differentiation among adolescents in these various communities varied from one place to another, although there was no correlation between the size of the high school and the number of groups identified by the students. While the same social type metaphors were often found in different communities, there were also some that were unique to particular localities. Similar social types in different communities were also identified by different metaphors. Occasionally more than one metaphor was used to refer to the same social type, and sometimes the same metaphor was used to identify different types.[5] Also, students sometimes

Table 17.1 Common Adolescent Groups

	1983–1988	1997–2002
	(N = 42)	(N = 129)
Socialite Groups		
Jocks	79%	96%
Preppies/Preps	24%	55%
Streetcorner Groups		
Freaks	40%	16%
Dirtballs/Dirties	17%	17%
Burnouts/Burnies	9%	9%
Druggies	7%	16%
Stoners	0%	12%
Gangs/gangsters	7%	27%
Wannabes	0%	7%
Wiggers	0%	6%
Intellectual Groups		
Brains	17%	12%
Geeks	14%	25%
Nerds	9%	16%
Other Groups		
Normals/Floaters/Drifters/In-Betweens	17%	19%
Rednecks/Hicks/Farmers/Cowboys	7%	13%
Punkers/Punks/Heavy Metalers/Goths	2%	17%
Skaters	0%	9%

identified male and female versions of the same term, such as *Jocks* and *Jockettes,* or groups of males and females such as *Jocks* and *Cheerleaders* or *Rah-
rahs* who hung out together.

In an earlier article I reported on the 1983–1988 cohort (see Berger 1996).
This chapter expands upon this earlier piece with data from the 1997–2002 cohort, with an eye toward examining the continuity and change in Wisconsin
adolescent subcultures over time. Table 17.1 indicates the percentage of student respondents who identified particular groups in their high schools.[6] Only
the most common groups, or groups that are indicative of change over time,
are included in this table. The most prevalent divisions within the high schools
parallel Chambliss's (1973) Saints and Roughnecks and the Schwendingers'
(1985) socialite, streetcorner, and intellectual types, but also include an array
of other groups.

Socialite Groups

Jocks was the most common metaphor used to refer to the socialite groups, a
designation that has increased over time: all but 5 of the 129 1997–2002 students writing papers for this study mentioned Jocks in their high schools. This
increase suggests that the *athletic* variation of the socialite adolescent type has

378 LAW-VIOLATING YOUTH GROUPS AND GANG DELINQUENCY

become even more entrenched over the years. Although the Jocks were involved in a considerable amount of "garden variety" delinquencies, they were perceived by the community to be basically "good" kids. Jocks were generally from the more affluent families in the community and were among the most popular students. One student referred to them as "your basic student," in part because they maintained a "B" or "C" average in school. (Only one student referred to the Jocks as "dumb.") Another student said that Jocks "were among the better students because if they did not pass their classes, they could not play in games." Some Jocks were known for "brown-nosing" teachers who typically gave them the "benefit of the doubt" and accepted their excuses for missing class. In addition, athletic coaches were known to intervene on Jocks' behalf to get them out of trouble and help them maintain their eligibility for school sports. One student said that the Jocks "could get away with almost anything." Another said that "they never got in trouble with the law because their football coach was one of the commanding officers of the local police department."

The Jocks were considered "stylish" and tended to dress neatly and keep their hair short. According to one student, they dressed "casual, but with taste, the sporty look." Sometimes they wore expensive designer clothes, but more often they wore athletic sweaters, lettermen jackets, Levi's, t-shirts, and "brand name" tennis shoes, frequently high-tops. While the Jocks generally behaved themselves within school grounds, they were frequently truant and engaged in drinking, using and selling drugs (especially marijuana), driving under the influence, and vandalism. But because they were more likely to have cars that enabled them to conduct their delinquencies outside of the area, or because they had access to homes when parents were vacationing or out for the evening, much of the Jocks' activities remained invisible to the community.

The Jocks were especially known for their heavy drinking. One student remarked that the boys on the football team probably drank "more than the entire school combined." Another student indicated that the Jocks' parents seemed to have "accepted the fact that their children went out, partied, and got drunk"—their main concern was that "their child did not get caught doing it." Still another described weekly parties on Friday and Saturday nights that were held at houses selected according to whose parents were not present. At these parties, they "drank to get drunk," and a youth was considered a "loser" and would not be invited again if he or she did not drink. Being seen at these parties increased one's popularity and prestige among peers so that one "could then date all the right people or join all of the popular clubs in school" (quotes from student papers). One student noted that Jocks "always had women flocking over them." In one community some Jocks were also called the *Studs,* because they were known for both their athletic and sexual prowess.[7]

As the Schwendingers (1985) found, the Wisconsin students identified a number of complementary or interrelated social types. For example, depending on the city or town, the behavioral traits of the Jocks were similar to what students in other communities observed in the *Preppies, Preps, Collegiates, Populars, Sportos, The Clique,* and *The Elite.* Other than Jocks, Preppie or Preps was the most common term used to describe these socialite groups, one with an increasing presence over the years. The similarity of these socialite groups was especially apparent when the students were from affluent families. One student said that "the Jocks and Preppies have almost everything in common. . . . Their parents bought them whatever they wanted and everything was given to them on a silver platter."

The term Jocks, of course, denotes members' involvement in school athletics. Female Jocks, Jockettes, Cheerleaders, or Rah-rahs were students involved in athletics or cheerleading or who merely associated with male Jocks. In some communities they were included among the "top dogs of the school" (quote from student paper). In other cases, however, they might be resented as "prissy females . . . [who] walked around with their noses stuck in the air" (quote from student paper).

While these socialite groups were considered the "top dogs," Preppies (or Preps) who were not involved in sports were typically differentiated from Jocks. They were identified by a distinct dress (e.g., polo shirts, khakis, Docksider shoes or penny loafers, with or without argyle socks), and in some cases, they were viewed in decidedly negative terms such as *Preppie Faggots* or *Fontana Fags.* These derogatory metaphors were used by students who resented the Preppies' affluence and social privilege. Preppies may also have been resented when they were "A" students or were perceived as hypocrites. As Milner (2004) explains, the Preppies are in somewhat of a precarious position.

> [They] may or may not care about learning . . . but they are concerned about getting decent grades. . . . The most successful students are often very disciplined and work exceedingly hard. But if they want to avoid being labeled a brain . . . [or] a nerd, they must also learn to "have a good time." This cannot be simply a private experience . . . [but] must be publicly displayed. This is one of the reasons that partying is such a central feature of prep life. It provides an opportunity to publicly display your willingness and ability to "let go," to "go wild," to "get bombed." But this form of hedonism must be limited to weekends and special events if it is not to incapacitate the producing self. (pp. 175–76)

Streetcorner Groups

Turning to the streetcorner youths in this study, Table 17.1 indicates that Freaks and Dirtballs (also known as *Dirties*) were among the most common metaphors for this type of adolescent. During the 1960s, the Freak type originated with the Hippie movement as a nonderogatory affirmation of rebellion, and there is a contemporary connotation of this term that refers to "artsy," "nonconformist," and "alternative" youths whose physical appearance was described similarly to Punks or Goths (to be discussed below).[8] Nonetheless, the fact that the Freak social type now overlaps with a derogatory type like Dirtballs suggests the precipitous decline in the positive valence associated with it. In contrast to Jocks, Freaks and Dirtballs were more likely to come from lower- and working-class families. They tended to wear torn and faded jeans, rock-and-roll or concert t-shirts, blue jean jackets, flannel shirts, and hiking boots. They were also more likely than other students to have long hair and beards. The Freaks and Dirtballs were generally unable to participate in school athletics because of their poor academic records, although one student identified a group called the *Frocks* who were "freaks who played sports" (quote from student paper).

Some students indicated that Freaks and Dirtballs used more drugs and engaged in more petty thievery than the socialite groups, but others thought that they were actually less delinquent. Regardless of their actual rates of delinquency, the Freaks and Dirtballs had reputations as "bad kids" who were overly specialized, preoccupied, or "burned out" with drugs (especially marijuana). The same was true of other drug-using groups such as the *Burnouts* (or *Burnies*), *Druggies,* and *Stoners.* Although the percent of students who identified Burnouts/Burnies in the 1983–1987 and 1997–2002 cohorts remained similar, the percent identified as Druggies and Stoners increased considerably (no one in the earlier cohort used the term Stoners). All told, an additional 21 percent of students referred to Druggies or Stoners, a percentage that corresponds to the 24 percent decline in the reference to Freaks per se. This change is further evidence of the declining social status of the Freak social type, whom the Wisconsin students also called *Heads, Potheads, Hippies, Junkies, No Minds,* and *Zoners.*

These low-status groups were also associated with smoking cigarettes in specific locations such as parking lots, school bathrooms, a corner of the auto shop, under the bleachers, or between two high school buildings. These places were sometimes referred to by names such as the "smoking lounge" or "cancer corner." One group of Dirtballs was also known as the *B-Wingers* because members hung out in the B-wing of a school building. In another case, Freaks often smoked cigarettes (and even marijuana) in a building known as "Freak Hall." At this school, they were also observed occasionally snorting cocaine behind a raised book in the classroom. This practice was called "sneak-a-toke."

In addition, some of the streetcorner groups were also known to be involved with cars or motorcycles (whom a couple of students in the 1997–2002 cohort called *Gearheads*) and were described similarly to Greasers. Greasers is a metaphor carried over from the 1950s, and there were still groups in more recent years that were identified by this term because of their tendency to grease down their hair and wear black leather jackets (the same was true of the *Greaseballs* and the *Hoods*). In one community, a similar group of Hispanic boys were labeled *Low-riders* because they drove cars that were "jacked up" in the back and low in the front.

The large majority of students writing papers for this study (especially in the earlier 1983–1988 cohort) were white. They often described students of color simply as *Blacks* or *Africans* and as *Mexicans, Hispanics,* or *Latinos.* No Asian groups were identified in the earlier cohort, but *Asians* and *Hmongs* were identified by a handful of students in the 1997–2002 cohort. (The Hmong has been a growing population in Wisconsin.) One black student, in turn, described some students in her school simply as *Whites.* The students of color, who generally resided in the larger metropolitan areas—particularly Milwaukee but also Beloit, Madison, Kenosha, and Sheboygan—were described by the white students who mentioned them as coming from the inner city and/or lower-class areas (sometimes through busing) and as having some members who were particularly prone to thievery or violence. Black females were also believed to be more likely to get pregnant. One group of black students, the *Breakers,* were known for their break-dancing. Outside of an occasional confrontation with whites, these groups were generally described as keeping to themselves.

One of the most notable changes between the 1983–1988 and 1997–2002 cohorts was the greater number of gangs and gang members mentioned by students. In the earlier cohort, 7 percent of the students identified adolescent groups associated with specific street gang names such as the *Vicelords, Black Gangster Disciples, Latin Kings,* and *Spanish Cobras,* as well as various gangs identified by street numbers such as the *2–4s* and *2–7s.* In the 1997–2002 cohort, however, 27 percent of the students identified such groups in a larger array of communities.

For the most part, gangs in Wisconsin first emerged in the city of Milwaukee in the late 1970s and early 1980s, which Hagedorn (1988) attributes to the growing racial segregation of the city and the declining manufacturing base of the local economy. But over the years youths claiming membership in gangs has become increasingly noticeable in other communities, even in small towns and rural communities, although much of this is attributable to the cultural diffusion of urban gang names, symbols, and folkways rather than to specific organizational ties between youths in different areas who claim membership in a gang of the same name (Stoneall 1997; Takata and Zevitz 1990).

This cultural diffusion has led to the emergence of the gang *wannabe* phenomenon.[9] Wannabe youths were not mentioned at all by the earlier cohort of students, but they were noted by 7 percent of the students in the more recent cohort; and an additional 6 percent of students mentioned a group they called *Wiggers,* which, as noted earlier, is a contraction of "white niggers." Wannabes is a derogatory term used to describe those (primarily white) youths who were viewed by other youths as only "playing" (or posing) at being in a gang. According to one student, these youths were "the ones who were always in fights with each other, other clique members, or staff. . . . [There was] one incident where a teacher was hit by a 'wannabe' because the teacher embarrassed him in front of the class." Another student described the Wiggers as youths who "acted as if they were black gang members. They tried to talk, dress, and act black. None of these teenagers . . . were involved in a gang, but they tried to act like they were. The other students made the Wiggers the laughing stock of the high school." Another student described the Wiggers as youths who "wore sport clothes and jerseys . . . about two sizes too big. The bigger the better, and their wardrobe wasn't complete without hats and lots of heavy jewelry." In a couple of instances, the students referred to such youths as *Homies,* "the ones that everyone ripped on because they would dress and talk like they were black, even though they were white." Still another referred to this type of youth as *White Trash* who "would talk about how great the black nation is and would cut down the white nation. They would dress in black designer clothing and wear necklaces with their names on them. They would walk with a stride of a typical gangster you see in a movie."[10]

Although high school youths tend to mock "wannabe" youths, law enforcement officials are not so sanguine about them. As one small-town police officer told me, "If the youths claim to be in a gang, we assume they are in a gang and treat them accordingly." Similarly, a former gang member, now a probation officer in the city of Madison, told me:

> I've become rather skeptical of those who dismiss or trivialize the trouble-makers as "wannabes," as not "real" gang members. . . . [These youths] are still doing some of the same things as the so-called real members. Some of them are even more dangerous because they feel that they have something to prove. Their friends tell them, "You ain't shit. You're too scared to do this." (Juette and Berger 2008:120)

Intellectual Youths

As the Schwendingers found, the intellectual social type was labeled with derogatory metaphors such as *Bookworms, Eggheads, Pets, Think-Tanks,* and *Academy Fags* and *Bitches. Brains, Geeks,* and *Nerds* were the most common designations for these groups, with the percentage of students identifying Brains declining, and the percentage of students identifying Geeks and Nerds increasing, over the years. These intellectual types were seen as "teacher's pets," "brown-nosers," "study bugs," or "goody-two-shoes." They were "smart kids who didn't have any social life," who had an overly "strict attitude" toward school, and who wore "out of date clothes that the Preps just got rid of" (quotes from student papers). One student described the Brains as "the ones who scuttle down the hallway, carrying more books than they can handle, while pushing their glasses up onto their noses as they walk." Some of the intellectuals were characterized as overly specialized in their interests. The *Computer Geeks,* for example, were "totally engrossed with computers," had "absolutely no social life outside of their computers," and had personalities "like wet fishes" (quotes from student paper). The *Pets,* on the other hand, were seen as more well-rounded academically (though still of low status) since they were good in subjects other than science and math.[11]

The relatively low status of the intellectual social types is further indicated by the fact that a metaphor such as *Nerds* could be used to describe students who were "either very bright or very dumb" (quote from student paper). Similarly, the term *Dorks* might be used to describe both "A" students as well as students who were dubbed *Losers.*[12] Not surprisingly, the intellectual students were the least likely to engage in delinquency.

Other Groups

Milner observes that the top and bottom groups in most stratification systems "are more clearly defined than those who rank in the middle" (2004:43), and to some extent the status of intermediary groups in Wisconsin reflects a more ambiguous ranking, too. This is true of the group of students—whose proportion (just under 20 percent of the student papers) remained fairly constant across the two cohorts—who were referred to variously as *Normals, Floaters, Drifters,* and *In-Betweens.* For the most part these students were viewed positively because they were "flexible" and "able to interact and belong to more than one group at a time," or neutrally because they "floated from group to group without committing to just one" (quotes from student papers). However, one student said they were viewed negatively because they were unable to "fit into any group."[13]

One intermediary group, which was identified by a larger proportion of students in the 1997–2002 cohort than the 1983–1988 cohort were variously called *Farmers, Rednecks, Hicks,* and *Cowboys,* which more generically reflect a "country" identity. In the earlier cohort, only Farmers and Rednecks were used to identify these groups, and at that time they generally had a derogatory connotation. Youths from farm families and who were involved in Future Farmers of America (FFA), for instance, were perceived by others "as not amounting to much except for farmers or their wives" (quote from student paper). One student referred to the FFA youths as *FFARMs,* which stood for *Future Farmers (Fuckers) of America Rural Manure.* The status of the Rednecks, on the other hand, was more ambiguous, being seen as "swaying" between the "outside borders of the Jocks and Hoods" (quote from student paper). Rural delinquencies attributed to these youths included "road tripping," the practice of driving around on rural roads while drinking, and "mailbox baseball," the practice of driving by roadside mailboxes and vandalizing them with baseball bats.[14]

In the 1997–2002 cohort, Hicks and Cowboys were terms that were also used to identify this "country" adolescent type, but whatever they were called, the status of these youths had clearly improved over the years, perhaps in part due to the growing popularity of country music and the broader cultural system to which it is connected. Whereas one student described the Hicks as among the lowest on the "totem pole" at his high school, another described the Hicks more positively as accounting for the "vast majority" of the students.[15]

> Most of the youths . . . from this group live on farms . . . or in the country. [They are] very laid back and easy to get along with. They do enough homework to just barely pass. But that is all that matters—that they pass. Most of the Hicks wear old blue jeans, t-shirts, baseball hats, work boots and of course, the traditional flannel shirt. . . . They listen to country, hard rock, and alternative. For fun they like to go to certain places in the country to party. On [weekend] nights, they are found huddled around a bonfire, listening to music and consuming large amounts of "barley pop." The only delinquent activity that they participate in is underage consumption of alcohol and underage smoking of cigarettes. During the week, most have part-time jobs and work all night. Their parents make them work so they can buy their own things. They buy their own clothes, cars, and pay for their own insurance. . . . [M]ost drive 4 x 4 pickup trucks. They also like to drive older cars that they can convert into fast muscle cars.

Similarly, another student described the more recent cohort of Farmers as follows:

> The kids who were considered farmers were those who participated in FFA and who took agricultural classes in school. . . . This group consisted mostly of males of lower- to middle-class backgrounds. They were not necessarily kids who lived on farms, but in many cases that was where they were raised. The Farmers were for the most part popular. . . . They were well-liked by school staff, the community, and other groups. . . . They often doubled as jocks, participating in football and wrestling, etc. . . . They were not always the best dressed, usually in jeans and t-shirt. They often were the kids listening to country music and driving pickup trucks to school. They tended to stay out of trouble. . . . However, some displayed bullying type behavior. They were rarely if ever punished.

An additional group of youths, whose presence has increased considerably other the years (from 2% to 17% of student papers in the respective cohorts), were variously called *Punks* or *Punkers,* as well as *Heavy Metalers* and *Goths.* These groups tended to be described similarly, with minor variations, but were differentiated from one another by their particular musical tastes. They tended to be viewed disparagingly by other students, but not necessarily so. One student described the Punks as youths who "don't care what anyone thinks about them. . . . [They] get good or decent grades in school, but are looked down upon because of their physical appearance. . . . [They listen to] bands that punks can slam-dance to, which is what they like to do for fun. They wear combat boots, have tattoos, and wear lots of chains and have many piercings all over their bodies." In addition to tattoos and piercings, which arguably have become more mainstream nowadays, other students mentioned

Punks' tendency to dye their hair in bright colors. One student noted that some of the Punks in his high school were also considered to be Druggies and Dirtballs. Goths, who were not mentioned in the earlier cohort of student papers, were described by one student as those youths who "wore all black clothing, black lipstick, black nail polish, chains and dog collars. Some even used white powder to make their faces paler. These kids . . . were quiet and stuck to themselves. Some were good students and some were not." A couple of students referred more generally to this group of youths (Punks/Punkers, Heavy Metalers, Goths) as the *Alternatives,* which also included a variant of the Freak social type I described earlier.[16] According to one student:

> Everyone in the alternative group centered around music and the arts. Most were part of the school band, created their own rock bands, and took art classes. The extreme alternative kids were characterized by black clothes, black make-up and fingernails, weird haircuts, combat boots, and very odd clothing styles. They often had body piercings and/or tattoos, . . . [and] were involved in odd behavior such as the game Dungeons and Dragons, . . . non-Christian [Satanic] worship, . . . suicide attempts, self-mutilation, drug abuse, . . . [and] sexual promiscuity. (quote from student paper)

Still another group that is worth mentioning is the *Skaters,* who were identified in 9 percent of the 1997–2002 student papers but not in the earlier cohort. This group seemed to have had low status in the adolescent hierarchy (see also Milner 2004). One student called them the *Skater Fags,* who "along with skateboarding, smoking cigarettes and large amounts of marijuana was a major time killer. They always smelled like marijuana."

Finally, another group worth noting but who were too few in number to include in the table were students who wrote papers about parochial high schools. A couple of students noted that their school had the same groups as can be found in public high schools, but one in the 1983–1988 cohort stood out because of the metaphors that were unique to this school. What is fascinating about this high school is the degree to which students managed to create a differentiated adolescent subculture in spite of authorities' attempts to induce rigid conformity among students. In this school, authorities' tolerance for deviation was low. Minor variations on dress or hair length, listening to rock-and-roll music, and conversing with members of the opposite sex were viewed by adults as indications of delinquent tendencies. The group of students known as the *Reps* (for Reprobates) were the most likely to engage in such activities. Included in this group was a subgroup known as the *Tumbleweeds* who were the heavy drinkers and more likely to use marijuana, occasionally steal, be sexually active, and get pregnant. The *Zoobies* were described as students with emotional problems that were curiously connected to their religious beliefs.[17] The conformists, on the other hand, included the *Bible-Bangers*—the parochial school equivalent of the intellectuals found in public schools. These youths felt "a definite 'call' from God" to be attending the school, collected "biblical notes and books much as a chipmunk gathers nuts," and had visiting preachers sign their Bible (quotes from student paper). This group was further divided among the *Missionary Kids* and *Preachers' Kids,* those whose parents were missionaries or preachers, and the *Stickers,* those whose "holier than thou" attitude led them to continuously report other students' transgressions to the school authorities (quote from student paper).

■ Conclusion

I began this chapter by suggesting that the phenomenon of gang delinquency should be expanded in terms of a broader conceptualization of adolescent subcultures. It is unfortunate that criminologists have been so preoccupied with gangs that they have neglected these more common adolescent groups. After reviewing previous research, I presented data on the social type metaphors used by Wisconsin youths in two cohorts (1983–1988 and 1997–2002) to delineate the status hierarchy of adolescent social relations, with an eye toward examining the continuity and change in Wisconsin adolescent subcultures over time. The findings are consistent with earlier research that examined the ways in which this "semantic domain" constructs and maintains the boundaries of expected behavior within and between youths (Schwartz and Merten 1967:455).

Although the data indicate considerable stability in Wisconsin adolescent subcultural types over time, some notable changes have occurred. These include increased identification of the Jocks social type, declining use of the Freaks metaphor and corresponding increase in use of the terms Druggies and Stoners, increased presence of both "real" gangs and "wannabe" gang members (the latter most notably among white youths), increased use of the Geeks and Nerds metaphors, increased presence and less derogatory characterizations of "country" types (Rednecks/Hicks/Farmers/Cowboys), and increased identification of Punks/Punkers/Heavy Metalers/Goths and Skaters social types.

Milner notes that an adolescent's social rank is primarily determined during the first year of high school, and by the sophomore year upward mobility in the status hierarchy tends to be restricted as the higher-status youths dictate who is "going to be 'cool' for the next three years" (2004:83). During the last year of high school, however, the elevated status of "seniors" more generally allows for some reassimilation of youths who had previously been devalued or marginalized. The process is facilitated by "the extensive common activities and rituals of solidarity during the senior year . . . [and] a whole array of graduation-related events" (p. 96). At this time, students also begin to acquire and anticipate new sources of power (e.g., they are courted by colleges or offered scholarships) and "hence the relevance of the high school status system" begins to decline (p. 96). Thus the intellectual students, for example, who have been devalued in high school, may go on to achieve greater educational and occupational success than the students who once made fun of them—the "revenge of the nerds" so to speak.

The data I discussed in this chapter are largely descriptive, and I did not investigate the adult or broader community reactions to the law-violating behaviors of these youths, nor did I investigate their post–high school experiences. Nevertheless, the stratified adolescent networks that I have described play a crucial role in reproducing the larger community social structure and mediating the relationship between social class background and particular patterns of delinquent behavior and later-life experiences (legal and illegal). For the most part, as Chambliss (1973) noted in "The Saints and the Roughnecks," upon leaving adolescence youths like the Saints can be expected to "follow the expected path, settling into the ways of the middle class, remembering fondly the delinquent but unnoticed fling of their youth." Youths like the Roughnecks, on the other hand, might "turn around," but more likely "their noticeable deviance will have been so reinforced by the police and community that their lives will be effectively channeled into careers consistent with their adolescent background."

Corsaro and Eder note that a major feature of the socialization process involves young people's "participation in a series of peer cultures in which childhood knowledge and practices are gradually transformed into the knowledge and skills necessary to participate in the adult world" (1990:214). Adolescent subcultural preferences and the societal reaction to them play a key role in determining long-term life course trajectories (Hagan 1991). Among relatively affluent males, delinquent subcultural activity may not only be without negative consequences, but apart from its academic distractions, it may actually yield tangible benefits insofar as participation in these "mildly disreputable pleasures"[18] helps socialize youths to anticipate the kinds of male-bonded pursuits that establish and consolidate "old-boy" and "new-boy" networks in the adult occupational world (p. 571).[19] Among lower- and working-class youths, on the other hand, delinquent subcultural activity may at best bring short-term status and material benefits within their peer groups, but at the expense of accumulated cultural deficits that greatly impede their later-life chances.

Notes

1. In this article, the concept of adolescent subcultures refers to adolescents in general and is not restricted to the delinquent sphere of activity.

2. Nowadays, however, the Internet has created an atmosphere where both boys and girls engage in verbally aggressive repartee with one another, leading to a phenomenon some have dubbed as "cyberbullying"—"[s]ending or posting of harmful material or engaging in other forms of social aggression using the Internet or other digital technologies" (Willard 2007:1). And whether on the Internet or in person, it is worth noting that girls can be as much (or more) emotionally abusive to one another as boys (see Wiseman 2002).

3. For example, Hirschi (1969) and Wiatrowski, Griswold, and Roberts (1981) found that the least delinquent youths were those who were most involved in academic activities.

4. For other early studies see Blumer et al. (1967), Eckert (1988), Friedman (1969), Gitchoff (1969), Kinney (1989), Lesko (1988), Poveda (1970), Riggle (1965), Schwartz (1987), and Weis (1969).

5. In one community, for example, the *Space-Cadets* were like *Greasers* who were "spaced out" on drugs, while in another they were girls who "did terrible in school, . . . acted like they had no idea of what was going on, . . . [and] spent most of their time worrying about their hair and makeup" (quotes from student paper).

6. A few students were from out of state, mainly from Illinois, and their responses are included in the analysis. Mark Urick and Carrie Walby assisted in the tabulation of the groups that appear in Table 17.1.

7. One group of southern California Jocks discussed in Wooden and Blazak's (2001) study is the *Spur Posse,* which consisted of 20 to 30 top high school athletes who were preoccupied with "hooking up" (having sex) with as many girls as possible. They competed with each other to see who could "score" with the most girls, and they often took turns having sex with the same ones. The boys boasted of their conquests but considered the girls "sluts" (see Tanenbaum 2000).

Among the Wisconsin students, the *Studs* were males who "had been with a lot of girls," and the *Wimps* were males who "hadn't been with anybody." In addition, females were classified as *Sluts, Virgins,* and *Serious Girls.* The Sluts "hopped around from one guy to the next in a short period of time," the Virgins "didn't go out with any guys and kept up their studies," and the Serious Girls "stayed with one guy for a long period of time" (quotes from student paper).

8. *Theater Freaks* "were the kids who were in all of the school plays. They walked around in flamboyant clothing and tried to talk as if they were entirely too sophisticated for the rest of the student body. They were the kids that wanted to experiment with everything and most of the other students referred to them as being 'out there' [strange]" (quote from student paper).

9. See Brotherton (1994), Hutchinson and Kyle (1993), and Monti (1993) for studies of the effect of neighborhood street gangs on the culture of schools. See Kitwana (2002) and Chapter 19 in this book for a discussion of black "hip hop" music and culture.

10. Another derogatory metaphor used to describe white youths is *Trailer Trash.*

11. A related group, though not intellectual per se, includes youths who participated in school band. These groups were sometimes called the *Band Kids* or more derogatorily the *Band Fags* or *Band Nerds.* As Milner observes, "To play a musical instrument even reasonably well requires years of disciplined practice under the supervision of adults," and for males musical activity may be considered "'unmanly,' an activity for 'sissies,' or 'fags and queers'" (2004:77). In the 1997–2002 cohort, a couple of students also mentioned a group of youths who were identified specifically by their sexual orientation as *Gays* or *Lesbians.*

12. Students with learning disabilities, as well as physical disabilities, were sometimes referred to as *Speds* (for Special Education) or identified with derogatory metaphors such as *Retards* or *Vegetables.*

13. One of these latter groups was called the *Fruits.*

14. A youth from Tennessee in the 1997–2002 cohort described the practice of "cow tipping," which "consists of going onto private property and tipping over standing and sleeping cows" (quote from student paper).

15. One student described the Rednecks as racist and the Hicks as not racist. Regarding racism, one *Skinheads* group (not one of the "country" groups) was mentioned: "People who were all white power [some with Satanic interests] . . . and were involved

in animal killing—catching a dog and tearing it apart or getting road kill and cutting it up in the backyard" (quote from student paper; see also Hamm 1993; Wooden and Blazak 2001).

16. One group, the *NINS,* was named after the music group Nine Inch Nails and was described by one student as "a branch of the freaks." Another student mentioned a group of girls, the *NIN Whores,* who "dress in all black and wear fishnet stockings. They have very black or bleached blonde flat hairstyles. They wear black lipstick and black painted fingernails. Behind their appearance, they are mostly higher achievers." Another group of students called the *Children of the Sun* dressed in all black and were compared to the *Trenchcoat Mafia* of Columbine fame.

17. One student saved bottles of water under his bed because of the *Book of Revelation* prediction that the "rivers will turn to blood."

18. Matza and Sykes (1961) noted a convergence between delinquency and the "subterranean" traditions of American society that include risk-taking or thrill-seeking activities such as gambling, drinking, and the pursuit of sexual conquests.

19. In addition, fraternity-related bonding among college males, known for its role in developing occupational networks, is also the site of socialization for male aggression, including fraternity gang rapes (Martin and Hummer 1989). Of course, male socialization for sexual aggression occurs at an earlier age (Ageton 1983).

▥ References

Ageton, Suzanne S. 1983. *Sexual Assaults among Adolescents.* Lexington, MA: Lexington Books.

Berger, Ronald J. 2001. "Adolescent Subcultures, Community Ecology, and Delinquency." In M. Maume and R. Matthews (eds.), *Syllabi and Instructional Materials for Courses in Juvenile Delinquency.* Washington DC: American Sociological Association.

———— (ed.). 1996. *The Sociology of Juvenile Delinquency.* Chicago: Nelson Hall.

Blumer, Herbert, Alan Sutter, Samir Ahmen, and Roger Smith. 1967. *The World of the Youthful Drug User.* ADD Center Final Report, School of Criminology, University of California, Berkeley.

Brotherton, David C. 1994. "Who Do You Claim? Gang Formations and Rivalry in an Inner City Public High School." In J. Holstein and G. Miller (eds.), *Perspectives on Social Problems,* vol. 5. Greenwich, CT: JAI Press.

Bynum, Jack E., and William E. Thompson. 1992. *Juvenile Delinquency: A Sociological Approach.* Boston: Allyn & Bacon.

Campbell, Anne, and Steven Muncer. 1989. "Them and Us: A Comparison of the Cultural Context of American Gangs and British Subcultures." *Deviant Behavior* 10: 271–88.

Chambliss, William J. 1973. "The Saints and the Roughnecks." *Society* 11:24–31.

Corsaro, William A., and Donna Eder. 1990. "Children's Peer Culture." *Annual Review of Sociology* 16:197–220.

Eckert, Penelope. 1988. "Adolescent Social Structure and the Spread of Linguistic Change." *Language & Society* 17:183–208.

Eder, Donna. 1985. "The Cycle of Popularity: Interpersonal Relations among Female Adolescents." *Sociology of Education* 58:154–65.

Eisenstadt, Stuart N. 1956. *From Generation to Generation: Age Groups and Social Structures.* New York: Free Press.

England, Ralph W. 1967. "A Theory of Middle Class Juvenile Delinquency." In E. Vaz (ed.), *Middle Class Juvenile Delinquency.* New York: Harper & Row.

Erickson, Maynard L., and Gary F. Jensen. 1977. "Delinquency Is Still Group Behavior: Toward Revitalizing the Group Premise in the Sociology of Deviance." *Journal of Criminal Law and Criminology* 68:388–95.

Espelage, Dorothy L., and Susan M. Swearer (eds.). 2004. *Bullying in American Schools: A Social-Ecological Perspective on Prevention and Intervention*. Mahwah, NJ: Lawrence Erlbaum.

Everhart, Robert. 1983. *Reading, Writing and Resistance: Adolescence and Labor in a Junior High School*. Boston: Routledge.

Friedman, Stanley D. 1969. *A Typology of Adolescent Drug Users*. M.A. thesis, University of California, Berkeley.

Gitchoff, G. Thomas. 1969. *Kids, Cops and Kilos: A Study of Contemporary Urban Youth*. San Diego: Malter-Westerfield.

Gottdiener, Mark, and Donna Malone. 1985. "Group Differentiation in a Metropolitan High School: The Influence of Race, Class, Gender, and Culture." *Qualitative Sociology* 8:29–41.

Greenberg, David F. 1981. "Delinquency and the Age Structure of Society." In D. Greenberg (ed.), *Crime and Capitalism: Readings in Marxist Criminology*. Palo Alto, CA: Mayfield.

Gubrium, Jaber F., and James A. Holstein. 1997. *The New Language of Qualitative Method*. Oxford: Oxford University Press.

Hagan, John. 1991. "Destiny and Drift: The Risks and Rewards of Youth." *American Sociological Review* 56:567–82.

Hagedorn, John M. 1988. *People and Folks: Gangs, Crime, and the Underclass in a Rustbelt City*. Chicago: Lake View Press.

Hamm, Mark S. 1993. *American Skinheads: The Criminology and Control of Hate Crime*. Westport, CT: Praeger.

Hirschi, Travis. 1969. *Causes of Delinquency*. Berkeley: University of California Press.

Hutchinson, Ray, and Charles Kyle. 1993. "Gangs in Schools." In S. Cummings and D. Monti (eds.), *Gangs: The Origins and Impact of Contemporary Youth Gangs in the United States*. Albany: SUNY Press.

Jessor, Richard J., John E. Donovan, and Frances M. Costa. 1993. *Beyond Adolescence: Problem Behavior and Young Adult Development*. New York: Cambridge University Press.

Juette, Melvin, and Ronald J. Berger. 2008. *Wheelchair Warrior: Gangs, Disability, and Basketball*. Philadelphia: Temple University Press.

Kinney, David A. 1989. *Dweebs, Headbangers, and Trendies: Adolescent Identity Formation and Change Within Socio-cultural Contexts*. Ph.D. diss., Indiana University, Bloomington.

Kitwana, Bakari. 2002. *The Hip Hop Generation: Young Blacks and the Crisis in African-American Culture*. New York: Basic Civitas.

Larkin, Ralph. W. 1979. *Suburban Youth in Cultural Crisis*. New York: Oxford University Press.

———. 2007. *Comprehending Columbine*. Philadelphia: Temple University Press.

Lesko, Nancy. 1988. *Symbolizing Society: Stories, Rites, and Structure in Catholic High School*. Philadelphia: Falmer.

Majors, Richard, and Janet Mancini Billson. 1992. *Cool Pose: The Dilemmas of Black Manhood in America*. New York: Lexington.

Martin, Patricia Yancey, and Robert A. Hummer. 1989. "Fraternities and Rape on Campus." *Gender & Society* 3:457–73.

Matza, David, and Gresham M. Sykes. 1961. "Juvenile Delinquency and Subterranean Values." *American Sociological Review* 26:712–20.

McCall, Nathan. 1994. *Makes Me Wanna Holler: A Young Black Man in America.* New York: Vintage.

Miller, Walter B. 1980. "Gangs, Groups, and Serious Youth Crime." In D. Shichor and D. Kelly (eds.), *Critical Issues in Juvenile Delinquency.* Lexington, MA: Lexington Books.

Milner, Murray, Jr. 2004. *Freaks, Geeks, and Cool Kids: American Teenagers, Schools, and the Culture of Consumption.* New York: Routledge.

Monti, Daniel J. 1993. "The Culture of Gangs in the Culture of the School." *Qualitative Sociology* 16:383–404.

Poveda, Anthony. 1970. *Drug Use among the Major Social Types in High School.* Ph.D. diss., University of California, Berkeley.

Riggle, William. 1965. *The White, the Black, and the Gray: A Study of Student Subcultures in a Suburban California High School.* Ph.D. diss., University of California, Berkeley.

Schwartz, Gary. 1987. *Beyond Conformity or Rebellion: Youth and Authority in America.* Chicago, IL: University of Chicago Press.

Schwartz, Gary, and Don Merten. 1967. "The Language of Adolescence: An Anthropological Approach to the Youth Culture." *American Journal of Sociology* 72:453–68.

Schwendinger, Herman, and Julia Siegel Schwendinger. 1985. *Adolescent Subcultures and Delinquency.* New York: Praeger.

Stafford, Mark. 1984. "Gang Delinquency." In R. Meier (ed.), *Major Forms of Crime.* Beverly Hills, CA: Sage.

Stoneall, Linda 1997. "Rural Gang Origins: A Wisconsin Case Study." *Sociological Imagination* 34:45–58.

Takata, Susan R., and Richard G. Zevitz. 1990. "Divergent Perceptions of Group Delinquency in a Midwestern Community: Racine's Gang Problem." *Youth and Society* 21:282–305.

Tanenbaum, Leora. 2000. *Slut: Growing Up Female with a Bad Reputation.* New York: Perrenial.

Weis, Joseph G. 1969. *A Social Typology of Adolescent Drug Use.* M.A. thesis, University of California, Berkeley.

———. 1973. *Delinquency among the Well-to-Do.* Ph.D. diss., University of California, Berkeley.

Wiatrowski, Michael D., David B. Griswold, and Mary K. Roberts. 1981. "Social Control Theory and Delinquency." *American Sociological Review* 46:525–41.

Willard, Nancy E. 2007. *Cyberbullying and Cyberthreats: Responding to the Challenge of Online Social Aggression, Threats, and Distress.* Champaign, IL: Research Press.

Wiseman, Rosalind. 2002. *Queen Bees and Wannabes: Helping Your Daughter Survive Cliques, Gossip, Boyfriends and Other Realities of Adolescence.* New York: Three Rivers Press.

Wooden, Wayne S., and Randy Blazak. 2001. *Renegade Kids, Suburban Outlaws: From Youth Culture to Delinquency.* Belmont, CA: Wadsworth.

Yinger, J. Milton. 1960. "Contraculture and Subculture." *American Sociological Review* 25:625–35.

———. 1982. *Countercultures: The Promise and Peril of a World Turned Upside Down.* New York: Free Press.

18

Urban Street Gangs:
Class, Race/Ethnicity, and Gender
Ronald J. Berger

*Ronald Berger illuminates the phenomenon of urban street gangs in the
United States, both historically and contemporarily. In particular, he
examines the social dimensions of gangs that are related to class,
race/ethnicity, and gender.*

PARTICIPATION IN LAW-VIOLATING YOUTH GROUPS—WHETHER OR NOT
these groups are called gangs—is a common experience for young people of
all class and racial/ethnic backgrounds (see Chapter 17). As Huff notes, "It is
important to acknowledge that it is normal and healthy for adolescents to want
to be with their peers . . . and gangs represent an extreme manifestation of that
age-typical emphasis on being together and belonging to something" (1993:6).
In Sanders's opinion (1994), however, it is the violence that distinguishes gangs
from other adolescent groups. This chapter reviews some of the basic features
of urban street gangs in the United States, both historically and contemporarily,
that are related to the social dimensions of class, race/ethnicity, and gender.

■ Class, Race/Ethnicity, and Gangs

Frederic Thrasher's (1927) classic study of Chicago youth gangs of an earlier
era offers a useful point of departure for a consideration of contemporary urban
gangs.[1] Youth gang members in the 1920s were largely the children of economically disadvantaged, white European immigrants—primarily Irish, Italians,
and Poles, but also Germans, Jews, Slavs, and Swedes. Most gang members
started out in thievery, which they engaged in as much for sport as for economic
gain. Gangs that formed more or less spontaneously as ordinary streetcorner
groups were consolidated through rivalry and strife. As Skolnick observes:

> Thrasher traced the rise of gangs to . . . the disintegration of family life,
> schools, and religion, . . . [the lack of] wholesome alternatives, . . . [and] the
> corruption and indifference of local politicians. The employment opportunities

available to these [youths] usually involved monotonous jobs with low wages that could scarcely compete with the rewards of the gang or with the fun of bonding and stealing. (1992:111)

In many respects, Skolnick adds, contemporary gangs have not changed in fundamental ways. Youths still join gangs for fun and recreation, to enhance their ability to make money, for physical protection, and for a sense of belonging to a community or alternative family (Sanchez Jankowski 1991). In some Chicano barrios of Los Angeles, "children, parents, and even grandparents have belonged to the same gang [for decades]. Although the adults fear and disapprove of the violence of today's gangs, they take pride in the tradition of gang membership" and expect the younger generation to preserve and uphold the neighborhood gang name (Skolnick 1992:114). More generally, gangs (whatever their race or ethnic background) are often tolerated in their communities because gang youths are not social outsiders among residents; they are sons and daughters, grandchildren, nieces and nephews, the neighbors' kids. The majority of their time is not spent in law-violating activities, and their behavior is appropriate in most social situations (Horowitz 1987; Shelden, Tracy, and Brown 2004; Venkatesh 1997; see Chapter 19).

In his urban ethnography, Sullivan (1989) studied three neighborhoods in Brooklyn, New York, in the early 1980s: Projectville was a largely black community, Hamilton Park was predominately white, and La Barriada was a mixture of Hispanics and whites. Projectville had the highest rate of poverty (52 percent living under the poverty level), followed by La Barriada (43 percent), and Hamilton Park (12 percent). Projectville also had the highest overall crime rate, and Hamilton Park the lowest, while La Barriada had the highest rate of violent crime.

In all three neighborhoods, nevertheless, Sullivan found that male youths progressed through a series of life stages that influenced their involvement in and commitment to crime. During the early to mid-teen years, youths from the same neighborhood began hanging out together in loosely-knit groups and participating in turf fights with youths from surrounding areas. They also stole items like radios, bicycles, and clothes, primarily for use rather than for sale on the open market; and when they did sell stolen property they had no idea of its actual market value. Importantly, however, these early-life forays into crime prepared them for more serious later-life criminality. Engaging in theft helped them revise their conception of "property rights . . . [as] no longer fixed but . . . [as] something over which [they] could exert control" (Robinson 1993:317). And from fighting they learned how to acquire and use weapons in violent crimes.

By the middle teenage years, the youths had acquired more experience in crime. They were now physically stronger and had a greater desire to consume commodities.

[They also] learned more about the value of stolen items and about the networks for converting them to cash; they were better able to weigh the risks and benefits between types of crime, as well as between crime and legitimate employment. The motivation for crime now became economic, a means of support rather than an occasional excursion to vary the day-to-day boredom of just hanging out . . . and as a youth took on crime as his main source of income, he dropped out of street fighting. (Robinson 1993:317)

Along the way, opportunities for legitimate employment, when available, reduced the incentive to engage in crime. The Hamilton Park white youths in particular had somewhat greater access to networks of legitimate employment and were thus the most likely to opt out of crime. Overall, Sullivan (1989) found that by their late teens most youths chose to desist from crime because escalating criminality increased their risk of apprehension. For example, the housing projects where the Projectville black youths lived afforded limited opportunities for profitable theft. When these youths began committing robberies and purse snatchings outside of their own neighborhoods, they increased their exposure and hence their chances of getting caught. Some who became disillusioned with violent theft, however, became attracted to drug sales instead.

In his ethnography of Puerto Rican gangs in Chicago, Padilla (1992) reports that youths often began their involvement in the drug trade as "runners" or "mules," but they soon realized that the distributors made most of the profits. Sullivan (1989) found that it was fairly easy for Brooklyn youths to obtain drugs on consignment until they acquired enough capital to stake themselves out. But even though a competent drug dealer could earn between $500 and $1,000 a week in the early 1980s, the life chances of these youths remained for the most part dismal. As one youth remarked,

I'm a good businessman. . . . I know how to buy and sell. But I've been ripped off, cut, and arrested. Now, I'm on probation and I won't get off so easy next time. But how am I gonna get a job now? . . . I can't go up to somebody and say, "Listen, I know how to buy and sell. . . . I've been buying and selling for years." (p. 175)

Gangs today include more older youths who have fewer opportunities to mature out of the gang than they did in Thrasher's day (Skolnick 1992). Hence some graduate to organized crime. Observers of the gang scene report that as early as the late 1960s and early 1970s, gangs in some large metropolitan areas, most notably in Chicago and New York, were beginning to be transformed "from territorially oriented younger members to commercially oriented older (19 plus) members" (Robinson 1993:312). Some African-American and Latino groups, for instance, began to muscle in on the territory previously controlled by Italian-American crime organizations. Needless to say, this transition of control has not always been peaceful.

Ironically, since the 1970s, incarceration of gang members has facilitated gang organization by bringing together a captive population of similarly situated offenders who can be easily recruited into larger, more powerful organizations (Hayden 2004; Irwin 1980; Jacobs 1977). For instance, Jeff Fort, a leader of Chicago's *Black P Stones Nation*—the P stands for Peace—formed the *El Rukns* while he was imprisoned in 1978. According to Robinson:

> Soon after his release, [Fort] met with representatives of the Italian syndicate having vice interests in El Rukn territory. Reputedly, the Italian group ordered Fort to keep hands off. After burning down the mob restaurant where the warnings were given, Fort, in turn, ordered the syndicate out of El Rukn territory. . . . By 1981, the El Rukns were investing their drug profits in real estate and other legitimate businesses and were employing pharmacists, doctors, accountants, and lawyers. Satellite clubs or alliances were [also] formed in other parts of the country. (1993:313)

Sanders (1994) studied gangs in San Diego, California, through the 1980s. He found that African-American gangs were more likely to sell (but less likely to use) drugs than their Chicano counterparts. Sanders did not find San Diego gangs to be particularly well organized; gang cohesiveness was rooted more in "the strengths of neighborhood . . . solidarity and loyalty" than in a formally structured organization (p. 145). However, Sanchez Jankowski (1991)—who studied 37 gangs in Boston, Los Angeles, and New York—argues that most gangs that are in a mature stage of development have identifiable leadership positions and established codes of conduct. Moreover, Sanchez Jankowski and others have concluded that by the late 1980s gang organizations of a variety of racial and ethnic backgrounds had become more entrepreneurial in nature, shifting away from turf-fighting toward more "systematic involvement in drug distribution" (Padilla 1992; Taylor 1990; Venkatesh 1997:84).

Research also suggests that Asian-American gangs are among the most highly entrepreneurial gangs in the country. Chinese gangs in particular, which can be found primarily in Boston, Los Angeles, New York, and San Francisco (as well as Toronto and Vancouver), have a well-defined hierarchical structure, are well-connected with adult crime groups and fraternal organizations, and have invested in legitimate businesses (Chin 1990; Shelden, Tracy, and Brown 2004).

In interviews conducted by Skolnick and colleagues (1993), African-American gang members from Los Angeles indicated that perceived economic benefit has increasingly become the primary reason for joining gangs. Skolnick and colleagues attribute the change in Los Angeles, in part, to the expanded cocaine importation that has dramatically decreased the wholesale cost of the drug. Prospective gang members are now evaluated in terms of their ability to sell drugs. The gang provides members with access to and control of drug markets within the gang's territory, shared information about the drug market (e.g., sellers, prices, out-of-town markets), protection from competitors and the police, as well as cash, loans, and "fronting" of drugs, weapons, clothes, and cars.

While African-American gangs in Los Angeles appear to have first emerged in the 1950s, the infamous supergangs or gang "nations"—the *Crips* and the *Bloods*—did not emerge until the late 1960s (Williams 2007). These gangs are said to be "deep," consisting of a large number of sets or factions. In 1991 Bing reported the existence of 56 Crip sets and 43 Blood sets. In 1993 Skolnick and colleagues reported that Crip or Blood crack-cocaine operations could be found in 22 states and at least 28 cities in regions all over the country. Gang members indicated that around 1986 they began traveling extensively to expand their drug business. This expansion was motivated, in part, by pressure from police crackdowns in Los Angeles, saturation of the Los Angeles drug market, and higher prices that could be charged in out-of-town markets. Other observers, however, believe that large-scale drug operations are still generally conducted by "individuals and small groups acting on their own rather than for the gang" as a whole (Reiner 1992:72; Shelden, Tracy, and Brown 2004).

In his San Diego study, Sanders (1994) found that African-American gangs (including Crip and Blood sets) extended their activities over a broad territory, while Chicano gangs were more confined to the barrio and lacked allegiances outside their community. On the other hand, Moore and colleagues characterized Los Angeles Chicano gangs as having a "widespread pattern of nonresident gang membership" and documented several ways in which such nonresident membership developed (1983:182). Sometimes gang membership was extended to relatives who lived outside the neighborhood. At times, families of gang members moved, but youths maintained affiliation with their original gang. Gangs also formed fighting alliances with gangs in other areas, or factions split apart and affiliated with other groups. Nonresident youths sometimes sought to join a gang because of its activities or reputation. Occasionally the borders of a barrio may have been unclear, leaving some members living in disputed areas, or freeway construction may have altered the community ecology, dividing a previously contiguous neighborhood.

In the Chicago area, both African-American and Latino (primarily Puerto Rican) gangs have grouped around the larger *People* and *Folks* gang nations or organizations (Bensinger 1984; Padilla 1992). These Chicago gangs can be traced to the late 1950s and early 1960s. Like the Crips and Bloods, People and Folks claim membership in multiple cities. Hagedorn (1988), for example, documented the emergence of People and Folks sets in Milwaukee, Wisconsin, around 1980. Hagedorn emphasizes that gangs develop primarily in response to local conditions. Only four of the original 19 Milwaukee gangs that he studied were started by former gang youths from Chicago, although an additional four gangs did have former Chicago gang youths as founding members. These migrant youths may bring drug and gun connections to the new gang and "act as cultural carriers of the folkways, mythologies, and other trappings of more sophisticated urban gangs" (Maxson 2006:111).

Gangs now appear to be forming in smaller cities, towns, and even rural areas (Skolnick, Bluthenthal, and Correl 1993; Takata and Zevitz 1990). In a study of rural/small-town gang origins in southeastern Wisconsin, Stoneall (1997) offers several hypotheses for the diffusion of youth gangs. Whereas Hagedorn (1988) traced the rise of gangs in Milwaukee (a city of about 650,000) to the deindustrialization and persistent racial segregation of that city, Stoneall suggests that economic development in smaller communities increases the size and diversity of the population in ways that can facilitate gang activity. As families of gang members move, often to escape the problems of large gang cities, youths bring with them gang experience and connections. Or at times youths with gang ties are dispersed through foster-home placements. Stoneall also suggests, like Skolnick, Blumenthal, and Correl (1993), that gang members are reaching out to new areas to expand their drug markets. In addition, school busing has contributed both to the diffusion of gangs and to a pattern of nonresident gang membership (Hagedorn 1988). At the same time, Stoneall argues, much of the apparent gang activity in small communities may simply be due to cultural diffusion and youth fads—the media exposes nongang youths to the broader gang subculture, and local peer groups emulate neighboring gang names, symbols, and styles. Adolescents who refer to themselves by the same gang name may not actually be in the same gang, or may not be in a gang at all; they may be a group of ordinary law-violating peers who are merely "playing" at being a gang (see also Chapter 17).

The diffusion of gangs from urban to rural areas has also been noted in research on Native-American youths. According to Melton:

> [A] 1994 Bureau of Indian Affairs (BIA) Law Enforcement Division Survey of 75 tribal and BIA law enforcement officers in 31 states . . . identified 181 gangs active on or near Indian country. . . . The largest Indian tribe, the Navajo Nation, has reported the existence of more than 28 gangs in 13 of its tribal communities. . . . The infiltration of gangs appears similar to the migration of gangs from large metropolitan cities like East Los Angeles into such cities as Albuquerque [New Mexico] and Phoenix [Arizona]. . . . It is suspected that some of the gang organizing is being initiated by Indian teenagers who have returned to the reservation, village, or pueblo after being raised in a city. (2002:166)

While criminologists continue to debate the distinction between gangs and other law-violating youth groups, it is clear that in some communities gangs have become "a recognized, albeit internally contradictory, community institution, performing a range of 'positive functions' while simultaneously engaging in behavior that has disrupted community social life" (Venkatesh 1997: 107). In his ethnography of the Saints, an African-American Chicago street gang, Venkatesh (1997) reported that the gang has been channeling some of its drug profits to the resident population in order to integrate itself into the social fabric of the Blackstone housing project in which it is based. The gang has distributed groceries and clothing, lent residents money (both interest-free and at exorbitant rates), paid the bail bond for jailed residents, replaced playground equipment, encouraged younger gang members to attend school, and offered protection from other gangs and criminal predators. The residents, in turn, have provided the Saints cover, withholding information from the police and refusing "to allow police to enter their apartments without search warrants" (p. 95). As one resident, a prominent leader on a tenant council, remarked:

> [We] stopped cooperating with police a long time ago, 'cause [the police] ha-
> rass us so much and they don't do a damn thing anyway. At least the gangs
> is giving us something, so lot of us prefers to help them 'cause we can *always*
> go to them and tell them to stop the shooting. Police don't do anything for us
> and they can't stop no shooting anyway. . . . [The Saints] is the one provid-
> ing security around here. . . . We all niggers anyway when it come down to
> it. (p. 95)

Some residents admit that the Saints "make our lives miserable, but if we piss them off, police ain't gonna come 'round here and help us out. And, shit, I gotta tell you, that most of the time it's nice, 'cause they make sure I don't get robbed up in here, they walk through the buildings like . . . police never did that!" (p. 103). Another put it this way: "We have to listen to [the Saints], 'cause when the police leave, [Saints members] are the ones who'll let you know if shootings gonna start up again, you know, they'll tell you if it's safe to go outside at night, or if you can go up north . . . or if you should just stay in the building" (p. 103). In the words of one Saint gang member, "We [want] to be part of the community, help our community, 'cause we're here to stay" (p. 108).

▨ Girls in Gangs

In her research on girls in gangs, Campbell (1987, 1991) interviewed lower-class minority youths in New York City (see Chapter 9). One cannot listen to these young women's accounts without questioning the adequacy of conventional gender explanations that emphasize the differences between females and males. The conventional assumption that males are more violent than females does not necessarily hold among these youths (Messerschmidt 1997; Simpson 1991). As one girl explained: "Round here you have to know how to fight. I'm glad I got a reputation. That way nobody will start with me. . . . They're going to come out losing. Like all of us. . . . We're crazy. Nobody wants to fight us. . . . They say, 'No, man. That girl might stab me or cut my face'" (Campbell 1987:462–63).

Overall, the self-reported delinquency of female gang members is lower than that of male gang members but higher than that of nongang males (Es-bensen and Huizinga 1993; Esbensen and Winfree 1998; Fagan 1990; Miller and Brunson 2000).[2] In a study of gang membership among eighth-grade students in

11 cities that is included in Chapter 5 of this book, Peterson and colleagues (2001) uncovered a more complex pattern. They found that 10 percent of gang members were involved in *all male* gangs and 37 percent of gang members were involved in *majority male* gangs, while only 3 percent of gang members were involved in *all female* gangs and 2 percent in *majority female* gangs. (*Majority male* and *majority female* gangs were defined as those having at least two-thirds of the members as male or female, respectively.) Nearly half of gang members were involved in *gender balanced* gangs. Peterson and colleagues also found that gender patterns of gang offending varied according to the gender composition of the gangs, with boys in majority-male gangs having the highest rates of delinquency and girls in all-female and majority-female gangs having the lowest rates.

Messerschmidt (1997) views the gang milieu as an environment in which girls experiment with and reconfigure the boundaries of femininity. Conventional femininity is the culturally dominant ideal that is associated primarily with middle-class, white, heterosexual women and that is organized around "the display of sociability rather than technical competence, fragility in mating scenes, compliance with men's desire for titillation and ego-stroking . . . [and] acceptance of marriage and childcare" (Connell 1987:187). According to Messerschmidt, when gang girls act tough and are violent they are not "doing masculinity" but are constructing an "oppositional femininity" that challenges the notion of femininity as a trait entirely distinct from masculinity.

Giordano and Cernkovich (1979) observe that gang girls are capable of identifying with and participating in aspects of both traditional and nontraditional gender roles. Elements of traditionalism still permeate the gang milieu. Girls, for instance, are most often involved in gangs as girlfriends of male gang members or as "little sister" subgroups or female auxiliaries that take their name from the male gang (e.g., Latin Kings and Queens) (Shelden, Tracy, and Brown 2004). One New York City gang girl told Campbell (1991) that when the boys were not around, they could do what they wanted. When the guys were there, however, they were "not allowed" to do as they pleased (p. 244). Similarly, a Los Angeles Chicana told Quicker, "If it wasn't for [the boys] we wouldn't be around 'cause the guys started [the gang]. . . . The girls never start the gang; the guys do. And the girls that like them or back them up started it with their permission" (1983:101).

In her study of Chicano gangs in Los Angeles, Moore found that the boys often treated the girls as possessions, "like a piece of ass." As one boy remarked, "It's just there . . . when you want a *chapete* (fuck). . . . The guys treat them like shit. . . . Just to have a partner for the time. . . . And then when they want something you know, get it—wham bam. . . . We used to . . . throw a *linea* (lining up to have sex with a girl), you know what I mean" (1991:54–55). Similarly, in her study of African-American gangs in Fort Wayne, Indiana, Burris-Kitchen (1995) found that girls had difficulty getting the respect they felt they deserved. As one young woman said, "Guys around here don't respect women much. I think it is because of all the rap music bashin' women. I listen to some of this music calling women bitches and ho's and it upsets me. I think the guys around here think sex is all we're good for" (p. 104).

Other females noted a double standard: "Most women get respect if they sellin' drugs, but not if they using. It's ok for guys to use, but not us" (Burris-Kitchen 1995:104). And although gang males express pride over female members' willingness to fight, they are sometimes uncomfortable with or ambivalent about female aggression. One of Quicker's respondents explained,

> "I've asked my boyfriend and they all come up with the same answer. 'I don't think a girl should be in . . . the fights.' . . . They say it's right for a guy, but it's not right for girls. . . . That's what they all say, yet they are happy to have their own girls. They're proud. They say our girls do this, our girls are bad. . . . [So] I don't know what they're talking about." (1983:12)

Gang girls—largely lower-class, minority youths—have few opportunities to make it in mainstream society. They come from families in which they often have experienced physical and sexual abuse, from families that are frequently "held together by their mothers who are subsisting on welfare. Most have dropped out of school and have no marketable skills" (Joe and Chesney-Lind 1995:413). The gang represents an alternative family, a social support system that buffers the dismal future that awaits them. But gang girls also recognize that they must negotiate a gender-stratified street environment dominated by males. As one said, "Females who are soft won't make it. . . . Someone think you weak, they goin' take from ya'. Even if you female you got to be willing to shoot" (Burris-Kitchen 1995:93). Campbell (1993) notes that gang girls know what it is like to be victimized:

> They know that, to survive, force must be met with more than unspoken anger or frustrated tears. Less physically strong and more sexually vulnerable than boys, they find that the best line of defense is not attack but the threat of attack. The key to this is the development of a reputation for violence, which will ward off opponents. There is nothing so effective as being in a street gang to keep the message blaring out: "Don't mess with me—I'm a crazy woman." (p. 133)

Females who are unwilling or unable to fight are thus viewed disparagingly. As one girl said, "Tramps. All they think about is screwing. . . . They don't fight. They don't go to rumbles with their guys. . . . They're a bunch of punks" (Campbell 1987:463). Another girl remarked, "You can belong as long as you can back up your shit and don't rat on your homegirls or back away [from a fight. You have to be] able to hold up the hood" (Harris 1988:109).

Although not equal in power, auxiliary female gangs are not mere appendages of male gangs. Girls in gangs have their own leaders and make most of their routine decisions without the boys (Bowker and Klein 1983; Giordano 1978). They take pride in their claims of autonomy and reject "any suggestion that they could be duped or conned by males" (Campbell 1987:460). In a study of San Francisco gangs, Lauderback and colleagues (1992) found that African-American females were less likely than Latinas to be affiliated with male groups. One African-American gang, the Potrero Hill Posse, started out as a mixed-gender group, with girls selling drugs for their boyfriends. Eventually, however, the females disaffiliated themselves from the males and formed a gang of their own, requiring members to be adept at either selling drugs (crack) or shoplifting.

Moore (1991) found that female gangs were not as closely bound to the barrio as male gangs and that girls often partied with boys from other gangs. Boys, however, were more likely to date girls who were not in gangs, expressing preference for those girls they perceived as more likely to fulfill traditional gender roles in the future. As one boy said, "You know that they are going to be good. You know they going to take care of business and . . . be a good housewife" (p. 75).

Some girls clearly rejected the traditionalism of male constructions of gender. "Not *me*," said one of Moore's informants, "they didn't treat me like that. They think we're possessions, but we're not. No way, I pick my own boyfriends. . . . You don't tell *me* who to be with" (Moore 1991:55). Similarly, some members of the Vice Queens, an African-American gang in Chicago, constructed a nontraditional oppositional femininity by unabashedly placing themselves at the boys' disposal, openly encouraging them to fondle them and have sex with them. Although the boys viewed the girls as mere sex objects, the girls gained status among their female peers by "being able to keep four or five boys 'on the string' without any boys knowing of the others, but at the same time, avoiding sexual relationships with too many boys at one time" (Fishman 1988:21). Orenstein suggests, however, that such girls have simply learned to derive whatever pleasure they can from their subordinate and exploitative position vis-à-vis boys and have "recast mistreatment as excitement" (1994:209).

Sikes (1997) interviewed Latina gang girls in San Antonio, Texas. She learned that "trains" (sex with a number of gang males in succession) were an option to "jump ins" (physical beatings by gang members) in gang initiation rituals. (Trains were not an option for male initiates.) The girls did not view the trains as rape but considered them "the coward's way in—after all, gang logic goes, all the girl does is lie down and spread her legs" (p. 110). Sikes found that most girls chose the "jump in" option.

Nevertheless, Campbell (1987) observes that serial monogamy, not promiscuity, is the norm for most gang girls and that girls who have sex outside of a steady relationship are often condemned. Gang girls may even avoid associating with "'loose' girls whose reputation might contaminate them by association" (p. 452). But once they are involved in a relationship, boys often attempt to exert control over their girlfriends' public appearance and behavior, not allowing them to wear shorts or low-cut blouses, to get "high," or to flirt with other guys. Males, on the other hand, reserve their prerogative to have other relationships. Masculinity norms make it difficult for boys to turn down an opportunity for sex, as this would be considered tantamount to an admission of homosexuality. Girls also accept this view of masculinity and blame other girls for "putting it in his face." In this way, romantic disputes between girls and boys are settled between girls. Nevertheless, the girls' main objective is not so much to "hold on to their man" as to gain other girls' respect (Campbell 1991; Sikes 1997).

Occasionally gang girls fight to defend territorial turf and gain recognition for their group. However, much of their fighting occurs in response to competition over boyfriends, assessments of beauty (who is "the cutest"), and negative gossip regarding one's reputation or that of a family member—their mother especially. Fighting among girls is generally less lethal than among boys, since it usually involves fists or knives rather than guns, but gun use among females does seem to have increased (Anderson 1994; Campbell 1993; Harris 1988).

Gang girls who fight or who are willing to use violence are not rejecting femininity but are constructing an alternative femininity that combines traditional and nontraditional gender traits. Although participation in a street fight involves physical aggression against rival gang members, it is also defined as an act of *caring* for one's gang and the "hood." Thus "what is usually considered atypical feminine behavior outside this situation is, in fact, *normalized* within the social context of interneighborhood conflict; girl-gang violence in this situation is . . . permitted and . . . encouraged . . . by *both* boys and girls as appropriate feminine behavior" (Messerschmidt 1997:82). Hence, doing femininity—"bad girl" femininity—can mean doing violence. Yet girls also play many of the more conventional feminine roles within the gang: child care, cooking, and preparing food and drink for parties. In addition, gang girls are very fussy about their physical appearance—their hair, makeup, wearing the right brand-name clothing—and they are disparaging of their peers who look drab or slovenly. Outside of the gang milieu they are unambiguously feminine. Campbell says that gang girls' concern "with their appearance [and] their pride in their ability to attract men . . . left me in no doubt that they enjoyed being women. They didn't want to be like men and, indeed, would have been outraged at such a suggestion" (1993:113).

At the same time, gang girls are often uninformed or misinformed about birth control, and rarely do they or their partners use it. Instead, they view pregnancy as an occupational hazard of sorts. Many of them get pregnant within a year after becoming sexually active, which may begin at or even before puberty. Becoming a mother does not require leaving the gang, and it offers girls an alternative source of status. Motherhood is valued, provided that the mother accepts responsibility for her child's welfare. The ability to care for children, however, often depends on parental or grandparental support and on the (diminishing) availability of governmental welfare. Abortion is generally condemned for the first pregnancy but is increasingly accepted after that. Wholehearted support for abortion, which might jeopardize their reputations as mothers, is uncommon (Campbell 1987; Moore and Hagedorn 1996; Williams and Kornblum 1985).

In their research in Milwaukee, Wisconsin, Moore and Hagedorn (1996) found that Latina girls had higher hopes of getting married than their African-American counterparts. Forty-three percent of Latina gang members and 75 percent of African Americans agreed with the statement, *"I'd rather raise my kids by myself,"* and 29 percent of the Latinas and none of the African Americans agreed that *"All a woman needs to straighten out her life is to find a good man"* (pp. 216–17). Male gang members, however, rarely marry the mothers of their children or contribute financially to their support, although they do take pride in their ability to father children, considering it a public demonstration of their masculinity. As one Potrero Hill gang member explained, speaking of her child's father, "They just get you pregnant and . . . go on about their business with somebody else" (Lauderback, Hansen, and Waldorf 1992:69). Moore and Hagedorn (1996) note that Latinas have been subjected to more traditional gender expectations than African-American women, who for generations have been forced to assume independent economic and familial roles. Yet Bourgois, in his study of a Puerto Rican neighborhood in New York, says that one of the problems facing inner-city communities today is the increasing number of mothers who are following "the paths of fathers in seeking independent lives in the underground economy or in substance abuse . . . [leaving no one] to cushion the fragmentation of the family unit" (1995:276).

Notes

1. Thrasher was part of the social disorganization tradition associated with Shaw and McKay that I discussed in Chapter 14.

2. More generally, Steffensmeier and Allen (1988) found that within the same racial group, female rates were consistently lower than male rates. But female rates were often higher than male rates for different subgroups of the population. For example, the black female rate was higher than the white male rate for crimes against persons, the urban female rate approximated or exceeded the rural male rate for minor property offenses, and the younger female rate was higher than the older male rate for both serious and minor property crimes.

References

Anderson, Elijah. 1994. "The Code of the Streets." *Atlantic Monthly,* May:81–94.

Bensinger, Gad J. 1984. "Chicago Youth Gangs: A New Old Problem." *Crime and Justice* 7:1–16.

Bing, Léon. 1991. *Do or Die.* New York: HarperCollins.

Bourgois, Philippe. 1995. *In Search of Respect: Selling Crack in El Barrio.* Cambridge, UK: Cambridge University Press.

Bowker, Lee H., and Malcolm W. Klein. 1983. "The Etiology of Female Juvenile Delinquency and Gang Membership: A Test of Psychological and Social Structural Explanations." *Adolescence* 13:739–51.

Burris-Kitchen, Deborah J. 1995. *Sisters in the Hood.* Ph.D. diss., Western Michigan University.

Campbell, Anne. 1987. "Self Definition by Rejection: The Case of Gang Girls." *Social Problems* 34:451–66.

———. 1991. *The Girls in the Gang.* Cambridge, MA: Basil Blackwell.

———. 1993. *Men, Women, and Aggression.* New York: Basic.

Chesney-Lind, Meda, and Randall G. Shelden. 2004. *Girls, Delinquency, and Juvenile Justice.* Belmont, CA: Wadsworth.

Chin, Ko-Lin. 1990. *Chinese Subculture and Criminality: Non-Traditional Crime Groups in America.* Westport, CT: Greenwood.

Connell, R. W. 1987. *Gender and Power: Society, the Person, and Sexual Politics.* Stanford, CA: Stanford University Press.

Esbensen, Finn-Aage, and David Huizinga. 1993. "Gangs, Drugs, and Delinquency in a Survey of Urban Youth." *Criminology* 31:565–87.

Esbensen, Finn-Aage, and L. Thomas Winfree. 1998. "Race and Gender Differences Between Gang and Non-Gang Youth: Results from a Multi-Site Survey." *Justice Quarterly* 15:505–25.

Fagan, Jeffrey A. 1990. "Social Processes of Delinquency and Drug Use Among Urban Gangs." In C. Huff (ed.), *Gangs in America.* Newbury Park, CA: Sage.

Fishman, Laura T. 1988. "The Vice Queens: An Ethnographic Study of Black Female Gang Behavior." Paper presented at the annual meeting of the American Society of Criminology, Chicago.

Giordano, Peggy C. 1978. "Girls, Guys, and Gangs: The Changing Social Context of Female Delinquency." *Journal of Criminal Law and Criminology* 69:126–32.

Giordano, Peggy C., and Stephen A. Cernkovich. 1979. "On Complicating the Relationship Between Liberation and Delinquency." *Social Problems* 26:467–81.

Hagedorn, John M. 1988. *People and Folks: Gangs, Crime, and the Underclass in a Rustbelt City.* Chicago: Lake View.

Harris, M. G. 1988. *Cholas: Latina Girls and Gangs.* New York: AMS Press.

Hayden, Tom. 2004. *Street Wars: Gangs and the Future of Violence.* New York: New Press.

Horowitz, Ruth. 1987. "Community Tolerance of Gang Violence." *Social Problems* 34: 437–50.

Huff, C. Ronald. 1993. "Gangs in the United States." In A. Goldstein and C. Huff (eds.), *The Gang Intervention Handbook.* Champaign, IL: Research Press.

Irwin, John. 1980. *Prisons in Turmoil.* Boston: Little, Brown.

Jacobs, James B. 1977. *Stateville: The Penitentiary in Mass Society.* Chicago: University of Chicago Press.

Joe, Karen, and Meda Chesney-Lind. 1995. "Just Every Mother's Angel: An Analysis of Gender and Ethnic Variations in Youth Gang Membership." *Gender and Society* 9:408–30.

Lauderback, David, Joy Hansen, and Daniel Waldorf. 1992. "Sisters Are Doin' It for Themselves: A Black Female Gang in San Francisco." *Gang Journal* 1:57–72.

Maxson, Cheryl L. 2006. "Gang Members on the Move." In A. Egley, C. Maxson, J. Miller, and M. Klein (eds.), *The Modern Gang Reader.* 3rd ed. Los Angeles: Roxbury.

Melton, Ada Pecos. 2002. "Traditional and Contemporary Tribal Justice." In C. Mann, and M. Zatz (eds.), *Images of Color, Images of Crime.* Los Angeles: Roxbury.

Messerschmidt, James W. 1997. *Crime as Structured Action: Gender, Race, Class, and Crime in the Making.* Thousand Oaks, CA: Sage.

Miller, Jody, and Rod K. Brunson. 2000. "Gender Dynamics in Youth Gangs: A Comparison of Males' and Females' Accounts." *Justice Quarterly* 17:419–48.

Moore, Joan W. 1991. *Going Down to the Barrio.* Philadelphia: Temple University Press.

Moore, Joan W., and John M. Hagedorn. 1996. "What Happens to Girls in the Gang?" In C. Huff (ed.), *Gangs in America.* Thousand Oaks, CA: Sage.

Moore, Joan W., Diego Vigil, and Robert Garcia. 1983. "Residence and Territoriality in Chicano Gangs." *Social Problems* 31:182–94.

Orenstein, Peggy. 1994. *School Girls.* New York: Doubleday.

Padilla, Felix. 1992. *The Gang as an American Enterprise.* New Brunswick, NJ: Rutgers University Press.

Peterson, Dana, Jody Miller, and Finn-Aage Esbensen. 2001. "The Impact of Sex Composition on Gangs and Gang Member Delinquency." *Criminology* 39:411–39.

Quicker, John C. 1983. *Homegirls: Characterizing Chicana Gangs.* San Pedro, CA: International Universities.

Reiner, Ira. 1992. *Gangs, Crime and Violence in Los Angeles.* Arlington, VA: National Youth Gang Information Center.

Robinson, Cyril D. 1993. "The Production of Black Violence in Chicago." In D. Greenberg (ed.), *Crime and Capitalism.* Philadelphia: Temple University Press.

Sanchez Jankowski, Martin. 1991. *Islands in the Street: Gangs and American Urban Society.* Berkeley: University of California Press.

Sanders, William B. 1994. *Gangbangs and Drive-Bys: Grounded Culture and Juvenile Gang Violence.* New York: Aldine de Gruyter.

Shelden, Randall G., Sharon K. Tracy, and William B. Brown. 2004. *Youths Gangs in American Society.* Belmont, CA: Wadsworth.

Sikes, Gini. 1997. *8 Ball Chicks: A Year in the Violent World of Girl Gangs.* New York: Anchor.

Simpson, Sally S. 1991. "Caste, Class, and Violent Crime: Explaining Difference in Female Offending." *Criminology* 29:115–35.

Skolnick, Jerome H. 1992. "Gangs in the Post-Industrial Ghetto." *American Prospect,* Winter:109–20.

Skolnick, Jerome H., Ricky Bluthenthal, and Theodore Correl. 1993. "Gang Organization and Migration." In S. Cummings and D. Monti (eds.), *Gangs: The Origins and Impact of Contemporary Gangs in the United States.* New York: SUNY Press.

Steffensmeier, Darrell J., and Emile Anderson Allen. 1988. "Sex Disparities in Arrests by Residence, Race, and Age: An Assessment of the Gender Convergence/Crime Hypothesis." *Justice Quarterly* 5:53–80.

Stoneall, Linda. 1997. "Rural Gang Origins: A Wisconsin Case Study." *Sociological Imagination* 34:45–58.

Sullivan, Mercer L. 1989. *Getting Paid: Youth Crime and Work in the Inner City.* Ithaca: Cornell University Press.

Takata, Susan R., and Richard G. Zevitz. 1990. "Divergent Perceptions of Group Delinquency in a Midwestern Community: Racine's Gang Problem." *Youth and Society* 21:282–305.

Taylor, Carl S. 1990. *Dangerous Society.* East Lansing: Michigan State University Press.

———. 1993. *Girls, Gangs, Women, and Drugs.* East Lansing: Michigan State University Press.

Thrasher, Frederic M. 1927. *The Gang.* Chicago: University of Chicago Press.

Venkatesh, Sudhir Alladi. 1997. "The Social Organization of Street Gang Activity in an Urban Ghetto." *American Journal of Sociology* 103:82–111.

Williams, Stanley Tookie. 2007. *Blue Rage, Black Redemption: A Memoir.* New York: Touchstone.

Williams, Terry, and William Kornblum. 1985. *Growing Up Poor.* Lexington, MA: D.C. Heath.

19

Gangstas, Thugs, and Hustlas: Identity and the Code of the Street in Rap Music

Charis E. Kubrin

Charis Kubrin explains "how structural conditions in inner-city communities have given rise to cultural adaptations—embodied in a street code—that constitute an interpretive environment where violence" as a means of acquiring respect is accepted, if not encouraged. Through a content analysis of rap music lyrics, she shows how rappers "actively construct violent identities for themselves and for others," hence legitimizing "certain aspects of the street code while ignoring . . . more positive aspects of urban life."

RECENT YEARS HAVE WITNESSED A RESURGENCE OF SOCIOLOGICAL research on identity, culture, and violence in inner-city black communities (Anderson 1999; Bruce et al. 1998; Fagan & Wilkinson 1998; Krivo & Peterson 1996; Kubrin & Wadsworth 2003; Kubrin & Weitzer 2003; Sampson & Wilson 1995). This work portrays a black youth culture or "street code" that influences the identity and behavior of residents, particularly with respect to violence. Typically ethnographic in nature, this literature describes how the code supplies compelling elements of local culture, a culture of the streets in which violence is rendered accountable and even normative.

One complementary medium for studying these issues that has not been fully exploited is rap music, a genre consistently noted for its focus on masculinity, crime, and violence. An aspect of hip-hop culture (Guevara 1996; Kelley 1996; Krims 2000), rap is "a musical form that makes use of rhyme, rhythmic speech, and street vernacular, which is recited or loosely chanted over a musical soundtrack" (Keyes 2002:1). Rap emerged from the streets of

"Gangstas, Thugs, and Hustlas: Identity and the Code of the Street in Rap Music," *Social Problems* 52, no. 3 (2005): 360–378. Reprinted by permission of the author and the University of California Press.

inner-city neighborhoods, ostensibly as a reflection of the hopes, concerns, and aspirations of urban black youth. When the genre first appeared in the 1970s, critics predicted a quick demise, but rap music flourished and has reshaped the terrain of American popular culture.

Rap music has undergone major transformations in the last two decades. One of the most significant occurred in the early 1990s with the emergence of "gangsta rap." The *St. James Encyclopedia of Popular Culture* identifies gangsta rap as the most controversial type of rap music, having received global attention for "its vivid sexist, misogynistic, and homophobic lyrics, as well as its violent depiction of urban ghetto life in America" (Abrams 2000:198). Its roots can be traced to early depictions of the hustler lifestyle and blaxploitation movies of the 1970s, which glorified blacks as criminals, pimps, pushers, prostitutes, and gangsters. Mainly associated with West Coast artists (Keyes 2002), gangsta rap is considered a product of the gang culture and street wars of South Central Los Angeles, Compton, and Long Beach, and the resurgence of the retromack culture (pimp attitude and style) of East Oakland (Perkins 1996). Since its early pioneers were gang members, gangsta rap relates to the life experiences of the rappers themselves, and its lyrics portray gang and ghetto life from a criminal's perspective (Krims 2000).

Gangsta rap departed from earlier rap forms, which were often characterized as socially conscious and more politically Afrocentric (Keyes 2002; Martinez 1997; Perkins 1996). Even today, gangsta rap differs from other types of rap mainly in that it is the musical expression of ghetto centricity, an expression that engages the "black youth cultural imagination that cultivated varying ways of interpreting, representing, and understanding the shifting contours of ghetto dislocation" (Watkins 2001:389). Scholars agree that other rap forms reflect a generic concern for chronicling the "black" experience, while gangsta rap is specifically interested in the black underclass in the ghetto (Keyes 2002; Rose 1994; Smith 1997). Today gangsta rap purportedly provides an insiders' look into black urban street life via crime and violence (Keyes 2004; Kitwana 1994).[1]

Sociological scholarship on identity, culture, and violence in inner-city communities has largely overlooked rap music. Much of the existing literature assumes that the street code is a product of neighborhood processes and neglects additional sources such as popular culture which may reflect, reinforce, or even advocate street-code norms. This study builds on the existing literature through a content analysis of rap music that explores how the code is present not only in "the street," but also in rap music. This research, however, does not suggest that rap directly causes violence; rather, it examines the more subtle discursive processes through which rap helps to organize and construct violent social identity and account for violent behavior.

Theoretically, the study considers how structural conditions in inner-city communities have given rise to cultural adaptations—embodied in a street code—that constitute an interpretive environment where violence is account-able, if not normative. It focuses on the complex and reflexive relationship be-tween the street code, rap music, and social identity. Empirically, the study ex-amines how rappers' lyrics actively construct violent identities for themselves and for others. It explores the ways in which violence is justified and ac-counted for in terms that clearly resonate with the code of the street. I address these issues through a content analysis of 403 songs on rap albums from 1992 to 2000. As I will argue, the lyrics offer portrayals of violence that serve many functions including establishing identity and reputation and exerting social control.

■ Social-Structural Conditions in Inner-City Communities:
The Context

Whereas studies of violent crime typically have been situated within an exclu-sively structural or subcultural theoretical framework, recent research argues that the causes of violence are both socio-structural and situational (Bruce et al. 1998; Fagan & Wilkinson 1998; Kubrin & Wadsworth 2003; Kubrin & Weitzer 2003; Sampson & Wilson 1995). Growing recognition of the utility of an inte-grative approach has led researchers to consider the relationship between struc-tural disadvantage, cultural and situational responses to such disadvantage, and the perpetuation of violence within African-American communities.

Structurally, the combined effects of poverty, unemployment, family dis-ruption and isolation from mainstream America define the neighborhood con-text for residents in many inner-city neighborhoods. These "concentration effects" contribute to social disorganization (Sampson & Wilson 1995) and vi-olence (Krivo & Peterson 1996; Kubrin & Weitzer 2003). The social, political, and economic forces that have shaped these conditions include, among other things, globalization and deindustrialization (Rose 1994; Wadsworth 2004; Wilson 1996), residential segregation (Keyes 2002; Massey & Denton 1993), punitive criminal justice policy (Tonry 1995), and a legacy of slavery and dis-crimination (Hawkins 1985). The concentrated disadvantage found in many urban African-American communities is not paralleled in predominantly white neighborhoods.

An important element of such disadvantaged communities is the opportu-nity structure available for residents. The inner city affords limited avenues for adolescents to obtain the types of social status and social roles available to youth in other environments (Rose 1994). Street-oriented peer groups domi-nate social roles, and few opportunities exist for broader participation in com-munity life, such as after-school groups, volunteer organizations, or super-vised athletics. Alternatives to conventional status attainment are thus limited to manifestations of physical power or domination, verbal agility, or displays of material wealth (Wilkinson 2001).

At the same time, illegitimate avenues for success abound. For many poor, young, black males, the opportunity for dealing drugs is literally just around the corner (Anderson 1999; Keyes 2002) and represents one of the most viable "job" options in the face of limited employment opportunities (Kitwana 2002). This is not to say that impoverished blacks bypass hard work as a prerequisite for success in life; young blacks, like most Americans who are given the opportunity to work, have demonstrated their willingness to do so (Newman 1999). But the continual demand for economic and social success, coupled with limited legitimate avenues and numerous illegitimate avenues by which to attain it, creates a unique situation unparalleled in white and middle-class black communities (George 1998).

The prevalence of drugs—and of crack cocaine in particular—generates more than increased illegitimate opportunities. Crack and the drug trade create neighborhood battles for the control over markets where violence is used as social control (George 1998; Keyes 2002). Elijah Anderson explains this phenomenon in his ethnography of Northton, a poor, urban, black community:

> Dealers have certain corners and spaces "sewed up," marked off as their own territory, and may prevent other dealers from selling either at a particular corner or even in the general area. At times these corners are bought and sold, leading to turf disputes and violence to decide who owns them. A "king of the hill" competition may ensue, awarding the corner to whoever can claim it. (1990:85)

Contributing to the violence, the ready availability of guns in these communities increases the stakes, often turning what would have been an assault into a homicide (Fagan & Wilkinson 1998; Wilkinson 2001).

Tenuous police-community relations contribute to these problems (see especially Anderson 1990). Residents of disadvantaged black communities, arguably those most in need of police protection, tend to be wary of the police, in part because of concerns about racial profiling and the possibility of being wrongfully accused. These practices cause residents who might otherwise assist the police to avoid them, to not cooperate with investigations, to assume dishonesty on the part of officers, and to teach others that such reactions are prudent lessons of survival on the streets (Kennedy 1997; Kubrin & Weitzer 2003). Anderson notes:

> Because the young black man is aware of many cases when an "innocent" black person was wrongly accused and detained, he develops an "attitude" toward the police. He becomes concerned when he notices "the man" in the community. . . . The youth knows . . . that he exists in a legally precarious state. Hence he is motivated to avoid the police and his public life becomes severely circumscribed. (1990:196)

For many poor and working-class blacks, police and brutality are synonymous (Rose 1994).

Scholars have documented the disparities between black and white communities. In many cities, racial differences in poverty, joblessness, and family disruption are so great that the worst urban contexts in which whites reside are considerably better than the average context of black communities (Sampson 1987). These inequalities are even greater considering that incarcerated blacks, typically the most economically and socially disadvantaged social bloc, are not included in census counts (Western 2002).

In addition to racial inequality, patterns of economic bifurcation within the African-American community have become more pronounced: "At one end of this bifurcated class structure are poor and working class blacks in ghetto communities that experience social, economic, spatial, and demographic isolation. On the other end is a black middle and lower-middle class buoyed by increased access to higher education and professional employment" (Watkins 2001:381). Although black middle-class residents may fare better than their lower-class counterparts, Pattillo-McCoy (1999) finds that almost half of the black middle class is concentrated in the lower-middle-class region, distinguished by its close proximity to the black working poor. Moreover, she finds that middle-class blacks do not perform as well as similarly situated whites on standardized tests, are more likely to be incarcerated for drug offenses, are less likely to marry and more likely to be single parents, and are less likely to be working. Thus, we should be cautious in celebrating the achievements of the "fragile black middle-class" (Kitwana 2002:42).

In sum, the extreme, concentrated disadvantage and isolation of black inner-city communities coupled with the quantity and potency of drugs and availability of guns have created a situation unparalleled in American history; such conditions represent "previously unseen challenges in African-American life" (Kitwana 1994:45; 2002:xx). These are the socio-structural community characteristics from which a "code of the street" has emerged.

▧ The Code of the Street and Neighborhood Subculture

In his ethnography of the moral life of the inner city, Anderson (1999) argues that a street code provides the principles governing much interpersonal public behavior. Given the bleak conditions, black youth in disadvantaged communities have created a local social order complete with its own code and rituals of authenticity (Anderson 1999; Henderson 1996; Keyes 2002; Kitwana 2002; Perkins 1996). This street code articulates powerful norms and characterizes public social relations among residents, particularly with respect to violence. Neighborhood structural conditions generate the subculture, so cultural differences reflect adaptations to structural inequality.

Social identity and respect are the most important features of the code. Respect—defined as being treated right or granted the deference one deserves—often forms the core of a person's self-esteem (Anderson 1999). One way to acquire respect is by developing a reputation for being violent, by creating a self-image based on "juice." On the streets, the image one projects is paramount, and at the top of the hierarchy is the "crazy," "wild," or "killer" social identity (Wilkinson 2001). A person's public bearing must send the message that he or she is capable of violence when necessary. In his study of inner-city Philadelphia communities, Anderson (1999) found that youth often created altercations with the sole purpose of building respect. Similarly, Wilkinson (2001) found that young men committed robberies in order to impress their peers and upgrade their social status. A third study found that youth from inner-city New York communities used violence for recognition (Fagan & Wilkinson 1998). In short, violence is thought to be the single most critical resource for achieving status among those who participate in street culture (Wilkinson 2001).

In this context, the gun becomes a symbol of power and a remedy for disputes. Since the 1970s, guns have been a central part of the changing character of youth violence (Fagan & Wilkinson 1998). For those who subscribe to the code, guns are the tactical choice for settling scores and asserting dominance in matters of honor, territory, and business (George 1998). The easy accessibility of guns in the inner city has raised the stakes of the street code even higher. Fagan and Wilkinson (1998) found that guns dominated social interactions; youth reported having one close by in case it would be needed during a conflict. Regarding one youth [they] state, "It was understood that using a gun to harm his opponent was the best way to handle the situation both in terms of what was expected on the street and what an individual had to do to maintain a respected identity" (p. 139). For many youth, guns have become symbols of respect, identity, and power in addition to having strategic survival value.

Building a violent reputation not only commands respect but also serves to deter future assaults. For those invested in street culture, or for those who simply wish to survive (Keyes 2002), a key objective of their demeanor is to discourage others from "testing" or "challenging" them. In some cases, manifest nerve—stealing another's possessions, mouthing off, pulling a trigger—builds a reputation that will prevent future challenges. However, when challenges arise or transgressions occur, violence is viewed as acceptable, appropriate, and even obligatory: "In the most socially isolated pockets of the inner city, this situation has given rise to a kind of people's law based on a form of social exchange whose byproduct is respect and whose caveat is vengeance or payback" (Anderson 1999:66). If a person is assaulted, for instance, it is essential in the eyes of his peers and others for him to seek revenge, otherwise he risks being victimized. Walking away from conflict is risky to one's health:

> To run away would likely leave one's self-esteem in tatters, while inviting further disrespect. Therefore, people often feel constrained to pay back—to seek revenge—after a successful assault. Their very identity, their self-respect, and their honor are tied up with the way they perform on the streets during and after such encounters. And it is this identification, including a credible reputation

for payback, that is strongly believed to deter future assaults. (Anderson 1999)

In instances of payback, violence is considered an appropriate reaction to crime, not a crime itself, and the offender operates on the assumption that the victim provoked his own injury (or death) through an act of wrongdoing. As Black (1983) explained decades ago, much crime is moralistic and involves the pursuit of justice; it is a mode of conflict management, a form of punishment—in some cases, it may even be capital punishment (see also Polk 1994). Much inner-city violence involves residents who characterize their conduct as a perfectly legitimate exercise of social control, as vengeful "self-help" (Kubrin & Weitzer 2003). These residents are determined to show that justice is done, even if this means they will be defined as criminals; they do what they think is right and willingly suffer the consequences.

Violent social control is directly related to the availability (and effectiveness) of authoritative agents of dispute resolution such as the police—vengeful self-help emerges in the absence or weakness of third-party control (Black 1983; Horwitz 1990). In other words, crimes of self-help are more likely where the law is less accessible, such as, for example, in poor minority communities where residents have relatively less legal protection. When called, the police may not respond, which is one reason many residents feel they must be prepared to defend themselves and their loved ones (Anderson 1999). Indeed, a study of extremely disadvantaged communities in St. Louis found that problems confronting the residents were often resolved informally—without calling the police—and that neighborhood cultural codes supported this type of problem solving, even when the "solution" was a retaliatory killing (Kubrin & Weitzer 2003). That residents frequently bypass the police to resolve disputes on their own confirms the street code as a "people's law based on street justice"; the code begins where the influence of the police ends and the personal responsibility for one's safety picks up (Anderson 1999).

Finally, the code of the street encompasses other related dimensions of street life in inner-city communities. For example, the code highlights the appreciation for material wealth as another way to establish self-image and gain respect. Nice cars, expensive jewelry, and the latest clothing fashions not only reflect one's style, but also demonstrate a willingness to possess things that may require defending. Likewise, respect and recognition are gained through sexual promiscuity and conquest. For young men, sex is considered an important symbol of social status, which results in the objectification of women. The more women with whom a young man has sex, the more esteem he accrues. And given the harsh conditions in extremely disadvantaged communities, the street code recognizes a growing sense of nihilism in black youth culture, an outgrowth of living in an environment filled with violence and limited opportunities. Clearly these dimensions of the street code reinforce, and are reinforced by, respect and violence.

In sum, worsening conditions in inner-city communities over the last several decades have given rise, in large part, to the street code. These same conditions also define the context in which rap music has emerged. In studying rap, scholars maintain that "popular forms of music contain significant cultural traditions that cannot be severed from the socio-historical moment in which they take place" (Rose 1994:xiv; see also Keyes 2002; Watkins 2001). The production of rap, and gangsta rap in particular, corresponded with crucial shifts in the material worlds inhabited by young minority males. . . . "[T]he hyper-segregated conditions of the postindustrial ghetto became a fertile reservoir of cultural production" (Watkins 2001:389). Rap music "anticipated the racial mood shifts and growing discontent of a generation of young black Americans who were either disillusioned by the racial hostilities brought on by participation in the societal mainstream or dislocated from the center of social and economic life altogether" (Watkins 2001:381). A question arises: What is the connection between inner-city life, the code of the street, rap music, and social identity? This is the focus of the next section.

The Street Code, Rap Music, and Social Identity

A naturalistic approach to understanding the culture-music-identity nexus would treat the street code as an explanation of behavior that operates much like a set of subcultural directives (see Gubrium & Holstein 1997; Holstein & Jones 1992). The subculture shapes and constrains residents' behaviors, particularly with respect to violence. From this point of view, the code would be viewed as a source of motivations and sanctions that lead to violence (see Anderson 1999) and, as such, behavior would stem from rule compliance, or noncompliance, with the tenets of the code (see Part I of Wieder 1988). From this perspective, the street code projects a compelling normative order, and rap lyrics would be viewed as reproductions of the code offered up to describe black urban street life. Put most simply, the street code could be viewed naturalistically as a source or inspiration for rap lyrics; the code-inspired lyrics would then be understood to reflect—whether accurately or inaccurately—black urban youth culture. An analysis using this approach would treat rap lyrics as more or less verifiable reports of street life and violence in poor urban communities (e.g., see Allen 1996).

Alternatively, one could frame the street code as an interpretive resource used to constitute what is and what is not deviant (Gubrium & Holstein 1997; Part II of Wieder 1988). This "constitutive" perspective treats the code as a source of indigenous explanation whereby reality is organized and made sensible through language use: "It is a form of social action through which social actors assemble the intelligible characteristics of their own circumstances. Descriptions, accounts, or reports, then, are not merely about some social world as much as they are constitutive of that world" (Holstein & Jones 1992:305).

Such an approach has been applied to studies of inmate accounts of "doing time" (Holstein & Jones 1992) and the informal code that permeates talk and conduct in a halfway house for convicted substance abusers (Wieder 1988).

In the latter work, Wieder (1988) treats the convict code as a set of locally developed instructions for understanding resident conduct. In describing this approach, Gubrium and Holstein explain:

> It became clear to Wieder that residents were doing much more than merely reporting on the features of their lives when they "told the code." They were trying to accomplish things in the telling, "doing things with words" to create the very social structures they were otherwise apparently just describing. They were, in practice, actively marking the border between deviance and nondeviance through talk and interaction. (1997:49)

Wieder recognized that the code represents more than a normative structure available to members of a setting as well as to the researcher of their behavior: it is a set of interpretive guidelines that was variably conjured up by the residents themselves who used it to account for matters that required explanation. In other words, "the code was a living embodiment of social control, serving as a shared accountability structure for residents' actions" (Gubrium & Holstein 1997:49–50).

Applying this perspective to the current study, I argue that both the street code and rap lyrics are constitutive elements of contemporary black urban culture. Here culture is akin to an interpretive tool kit (Swidler 1990) that is useful for understanding residents' experiences. As I will demonstrate, rap lyrics are discursive actions or artifacts that help construct an interpretive environment where violence is appropriate and acceptable. The lyrics—like the street code in Anderson's (1999) study—create the sense of a normative climate of violence. They provide sometimes graphically detailed instructions for how to interpret violent, degrading conduct and in so doing create possibilities for social identity in relation to violence. From this point of view, a lyrical analysis is less concerned with how well rappers' accounts comport with objective reality and instead focuses on how such accounts are used by rappers to reflexively accomplish a sense of reality—for themselves and for others. In the process, rappers articulate "vocabularies of motive" (Mills 1940) and "grammars of motive" (Burke 1945) to explain and account for street reality. In line with these classic approaches to rhetorical analysis, the constitutive approach is concerned with how words and grammar are used to constitute rather than report historical reality and its causes. Thus, for the purpose of analysis, I suspend belief (or doubt) in the motivations and explanations rappers offer for events and actions, and focus instead on account making as a persuasive project that constitutes situated realities.

This is not to suggest that the street code is insubstantial or without explanatory value. But neither the code nor culture more generally is deterministic. The code and rap music do not cause violence; violent conduct is far more complex than that. Because listeners interpret music in multiple ways, rap and its lyrics are appropriated and embedded into specific individual, familial, and community fields of reference. That rap music is a "localized form of cultural expression" is clearly evident in the work of Bennett (1999a, 1999b) and of Rose (1994), who explains how

> Los Angeles County, Oakland, Detroit, Chicago, Houston, Atlanta, Miami, Newark and Trenton, Roxbury, and Philadelphia developed local hip-hop scenes that link various regional postindustrial urban experiences of alienation, unemployment, police harassment, social, and economic isolation to their local and specific experience via hip-hop's language, style, and attitude. (p. 60)

Lyrics have situational and situated meaning. Moreover, their reception may be oppositional. For example, Negus and Velazquez (2002) point out that listeners may disagree with or reject lyrics resulting in disaffiliation, ambivalence, and disengagement with (rap) music.[2] Anticipated disaffiliation may even be part of the lyrics' design (as in instances of irony, sarcasm, or hyperbole). That media content has multiple meanings and that audiences actively construct this meaning implies no direct relationship between music and identity (or behavior). The street code and rap music lyrics do not compel one to act, but they do provide an accountability structure or interpretive resource that people can draw upon to understand violent identity and conduct.

That listeners of rap music are "actively involved in the construction of meaning" (Bennett 1999b:86) implies a complex and reflexive culture-music-identity relationship, as Frith (1996), Negus and Velazquez (2002), and Danaher and Roscigno (2004) all suggest. Instead of music lyrics reflecting preexisting identities, in this view, they help to organize and construct identity. Frith states, "The issue is not how a particular piece of music reflects the people, but how it produces them, how it creates and constructs an experience" (1996:109). Likewise, the development of cultural forms will be structured by the reciprocal and mutually influential dynamics of production and reception (Danaher & Roscigno 2004).

In short, rap lyrics instruct listeners in how to make sense of urban street violence and how to understand the identities of those who participate in (or avoid) it. They do so in ways that resemble what Anderson's (1999) informants told him about street violence. Both sets of instructions—the everyday telling of the code by residents and the rappers' telling of the code in music lyrics—provide potent and complementary sources of local culture. Through the telling of the code, both in the streets and in the music, residents and rappers actively construct identities and justify the use of violence. As I will show, the rap lyrics provide vivid "vocabularies of motive" (Mills 1940), which structure violent identities and justify violent conduct, providing a way for listeners to understand and appreciate violent conduct.

▨ Data, Methods, and Analysis

To examine the street code in rap lyrics, I identified rap albums from 1992 to 2000 that had gone platinum (that is, had sold over 1,000,000 copies) during that period (N = 130).[3] I examined rap albums generally, rather than only gangsta rap albums, because rap albums typically mix genres (Krims 2000), and many songs with street code elements would have been excluded from the analysis if only gangsta rap albums had been included. The criterion that an album had sold over 1,000,000 copies ensured that the music had reached a wide segment of the population.[4]

The 1992 to 2000 period was chosen because gangsta rap emerged in the late 1980s/early 1990s (Kelley 1996; Keyes 2002; Kitwana 2002; Krims 2000; Smith 1997; Watkins 2001), and while still popular today, beginning around 1999, it became highly commercialized (Kitwana 1994; Krims 2000; Smith 1997; Watkins 2001). Therefore, the year 2000 represents a turning point in the rap music industry whereby production values more clearly addressed commercial competition, pushing cultural production and reproduction aside. I chose to examine this time frame to capture a period when the fiscal priorities of the music industry were not so clearly dominating cultural commentary.[5]

The 130 albums had 1,922 songs. For the analysis I drew a simple random sample of 632 songs (roughly 1/3rd of the sample) and coded each song in two stages. First, I listened to a song in its entirety while reading the printed lyrics in order to get an overview of the song.[6] Second, I listened to the song again and coded each line to determine whether six street code elements were present (0 = no, 1 = yes): (1) respect, (2) willingness to fight or use violence, (3) material wealth, (4) violent retaliation, (5) objectification of women, and (6) nihilism.[7] These elements were identified based upon a close examination of Anderson's (1999) work. They encompass the major points raised throughout his general discussion of the "code of the street." Although this article's focus is violence, I report the percentage of songs that discussed related themes for comparison. I coded the data conservatively, identifying themes only where it was clear that the lyrics reflected the street code. In cases of uncertainty about the meaning of a word or phrase, I consulted *The Rap Dictionary,* a comprehensive online dictionary of rap and hip-hop terms. As most themes are intricately linked, in those instances where lyrics referred to more than one theme at a time, each scored a "1" to create overlapping categories. Finally, in the relatively few cases where lyrics criticized or made light of the street code, I scored those as "0" so as to include only statements that endorsed the code.[8]

The findings are based on a sample size of 403 songs (64 percent of the total sample). During the course of coding, after song 350, I no longer encountered lyrics that described new aspects of the street code themes. I coded another 53 songs to ensure that I had reached saturation (Glaser & Strauss 1967). In all, 1,588 minutes of music were coded for the analyses.

To assess intercoder reliability, an independent researcher identified a random subset of the sample (N = 64, 16% of the final sample) and listened to the songs, read the lyrics, and coded the cases. Agreement percentages were computed, which reflect how often the researcher and I agreed that the street code theme was present (or absent) in the lyrics. Although the percentages vary slightly by theme, overall they suggest fairly strong agreement: 70.3 percent for respect, 79.7 percent for willingness to fight or use violence, 75 percent for material wealth, 82.8 percent for retaliation, 73.4 percent for objectification of women, and 87.5 percent for nihilism.

The first analyses I present are quantitative and describe the occurrence of violence (and the other themes) in the sample. The second analyses are qualitative and determine how rappers portray violent identities—both their own and those of others—and account for the use of violence in everyday street lives. Using content analysis, I looked for instances of violence (and related issues) in the lyrics and illustrate the results using representative quotations. During coding, I looked for evidence of violence, respect for being violent, the role of guns and other weapons, violent personae, violent retaliation, justification for the use of violence, and community support for violence. Since subthemes did arise in the process of coding the lyrics (e.g., violent retaliation for snitching, projecting a mentally unstable violent persona), I carefully searched for additional meanings in the data and incorporated them into the findings. In this way, the findings not only address how violence is characterized in rap music, but they also contribute to the theoretical framework for understanding the street code.

▨   The "Street Code" in Rap Lyrics

The street code is clearly a staple of rap music lyrics. I found each street code theme prominently represented in the lyrics, albeit to varying degrees. Respect was the most commonly referenced theme (68% of the songs), followed closely by violence (65%). Material wealth and violent retaliation were mentioned in 58 percent and 35 percent of the songs, respectively. Finally, nihilism was present in 25 percent, and only 22 percent had references to the objectification of women, despite the common assumption that misogyny pervades rap music.

The qualitative review of the data underscores the centrality of violence in rap music and suggests that violence has several components. The discussion below considers the two most prominent functions served by violent imagery in rap lyrics: (1) establishing social identity and reputation, and (2) exerting social control. The discussion below includes 45 direct quotations by 21 different rappers. These quotations do not exhaust the universe of violence examples, but are representative.

Constructing Violent Social Identity and Reputation

In extremely disadvantaged neighborhoods, residents learn the value of having a "name," a reputation for being violent, as a means of survival. To build such a reputation is to gain respect among peers (Anderson 1999). Accordingly, rappers often project images of toughness in their music, referring to themselves and others as assassins, hustlers, gangstas, madmen, mercenary soldiers, killas, thugs, and outlaws. Some rappers are even more colorful in their depictions: "untamed guerillas" (Hot Boys, "Clear Da Set"), "3rd world nigga" (Master P, "Making Moves"), "thuggish, ruggish niggas" (BTNH, "2 Glocks"), "hellraiser" (2Pac, "Hellrazor"), "trigger niggas" (Master P, "Till We Dead and Gone"), "the nigga with the big fat trigger" (Ice Cube, "Now I Gotta Wet'Cha"), "no limit soldier" (Silkk the Shocker, "I'm a Soldier"), "young head busta" (Hot Boys, "'Bout Whatever"), "wig splitas" (Juvenile, "Welcome 2 the Nolia"), "cap peelers" (Mystikal, "Mystikal Fever"), "grave filler" (Juvenile, "Back that Ass Up"), "gat buster" or "trigger man" (Jay-Z, "It's Hot"), "raw nigga" (Layzie Bone, "2 Glocks"), and "Sergeant Slaughter" (Killer Mike, "Snappin' and Trappin'").

To bolster this image of toughness, rappers describe how dangerous they and others are—or can be, if necessary. The Notorious B.I.G. raps, "Armed and dangerous, ain't too many can bang with us," while 2Pac boasts, "A little rough with a hard core theme / Couldn't rough something rougher in your dreams / Mad rugged so you know we're gonna rip / With that roughneck nigga named 2Pacalypse" (2Pac, "Strugglin'"). Cypress Hill references 187, the California Penal Code for murder, as a way to drive home their violent image: "1 for the trouble, 8 for the road / 7 to get ready when I'm lettin' off my load / I'm a natural-born cappeela', strapped [armed] illa / I'm the West Coast settin' it on, no one's reala'" (Cypress Hill, "Stoned Raiders"). Master P describes the viciousness of his posse:

> We couldn't run from niggas cause we 'bout it 'bout it
> I'm from the set where my niggas get rowdy rowdy
> We gon' hang niggas
> We gon' bang niggas
> We gon' slang niggas
> Cause we trigger niggas. (Master P, "Till We Dead and Gone")

In projecting a tough image, rappers allude to violent reputations whether for "kickin' ass" or for "keepin' an extra clip" in their gun: "I'm an assassin known for kickin' ass / Show me who them niggas are, and watch me start blastin' / It's Mr. Magic, known for causin' havoc / As long as I'm on your side, see there's no need for panic" (C-Murder, "Watch Yo Enemies"); "I was born and raised for this gangsta shit / C-Murder be known for keepin' an extra clip / My pops say look 'em in the eye before I kill 'em / P crank the 'llac [Cadillac] up and let's go get 'em" (C-Murder, "How Many").

Young inner-city males take reputation or "rep" seriously and exert effort into building it in order to gain respect (Fagan & Wilkinson 1998). Often rappers will instruct listeners on how to develop "rep" on the street: "Rep in New York is the cat burglar, the fat murderer / Slippin' the clip in the Mac [Mac 10 submachine pistol] inserterer / Hurtin' your pockets, droppin' your stock to zero profit / Holding heroes hostage and mansions for ransom like DeNiro mob flicks" (Big Punisher, "Fast Money"); "Sterling [B.G.'s friend] lived a soldier, died a soldier / Had respect for knockin' heads clean off the shoulder" (B.G., "So Much Death"); "Kickin' niggas down the steps just for rep" (Notorious B.I.G., "Ready to Die"). In these examples, rappers authorize the use of violence to establish identity. In other words, the lyrics "accomplish [identity] in the telling" (Gubrium & Holstein 1997:49).

At the top of the hierarchy is the "crazy" or "wild" social identity (Fagan & Wilkinson 1998). As a way to display a certain predisposition to violence, rappers often characterize themselves and others as "mentally unstable" and therefore extremely dangerous. Consider Snoop Dogg and DMX, both of whom had murder charges brought against them in the 1990s: "Here's a little something about a nigga like me / I never should have been let out the penitentiary / Snoop Dogg would like to say / That I'm a crazy motherfucker when I'm playing with my AK [AK-47 assault rifle]" (Snoop Dogg, "DP Gangsta");

> Since I run with the devil, I'm one with the devil
> I stay doin' dirt so I'm gonna come with the shovel
> Hit you on a level of a madman, who's mind's twisted
> Made niggas dreams caught the last train, mines missed it,
> Listed as a manic, depressin' with extreme paranoia,
> and dog I got somethin' for ya!
> Have enough of shit, startin' off hard then only gettin' rougher!
> Tougher, but then came the grease, so if you wanna say peace,
> Tame the beast! (DMX, "Fuckin' Wit' D")

An important element of the "crazy" persona is having a reputation for being quick tempered (Katz 1988). In the chorus of "Party Up," DMX warns others that even when he's at the club partying, the slightest thing may set him off: "Y'all gon' make me lose my mind (up in here, up in here) / Y'all gon' make me go all out (up in here, up in here) / Y'all gon' make me act a fool (up in here, up in here) / Y'all gon' make me lose my cool (up in here, up in here)" (Chorus, DMX, "Party Up"). These lyrics show how the code is brought into play to account for matters that require explanation, in this case, for explaining a mood shift that may result in violence. DMX and others account for their violent behavior, which they render acceptable and appropriate given the circumstances. The lyrics supply a vocabulary of motive which, Mills argues, offers "accepted justifications for present, future or past programs or acts" (1963:443).

Verbal assertions of one's violent tendencies are important in establishing identity, but physical assertions are necessary as well (Anderson 1999). So, while projecting the right image is everything, backing up the projection with violent behavior is expected. For this reason, some rappers project images of toughness by describing acts of violence that they have perpetrated on others.

The Notorious B.I.G. explains how he point blank kills someone: "As I grab the glock, put it to your headpiece / One in the chamber, the safety is off release / Straight at your dome [head] homes, I wanna see cabbage / Biggie Smalls the savage, doin' your brain cells much damage" (Notorious B.I.G., "Ready to Die"). It is common for rappers to provide detail when describing violent situations. Some songs contain literally dozens of lines describing in rich detail incidents that precipitate violence, the persons involved, violent acts, weapons, ammunition, and the bloody aftermath. The descriptions often make explicit reference to elements of the street code: "Must handle beef, code of the street / Load up the heat, if these niggas think they could fuck around / Real niggas do real things / By all means, niggas knowin' how we get down" (Nas, "Shoot 'Em Up"). Here the rapper, Nas, accounts for his violent actions in ways analogous to what Wieder (1988) reported in his study of a halfway house. Wieder explains, "It [the code] was a device for accounting for why one should feel or act in the way that one did as an expectable, understandable, reasonable, and above all else acceptable way of acting or feeling" (p. 175). Nas's notion that one "must handle beef" not only accounts for his violent conduct; it also instructs listeners how to understand violent circumstances and violent responses, given the situation.

Firearms are often used to claim the identity of being among the toughest. In fact, guns—referred to by rappers as street sweepers, heaters, ovens, and pumps—have become the tactical choice for demonstrating toughness and for settling scores, as suggested by the Notorious B.I.G., "Fuck tae kwon do, I tote the fo'-fo' [.44 magnum]" ("One More Chance") and Dr. Dre, "Blunt in my left hand, drink in my right, strap [gun] by my waistline, cause niggas don't fight" ("Ackrite"). Both rappers acknowledge the important role of the gun in the ghetto and justify its use.

Further, rappers acknowledge an increase in gun use by showing how times have changed in the inner city (George 1998). Fagan and Wilkinson (1998) found that inner-city young males often characterized their neighborhood as a "war zone" and described the streets as dangerous and unpredictable, a sentiment echoed in many of the songs. For example, in "Things Done Changed" the Notorious B.I.G. reminisces about the past as he explains how conditions in the ghetto have become much more violent:

    Remember back in the days, when niggas had waves,
    Gazelle shades, and corn braids
    Pitchin' pennies, honies had the high top jellies
    Shootin' skelly, motherfuckers was all friendly
    Loungin' at the barbeques, drinkin' brews
    With the neighborhood crews, hangin' on the avenues
    Turn your pagers to nineteen ninety three
    Niggas is gettin' smoked [killed] G, believe me.
        (Notorious B.I.G., "Things Done Changed")

The Notorious B.I.G. goes on to describe in detail how violence began to escalate as drugs, fighting, gambling, and general disorganization set in. Violent
circumstances and experiences are frequently offered as emerging norms as
rappers depict the "reality" of street life—for them and for others. When rappers portray life in the streets as dangerous and unpredictable, they implicitly
authorize the use of violence to establish identity and supply a vocabulary of
motives for describing and understanding violent conduct.

As a result of worsening conditions, guns have become an everyday ac-
cessory in the ghetto. One study found that most young males carry guns and
describe them as central to their socialization (Fagan & Wilkinson 1998). For
many, carrying a gun is as common as carrying a wallet or keys. Rapper 2Pac
makes this point clear in the chorus of "High Speed." He is asked, "Whatcha
gonna do when you get outta jail?" and answers matter-of-factly: "I'm gonna
buy me a gun." The lesson to learn is summed up in the chorus of C-Murder's
"Watch Yo Enemies": "Watch your motherfuckin' enemies / And you might
live a long time / Watch your motherfuckin' enemies / Stay strapped [carry a
gun] cause the ghetto is so wicked now." C-Murder both rationalizes his decision to carry a gun and instructs the listener that in everyday life one must "stay
strapped" to stay secure. The lyrics are implicit, interpretive instructions for understanding "life in the streets"—not just for rappers, but for others as well.

Collectively, rap lyrics show how toughness and a willingness to use violence are articulated as central features of masculine identity and reputation.
The rappers implicitly and explicitly use the code of the street to construct
identities and in so doing they resemble Anderson's (1999) respondents from
inner-city communities in many important respects. As the above passages illustrate, rappers typically characterize life on the streets as violent and unpredictable and implicate this violence and their participation in it in their own
identity work. The lyrics provide an implicit recipe for how to create a violent,
but viable, street identity. The lyrics suggest that one learns the value of having a reputation for being tough in order to survive. The lyrics also enlist guns
as signs of toughness; their possession is a significant identity marker. The
lyrics tout "rep" as a means of gaining and sustaining respect among peers and
preventing future challenges. In sum, the lyrics provide both a formula and a
justification for violent street identities.

Portraying Violence as Social Control

As the problems of the inner city become more acute and police-community
relations grow increasingly tentative, residents claim they must assume primary responsibility in matters of conflict (Kubrin & Weitzer 2003). This often
results in violence intended as punishment or other expression of disapproval.
Most frequently violent social control is precipitated through disrespect. Rappers are virtually fixated on "respect"; they tell listeners that no one should

tolerate disrespect and are clear about the consequences of such behavior, which can include death for the "perpetrator." Whether referenced only in passing or explained in more detail, the message is clear. There may be severe penalties for disrespect:

> Y'all punk muthafuckas ain't got no nuts
> I only be dealin' with real niggas
> Them other niggas, they get they ass put in check
> When they try to flex and disrespect me
> And that's when I gotta get even with niggas, retaliation.
>   (Krayzie Bone, "Thugz All Ova Da World")

> Gotta push the issue
> On the fools that dis you
> Whether pump or pistol
> When it's up in yo' gristle [face]
> Hand yo' mama a tissue
> If I decide to kiss [kill] you.
>   (Ice Cube, "Ask About Me")

In the latter passage, Ice Cube not only warns others about the repercussions of disrespecting him, but also makes explicit the rules of the game concerning disrespect: payback is a must. Cube's lyrics instruct listeners that on the streets when one is disrespected one responds with violence. In this way, he constructs an interpretive environment where violence is accountable and acceptable, as both a means of constructing identity and of enforcing social control on the street.

Disrespect can come in a variety of flavors including disrespect by testing or challenging someone, disrespect through victimizing—usually robbing—someone, and disrespect by snitching. Each was serious enough to warrant violent self-help again and again in rap songs.

Responding to Challenges. Rappers are often vague [about] what constitutes being "tested" or "challenged"—two words commonly encountered in the lyrics. What they make very clear, however, is the reaction to being "tested" or "challenged," summed up succinctly by the Notorious B.I.G., "Fifty-shot clip if a nigga wanna test," and Bone Thugs-N-Harmony, "A nigga wanna test, catch slugs, put 'em in the mud"; "187 is a lesson for them niggas that want to test, bring more than one cause me shotgun will be buckin' your chest."

One form of testing or challenging involves "fucking with" someone or with his or her family, friends, or "posse." To do so, according to the code, is to invite a virtual death sentence. In "It's On," Eazy-E bluntly states, "You try to fuck with E nigga run run run, cause if it's on motherfucker, then it's on G." DMX describes the implications of "fuckin' wit' D": "Fuckin' wit' me, y'all know somebody has / Told you about fuckin' wit' D, stuck in / A tree is what you will be, like a cat / And I'm the dog at the bottom, lookin' up" (DMX,

"Fuckin' Wit' D"). In a song appropriately titled "Murder III," Mystikal is furious as he recounts the story of his sister's death at the hands of her boyfriend. Mystikal tells the boyfriend, "I'm living for revenge"; "I know what you did, I'm comin' to get'cha, you cannot live / Look, you sleep forever is the fuckin' price / Shit, a throat for a throat, a life for a life" (Mystikal, "Murderer III"). And consider the lyrics from a Juvenile song: "I ain't gonna let a nigga disrespect my clique / And I ain't gon' let a nigga come and take my shit / That'll make me look like a stone cold bitch / So ain't no way I ain't gon' grab my AK and let my shit spit" (Juvenile, "Guerilla"). Note Juvenile's reference to looking like a "stone cold bitch" if he does not respond to "niggas disrespecting his clique." Here he strongly justifies the use of violent social control in order to not lose respect—a fundamental aspect of the code. As such, the lyrics serve as a vehicle by which Juvenile and other rappers explain and justify their actions. The message that one is not a pushover must be loud and clear. In this context, projecting the right image is everything, an image that must be substantiated with violent behavior (Fagan & Wilkinson 1998).

The code in the lyrics justifies a reciprocal exchange of punishments in cases where one's friends and family are victimized. This position is not difficult to justify. According to the street code, even verbal disrespect cannot go unpunished (Kubrin & Weitzer 2003). This seemingly mild form of disrespect is enough to provoke violent retaliation in numerous songs: "Talk slick, you get your neck slit quick / Cause real street niggas ain't havin' that shit" (Notorious B.I.G., "Machine Gun Funk"). In another song, Ice Cube warns that you should "check yo self"—watch what you say and do—because otherwise the consequences will be "bad for your health"; "So come on and check yo self before you wreck yo self / Check yo self before you wreck yo self / Yeah, come on and check yo self before you wreck yo self / Cause shotgun bullets are bad for your health" (Chorus, Ice Cube, "Check Yo Self").

Resisting Victimization. Inner-city communities pose high levels of risk for victimization. Yet an important part of the street code is not to allow others to "get over on you," to let them know that you are not to be messed with. So those who want to present themselves as streetwise signal to potential criminals (and anyone else) that they are not the ones to be targeted for victimization (Anderson 1999). Rap lyrics invoke such signals, letting listeners know that being disrespected through robbery victimization is a costly transgression: "You play with my life when you play with my money / Play around but this'll be the last time you think somethin's funny" (DMX, "One More Road to Cross"). Method Man insists that violent retaliation is an automatic response to robbery: "Niggas try to stick [rob] me, retaliation, no hesitation" ("Sub Crazy"). And the Wu-Tang Clan warns others that they can get "wild with the trigger" if need be: "Shame on a nigga who try to run game on a nigga / Wu buck wild with the trigger! / Shame on a nigga who try to run game on a nigga / We buck—I fuck yo' ass up! What?" (Wu-Tang Clan, "Shame on a Nigga"). Rappers' lyrics actively define the border between what is acceptable and unacceptable behavior—in other words, what will or will not provoke violent retaliation, as well as what is an appropriate and warranted response. By invoking rules and elaborating their application to specific cases, these rappers describe and constitute their activities as rational, coherent, precedented, and orderly (Gubrium & Holstein 1997). The concluding message to the would-be offender: "If you ever jack [rob] this real nigga, you'd besta kill me or pay the price" (C-Murder, "Ghetto Ties").

Don't Snitch. Violence as social control is perhaps best personified in cases of snitching, where rappers are not at all reluctant to administer capital punishment: "My next door neighbor's having a convo with undercovers / Put a surprise in the mailbox, hope she get it / Happy birthday bitch, you know you shouldn't a did it" (2Pac, "Only Fear of Death"). In many rappers' eyes, the worst case scenario is to "end up Fed": "And I don't know who the fuck you think you talkin' to / No more talkin'—put him in the dirt instead / You keep walkin'—lest you end up red / Cause if I end up Fed, y'all end up dead" (DMX, "Party Up"). DMX concludes with, "Sun in to sun out, I'ma keep the gun out, Nigga runnin his mouth? I'ma blow his lung out." Entire songs may be devoted to warning others about the repercussions of snitching and testifying, as is Nas's song "Suspect" with the chorus: "To the suspect witness don't come outside / You might get your shit pushed back tonight" (Nas, "Suspect").

These excerpts provide a glimpse of why, after a violent incident, residents of extremely disadvantaged communities are often unwilling to cooperate with the police out of fear of retribution (Kubrin & Weitzer 2003). The lyrics virtually instruct observers to keep quiet and perpetrators to enforce silence. The code in the lyrics is strikingly similar to the one Anderson observed, whereby people "see but don't see" (1999:133). The neighborhood mantra is "Niggas do unto these snitches before it's done unto you" (2Pac, "Hell 4 a 'Hustler'"), which clearly conveys that snitching is unacceptable and offers guidelines for how one should respond when encountering a snitch. Again, the theme of justified violence is clear.

Retaliation. In cases of snitching or disrespect, violent retaliation is portrayed as punishment and is characterized as an acceptable and appropriate response as part of the street code. In many instances violent retaliation is claimed to be not only appropriate but also obligatory: "You fucked with me, now it's a must that I fuck with you" (Dr. Dre, "Fuck with Dre Day"); "Otis from the thirteenth bit the dust / It's a must we strap up and retaliate in a rush" (B.G., "So Much Death"). In "Retaliation," B.G. describes acts of retaliation and expresses the sentiment that retaliation is expected, a given, known to all, and therefore, clearly justified. It's simple: "You done took mine, I'ma take yearn": "Ain't that cold? I heard a nigga downed my nigga / My partner just paged me and say they found my nigga / It's a bust back thang can't be no hoes / I got a hundred rounds plus for my Calico." And later in the song: "You sleep six feet I tear down the whole street / Bust ya head up leave ya deader yo blood redder / Nigga what, keep ya mouth shut retaliation is a must." Ms. Tee warns all in the chorus: "Niggas . . . they comin' to get'cha / You betta watch ya back before they muthafuckin' split cha" (B.G., "Retaliation"). Retaliation, of course, builds "juice." According to the lyrics, it is also a way to deter future assaults, as Rappin 4-Tay explains to 2Pac: "Pac I feel ya, keep servin' it on the reala / For instance say a playa hatin' mark is out to kill ya / Would you be wrong, for buckin' a nigga to the pavement? / He gon' get me first, if I don't get him— fool start prayin'" (2Pac, "Only God Can Judge Me"). Again, we see how rappers justify the use of violence, this time as a deterrent.

Anderson (1999) suggests that everyone knows there are penalties for violating the street code. In their music, rappers use the implicit rules of the code as explanations for street behavior. By reference to aspects of the code, the lyrics mark what is acceptable and unacceptable behavior (e.g., don't challenge, victimize, snitch). The lyrics make sense of violence as an arguably accountable response to a wide variety of "offenses," while simultaneously identifying just what those "offenses" might be. The above passages show how the code is variably conjured up by rappers to instruct listeners on how to understand and account for their own and others' everyday actions. In this way, the code becomes a living embodiment of social control as it both serves to define offensive behaviors and accounts for the violence that might be forthcoming in response (Gubrium & Holstein 1997).

■ Rap Music and Cultural Codes

That violence constitutes a large part of rap music, particularly gangsta rap, is axiomatic. This study found that nearly 65 percent of the songs sampled make reference to some aspect of violence and many songs were graphic in their violent depictions. It is precisely for this reason that gangsta rap is controversial and unpopular with some segments of the population. Still, rappers tell important stories through their music. Some use their street knowledge to construct first-person narratives that interpret how social and economic realities affect young black men in the context of deteriorating inner-city conditions. Other narratives may be more mythical than factual. Regardless of their source or authenticity, rap lyrics serve specific social functions in relation to understandings of street life and violence.

In rap music, social identity and respect are the most important features of the street code. Lyrics instruct listeners that toughness and the willingness to use violence are central to establishing viable masculine identity, gaining respect, and building a reputation. As Anderson might suggest, the lyrics show how violent confrontations settle the question of "who is the toughest and who will take, or tolerate, what from whom under what circumstances" (1999:69). As was evident in many passages, references to guns are used to bolster these violent identities.

In cases of disrespect, the code—as evident in the lyrics—makes clear that payback is imminent. Rappers' lyrics delineate the rules and actively mark the border between acceptable and unacceptable behavior. Moreover, the lyrics teach listeners how to appropriately respond in the event that rules are violated; they authorize the use of violent retaliation in certain situations and thereby prescribe violent self-help as a method of social control. As the lyrics showed, the code requires constant application and articulation with concrete events and actions in order to make the events and actions meaningful and accountable.

In examining how rappers use violence to establish social identity and reputation and exert violent social control, the study has carefully considered the relationship between the street code, rap music, and identity and behavior. As argued earlier, one approach is to treat the code as an explanation of behavior that operates much like subcultural counter-directives. From this view, the street code is a compelling normative order and rap lyrics are reproductions of the code that describe black urban street life. Any examination, therefore, would treat the lyrics as more or less accurate reports of street life and violence in poor urban communities.

The current analysis provides a different framing. Rather than encouraging residents to be deviant, here the code is seen as an interpretive resource—as a source of indigenous explanation whereby reality is organized and made sensible through language use—in this case, lyrics. As explained earlier, the code supplies an interpretive schema for seeing and describing violent identity and behavior, and the lyrics are treated as reality-producing activities. In terms of analysis, this has led us beyond the artists' own explanations (the simple telling of the street code) in order to determine what is accomplished by the use of the code as an explanation of behavior. In other words, the focus has shifted from what is said by rappers to how they say it and what is socially realized in the process. I have bracketed rappers' claims about the causes of behavior in order to examine what is accomplished by making the claims. This has meant suspending belief in whether or not rappers' claims are true (Burke 1945; Gubrium & Holstein 1997). My analysis is indifferent to whether the reality rappers portray in their lyrics is an "actual" or "literal" one. What is important is that rap artists create cultural understandings of urban street life that render violence, danger, and unpredictability normative.

Of course, this cultural understanding legitimizes certain aspects of the street code while ignoring other important and arguably more positive aspects of urban life. Anderson devotes a significant portion of his book to discussing "decent" families and daddies and reminds us "to be sure, hustlers, prostitutes, and drug dealers are in evidence, but they coexist with—and are indeed outnumbered by—working people in legitimate jobs who are trying to avoid trouble" (1999:24). But what we mostly hear in rap lyrics are rappers touting the virtues of violence with little of the more mundane, yet positive, elements that emanate from the black community. This is not to say that the lyrics are inaccurate. But as a cultural force, gangsta rap music offers a particular characterization of urban life. While this version of local culture may be at odds with other versions, it is the one that gets the most "air play," so to speak. In that sense, it widely promotes an accountability structure in which violence is legitimized and condoned.

This raises another important issue: the characterization of rap music and its messages in the context of mainstream culture. Although Martinez (1997) and others (e.g., Negus 1999) recognize rap as a resistant, oppositional, countercultural form of expressive culture, they also argue that this culture "may be embedded within and even contribute to a dominant hegemonic framework" (Martinez 1997:272). I agree wholeheartedly. Rap music does not exist in a cultural vacuum. Rather, it expresses the cultural crossing, mixing, and engagement of black youth culture with the values, attitudes, and concerns of the white majority. Many of the violent (and patriarchal, materialistic, sexist, etc.) ways of acting that are glorified in gangsta rap are a reflection of the prevailing values created, sustained, and rendered accountable in the larger society. Toughness and a violent persona have been central to masculine identity in myriad American social contexts. And young men come to identify the connections between masculinity-power-aggression-violence as part of their own developing masculine identities (Messerschmidt 1986). In short, gangsta rap is just one manifestation of the culture of violence that saturates American society as a whole—in movies, video games, sports, [professional] wrestling, and other venues. Therefore, it is important to recognize that the values that underpin some rap music are very much byproducts of broader American culture.

Indeed, in some cases rap music does not warrant the excessive criticism it receives. Recall that one finding from the analysis is that "objectification of women" or "misogyny" is not as pervasive in rap lyrics as originally thought. Likewise, it does not appear to be a significant part of the rappers' code— nowhere near as central as respect and violence. Of all the street code themes, "objectification of women" was least prominent in the lyrics. A greater percentage of the songs mentioned issues related to nihilism, a topic frequently overlooked in the literature and by critics. This is not to suggest that rappers be "let off the hook" for their violent and misogynistic lyrics but that critics recognize that rap music and misogyny are not synonymous and acknowledge the variability in topics covered by rappers.

Findings from this study suggest that violence researchers might look beyond traditional data sources (e.g., census reports and crime statistics) for the empirical traces of "culture in action" (Swidler 1990) that render violence acceptable. As I have argued, rap music does not cause violence but extends the purview of the street code of violence and respect. Rappers' telling the street code in their music in conjunction with the everyday telling of the code by inner-city residents in community research (Anderson 1999; Fagan & Wilkinson 1998; Kubrin & Weitzer 2003) provide two potent sources of local culture—a culture of the streets in which violence is cast as a way of life.

■ Notes

1. See Krims (2000) for a detailed description of differences in themes, flow, and musical style between other rap forms and gangsta rap.

2. Press (1994) raises a similar point in her review of the cultural reception literature when she describes a sophisticated model of reception as a site of struggle between cultural industries, critics, and receivers. According to Press, "this model emphasizes both the importance of cultural judgments of authority, and the responses of groups with differential power in relation to these judgments" (p. 230). In essence, this approach fully incorporates the varied experiences and interpretations of those consuming popular culture.

3. Not included are movie soundtrack and compilation albums.

4. One might ask whether such artists are the best "spokespersons" for the street code. Given their success, one could argue that these rappers may be removed from disadvantaged urban areas and not engaged in crime and violence, so that the authenticity of the imagery they construct is questionable. On the other hand, one could argue that the music industry highlights the outlaw character of rappers to establish their "street cred." To explore these issues, I determined the number of rappers/rap groups in my sample (N = 61) that had been charged with and/or convicted of a felony. As criminal records are not publicly available, I obtained this information by reading magazine articles and articles on the web that provided information on the criminal records of rap artists. I was able to find numerous articles mostly from MTV.com, which has a news archive link with information on rappers dating back to the early 1990s. I created a database that recorded whether each artist, or any of the artists in a rap group, had been charged with and/or convicted of a felony along with the type of felony. I was conservative and coded "no" if unable to find any information on a rapper/group. The results show that nearly half (46%) of the rappers have been charged with and/or convicted of a felony and another 8 percent have been charged with and/or convicted of a serious misdemeanor. Some of the charges/convictions include: murder, stabbing, robbery, sexual assault, assault with a deadly weapon, aggravated rape, narcotics, terrorist threats, and bribery. These results are consistent with researchers' general claims about rap artists' brushes with the law (Keyes 2002). Ultimately, however, it makes no difference to my analysis since I am interested in the identity construction process and am indifferent to the authenticity of identity claims. In this article I examine cultural reproduction not reality reproduction.

5. Critics argue that the record companies have exaggerated the violence in today's rap music as a marketing ploy. Watkins (2001) points out that whereas the early stages of production were managed by small independent record labels, the genre's success led to stronger ties, and consequently greater obligations, to the major record labels. Still, even as rap continues to make inroads into the commercial sphere of popular entertainment, it retains a strong identification with the street and the ethos of grass roots expression (Bennett 1999b; Rose 1994). Many rap artists strive to remain "underground," refusing to identify with a pop market and insisting that staying "real" necessitates

authenticity and a continued connection with the streets (Keyes 2002). Still, it is important to remember that rap music cannot be fully severed from the ties of the record industry, which has implications for a lyrical analysis. However, to minimize the influence of the record industry, I end my analysis in 2000.

6. Lyrics were obtained from *The Original Hip-Hop/Rap Lyrics Archive.*

7. "Nihilism is the belief that all values are baseless and that nothing can be known or communicated. It is often associated with extreme pessimism and a radical skepticism that condemns existence" (Pratt n.d.). To capture nihilism while coding I looked for evidence of such things as bleak outlook on life, perceived or real sense of powerlessness, frustration and despair, fear of death and dying, and resignation or acceptance of death.

8. Although infrequent, examples of lyrics that denounced and/or made light of the street code include: "If others disrespect me or give me flack / I'll stop and think before I react / Knowing that they're going through insecure stages / I'll take the opportunity to exercise patience / I'll see it as a chance to help the other person / Nip it in the bud before it can worsen" (Beastie Boys, "Bodhisattva Vow"); "Get off your high horse or die off like extinction / Boriquans are like Mohicans, the last of the Po'Ricans / We need some unity, fuck all the jeeps and jewelry / The maturity keeps me six feet above obscurity" (Big Punisher, "Capital Punishment");

> I tell you life is too short for it to be like that
> We gotta be leaders, can't follow the pack
> With all them fiends in the streets smokin' crack
> What you give life is what it gives you back
> Cause money in the ghetto ain't nothin' new
> But when you make the money you gotta know what to do
> Buy you a business or buy you a house
> Just so the police can't wipe you out
> I heard it in the streets, they say you the man
> So try to help your brothers and lend a helpin' hand.
>   (Too Short, "Thangs Change")

■ References

Abrams, Nathan. 2000. "Gansta Rap." In T. Pendergast & S. Pendergast (eds.), *St. James Encyclopedia of Popular Culture*. Farmington Hills, MI: Thomson-Gale.

Allen, Ernest, Jr. 1996. "Making the Strong Survive: The Contours and Contradictions of Message Rap." In W. Perkins (ed.), *Droppin' Science: Critical Essays on Rap Music and Hip Hop Culture*. Philadelphia: Temple University Press.

Anderson, Elijah. 1990. *Streetwise: Race, Class and Change in an Urban Community*. Chicago: University of Chicago Press.

———. 1999. *Code of the Street*. New York: Norton.

Bennett, Andy. 1999a. "Rappin' on the Tyne: White Hip-Hop Culture in Northeast England—an Ethnographic Study." *Sociological Review* 47:1–24.

———. 1999b. "Hip Hop am Main: The Localization of Rap Music and Hip Hop Culture." *Media, Culture & Society* 21:77–91.

Black, Donald. 1983. "Crime as Social Control." *American Sociological Review* 48:34–45.

Bruce, Marino A., Vincent J. Roscigno & Patricia L. McCall. 1998. "Structure, Context, and Agency in the Reproduction of Black-on-Black Violence." *Theoretical Criminology* 2:29–55.

Burke, Kenneth. 1945. *A Grammar of Motives.* New York: Prentice Hall.

Danaher, William F. & Vincent J. Roscigno. 2004. "Cultural Production, Media, and Meaning: Hillbilly Music and the Southern Textile Mills." *Poetics* 32:51–71.

Fagan, Jeffrey & Deanna Wilkinson. 1998. "Guns, Youth Violence, and Social Identity in Inner-Cities." *Crime & Justice* 24:105–88.

Frith, Simon. 1996. "Music and Identity." In S. Hall & P. Gay (eds.), *Questions of Cultural Identity.* London: Sage.

George, Nelson. 1998. *Hip Hop America.* New York: Viking.

Glaser, Barney G. & Anselm L. Strauss. 1967. *The Discovery of Grounded Theory: Strategies for Qualitative Research.* Chicago: Aldine.

Gubrium, Jaber F. & James A. Holstein. 1997. *The New Language of Qualitative Method.* Oxford: Oxford University Press.

Guevara, Nancy. 1996. "Women Writin' Rappin' Breakin'." In W. Perkins (ed.), *Droppin' Science: Critical Essays on Rap Music and Hip Hop Culture.* Philadelphia: Temple University Press.

Hawkins, Darnell F. 1985. "Black Homicide: The Adequacy of Existing Research for Devising Prevention Strategies." *Crime & Delinquency* 31:83–103.

Henderson, Errol A. 1996. "Black Nationalism and Rap Music." *Journal of Black Studies* 26:308–39.

Holstein, James A. & Richard S. Jones. 1992. "Short Time, Hard Time: Accounts of Short-Term Imprisonment." *Perspectives on Social Problems* 3:289–309.

Horwitz, Alan V. 1990. *The Logic of Social Control.* New York: Plenum Press.

Katz, Jack. 1988. *Seductions of Crime.* New York: Basic.

Kelley, Robin D. G. 1996. "Kickin' Reality, Kickin' Ballistics: Gangsta Rap and Postindustrial Los Angeles." In W. Perkins (ed.), *Droppin' Science: Critical Essays on Rap Music and Hip Hop Culture.* Philadelphia: Temple University Press.

Kennedy, Randall. 1997. *Race, Crime and the Law.* New York: Vintage Books.

Keyes, Cheryl L. 2002. *Rap Music and Street Consciousness.* Chicago: University of Illinois Press.

Kitwana, Bakari. 1994. *The Rap on Gangsta Rap.* Chicago: Third World Press.

———. 2002. *The Hip Hop Generation: Young Blacks and the Crisis in African American Culture.* New York: Basic.

Krims, Adam. 2000. *Rap Music and the Poetics of Identity.* Cambridge: Cambridge University Press.

Krivo, Lauren J. & Ruth D. Peterson. 1996. "Extremely Disadvantaged Neighborhoods and Urban Crime." *Social Forces* 75:619–50.

Kubrin, Charis E. & Tim Wadsworth. 2003. "Identifying the Structural Correlates of African-American Killings: What Can We Learn from Data Disaggregation?" *Homicide Studies* 7:3–35.

Kubrin, Charis E. & Ronald Weitzer. 2003. "Retaliatory Homicide: Concentrated Disadvantage and Neighborhood Culture." *Social Problems* 50:157–80.

Martinez, Theresa A. 1997. "Popular Culture as Oppositional Culture: Rap as Resistance." *Sociological Perspectives* 40:265–86.

Massey, Douglas S. & Nancy A. Denton. 1993. *American Apartheid: Segregation and the Making of the Underclass.* Cambridge, MA: Harvard University Press.

Messerschmidt, James W. 1986. *Capitalism, Patriarchy, and Crime: Toward a Socialist Feminist Criminology.* Totowa, NJ: Rowman & Littlefield.

Mills, C. Wright. 1940. "Situated Actions and Vocabularies of Motive." *American Sociological Review* 5:904–13.

———. 1963. *Power, Politics and People.* New York: Oxford University Press.

Negus, Keith. 1999. *Music Genres and Corporate Cultures.* London: Routledge.

Negus, Keith & Patria Roman Velazquez. 2002. "Belonging and Detachment: Musical Experience and the Limits of Identity." *Poetics* 30:133–45.

Newman, Katherine S. 1999. *No Shame in My Game: The Working Poor in the Inner City.* New York: Vintage Books.

The Original Hip-Hop/Rap Lyrics Archive. 2002. Retrieved April 24, 2005 (http://www .ohhla.com/all.html).

Pattillo-McCoy, Mary. 1999. *Black Picket Fences: Privilege and Peril among the Black Middle Class.* Chicago: University of Chicago Press.

Perkins, William Eric (ed.). 1996. *Droppin' Science: Critical Essays on Rap Music and Hip Hop Culture.* Philadelphia: Temple University Press.

Polk, Kenneth. 1994. *Why Men Kill: Scenarios of Masculine Violence.* Cambridge: Cambridge University Press.

Pratt, Alan. n.d. "Nihilism." *The Internet Encyclopedia of Philosophy.* Retrieved April 23, 2005 (http://www.iep.utm.edu/n/nihilism.htm).

Press, Andrea. 1994. "The Sociology of Cultural Reception: Notes toward an Emerging Paradigm." In D. Crane (ed.), *The Sociology of Culture.* Cambridge, MA: Blackwell.

The Rap Dictionary. Edited by Patrick Aloon. March 21, 2005. Retrieved April 24, 2005 (http://www.rapdict.org/ Main_age).

Rose, Tricia. 1994. *Black Noise: Rap Music and Black Culture in Contemporary America.* Hanover, NH: Wesleyan University Press.

Sampson, Robert J. 1987. "Urban Black Violence: The Effect of Male Joblessness and Family Disruption." *American Journal of Sociology* 93:348–82.

Sampson, Robert J. & William Julius Wilson. 1995. "Toward a Theory of Race, Crime and Urban Inequality." In J. Hagan & R. Peterson (eds.), *Crime and Inequality.* Stanford, CA: Stanford University Press.

Smith, Christopher Holmes. 1997. "Method in the Madness: Exploring the Boundaries of Identity in Hip Hop Performativity." *Social Identities* 3:345–74.

Swidler, Ann. 1990. "Culture in Action." *American Sociological Review* 51:273–86.

Tonry, Michael. 1995. *Malign Neglect: Race, Crime and Punishment in America.* Oxford: Oxford University Press.

Wadsworth, Tim. 2004. "Industrial Composition, Labor Markets, and Crime." *Sociological Focus* 37:1–24.

Watkins, S. Craig. 2001. "A Nation of Millions: Hip Hop Culture and the Legacy of Black Nationalism." *The Communication Review* 4:373–98.

Western, Bruce. 2002. "The Impact of Incarceration on Wage Mobility and Inequality." *American Sociological Review* 67:526–46.

Wieder, Lawrence D. [1974] 1988. *Language and Social Reality.* Landham, MD: University Press of America.

Wilkinson, Deanna. 2001. "Violent Events and Social Identity: Specifying the Relationship between Respect and Masculinity in Inner-City Youth Violence." *Sociological Studies of Children & Youth* 8:231–65.

Wilson, William J. 1996. *When Work Disappears: The World of the New Urban Poor.* New York: Vintage.

20

Community Tolerance
of Gang Violence

Ruth Horowitz

*In this ethnography of a lower-class Chicano community in Chicago,
Ruth Horowitz shows how community tolerance of gang violence is a
negotiated and tenuous phenomenon. On the one hand, gang youths are
tolerated by adults because they are not social outsiders, and they behave
appropriately in most social situations. On the other hand, this tolerance
of gangs breaks down when youths disrupt community functions or directly
implicate a family in violence. At such times, the negotiated sense of order
is no longer tenable and the incongruence between gangs and legitimate
community norms becomes more salient.*

ALL SOCIAL GROUPS ARE OCCASIONALLY CONFRONTED BY TROUBLE-
some behavior, and the reactive strategies they employ to define, punish, or
treat such behavior as "deviant" have been a fertile ground for research. However, much less attention has been devoted to the phenomenon of tolerance of
threatening or disturbing behavior. How and why people tolerate actions they
do not support are complex questions. Tolerance of disapproved conduct may
vary in degree. For instance, Lofland (1983) distinguishes between negative
and positive toleration. Negative toleration is the ability "to put up with" another's differences or potentially problematic conduct simply because of lack
of awareness or limited contact between self and other. On the other hand, positive toleration involves the ability to maintain a relationship with another in
open awareness and "with at least a mild appreciation" of their personal or behavioral differences (p. 5).

This article presents a case study of these and other tolerant responses to
the violent behavior of gangs in a Chicago Chicano community. I focus on the

"Community Tolerance of Gang Violence," *Social Problems* 34, no. 5 (1987): 432–450. Reprinted
by permission of the author and the University of California Press.

processes through which violent acts and their meaning are interactionally negotiated and mutually understood among gang members, nongang youths, and adult members of the community. By analyzing how these groups collaborate to maintain a sense of predictability and safety in their families and neighborhood (Wallace 1980)—and by examining occasions where this tenuous sense of order collapses—I attempt to show why community members are generally able to tolerate conduct that outsiders condemn as senseless acts of violence.

■ Tolerance and Negotiated Order

Few studies of violent gangs have considered the question of community tolerance. Some research on other forms of troublesome behavior indicates that the smaller the social distance between the actor and the audience, the greater the reluctance of the audience to categorize the actor as deviant (Pfuhl 1978; Rubington & Weinberg 1978; Yarrow et al. 1955). Such findings highlight a need to examine how tolerant or intolerant reactions to gang violence are contingent on the relationships between gang members and various community audiences.

More specifically, the ability of community members to maintain a tolerant stance toward the potentially disturbing or life-threatening behavior of gangs may depend fundamentally on the different "awareness contexts" that characterize their relationships to gang members. As Glaser and Strauss describe it, an awareness context is "the total combination of what each interactant in a situation knows about the identity of the other and his own identity in the eyes of the other" (1964:67). Even in close relationships, such as between family members, all parties may not be fully or equally aware of each others' identities outside of the relationship. Levels of tolerance may be affected not only by the degree of awareness (i.e., aware, suspicious, unaware) in a relationship, but also by the extent to which interactants acknowledge their awareness of others' identities (i.e., pretense or no pretense). For example, parents may openly acknowledge an awareness that their son is a "good boy" at home while being unaware or covertly suspicious of his identity on the street as a gang member. However, awareness contexts are always subject to revision or dramatic change in the face of new evidence about alternative identities—for example, if parents discover their son was involved in a street fight.

In stressing the importance of awareness contexts, I do not mean to imply that tolerance simply amounts to a passive state of ignorance about gang members' behavior and identities. All parties to such relationships actively participate in the construction and maintenance of negative as well as positive toleration (Lofland 1983). In this respect, my approach is similar to Becker and Horowitz's (1972) study of civility in San Francisco, where they found that toleration of a wide range of conduct and groups was based on mutual accommodations worked out between actors and audiences through a process of negotiation.

Furthermore, I will focus on the negotiated character of moral judgments about the violent acts of gangs in relation to community standards of conduct. Here, my analysis contrasts with Lemert's early conception of community tolerance, which treated the relationship between acts and cultural standards as basically unproblematic: "societal reaction tends to be a pure function of the interaction of deviation and the norms of the groups which are transgressed" (1951:54; see also Scott 1972). A view of community reaction as a direct function of rule-violations fails to account for the active manipulation of standards or situational maneuvers involved in the interactional construction of tolerance. For instance, analysts of urban life point out that tolerance may be maintained by avoiding contact with groups whose conduct is problematic (Karp et al. 1977; Lofland 1973; Suttles 1972)—in a sense, avoidance ("spatial myopia") mediates between standards and conduct. However, as Stokes and Hewitt point out, even when contacts between groups or with potentially disruptive behavior are unavoidable, audiences and actors often collaborate in "aligning actions" that "sustain a relationship (but not necessarily an exact correspondence) between ongoing conduct and culture in the face of recognized failure of conduct to live up to cultural definitions and requirements" (1976:844). Accordingly, I deal with tolerance and other community reactions to gang violence as a process of negotiation "among people interacting with one another and not simply [as] a question of applying rules or principles to conduct" (Stokes & Hewitt 1976:844).

The people I studied—Chicano gang members, nongang youths, and adults on 32nd Street—routinely collaborated to maintain a sense of order and mutual tolerance in their community. I will examine how most community members were generally able to avoid awareness of the violent acts of their sons and neighbors or to align such acts with cultural standards of honor. However, as I will also show, the presumption of order was precarious and subject to collapse on those occasions where accommodations between gangs and their neighbors failed, and violence intruded into the affairs of the rest of the community. People become baffled, upset, and shocked when the routine flow of events is disrupted (see Scott 1972)—and they may focus their fear and outrage toward the source of this disorder. Just as tolerance is embedded in a cultural and social order that is continually negotiated, a breakdown of this negotiated order can lead to intolerance of gang violence.

■ Setting and Methods

On 32nd Street, violent gangs were prevalent: they had guns; they shot at or stabbed each other and, occasionally, nongang youths; and they sometimes killed people. The majority of community residents were poor and poorly educated. According to census data, there were 44,000 residents in the approximately 150 square block area, but some local estimates ranged as high as

70,000.[1] Some people chose to stay in the neighborhood; others were unable to move because of their ethnic status or lack of income. However, most residents did not retreat behind heavily barricaded doors; in fact, people spent a good deal of time outdoors and walked around the community at all hours of the day and night.

Some local residents estimated that close to 70 percent of the male population, at least for a short period (a few months), joined one of the eight major gangs. Most of the gangs were divided into age-graded groups such as the Tinys, Midgets, Littles, Juniors, and Seniors. Acts of expressive violence by one or more gang members were relatively common, and the chances that other community residents would witness such violent events were quite high. Most conflicts did not end in a death; however, the number of gang-related deaths averaged about five per year during the period of my research.[2]

My research was conducted over a three-year period using participant-observation techniques. I spent long periods daily with the gang members in the streets, on their park bench, at dances, at parties, and in their homes while I was living in the community. I developed very close ties with some gang members and was often invited to their basement clubhouse while some members of their gang were excluded. Many of them would talk to me individually about their lives, but others never spoke to me privately. If there were questions about an event, someone would say, "Ask Ruth, she's writing it all down." I also spent considerable time with many unaffiliated male youth and with a variety of female groups (see Horowitz 1983, 1986 for further details).

Most of the gang data reported here concerns the Lions, which had approximately 30 core members. When I started the research, the Lions were 15 to 18 years old and made up the "Littles" segment of the gang. They split up a year later into the "Littles" and "Juniors"; however, they remained closely affiliated and continued to spend time on the same bench. When I returned to do a restudy seven years after the first meeting with the group, most of the original group were Seniors, who were married, were working, and had children. They still spent many of their evenings on the same bench. When I showed up at the park, the first thing anyone said was, "Ruth, where have you been?" It immediately seemed as though I had never left.

In the following analysis, I first explore the meaning of gang violence to gang members and other community members and the processes by which groups (nongang males and family) in varying relationships to gang members construct and maintain their presumption of order. Second, I examine the conditions under which gang violence becomes the solvent that destroys the apparent safety and order of the neighborhood. Third, I focus on how the distinct meanings attributed to gang violence by outsiders create a situation in which violence is not understood or tolerated. Finally, I consider some of the reasons why gang violence continues to be tolerated by parents.

■ Honor, Violence, and Etiquette

The cultural framework of honor and its extensive pattern of moral meanings permeate many of the social relationships on 32nd Street. A strong emphasis on the value and symbols of personal honor is generally found in Mediterranean and Latin societies (Peristiany 1966). On 32nd Street the man of honor supports his family, accumulates no long-standing debts, protects the chastity of his women,[3] and guards against any aspersions on his masculinity. He is independent and dominant. These criteria are generally understood by community residents as a basis for evaluating actions. Should a man's honor be questioned publicly, violence is an expected response. On such occasions residents know the meaning of others' actions, where violence fits into the scheme of things, and what options are available and sensible.

Honor revolves around a man's ability to command deference in interpersonal relations. An individual suspects he is viewed as weak when he believes he has been publicly humiliated—that is, his right to deferential treatment in public has been challenged. In order not to test another man's claims to precedence inadvertently, men follow strict rules of etiquette in daily life: hands are shaken in greeting, bumping into others is assiduously avoided, and staring is eschewed. Polite and proper interactions indicate respect for others and allow unproblematic interaction to occur. Any violation might be regarded as an intended slight. A situation defined as a test of honor or a character contest is a fateful situation, a situation consequential to the participants with a problematic outcome (Goffman 1967).

If contests of honor are to be avoided, adherence to the rules of courtesy and etiquette is essential. Following the rules of etiquette allows for safe management of face-to-face interaction and is expected during all social occasions. There is often at least one large, formal social occasion in the community every week. Weddings and *quinceañeras* (a 15-year-old girl's birthday party) tend to be elaborate affairs planned months in advance; frequently more than 200 guests attend, and those who stand up as part of the bridal party or escort the 15-year-old wear formal, matching attire. The families serve dinner and typically have an open bar. Gang members attend such affairs regularly, often as escorts in rented tuxedos, and behave appropriately. Politeness demonstrates respect.

Moreover, the social skills learned and used in the family are employed on the job and in school. Many of the gang members work, and they are well aware of the different cultural interpretations of interaction in different settings. They carefully separate their behavior and identities on the job from their activities in the streets so that employers remain ignorant of their gang membership. A striking example of this involved a member of the Lions who worked at a large downtown bank as a computer operator. For several months he had not missed a single day of work, was on time, and always wore a tie.

The bank management regarded him as one of their best trainees until they discovered that he was charged with a felony for carrying a gun on 32nd Street. He could not understand why they fired him because, as he explained it, it was unnecessary to take a gun into the bank. On 32nd Street on a Saturday when the Lions were expecting "trouble," it was.

This ability to understand varying audience definitions of gang violence allows gang members to adjust their conduct towards the audience found in a particular setting. In return, by defining gang violence within a framework of honor, community members are able to understand such violence and to construct a partial basis for its toleration. However, this negative toleration does not amount to approval because gangs have changed the traditional notion of honor. Therefore, audiences must construct their own appraisals and evaluations of situations in which they encounter gang violence. Different audiences employ different strategies to maintain their presumption of order and achieve varying degrees of tolerance.

Gang Violence as an Extension of Honor: Acceptance and Tolerance

Gang-Gang Interaction: Acceptance

In the process of developing a distinctive social identity, gang members have distorted the traditional notion of honor. In general, the man of honor on 32nd Street is sensitive to challenges; however, gang members view the means of maintaining honor—displays of toughness—as an essential criterion of status and as a prime reason for involving one's self in such situations.[4] That is, gang members seek out and initiate challenges to another's honor as one way of publicly asserting their claim to precedence and enhancing their reputation by demonstrating their toughness. Other gang members almost routinely accept that definition of the situation and respond violently.

While it may be the intent of the initiator of a challenge to demean the other (requiring an immediate response of violence), the normative ambiguity of such encounters allows for alternative responses. The challenge may be defined as an intended insult and a character contest ensues. However, it is also possible that the individual who is insulted may view the actions of the initiator as the result of poor manners and as unintentional, allowing him to place the onus on the properties of the situation and to ignore or excuse the actions of the initiator. Here the situation is defined as routine, inconsequential, and unproblematic. The initiator then may leave the scene, if excused, or make further provocative actions if he wants the other to see his actions as demeaning. This negotiation process may terminate rapidly or continue until a fight is finally provoked. For example, on one occasion after a dance, someone knocked into Gilberto, President of the Lions; but Gilberto said, "Excuse me," and walked away. The young man looked as though he would pursue the encounter, but he turned away and melted into the crowd. I asked Gilberto about the incident, and he explained that there would have been no contest. The young man was no one important, no one worth fighting.

When the gang members define an act as intentional and demeaning, they respond with violence. These encounters may occur in the streets, parks, or club houses. Most terminate with a few bruises, but they occasionally end in death. After one encounter in which two of the Lions were jumped and beaten up in an alley, the other members gathered to discuss how they could regain the reputation they had lost when their two members were beaten. Several weeks later, there was a fight after a dance and the Lions declared themselves on top again. The potential combatants know what options are available and know the possible consequences of each move. The presumption of orderliness, there-fore, remains intact. While gang members generally agree on the kind of inci-dents that can be defined as demeaning, the exact meaning of each incident must be negotiated by the immediate participants. This process is crucial, for the ordering of social relationships may hinge on the outcome of each new en-counter (Anderson 1978). While gang members may not approve of any one member's construction of a particular encounter, in general, violence as a re-sponse is approved and demonstration of toughness is one means of achieving status.

Nongang Youth: Positive Toleration

Gang membership does not define the boundaries of friendship, although it generally delimits the boundary of complete approval of gang violence. There are youths who spend time in the same settings as gang members and interact with them freely and fairly frequently; however, they generally do not actively seek situations in which they can challenge the reputation of others in order to enhance their own status. While they may defend their honor when provoked, developing a reputation as "tough" is generally not a central concern.

During my field work, many nongang youths spent time at one of the parks where two of the reportedly toughest gangs (Lions and Senior Greeks) were lo-cated. Several of these young men talked constantly with the gang members and attended the same classes and parties. War stories of previous fights were shared and thoroughly discussed. However, unaffiliated young men did not fully approve of gang members' activities and sometimes referred to them as "crazy" (fighting too much over small incidents) or explained that they would never instigate fights like gang members did. Yet, they understood gang vio-lence; it is intelligible, sensible, and, in its context, proper. They concluded that they rarely would be challenged to fight and could remain safely watching an incident evolve, leave the area or, on certain occasions, voluntarily become involved.

Generally, nongang youths relate to members in an atmosphere of positive toleration. Some even swear allegiance to come to the aid of a threatened gang. At one private party, the members of the Lions gang expected the arrival of one of the gangs with whom they were "at war." Several unaffiliated young men volunteered to help out, and all waited at the party until long past midnight when everyone finally staggered home. Yet, on another occasion, they left the park when the Lions were expecting to fight some Junior Greeks.

These young men understand that they generally can remain as an uninvolved audience because gang members symbolically segregate themselves from nongang youth. Gang members evaluate themselves as having the highest status and no one of high status gains much by challenging someone of lesser status. As members of a gang, they cannot issue a challenge in the name of the gang to a nongang individual. With no one to back up the person challenged, the fight would be too unequal and little would be gained by the gang member. One peripheral member of the Lions challenged a nongang member and lost. When he asked for assistance from the group, they laughed at him and he stopped hanging around. Moreover, even if a nongang youth interprets the actions of a gang member as casting aspersions upon his honor, the situation evolves in a sensible and fitting manner; they fight to maintain their honor. For example, a gang member may question the nongang youth's toughness. On the one hand, the nongang member may choose not to interpret the behavior of the other as offensive and walk away. On the other hand, he may interpret the action of the other as demeaning and react violently. On one occasion, Jamie, an unaffiliated youth, and a Junior Greek fought after the Junior Greek publicly called Jamie a name. Jamie felt that his heroic effort in the fight was sufficient to maintain his honor. There also were fights between gang and nongang youths over questions of chastity: "I'll get him if he ever says that about my sister in my presence." The meaning of such actions, from the perspective of the nongang member, is one of upholding his honor, not of gaining a reputation as a tough man.

While unaffiliated young men do fight, most define those situations as defending their honor, not as asserting their toughness and developing their reputation. Although they regard gang members' efforts to develop a reputation with admiration or, at least, sympathy, these young men remain symbolically separate from gang members and generally refrain from openly challenging others.

The Family: Negative Toleration

Considerable work is often required on the part of both parents and gang members to insure the parents' presumption of order and their continued toleration of gang violence. While most parents do not approve of fighting to better one's reputation, they understand the use of violence to uphold one's honor. While few parents would acknowledge that they think it important or good for their son to be a gang member or want him to be constantly fighting,[5] most would see violence—and, occasionally, deadly violence—as a proper and justifiable response to offenses against family honor. In one instance a gang member shot and killed his father after finding him a number of times with several different young girls. Not only did the father publicly flaunt his infidelities, but he was often out of work and did not support his family well. There was considerable support for the son's actions within the community and his mother fought for his release. Fighting to maintain one's honor is understood and generally approved under certain conditions, particularly if a man or his family is demeaned publicly.

The use of violence by gang members to enhance reputation has a different quality than violence to defend honor. When violent acts are employed as a means to demonstrate toughness, most parents do not approve of such activities. One father referred to all gang members as hoodlums. To maintain their presumption of order, parents may steadfastly avoid acknowledging that their sons are in gangs and that young men are hurt or even killed within a few blocks of their homes. They actively strive to maintain their negative toleration; they will put up with gang violence as long as it does not enter their social world. However, the gang members must cooperate for the parents' unawareness to continue.

Parents often can maintain the fiction of their son's conventional conduct outside the home if he behaves properly when at home. An honorable son respects his parents and elders by deferring to them and behaving according to the rules of etiquette. What he does in the street need not be consistent with his behavior at home. The possibility of segmenting actions by social setting is supported by the expectations that men be independent. Parents encourage their male children from an early age to play away from the house, partly to encourage independence and to compensate for lack of space. Consequently, what boys do outside the home may not interfere or be consistent with their home life. A boy who is a "good son"—who respects his parents and behaves appropriately at home—can also be a tough gang member. Most gang members agree that street behavior should not be brought into the home. One of the Lions explained that he deserved to be beaten by his mother for coming home drunk and rowdy. Inebriation was appropriate, but he thought that he should not have gone home while drunk.

While some parents appear to remain largely ignorant of what occurs in the streets, other parents, if pressed, acknowledge suspicions about their son's involvement in gang violence. However to make his behavior more consistent with their standards, they may argue that he never starts any fights and that his particular gang is really a group of nice young men. For instance, the mother and aunt of a member who had a reputation as one of the toughest members of a wild gang told me that his gang was just a few young men who had grown up together. Parents are never told stories of fights and participants rarely receive severe wounds that cannot be explained away. Gang members' accounts for injuries were sometimes outrageous, but parents rarely questioned their sons. One son explained that the large gash over his eye was a result of falling against a locker, and another explained that the ugly wound on his shin was a result of falling. In fact, he had been hit with a bat.

The generally held expectation that sons grow out of gang membership helps parents remain tolerant. Parents can refer to examples of gang members who have grown up and obtained a good job or attended college. When confronted by a son's gang membership, parents often argue that "Boys will be boys" or "He'll grow out of it."

While parents and gang members have developed techniques that facilitate the routine flow of activities, both adults and young gang members must work especially hard to maintain the parents' presumption of order at some social occasions. For example, parents sometimes talk about minimizing the number of gang members invited to wedding[s] and *quinceañeras.* Exclusion, however, is generally impossible. When anyone is asked to be part of the bridal or *quinceañeras* party, the entire family is invited. Additionally, many of the gang members are sought as escorts and people often attend uninvited.

Gang members also work to see that such events progress as planned. Respect for and knowledge of the rules of etiquette allow the gang members to work towards this smooth construction of an event. Gang members generally behave appropriately, find chairs for ladies, drink enough to get drunk but not enough to become too rowdy, and wear their best clothes. During the many public dances I attended over a two-year period, male gang members never fought inside a dance—only girls did. Although guns were passed in to the people at the dances and there were many rumors of impending fights, the fights usually occurred outside the dance or party and away from any crowds. Rumors of potential fights also circulated during many of the weddings and *quinceañeras,* but few of the rumored conflicts materialized. Two gangs who were "at war" attended a wedding. Each claimed that they were going to "get the others"; but they managed to stay on either side of the room, explained that they had to get more of their men, and claimed they did not have enough guns to fight. In all these situations, the events evolved as planned, and the presumption of order was maintained. The gang members and other guests collaborate so that everyone experiences the situation as orderly and routine.

Additionally, spatial segregation allows gang fights to occur without disrupting others' presumptions. Fights rarely last very long; the majority of time is spent talking about a fight, making preparations, and waiting for it to occur. Fights are confined generally to public places (streets, alleys, and parks) that allow others to leave the setting. When several gangs held a peace conference at the park, no one was sure what was going to occur. All girls and unaffiliated males disappeared from the park that Sunday afternoon about 15 minutes before most of the gang members arrived. Whenever the Lions were expecting "trouble," the girls would leave. Sometimes parents admonish smaller children not to hang around locations where gang members have their fights. Moreover, there is typically some warning before a fight. If a large number of young men wearing their colors walk intently down the street, and if people do not want to see a fight, they need not follow them. Only people whose homes border the area where the fight occurs may be forced to observe it.   ·

Another form of gang violence involves the use of a car—riding by some enemy group and shooting at them. This is done quickly and is observed only by the people who happen to be in the immediate vicinity. Other chance encounters may occur in back alleys, but these are typically observed by few. Segregation of violent conduct and parents' work at explaining the conduct of their children help to permit the adults to maintain their presumption of order. They do not want to know about violence or see it; however, this is not always possible. The presumption of order is fragile and sometimes evolves into disorder.

■ Segregation Failures: Intolerance

Gang violence does not always develop in a manner that others can understand or think of as proper. Life is disrupted when violence occurs where people think it ought not to impinge. It can be terrifying and change the lives of family, friends, and the gang members themselves.

The Family: Awareness

Gang members generally work hard to avoid fights on social occasions so that others can maintain their presumption of order. However, gang members find that this is not always possible. At times they must fight; it is sensible and appropriate from their perspective.

The setting of the fight is critical. When a fight occurs at a party, there is no way for the audience to escape. During the period of observation, most weddings and *quinceañeras* proceeded smoothly. In other instances, however, major battles took place. During a *quinceañeras* a small girl was shot accidentally when two gangs clashed. At one wedding the groom was arrested for assault. When several members of the wedding party were arrested along with the groom, some of the girls in the party became hysterical along with the bride and the couple's family. The only people who remained calm were some older gang members who were uninvolved in the fight. When fights occur indoors, they disrupt the flow of regularly occurring talk and activity. While gang members feel they have made a valid choice, others are angry at the disturbance and fear that they or their families might be hurt. Their co-presence makes escape impossible and such an abrupt intrusion of violence into community affairs is neither expected nor evaluated as fitting by others. The presumption of order cannot be maintained and the audience becomes terrified.

A fight is also viewed as insulting to the family giving the party. People who spend the money, time, and effort to make a nice affair deserve respect from their guests and violence demonstrates lack of respect. Talk after a fight focuses on the incident, not on the social occasion. People sometimes place the blame on the family. One young girl cried several days after a fight at her *quinceañeras*. She was convinced that her family would lose respect after failing to control the guests.

Moreover, when relatives are involved in a serious fight, families can no longer remain unaware or maintain the pretense that a family member is not a gang member. Parents become baffled, upset, confused, and angry at the sudden failure of the social arrangements that allow them to tolerate conduct they do not fully approve.

However, the evolution from order to disorder may also proceed more slowly. Occasions do occur when families must begin to deal with the knowledge that a young man may not be a "nice boy" as distinct from "one of those gang members." Families are sometimes struck by the disjuncture between street life and the conventional world when a son is arrested or hurt badly or when a family member is threatened. The conflict is explicit and has to be faced or explained away. Many families continue to attempt to view their son as a "good son," unwittingly and unwillingly pulled into trouble by bad youth. This makes the conduct comprehensible. Sometimes the problem is managed by sending him to relatives in another state or Mexico. The work to maintain the presumption of order may continue for an extensive period. One mother, who had her 18-year-old son released from detention over 20 times, finally refused to bail him out on his 27th (by his own count) arrest. This is an extreme case, but it is interesting that his mother bailed him almost every time before the last when he moved permanently to another state. To account for her long history of tolerance for her son's arrests, she explained that he was a "good boy."

Occasionally, a family member is threatened by a gang and the conflict is brought into the home. In one such instance, an enemy of the Lions threw a brick through the window of the home of a Lion's mother. She was very upset and could not understand why someone would want to hurt her family. Threats are sometimes made toward family members who are supposed to relay them to their brothers. The family cannot help but experience disruption in their lives and come to feel that gangs are dangerous and that their activities should be stopped. The father of a 16-year-old girl's child was involved in a conflict with an enemy gang. When the gang came looking for him at her house, her family, very upset by their involvement, sent the young woman to live with relatives and carefully watched the streets for several weeks. The discovery that a "nice boy" is involved in violent activities peels away the carefully constructed barriers that most relatives employ to maintain a presumption of orderliness. When someone else's son is hurt, he might have been "no good"; but kin are viewed generally as "good boys." However, except for sending sons away, parents make few efforts to control them.

Nongang Youth: Perhaps You Are Tough

Many of the nongang youth are good fighters, and some are viewed as "tough warriors" by gang members. Consequently, such nongang members are always at risk of being challenged by individual gang members who could improve their status by winning a fight. One young man transferred to a private school after being challenged more than five times in one semester. It was a great sacrifice for his family, and he started to work after school and on weekends to pay the tuition.

The symbolic segregation of gang and nongang youth is tenuous. There is always a possibility that gang members may choose to redefine the identity of the nongang male as a potential gang member, making the presumption of order difficult for the nongang individual. For example, one young man who socialized frequently with the Lions was challenged by some of the Lions to fight. They told him that he had to become a member because he knew too many of their secrets. Several gang members beat him up. To avoid further confrontations, he enlisted in the military. When a gang redefines the symbolic boundaries between gang members and others, the situation, from the perspective of nongang youth, no longer evolves as expected or in a proper and fitting manner; they cannot tolerate such behavior.

Gangs: What Makes an Honorable Man?

Fighting in schools disallows the presumption of order for some gang members. Much work by some gang members goes into avoiding such confrontations. Gang members, in order to avoid being so identified, may transfer to public schools outside the community or to parochial schools. Some even quit school to avoid fights. For example, Carlos, a gang member, dropped out his junior year claiming: "Shit, I nearly was blown away in school yesterday. This dude pulls out a .45 and sticks it in my stomach. You know you can't trust them chicks. They pack the heats for the dudes. That chick [who handed the gang member the gun] was supposed to be going out with a friend of ours." For gang members like Carlos, becoming a participant can have serious consequences—being expelled or arrested—that might disrupt their futures. They want their lives to evolve as planned and seek to avoid settings where a fight might jeopardize future plans.

Even the young men who remain gang members as they mature begin to feel that gang violence is less acceptable. They are no longer sure that they should remain symbolically segregated from other adults. They begin to tolerate rather than approve of violence. While the majority of youth drop out of the gangs by 18 or 20, some maintain their affiliation as Seniors along with marriage, fatherhood, and steady employment (Horowitz 1982). Several of the gangs on 32nd Street had Senior groups. The Lions gang continued to fight as the members entered their twenties even though they individually began to think that they were too old to use toughness and their identities as warriors as indicators of status. When one member of the Lions who had been institutionalized for two years returned to the street, he failed to notice that the others had changed. He wanted to start fights and the others kept putting him off. Such "trouble" held increasing risks and older members rarely instigated fights.

Over their years together, gang members had developed very close ties and depended upon each other, a potentially dishonorable situation. In an honor-based subculture, suspicions of dependency may be evaluated as weakness and, to gang members, these suspicions can only be mitigated by demonstrated toughness. They were, in fact, dependent upon each other; therefore, to remain together as men with claims to being tough, they publicly had to declare a willingness to fight. The tension between maintaining identity in the street world of juvenile gangs and developing an image as a responsible adult began to make the presumption of orderliness more difficult to maintain. Adulthood and demonstrations of toughness began to appear increasingly incongruous.

Yet, the older gang members' sense of self-worth remained partly dependent on interaction with peers who remained in the streets, and they continued to act to maintain the respect of street peers (Horowitz 1982). They did not feel free to discuss the ambivalence they were experiencing about toughness: now they were tough only so that they could remain together rather than hanging together because they are tough. Although each privately began to experience a lack of order in his own life, the basis upon which gang members evaluated social relationships remained almost the same. They felt that they had to fight even if they were no longer entirely sure it was fitting.

■ Outsiders' Views of Gang Violence: Intolerance

While most of the community residents I have discussed are situationally intolerant of gang violence, some groups are intolerant of gang activities in any context. The framework of honor does not inform their interpretation of gang violence. For teachers and other outside "helping" personnel, the meaning of the youth's violence is obscure. Young people are feared and violence is not understood and never develops as expected; there is no presumption of order.

Law enforcement officials and the public often regard gangs as a symbol of disorder. The police in many cities have "gang intelligence units," and the government has funded many gang prevention and intervention programs—for example, the Chicago Area Project (Kobrin 1959) and the Mid-City Project

(Miller 1962). Juvenile justice workers and police surveyed in many major cities still see gang violence as a major problem (Miller 1975).

Such outsiders view the world of the young people on 32nd Street as dangerous and unappealing. One of the youth centers run by social workers from outside the community did not permit teens to use its facilities, because "They are all just troublemakers." Many teachers avoided "unnecessary contact" with students by retreating from the community as quickly as possible at the end of each working day. During my field work, few teachers attended events in the neighborhood. High school dances were held in the afternoons because school authorities were afraid of what might happen at night.

Some teachers have so little understanding of honor and violence that they fail to see how their own behavior is interpreted by students. A counselor expelled Jesus from high school on his 16th birthday for extended absences. Jesus called his mother and told her about his situation. The counselor, overhearing the conversation, laughed at him and Jesus punched him. Jesus could have ignored the laugh, defining the counselor as ignorant, but it told him that the counselor had no respect for him. Jesus felt that the only way he could regain his dignity was to punch him.

Teachers fail to distinguish gang members from nongang individuals and to acknowledge any differences. One teacher said, "They should all be frisked every day." Most of the members neither wear their insignia, advertise their affiliations, nor act differently than others in school, and most school personnel rarely venture into the community. Gang members are generally pushed and pulled out of school by their lack of interest and the possibility of excitement in the streets. For example, most of the eighth-grade teachers were unaware that the boy chosen as the best dressed by his class was an active member of the Lions. He was outside drinking when his prize was announced at the graduation dinner-dance. He left school the following year for lack of interest—not misbehavior. For many teachers, their lack of understanding of gangs and other young people in the community leads to a fundamental intolerance of youth. The community is defined as a dangerous place, one to be avoided, whenever possible.

■ Conclusion

In the Chicano community I studied, gang members are not cut off from the adult world, nor do they reject adult authority. On the other hand, their behavior is neither completely acceptable to adults, nor are they completely integrated into the social world of adults. While parents do not approve of gang violence, it is understood as a distortion of their notion of honor. As individuals, gang members are part of community and family life and accept the more conventional world of adults. Chicano youth act independently from their parents yet participate in many of the same social events and accept the authority of their parents in the home. However, in other communities the relationship between these social worlds appears to be simpler. Short and Strodtbeck (1965) found that black gangs were acceptable to community adults and integrated into the adult world, whereas white gangs were cut off from their parents and rejected adult authority. My analysis suggests that the cultural link between the street world and the conventional world—particularly the framework of honor—at least partially accounts for the Chicano gang's complex relationship to parents and other community members.

While the presumption of order is precariously maintained for most community members, it is unclear whether families' tolerant responses to violence are embedded in a context of freedom of choice or are indications of powerlessness. Can parents exercise sufficient control over their sons' behavior and their own actions that they need not openly condemn gang violence? Or is toleration one of the few options available to parents who are unable to control the behavior of youth but unwilling to hand them over to the authorities?

Part of the difficulty in answering these questions is that the gang members are neither perceived as dangerous strangers (Merry 1981) nor are they protecting the local area from strangers (Suttles 1968, 1972), which might give them some legitimacy. The issue exists because gang members are not strangers; they are relatives and friends. Family and neighborhood networks are too extensive to pretend that gang members do not belong. Their activities are dangerous but they are not regarded as dangerous people.

Controlling the gang members' activities appears almost impossible and moving away from gang territories is usually too costly, both financially and socially. Close supervision of sons' activities runs against parents' own cultural understandings of honor. An honorable man is supposed to be independent and the honor of the family is embedded in the conduct of all its members. Thus, parents are caught in a cultural dilemma. On the one hand, a young man must be taught to be independent. He should, therefore, be on his own outside the home and ought to stand up to others' claims of precedence. On the other hand, to jeopardize the honor of the family by continuously fighting and getting into trouble with the law is not right. While they do not approve of their sons' gang activities, parents often feel that to try to control those activities is to fail to turn their sons into men. However, to call in outside agents (police) to control gang violence is not a viable solution because to question publicly a son's moral character is to question the honor of the family. While parents often punish daughters by keeping them indoors for untoward behavior, they rarely do that to sons. Occasionally, if things get very bad, they send a son out of the state or country to relatives. Beyond this, parents feel that there is little they can do—the pull of the streets is too strong.

When there is little they feel that they can do to deter violence and the perpetrators are people whom they love, parents have little choice but to cooperate with the gang members in negotiating a sense of order. As long as violence is ecologically segregated from "parental space," parents can do their part to maintain a pretense of unawareness of the gang identity of their children. Even when parents become aware of conduct that fails to measure up to their standards, they work to align such actions with the cultural framework of honor and their familial conception of a "good son." This cannot be achieved without the cooperation of the gang members who respect the need to segregate their violent actions by time and place and who offer reasonable accounts for their conduct that can be accepted by their parents.

In contrast to studies that have ignored the relationship of gangs to other community residents, this analysis has shown how nongang community residents, but not outsiders, manage to coexist successfully with violent gangs. If community audiences were to react to gang members as deviant, they would be faced with several dilemmas. Above all, they would have to reject beloved family members. To control gang violence, they would have to call in the authorities, thus publicly questioning family honor. The cultural and existential solution is to work with gang members to maintain a relationship of mutual toleration and to engage in negotiations which allow community life to proceed in an orderly, if tenuous, fashion.

■ Notes

1. Arguments have been made that the Spanish-speaking population is greatly undercounted in the US census. In part this may be explained by language barriers and fear of immigration officials.

2. According to Chicago police department statistics, the Hispanic neighborhoods had the highest rates and numbers of gang-related homicides. The rates have remained fairly stable over the years. During the period of 1971–1975, I could account for four or five gang-related deaths each year. There were 16 homicides in the 1978–1981 period on 32nd Street, and 20 additional murders during the same period in a continuous neighborhood (Spergel 1984). Many of these may have involved residents from 32nd Street or relatives as there is much interaction between the two communities. The five Hispanic areas comprise 12.4 percent of the city population and 51.9 percent of all gang homicides (Spergel 1984). Local leaders often place the estimated number of gang-related murders higher than police estimates, due in part to different definitions of "gang-related." However, this number sometimes may be inflated for political purposes such as demands for additional resources. More people are directly affected than just the families of victims, as there is often more than one perpetrator of the murder. This is important for the individuals and families not only if caught, but as potential victims of revenge attacks.

3. A woman's shame (a premarital loss of virginity or an extramarital affair) reflects on the male family members, as it indicates a man's inability to control the lives of his women and a failure to maintain his dominant position.

4. Erlanger (1979) argues that violence is not the only means of maintaining machismo and that it is a result of estrangement. My data also support the notion that a gang member may gain status in a variety of ways; however, I have discussed this topic elsewhere (Horowitz 1983; Horowitz & Schwartz 1974).

5. Many of the parents of these young people grew up outside of Chicago and were not in gangs. However, there was at least one father of one of the Lions who was

very young, had been a gang member in a nearby neighborhood, and came to the park on a number of occasions to gossip with the young men. He occasionally applauded their efforts. This appeared atypical in this relatively newly formed neighborhood with a short history of gangs. In Los Angeles, where gangs have long histories and where sons may follow fathers into a gang, such behavior might be more common (Moore 1978).

■ References

Anderson, Elijah. 1978. *A Place on the Corner.* Chicago: University of Chicago Press.

Becker, Howard & Irving L. Horowitz. 1972. *Culture and Civility in San Francisco.* New Brunswick, NJ: Transaction.

Erlanger, Howard. 1979. "Estrangement, Machismo and Gang Violence." *Social Science Quarterly* 60:235–48.

Glaser, Barney & Anslem Strauss. 1964. "Awareness Contexts and Social Interaction." *American Sociological Review* 29:669–79.

Goffman, Erving. 1967. *Interaction Ritual.* New York: Doubleday.

Horowitz, Ruth. 1982. "Masked Intimacy and Marginality: Adult Delinquent Gangs in a Chicano Community." *Urban Life* 11:3–26.

———. 1983. *Honor and the American Dream.* New Brunswick, NJ: Rutgers University Press.

———. 1986. "Remaining an Outsider: Membership as a Threat to Research Rapport." *Urban Life* 14:409–30.

Horowitz, Ruth & Gary Schwartz. 1974. "Honor, Normative Ambiguity and Gang Violence." *American Sociological Review* 39:238–51.

Karp, David H., Gregory P. Stone & Willam C. Yoels. 1977. *Being Urban: A Social Psychological View of City Life.* Lexington, MA: D. C. Heath.

Kobrin, Solomon. 1959. "The Chicago Area Project: A Twenty-five Year Assessment." *Annals of the American Academy of Political & Social Science* 322:1–29.

Lemert, Edwin. 1951. *Social Pathology.* New York: McGraw Hill.

Lofland, Lyn. 1973. *A World of Strangers.* New York: Basic Books.

———. 1983. "Urban Relationships and Urban People: Creating Cosmopolitans." Paper presented at the annual meeting of the Society for the Study of Symbolic Interaction, Detroit.

Merry, Sally. 1981. *Urban Danger.* Philadelphia: Temple University Press.

Miller, Walter B. 1962. "The Impact of a 'Total-community' Delinquency Control Project." *Social Problems* 10:168–91.

———. 1975. "Violence by Youth Gangs and Youth Groups as a Crime Problem in American Cities." US Department of Justice, Washington, DC: US Government Printing Office.

Moore, Joan W. 1978. *Homeboys.* Philadelphia: Temple University Press.

Peristiany, J. G. 1966. *Honor and Shame.* Chicago: University of Chicago Press.

Pfuhl, Edwin. 1978. "The Unwed Father: A 'Non-deviant' Rule Breaker." *Sociological Quarterly* 19:113–28.

Rubington, Earl & Martin Weinberg (eds.). 1978. *Deviance: The Interactionist Perspective.* New York: Macmillan.

Scott, Robert A. 1972. "A Proposed Framework for Analyzing Deviance as a Property of Social Order." In R. Scott & J. Douglas (eds.), *Theoretical Perspectives on Deviance.* New York: Basic.

Short, James & Fred Strodtbeck. 1965. *Group Process and Gang Delinquency.* Chicago: University of Chicago Press.

Spergel, Irving. 1984. "Violent Gangs in Chicago: In Search of Social Policy." *Social Service Review* 58:199–226.

Stokes, Randall & John Hewitt. 1976. "Aligning Actions." *American Sociological Review* 41:838–49.

Suttles, Gerald. 1968. *Social Order of the Slums*. Chicago: University of Chicago Press.

———. 1972. *The Social Construction of Community*. Chicago: University of Chicago Press.

Wallace, Samuel E. 1980. *The Urban Environment*. Homewood, IL: Dorsey Press.

Yarrow, Marion & Leila Deasy. 1955. "Psychological Meaning of Mental Illness in the Family." *Journal of Social Issues* 4:12–24.

PART 6

The Contemporary Juvenile Justice System

EVERY STATE IN THE UNITED STATES HAS A JUVENILE CODE AND A SPE-
cialized court structure that deals with the problems of children and youths in
trouble with the law. There are more than 3,000 juvenile court jurisdictions
throughout the country, however, and these systems are not uniform or standardized but vary from one jurisdiction to another (Krisberg, Litsky, and
Schwartz 1984). Moreover, juvenile courts deal with three general categories
of youths. **Delinquents** are those who violate criminal laws for which adults
could be charged. **Status offenders** are those who commit acts for which
adults could not be charged, for example, running away, truancy, curfew violations, and even vague transgressions such as "incorrigibility," "habitual disobedience," and "immoral behavior" (see Part 1). **Dependent children** are
those who have been so neglected or abused that they need to become wards
of the court. In addition, "the legal activities involved in adoptions, in setting
and enforcing child support orders which result from divorce, and in hearing
requests for the termination of parental rights are generally the responsibility
of juvenile courts" (Waegel 1989:154).

■ The Stages of Juvenile Justice
In spite of this diversity, it is possible to make some generalizations about the
stages of the juvenile justice system through which young people are
processed in the United States. Although youths may be referred to juvenile
court by parents, schools, social service agencies, and other sources, the large

majority of cases are referred by the police. At every stage, however, including the police stage, youths are screened out of the system and are either released outright or diverted to an alternative agency for assistance. Indeed, about a third of the youths who are arrested are not referred to juvenile court (Snyder and Sickmund 2006; Stahl et al. 2007).

Following police or other referral to the juvenile court, youths go through the **intake** stage where they are screened by an intake officer who determines whether the youth should be released, handled through alternative or informal means, or required to appear at a formal hearing before a juvenile court judge. More than half of all youths who are referred to intake are processed with the filing of a formal petition that requires court appearance. Among those who are not, many admit to the charges and agree to meet the conditions of an **informal disposition,** such as a requirement to receive counseling, or else a formal petition is filed at a later date. Minor (especially first-time) offenders, or those for whom there is insufficient evidence to proceed, may be released outright. Among those who remain under court jurisdiction, most are released into the custody of their parents while waiting to appear before a judge, but some may be held in **detention** or preventive custody. Typically, a decision to detain a youth in custody must be reviewed by a judge at a detention hearing in which the youth "has a right to counsel and other procedural safeguards" (Siegel and Welsh 2009:444; Stahl et al. 2007).[1]

Juvenile codes in most states also contain provisions whereby some serious offenders (typically at least 14 years of age or older) can be waived or transferred to an adult criminal court for prosecution. This decision is made at intake, and since the 1966 US Supreme Court decision in *Kent v. U.S.,* youths under consideration for transfer are entitled to be represented by counsel at a **waiver** hearing, where the judge must provide justification for transfer. Some states have attempted to bypass the uncertainties of a waiver hearing, however, by presumptively allowing or even requiring youths who are charged with particular types of offenses to be prosecuted as adults. Overall, fewer than 1 percent of all petitioned delinquency cases are waived (Feld 1993; Siegel and Welsh 2009; Stahl et al. 2007).[2]

After a petition is filed by the intake officer, youths appear before a judge for an **adjudication** hearing. Since the 1967 US Supreme Court decision in *In re Gault,* youths who are adjudicated for a delinquency violation are entitled to most of the procedural safeguards given to adult offenders, including "the right to counsel, freedom from self-incrimination, [and] the right to confront and cross-examine witnesses" (Siegel and Welsh 2009:445). At the beginning of the hearing, the judge asks the youth if he or she admits or denies the petition—in essence, if the youth pleads guilty or not guilty. In most cases the youth admits to the charge in order to make a favorable impression on the judge.[3] A large majority of youths who are processed at this stage are adjudicated "delinquent" or are otherwise found to be "in need of supervision."

Some cases are dismissed because of insufficient evidence, and others are held in abeyance pending completion of an informal disposition known as a **consent decree** that is ordered by the judge. If the youth does not meet the terms of the informal disposition, he or she will be brought back before the judge for formal adjudication (Butts and Sickmund 1992; Stahl et al. 2007).

After a youth is adjudicated delinquent or found to be "in need of supervision," the judge must make a determination as to the **disposition** or sentence. Typically, a probation officer prepares a predisposition report based on criteria such as the youth's prior record, family situation, school performance, and psychological profile. At an ensuing disposition hearing, the judge generally follows the probation officer's recommendations. The range of dispositions "available to a court typically includes commitment to an institution [and] placement in a group or foster home or other residential facility," but most often the dispositions entail in-home placements such as "probation (either regular or intensive supervision); referral to an outside agency, day treatment, or mental health program; or imposition of a fine, community service, or restitution" (Stahl et al. 2007:2).

■ Due Process Rights of Juveniles

In Part 1 we noted the philosophy of informality—*parens patriae*—that was associated with the early juvenile courts, which was a means by which the state expanded its jurisdiction over an increasing number of youths without providing them with constitutional due process protections against unwarranted governmental intrusion in their lives. The problems associated with this system came to a head in the 1960s following a number of US Supreme Court decisions that expanded the rights of adult criminal defendants.[4]

The landmark US Supreme Court decision regarding the rights of juveniles was the 1967 case of *In re Gault.* Binder, Geis, and Bruce (1988) provide the following summary of the case:

> Fifteen-year-old Gerald Gault and a friend were arrested by a deputy sheriff in Gila County, Arizona, on the basis of a complaint by a neighbor . . . about a telephone call that involved lewd and indecent remarks. . . . When arrested for the call, Gault was under probation [for] . . . having been in the company of another boy who had stolen a wallet. After his arrest, Gault was taken to a detention home where he was kept for several days. His parents were not notified of the arrest, of his custody in the home, or of a petition filed with the juvenile court for an initial hearing. In a subsequent adjudicatory hearing, Gault and his parents were not formally notified of the charges against him, there was no right to counsel, there was no right to confrontation and cross-examination (the offended woman never even appeared at the hearing), there was no privilege against self-incrimination (Gault's admission of guilt was accepted with an absence of procedural safeguards), and there was no right either to a transcript of the proceedings or to appeal to a higher court in Arizona. As a result . . . Gault was committed to an institution for six years. (pp. 250–251)

Binder, Geis, and Bruce add that the maximum penalty for an adult committing a similar offense at the time in Arizona was a fine of $50 or a jail term of not more than two months!

Gault and his parents appealed the case, which eventually reached the US Supreme Court. In its decision, the Court ruled that the due process clause of the Fourteenth Amendment applied to delinquent proceedings that could result in institutional confinement. More specifically, the Court ruled that under such circumstances juveniles should be granted "the right to an adequate notice of charges, the right to counsel, the right to confront and cross-examine witnesses, the right against self-incrimination, the right to a transcript of the proceeding, and the right to appellate review" (Thornton, Voigt, and Doerner 1987:313).

Although the court was willing to expand the rights of youths in other areas of law (see Table 21.1), it did not desire to abolish entirely the *parens patriae* philosophy of the juvenile court. In its 1971 decision in *McKiever v. Pennsylvania,* for instance, the Court ruled that youths did not have a constitutional right to a trial by jury (although individual states could grant this right if they so desired). The Court reasoned that a jury trial was not necessary for a fair and equitable hearing of fact—the fact-finding capacity of the court— and that granting youths this right would transform the juvenile justice system into an adversarial process that would mark the end of *parens patriae.*

Table 21.1 Important US Supreme Court Juvenile Justice Decisions

Kent v. United States (1966): Juveniles are entitled to a waiver hearing, with access to legal counsel, before being transferred to adult court.

In re Gault (1967): Juveniles adjudicated for a delinquency petition are afforded most, but not all, of the due process protections given to adults, including: notification of charges, right to legal counsel, right to confront and cross-examine witnesses, privilege against self-incrimination, right to a transcript of the hearing, and right to appellate review.

In re Winship (1970): "Proof beyond a reasonable doubt" rather than a "preponderance of the evidence" is necessary to adjudicate a juvenile as a delinquent.

McKiever v. Pennsylvania (1971): Juveniles do *not* have a constitutional right to a trial by jury.

Breed v. Jones (1975): Waiver proceedings do *not* constitute a violation of a juvenile's protection against "double jeopardy," but a youth cannot be transferred to adult court after being adjudicated in juvenile court. The judge at the waiver hearing and the adult court trial must be different.

Fare v. Michael C. (1979): A juvenile's request to see his probation officer at the time of interrogation does *not* revoke the right to remain silent.

Schall v. Martin (1984): Juveniles may be detained before trial for their own protection or the protection of the public.

New Jersey v. T.L.O. (1985): "Reasonable suspicion," not "probable cause," is the minimum standard governing searches of students' lockers by school officials.

Vernonia School District v. Acton (1995): Required drug testing of students choosing to participate in interscholastic athletics is constitutional.

Roper v. Simmons (2005): Capital punishment for juveniles who committed their crimes when they were under 18 years of age is unconstitutional.

Although *Gault* and other court rulings have made juvenile justice professionals more cognizant of due process issues (Binder and Geis 1982), many
observers question its impact on providing youths with equal protection under
the law, noting that youths and their parents are often discouraged from exer-
cising their privilege against self-incrimination and their right to an attorney
(Aday 1986; Bortner 1982; Grisso 1981). Feld (1988), a leading critic of the
juvenile justice system, found that large urban states were the most likely to
provide juveniles with the right to counsel and that within states there was considerable county-by-county variation, with ranges from less than 10 percent to
more than 90 percent of youths provided with counsel (see also Feld 1984,
1990, 1993). Feld considered several possible explanations for the all-too-fre-
quent low representation of attorneys: "parental reluctance to retain an attorney; a judicial encouragement of and readiness to find waivers of the right to
counsel in order to ease administrative burdens on the courts; a continuing judicial hostility to an advocacy role [for attorneys] in a traditional, treatment-
oriented court; or a judicial predetermination of dispositions with nonappoint-
ment of counsel where probation is the anticipated outcome" (1988:395).

■ Discretion and Intervention

As each point in the juvenile justice system, beginning with referral by the police or other authorities, through intake, adjudication, and disposition, officials
make discretionary decisions and choose among a variety of available options.
Such discretion is inevitable when decisionmakers apply general rules pertaining
to juvenile law (both substantive and procedural) to specific, concrete cases.
Juvenile justice officials are not "decision-making automatons . . . with little
latitude for subjective judgments" (Waegel 1989:130).

One of the most important issues in the sociology of juvenile justice involves the question of how these discretionary decisions are made. Are they
made primarily on the basis of legal criteria such as the seriousness of the offense and prior record of the youth? Or are they based on social or extralegal
factors such as race, class, gender, or other criteria? In Chapter 21, "Legal and
Extralegal Factors in Police and Court Processing of Juveniles," Ronald
Berger reviews the research literature on this issue and concludes "that legal
factors alone cannot explain how youths are processed through the juvenile
justice system." Next, in Chapter 22, "Gang Members and the Police," Carl
Werthman and Irving Piliavin's interviews with youths who have encountered
the police illuminate the dynamics of police-juvenile interaction in "situations
of suspicion." Werthman and Piliavin show how racial and ethnic status, as
well as other personal attributes, are used by police to identify "suspicious"
youths and levy charges against them. Next, in Chapter 23, "Judging Delinquents," Robert Emerson's ethnography highlights the ways in which juvenile
court personnel attempt to distinguish cases of genuine "trouble" that warrant
official intervention from cases that do not warrant "doing something" about

the youths who are brought to their attention. Emerson examines the ways in which official assessments of youths' moral character and the dynamics of denunciations and counterdenunciations influence juvenile court outcomes.

Turning to the dispositional stage of the juvenile justice system, the last three chapters focus on issues pertaining to the treatment of youths in various correctional settings and under varying levels of supervision. In Chapter 24, "A Comparative Analysis of Organizational Structure and Inmate Subcultures in Institutions for Juvenile Offenders," Barry Feld evaluates different organizational structures and treatment modalities that are used in juvenile correctional institutions and their effect on both staff and inmates. In particular, Feld's research demonstrates that correctional institutions that emphasize rehabilitative treatment over custody, especially those that utilize group-oriented strategies, are better able to reduce the violence that all too often permeates inmate institutional subcultures.

Many observers believe that community-based alternatives to secure correctional institutions offer a more constructive and promising response to juvenile delinquency. Community corrections span a gamut of approaches, from traditional probation to group homes and other treatment centers where juveniles receive a variety of mental health, counseling, chemical dependency, and academic, vocational, and recreational services aimed at the rehabilitation rather than the mere punishment of juveniles. In Chapter 25, "Viable Options: Intensive Supervision Programs for Juvenile Delinquents," William Barton and Jeffrey Butts note that the results of research on "the relative effectiveness of community-based correctional alternatives . . . have been occasionally encouraging but often discouraging or inconclusive." More specifically, however, Barton and Butts are concerned with the effectiveness and cost of home-based intensive probation services involving small caseloads and frequent worker-client contact, and their study offers an example of how three such programs (combined) in "Wayne County, Michigan, a large, urban county that includes the city of Detroit," were evaluated. Utilizing two-year follow-up data from official delinquency records and self-report measures, Barton and Butts found that the criminal recidivism rates of youths receiving intensive probation were comparable to the rates of a comparison or control group of youths who "were subject to a variety of [other] placement options, including [conventional] in-home supervision, . . . shelter and group home placements, camps, and large public or private institutions" and at less cost. (About 80 percent of the latter placements were out-of-home dispositions, and 90 percent of these were in large institutions.) Barton and Butts's evaluation suggests that community-based programs can provide a viable alternative for many youths who otherwise would have been candidates for out-of-home placement. The researchers do not claim that community-based corrections necessarily work better than more severe dispositions, but that they *work as well for less cost.* Overall, the intensive supervision programs they evaluated saved the state of Michigan $8.85 million over the period of evaluation.

In Chapter 26, "Evaluating Juvenile Drug Courts: Shedding Light into the Theoretical Black Box," Paul Gregory, Kristen DeVall, and David Hartmann consider another community alternative that has garnered increasing attention in recent years. Juvenile drug courts, as the authors note, "streamline drug cases away from traditional processing and punishment" and place substance-abusing offenders in specialized court-monitored treatment programs (Senjo and Leip 2001:68). Gregory, DeVall, and Hartmann discuss the philosophy underlying drug courts as well as the elements of effective evaluation and the difficulty of meeting these criteria. They also review previous evaluation studies and present the results of their own evaluation of the Midwest Juvenile Drug Court Program (a pseudonym) that covers a period of nine years. The results, as is often the case with correctional treatment evaluations more generally, are mixed, but sufficiently encouraging to persuade Gregory, DeVall, and Hartmann to continue to "find ways of improving both the operation and evaluation" of such programs. The authors' primary objective, however, is not just to evaluate their program but to use it to illuminate the methodological complexity of the evaluation process and to note the need for more theoretically informed research that can elucidate more clearly why and how drug courts should be expected to change young people's behavior.

Gregory, DeVall, and Hartmann offer suggestions for what a theoretically informed drug court and theory-dependent evaluation process would entail.[5] Other scholars, more generally, have offered criteria that identify the ingredients of effective correctional treatment. Andrews and colleagues (1990a, 1990b), for example, believe that the most effective correctional interventions utilize behaviorist and social learning principles (see Part 2 and Chapter 7), are carefully matched to offenders' particular learning styles and psychological needs, and are designed to enhance aggression management and stress management skills as well as academic and vocational skills, change antisocial attitudes and ways of thinking, reduce chemical dependencies, foster familial bonds, modify peer associations and role models, and help access appropriate service agencies (see also Cullen and Applegate 1997; Gibbons 1999; Pearson et al. 2002).[6]

Others also advocate greater use of **restitution,** whereby youthful offenders are required to compensate victims or recompense the community through some form of monetary payment or service (e.g., working at a nursing home or hospital, performing grounds work at a city park, cleaning up graffiti). The purpose of restitution is not simply to compensate victims or punish law violators but to make offenders accountable to the *people they have harmed,* thereby erasing "one of the strongest defenses . . . to wrongdoing, [the] inability to empathize . . . with those who have suffered" (Binder, Geis, and Bruce 1988:562). By requiring the sacrifice of time and convenience, the expenditure of effort, and the performance of meaningful tasks, it is hoped that offenders will acknowledge and understand their personal and social responsibilities. As Karmen notes, "By making fiscal atonement or contributing services, they can feel cleared of guilt, morally redeemed, and reaccepted into the fold" (2004:

295; see also Schneider 1986; Schneider and Finkelstein 1998). As such, restitution is consistent with Braithwaite's concept (1989) of **reintegrative shaming,** in which offenders receive social disapproval that is designed to invoke remorse. If they are remorseful and willing to right their wrongs, however, they are forgiven and welcomed back into the community.[7]

Earlier in this book, Ferdinand argued in Chapter 3 that "treatment programs for juveniles with psychological or social needs are . . . essential [elements of a] civil society. . . . Treatment has worked only haphazardly because it has not been championed consistently by experienced agencies with roots in local communities." We also need to appreciate, as Bortner reminds us, that much of what young people seek is what most adults seek—"a sense of meaningful contribution to society, a sense of community and friendship, love and support and a measure of individual autonomy" (1988:378). The inability of adults to assist the young "in their transition from infancy to adulthood relates not only to the complexity of such a transition in contemporary society, but . . . to the crisis that plagues most adults. The relationships and roles essential to the well-being of [the] young . . . do not exist in the lives of many adults, including . . . parents, teachers, jailers, or the gods of mass culture."

◼ Notes

1. In some jurisdictions, prosecutors have become more involved in the intake process to provide for early legal review of the case in the event that the youth intends to deny the charges when later appearing before a judge (Rubin 1980).

2. A study of the nation's 75 largest counties found that about two-thirds of transferred juveniles were charged with violent crimes, about two-thirds of those transferred were convicted, and about two-thirds of those convicted received prison or jail terms (Strom, Smith, and Snyder 1998). In some states or counties, however, a majority of transferred juveniles were nonviolent offenders—offenders who often received lighter penalties than they might have received had they remained in the juvenile system because in the adult system they were considered "lightweight" (Bishop, Frazier, and Henretta 1989; Howell 1996; Osbun and Rode 1984).

3. Plea bargaining—the exchange of prosecutorial concessions for a defendant's guilty plea—is also practiced in the juvenile justice system, although not as often as in the adult system (Sanborn 1992, 1993; Siegel and Welsh 2009).

4. As Thornton, Voigt, and Doerner (1987:311) summarize: "The court ruled . . . that the Constitution protected adult citizens from unreasonable search and seizure (*Mapp v. Ohio,* 1961), afforded accused persons the right to an attorney (*Escobedo v. Illinois,* 1964; *Gideon v. Wainwright,* 1963), prohibited cruel and unusual punishment (*Robinson v. California,* 1962), allowed citizens the privilege against self-incrimination (*Wong Sun v. U.S.,* 1963), set down guidelines concerning pretrial identification (*Gilbert v. California,* 1967; *U.S. v. Wade,* 1967), specified stop-and-frisk practices (*Terry v. Ohio,* 1968), and established proper warnings to be given prior to a custodial investigation (*Miranda v. Arizona,* 1966)."

5. Their preference is for social learning theory; see Chapter 7.

6. Andrews et al. (1990a, 1990b) challenge those who have concluded that "nothing works" in the field of correctional treatment (e.g., see Lab and Whitehead 1988,

1990; Whitehead and Lab 1989). It is perhaps the case that some analysts think the "glass is part empty" and other analysts think the "glass is part full."

7. Reintegrative shaming may be contrasted with disintegrative shaming, whereby the offender continues to be treated as an outsider, is not forgiven for past sins, and thus is more likely to relapse into crime after having difficulty reentering the community (Braithwaite 1989). Restitution programs are often associated with the restorative justice movement, a community correctional response that attempts to enlist participation of all "parties with a stake in a particular offense [who] come together to resolve collectively how to deal with [its] aftermath . . . and its implications for the future" (Zehr and Mika 1998:54).

Victim-offender mediation (VOM) may be part of this process. This entails bringing offenders and victims together to work out a fair arrangement under the guidance of a trained mediator or counselor. Beyond restitution, VOM gives victims the opportunity to express their anger, indignation, anxieties, and fears and to get answers to such lingering questions as "Why did you choose to attack me?" or "How did you gain entrance to my home?" or "How could I have avoided this?" Through this process victims may be helped to achieve some psychological closure to their experience. Offenders, in turn, are given the opportunity to accept responsibility for what they did, express genuine remorse, and agree to do as much as they can "to try to restore the victim to the condition he or she was in before the crime occurred" (Karmen 2004:347).

■ References

Aday, David P. 1986. "Court Structure, Defense Attorney Use, and Juvenile Court Decisions." *Sociological Quarterly* 27:107–119.

Andrews, D. A., et al. 1990a. "Does Correctional Treatment Work? A Clinically Relevant and Psychologically Informed Meta-analysis." *Criminology* 28:369–404.

———. 1990b. "A Human Science Approach or More Punishment and Pessimism: A Rejoinder to Lab and Whitehead." *Criminology* 28:419–429.

Binder, Arnold, and Gilbert Geis. 1982. "*Ad Populum* Argumentation in Criminology: Juvenile Diversion as Rhetoric." *Crime and Delinquency* 30:309–333.

Binder, Arnold, Gilbert Geis, and Dickson D. Bruce. 1988. *Juvenile Delinquency: Historical, Cultural, and Legal Perspectives.* New York: Macmillan.

Bishop, Donna M., Charles E. Frazier, and John C. Henretta. 1989. "Prosecutorial Waiver: Case Study of a Questionable Reform." *Crime and Delinquency* 35:179–201.

Bortner, M. A. 1982. *Inside a Juvenile Court: The Tarnished Ideal of Individualized Justice.* New York: New York University Press.

———. 1988. *Delinquency and Justice: An Age of Crisis.* New York: McGraw-Hill.

Braithwaite, John. 1989. *Crime, Shame, and Reintegration.* New York: Cambridge University Press.

Butts, Jeffrey A., and Melissa Sickmund. 1992. *Offenders in Juvenile Court, 1989.* Washington, DC: Office of Justice and Delinquency Prevention.

Cullen, Francis T., and Brandon K. Applegate (eds.). 1997. *Offender Rehabilitation: Effective Treatment Intervention.* Aldershot, UK: Ashgate.

Feld, Barry C. 1984. "Criminalizing Juvenile Justice: Rules of Procedure for Juvenile Court." *Minnesota Law Review* 69:141–276.

———. 1988. "*In re Gault* Revisited: A Cross-state Comparison of the Right to Counsel." *Crime and Delinquency* 34:393–424.

———. 1990. "The Punitive Juvenile Court and the Quality of Procedural Justice." *Crime and Delinquency* 36:442–466.

————. 1993. "Juvenile (In)justice and the Criminal Court Alternative." *Crime and Delinquency* 39:403–424.

Gibbons, Don C. 1999. "Review Essay: Changing Lawbreakers—What Have We Learned Since the 1960s?" *Crime and Delinquency* 45:272–293.

Grisso, Thomas. 1981. *Juveniles' Waiver of Rights: Legal and Psychological Competence.* New York: Plenum.

Howell, James C. 1996. "Juvenile Transfers to the Criminal Justice System: State of the Art." *Law and Policy* 18:17–60.

Karmen, Andrew. 2004. *Crime Victims: An Introduction to Victimology.* Belmont, CA: Wadsworth.

Krisberg, Barry, Paul Litsky, and Ira Schwartz. 1984. "Youth in Confinement: Justice by Geography." *Journal of Research in Crime and Delinquency* 21:153–181.

Lab, Steven P., and John T. Whitehead. 1988. "An Analysis of Juvenile Correctional Treatment." *Crime and Delinquency* 34:60–83.

————. 1990. "From 'Nothing Works' to 'The Appropriate Works': The Latest Stop on the Search for the Secular Grail." *Criminology* 28:405–417.

Osbun, Lee Ann, and Peter A. Rode. 1984. "Prosecuting Juveniles as Adults: The Quest for 'Objective' Decisions." *Criminology* 22:187–202.

Pearson, Frank S., Douglas S. Lipton, Charles M. Cleland, and Dorline S. Yee. 2002. "The Effects of Behavioral/Cognitive Programs on Recidivism." *Crime and Delinquency* 48:476–496.

Rubin, H. Ted. 1980. "The Emerging Prosecutor Dominance of the Juvenile Intake Court Process." *Crime and Delinquency* 26:299–318.

Sanborn, Joseph B. 1992. "Pleading Guilty in Juvenile Court: Minimal Ado About Something Very Important to Young Defendants." *Justice Quarterly* 9:127–150.

————. 1993. "Philosophical, Legal, and Systemic Aspects of Juvenile Court Plea Bargaining." *Crime and Delinquency* 39:509–527.

Schneider, Anne. 1986. "Restitution and Recidivism Rates of Juvenile Offenders: Results from Four Experimental Studies." *Criminology* 24:533–552.

Schneider, Peter R., and Matthew C. Finkelstein (eds.). 1998. *RESTTA National Directory of Restitution and Community Service Programs.* Bethesda, MD: Pacific Institute for Research and Evaluation.

Senjo, Scott R., and Leslie A. Leip. 2001. "Testing and Developing Theory in Drug Court: A Four-part Logit Model to Predict Program Completion." *Criminal Justice Policy Review* 12:66–87.

Siegel, Larry J., and Brandon C. Welsh. 2009. *Juvenile Delinquency: Theory, Practice, and Law.* Belmont, CA: Wadsworth.

Snyder, Howard N., and Melissa Sickmund. 2006. *Juvenile Offenders and Victims: 2006 National Report.* Pittsburgh, PA: National Center for Juvenile Justice.

Stahl, Ann L., et al. 2007. *Juvenile Court Statistics 2003–2004.* Pittsburgh, PA: National Center for Juvenile Justice.

Strom, Kevin J., Steven K. Smith, and Howard N. Snyder. 1998. *Juvenile Felony Defendants in Criminal Courts.* Washington, DC: US Department of Justice.

Thornton, William E., Lydia Voigt, and William G. Doerner. 1987. *Delinquency and Justice.* New York: Random House.

Waegel, William B. 1989. *Delinquency and Juvenile Control: A Sociological Perspective.* Englewood Cliffs, NJ: Prentice-Hall.

Whitehead, John T., and Steven P. Lab. 1989. "A Meta-analysis of Juvenile Correctional Treatment." *Journal of Research in Crime and Delinquency* 26:276–295.

Zehr, Howard, and Harry Mika. 1998. "Fundamental Concepts of Restorative Justice." *Contemporary Justice Review* 1:47–55.

21

Legal and Extralegal Factors in Police and Court Processing of Juveniles

Ronald J. Berger

One of the most important issues in the sociology of juvenile justice involves the question of how officials make discretionary decisions and choose among a variety of available options when dealing with youths who come to their attention. Are these decisions made on the basis of legal variables such as the seriousness of the offense and prior record of the juvenile? Or are they based on social variables or extralegal factors such as race/ethnicity, class, gender, or other criteria? Ronald Berger reviews the research literature on the issue and concludes "that legal factors alone cannot explain how youths are processed through the juvenile justice system."

THIS CHAPTER REVIEWS RESEARCH THAT HAS EXAMINED THE IMPACT of legal and extralegal factors on police and court processing of juveniles. Especially controversial have been studies that have suggested bias against individuals of particular racial/ethnic backgrounds, which raises the specter of discrimination and "racial profiling." Of course, a finding of disparity does not necessarily imply discrimination: *disparity* occurs when legally relevant factors are applied but "have different results for different groups," while *discrimination* occurs when decisions are based on an individual's social status rather than on legally appropriate criteria (Petersilia and Turner 1988:92). Nevertheless, the research on group variations has not always been consistent, and some researchers suggest that the mixed results may reflect actual differences among departments and the "jurisdictional fragmentation" that characterizes the juvenile justice system (Pope and Feyerherm 1990:328), which some have dubbed "justice by geography" (Feld 1991; Krisberg, Litsky, and Schwartz 1984). In addition, inconsistent findings may also stem from the different time frames of studies (e.g., pre-*Gault* vs. post-*Gault* era), as well as from varying research designs and methodologies that are employed—differences in the way variables are operationalized, in the types of statistical techniques that are used, in the types of control variables (if any) that are included in multivariate analyses, in the use of cross-sectional versus longitudinal designs, and in the focus on variations within or between jurisdictions. Pope and Feyerherm (1995) also suggest that use of data from states or counties that aggregate cases from different localities may mask the discriminatory processes that occur in particular places.

■ The Police

Most of the research on juveniles and the police has focused on the criteria used by law enforcement to make decisions about whether or not to arrest or release with only a reprimand or warning juveniles who are suspected of violating the law. Research has indicated that most juvenile encounters with the police (excluding traffic offenses) are initiated in response to a citizen complaint, with most of these encounters involving nonfelony offenders. While arrest is "virtually automatic" with felonies, "informal resolution" is more likely in other cases (Binder, Geis, and Bruce 2001; Waegel 1989:32).

Race/Ethnicity and Class

While black youths are more likely than white youths to be arrested, some researchers explain this in terms of black youths' greater involvement in serious crimes and prior arrest records, or to the higher victimization rates among black residents, whom studies have found are more likely than whites to "lobby for formal police action" (Lundman, Sykes, and Clark 1978:88; see also Black and Reiss 1970; Smith and Visher 1981). Binder and colleagues conclude that "while there does seem to be differential disposition of youths on the basis of race in some departments, there is no evidence that it is a common or widespread phenomenon" (2001:253; Waegel 1989).

At the same time, a number of studies have pointed to racial bias in arrest decisions while taking into account the seriousness of offending and prior record of black and white youths. Dannefer and Schutt (1982), for example, found racial bias related to the proportion of the population that belonged to a minority group. As a minority group's presence increased, they argued, police may have greater fear of residents "getting out of their place" (p. 1115).[1] In a comparison of *Uniform Crime Reports* arrest data and *National Youth Survey* self-report data, Huizinga and Elliott concluded that nonwhite youths were at greater risk of "being charged with more serious offenses than whites involved in comparable levels" of delinquency (1987:221). Blumstein (1993) was particularly critical of the "war on drugs" campaign that began in the mid-1980s. Between 1965 and 1980, he observed, the drug arrest rates for white and nonwhite youths were comparable—and even somewhat higher for whites during the 1970s. Arrest rates declined for both groups from the mid-1970s to early 1980s (due to the decriminalization of marijuana in some jurisdictions), but, significantly, the rates for black youths accelerated annually by 20–25 percent in the latter part of the decade while the rates for white youths declined. Insofar as self-report studies indicate that black youths do not use more drugs than white youths—and there is some evidence that white youths use more drugs (US Department of Health and Human Services 2007)—a conclusion of discrimination would seem warranted (Berger, Free, and Searles 2009).

Furthermore, research finds that police are more likely to invoke their power to arrest when the suspect is disrespectful, and minority youths are more likely to respond in ways that are perceived this way (Black 1980). But it is also likely that their disrespectful reactions stem from the hostile treatment and shakedowns they not uncommonly receive from police. As Mann observes, people of color "may be stopped for questioning in sections of cities where they are not often seen, or for driving a car which seems beyond their means or is assumed by the police to be of doubtful legal possession; [indeed] minorities are often hassled simply for having a conversation on the street" (1993:138; see Chapter 22).

Like the evidence on race, the research on class bias in police processing of juveniles has been inconsistent. In an important study, however, Sampson found that class, as measured by neighborhood socioeconomic status, had an "inverse effect on police contacts independent of actual law-violating behavior as measured by self-reported delinquency" (1986:876). Moreover, this relationship persisted while controlling for "prevalence, frequency and type of delinquency, race, family structure, delinquent peers, and gang membership."

Sampson argued that the police do, in fact, behaviorally orient themselves to patrolling in lower-class communities and that officers view youths in lower-class areas as more prone to delinquency than youths in higher-class areas. Yet Sampson emphasized that

> a large part of any effect of individual [socioeconomic status] on arrests is spurious and reflects an ecological bias in police perceptions rather than a bias directed solely at lower-class juveniles in actual police encounters. . . . The police may be equally likely to arrest juveniles given an encounter for a particular offense, but are more likely to detect offenses and initiate encounters in contexts where youth are more heavily scrutinized. (1986:877–78)

In addition, lower-class areas have a more active street life than middle-class communities, largely because residents have less access to private space. "Since the regulation of public places is a central task of policing, . . . people in lower-class areas are subjected to greater surveillance" (1986:878). Ultimately these processes translate into a greater likelihood of lower-class youths—including minority youths—accumulating a prior record of offending, even if only for minor offenses (Chambliss 1994). Thus research that finds that prior record predicts likelihood of subsequent arrest ignores the possibility that earlier biases may affect later outcomes whether or not bias is present in these later situations.

Furthermore, Chambliss (1994) suggests that intensive police surveillance of low-income minority communities is also political. Law enforcement organizations are "self-perpetuating bureaucracies" concerned with justifying "their claim to more and more of the taxpayer's dollars" (p. 191). "In a class society, the powerless, the poor, and those who fit the public stereotype of 'the criminal'"—what Skolnick (1994) called a "symbolic assailant"—"are the human resources needed by law enforcement agencies to maximize rewards and minimize strains. . . . [They are] a population without political clout, with few resources to successfully defend against criminal charges" (pp. 191–92).

Gender

Gender is another social variable that has been examined in studies of police decisionmaking. There is some evidence that girls have been the beneficiaries of police "chivalry" when they display traditional gender role characteristics, appear to "know their place," and are "apologetic, submissive, and deferential" to the police (Waegel 1989:137). These females are more likely to receive preferential treatment than those who are less traditional in their demeanor, and white females are more likely to be treated in this way than blacks (Visher 1983).

On the other hand, while some research finds that females have been treated more leniently than males for criminal offenses, they have been treated more severely for status offenses (Binder, Geis, and Bruce 2001; Chesney-Lind and Shelden 2004). In these latter circumstances, police may feel that further intervention is necessary to "help the girl" and prevent her from getting into more trouble (Waegel 1989:137). Girls have also been victims of a "double standard" insofar as boys have been expected to "sow their wild oats" while girls have been expected to show restraint, especially regarding sexual matters. Moreover, police arrest of female status offenders appears to have reflected parental preferences for legal assistance in controlling daughters more than sons (Chesney-Lind 1987, 1989; Chesney-Lind and Shelden 2004).

Other Factors

Klein and colleagues (1975) suggest that one reason for variation in police practices from one jurisdiction to another is that most police departments don't have written guidelines for the handling of juveniles. This heightens "the influence of informal intradepartmental and personal forces on decision making" (Binder, Geis, and Bruce 1988:275). Departments vary by different "operating codes" or "organizational styles" of policing (Wilson 1968). For instance, departments that operate according to a "legalistic style" adopt a more professional or "by the book" approach that results in higher arrest rates but that minimizes discretion and bias. On the other hand, "watchman style" departments emphasize the maintenance of order that can often be accomplished without resort to arrest, but which also gives officers more discretionary authority that may result in greater bias or discriminatory treatment of certain groups of youths.[2]

■ The Juvenile Court

In addition to research on the police, numerous studies have examined discretionary decisions at the intake and disposition stages of the juvenile justice system. At the intake stage, the intake officer must decide whether to detain or release a juvenile, refer him or her to another agency, or file a petition for formal court processing. At the disposition stage, the judge, who takes into account a probation officer's recommendation, must decide whether to grant an adjudicated youth probation or other community supervision, remove the youth from his or her home, or place the youth in a correctional facility.

Race/Ethnicity and Class

Studies of legal and extralegal influences on juvenile court decisions have produced results parallel to those of police processing of juveniles. Binder and colleagues (2001) concluded that no general pattern of discrimination has been found, but this conclusion is contradicted by other research. Dannefer and Schutt (1982), for example, found evidence of racial bias, although much less so than at the police stage. They argued that racial bias may decrease at the later stages of juvenile justice processing as police "bias may be compensated for, to some extent, by the courts" (p. 1113; see also Pope and Feyerherm 1995; Rodriguez 2007). Palazzari (1982) found such compensation at intake, where black youths were more likely than whites to be released.[3] However, for those who remained in the system, she found that blacks received harsher treatment at the disposition stage. Other studies also indicated that black youths were more disadvantaged at the later stages of the system, suggesting that as the cohort of processed offenders becomes more homogeneous with respect to legal criteria, the influence of extralegal factors becomes more pronounced (Bishop and Frazer 1988; Fagan, Slaughter, and Hartstone 1987; McCarthy and Smith 1986). Some researchers have noted an "accumulation of disadvantage" for minority youths as they move through the various decision points in the system, with the risks compounded at each successive stage (McCord, Widom, and Crowell 2002; Pope and Feyerherm 1995:3).[4]

In a study of juvenile court data drawn from 159 counties in 17 states between 1985 and 1989, McGarrell found that "non-white youths were more likely to be referred to and petitioned in court, to be detained, and to be placed outside the home," and that the disparity between nonwhite and white youths increased between 1985 and 1989, especially for drug offenses (1993:29; see Blumstein 1993). However, there were significant variations by counties, indicating that these trends were by no means universal. Other studies have found more se-vere outcomes for youths in counties with a higher percentage of the popula-tion that was nonwhite (Armstrong and Rodriguez 2005; Tittle and Curran 1988).

As with research on race/ethnicity, some studies have found that lower-class youths receive harsher juvenile court treatment while other studies have not. Carter and Clelland (1979) found evidence of class bias, but only for less serious offenders. Research findings have also been inconsistent over the ques-tion of whether class bias increases or decreases at later stages in the system (Clarke and Koch 1980; Cohen and Kluegel 1978; McCarthy and Smith 1986; Palazzari 1982).

Sampson and Laub (1993) tested propositions derived from conflict the-ory that indicated an influence of race and class on community-level variations in juvenile justice processing. They hypothesized that "all else being equal, counties characterized by racial inequality and a large concentration of the 'underclass' . . . are more likely . . . to be perceived as containing offensive and threatening populations and, as a result, are subject to increased social control by the juvenile justice system" (p. 293). In a multivariate analysis of over 500,000 juvenile case records that were aggregated from over 300 counties across the country for 1985, Sampson and Laub found support for their hypothesis—that is, measures of racial inequality and the percent of the population that was un-derclass were associated with a greater likelihood of youths being formally pe-titioned to court, being detained before adjudication, and receiving out-of-home placements. Sampson and Laub also reported more severe juvenile court outcomes for black youths than for white youths.

Gender

The results of research on gender and juvenile court processing have been sim-ilar to those on gender and the police. Although some studies have not found gender to be a significant factor, others indicate that girls have been treated more severely than males for status offenses but less severely for criminal of-fenses (Bishop and Frazer 1992; Chesney-Lind and Shelden 2004; Cohen and Kluegel 1979; Hagan, Simpson, and Gillis 1979).

In a study of over 36,000 juvenile court referrals in a midwestern state be-tween 1975 and 1983, Johnson and Scheuble (1991) found that the gender-dis-position relationship was complicated by both the type of offense and the type of disposition.

> The analysis of the total sample found that boys were more likely to be put on probation or locked up than girls, and girls were more likely than boys to be dismissed. . . . For the less serious misdemeanor offenses, girls were more likely to be dismissed and boys put on probation or locked up. For property felons, girls were also more likely to be dismissed and boys put on probation.

No significant gender differences were found for the more punitive dispositions although they were in the direction of greater odds of custody transfer
for girls and lock-up for boys. For the more serious personal offenses, this
pattern was contradicted—girls had greater odds of lock-up than boys, but
the differences were not statistically significant. (pp. 693–94)

Johnson and Scheuble also reported a trend over time toward greater odds of
girls being dismissed and of boys receiving probation or lockup. In addition,
the bias toward leniency for girls was greater in urban areas than in rural areas.

Other Factors

With regard to legal factors that affect juvenile court outcomes, the most consistent finding across all jurisdictions has involved the influence of a juvenile's
prior record. On the other hand, offense seriousness has appeared less related
to court outcomes because of differences in courts' treatment of particular types
of offenses. For instance, in some jurisdictions, status offenders have had a
higher probability of being retained because of their adverse family situations
and in other jurisdictions they have not (Binder, Geis, and Bruce 2001; Smith,
Black, and Weir 1980; Waegel 1989).

Just as different organizational styles influence police processing of juveniles, varying juvenile court philosophies affect the relative influence of legal
and extralegal factors. Juvenile court philosophies range from a more informal
parens patriae or treatment orientation to a more formal or legalistic one (Stapleton, Aday, and Ito 1982; see Chapters 1–3). The former may emphasize social
criteria (e.g., family background, school achievement) in evaluating a youth's behavior, while the latter may focus on legal issues (e.g., prior offenses, whether
there is sufficient evidence to convict). Some studies found that variables related to a juvenile's family life and school and employment record were used
by officials to decide whether an offense was "a direct manifestation of a delinquent character and thus a sign of future trouble, or simply incidental to a juvenile's character and thus unlikely to occur again" (Liska and Tausig 1979:
203; see also Clarke and Koch 1980; Cohen and Kluegel 1978; Smith, Black,
and Weir 1980). Pope and Feyerherm suggest that family circumstances, especially, "may be one mechanism through which race indirectly affects outcome
decisions," since youths from single-parent homes, especially from female-
headed households, "often face more severe dispositions," and black youths
are more likely than white youths to reside in such homes (1995:11).

In addition, Hasenfeld and Cheung (1985) identified a number of other
contextual factors that influenced juvenile court decisions. At intake, for example, the likelihood that juveniles would be held for formal court processing
was increased if there was pressure from the referral agency (e.g., police,
school). On the other hand, the likelihood of formal processing was decreased
if the juvenile court was part of a "court of general jurisdiction rather than a

court of limited jurisdiction" (p. 806). Because they have appellate review, courts of general jurisdiction tend to adopt a more legalistic orientation. Such courts are "less likely to process formally cases lacking legal merit and more inclined to process them nonjudicially, thus freeing themselves of . . . [appellate] review. Moreover, courts of general jurisdiction encounter more diverse cases and must establish priorities and are more likely, therefore, to use nonjudicial handling to screen out 'minor' cases" (pp. 806–7). Hasenfeld and Cheung also found that the likelihood of formal processing was less in communities with greater economic resources, higher volumes of referrals, and more available youth services.[5] As for judges' dispositional decisions, juveniles received harsher sentences from judges who were elected (as opposed to appointed) and lighter sentences from judges who focused on "due process" issues. Presumably, elected judges were more sensitive to public demand to "crack down" on juvenile crime, while due process judges were concerned with protecting the rights of juveniles.

Waiver and Representation by Counsel

A few studies have also examined legal and extralegal factors in the decision to waive or transfer a case from juvenile court jurisdiction to adult criminal court and in the effects of being represented by counsel. For instance, Bortner (1986) found that black youths were overrepresented in waived cases, but Fagan, Forst, and Vivona (1987) reported that age and type of offense were the best predictors of waiver. Older youths and youths convicted of murder or rape were the most likely to be transferred to adult court; and the overrepresentation of minority youths appeared to be due to their greater likelihood of being charged with murder. Eigen (1981) found that black youths who murdered whites were especially likely to be waived.

In a multivariate study that examined a large number of variables, Poulos and Orchowsky (1994) found that prior property crime convictions were the single best predictors of transfer from juvenile court. They also identified a list of other factors that increased the likelihood of waiver: the current offense involved murder, manslaughter, rape, drug sales, or use of a firearm; the offender had a previous felony conviction or juvenile commitment; the offender was 17 years old or had at least a ninth-grade education; and the case was handled by a metropolitan court. When controlling for these variables, race and gender were not related to the transfer decision.

Finally, a number of studies on representation by counsel in the post-*Gault* era indicated that juveniles who had attorneys actually received more severe dispositions than juveniles who were not represented (Bortner 1982; Burruss and Kempf-Leonard 2002; Clarke and Koch 1989; Feld 1988, 1989), and that this association was more pronounced for nonwhite youths than for white youths

(Guevara, Spohn, and Herz 2004). Feld considered several possible explanations for these findings:

> Attorneys in juvenile court . . . [may be] incompetent and prejudice their clients' case. . . . Public defender offices . . . [may] in many jurisdictions assign their least capable lawyers or newest staff attorneys to juvenile courts to get trial experience. . . . Court-appointed counsel may be beholden to the judges who select them and more concerned with maintaining an ongoing relationship with the court than vigorously protecting the interests of their clients. . . . It may be that presence of lawyers antagonizes traditional court judges . . . [or] that early in a proceeding, a juvenile court judge's greater familiarity with a case may alert him or her to the eventual disposition that will be imposed and counsel may be appointed . . . [in cases] of more severe consequences. . . . [Also] judges may treat more formally juveniles who appear with counsel . . . [and] may feel less constrained when sentencing a youth who is represented. (1988:405, 419–20)

■ Conclusion

The interaction between legal and extralegal variables is complex, and it is difficult to tease out their relative effects at different points in the police and court processing of juveniles. It is especially difficult to determine whether a finding of disparity necessarily entails bias or discrimination. Moreover, the complexity of the interdependence may be lost by focusing on only one decision point at a time, as has been the case with many studies, particularly if one is trying to pinpoint whether discrimination occurs at particular stages and for particular types of offenses. For example, Pope and Feyerherm suggest three possible variations:

1. When disparity exists, it may be present at any decision point in the juvenile justice system. Moreover, it may exist at wholly different points in different jurisdictions.
2. Disparity may comprise either large differences in processing at some stage in the system, or more likely, a series of accumulations of relatively small differences in processing, with a relatively large net effect.
3. Because each jurisdiction may set out many of its own specific rules and practices, the search for disparity may require identifying jurisdictions that may need more intense scrutiny. Each locality, in essence, has its own version of the juvenile justice system and each behaves differently. (1995:5)

In any case, as this review indicates, it is quite clear that legal factors alone cannot explain how youths are processed through the juvenile justice system. Analyses that take into account the extralegal or social factors that influence the discretionary decisions of juvenile justice autho rities are necessary if one really wants to understand how the system operates.

▨ Notes

1. The pattern has been interpreted in terms of minority-group threat (or power threat) theory (Blalock 1967).

2. Wilson (1968) also identified "service style" departments that may be found in middle-class communities. The relative absence of serious criminality in these areas reduces police reliance on arrest as a means of resolving problems and increases their service, social welfare, or guidance function.

3. In one early study, Scarpitti and Stephenson found harsher dispositions for whites because, the researchers argued, "black boys had to exhibit a much greater delinquency commitment before the most punitive alternative was selected" (1971:48). Leiber (1994) found that nonwhite youths generally received more severe dispositions than whites, but Native-American youths received less severe dispositions than blacks.

4. Preadjudicated detained youths are more likely to be petitioned to juvenile court and to receive more severe dispositions than nondetained youths, and nonwhite youths are more likely to be detained (Bishop and Frazer 1996; Bortner and Reed 1985; Clarke and Koch 1980; Leiber and Fox 2005; McCarthy and Smith 1986).

5. Krisberg, Litsky, and Schwartz (1984) reported that availability of bed space was the best predictor of pretrial detention, and Feld (1991) found that urban courts, which were more highly bureaucratized and inclined toward formal social control, issued more severe dispositions.

▨ References

Armstrong, Gaylene S., and Nancy Rodriguez. 2005. "Effects of Individual and Contextual Characteristics on Preadjudication Detention of Juvenile Delinquents." *Justice Quarterly* 22:521–39.

Berger, Ronald J., Marvin D. Free, and Patricia Searles. 2009. *Crime, Justice, and Society: An Introduction to Criminology,* 3rd ed. Boulder, CO: Lynne Rienner.

Binder, Arnold, Gilbert Geis, and Dickson D. Bruce. 1988. *Juvenile Delinquency: Historical, Cultural, and Legal Perspectives.* New York: Macmillan.

———. 2001. *Juvenile Delinquency: Historical, Cultural, and Legal Perspectives.* 3rd ed. Cincinnati, OH: Anderson.

Bishop, Donna M., and Charles S. Frazer. 1988. "The Influence of Race in Juvenile Justice Processing." *Journal of Research in Crime and Delinquency* 25:242–63.

———. 1992. "Gender Bias in Juvenile Justice Processing: Implications of the JJDP Act." *Journal of Criminal Law and Criminology* 82:1162–86.

———. 1996. "Race Effects in Juvenile Justice Decision-Making: Findings of a Statewide Analysis." *Journal of Criminal Law and Criminology* 86:392–414.

Black, Donald J. 1980. *Manners and Customs of the Police.* New York: Academic Press.

Black, Donald J., and Albert J. Reiss. 1970. "Police Control of Juveniles." *American Sociological Review* 35:63–77.

Blalock, Hubert. 1967. *Toward a Theory of Minority-Group Relations.* New York: Wiley.

Blumstein, Alfred. 1993. "Making Rationality Relevant." *Criminology* 31:1–16.

Bortner, M. A. 1982. *Inside a Juvenile Court: The Tarnished Ideal of Individualized Justice.* New York: New York University Press.

———. 1986. "Traditional Rhetoric, Organizational Realities: Remand of Juveniles to Adult Court." *Crime and Delinquency* 32:53–73.

Bortner, M. A., and Wornie L. Reed. 1985. "The Preeminence of Process: An Example of Refocused Justice Research." *Social Science Quarterly* 66:413–25.

Burruss, George W., and Kimberly Kempf-Leonard. 2002. "The Questionable Advantage of Defense Counsel in Juvenile Court." *Justice Quarterly* 19:37–67.

Carter, Timothy J., and Donald Clelland. 1979. "A Neo-Marxian Critique, Formulation and Test of Juvenile Dispositions as a Function of Social Class." *Social Problems* 27:96–108.

Chambliss, William J. 1994. "Policing the Ghetto Underclass: The Politics of Law and Law Enforcement." *Social Problems* 41:177–94.

Chesney-Lind, Meda. 1987. "Female Offenders: Paternalism Reexamined." In L. Crites and W. Hepperle (eds.), *Women, the Courts, and Equality.* Newbury Park, CA: Sage.

———. 1989. "Girls' Crime and Woman's Place: Toward a Feminist Model of Female Delinquency." *Crime and Delinquency* 35:5–29.

Chesney-Lind, Meda, and Randall G. Shelden. 2004. *Girls, Delinquency, and Juvenile Justice.* Belmont, CA: Wadsworth.

Clarke, Stevens H., and Gary G. Koch. 1980. "Juvenile Court: Therapy or Crime Control, and Do Lawyers Make a Difference?" *Law and Society Review* 14:263–306.

Cohen, Lawrence E., and James R. Kluegel. 1978. "Determinants of Juvenile Court Dispositions: Ascriptive and Achieved Factors in Two Metropolitan Courts." *American Sociological Review* 43:162–76.

Dannefer, Dale, and Russell K. Schutt. 1982. "Race and Juvenile Justice Processing in Court and Police Agencies." *American Journal of Sociology* 87:1113–32.

Eigen, Joel P. 1981. "The Determinants and Impact of Jurisdictional Transfer in Philadelphia." In J. Hall et al. (eds.), *Major Issues in Juvenile Justice Information and Training.* Columbus, OH: Academy for Contemporary Problems.

Fagan, Jeffrey A., Martin Forst, and T. Scott Vivona. 1987. "Racial Determinants of the Judicial Transfer Decision: Prosecuting Violent Youth in Criminal Court." *Crime and Delinquency* 33:259–86.

Fagan, Jeffrey A., Ellen Slaughter, and Eliot Hartstone. 1987. "Blind Justice? The Impact of Race on the Juvenile Justice Process." *Crime and Delinquency* 33:224–58.

Feld, Barry C. 1988. "*In re Gault* Revisited: A Cross-state Comparison of the Right to Counsel." *Crime and Delinquency* 34:393–424.

———. 1989. "The Right to Counsel in Juvenile Court: An Empirical Study of When Lawyers Appear and the Difference They Make." *Journal of Criminal Law and Criminology* 79:1185–1346.

———. 1991. "Justice by Geography: Urban, Suburban, and Rural Variations in Juvenile Justice Administration." *Journal of Criminal Law and Criminology* 82:156–210.

Guevara, Lori, Cassia Spohn, and Denise Herz. 2004. "Race, Legal Representation, and Juvenile Justice: Issues and Concerns." *Crime and Delinquency* 50:344–71.

Hagan, John, John Simpson, and A. R. Gillis. 1979. "The Sexual Stratification of Social Control: A Gender Based Perspective on Crime and Delinquency." *British Journal of Criminology* 30:25–38.

Hasenfeld, Yeheskel, and Paul P. L. Cheung. 1985. "The Juvenile Court as a People-processing Organization: A Political Economy Perspective." *American Journal of Sociology* 90:801–24.

Huizinga, David, and Delbert S. Elliott. 1987. "Juvenile Offenders: Prevalence, Offender Incidence, and Arrest Rates by Race." *Crime and Delinquency* 33:206–23.

Johnson, David, and Laurie K. Scheuble. 1991. "Gender Bias in the Disposition of Juvenile Court Referrals: The Effects of Time and Location." *Criminology* 29:677–99.

Klein, Malcolm W., Susan Labin Rosenzweig, and Ronald Bates. 1975. "The Ambiguous Juvenile Arrest." *Criminology* 1:78–89.

Krisberg, Barry, Paul Litsky, and Ira Schwartz. 1984. "Youth in Confinement: Justice by Geography." *Journal of Research in Crime and Delinquency* 21:153–81.

Leiber, Michael J. 1994. "A Comparison of Juvenile Court Outcomes for Native Americans, African Americans, and Whites." *Justice Quarterly:* 257–78.

Leiber, Michael J., and Kristan A. Fox. 2005. "Race and the Impact of Detention on Juvenile Justice Decision Making." *Crime and Delinquency* 51:470–97.

Liska, Allen F., and Mark Tausig. 1979. "Theoretical Interpretations of Social Class and Racial Differentials in Legal Decision-Making for Juveniles." *Sociological Quarterly* 20:197–207.

Lundman, Richard L., Richard E. Sykes, and John P. Clark. 1978. "Police Control of Juveniles: A Replication." *Journal of Research in Crime and Delinquency* 15:74–91.

Mann, Coramae Richey. 1993. *Unequal Justice: A Question of Color.* Bloomington: Indiana University Press.

McCarthy, Belinda R., and Brent L. Smith. 1986. "The Conceptualization of Discrimination in the Juvenile Justice Process: The Impact of Administrative Factors and Screening Decisions on Juvenile Court Dispositions." *Criminology* 24:41–64.

McCord, Joan, Cathy Spatz Widom, and Nancy A. Crowell. 2002. *Juvenile Crime, Juvenile Justice.* Washington, DC: National Academy Press.

McGarrell, Edmund F. 1993. "Trends in Racial Disproportionality in Juvenile Court Processing: 1985–1989." *Crime and Delinquency* 39:29–48.

Palazzari, Therese A. 1982. *The Impact of Race and Socioeconomic Status on Juvenile Court Dispositions.* Unpublished M.A. thesis, University of Wisconsin–Milwaukee.

Petersilia, Joan, and Susan Turner. 1988. "Minorities in Prison: Discrimination or Disparity?" *Corrections Today* 50:92–94.

Pope, Carl E., and William Feyerherm. 1990. "Minority Status and Juvenile Justice Processing: An Assessment of Research Literature." *Criminal Justice Abstracts* 22:327–36 (part 1), 527–42 (part 2).

———. 1995. *Minorities and the Criminal Justice System: Research Summary.* Washington, DC: US Department of Justice.

Poulos, Tammy Meredith, and Stan Orchowsky. 1994. "Serious Juvenile Offenders: Predicting the Probability of Transfer to Criminal Court." *Crime and Delinquency* 40:3–17.

Rodriguez, Nancy. 2007. "Juvenile Court Context and Detention Decisions: Reconsidering the Role of Race, Ethnicity, and Community Characteristics in Juvenile Court Processes." *Justice Quarterly* 24:629–55.

Sampson, Robert J. 1986. "Effects of Socioeconomic Context on Official Reactions to Delinquency." *American Sociological Review* 51:876–85.

Sampson, Robert J., and John H. Laub. 1993. "Structural Variations in Juvenile Court Processing: Inequality, the Underclass, and Social Control." *Law and Society Review* 27:285–311.

Scarpitti, Frank R., and Richard M. Stephenson. 1971. "Juvenile Court Dispositions: Factors in the Decision-Making Process." *Crime and Delinquency* 17:142–51.

Skolnick, Jerome H. 1994. *Justice Without Trial: Law Enforcement in Democratic Society.* New York: Macmillan.

Smith, C. P., T. E. Black, and A. W. Weir. 1980. *Report of the National Juvenile Justice Assessment Centers. A National Assessment of Case Disposition and Classification in the Juvenile Justice System: Inconsistent Labeling, Vol II: Results of a Literature Search.* Washington, DC: US Government Printing Office.

Smith, David A., and Christy A. Visher. 1981. "Street-level Justice: Situational Determinants of Police Arrest Decisions." *Social Problems* 29:167–77.

Stapleton, Vaughan, David P. Aday, and Jeanne A. Ito. 1982. "An Empirical Typology of American Metropolitan Juvenile Courts." *American Journal of Sociology* 88:549–65.

Tittle, Charles R., and Debra A. Curran. 1988. "Contingencies for Dispositional Disparities in Juvenile Justice." *Social Forces* 67:23–58.

US Department of Health and Human Services. 2007. "Appendix G: Selected Prevalence Tables," available online at www.oas.samsha.gov.

Visher, Christy A. 1983. "Gender, Police Arrest Decisions, and Notions of Chivalry." *Criminology* 21:5–28.

Waegel, William B. 1989. *Delinquent and Juvenile Control: A Sociological Perspective.* Englewood Cliffs, NJ: Prentice-Hall.

Wilson, James Q. 1968. *Varieties of Police Behavior.* Cambridge, MA: Harvard University Press.

22

Gang Members and the Police

Carl Werthman and Irving Piliavin

Carl Werthman and Irving Piliavin's interviews with youths who have encountered the police illuminate the dynamics of police-juvenile interaction in a "situation of suspicion." Werthman and Piliavin show how racial and ethnic status, as well as other personal attributes, are used by police to identify "suspicious" youths and levy charges against them.

THE JUVENILE OFFICER [JUVENILE OFFICERS MAY WORK AS INDIVIDUAL specialists in a police department or as part of a specialized unit] exercises a good deal of discretion in deciding how to process offenders, a discretion that far transcends the measure of ambiguity ordinarily involved in legal assessments of motivation and intent. Although a truant may not be responsible for his behavior, he may be a touch rebellious, or he may be acting in complete and willful disregard for law, the nature and intent of this crime is not as important to a juvenile officer as what he learns about the attitude of the offender towards the idea of the law itself. For example, if an officer decides he is dealing with a boy who is "guilty but essentially good" or "guilty but sometimes weak," the probability is high that he will decide to let the boy go with a warning about the consequences of committing this crime again. He might feel that contact with the unsavory clientele of a juvenile hall would damage an otherwise positive attitude towards the law or that moral contamination in the eyes of parents and teachers as a result of being sent to jail might weaken an otherwise firm commitment to conventional behavior. On the other hand, if the officer decides that the offender is a "punk," a "persistent troublemaker," or some other version of a thoroughly bad boy, he may well decide to make an arrest.[1]

A "delinquent" is therefore not a juvenile who happens to have committed an illegal act. He is a young person whose moral character has been negatively assessed. And this fact has led some observers to conclude that the

Excerpt from *The Police: Six Sociological Essays,* edited by David Bordua (John Wiley and Sons, 1967). Reprinted by permission of John Wiley and Sons, Inc.

transformation of young people into official "delinquents" is best looked at as an organizational rather than a legal process since policemen, probation officers, and juvenile court judges often base their dispositions on a host of criteria that are virtually unrelated to the nature of the specific offense.[2]

The *magnitude of an offense,* of course, can become a factor in dispositions. One responsibly planned and willfully executed robbery, rape, or assault can ruin the moral status of a juvenile indefinitely. Since 90 percent of the crimes committed by juveniles are minor offenses, however, this criterion is only rarely used.

The number of *previous contacts with police* has a more important effect on dispositions. These contacts are typically recorded on easily accessible files, and these files contain everything from arrests and convictions to contacts made on the flimsiest of contingent grounds. If a boy confesses to a crime and is not known to the police, he is often released. If he is caught for a third or fourth time, however, the sum total of previous contacts may be enough to affect a judgment about his moral character adversely, regardless of the nature or magnitude of the present offense and regardless of the reasons he was previously contacted. For example:

> Like last night, man, me and Willy got busted for curfew. I mean I got busted for curfew. We was walkin' towards home, and these cops pull up. It was a Friday night, man, so we didn't want no trouble. When the cops ask us what we was doing and what about our names we was all nice. So then the cop gets on that radio and checks us out. There was a whole bunch of noise comin' over that box. I couldn't hear what they was sayin'. But then the cop comes out and says to Willy, "O.K., you can go." And I say, "What about me?" And the cop says, "You been in trouble before. We don't want you walkin' the streets at night. We going to take you down to the station for curfew." Then I got real mad. I almost ran. Lucky thing I didn't though. I woulda been in real trouble then.

There is even some evidence to suggest that assessments about the type and quality of *parental control* are even more important factors in dispositions than any of the offense-related criteria. One of the main concerns of a juvenile officer is the likelihood of future offense, and this determination is often made largely on the basis of "the kinds of parents" a boy happens to possess. Thus, the moral character of parents also passes under review; and if a house appears messy, a parent is missing, or a mother is on welfare, the probability of arrest increases. Similarly, a boy with a father and two older brothers in jail is considered a different sort of person from a boy whose immediate family is not known to the police. As Aaron Cicourel points out, these judgments about family life are particularly subject to bias by attitudes related to class.[3]

> See, like if you and maybe one of your brothers, say both of you, been to Y.A.,[4] or your sister, every time they see you they get on your back. They

know all your family. If they ever pick you up and look at your records, they automatically take you in. They see where your sister been to jail, your brother, or if you ever went to jail. And they start saying, "Your whole family is rotten. Your whole family is jailbirds." Shit like that. And this is what really make you mad, when they tell you your mother don't know how to read!

Although the family situation of a boy and his record of prior police contacts both enter into dispositions, the most important factor affecting the decision of juvenile officers is the attitude displayed by the offender, both during and after the confession itself. Cicourel, for example, found that juvenile officers were strongly influenced by the style and speed with which the offender confessed.[5] If a boy blurts out his misdeeds immediately, this behavior is taken as a sign that the boy "trusts" authority and is therefore "under control." If the boy proves to be a "tough nut to crack," however, he is viewed with suspicion. As soon as a juvenile is defined as "hardened," he is considered no less dangerous to society than the adult criminal.

Similarly, the boys who appear frightened, humble, penitent, and ashamed are also more likely to go free. They are often defined as "weak, troubled, and the victim of circumstances" but basically "good boys," an assessment of moral character that may win them a release.

On the other hand, if a boy shows no signs of being spiritually moved by his offense, the police deal harshly with him. Not only has he sinned against a legal rule, but he has also symbolically rejected the normative basis for conforming to it in the first place; and it is this double deviation that has fateful consequences for the way he is treated by the police. Once he gets himself defined as "the kind of person who doesn't respect the law," he becomes a perfect candidate for arrest, detention, and eventual incarceration. Most of the juvenile officers we interviewed felt that the attitude of the offender was the major determinant of dispositions in 50 percent of their cases, and Nathan Goldman reports that "defiance on the part of a boy will lead to juvenile court quicker than anything else."[6]

It is hardly necessary to describe the way most gang boys feel about the equity of these dispositions. One only needs to imagine the look on a boy's face when he is told that he is about to spend a year in jail for an offense committed with a friend who was sent home when he promptly confessed.

■ The Situation of Suspicion

. . . Policemen develop indicators of suspicion by a method of pragmatic induction. Past experience leads them to conclude that more crimes are committed in the poorer sections of town than in the wealthier areas, that blacks are more likely to cause public disturbances than whites, and that adolescents in certain areas are a greater source of trouble than other categories of the citizenry. On the basis of these conclusions, the police divide the population and physical territory under surveillance into a variety of categories, make some initial assumptions about the moral character of the people and places in these categories, and then focus attention on those categories of persons and places felt to have the shadiest moral characteristics. As one patrolman states:

> If you know that the bulk of your delinquency problem comes from kids who, say, are from 12 to 14 years of age, when you're out on patrol you are much more likely to be sensitive to the activities of juveniles in this age bracket than older or younger youth. This would be good law enforcement practice. The logic in our case is the same except that our delinquency problem is largely found in the black community and it is these youth toward whom we are sensitized.[7]

According to both gang members and patrolmen, residence in a *neighborhood* is the most general indicator used by the police to select a sample of potential law violators. Many local patrolmen tend to consider all *residents* of "bad" neighborhoods rather weakly committed to whatever moral order they make it their business to enforce, and this transforms most of the people who use the streets in these neighborhoods into good candidates for suspicion. . . .

Although many patrolmen believe that some entire neighborhoods are morally inferior to others, they do not enforce their standards with the same severity in all parts of "poor" neighborhoods. According to gang members, the "territory" contains both safe spots and danger spots. The *danger spots* tend to be public places of business, such as outdoor drive-in hamburger stands or pool halls, where a great many young people in the neighborhood often congregate and where fights and arguments frequently break out. The probability of being defined as suspicious by the police in these places is quite high, and thus physical presence is more of a risk than in other spots. . . .

Although the police seem to create a few "safe spots" within "bad neighborhoods," gang members report that the *boundaries of neighborhoods* are patrolled with great seriousness and severity. The police are seen as very hard on "suspicious looking" adolescents who have strayed from home territory.

> (Do you guys stay mostly at Hunters Point or do you travel into other districts?) If we go someplace, they tell us to go on home. Because every time we go somewhere we mostly go in big groups and they don't want us. One time we was walking on Steiner Street. So a cop drove up and he say, "Hey! Hanky and Panky! Come here!" And he say, "You all out of bounds, get back on the other side of Steiner Street." Steiner Street is supposed to be out of bounds. (What's on the other side of Steiner?) Nothin' but houses.

Gang members interpret the policy of trying to stop them from traveling into other lower-class neighborhoods as a tactic to stop gang wars, and our research on the police suggests that the boys are right. The police do tend to see all sojourns into neighboring territories as potential attacks on rival gangs. . . .

In addition to preventing gang members from traveling into neighborhoods of the same class and ethnic status as their own, the police are equally as stringent about preventing the boys from crossing boundaries into neighborhoods of a higher status or a different color. Although the policy of the police is the same in both cases, they attribute different motives to the boys for wanting to enter higher-status areas. When gang members visit other lower-class neighborhoods, the police suspect them of instigating war; when they are found in middle- or upper-class neighborhoods, the police suspect them of intentions to commit robbery or rape.

> Me and a friend of mine, we went to a girl's house name of, ah, no, I ain't gonna say her name. You might know her. She was stayin' in a white district. So when we was up there, I guess they saw we was [black]. You know, not mostly [black] people stay up there. It was about 10 o'clock 'cause we was leaving the girl's flat. Just walked out the door. Comin' out the door, and here's the curb. We right there by the curb. Gonna go down the block. Cops come around the corner with an orange light. I believe they just sitting there waiting to nab us. They probably seen us go in there. They come and pull us out. Shake us down. All the way down, too, man. They shake us all the way down. And ask us what we doing over here. We tell them we came out to this girl's house. He say, "Where'd you stay?" I say, "Well, you just saw us come out the house 'cause I saw you right around the corner." He say, "Well, she's [black]." So they say, "Some girl got raped up here." Or something like that. Some old lie. Then he say, "Where you live?" I say, "Hunters Point." He say, "I'm gonna give you about 10 or 15 minutes to catch the bus, and if you're not off this corner, if I see you over here, I'll bust you." Just like that. If the police catch you walkin' with a white girl, boy, you in big trouble.

Race thus becomes a particularly salient indicator of "suspiciousness" when blacks or Hispanics are found in white neighborhoods. Being a black per se (or being a black in a black neighborhood) is apparently not as important a criterion of suspiciousness as being a black who is "out of place." "If boys from Hunters Point or Fillmore (black neighborhoods in San Francisco) go in all white districts, the police will stop you and ask you where you from. If you say Fillmore or Hunters Point, they'll take you down to the station, and run checks on you. Any burglaries, any purse snatchings, anything." . . .

In addition to the variety of *places* used to draw samples, however, the police also seem to rely on a number of physical or material *individual attributes*. Certain kinds of clothing, hair, and walking styles seem intrinsically to trigger suspicion. The general description of these styles had best be left to the boys themselves.

> (Why do you think the cops pick you up all the time?) Why do they pick us up? They don't pick everybody up. They just pick up the ones with the hats on and trench coats and conks.[8] If you got long hair and hats on, something like this one, you gonna get picked up. Especially a conk. And the way you

dress. Sometimes, like if you've got on black pants, better not have on no black pants or bends.[9] . . . They think you going to rob somebody. And don't have a head scarf on your head. They'll bust you for having a head scarf.[10] (All right, so they bust you for clothes. That's one thing. Is there anything else?) The way you walk sometimes. If you walk pimp. Don't try to walk pimp. Don't try to be cool. You know. They'll bust you for that. (Could you tell me how you walk pimp?) You know. You just walk cool like. Like you got a boss high.[11] Like you got a fix or something. Last night a cop picked me up for that. He told me I had a bad walk. He say, "You think you're bad." You know.

Finally, the police also use themselves as an instrument for locating suspicious people. Every time an officer makes visible contact with a citizen, the citizen is forced to confront his status in the eyes of the law, and the police soon learn to rely on hostile looks and furtive glances as signs of possible guilt. A policeman's uniform is a potent symbolic device. It sometimes has the power to turn a patrolman into a walking test of moral identity.

It should not be construed from the above discussion that the process of locating a population of potential offenders always proceeds on such slim grounds. There are a variety of "scenes" that constitute much more obvious bases for investigation. However, since policemen rarely stumble on armed men standing over dead bodies, much of their activity involves a subtle and exceedingly tenuous reading of both appearances and events. For example, when dealing with people who possess the ecological and personal indicators of suspiciousness outlined above, patrolmen may turn a screwdriver into a "deadly weapon" and a scratch on the neck into evidence of rape.

> Like you be walking. Just come from working on the car or something. And if you've got a screwdriver or something in your back pocket, hell, they may beat the shit outa you. They talk about you got a burglary tool or you got a deadly weapon on you. Remember the time when we was getting ready to go up to the gym? We came home from school one day. He had some scratches on his neck, and the cop pull over and say, "Turn around!" The cop grabbed him. I didn't say nothing. I was walking. I got to the top of the stairs, and the cop holler "Turn around" at me too. So I turn around. And the cop look at my neck and he say, "Yeah. You too. You got scratches on your neck too." So he took us down to the police station. It seems like some girl way over in another district got raped. And the girl say, "I think they live over at Hunters Point and I scratched one of them on the neck." Some stuff like that.

Gang members are very much aware of their moral status in the eyes of the police. On most occasions, they are likely to know that the police have singled them out for interrogation because of the neighborhood they live in, because of their hair styles, or perhaps because they are temporarily "out of place." They know how the police operate, and they are particularly aware of the role played by judgments about moral character in this methodology. . . .

■ Outcomes

If a juvenile being interrogated in the situation of suspicion refuses to proffer the expected politeness or to use the words that typically denote respect and if no offense has been discovered, a patrolman finds himself in a very awkward position. He cannot arrest the boy for insolence or defiance, since for obvious reasons no charges of this nature exist. The patrolman is thus faced with the choice of three rather unpleasant alternatives.

First, he can back down, thereby allowing his authority to evaporate. If a patrolman allows his authority to escape, however, there is no guarantee that it can be recaptured the next day or any day thereafter. Since patrolmen are structurally locked into the authority role over long periods of uninterrupted time, any fleeting defeat at the hands of a gang member has the prospect of becoming permanent. In a certain sense, then, gang members have a great deal of power. With the mere hint of impiety they can sometimes manage to strip a patrolman symbolically of his authority.

For these reasons, if a patrolman does decide to back down, he must be careful to retreat strategically by withdrawing from the encounter without a public loss of face. This is usually done by communicating to the juvenile that his innocence is fortuitous, that he is the kind of person who could have committed an offense, and that he owes his release to the grouchy good graces of the interrogating officer. If executed artfully, comments such as "keep your nose clean or we'll run you in next time" can pave the way out of a potentially damaging encounter. From the point of view of the boys, of course, this technique simply constitutes an additional insult to moral character.

If a patrolman chooses to press his claims to authority, however, he has only two sanctions available with which to make these claims good. On the one hand, he can attempt an arrest.

> One day we were standing on the corner about three blocks from school and this juvenile officer comes up. He say, "Hey, you boys! Come here!" So everybody else walked over there. But this one stud made like he didn't hear him. So the cop say, "Hey punk! Come here!" So this one stud sorta look up like he hear him and start walking over. But he walking over real slow. So the cop walk over there and grab him by the collar and throw him down and put the handcuffs on him, saying, "When I call you next time, come see what I want!" So everybody was standing by the car, and he say, "All right you black mother fuckers! Get your ass home!" Just like that. And he hand-cuffed the stud and took him to juvenile hall for nothing. Just for standing there looking at him.

On the other hand, there are a variety of curfew, vagrancy, and loitering laws that can also be used to formally or officially prosecute the informal violation of norms governing deportment in the situation of suspicion.

> I got arrested once when we were just riding around in a car. There was a bunch of us in the car. A police car stopped us, and it was about ten after ten

when they stopped us. They started asking us our names and wanted to see our identification. Then they called in on us. So they got through calling in on us, and they just sit in the car and wait 'til the call came through. Then they'd bring back your I.D. and take another one. One at a time. They held me and another boy till last. And when they got to us it was five minutes to eleven. They told everybody they could go home, but they told us it didn't make no sense for us to go home because we was just riding around and we'd never make it home in five minutes. So they busted us both for curfew.

In addition to these laws, a boy can also be charged with "suspicion" of practically anything. When the police use suspicion as a charge, however, they usually try to make the specific offense as serious as possible. This is why the criminal records of many gang boys are often heavily laced with such charges as "suspicion of robbery" and "suspicion of rape."

(Could you tell me some of the things you have been busted for?) Man, I been charged with everything from suspicion of murder to having suspicious friends. I think they call it "associates!" (laughter) They got me on all kinda trash, man, and they only make but one thing stick. (What's that?) A couple of years ago they caught me stone cold sittin' behind the wheel of a '60 Pontiac. I said it belong to my uncle, but it turn out that the name of the registration was O'Shaunessee or O'Something, some old fat name like that. The cop knew there wasn't no bloods [blacks] named things like that.

Gang boys are aware that the police have a very difficult time making these illusory charges stick. They can always succeed in sending a boy to jail for a few hours or a few days, but most of these charges are dismissed at a preliminary hearing on recommendations from probation officers. Moreover, gang members also understand the power of probation officers, and by behaving better in front of these officials they can often embarrass the local authority of patrolmen by having decisions to arrest reversed over their heads. As far as the patrolmen are concerned, then, the boys can make a mockery of false charges as a sanction against impertinence in the situation of suspicion.

Perhaps more important, however, a patrolman's sergeant also knows that most trivial or trumped up charges are likely to be dropped, and thus the police department itself puts a premium on ability to command authority without invoking the sanction of arrest. Unlike the juvenile officer who is judged by his skills at interrogation, a patrolman's capacity to gain respect is his greatest source of pride as well as his area of greatest vulnerability. If he is forced to make too many "weak" arrests, he stands to lose prestige among his peers and superiors on the police force and to suffer humiliation at the hands of his permanent audience of tormentors on the beat.

It is largely for these reasons that many patrolmen prefer to settle a challenge to authority on the spot, an alternative that necessarily poses the prospect of violence. As William Westley has pointed out, in the last analysis the police can always try to "coerce respect."[12]

They don't never beat you in the car. They wait until they get you to the station. And then they beat you when the first shift comes on and they beat you when the second shift comes on. I've seen it happen. I was right there in the next cell. They had a boy. His name was Stan, and they had beat him already as soon as they brought him in. And then when they was changing shifts, you know, the detective came and looked on the paper that say what he was booked for, I think it was robbery or something like that, and they started beating on him again. See, the police are smart. They don't leave no bruises. They'll beat you somewhere where it don't show. That's the main places where they look to hit you at. And if it did show, your word wouldn't be as good as theirs. They can lie too, you know. All they have to say is that you was resisting and that's the only reason they need for doing what they do.

Resisting arrest is the one charge involving violence that seems uniquely designed to deal with improper deportment in the situation of suspicion. A policeman interviewed by Westley suggests that when the challenge to authority is not sufficiently serious to warrant this charge, the police may continue to provoke the suspect until the level of belligerence reaches proportions that legitimate invoking this category of offense.

For example, when you stop a fellow for a routine questioning, say a wise guy, and he starts talking back to you and telling you that you are no good and that sort of thing. You know you can take a man in on a disorderly conduct charge, but you can practically never make it stick. So what you do in a case like this is to egg the guy on until he makes a remark where you can justifiably slap him, and then if he fights back, you can call it resisting arrest.[13]

And from a gang member's point of view:

Another reason why they beat up on you is because they always have the advantage over you. The cop might say, "You done this." And you might say, "I didn't!" And he'll say, "Don't talk back to me or I'll go upside your head!" You know, and then they say they had a right to hit you or arrest you because you were talking back to an officer or resisting arrest, and you were merely trying to explain or tell him that you hadn't done what he said you'd done. One of those kinds of things. Well, that means you in the wrong when you get downtown anyway. You're always in the wrong.

Unlike encounters between gang members and patrolmen, the confrontations between gang members and juvenile officers rarely end in violence. This is because the ability to command respect is not as crucial to a juvenile officer as it is to a patrolman. A juvenile officer is not judged by his capacity to command authority on a beat, and he can therefore leave a situation in which his authority has been challenged without having to face the challenger again the next day. Since he is evaluated largely by his skill at interrogation, he rarely finds himself structurally predisposed to "coerce respect."

■ Notes

1. For a more complete discussion of police discretion in dealing with juveniles, see Irving Piliavin and Scott Briar, "Police Encounters with Juveniles," *American Journal of Sociology* 70 (1964):209–11.

2. The problem of discretion has been formulated and studied by Aaron Cicourel in these terms. See Aaron V. Cicourel, *The Social Organization of Juvenile Justice* (New York: Wiley, 1968).

3. Aaron Cicourel, "Social Class, Family Structure and the Administration of Juvenile Justice," Center for the Study of Law and Society, University of California at Berkeley, Working Paper.

4. The detention facilities administered by the California Youth Authority.

5. Cicourel, *The Social Organization of Juvenile Justice,* op. cit.

6. Nathan Goldman, *The Differential Selection of Juvenile Offenders for Court Appearances,* National Council on Crime and Delinquency (1963), p. 106.

7. Irving Piliavin and Scott Briar, op. cit., p. 212.

8. A "conk" is a hair straightening process used by blacks that is similar in concept to the permanent wave.

9. "Bends" are a form of the bell-bottom trouser which, when worn effectively, all but obscure the shoe from the vision, thus creating the impression that the wearer is moving down the street with an alarmingly irresponsible shuffle.

10. Head scarves (sometimes called "mammy rags") are worn by blacks around the forehead to keep "conk jobs" in place.

11. "Boss" is a synonym for "good."

12. The above analysis of why policemen retaliate when the legitimacy of their authority is challenged differs somewhat from Westley's analysis of why a large percentage of the policemen he studied "believed that it was legitimate to use violence to coerce respect." Westley argues that disrespectful behavior constitutes a threat to the already low "occupational status" of policemen and therefore comes as a blow to their self-esteem. Westley's hypothesis would suggest, however, that those policemen who accepted their low occupational status would therefore allow their authority to be challenged. Although Westley's variables no doubt affect the behavior of patrolmen, there also seems to be more at stake than status as a workman when claims to authority are ignored. In a sense the patrolman whose authority has been successfully called into question has already abdicated a sizable chunk of his honor as well as his job. See William A. Westley, "Violence and the Police," *American Journal of Sociology* 59 (1953):34–41.

13. Ibid., p. 39.

23

Judging Delinquents

Robert M. Emerson

Robert Emerson's ethnography highlights the ways in which juvenile court personnel attempt to distinguish cases of genuine "trouble" that warrant official intervention from cases that do not warrant "doing something" about the youths who come to their attention. Emerson examines the ways in which official assessments of youths' moral character and the dynamics of denunciations and counterdenunciations influence juvenile court outcomes.

■ "Trouble"

. . . [Y]ouths brought before the juvenile court generally represent "trouble" for some caretaking or control institution. In this sense every delinquent is "trouble" for someone, . . . [and] every delinquency complaint represents a plea that the court "do something" to remedy or alleviate that "trouble." Hence, one fundamental set of problems and demands confronting the juvenile court arises from the pressures and expectations of those initiating court action that "something be done." In this sense the court must work out practical solutions to cases that satisfy, or at least take some cognizance of, the concerns of complainants.

But not all cases represent "trouble" in the eyes of the court; the court does not automatically accept the contentions of complainants. Rather the court makes an independent assessment of "trouble" and of the necessity of "doing something," an assessment that reflects its own organizational priorities and "problem relevances" (Schutz 1964:235).

These distinctive problem relevances turn on two fundamental features of the court situation. First, the time, personnel, and resources available for dealing with delinquency cases are severely limited. Consequently, court operations are subject to strict economy in the uses of resources and personnel. Second, court personnel have a higher tolerance of "delinquency" than most

---

Excerpt from *Judging Delinquents,* by Robert M. Emerson (Aldine, 1969). Reprinted by permission of the author.

complainants. Routinely encountering a wide range of youthful misconduct, the court develops a relatively narrow definition of delinquency. This definition generally requires quite frequent and serious manifestations of disturbing conduct before a youth will be categorized as "really delinquent." As a result, court workers often feel that complainants' "troubles" are exaggerated and that the kinds of official responses they seek are inappropriately drastic.

The court thus comes to follow a principle of conservatism in case management. This in turn requires it to separate "serious" cases where there is "real" trouble, from those where the "trouble" is "mild" or "normal," requiring little attention.[1]

The search for "real" trouble emerges as a recurring theme throughout court staff's explanations of their work. For example, the judge described his orientation toward the conduct of formal hearings in the following terms: "We look for tip-offs that *something is really wrong.* We get some tip-offs just from the face-sheet; truancy, school attendance, conduct, and effort marks. . . . *If you get something wrong there, you know there's trouble.* When you get truancy or bad conduct plus delinquency, there's definitely something wrong [emphasis added]."

Similarly, a woman probation officer in talking about girl shoplifting cases said:

> Shoplifters are the simplest and most promising kind of girls I have. Often they come from good families. But there may also be *"a very serious problem"* involved. Sometimes while taking the face-sheet you can see how "serious" it is. But usually these cases are continued without a finding in order to determine if there is any "serious problem." . . . Then again, some are dealt with more severely, "depending on the girl's attitude." For some of the cases are more *"severe"* and have to be dealt with accordingly. [emphasis added]

By this sifting process the court begins to allocate its time, efforts, and resources among delinquency cases. On the one hand, the court locates cases where "something has to be done," where special handling is required; on the other hand, it finds cases which can be "let go." The great majority of the court's cases are of the latter sort—"untroubled"—and require staff to devote only a minimum of time and effort to overseeing and changing the life circumstances of the delinquent. A woman probation officer, for example, commented on the unserious nature of girl shoplifters by noting: "I don't see them any more [after their hearing]." On the other hand, in cases where "trouble" is found, where "something wrong" is noted, the court more actively intervenes, concentrating its efforts and resources for change. Extraordinary measures are taken in managing these cases, and much effort is devoted to working out some adequate remedy.

In general, a case brought to juvenile court under a definition of "trouble" has three possible outcomes. First, complainant and court definitions of trouble may more or less coincide; the court then seeks some satisfactory remedy for the case. Second, complainant and court definitions of trouble may diverge. Usually this disparity reflects a judgment of a lesser degree of trouble by the court, for the reasons discussed previously. In this situation the court initially tries to convince the complainant that it has no power to do anything or that nothing need be done. This may require special efforts to satisfy the complainant, to persuade him not to press for special action, or to induce him to accept some less drastic solution than he originally envisioned.[2]

Finally, the court may feel there is no trouble, but be unable to "cool out" the complainant. In this situation the court may be moved to "do something" even though it feels such action is not really necessary. A course of events leading to such an outcome occurred in the following case:

> A 16-year-old black boy was brought to court for assaulting a fire chief. The previous night the boy's best friend had been knifed during a fight and a fire department "ambulet" called to the scene. When the fire chief directing the operation had refused to let the defendant accompany his critically wounded friend to the hospital in the ambulance, the youth had punched him. As a result, the chief had insisted that the police take out the assault complaint.
>
> In court, a social-worker sponsor of the youth reported that the police had expected the case to be settled with an apology by the boy, but that the chief had refused to drop his complaint. The police officer acting as prosecutor outlined the alleged facts briefly, requested a two-week continuance before the hearing, and concluded by stating, "the boy came here on his own volition this morning," suggesting that bail would not be required. Outside the courtroom, in discussing this continuance with me, the police officer noted: "We let it cool. Let the chief cool off."
>
> When the hearing was finally held, the judge placed the youth on a suspended sentence after finding him delinquent on the assault complaint. At the same time, the judge complemented this relatively severe judgment with special efforts to soothe the fire chief's indignation.

As this case suggests, the strength of a complainant's demands to "do something" may constitute a crucial factor in the court's identification of "trouble." Strong demands create a presumption that "something has to be done" and demonstrate the existence of behavior intolerable to someone with responsibility for controlling the delinquent. . . .

■ The Relevance of Moral Character

In seeking practical solutions to cases felt to involve "trouble," the juvenile court is largely guided by its judgments and inferences regarding the nature of the delinquent actor involved. That is, the solution to the problem—what can and what must we do with this case?—generally depends on the answer to: what kind of youth are we dealing with here? This involves a process of inquiry into the youth's *moral character.* . . .

If the court decides that there is no trouble in a case, it assumes that the delinquent involved is *normal* in character. If trouble is located, however, character is rendered *problematic*. This initiates more intensive court involvement with the case, as well as more intensive concern with accounting for the youth's behavior. Upon examination, it may be felt that the delinquent is really possessed of normal character despite indications of trouble. As a result, assessments of normal character may occur at either initial or subsequent stages of the court sorting process.

Similarly, damaged character may not be identified on first contact but begin to "emerge" in subsequent encounters. For example, a case may be treated as routine until the delinquent appears in court for a second or third time within a period of several months. Such reappearances cast doubt on the previously assumed normality of character. Initial judgments may fall before a variety of factors. At almost any point in a court career, doubts cast on character may be minimized or dismissed or, alternatively, confirmed and explained as expressions of some discredited kind of moral character. The court builds up experience with an individual delinquent and accumulates a biographical file on him so that its assessments of his character become stable. Yet this view is nearly always open to some modification: while an assessment of poor character is not easily removed, it may at least be reinterpreted as of a different kind. . . .

■ A Note on Total Denunciation

Consideration of the structural features of total denunciation provides additional insight into the processes of establishing moral character in the juvenile court. For a successful total denunciation must transcend routine denunciation by *foreclosing* all possible defenses and by *neutralizing* all possible sources of support.

Foreclosure of defenses available to the delinquent . . . has two related elements. First, in order to discredit moral character totally, it must be clearly demonstrated that the denounced delinquent has been given a great many "breaks" or "chances" which he has, however, rejected and spoiled. Such a demonstration is necessary to prove that the case is "hopeless," that the delinquent youth's character is so ruined as to preclude any possibility of reform. The role of the disregarded "chance" is clearly seen in the following case, where a probation officer convinces both judge and public defender to go along with his punitive recommendation by proving that the youth has received chances not even officially reported:

> Two escapees from reform school were brought into court on a series of new
> complaints taken out by the police. Public defender argued that these com-
> plaints should be dismissed and the boys simply returned to the school. The
> probation officer, however, argued strongly that the boys should be found de-
> linquent on the new complaints (this would require reconsideration of their

cases by the Youth Correction Authority, perhaps leading to an extension of their commitment). The probation officer described how one of his colleagues had worked hard on one of these cases earlier, giving the boy a great many chances, none of which did any good. The judge accepted the probation officer's recommendation.

After the hearing, the public defender admitted that he felt the probation officer had been right, acknowledging the validity of his picture of the character of this boy: "I did not realize he was such a bastard. . . . Apparently one of the probation officers had given him a lot of breaks. He had him on so many cases that he should be shot."

Second, it must be made to appear that the delinquent himself "messed up" the chances that he had been given. It should be established not only that the youth misbehaved on numerous occasions, but also that he did so in full knowledge of the possible consequences and with no valid excuse or extenuating circumstances. In this way, responsibility or "fault" for the imminent incarceration must fall completely on the denounced delinquent. Any official contribution to the youth's "messing up" (e.g., an official's intolerance) must be glossed over so that the delinquent bears total blame.

Court probation is in fact constructed so that responsibility for "messing up," should it occur, unavoidably falls on the delinquent. . . . Probationers are constantly warned that they will be committed if there is any further misconduct, and they are given a number of "breaks" on this condition. As one probation officer commented about a youth who had been "given a break" by the judge: "This way, if he gets committed, he knows he has it coming." Furthermore, the constant warnings and lectures against getting into trouble that occur throughout probation tend to undermine in advance the possibility of defending subsequent misbehavior. For example, it is difficult for a youth to excuse a new offense as the product of peer group influence when he has continually been warned to stay away from "bad friends."

[Another] key element in a successful total denunciation is the neutralization of all possible sources of support. There are several components in this neutralization. First, the assessment of discredited and "hopeless" character must be made to appear as a general consensus among all those concerned in the case. A delinquent without a spokesman—with no one to put in a good word for him—stands in a fundamentally discredited position.

Here the stance taken by the delinquent's lawyer, normally a public defender, becomes crucial. A vigorous defense and pitch by a lawyer often might dispel the appearance of consensus and weaken the denunciation. This occurs very rarely, however, because of court cooptation of the public defender. Working closely with the probation staff, the public defender comes to share their values and indexes of success and failure in delinquency cases. Consequently, he will generally concur with the court's highly negative assessments of delinquent moral character. As a public defender noted in response to a question about how he usually handled his cases in the juvenile court:

> Generally I would find the probation officer handling the case and ask him: "What do you have on this kid? How bad is he?" He'll say: "Oh, he's bad!" Then he opens the probation folder to me, and I'll see he's got quite a record. Then I'll ask him, "What are you going to recommend?" He'll say, "Give him another chance. Or probation. Or we've got to put him away."
>
> But probation officers don't make this last recommendation lightly. Generally they will try to find a parent in the home, "someone who can keep him under control, someone who can watch him." But if the probation officer has given the kid a number of chances, it is a different story: "He's giving the kid chances and he keeps screwing up. . . . [Commitment will then be recommended.] And I say the kid deserves it. Before a kid goes away he's really got to be obnoxious—he will deserve it."

Adoption of probation standards for assessing delinquent character becomes crucial in total denunciation. The public defender is then in the position of arguing on behalf of a youth whose moral character has been totally discredited in his eyes and who he feels should indeed be committed. His courtroom defense will generally reflect this assessment. He will make only the most perfunctory motions of arguing that the delinquent be let off, and he will do so in a way that communicates an utter lack of conviction that this is a desirable course of action. Or, as in the following case, he will not even go through the motions of making a defense but will explicitly concur with the recommended incarceration and the grounds on which it rests:

> A policeman told of finding an 11-year-old black boy in a laundry where a coin box had been looted. The officer reported that the boy had admitted committing the offense. Public defender waived cross-examination, and the judge found the youth delinquent.
>
> Probation officer then delivered a rather lengthy report on the case. The boy had been sent to the Boys' Training Program and, while no great trouble, did not attend regularly. He had also recently been transferred to the Harris School and had been in trouble there. Probation officer recommended that the prior suspended sentence be revoked and the boy committed to the Youth Correction Authority.
>
> Judge then asked the public defender if he had anything he wanted to say. Public defender: "The record more or less speaks for itself. He does not seem to have taken advantage of the opportunities the court has given him to straighten out." Then, after briefly reconferring with the probation officer, the judge ordered the commitment. Public defender waived the right of appeal.

Second, the denouncer must establish that in "messing up" and not taking advantage of the chances provided him, the denounced has created a situation in which there is *no other alternative open* but commitment to the Youth Correction Authority. In some cases, this may involve showing that the youth is so dangerous that commitment to the Authority is the only effective way he can be restrained; in others, demonstration that by his misbehavior the youth has completely destroyed all possible placements, including the one he has been in. It is only by dramatically showing in these ways that "there is nothing we can do with him" that the proposed commitment can be made to appear as an inevitable and objective necessity.

The fact that many total denunciations concentrate on proving that nothing else can be done with the case reflects the court's basic resistance to unwarrantable agency attempts to "dump" undesirable cases onto them for incarceration. The court feels that most of these institutions are too ready to give up on cases that from the court's point of view are still salvageable. To overcome this suspiciousness, the denouncer must not only present the youth's character as essentially corrupt and "hopeless," but also show that every effort has been made to work with him and every possible opportunity afforded him. The denouncer, in other words, must take pains to avoid appearing to be merely getting rid of a difficult and troublesome case simply to make his own work easier. This requires showing both that persistent efforts have been made to work with the case and that at the present time even extraordinary efforts cannot come up with anything as an alternative to incarceration.

A final aspect of demonstrating that there is no viable alternative to incarceration involves isolating the denounced delinquent from any kind of reputable sponsorship. In the usual case, where a parent acts as sponsor, successful total denunciation requires either that the parent be induced to denounce the youth and declare him fit only for incarceration or that the parent be discredited. In other cases, where the sponsor is a parental substitute, this sponsor must similarly be led to denounce the youth or be discredited. In this way, for example, sponsors who seek too aggressively to save delinquents considered overripe for commitment by other officials may encounter attacks on their motives, wisdom, or general moral character. This not only undermines the viability of any defense of character made by the sponsor, but also effectively isolates the delinquent by showing the unsuitability of his sponsorship as an alternative to commitment. . . .

■ Counter-Denunciation

As noted earlier, the courtroom proceeding routinely comes to involve a denunciation of the accused delinquent in the course of a confrontation between him and his accusers. This fact creates the conditions for the use of *counter-denunciation* as a defensive strategy. This strategy seeks to undermine the discrediting implications of the accusation by attacking the actions, motives and/or character of one's accusers.

The underlying phenomenon in counter-denunciation has been noted in a number of other contexts. McCorkle and Korn, for example, have analyzed the concept of the "rejection of the rejectors" as a defensive reaction to imprisonment (1964:520). Similarly, Sykes and Matza explain the "condemnation of the condemners" in the process of neutralization in the following terms: "The delinquent shifts the focus of attention from his own deviant acts to the motives and behaviors of those who disapprove of his violations" (1957:668). The concept of counter-denunciation, in contrast, focuses on the communicative work which accomplishes this shift of attention. Furthermore, it gains relevance as a defense against attempted character discrediting. Use of this strategy, however, is extremely risky in the court setting. While counter-denunciation may appear to the delinquent as a "natural" defense as he perceives the circumstances of his case, it tends to challenge fundamental court commitments and hence, even when handled with extreme care, often only confirms the denunciation.

It is striking that counter-denunciation has the greatest likelihood of success in cases where the complainant or denouncer lacks official stature or where the initiative rests predominantly with private parties who have clearly forced official action. Under these circumstances the wrongful quality of the offense can be greatly reduced if not wholly eliminated by showing that the initiator of the complaint was at least partially to blame for the illegal act. For example:

> A 16-year-old black boy, Johnny Haskin, was charged with assault and battery on two teenaged girls who lived near his family in a public housing project. Although a juvenile officer brought the case into court, he was clearly acting on the initiative of the two girls and their mother, for he had had no direct contact with the incident and did not testify about it. He simply put the two girls on the stand and let them tell about what happened. This was fairly confused, but eventually it appeared that Johnny . . . had been slapping the younger sister in the hall of the project when the older girl had pulled him off. He had then threatened her with a knife. The girls admitted that there had been fighting in the hall for some time, and that they had been involved, but put the blame on Johnny for starting it. Mrs. Haskin, however, spoke up from the back of the room, and told about a gang of boys coming around to get her son (apparently justifying Johnny's carrying a knife). And Johnny himself denied that he had started the fighting, claiming that the younger girl had hit him with a bat and threatened him first.
>
> Judge then lectured both families for fighting, and placed Johnny on probation for nine months, despite a rather long prior record.

In this case, by establishing that the girls had also been fighting, the boy was at least partially exonerated. The success of this strategy is seen in the fact that the judge lectured both families, and then gave the boy what was a mild sentence in light of his prior court record.

Similarly, the possibility of discrediting the victim, thereby invalidating the complaint, becomes apparent in the following "rape" case:

> Two black boys, ages 12 and 13, had admitted forcing "relations" on a 12-year-old girl in a schoolyard, the police reported. After a full report on the incidents surrounding the offense, the judge asked the policemen: "What kind of girl is she?" Officer: "I checked with Reverend Frost [the girl's minister

and the person instrumental in reporting this incident] and he said she was a good girl."

As the judge's query implies, the reprehensibility of this act can only be determined in relation to the assessed character of the girl victim. Had the police or the accused brought up evidence of a bad reputation or incidents suggesting "loose" or "promiscuous" behavior, the force of the complaint would have been undermined.

In the above cases, successful counter-denunciation of the complainants would undermine the moral basis of their involvement in the incident, thereby discrediting their grounds for initiating the complaint. But this merely shifts part of the responsibility for an offense onto the complaining party and does not affect the wrongful nature of the act per se. Thus, by denouncing the general character of the complainant and the nature of his involvement in the offense, the accused does not so much clear himself as diminish his guilt. If the offense involved is serious enough and the culpability of the complainant not directly related to the offense, therefore, this strategy may have little impact.

For example, in [a] homosexuality-tinged case of car theft, . . . both the accused and his father tried to support their contention that the car owner was lying by pointing to his discredited character. But the "victim's" homosexuality had no real connection with the act of stealing the car nor with the threatened physical violence it entailed, and hence did not affect the judge's evaluation of the act and of the delinquent's character. Under these circumstances, the soiled nature of the victim simply was not considered sufficiently extenuating to dissolve the reprehensibility of the act.[3]

In general, then, a successful counter-denunciation must discredit not only the general character of the denouncer but also his immediate purpose or motive in making the complaint. Only in this way can the counter-denunciation cut the ground out from under the wrongfulness of the alleged offense. For example:

> An 11-year-old black boy was charged with wantonly damaging the car of an older black man, Frankie Williams, with a BB gun. With the boy was his mother, a respectably dressed woman, a white lawyer, and a white couple who served as character witnesses.
>
> A juvenile officer brought the case in and then called Mr. Williams up to testify. The witness told of going outside to shovel his car out of the snow several weeks previously and finding his windshield damaged in several places. He had noticed the boy at this time leaning out of the window of his house with a BB gun. Lawyer then cross-examined, getting Williams to admit that he had been bickering with the family for some time, and that a year before the mother had accused him of swearing at her son and had tried to get a court complaint against him. (Judge ruled this irrelevant after Williams had acknowledged it.) Williams seemed flustered, and grew angry under the questioning, claiming that because of the boy's shooting he would not be able to get an inspection sticker for his car.

Juvenile officer then told judge that although he had not investigated the case, his partner reported that the marks on the windshield were not consistent with a BB gun. Williams had also admitted that he had not looked for any BB pellets. On the basis of this evidence, the judge found the boy not delinquent. He then severely warned all parties in the case: "I'm going to tell you I do not want any more contests between these two families. Do you understand?"

Here, by showing that the complainant had both a selfish motive for complaining about his damaged windshield (to help get it repaired) and a grudge against the defendant and his family, as well as bringing out the lack of concrete evidence to substantiate the charge, the lawyer was able to get the complaint totally dismissed.

Similarly, the circumstances of the following case were such as to suggest initially that complaints had been taken out to intimidate or at least get even with boys against whom there was some resentment:

Two teenaged black boys were brought to court for breaking windows. Case was continued, and policeman gave the following account of what had happened. Several weeks previously there had been a disturbance and some windows broken in a middle class section of the city. There were six boys apparently involved, including these two. One of the occupants of the home had come out and begun shooting at the boys, who were on the other side of the street, "allegedly to protect his property." One of these two boys had been hit in the leg, and another man (apparently a passerby) had also been hit. The shooter, named Barr, "is now up before the grand jury" for this, but meanwhile had taken out complaints against these two boys. A private attorney representing the two accused then took over, explaining how his clients had just been summoned to testify against Barr. Lawyer next questioned the cop about why complaints had been brought only against these two of the six boys, including the one who had been shot, and the other who had been a witness to the shooting. Cop replied that the other boys had been investigated, but there was nothing against them.

Here the boys' lawyer successfully established that the complaints against his clients had been initiated by the defendant in a related criminal action, suggesting an attempt to discredit in advance their testimony against him. The judge responded by continuing the case, releasing both boys to the custody of their parents, even though one had a long record.

Finally, successful counter-denunciation requires that the denounced provide a convincing account for what he claims is an illegitimate accusation. The court will reject any implication that one person will gratuitously accuse another of something he has not done. The youth in the following case can provide this kind of account:

Five young boys were charged with vandalism and with starting a fire in a public school. Juvenile officer explained that he had investigated the incident with the school principal, getting two of the boys to admit their part in the vandalism. These two boys had implicated the other three, all of whom denied the charge.

The judge then took over the questioning, trying to determine whether the three accused had in fact been in the school. In this he leaned heavily on finding out why the first two boys should lie. One of the accused, Ralph Kent, defended himself by saying he had not been at the school and did not know the boy who had named him. Judge asked how this boy had then been able to identify him. Kent replied that he had been a monitor at school, and one of his accusers might have seen him there. And he used to take the other accuser to the basement [lavatory] because the teacher would not trust him alone for fear he would leave the school.

The two other boys continued to deny any involvement in the incident, but could provide no reason why they should be accused unjustly. The judge told them he felt they were lying, and asked several times: "Can you give me a good reason why these boys would put you in it?" Finally he pointed toward Kent and commented: "He's the only one I'm convinced wasn't there." He then asked Kent several questions about what he did as a monitor. When it came to dispositions, Kent was continued without a finding while the four other boys were found delinquent.

In this situation an accused delinquent was able to establish his own reputable character in school (later confirmed by the probation report on his school record), the discredited character of one of his accusers, and a probable motive for their denunciation of him (resentment toward his privileges and position in school) in a few brief sentences. It should be noted, however, that this successful counter-denunciation was undoubtedly facilitated by the fact that denouncers and denounced were peers. It is incomparably more difficult for a youth to establish any acceptable reason why an adult should want to accuse and discredit him wrongfully.

Counter-denunciation occurs most routinely with offenses arising out of the family situation and involving complaints initiated by parents against their own children. Here again it is possible for the child to cast doubt on the parents' motives in taking court action, and on the parents' general character:

A black woman with a strong West Indian accent had brought an incorrigible child complaint against her 16-year-old daughter. The mother reported: "She never says anything to me, only to ask, 'Gimme car fare, gimme lunch money.' . . . As for the respect she gave me, I don't think I have to tolerate her!" The daughter countered that her mother never let her do anything, and simply made things unbearable for her around the house. She went out nights, as her mother claimed, but only to go over to a girlfriend's house to sleep.

This case was continued for several months, during which time a probation officer worked with the girl and the court clinic saw mother and daughter. The psychiatrist there felt that the mother was "very angry and cold." Eventually an arrangement was made to let the girl move in with an older sister.

In this case the daughter was effectively able to blame her mother and her intolerance for the troubled situation in the home. But in addition, counter-denunciation may also shift the focus of the court inquiry from the misconduct charged to the youth onto incidents involving the parents. This shift of attention facilitated the successful counter-denunciation in the following case.

> A 16-year-old white girl from a town some distance from the city was charged with shoplifting. But as the incident was described by the police, it became clear that this offense had occurred because the girl had run away from home and needed clean clothes. Police related what the girl had said about running away: She had been babysitting at home and was visited by her boyfriend, who had been forbidden in the house. Her father had come home, discovered this, and beaten her with a strap. (The girl's face still appeared somewhat battered with a large black-and-blue mark on one cheek, although the court session occurred at least three days after the beating.) She had run away that night.
>
> The rest of the hearing centered not on the theft but on the running away and the incident which precipitated it. After the police evidence, the judge asked the girl: "How did you get that mark on your face?" Girl: "My father hit me." Judge: "With his fist?" Girl (hesitating): "Yes, it must have been his fist." Later in the proceeding, the judge asked the girl specifically why she had run away. She emphasized that she had not tried to hide anything; the kids had been up until eleven and the boy had left his bike out front. "I didn't try to hide it. I told them he'd been there."
>
> With this her father rose to defend himself, arguing with some agitation: "... His clothes were loose. Her clothes were loose. Her bra was on the floor. ... She was not punished for the boy being in the house, but for what she did." Girl (turning toward her father): "What about my eye?" Father: "She got that when she fell out of the bed (angrily, but directed toward the judge)." Girl (just as angrily): "What about the black and blue marks?" Father: "Those must have been from the strap."

The relatively high probability of successful counter-denunciation in cases arising from family situations points up the most critical contingency in the use of this protective strategy, the choice of an appropriate object. Denouncers with close and permanent relations with the denounced are particularly vulnerable to counter-denunciation, as the accusation is apt to rest solely on their word and illegitimate motives for the denunciation may be readily apparent. But again, where relations between the two parties are more distant, counter-denunciation has more chance of success where the denouncer is of more or less equivalent status with the denounced. Thus, the judge can be easily convinced that a schoolmate might unjustly accuse one from jealousy, but will reject any contention that an adult woman would lie about an attempted purse-snatching incident.

While a denounced youth has a fair chance of successfully discrediting a complainant of his own age, and some chance where the complainant is a family member, counter-denunciations directed against officials, particularly against the most frequent complainants in the juvenile court, the police, almost inevitably fail. In fact, to attempt to counterattack the police, and to a lesser extent, other officials, is to risk fundamentally discrediting moral character, for the court recoils against all attacks on the moral authority of any part of the official legal system.

One reflection of this is the court's routine refusal to acknowledge complaints of *unfair* treatment at the hands of the police. On occasion, for example, parents complain that their children were arrested and brought to court while others involved in the incident were not. Judges regularly refuse to inquire into such practices:

> Two young Puerto Rican boys were charged with shooting a BB gun. After police testimony, their mother said something in Spanish, and their priest-translator explained to the judge: "What they've been asking all morning is why they did not bring the other two boys." The judge replied: "I can only deal with those cases that are before me. I can't go beyond that and ask about these other boys that are not here."

Similarly, in this same case the judge refused to inquire into a complaint of police brutality when the mother complained that one boy had been hit on the head, saying: "The question of whether he was injured is not the question for me right now."

But beyond this, the court will often go to great lengths to protect and defend the public character of the police when it is attacked during a formal proceeding. To accuse a policeman of acting for personal motives, or of dishonesty in the course of his duties, not only brings immediate sanctions from the court but also tends to discredit basically the character of the delinquent accuser. Accusations of this nature threaten the basic ceremonial order of the court proceeding and hence the legitimacy of the legal order itself.

■ Notes

1. Cavan (1966) employs the concept "normal trouble" to describe aspects of barroom behavior. "Normal trouble" involves "improper activities that are frequent enough to be simply shrugged off or ignored" and hence constitutes "a taken-for-granted aspect of the public drinking place" (p. 18). Cases where the juvenile court feels no special intervention is required involve "normal trouble" in this sense.

2. On occasion, however, the court may find itself in the position of pushing a more severe definition of "trouble" and a more drastic course of action upon some other party. This occurs when the court diagnoses "trouble" where the complainant feels there is none and, more frequently, when parents deny serious trouble in the case of their child.

3. Note, however, that even though this denunciation succeeded, the denouncer suffered both discrediting and penalty. Immediately after the delinquency case had been decided the police took out a complaint for "contributing to the delinquency of a minor" against him, based on his admitted homosexual activities with the youth. This "contributing" case was brought before the juvenile court later that same morning, complainant and accused changed places, and the first denouncer was found guilty, primarily from what he had revealed about his behavior earlier in establishing the delinquency complaint.

■ References

Cavan, Sherri. 1966. *Liquor License: An Ethnography of Bar Behavior.* Chicago: Aldine.

McCorkle, Lloyd W. & Richard Korn. 1964. "Resocialization Within Walls." In D. Dressler (ed.), *Readings in Criminology and Penology.* New York: Columbia University Press.

Schutz, Alfred. 1964. *Collected Papers, Vol. II: Studies in Social Theory.* Edited by M. Natanson. The Hague: Martinus Nijhoff.

Sykes, Gresham M. & David Matza. 1957. "Techniques of Neutralization: A Theory of Delinquency." *American Sociological Review* 22:664–70.

24

A Comparative Analysis of Organizational Structure and Inmate Subcultures in Institutions for Juvenile Offenders

Barry C. Feld

Barry Feld evaluates different organizational structures and treatment modalities that are used in juvenile correctional institutions and their effect on both staff and inmates. In particular, Feld's research demonstrates that correctional institutions that emphasize rehabilitative treatment over custody, especially those that utilize group-oriented strategies, are better able to reduce the violence that all too often permeates inmate institutional subcultures.

THE PENOLOGICAL DEBATE OVER THE ORIGINS, PROCESSES, AND CHARacteristics of inmate subcultures in correctional facilities has attributed the qualities of subcultures either to features of the formal organization or to preimprisonment characteristics of the incarcerated offenders.[1] Observers of adult and juvenile correctional facilities confirm the emergence of inmate subcultures within institutions, and most studies of prison cultures document their oppositional qualities, with the hostility and antagonism between inmates and staff subsumed in an "inmate code."[2]

The two competing explanations of the inmate social system are commonly referred to as the "indigenous origins" model and the "direct importation" model.[3] The former provides a functionalist explanation that relates the values and roles of the subculture to the inmates' responses to problems of adjustment posed by institutional deprivations and conditions of confinement[4] [the functionalist explanation suggests that the inmate subculture is a functional,

"A Comparative Analysis of Organizational Structure and Inmate Subcultures in Institutions for Juvenile Offenders," *Crime and Delinquency* 27, no. 3 (1981): 336–363. Reprinted by permission of Sage Publications, Inc.

or practical, adaptation to the deprivations of prison life]. Accordingly, the formal organization of the prison shapes the informal inmate social system. While earlier studies of adult maximum-security prisons described a monolithic inmate culture of collective opposition to staff values and goals,[5] more recent studies suggest that a modification of organizational structure in pursuit of treatment goals results in considerably greater variability in the inmate social system and the processes of prisonization.[6]

An alternative interpretation attributes the normative order of adult prisons to the identities, roles, and values held by the inmates before incarceration.[7] Accordingly, inmates' personal characteristics shape the subculture, and in a population of incarcerated offenders an oppositional, criminal value system predominates. Differences in social characteristics such as sex, race, or criminal involvement before incarceration influence both the subculture's qualities and any individual inmate's adaptations to it.[8]

■ Inmate Violence in Institutions

The prevalence of inmate violence and its significance for stratification, role differentiation, and subcultural processes represent a recurring theme.[9] However, the relationships between organizational variables, inmate violence, and other characteristics of the subculture have not been adequately explored.

Physical aggression, verbal abuse, or psychological intimidation can be used to create or reestablish relationships of domination and submission within the subculture.[10] Many maxims of the inmate code are attempts to regulate violence and exploitation among inmates, and many of the "argot" roles differentiate inmates on the basis of their use of or response to aggression.[11] For individual inmates, many of the "pains of imprisonment"—material deprivations, sexual isolation, and threats to status, self esteem, and personal security—cited in the functional explanations of subcultures can be alleviated by the use of violence. While imprisonment imposes deprivations, violence and exploitation provide at least some inmates with a potential solution, albeit at the expense of other inmates.[12]

The prevalence of inmate violence also reflects characteristics of the incarcerated. Many adult and juvenile inmates are drawn from social backgrounds or cultures that emphasize toughness, manliness, and the protection of one's own physical integrity.[13] Preincarceration experiences equip in different ways inmates from diverse social, economic, criminal, racial, or sexual backgrounds to participate in the violent subcultures within some institutions.[14] Thus, a predisposition to violence among the inmate subculture also reflects influences of cultural importation which organizational features may aggravate or mitigate.

Neither functionalist nor importation explanations alone adequately explain the characteristics of the inmate subculture or an inmate's adaptations to it. The functionalist model does not account for the influence of pre- and postimprisonment variables on inmates' adaptations, while the importation model does not fully explicate the connections between preprison characteristics and the subcultures that arise within institutions that are not custodial or punitive. Although some recent research attempts to integrate the two perspectives by identifying the ways in which preprison characteristics influence inmates' adaptations to adjustment problems created by the organization,[15] most subculture studies suffer from the common shortcoming of focusing on prisonization within only a single institution. In contrast, a comparison of organizations would permit a fuller exploration of the relationships between formal organizational structure and the ensuing inmate culture, as well as of the influence of preprison characteristics on the adaptations of inmates in diverse settings.[16] Controlling for the effects of preincarceration characteristics on inmates' perceptions and adaptations, this study presents a comparative analysis of the ways in which variations in organizational goals and intervention strategies in institutions for juvenile offenders produce differences in the informal inmate social system.

Organizational features affect the inmate subculture and the prevalence of inmate violence both by creating incentives for inmates to resort to violence and by providing inmates with opportunities to use violence. Organizational variations in the nature and extent of deprivations may motivate inmates in different ways to exploit others. Various organizational control strategies differ in the degree to which they provide an environment conducive to the use of violence to relieve these deprivations. The deprivations and control strategies also influence many other aspects of the subculture. This comparative analysis examines the variations in organizational goals, staff intervention strategies, and social control practices that influence the levels of violence and the structure of the inmate social system.

■ Correctional Typology

There are several descriptions of the organizational variations in juvenile and adult correctional facilities that can be used as tools to classify systematically and compare the relationships between organizational structure and inmate subculture.[17] A common classification distinguishes juvenile correctional organizations on the basis of their custody or treatment goals,[18] distinguishing differences in goals on the basis of the relative emphases staff place on custody and containment, and on vocational and academic education versus clinical or group treatment.[19] The intervention strategies used to achieve either custodial or therapeutic goals range from group-oriented practices to those more attuned to individuals' characteristics.[20] Group-oriented strategies reflect efforts to change or control an inmate through the group of which he is a member, while individualized methods of intervention focus more directly on the person, without comparable manipulation of the social environment.

Organizational goals—custody or treatment—and strategies of change—group or individual—may vary independently; thus, four different types of correctional organizations may be distinguished on the basis of both their correctional goals and the means used to attain those goals (see Figure 24.1).

Every juvenile correctional institution confronts the same necessity to explain both what its clients' problems are and how the clients should be rehabilitated.[21] The answers to the questions of cause and cure in turn determine the organizational goals and the intervention strategies and social control practices required to achieve them. The typology in Figure 24.1 illustrates four different kinds of correctional solutions to the problems of juvenile offenders. It also suggests several interrelated organizational variables: a staff ideology defining inmates and their needs, organizational goals serving those needs, intervention strategies implemented through programs and social control practices, and the structure of relationships between inmates and staff.

A degree of internal consistency among these organizational variables is necessary. Methods of intervention and social control practices must be complementary, since efforts to ensure compliance that alienate the inmate are incompatible with change strategies requiring commitment on the part of that inmate.[22] Compliance strategies and programs will vary with the correctional goals and

Figure 24.1 Correctional Typology

Organizational Goals

	Custody	Treatment
Organizational Means		
Group-Oriented Intervention Strategy	Group Custody Custodial[a] Obedience/Conformity[b] Protective custody[c]	Group Treatment Group treatment[a] Treatment[b] Therapeutic community[c]
Individual-Oriented Intervention Strategy	Individual Custody Educational[a] Reeducation I/ Development[b] Protective custody[c]	Individual Treatment Psychotherapeutic[a] Treatment[b,c]

Notes: a. Organization corresponding to typology in Studt et al., *C-Unit,* p. 12 [see note 17].

b. Organization corresponding to typology in Street et al., *Organization for Treatment,* p. 12 [see note 6].

c. Organization corresponding to typology in Ohlin, "Organizational Reform in Correctional Agencies." p. 1000 [see note 18].

inmate changes sought and determine the kinds of relationships staff develop with inmates. Amitai Etzioni's compliance framework provides a basis for a comparative organizational analysis of staff control strategies and inmates' responses in coercive and normative-coercive settings.[23] The primary correctional social control strategies are (1) the threat or use of physical coercion, (2) the threat or use of transfer to less desirable units or isolation cells, (3) the use of a privilege system,[24] and (4) collaboration between inmates and staff, which may be either informal[25] or formal.[26]

■ Methods

The data for this study were collected in 10 cottage units located in four juvenile institutions administered by the Massachusetts Department of Youth Services before the closing of the training schools.[27] A process of institutional decentralization initiated to transform the various cottage settings into small, therapeutic communities[28] provided considerable autonomy and independence for each individual unit. Clinical, vocational, academic, and cottage personnel either formed staff teams or were assigned to cottages to develop coordinated treatment programs. Decentralization resulted in a number of diverse "mini-institutions" in which staff pursued a variety of goals using different intervention strategies.

Since inmate assignments to the various cottages were not randomized, the 10 cottages studied were selected to maximize the comparability of inmate populations and the variety of treatment strategies used. The 10 cottages studied included seven units for males, two for females,[29] and one coeducational facility, located in four different state institutions. Cottage populations were matched on the basis of age, race, past criminal histories (both official and self-reported), present commitment offense, age at initial contact and number of prior juvenile court appearances, and prior commitments to institutions. . . . The cottages sampled produced comparable inmate groups. Although cottage assignments were not randomized, there was no systematic effort by administrators to match inmate "needs" with particular treatment programs, and the primary determinants were the availability of bed space and the need to maintain a population balance among the various cottages. [Tables from the original article have been omitted.]

In addition to the matching of populations, statistical controls for the effects of background characteristics within each cottage were used to establish cottage comparability. Controls for each background variable were used to determine whether a particular characteristic was systematically associated with differences within each cottage population and whether the differences among cottages were a product of these population differences. In addition to tests for relationships between background variables and attitudes, [statistical] tests were used to allow for interaction effects between inmates' characteristics and cottage

treatment strategies. Despite some variations in the respective cottage populations, these techniques support the conclusion that the substantial differences
between cottages were not a function of variations in the inmate populations
and are properly attributed to the cottages' social structures.[30] In institutions
with young populations (averaging approximately 16 years of age), who are
presumably less committed to criminal careers than are imprisoned adults and
who are incarcerated for an average of four months, it is not surprising that
background characteristics or preimprisonment experiences are subordinate to
the more immediate, organizational imperatives. . . .

Data were collected in each of the 10 cottages by a team of five trained
researchers who spent about six weeks in each unit administering questionnaires and interview schedules to both staff members and residents. Between
90 and 100 percent of the staff and residents in each cottage completed hour-
long closed-ended questionnaires and equally extensive open-ended structured
interviews. Most of the researchers' time was spent in participant observation
and unstructured interviews, with field notes transcribed onto standardized
forms to simplify analysis, coding, and comparison of observations from different settings.

Findings

Organizational Structure

Although the administrators of the Massachusetts Department of Youth Services told the institutional staff to "do good things for kids," they did not specify what the staff members should do or how they should do it. The process of
institutional decentralization allowed staff to pursue a variety of goals using
diverse treatment strategies within the autonomous cottages. In structuring programs for how their clients should be handled and changed, staff were guided
by their own assumptions about the causes of and cures for delinquent behavior. Although there was some diversity among staff within the respective cottages, recruitment, self-selection, and cottage assignments resulted in relatively
homogeneous correctional ideologies among cottage personnel; the focus of
this study is on the substantial differences among the various units in programs
and goals that emerged and the effects of these differences on the respective inmate cultures.

Cottage Programs and Social Control Strategies

Maximum Security (Group Custody). Cottage Nine was a unit used for juveniles who had run away from the institution and for youths who had committed other disciplinary infractions. About half of all residents escaped from the

institution at some time during their stay; there were no significant differences between those who absconded and those who did not. There was no vocational training, academic education, or clinical program in the maximum-security setting. Intervention consisted of punishment and deprivation, with periods of enforced idleness interrupted only for meals, routine clean-up, and cottage maintenance. All the cottage activities took place in a highly controlled, structured environment, and virtually all activities occurred in a group setting. Staff attempted to coerce inmate conformity and obedience, and punished recalcitrance or resistance. As a result, a typical three- to four-week stay in Cottage Nine before return to an open cottage was an unpleasant experience which residents had little choice but to endure.

Staff used physical coercion and isolation cells—"the Tombs"—to enforce obedience, conformity, and respect. These techniques were feasible since there was no program in which staff needed to obtain active inmate participation, and the staff's physical domination made coercion practicable. Staff members used their limited repertoire of controls to counter major forms of deviance such as riots and fights, as well as inmate provocation, disrespect, or recalcitrance. They also used mass lockups and other forms of group punishment. Other control techniques were virtually absent, since there were no amenities or privileges that might be lost, and strategies designed to ensure group control precluded the development of individualized relationships necessary for collaborative controls. The use of coercive tactics alienated inmates, who minimized contacts with staff. Personnel ignored considerable inmate misbehavior that did not challenge their authority, and did not encourage inmates to report deviance that occurred outside the presence of staff members.

Industrial Training School (Individual Custody). Despite considerable program diversity, each of the individual custody settings—Cottage 8, Elms, Westview, and the Lancaster Industrial School for Girls—used vocational training as the primary strategy of change. Most of the trades programs consisted of either institutional maintenance or services for residents—a cafeteria program, laundry program, institutional upkeep, painting, landscaping and groundskeeping, and the like. There were limited academic and clinical programs in some of the cottages. However, individual counseling sessions were not scheduled regularly, and inmates initiated contact with clinical staff primarily to secure a weekend furlough or early parole.

Compared with those in the maximum-security unit, residents of the training school cottages enjoyed greater physical freedom within the institution, which rendered staff control more difficult. Inmate cooperation in the work programs was also problematic. Staff used a privilege system to induce conformity, coupling this with the threat of transfer to more punitive, maximum-security settings. The privilege system was a security-graded progression, with inmates at different levels accorded different privileges or governed by different restrictions. Passage from one level to another reflected the amount of time served and an inmate's general behavior and conformity. Because of the relatively limited privileges available, staff members exercised considerable discretion in the rules they enforced, against whom, and under what circumstances. The staff also collaborated informally with inmate leaders to maintain order, manipulating the privilege system to confer additional status and rewards on the elite. Informal collaboration between staff members and the inmate elite is a common training school control strategy because of the availability of privileges, the discretionary bases upon which rewards are manipulated, and the problems of maintaining order posed by program individualization, the need to secure cooperation, and increased inmate freedom.[31]

Individual Treatment. The individual treatment program used all types of clinical treatment, including both individual counseling and individual therapy in a group setting. The cottage program was free and open with few restrictions. Staff minimized deprivations and maximized amenities to encourage inmate commitment and involvement in the clinical process. Staff eschewed universal rules, responding to each inmate on the basis of individualized therapeutic considerations.

Staff relied almost exclusively on a rich privilege system to secure the cooperation and participation of inmates. Although the threat of transfer to a less desirable setting was a possibility, the penalty was never invoked. There was virtually no physical coercion or informal collaboration used to obtain conformity or obedience. In response to inmate deviance, additional clinical sessions were prescribed to reinforce the privilege system—not as sanctions, but to provide additional supports for the recalcitrant resident.

Group Treatment. All of the group treatment cottages used a therapeutic community treatment model,[32] which was supplemented with either vocational or academic educational programs. The therapeutic community treatment model used both daily staff-inmate community meetings and group therapy sessions. A daily log provided the agenda for cottage community discussions, with staff and residents encouraged to record incidents that required the community's attention. At these meetings, staff integrated observations of residents on work, school, or cottage living. They then divided the cottage populations into smaller treatment groups and used a type of guided group interaction to deal with interpersonal problems or to resolve issues raised during the community meetings.

Formal collaboration between staff and inmates was the primary means of social control. Staff used the group problem-solving process to define and enforce cottage norms and to mobilize group pressures to deal with specific instances of deviance. Rules and consequences were elaborated in a privilege system that was jointly enforced; each inmate's privileges and freedoms were more dependent upon performance and participation and were less a function of the length of time served than was the case in the more custodial settings. The gradations of privileges and freedom and the responsibilities associated with each level were consistently and energetically enforced.

The strength of the formal collaboration process was the pressure staff placed upon residents to motivate other inmates to change. The concept of "responsibility" was crucial, and residents were responsible both for their own progress and behavior and for that of others. This principle of third-party responsibility provided a therapeutic rationale that significantly transformed subcultural norms governing informing and greatly increased the amount of information received by staff about the inmate group.

The Relationship between Staff Correctional Ideology and Cottage Program Characteristics. The differences in correctional programs and control strategies stemmed from various assumptions staff made about appropriate ways to treat inmates. Since staff members were allowed to form their own cottage teams, there was substantial interpersonal and ideological compatibility within units. For purposes of explaining the diversity in the cottage programs and subcultures, the more important differences were among the different units. . . .

One component of a correctional ideology is the emphasis placed by staff on inmates' obedience, respect for authority, and submission to external controls. Custodial staff were much more concerned with obedience and respect than were treatment personnel, and subscribed more extensively to the use of external controls to achieve inmate conformity.

Cottage staff members also differed in their views of deviance. Personnel in the treatment-oriented cottages attributed delinquency to emotional or psychological problems, while custody staff rejected psychopathology or emotional dysfunction, emphasizing as a cause of delinquency such factors as a youth's exercise of free will, which could be deterred by punishment. Because the custody staff rejected psychological interpretations, they found delinquent or bizarre inmate behavior considerably more difficult to understand than did treatment staff. Staff members also disagreed over whether delinquents were capable of establishing "normal" relationships, with those emphasizing custody far more likely than treatment personnel to regard the inmates in their cottages as "hard-core delinquents" who were dangerous and untrustworthy.

A correctional ideology both rationalizes deviance and its control and describes the end result sought—the "changed" inmate. Institutional behavior provides the staff with an indicator of an inmate's "rehabilitation" and readiness to return to the community. Custody staff strongly preferred inmates who followed orders, kept to themselves, and stayed out of trouble, which reflected their greater emphasis on external conformity rather than internalized controls. Their more negative perceptions of inmates and apprehension about collusion also led the custody staff members to disrupt informal inmate associations and encourage self-isolation, while treatment personnel encouraged inmate involvement with other inmates.

These alternative analyses of delinquency led staffs to pursue different correctional goals. When personnel were asked to choose among various correctional goals for incarcerated delinquents, significantly more of the custody-oriented staff members subscribed to custodial institutional objectives—isolation, respect and discipline, and training and educating—than did treatment personnel. Allocation of institutional resources provides another indicator of organizational goals; in juvenile institutions, personnel are the primary resource. Organizations pursuing custodial goals assign personnel to control and containment, or vocational and educational functions; treatment-oriented organizations, in contrast, assign more staff members to clinical and treatment functions. The greatest proportion of personnel in the custodial cottages served as guards, work supervisors, and academic instructors, while the treatment-oriented cottages assigned a larger percentage of the staff to treatment roles, with a corresponding reduction in purely supervisory personnel.

The Inmate Subcultures

An inmate subculture develops within the confines of a correctional institution, and its norms and values reflect the focal concerns of institutional life and the inmate population. Inmate roles and subculture stratification reflect conformity to or deviation from these norms, and newly entering inmates are socialized into this system and adapt to the expectations of their fellow inmates. The informal social system often mediates the effectiveness of the formal organization, aiding or thwarting staff members in the pursuit of their goals.[33]

A feature of correctional organization that influences the character of the inmate social systems is the extent to which staff members successfully control inmate violence and exploitation. Institutional characteristics influence the prevalence of inmate aggression by varying the levels of deprivation, a condition that gives some inmates an incentive to direct predatory behavior at others, and by providing the opportunities under which such exploitation may be carried out successfully. Inmate violence is directly related to the quality of relations between inmates and staff and to the information available to personnel about the workings of the subculture. Thus, controlling violence is a *sine qua non* of effective correctional programming and administration.

There was a clear relationship between the type of formal organization and the informal inmate culture. In the punitive, group custody setting, inmates experienced the greatest deprivation and were the most alienated from other inmates and staff members. Inmate alienation prevented the development of effective staff controls and allowed aggressive inmates to exploit their fellows through diverse forms of violent behavior. In the training school settings, the staff members used a privilege system coupled with informal cooperation of the inmate elite to bring potentially aggressive inmates under some degree of control. This reduced the effectiveness of inmate violence and exploitation, although aggression remained the dominant mode of interaction within the subculture. In the treatment-oriented cottages, especially in the group treatment programs, formal collaboration between inmates and staff members reduced the level of inmate violence and provided a therapeutic rationale for informing that made the workings of the subculture more visible to staff. The greater visibility, combined with significantly reduced deprivation, lowered the necessity for and effectiveness of inmate aggression and exploitation and allowed for the emergence of a more positive inmate culture.

Inmate Perceptions of Staff and Inmates. Problems of institutional living influence inmates' motives for interaction and the types of solutions they can develop. Just as correctional personnel structure their relationships with inmates, residents attempt to structure and control their relationships with staff and other inmates to resolve the problems of the informal organization. The types of relationships and collective solutions available depend upon the inmates' perceptions of the program, staff, and other inmates. Inmate cooperation with staff augers [*sic*] for a more open, visible, and manageable social system. If staff cannot obtain inmate cooperation through either formal or informal collaboration, then a more closed, subterranean, and violent social system emerges.

Cottage Purposes. The cottage goals and programs define the organizational context to which inmates must adapt. . . . When asked about cottage purposes and staff expectations, residents of the custody-oriented cottages described the cottages as places for punishment, while inmates in the treatment-oriented settings regarded the cottages as places for rehabilitation and for gaining self-awareness. As a further indicator of organizational purposes and adaptive constraints, inmates were asked whether staff encouraged them to conform or to gain insight into their own motivation and behavior. Responding to staff expectations, . . . inmates in the custody-oriented settings were more than twice as likely to view the staff as demanding obedience and conformity as were those in the treatment cottages, while the latter were almost three times as likely as the residents of custody-oriented settings to describe staff expectations in terms of treatment and self-understanding.

A corollary of the differences in custodianship and punitiveness was the "pain of imprisonment" that inmates described. While some of the problems inmates confront are inherent in incarceration—loss of liberty, separation from family and friends, increased dependency and submission to authority, and the like—other pains of confinement, such as material deprivations, are attributable to characteristics of a particular setting. By virtually every measure, the inmates in the custody-oriented cottages reported far more extensive and severe problems associated with their confinement—boredom, living with other residents, and material deprivations—than did the inmates in the treatment cottages. These reported differences in institutional amenities resulted from staff actions, since treatment personnel tried to minimize the unpleasant, alienating aspects of incarceration to a greater extent than did custody-oriented staff.

Inmate Perceptions of Staff. Inmates' views of staff paralleled staff members' perceptions of inmates. In those settings where staff had negative views of inmates, describing them as dangerous, unreliable, abnormal, or incorrigible, the inmates held correspondingly negative views of staff, regarding them as untrustworthy, unhelpful, or indifferent. In those settings where the staff expressed more favorable views of inmates, residents shared more positive views of the staff. Virtually every inmate in the maximum-security setting and over half the inmates in the individual custody settings, as contrasted with only about one-fifth of those in the treatment settings, regarded staff as neither concerned nor helpful. Inmates readily equated punitive programs with unconcerned staff and therapeutic programs with committed staff. Likewise, residents of the custody-oriented cottages initiated fewer contacts with personnel and talked with them less about personal problems than did those in the treatment settings.

Inmate Perceptions of Other Inmates. Characteristics of the inmate social system also reflect the extent to which inmates can cooperate with one another to ease the hardship of adjusting to the institution. The residents of the custody-oriented cottages reported substantially lower levels of trust and concern on the part of other inmates than did those in the treatment-oriented settings. Residents of the treatment cottages also reported greater inmate solidarity than did their custody cottage counterparts. Since predatory behavior and subcultural violence were more prevalent in the custody-oriented settings, the differences in inmate perceptions also reflect the extent to which inmates were exploited and victimized by others.

Inmate Adaptations. Differences among the programs in staff expectations constitute an additional organizational constraint on inmates' adaptations. Custodial staff emphasized inmate conformity and obedience, whereas treatment staff emphasized gaining insight and solving personal problems. . . . In response, inmates in the custody-oriented settings chose either overt conformity and covert deviance or obedience and conformity as adaptive strategies, while those in the treatment-oriented settings chose self-understanding. Similarly, adaptations reflecting elements of prisonization—prompt obedience, conformity, and self-isolation—were chosen by twice as many residents of custody-oriented settings as those in treatment programs, closely paralleling the staff expectations.

Social Structure of the Inmate Subculture. Inmates interact more frequently and intensely with residents of their own cottage than they do with those in other settings, and a set of norms and roles based upon those norms govern their interactions with other inmates and staff. Differences in staff intervention practices are strongly related to variations in inmates' perceptions of other inmates, staff, and institutional adaptation, and to corresponding differences in inmate norms, subculture roles, and interaction patterns.

The inmates' and staff's responses to violence and aggression are among the most important determinants of subculture processes. In the absence of effective controls, violence and aggression underlie most interactions within the inmate subculture.[34] Direct action, toughness, and defense of personal integrity are focal concerns of many delinquent inmates,[35] and even a few aggressive inmates can immediately make the control of violence a major concern within the institution. Moreover, the prevalence of violence is closely related to other subcultural norms, particularly those related to informing.

Inmate norms governing interactions with staff and the acceptability of informing personnel of other inmates' activities have been frequently described.[36] Informing and subcultural violence are closely linked, since uncontrolled violence can deter informing, while informing, if properly encouraged by staff, can reduce it. The regulation of the flow of information between inmates and staff thus emerges as a critical determinant of inmate roles and subculture structure.

Inmates' views of staff and inmates and their adaptations to the institution influence the amount of information staff members receive about the inmate social system, which in turn conditions the staff members' ability to control subcultural violence. Residents of the treatment cottages held relatively favorable views of other inmates and staff. Because of the greater availability of privileges and amenities, they had less incentive to engage in covert deviance to relieve deprivations and thus had less to hide. Almost three times as many inmates in the treatment settings as in the custody-oriented settings approved of informing. In fact, a virtual majority of residents of the former approved of informing.

As indicated previously, the treatment inmates' support for informing stemmed, in part, from the staff members' redefinition of informing as "helping" or "being responsible for others" as part of the treatment program. Formal collaboration reinforced the therapeutic rationale for informing and gave inmates greater protection from intimidation by increasing the visibility of informal pressures by other inmates. By legitimating and fostering informing, staff members received an enormous amount of information about the hidden processes of the subculture, which better enabled them to control inmate violence.

Participant observation and structured interviews provided an insight into "strong-arming" and "bogarting"—the subterranean violence among residents. "You have to fight" was a norm in the custody-oriented cottages, and the levels of verbal abuse and physical violence were considerably higher there than in the treatment-oriented settings. Inmates emphasized toughness, resisting exploitation or provocation, and maintaining one's position in the subculture through physical means. Physical and verbal testing and scuffles were daily occurrences, although actual fights were less frequent. The inmate did not have to be a successful fighter, but a willingness to fight to protect himself, his position, and his property was essential. Fighting and defending against exploitation were as important for female inmates as for males in comparable custodial cottages.

An inmate's readiness and ability to defend personal integrity and property were tested very early during confinement as new residents were subtly or overtly challenged for whatever material goods they possessed. As mentioned above, the greater deprivation in the custody-oriented settings made exploitation a profitable strategy for the more aggressive inmates. Residents who fought back could insulate themselves from chronic exploitation, while failure to do so left them and their possessions vulnerable.

There was significantly less exploitation in the treatment-oriented cottages than in the custody-oriented cottages. The field observers recorded fewer incidents of fights, physical confrontations, or expropriation of property. All the observers commented on the virtual absence here of "ranking"—verbal abuse—as compared with the custody cottages. There was less normative support for fighting, and when it did occur most of the inmates condemned it in the community meetings.

The differences in subcultural violence resulted from the steps staff took to control it. In the custody cottages, inmates retaliated with violence to punish those who informed to staff and to discourage other inmates from doing so. Given their limited social control repertoire, custody staff did not encourage inmates to inform, since it only forced them to confront violent inmates directly. When staff members learned of inmate violence or victimization, they seldom took steps to prevent its recurrence. More frequently, they reinforced the values of the violent subculture by encouraging the resident to fight back and defend himself. In view of the unsympathetic and unsupportive staff response to complaints and the retaliatory inmate violence that followed, inmates had little incentive to cooperate with staff. Custody staff were isolated from the workings of the subculture, and unable to combat the violence that stifled the flow of information. In the treatment-oriented cottages, formal collaboration and inmate support for informing provided channels of communication and a mechanism for coping with incidents of violence.

While inmate approval of informing afforded greater control over inmate violence, there were differences in other subcultural norms as well. Responses to a series of hypothetical stories concerning common incidents in correctional institutions demonstrated a further contrast in the norms that prevailed in the various cottages. About two-thirds of the inmates in the treatment-oriented settings, as compared with less than half of those in the custody-oriented settings, supported "positive" inmate behavior—cooperation with staff, refusal to aid escapes, and the like.

Different inmate roles and subculture stratification accompanied the differences in cottage norms. In the more violent custodial cottages, the roles of superior and inferior were allocated on the basis of an inmate's ability to "out-fight, out-think, or out-talk" fellow inmates. Since most inmates were neither complete successes nor complete failures in out-fighting, out-thinking, or out-talking their peers, the distribution of roles resulted in a stratification system with a few aggressive leaders at the top, a few "punks"—chronic victims—at the bottom, and most of the inmates occupying a more intermediate status, neither "one-up" nor "one-down." In the treatment-oriented settings, inmate roles and stratification were not as tied to physical or verbal prowess.

The differences in cottage norms and inmate relations were reflected in the characteristics of the inmate leadership as well. A majority of inmates in the custody-oriented cottages, as contrasted with about one-quarter of the residents of the treatment cottages, described the leaders as filling a negative and violent role in cottage life. Both observation and interviews revealed that leaders were those inmates who "strong-armed" and exploited lower-status inmates. There was greater normative support for negative inmate behavior in these cottages, and the leaders reflected and perpetuated the dominant values of the subculture.

Norms governing violence and informing constrained inmate leaders in the treatment-oriented cottages. Formal collaboration between inmates and staff reduced the leaders' ability to maintain covert physical control over the inmate group, and they played a more positive and supportive role in the institution. Formal collaboration increased their visibility and required that they at least appear to adopt a cooperative attitude in their relations with staff, which enabled other inmates to establish more positive relationships with inmates and staff.

At the bottom of the custody cottages' social structure were the "punks," inmates who were bullied and exploited and who acquiesced in the role of victim. Since the first rule of survival in the violent subculture was to defend oneself, inmates who were unable or unwilling to fight were at the mercy of those who would do so. Punks were chronically victimized, both psychologically and physically, and were the victims of merciless taunting and pummeling. In the custodial settings, the strong norm against informing prevented either the victims or other inmates from revealing what occurred. The inability of staff to control the violence prevented inmates from revealing their victimization and left them at the mercy of their exploiters.

Homosexual rape was the ultimate act of physical aggression by tough cottage leaders against punks. More than exploitative sexual satisfaction, rape entailed conquest and domination of the victim by the aggressor.[37] Every incident of homosexual assault discovered during this study could be analyzed in terms of leader-punk role relationships; such assaults occurred only in the violent custody-oriented cottages.

In the treatment-oriented settings, punks did not suffer as much physical or verbal abuse. Although other inmates regarded them as weak, immature, and lacking self-respect, formal collaboration provided a substantial check on the extent of their victimization. At least by contrast with those in the custody-oriented settings, low-status inmates in the treatment cottages enjoyed a comparatively benign incarceration experience.

■ Discussion and Conclusions

Organizational structure has a major effect on the informal inmate social system. The cottage programs varied in both the levels of deprivation and the effectiveness of staff controls and confronted the inmates with markedly different organizations to which to adapt. The respective cottage cultures reflected these differences in inmates' perceptions of cottage purposes and goals, in their adaptations to the institution, in their views of staff and other inmates, and in their norms, values, and interaction patterns.

Punishment and isolation were the reasons given by the inmates in maximum security for their incarceration. They suffered the greatest deprivation within the institution, which gave them the greatest incentive to improve their circumstances through violent exploitation and covert deviance. Staff sought inmate obedience and conformity and used physical control to obtain compliance and suppress challenges to their authority. Inmates were alienated by the staff's repressive controls, and the absence of programs prevented the development of individualized relationships, perpetuating the negative stereotypes of one another held by inmates and staff. Motivated by their poor opinion of inmates, staff attempted to disrupt informal groups. The inmates' isolation hindered them from cooperating with one another in the institutional adjustment or in resisting exploitation, while predatory violence reinforced inmates' negative views of one another. Inmates adapted by isolating themselves, avoiding other inmates and appearing to obey staff. In developing covert deviant solutions to relieve their material deprivation, particularly in exploiting weaker inmates for their possessions, tough inmates reinforced their own dominant status and provided themselves with a measure of safety and security. They discouraged inmate contact that would reveal their own deviant and violent behavior and physically punished inmates who informed to discourage the communication of information that would improve staff control. And the dominance of aggressive inmates reinforced staff efforts to isolate inmates within the culture by making inmates distrustful and fearful of one another. The inmates' ability to use violence determined their various roles within the group, and prevented them from engaging in positive forms of social behavior. The failure of staff to support informing or to control violence forced the inmates to seek accommodation with the primary source of power, the aggressive inmate leaders. This, in turn, reinforced their alienation from one another, precluded collective resistance to aggression, and left each individual inmate at the mercy of those who were more aggressive.

Subculture characteristics in the training school cottages were similar to those in maximum security, although organizational differences reduced the extremes of staff-inmate alienation and antagonism. Program individualization engendered more contacts between staff and inmates that tempered somewhat their negative perceptions of one another. The use of vocational programs required staff to obtain the active cooperation of inmates in productive work. Staff induced at least minimal cooperation and participation in work programs through privileges and rewards that reduced the levels of institutional deprivation. The necessity to obtain voluntary compliance limited the utility of punitive forms of social control, and a privilege system provided staff with a more flexible means of responding to inmates than did the use of force and isolation cells. The forms of adaptation among inmates reflected staff members' primary emphasis on obedience and conformity. Staff informally collaborated with and co-opted the potentially violent inmate elite, and thus obtained some control over aggression within the subculture. By co-opting the inmate leaders through informal collaboration, staff enlisted their aid in maintaining order within the subculture. In the course of protecting their privileged status, the leaders informally maintained control for staff, suppressed some forms of anti-institutional activities, and reduced the levels of violence within the inmate group. The privileges available reduced the levels of deprivation, and covert inmate deviance declined accordingly. With less to hide, there was less need among the inmates to restrict contact with staff. Although inmates disapproved of informing, this was not as ruthlessly suppressed as was the case in maximum security. The lesser degree of deprivation and violent exploitation reduced the inmates' isolation and alienation from one another.

The differences in organizational goals and intervention strategies in the treatment-oriented cottages had a significant effect on the inmates' incarceration experience. Staff both elevated treatment expectations over custodial considerations and successfully communicated their expectations to inmates. Rehabilitation, gaining insight, and solving personal problems were seen as the purposes of incarceration, and these goals required change rather than simply conformity. Staff emphasized more rewarding experiences and privileges, and residents of the treatment settings suffered less punishment, deprivation, or alienation than did their custody cottage counterparts. The reduced material deprivation also lowered inmates' incentive to engage in deviant activities within the institution.

In both the individual and group treatment settings, positive contact between staff and inmates was considerable, occurring in individual counseling and through formal collaboration, resulting in markedly more favorable inmate perceptions of staff than in the other settings. Formal collaboration allowed inmates and staff to make decisions collectively about cottage life and provided them with a common context in which to meet. Formal collaboration fostered greater equality among staff members, between staff and inmates, and among inmates, and reduced inmates' alienation from staff and encouraged more favorable views of fellow inmates.

Formal collaboration coupled with individual and group treatment increased the visibility of the inmate subculture and provided staff and inmates with a mechanism for controlling inmate violence. Staff provided a rehabilitation-based rationale for informing, enabling the norm governing this behavior to become more positive than was the case in the custody cottages. Equally important, staff members defined the program itself in such a way as to convince the inmates that personnel were committed to treatment rather than punishment. The increased communication of information enabled staff to control inmate violence, which reinforced this communication. The reduced deprivation, increased freedom, and support provided by formal collaboration for controlling inmate violence combined to foster more positive, less exploitative inmate relationships.

▨ Notes

1. See Hugh Cline, "The Determinants of Normative Patterns in Correctional Institutions," in *Scandinavian Studies in Criminology,* vol. 2, Nils Christie, ed. (Oslo, Norway: Oslo University Press, 1968), pp. 173–84; Barry Schwartz, "Pre-institutional vs. Situational Influence in a Correctional Community," *Journal of Criminal Law, Criminology & Police Science,* Dec. 1971, pp. 532–42; Charles W. Thomas & Samuel C. Foster, "The Importation Model Perspective on Inmate Social Roles," *Sociological Quarterly,* Spring 1973, pp. 226–34; Charles W. Thomas, "Theoretical Perspectives on Alienation in the Inmate Society," *Pacific Sociological Review,* vol. 18 (1975), pp. 483–99; Charles W. Thomas & Matthew Zingraff, "Organizational Structure as a Determinant of Prisonization," *Pacific Sociological Review,* January 1976, p. 98.

2. Donald Clemmer, *The Prison Community* (Boston: Christopher, 1940); Nonnan S. Hayner & Ellis Ash, "The Prison as a Community," *American Sociological Review,* vol. 4 (1940), pp. 577–83; Howard Polsky, *Cottage 6* (New York: Russell Sage, 1962); David A. Ward & Gene Kassebaum, *Women's Prison: Sex and Social Structure* (Chicago: Aldine, 1965); Clemens Bartollas, Stuart J. Miller & Simon Dinitz, *Juvenile Victimization: The Institutional Paradox* (Beverly Hills: Sage, 1976).

3. Thomas, "Theoretical Perspectives on Alienation in the Inmate Society"; Charles W. Thomas, "Theoretical Perspectives on Prisonization: A Comparison of the Importation and Deprivation Models," *Journal of Criminal Law & Criminology,* March 1977, pp. 135–45.

4. Lloyd W. McCorkle & Richard Korn, "Resocialization with Walls," *Annals of the American Academy of Political & Social Science,* May 1954, pp. 88–98; Gresham Sykes, *Society of Captives* (Princeton, NJ: Princeton University Press, 1958); Gresham Sykes & Sheldon Messinger, "The Inmate Social System," in *Theoretical Studies in Social Organization of the Prison,* Richard Cloward et al., eds. (New York: Social Science Research Council, 1960), pp. 5–19; Irving Goffman, *Asylums* (Garden City, NY: Anchor, 1961).

5. Hayner & Ash, "Prison as a Community"; Clarence Schrag, "Leadership among Prison Inmates," *American Sociological Review,* vol. 19 (1954), pp. 37–42; Clarence Schrag, "Some Foundations for a Theory of Corrections," in *The Prison: Studies in Institutional Organization and Change,* D. Cressey, ed. (New York: Holt, Rinehart &

Winston, 1961), pp. 309–58; Gresham Sykes, "The Corruption of Authority and Rehabilitation," *Social Forces,* vol. 34 (1956), pp. 257–62.

6. Oscar Grusky, "Organizational Goals and the Behavior of Informal Leaders," *American Journal of Sociology,* vol. 65 (1959), pp. 59–67; Oscar Grusky, "Role Conflict in Organizations: A Study of Prison Camp Officials," *Administration Science Quarterly,* March 1959, pp. 452–72; Stanton Wheeler, "Socialization in Correctional Communities," *American Sociological Review,* October 1961, pp. 707–11; Mayer N. Zald, "Organizational Control Structures in Five Correctional Institutions," *American Journal of Sociology,* November 1962, pp. 335–45; Mayer N. Zald, "Comparative Analysis and Measurement of Organizational Goals: The Case of Correctional Institutions of Juveniles," *Sociological Quarterly,* Summer 1963, pp. 206–30; Peter G. Garabedian, "Social Roles and Processes of Socialization in the Prison Community," *Social Problems,* Fall 1963, pp. 139–52; Peter G. Garabedian, "Social Roles in a Correctional Community," *Journal of Criminal Law, Criminology & Police Science,* September 1964, pp. 338–47; Daniel Glaser, *The Effectiveness of a Prison and Parole System* (Indianapolis, IN: Bobbs-Merrill, 1964); Mayer N. Zald & David A. Street, "Custody and Treatment in Juvenile Institutions," *Crime & Delinquency,* July 1964, pp. 249–56; Bernard Berk, "Organizational Goals and Inmate Organization," *American Journal of Sociology,* March 1966, pp. 522–34; David A. Street, Robert D. Vinter & Charles Perrow, *Organization for Treatment* (New York: Free Press, 1966); Ronald L. Akers, Norman S. Hayner & Werner Gruniger, "Homosexual and Drug Behavior in Prison," *Social Problems,* vol. 21 (1974), pp. 410–22; Ronald L. Akers, Norman S. Hayner & Werner Gruniger, "Prisonization in Five Countries," *Criminology,* February 1977, pp. 527–54; Barry C. Feld, *Neutralizing Inmate Violence: Juvenile Offenders in Institutions* (Cambridge, MA: Ballinger, 1977) .

7. John Irwin & Donald Cressey, "Thieves, Convicts, and the Inmate Culture," *Social Problems,* Fall 1962, p. 142; Ward & Kassebaum, *Women's Prison.*

8. Ward & Kassebaum, *Women's Prison;* James Jacobs, "Stratification and Conflict among Prison Inmates," *Journal of Criminal Law & Criminology,* vol. 66 (1976), p. 476; Leo Carroll, *Hacks, Blacks, and Cons* (Lexington, MA: Lexington Books, 1974); Thomas & Foster, "Importation Model Perspective on Inmate Social Roles"; Thomas, "Theoretical Perspectives on Prisonization."

9. Polsky, *Cottage 6;* Bartollas et al., *Juvenile Victimization;* Jacobs "Stratification and Conflict among Prison Inmates."

10. Social control by inmates within the subculture may be maintained by verbal as well as physical manipulation. Verbal assaults—"ranking"—provide a mechanism by which relative status is fixed by verbal rather than physical aggression. Howard Polsky described ranking as "verbal, invidious distinctions based on values important to the group. . . . Ranking fixes antagonistic positions among three or more persons by placing one member in a target position" (*Cottage 6,* p. 62). David Matza describes the same process as "sounding," which entails an "imputation of negative characteristics . . . wherein the recipient concurs with the perpetrator in the negative evaluation of the substance of the remark" (*Delinquency and Drift* [New York: John Wiley, 1964], p. 43). This process of verbal denigration is prevalent in female inmate interactions as well (Rose Giallombardo, *Society of Women* [New York: John Wiley, 1966]; Rose Giallombardo, *Social World of Imprisoned Girls* [New York: John Wiley, 1974]). The target of scornful, mocking, or negative statements made in the presence of a social audience can either concur in the negative imputations, establishing subordination, or resist the characterization. Acquiescence or resistance defines relative social status.

11. Sykes, *Society of Captives;* Sykes & Messinger, "Inmate Social System."

12. Polsky, *Cottage 6;* Bartollas et al., *Juvenile Victimization;* Feld, *Neutralizing Inmate Violence.*

13. Walter Miller, "Lower Class Culture as a Generating Milieu of Gang Delinquency," *Journal of Social Issues,* vol. 14 (1958), pp. 5–19; Marvin Wolfgang & Franco Ferracuti, *The Subculture of Violence* (London, England: Tavistock, 1967).

14. Jacobs, "Stratification and Conflict among Prison Inmates"; Giallombardo, *Social World of Imprisoned Girls;* Feld, *Neutralizing Inmate Violence.*

15. Charles W. Thomas & Samuel C. Foster, "Prisonization in the Inmate Contraculture," *Social Problems,* Fall 1972, pp. 229–39; Thomas & Foster, "Importation Model Perspective on Inmate Social Roles"; Akers et al., "Homosexual and Drug Behavior in Prison"; Feld, *Neutralizing Inmate Violence.*

16. Street et al., *Organization for Treatment;* Akers et al., "Homosexual and Drug Behavior in Prison"; Feld, *Neutralizing Inmate Violence.*

17. Donald R. Cressey, "Prison Organization," in *Handbook of Organizations,* J. March, ed. (Chicago: Rand McNally), pp. 1023–70; Street et al., *Organization for Treatment;* Elliot Studt, Sheldon Messinger & Thomas Wilson, *C-Unit: Search for Community in Prison* (New York: Russell Sage, 1968).

18. Street et al.; Lloyd Ohlin, "Organizational Reform in Correctional Agencies," in *Handbook of Criminology,* D. Glaser, ed. (Chicago: Rand McNally, 1974), pp. 995–1020; Feld, *Neutralizing Inmate Violence.*

19. Zald, "Organizational Control Structures in Five Correctional Institutions"; Zald, "Comparative Analysis and Measurement of Organizational Goals"; Zald & Street, "Custody and Treatment in Juvenile Institutions."

20. Corresponding to distinctions between custody and treatment, there is also a tension in the organization between tendencies toward bureaucratization and tendencies toward individualization. The pressures of bureaucratization lead personnel to deal with inmates according to gross characteristics. The pull toward individualization leads to nonroutinized treatment with potentially disruptive consequences for the organization. The nonuniform nature of individual behavior results either in individualized, nonroutinized staff responses or in an effort to increase predictability through regimentation. While bureaucratization increases regimentation and clearly defined expectations for inmate behavior, individualization requires either specifying norms for every eventuality or delegating discretion and authority to low-level staff to enable them to deal with unpredictable situations and individual variations. The resolution of these countervailing pressures constitutes a primary source of variation in organizations. See Goffman, *Asylums;* Cressey, "Prison Organization."

21. Street et al., *Organization for Treatment.*

22. Amitai Etzioni, *A Comparative Analysis of Complex Organizations* (New York: Free Press, 1961/1975).

23. Ibid.

24. Goffman, *Asylums.*

25. Lacking complete physical domination of inmates, staff members rely upon the inmate elite to maintain social order, in return for which the staff allow the elite certain privileges and immunities. Richard Cloward describes one way in which this process occurs. He notes that the two primary groups in the prison—custodians and inmates—seek, respectively, social order and escape from deprivation. The custodian employs coercion and inducement, force and incentive to secure order from the inmates, but "in the absence of absolute force, the prisoner must be led to share in the process of social control." Disruptive behavior is avoided by guards who provide access to illegitimate means whereby the prisoners can reduce the deprivation. "The official system accommodates to the inmate system in ways that have the consequence of creating illegitimate opportunity structures." To some extent the guards can determine

which prisoners will have access to these opportunities, and in turn these prisoners maintain order for the guards as a means of protecting their own privileged positions. This occurs because "certain prisoners, as they become upwardly mobile in these structures, tend to become progressively conservative. . . . Seeking to entrench their relative advantage over other inmates, they are anxious to suppress any behavior that might disturb the present arrangements." Richard Cloward, "Social Control in Prison," in *Theoretical Studies in Social Organization of the Prison,* R. Cloward et al., eds. (New York: Social Science Research Council, 1960), pp. 20–48.

This process is also described by Richard McCleary, "Communication Patterns as Bases of Systems of Authority and Power," in *Theoretical Studies in Social Organization of the Prison,* R. Cloward et al., eds. (New York: Social Science Research Council, 1960), pp. 49–77; Richard McCleary, "The Governmental Process and Informal Social Control," in *The Prison,* D. Cressey, ed. (New York: Holt, Rinehart & Winston, 1961), pp. 149–88; and Sykes, *Society of Captives.* According to Sykes ("Corruption of Authority and Rehabilitation"), the guards must rely on the inmates to maintain order because of the "lack of a sense of duty among those who are held captive, the obvious fallacies of coercion, the pathetic collection of rewards and punishments to induce compliance, the strong pressures toward the corruption of the guard in the form of friendship, reciprocity, and the transfer of duties into the hands of trusted inmates—all are structural defects in the prison's system of power rather than individual inadequacies." The same processes operate in institutions for juvenile offenders. See Polsky, *Cottage 6;* Feld, *Neutralizing Inmate Violence;* Bartollas et al., *Juvenile Victimization.*

26. Formal collaboration between staff and inmates as a means of social control occurs when a social structure allows both to participate, at least to some degree, as members of a common group in defining deviance, determining the appropriate sanctions, or both. Formal collaboration differs from informal collaboration in a number of critical respects. It is explicit and overt, with parties visibly engaged in the process. Since the process is formalized and given organizational sanction, it is legitimate and consistent with the declared principles of the organization, rather than covert, *sub rosa,* and basically subversive of the formal organization. Formal collaboration is universalistic and democratic, with all members of both groups potentially involved, rather than elitist and particularistic, confined only to the inmate leadership.

27. Feld, *Neutralizing Inmate Violence;* Robert Coates, Alden Miller & Lloyd Ohlin, *Diversity in a Youth Correctional System* (Cambridge, MA: Ballinger, 1978); Craig McEwen, *Designing Correctional Organizations for Youth* (Cambridge, MA: Ballinger, 1978).

28. Maxwell Jones, *Beyond the Therapeutic Community* (New Haven, CT: Yale University Press, 1968); Maxwell Jones, *Social Psychiatry in Practice* (Baltimore, MD: Penguin Books, 1968).

29. The Lancaster Industrial Schools for Girls was not converted to a decentralized, cottage-based institution to nearly the same degree as were the Shirley Industrial School and the Lyman Schools. It still operated as a traditional training school and there were virtually no differences in the social structure of the individual cottages. . . .

30. Feld, *Neutralizing Inmate Violence,* pp. 207–11.

31. Polsky, *Cottage 6;* Bartollas et al., *Juvenile Victimization;* Feld, *Neutralizing Inmate Violence.*

32. Jones, *Beyond the Therapeutic Community;* Jones, *Social Psychiatry in Practice.*

33. Sykes & Messinger, "The Inmate Social System"; Sheldon Messinger, "Issues in the Study of the Social System of Prison Inmates," *Issues in Criminology,* vol. 4 (1970), pp. 133–44; Street et al., *Organization for Treatment.*

34. Polsky, *Cottage 6;* Bartollas et al., *Juvenile Victimization;* Feld, *Neutralizing Inmate Violence.*

35. Miller, "Lower Class Culture as a Generating Milieu of Gang Delinquency"; Wolfgang & Ferracuti, *Subculture of Violence.*

36. Sykes, *Society of Captives;* McCleary, "Communication Patterns as Bases of Systems of Authority and Power"; McCleary, "Governmental Process and Informal Social Control"; Sykes & Messinger, "Inmate Social System."

37. Susan Brownmiller, *Against Our Will: Men, Women and Rape* (New York: Simon & Schuster, 1975).

25

Viable Options: Intensive Supervision Programs for Juvenile Delinquents

William H. Barton and Jeffrey A. Butts

William Barton and Jeffrey Butts explore the value of community-based alternatives to incarceration for juvenile offenders. In particular, they examine the effectiveness and cost of home-based intensive probation services involving small caseloads and frequent worker-client contact through an evaluation of three such programs (combined) in Wayne County, Michigan. Barton and Butts found that the criminal recidivism rates of youths receiving intensive probation were comparable to the rates of a comparison or control group of youths who were subject to more severe and expensive dispositions. Barton and Butts do not claim that community-based corrections necessarily work better than more severe dispositions, but that they work as well for less cost.

... [A] NUMBER OF STUDIES HAVE EXPLORED THE RELATIVE EFFECTIVEness of community-based correctional alternatives for juvenile offenders (Austin et al. 1987; Empey & Erickson 1972; Empey & Lubeck 1971; Kobrin & Klein 1983; Murray & Cox 1979; Ohlin et al. 1977; Palmer 1974; Weeks 1958). The results of this research have been occasionally encouraging but often discouraging or inconclusive. Many studies have been criticized for using poor research designs, others for badly operationalizing important variables or misinterpreting results (see especially Lerman 1975 on Palmer 1974; Maltz et al. 1980 on Murray & Cox 1979).

... [Other] studies have provided at least suggestive evidence for the effectiveness of particular rehabilitation programs and intermediate sanctions such as intensive probation supervision, offender tracking, home detention, electronic monitoring, adventure programs, and vocational training (see Gendreau & Ross

---

"Viable Options: Intensive Supervision Programs for Juvenile Delinquents," *Crime and Delinquency* 36, no. 2 (1990): 238–256. Reprinted by permission of Sage Publications, Inc.

1987; Greenwood 1986; Greenwood & Zimring 1985; McCarthy 1987; Petersilia 1987). Yet, pervasive dissension among researchers has combined with remnants of the "nothing works" scare of the 1970s to forestall needed developments in juvenile corrections. With few exceptions, state policymakers seem to be pursuing incarceration-based criminal justice strategies as if no viable alternatives existed.

This article presents the major findings from a five-year evaluation of three home-based, intensive supervision programs for adjudicated delinquents in Wayne County, Michigan, a large, urban county that includes the city of Detroit. The evaluation employed a randomized design with a two-year follow-up period to compare youths assigned to the in-home programs with a control group of youths who were committed to the state. The study results have important implications for juvenile justice practitioners and policymakers grappling with the task of deploying scarce program resources.

■   Background of the Study

Short of transferring a juvenile to adult court, the most severe disposition available to Michigan juvenile courts is commitment to the state Department of Social Services (DSS) for supervision and placement. Once committed to DSS, the great majority of juvenile offenders are placed in training schools or comparable private institutions at considerable cost to taxpayers. In 1982, more than 700 youths were committed to the state by the Wayne County Juvenile Court, reflecting a higher per capita rate than that of any other Michigan county.

In response to a growing rate of commitments, the state limited the number of Wayne County juveniles it would accept to 500 per year as of 1983. The county, in turn, implemented three experimental programs designed to provide alternative services to some of the youths who otherwise would have been committed. While they differed somewhat in philosophical orientation, all three programs provided intensive probation services using small caseloads and frequent worker-client contact. One of the in-home programs, the Intensive Probation Unit (IPU), was operated by the juvenile court. The other two were run by private agencies under contract to the court—the Comprehensive Youth Training and Community Involvement Program (CYTCIP) and Michigan Human Services, Inc. (MHS).[1]

Implementation of the in-home programs included an evaluation to determine whether they were cost-effective alternatives to state commitment. Although effectiveness can be defined in various ways, the Wayne County evaluation focused on the programs' ability to contain or reduce delinquent behavior to the extent that their clients could remain in the community instead of being placed in correctional institutions. The goal of the evaluation was to weigh the programs' success in this endeavor against the costs associated with the alternative, that is, commitment to the state.

■ The Evaluation

The study randomly assigned equivalent groups of youths to each program and the control group. Between February 1, 1983 and March 5, 1985, every youth recommended by the juvenile court for commitment to the state was screened for program eligibility. Juveniles charged with very violent offenses, those with a documented history of psychiatric disturbance, and those with no potential home in the community (e.g., neglect wards) were automatically excluded from the study. Because very few females had been considered for commitment, the evaluation study was limited to males.

A total of 511 juveniles (about 40 percent of those screened) met the eligibility criteria and were randomly assigned to the evaluation. The three programs received 326 youths, while 185 state wards comprised the control group. Those assigned to the in-home programs had their commitment orders rescinded but remained wards of the court on probationary status. The control group youths were committed to DSS as they would have been prior to the introduction of the programs and the evaluation.

Strictly speaking, this study does not purport to test the intensive supervision programs as an alternative to incarceration per se, but rather as an alternative to commitment to the state. Committed youths were subject to a variety of placement options, including in-home supervision by DSS workers, shelter and group home placement, camps, and large public or private institutions. About 80 percent of committed youths from Wayne County, however, were placed out of the home, and about 90 percent of those were placed in large institutions.

Most of the study youths were black (68.7%) and from single-parent households (67.2%) in which no adult was employed (58.3%). Most were Detroit residents (76.3%), with the remainder living in suburban areas and outer Wayne County. Their average age at entry was 15.4 years old; only about a third were 16 or older. Most (68.9%) had been on regular probation before their most recent court appearance. They averaged 3.2 prior charges; many (23.5%) had five or more priors. About 9 percent had no prior charges. The majority (78.1%) entered the study as a result of a criminal charge, and for about half (51.3%) that charge could be considered quite serious (i.e., larceny, breaking and entering, auto theft, burglary, assault). Thus, the juveniles in the study sample were relatively serious and chronic, though not highly violent, offenders.

Each youth was followed for two years after randomization. The evaluation gathered data from several sources. The youths and their parents were interviewed on two or three occasions, depending on program assignment. An initial interview was conducted as soon as possible after assignment to the programs, an exit interview was completed upon a youth's termination from an in-home program, and a follow-up interview was scheduled for two years after random assignment. Control group cases received only the initial and follow-up interviews.[2] Demographic data and official offense data (e.g., most recent offense, prior offenses, recidivism) were obtained from juvenile court records examined upon assignment and again periodically throughout the two-year period. These data were supplemented by a check of adult court records for youths who came under the jurisdiction of the adult system during the two-year study period.

Records of the frequency and nature of contacts between the program staff and the youths were obtained from case files maintained by each youth's primary worker. These data were used to assess the quantity and quality of program effort. Program staff also responded to a questionnaire about the problems, progress, and prognosis of each youth, as well as a listing of the program's efforts on behalf of him or her. This questionnaire was completed upon each youth's termination from a program. Information regarding the cost of the programs and of DSS placements was obtained annually from juvenile court and DSS records. The juvenile court's annual reports provided other information regarding its commitment rates and overall offense patterns.

■ Results

The results of the evaluation are presented in three sections. The first section describes the activities of the programs. The next section examines recidivism in terms of official charges and self-reported delinquency. The third section compares the cost of the programs with the usual cost of commitment to the state. Together, these measures should produce the convergence of evidence advocated by researchers as the most effective method of evaluating program outcomes (Gray et al. 1978; Lipsey et al. 1981; Waldo & Griswold 1979). The results suggest that the programs were cost-effective, although implementation problems diluted their impact.

Program Activities

The programs were given considerable latitude in defining how "intensive" they would be and in deciding what to include in their repertoire of services. All three programs, however, restricted caseloads to between 6 and 10 youths per worker. Program workers supervised youths directly and either provided or arranged for the provision of whatever other services were deemed necessary. The programs were designed to have a capacity of about 50 cases. It was expected, but not formally required, that cases would remain in the programs for about one year, unless recidivism necessitated their earlier removal.

The program workers were required to keep a record of all contacts made with and on behalf of each youth. The various types of contact were classified as: home contacts, program site contacts (e.g., group sessions and office visits), other agency contacts (e.g., at schools or other service agencies, sometimes called "collateral" contacts), and telephone contacts.

Table 25.1 shows the average number of monthly contacts per case recorded by each program. The MHS workers appear to have made significantly more

Table 25.1 Average Monthly Contacts by Program

Index	MHS N = 93		IPU N = 95		CYT N = 102	F	p
All Contacts	13.77	>	10.81	=	10.44	7.80	<.001
At Clients' Homes	6.38	>	4.41	>	2.02	57.88	<.001
At Program Sites	1.63	=	1.50	<	5.39	42.36	<.001
At Other Agencies	2.49	>	1.83	>	0.70	40.67	<.001
Telephone Contacts	3.28	=	3.06	>	2.33	4.17	<.02

ANOVA results
> First mean significantly higher than second (p < .01)
= First and second means not significantly different
< First mean significantly lower than second (p < .01)

contacts than workers in the other two programs. MHS staff reported contacting each client an average of nearly 14 times each month, or about 3 1/2 contacts per week. The other two programs averaged between 10 and 11 contacts per month, or slightly fewer than 3 contacts per week. [See the book appendix for a brief explanation of the statistical techniques used in this chapter (e.g., analysis of variance (ANOVA), factor analysis, and regression (to control for "regression to the mean")).]

MHS staff reported the greatest frequency of home contacts (more than six per month); CYTCIP the least (about two per month). However CYTCIP reported significantly more contacts at their program site (more than five per month) than did the other programs (less than two per month). Differences in the other contact frequencies were smaller, although MHS's frequency of collateral contacts (2.49 per month) was significantly higher than that of IPU (1.83 per month) which, in turn, was significantly higher than that of CYTCIP (0.70 per month).

These patterns of contact are consistent with the agencies' avowed differences in program emphases. MHS, the most family-focused program, relied most upon home contacts. CYTCIP, with an on-site educational and recreational emphasis, relied most upon on-site contacts. IPU occupied a middle niche, with more home contacts than CYTCIP but fewer than MHS, an intermediate number of collateral contacts, and relatively many telephone contacts. Such a pattern is consistent with its emphasis on behavioral supervision, resembling regular probation but at a more intensive level.[3]

The three agencies attempted to provide a large array of services to the youths and their parents. Questionnaires completed by staff regarding each terminating case suggested the range of services used by the programs. All programs utilized behavioral supervision and individual counseling with nearly every youth; school placement assistance and social skills training were also used frequently. Otherwise, the programs' service delivery patterns reflected their different emphases. CYTCIP clients had the highest participation rate in youth groups, recreational activities, and camping, while MHS reported greater utilization of parent counseling, parent groups, and tokens/rewards. Both CYTCIP and MHS utilized job-related components more often that did IPU.

Although the three programs had distinct emphases in the delivery of services, they did not differ significantly from each other in case outcomes. Together, the programs successfully graduated just under half of their cases (46.3%). Program youths graduated when the staff were satisfied with their continued cooperation and behavioral improvements. Nongraduates were usually terminated for a new adjudication or for noncompliance with the program. MHS had the highest graduation rate at 51 percent while that of IPU was lowest at 41.6 percent. The apparent differences between programs, however, were not statistically significant.

Outcomes

Official charges. The evaluation carefully tracked the offenses charged against study youths during the two-year follow-up period. All alleged offenses, not just final charges or adjudications, were recorded. Data were collected from court records in both the juvenile and the adult system and at state and local levels. For each case the evaluation analyzed: the number of charges filed during the two-year period, the most serious offense charged, and the average seriousness of all the offenses charged.

During the two-year follow-up period, 78 percent of the in-home program youths and 53 percent of the control group youths reappeared in a juvenile or adult court at least once. To compare the groups, however, a number of other factors must be taken into account, such as the seriousness of their offenses and the relative amounts of time they were at large in the community during the two-year period. After adjusting for these considerations, the official recidivism of the program youths and the control group was quite similar.

Status offenses accounted for about one-fourth (24.7%) of all charges against the program youths, while violations of program rules accounted for an additional 5 percent. Other program youths were charged with auto theft (13%), breaking and entering (10%), and larceny (7.5%). Relatively few charges were for extremely violent crimes (7% for aggravated assault, 4.4% for armed robbery, 3% for rape, attempted murder, or murder). The control group youths were charged with proportionally fewer status offenses (10.3%) and more serious offenses (15% auto theft, 12% breaking and entering, 6.6% armed robbery, 7.5% for rape, attempted murder, or murder). Control group youths acquired fewer charges, but when they did appear they tended to be for more serious offenses.

The youth's offenses were grouped into six levels of seriousness, as shown in Appendix 25.1. Seriousness weights were assigned to each level and used to calculate the total seriousness and average seriousness of each youth's charges.

The charges against the youths were also weighted by the time they spent incarcerated during the two-year study period (in detention, institutional placement, jail, or prison). Time not incarcerated was considered to be time "at large." Control group youths averaged much less time at large (10.7 months) than did in-home program youths (18.3 months).

What would have happened had all the youths spent the full 24 months at large with the program youths receiving the in-home services? That question cannot be answered unequivocally, but one can derive a reasonable estimate by assuming that each youth's behavior while at large during the two-year study period was typical. The charges filed against the youths can be divided by the number of months each was at large to derive a rate of charges per month. That rate can be multiplied by 24 to yield an estimate of the number of charges that would be expected had the youth spent the full 24 months at large.

Table 25.2 presents the incidence and seriousness of official charges and estimates charges controlling for time at large in the community. The in-home program youths had significantly more charges (2.63 per case) than did the control group (1.31). If status offenses and technical violations are excluded, the average *number* of criminal charges per case still favors the control group (1.17 versus 1.85) although the difference is smaller. The average seriousness of the control group's charges, however, was significantly higher (4.19) than that of the program youths (3.44).

The groups' average time incarcerated indicates that the control group had significantly less opportunity to recidivate. The last two rows in Table 25.2 show the number of charges and criminal charges that would be expected had all the youths been at large for 24 months. Program youths would be expected to show 5.41 charges each versus 4.05 charges for the youths in the control group, a difference which is not statistically significant as indicated in Table 25.2. Regarding criminal charges only, the two groups show nearly identical expected rates: 3.69 charges per program youth and 3.58 charges per control group youth.

This last observation from Table 25.2 is the most telling, for it points to the essential similarity between the two groups. All of the apparent differences in recidivism favoring the control group can be attributed to two factors: (1) program youths were much more likely than control group youths to be charged with status offenses after their assignment to the study, and (2) program youths spent much more of the two-year study period at large in the community. When these two factors are controlled, the recidivism of the two groups, in terms of criminal charges, is nearly identical.

The evaluation's adjustment for the youths' time at large should not obscure the fact that commitment and placement by the state did "incapacitate" the study youths. The community was spared their behavior during the time the youths were under lock and key. Even among the control group, however,

Table 25.2 Comparison of Program and Control Cases on Charge Incidence, Charge Seriousness, and Time at Large During Two-Year Study Period

	Program	Control	F	p
Mean Number of Charges	2.63	1.31	40.47	<.0001
(N)	(326)	(185)		
Mean Number of Criminal Charges	1.85	1.17	13.73	<.001
(N)	(326)	(185)		
Mean Charge Seriousness	3.44	4.19	21.19	<.0001
(N)[a]	(254)	(99)		
Mean Number of Months Incarcerated	5.64	12.81	123.05	<.0001
(N)	(326)	(185)		
Mean Number of Months at Large	18.30	10.68	138.10	<.0001
(N)	(326)	(185)		
Mean Number of Weighted Charges[b]	5.41	4.05	3.26	.07 ns
(N)	(326)	(160)		
Mean Number of Weighted Criminal Charges	3.69	3.58	0.04	.85 ns
(N)[c]	(326)	(160)		

Notes: a. Number of cases is smaller because mean seriousness is based only upon cases with at least one charge.

b. Weighted charges are adjusted to compensate for case differences in months at large during the two-year study period. Weighted charges are the number of charges that would have been filed in 24 months at large, had the youth's frequency of being charged remained constant.

c. Excludes cases who were never at large during the two-year study period.

the average period of incarceration was just over a year. All but the most serious juvenile offenders will inevitably be released from the training school system and return to the community. How much is really accomplished by incarcerating young offenders in expensive facilities for a few months each if their prospects for long-term improvement are apparently no better than those of youths on probation? The effects of the control group youths' behavior were at best temporarily delayed by incarceration. If intensive supervision achieves the same long-term reduction in delinquency for one-third the cost, the question becomes one of cost-effectiveness.

Self-reported delinquency. One cannot assume, of course, that official charges perfectly reflect actual delinquent behavior. Self-report measures have been used in delinquency research for more than 30 years (Porterfield 1946; Short & Nye 1957). Researchers have found that when administered properly and collected under conditions of anonymity or confidentiality, as in the present study, information provided by youths concerning their own activities can be a reliable and internally consistent method of estimating delinquent behavior within some defined time span (Erickson & Empey 1963; Farrington 1973; Hardt & Peterson-Hardt 1977; Hindelang et al. 1979, 1981; Kulik et al. 1968).

In each of the interviews, the study youths were asked how often, during the preceding four months, they had engaged in any of 26 different behaviors, from status offenses (e. g., "skipping school without an excuse") to serious crimes (e.g., "injuring someone with a weapon"). Responses from the initial interview provided a profile of each youth's delinquent behavior in the four months preceding program entry. The exit interview measured delinquent activity during the four months prior to program termination. The final follow-up interview yielded self-reported delinquency for the last four months of the two-year study period.

Due to randomized assignment, program and control group youths did not differ initially in self-reported delinquency (SRD). Thus, the self-report measures can address a major question: Two years after their diversion from commitment, did program youths differ from the control group in SRD? As shown below, the answer is generally no, although the program youths did report committing significantly fewer *violent* crimes than the control group youths at the two-year follow-up.[4] This finding parallels the results of the analysis of official charges.

Rather than look at results for each of the 26 self-report items used in the interviews, the behaviors can be grouped into empirically and logically defined categories. A factor analysis of the SRD items in the initial interview produced four meaningful factors (as shown in Appendix 25.2). Indexes were created by adding the scores on the items within each grouping. Thus the *Minor Offense* index contains the number of times a youth ran away, skipped school, trespassed, etc. during the four months in question. The other three indexes summarize *Drug/Alcohol Offenses, Property Offenses,* and *Violent Offenses.* In addition to these four indexes, a *Total Delinquency* index was constructed by adding the responses on all 26 items.

A commonsense way to examine individual SRD change would be to look at the differences between the initial and follow-up interviews. Simple change scores, however, are plagued by the statistical artifact known as "regression to the mean," noted in previous evaluations of delinquency programs (see Murray & Cox 1979; Maltz et al. 1980). One way to adjust for this bias is to control statistically for an individual's initial score and derive an *adjusted* change score that represents change independently of the initial score. Technically, the raw change score (i.e., follow-up score minus the initial score) is regressed on the corresponding initial score for each index. The residuals of the regressions are the adjusted change scores.

Table 25.3 compares the adjusted SRD change scores on the various indexes. Most of the mean values are close to zero, suggesting very little overall difference. On every measure, however, the program youths reported a slight mean decrease while control group youths reported a slight mean increase. Overall, program youths reported a decrease of about three delinquent acts while the control group youths reported an increase of more than four. On the violent behavior index, the difference between the groups is statistically significant—the program youths mean adjusted change (–1.07) is significantly lower than that of the control group (+1.67), which increased slightly.

This pattern can be seen clearly by comparing the percentage of youths from the two groups that showed a reduction in SRD at follow-up. On every

Table 25.3 Adjusted Change Scores for SRD Indexes Between Initial and Follow-up Interview

Delinquency Index	N	Mean Change	Reduction		No Reduction	
			N	(%)	N	(%)
Minor						
Programs	143	−0.42	87	(60.8)	56	(39.2)
Control	71	0.54	39	(54.9)	32	(45.1)
Drug/Alcohol						
Programs	143	−0.42	80	(55.9)	63	(44.1)
Control	73	0.57	38	(52.1)	35	(47.9)
Property						
Programs	147	−0.61	108	(73.5)	39	(26.5)
Control	69	1.33	43	(62.3)	26	(37.7)
Violent						
Programs	141	−1.07*	99	(70.2)	42	(29.8)
Control	71	1.67*	42	(59.2)	29	(40.8)
Total						
Programs	124	−2.66	79	(63.7)	45	(36.3)
Control	65	4.32	32	(50.0)	32	(50.0)

Note: *Mean change of program cases is significantly lower (i.e., reflect greater reduction) than that of control group cases ($F = 4.8$; $p < .05$).

index, a slightly higher percentage of program youths reported a reduction. Overall, about 64 percent of the program youths reported reduced level of delinquency compared to 50 percent among those in the control group. On the relatively serious property and violent behavior indexes, more than 70 percent of the program youths reported reductions, compared to about 60 percent of control group youths.

The results thus far indicate that the in-home programs were no less effective at curbing recidivism than commitment to the state. A final indicator of program effectiveness is that the programs were able to maintain their successful cases in the community. Nearly 80 percent (78.1 percent) of program *graduates* were free of new charges after leaving the programs. Because the average tenure for successful cases was 13 months, this result reflects about one year of postprogram follow-up. Regardless of whether the programs merely allowed already success-prone youths to be successful, or in fact rehabilitated potential recidivists, all the study youths had been recommended for state commitment before being assigned to the programs. With the addition of intensive supervision, many were able to remain successfully in the community.

Cost Comparison
If in the absence of the programs all diverted youths would have been committed, the total cost of these avoided commitments can be used as an estimate of

fiscal savings attributable to the programs. Not all of these savings were realized, however, due to a steady rise in commitments from Wayne County. Following the introduction of the programs, the commitment rate increasingly exceeded what would have been projected from the volume of delinquency petitions brought before the court (Barton & Butts 1988). These extra commitments, otherwise known as net-widening, diluted the potential savings of the three programs.

In calculating the savings attributable to the programs, the basic unit of comparison is the cost of each "youth-day" spent in various types of placement. An average per diem rate was calculated for male delinquency wards from Wayne County during each year of the study. If one knows the total number of days a youth was successfully enrolled in a program, one can calculate the likely cost of state commitment for those days. A comparison of this estimated cost with actual program expenditures provides a gross indication of the commitment costs avoided by the programs.[5]

The method of analysis may be summarized by the following simple equations:

1. Commitment per Diem Cost x Program Youth Days
   = Comparable Cost of Commitment

2. Comparable Cost of Commitment – In-Home Program Expenditures
   = Commitment Costs Avoided

3. Commitment Costs Avoided – Additional Costs of Net-Widening
   = PROGRAM SAVINGS

Out-of-home placements varied greatly in cost, from less than $25 per day in some group homes to about $120 per day in the training schools and private residential facilities. The proportion of Wayne County wards that were in each type of placement on a given day was combined with the cost for these placements to calculate the average per diem cost of a delinquency commitment from Wayne County. The average per diem cost of out-of-home placements for males was estimated at $79.56 in 1983, rising to $104.20 by 1986. Then, because not all state wards are placed out of the home, this average cost was multiplied by the percentage of state wards from Wayne County who were placed out of the home.

During 1983, for example, 78 percent of the males were placed out of their homes during the first year of state wardship (all study youths were facing their first commitment). The estimated 1983 per diem cost of commitment for state wards from Wayne County, therefore, was $62.06 (or $79.56 x .78). Subsequent estimates were $68.88 in 1984, $81.02 in 1985, and $88.57 in 1986. The total number of program youth-days multiplied by these averaged commitment per diem rates produced estimates of the commitment costs avoided by the programs: $1.26 million in 1983, $2.62 million in 1984, $3.57 million in 1985, and $4.12 million in 1986.

Of course, the operational costs of the programs themselves must be subtracted from these figures to estimate program savings. In 1986, for example, IPU cost approximately $22.48 per youth per day; CYTCIP's per diem cost was $21.89, while MHS's was $31.38. Taken together, the per diem costs of the in-home programs averaged about $26 ($31 for females). Overall, each program youth-day cost about 31 percent of a comparable day of commitment. As shown in Table 25.4, the three in-home programs allowed the state and county to avoid more than $11.5 million in commitment costs between 1983 and 1986.

Net-widening. In the first years of the study, it was plausible to assume that one program youth-day saved one day of commitment costs. The study youths surely would have been committed in the absence of the in-home programs, and commitments from Wayne County were sharply reduced. Commitments rebounded in subsequent years, however, and the programs began to augment rather than substitute for commitment. The evaluation found that even when adjusting for the changing volume of petitions coming before the juvenile court, the number of commitments increasingly exceeded expectations. The excess was estimated to be 20 cases in 1983, increasing to about 42 cases in 1984, 50 cases in 1985, and approximately 78 cases in 1986 (see Barton & Butts 1988).

The cost of these "extra" commitments was subtracted from the cost of avoided commitments in order to refine the program savings estimate.[6] Table 25.4 indicates that the total cost of net-widening from 1983 to 1986 was estimated to be $2.7 million. Thus, according to the most conservative estimate, the use of intensive supervision as an alternative to commitment generated $8.85 million in savings between 1983 and the end of 1986.

■ Discussion

The results of this study can be generalized only to that portion of the juvenile commitment population that would meet the eligibility criteria for the intensive

Table 25.4 Estimated Program Savings, 1983–1986

Year	Commitment Costs Avoided	Estimated Cost of Net-Widening	Estimated Savings
1983	$1,258,875	$232,760	$1,026,115
1984	2,623,721	551,250	2,072,471
1985	3,569,448	714,350	2,855,098
1986	4,108,005	1,208,688	2,899,317
Total	$11,560,049	$2,707,048	$8,853,001

supervision programs, in other words, relatively serious but primarily nonviolent offenders facing their first state commitment. The results suggest that the programs offered a viable, alternative disposition for many such youths who would otherwise have been committed to the state. At about one-third the cost, the programs were no less effective than commitment in controlling subsequent offending or producing other measurable outcomes.[7]

The evaluation's longitudinal analysis of recidivism does not suggest that the in-home programs were dramatically successful in reducing delinquency. The programs did achieve a slight reduction in SRD activity, however, while commitment to DSS was accompanied by a slight increase in the average level of delinquent behavior. When controlling for the youth's time at large, the experimental and control groups were also similar in the number of official charges.

This conclusion of "no difference" may disappoint those who advocate in-home programming for young offenders. It is important to remember, however, that the programs were assessed as an alternative to the traditional means of handling adjudicated delinquents. Rather than applying some absolute standard that would suggest whether the programs "worked," the crux of the evaluation was to explore how they compared with what was already being done. Given their cost differences, a null finding might be interpreted as a clear success for the programs. Furthermore, the programs in this study were not perfectly implemented. With careful attention to case-screening procedures, flexible program development, and policies that curb net-widening, intensive supervision programs could be more cost-effective.

This study suggests that intensive supervision is a viable option that other jurisdictions should consider. States that rely heavily on incarceration could reallocate resources from institutional beds to in-home programs and provide more cost-effective services to more youths. In other states, the development of in-home alternatives could prevent the costly construction and operation of new beds. With careful implementation, intensive supervision programs could become a major component of the dispositional continuum in juvenile justice.

* * *

Appendix 25.1 Offense Category Definitions and Seriousness Weights

Offense Category	Seriousness Weight	Offenses
Status	1	Status Offenses (e.g., truancy, incorrigibility)
Program Offenses	1	Violation of Probation (unspecified) Program Offenses (e.g., failure to obey program rules)
Minor	2	Littering, Loitering, UPIS Disorderly Conduct Resisting Arrest, Fleeing, and Eluding
Drug	3	Drug Possession (except heroin) Heroin Possession Drug Sales
Medium	4	Vandalism, Malicious Destruction of Property Weapons Possession Receiving Stolen Property Fraud Simple Assault
Major 1	5	Larceny Auto Theft Breaking and Entering Aggravated Assault Unarmed Robbery
Major 2	6	Armed Robbery Arson Rape Sexual Assault Manslaughter Attempted Murder Murder

Appendix 25.2 Composition of Self-Report Delinquency Indexes Using Initial Youth Interviews (N = 412)

I. Drug and Alcohol Offenses (Alpha = .76)
   Drank beer, wine, or liquor without your parents' permission.
   Smoked marijuana (or hash).
   Used any drugs or chemicals to get high, except marijuana.
   Sold marijuana, drugs, or chemicals.
II. Property Offenses (Alpha = .86)
   Purposely damaged or messed up something not belonging to you worth more than $200.
   Purposely damaged or messed up something not belonging to you worth between $50
      and $200.
   Took something worth more than $200 that didn't belong to you.
   Took something worth between $50 and $200 that didn't belong to you.
   Broke into a house or a building.
   Took a car without the permission of the owner.
III. Violent Offenses (Alpha = .80)
   Injured someone with a weapon.
   Injured someone so that they had to stay in the hospital overnight or longer.

Injured someone so that they needed a doctor's care (but didn't stay in a hospital).
Injured someone so that you left a bruise or cut (but didn't need a doctor).
Threatened to hurt or injure someone with a weapon.
Took part in a fight where a bunch of your friends were against another bunch.
Carried a gun or knife besides an ordinary pocket knife.
Hit one of your parents.

IV. Minor Offenses (Alpha = .76)
Ran away from home (at least for a day or two).
Skipped a day of school without any real excuse.
Tried to get something by lying about who you were or how old you were.
Tried to get something by lying to a person about what you would do for him or her.
Purposely damaged or messed up something not belonging to you that was worth less than $50.
Took something worth less than $50 that didn't belong to you.
Threatened to hurt or injure someone without a weapon.
Trespassed on someone's property (not counting breaking in).

■ Notes

1. CYTCIP inherited its program from another agency that was unable to fulfill its initial contract after several months of operation. Although CYTCIP gradually replaced existing staff and revised the program to its own specifications, the evaluation cannot draw firm conclusions about CYTCIP's effectiveness with its particular program. Subsequent to the evaluation, Michigan Human Services changed its name to Spectrum Human Services.

2. Exit interviews were not sought with the control group cases because most of them experienced a variety of placements during their state wardship, so that it was not clear what would constitute an "exit" comparable to a termination from one of the in-home programs. Furthermore, this study made no attempt to evaluate the treatment afforded the control group.

3. The fact that these patterns conform to expectations about program characteristics lends credence to the use of the workers' contact reports for comparison purposes. Still, findings based upon these data must be interpreted cautiously, as records of contact may reflect organizational and management attributes of the programs (e.g., diligence in record keeping) as well as actual service delivery.

4. By the third interview, only half of the original sample participated fully. All analyses, however, were examined for nonresponse bias.

5. An alternative would be to multiply the average per diem by the control group's average length of placement under commitment status. This would not produce substantially different results, however, because the average program tenure was within one month of the control group's average placement duration.

6. Several steps were needed to estimate the average cost per *extra* commitment. The per diem costs of commitment were multiplied by 182.5 days to produce the average cost incurred in a given calendar year for each commitment made during that year. The 182.5 day figure (i.e., 365 ÷ 2) was used to account for the fact that commitments can occur at any time during the year. Separate costs were calculated for males and females and averaged according to their respective proportions of the commitment population (86% male). The resulting cost of a commitment in a given year, multiplied by the number of extra commitments occurring that year, provided the estimated net-widening costs. For example, the 78 extra commitments in 1986 cost an average of $15,946 each for a total cost of more than $1.2 million.

7. Outcomes other than recidivism were analyzed by the evaluation, including changes in family relationships, school attitudes, academic or occupational achievement, self-concept, etc. The results at the two-year follow-up showed essentially the same pattern found for recidivism: little or no difference between the in-home programs and commitment to the state.

■ References

Austin, James, Barry Krisberg & Karen Joe. 1987. *The Impact of Juvenile Court Intervention*. Draft Report. San Francisco: National Council on Crime & Delinquency.

Barton, William H. & Jeffrey A. Butts. 1988. "The Ever Widening Net: System Adaptations to the Introduction of New Programs in a Juvenile Court." Paper presented at the annual meeting of the American Society of Criminology, Chicago.

Empey, LaMar T. & Maynard L. Erickson. 1972. *The Provo Experiment: Evaluating Community Control of Delinquency*. Lexington, MA: Lexington Books.

Empey, LaMar T. & Steven G. Lubeck. 1971. *The Silverlake Experiment: Testing Delinquency Theory and Community Intervention*. Chicago: Aldine.

Erickson, Maynard L. & LaMar T. Empey. 1963. "Court Records, Undetected Delinquency, and Decision-Making." *Journal of Criminal Law, Criminology & Police Science* 54:456–59.

Farrington, David P. 1973. "Self-Reports of Deviant Behavior: Predictive and Stable?" *Journal of Criminal Law & Criminology* 64:99–110.

Gendreau, Paul & Robert R. Ross. 1987. "Revivification of Rehabilitation: Evidence from the 1980s." *Justice Quarterly* 4:349–407.

Gray, Charles M., C. Johnston Conover & Timothy M. Hennessey. 1978. "Cost Effectiveness of Residential Community Corrections: An Analytical Prototype." *Evaluation Quarterly* 2:375–400.

Greenwood, Peter W. 1986. "Promising Approaches for the Rehabilitation or Prevention of Chronic Juvenile Offenders." In P. Greenwood (ed.), *Intervention Strategies for Chronic Juvenile Offenders*. New York: Greenwood.

Greenwood, Peter W. & Franklin E. Zimring. 1985. *One More Chance: The Pursuit of Promising Intervention Strategies for Chronic Juvenile Offenders*. Santa Monica, CA: RAND.

Hardt, Robert & Sandra Peterson-Hardt. 1977. "On Determining the Quality of the Delinquency Self-Report Method." *Journal of Research in Crime & Delinquency* 14: 247–61.

Hindelang, Michael J., Travis Hirschi & Joseph G. Weis. 1979. "Correlates of Delinquency: The Illusion of Discrepancy Between Self-Report and Official Measures." *American Sociological Review* 44:995–1014.

———. 1981. *Measuring Delinquency*. Beverly Hills, CA: Sage.

Kobrin, Solomon & Malcolm W. Klein. 1983. *Community Treatment of Juvenile Offenders: The DSO Experiments*. Beverly Hills, CA: Sage.

Kulik, James A., Kenneth B. Stein & Theodore R. Sarbin. 1968. "Disclosure of Delinquent Behavior Under Conditions of Anonymity and Non-Anonymity." *Journal of Consulting & Clinical Psychology* 32:506–9.

Lerman, Paul. 1975. *Community Treatment and Social Control: A Critical Analysis of Juvenile Correctional Policy*. Chicago: University of Chicago Press.

Lipsey, Mark W., David S. Corday & Dale E. Berger. 1981. "Evaluation of a Juvenile Diversion Program: Using Multiple Lines of Evidence." *Evaluation Review* 5:283–306.

Maltz, Michael D., Andrew C. Gordon, David McDowall & Richard McCleary. 1980. "An Artifact in Pretest-Posttest Designs—How It Can Mistakenly Make Delinquency Programs Look Effective." *Evaluation Review* 4:225–40.

McCarthy, Belinda R. (ed.). 1987. *Intermediate Punishments: Intensive Supervision, Home Confinement and Electronic Surveillance.* Monsey, NY: Willow Tree Press.

Murray, Charles A. & Louis A. Cox. 1979. *Beyond Probation.* Beverly Hills, CA: Sage.

Ohlin, Lloyd E., Alden D. Miller & Robert B. Coates. 1977. *Juvenile Correctional Reform in Massachusetts.* Washington, DC: US Government Printing Office.

Palmer, Ted. 1974. "The Youth Authority's Community Treatment Project." *Federal Probation* 38:3–14.

Petersilia, Joan. 1987. *Expanding Options for Criminal Sentencing.* Santa Monica, CA: RAND.

Porterfield, Austin L. 1946. *Youth in Trouble.* Fort Worth, TX: Leo Potisham Foundation.

Short, James F. & F. Ivan Nye. 1957. "Reported Behavior as a Criterion of Deviant Behavior." *Social Problems* 5:207–13.

Waldo, Gordon & David Griswold. 1979. "Issues in the Measurement of Recidivism." In L. Sechrest et al. (eds.), *The Rehabilitation of Criminal Offenders: Problems and Prospects.* Washington, DC: National Academy of Sciences.

Weeks, H. Ashley. 1958. *Youth Offenders at Highfields: An Evaluation of the Effects of the Short-Term Treatment of Delinquent Boys.* Ann Arbor: University of Michigan Press.

26

Evaluating Juvenile Drug Courts: Shedding Light into the Theoretical Black Box

Paul D. Gregory, Kristen E. DeVall, and David J. Hartmann

Paul Gregory, Kristen DeVall, and David Hartmann consider community-based drug courts as an alternative correctional disposition for juvenile offenders. They discuss the philosophy underlying drug courts and the elements of effective evaluation. They also review previous evaluation studies and present the results of their own evaluation of the Midwest Juvenile Drug Court Program (MJDCP). The results are mixed but sufficiently encouraging to persuade Gregory, DeVall, and Hartmann to continue to "find ways of improving both . . . [the] operation and evaluation" of such programs. The researchers' main objective, however, is not just to evaluate the MJDCP but to use it to illuminate the methodological complexity of the evaluation process and to note the need for more theoretically informed research that can elucidate more clearly why and how drug courts should be expected to change young people's behavior.

THE USE OF ILLICIT DRUGS AND ALCOHOL BY YOUTH IN THE UNITED States continues to impact our country's juvenile justice system. The National Center on Addiction and Substance Abuse (2004) reports that more than half of the 2.4 million juvenile arrestees in 2000 tested positive for alcohol or drugs. Moreover, the number of juvenile crimes involving illegal substances appears to have increased; "juvenile arrests for drug abuse violations increased 19 percent . . . between 1994 and 2003" (Snyder 2005:1).

Numerous programs aimed at lowering substance use and criminal recidivism among juveniles have been instituted over the years with different levels of success. One of these programs is the juvenile drug court, which began in the early 1990s as a part of the larger adult drug court movement. Juvenile drug courts were created in response to the overwhelming number of drug-related criminal cases cycling through the court system and the consequent realization that law enforcement and imprisonment alone were not working to reduce the supply and demand of drugs (Goldkamp 1994; Hora, Schma, and Rosenthal 1999). These programs purport to fill a service gap in an ever-changing juvenile justice system, as the nature of criminal acts committed by juveniles has changed, becoming "far more complex, entailing more serious and violent criminal activity and escalating degrees of substance abuse" (Drug Court Clearinghouse and Technical Assistance Project 1998:1).

In the study reported in this chapter, we examine the impact of the Midwest Juvenile Drug Court Program (MJDCP) located in a medium-size Midwestern city.[1] The MJDCP is a long-standing drug court program with national recognition as an exemplary model. We offer the study as an example of a well-executed outcome-oriented evaluation. Like all evaluations, this one seeks to establish the quality and worth of the program under consideration (Scriven 1999). This effort is difficult enough to test our ingenuity as well as to occupy available time and budgetary resources, but an additional question—one that is often neglected in evaluation research and that we hope is subject to closer scrutiny—is the importance of not simply *describing* whether a program works or doesn't work but *explaining* why it works or doesn't work. This desire to understand the outcomes rather than simply describe them may generally be referred to as the "theory question" and is surprisingly contentious in the field of program evaluation even as it is almost sacrosanct in most social science research.

In what follows, we first provide a brief overview of the drug court movement, including the rationale behind the creation of juvenile drug court programs. Next, we address three components of effective program evaluation—the *who, what,* and *when* of evaluation—including a discussion of the rationale behind the MJDCP evaluation, and we report on the outcome measures for the first nine years of the program. Finally, with that empirical case at hand, we offer some observations on the pros and cons of explicitly using social science theory in this kind of work.

■ The Drug Court Movement

Drug courts, in essence, represent an integration of public-health and public-safety strategies for fighting crime and administering "justice." Marlowe notes that drug courts combine "community-based drug abuse treatment with ongoing criminal justice supervision" (2003:4). Senjo and Leip observe that drug courts are "specialized criminal court[s] that streamline drug cases away from traditional processing and punishment into an intensive drug treatment program" (2001:68). Although no two drug courts are alike, academics, researchers, and practitioners agree that drug courts are palpably different from the traditional model of criminal justice.

Table 26.1 identifies the key differences between traditional and drug court models of criminal justice. The traditional model focuses on legal issues of

Table 26.1   Criminal Justice Models: Traditional Versus Drug Court

Traditional Model	Drug Court Model
Legal dispute resolution	Problem-solving/therapeutic process
Adversarial	Collaborative
Case oriented	Needs-based oriented
Few participants/stakeholders	Multiple participants/stakeholders
Formal	Informal
Judge as arbiter	Judge as facilitator/coach

Source: Adapted and modified from Roger K. Warren, "Re-engineering the Court Process," Great Lakes Summit, Madison, WI, September 24–25, 1998.

guilt versus innocence and due process procedures. It is an adversarial process that emphasizes the legalistic manner by which participants, or stakeholders (e.g., the government, defendant, prosecutor, and defense attorney), are pitted against one another in a dispute resolution process. Particular cases are argued in a courtroom characterized by minimal discourse among the aforementioned parties, with dialogue that is highly routinized and regulated by strict courtroom procedures.

The drug court model, on the other hand, is more of a needs-based, problem-solving therapeutic process that incorporates the knowledge and expertise of multiple stakeholders. It focuses its efforts on assisting offenders in solving life problems that contribute to their illegal activity (and involvement in the criminal justice system). Instead of working against one another to determine guilt or innocence, the drug court model is a collaborative process whereby stakeholders cooperate to assist offenders in improving their lives. Additionally, drug courts utilize therapeutic counselors, educators, and other social agencies as an integral part of this collaboration. Although the discourse among these parties takes place in court, the atmosphere is less formal than in the traditional model and is guided by a judge who is viewed as a facilitator or coach.

More specifically, a *juvenile* drug court is defined as "a drug court that focuses on juvenile delinquency (e.g., criminal) matters and status offenses (e.g., truancy) that involve substance-abusing juveniles" (Drug Court Clearinghouse and Technical Assistance Project 1998:3). These programs are designed to be more holistic than traditional courts and hence depend on the collaboration among several organizations, including treatment, juvenile justice agencies, social service agencies, and the courts. With this collaboration and mutual effort, youths receive more appropriate referrals that are specific to their individual needs (McGee et al. 1998).

Juvenile Drug Court Strategies
The National Drug Court Institute (2003) has developed 16 juvenile drug court strategies to provide insight into the principles that collectively form the juvenile

drug court model: (1) collaborative planning, (2) teamwork, (3) clearly defined target population and eligibility criteria, (4) judicial involvement and supervision, (5) monitoring and evaluation, (6) community partnerships, (7) comprehensive treatment planning, (8) developmentally appropriate services, (9) gender appropriate services, (10) cultural competence, (11) focus on strengths, (12) family engagement, (13) educational linkages, (14) drug testing, (15) goal-oriented incentives and sanctions, and (16) confidentiality. Practitioners recognize that the structure of juvenile drug courts varies across jurisdictions. These elements are what define the nature of *therapeutic* juvenile drug court programs, however.

In order to garner support from multiple community agencies, drug court programs are normally facilitated by a team of individuals within the local community, including a judge, probation officer, substance abuse treatment counselors, school district personnel, law enforcement officer, prosecutor, defense attorney, and representatives of other community resource agencies. The frequent presence of the judge is one of the most important parts of the program, as she or he is expected to develop personal relationships with participants through frequent court hearings. (Many juvenile drug court programs require participants to attend weekly hearings with the judge.) Many times "the judge is the only constant in the youth's life, providing the structure and support that are otherwise absent" (National Drug Court Institute 2003:20). Juvenile drug court programs also utilize numerous resources within the justice system and local community, including case supervision, mental health and substance abuse services, as well as educational/vocational services in order to provide program participants (and their families) with holistic treatment and individualized supervision, which are underlying premises of the entire juvenile justice system. Moreover, unlike many traditional juvenile probation services, juvenile drug court participants receive intensive supervision, random and frequent drug testing, and individualized counseling services. Juvenile drug court programs employ objective assessment criteria for all participants in order to assess risk and needs and deliver more individualized treatment services. Last, program evaluation is an important part of juvenile drug court programs.

Therapeutic Jurisprudence

Although not explicitly created around a theoretical perspective, drug court programs are often viewed as an application of the legal theory known as "therapeutic jurisprudence." The premise underlying therapeutic jurisprudence is that a legal rule or practice can be studied to determine whether or not it benefits those it is intended to help. Hora, Schma, and Rosenthal proposed the establishment of "therapeutic jurisprudence as the DTC [drug treatment court] movement's jurisprudential foundation" (1999:440). The idea is to use therapeutic jurisprudence to provide a theoretical justification underlying the implementation of drug courts throughout the country as well as to provide a theoretical framework for modifying and evaluating existing drug courts. Whether and how well it has served these purposes will be discussed below.

Funding of Juvenile Drug Courts

Juvenile drug court programs have grown considerably since their inception. The first juvenile drug court originated in 1993 in Key West, Florida (Belenko 2001). In October 1996 there were 19 juvenile drug court programs in operation or in the planning stage in 12 states (Drug Court Clearinghouse and Technical Assistance Project 1996). By December 2000 there were 131 juvenile drug courts in operation in 46 states, and by May 2001 the number had increased to 158 (Belenko 2001). More recently, the National Drug Court Institute identified 455 juvenile drug courts currently operating in the United States (Huddleston, Marlowe, and Casebolt 2008).

The drug court movement has generally received support from the federal government. The US attorney general has awarded grants to states, state courts, local courts, units of local governments, and Indian tribal governments for the purpose of establishing drug courts under Title V of the Violent Crime Control and Law Enforcement Act of 1994 (Roberts, Brophy, and Cooper 1997). In 1998 President Bill Clinton earmarked $27 million in continued support for the drug court movement, and in 1999 Congress appropriated $40 million for drug court grants to be utilized for planning, implementation, and enhancement (Senjo and Leip 2001). Additional funding to expand existing programs or to plan the creation of new ones in the amount of $14 million was distributed to 147 jurisdictions for fiscal year 1999 (Office of Justice Programs 1999).

In the last several years, however, funding for drug courts has been reduced as a result of the ever-shrinking federal appropriations. More specifically, in fiscal years 2006 and 2007, drug courts received $10 million, which represents a 75 percent decrease from 2005 appropriations. The fiscal year 2008 appropriation was $15.2 million, which was a 50 percent increase from 2007, but less than what was hoped for and projected during early negotiations with legislative officials (National Association of Drug Court Professionals 2008). What these trends illustrate is that even though the number of drug courts in the planning, operation, and expansion stages continues to grow exponentially, the funding for drug courts continues to decrease. Proponents of the drug court movement are hopeful that funding for drug courts will be restored in the future.

■ The Who, What, and When of Program Evaluation

Effective evaluation provides answers to the questions of *who*, *what*, and *when* to evaluate. The question of "who" to evaluate involves the identification of two important groups: a target population for the program's experimental or treatment group and the creation and maintenance of a control or comparison group. The treatment group refers to the cultivation of a strategic sense of the specific individuals who will be placed in the drug court program, whereby logistical (administrative and political) control over specific entry decisions is balanced against the broader "types" of persons in need of the program or for whom one wishes to draw inferences. Criminal history and treatment intensity are two key issues to be considered here. Regarding criminal history, will the program recruit juveniles with extensive criminal histories, first-time offenders, or others who are in between? Regarding treatment intensity, DeMatteo, Marlowe, and Festinger note that "the services provided in many drug court programs may be clinically contraindicated for a sizeable proportion of clients who do not have a diagnosable or clinically significant substance use disorder" (2006:131). As a result, one must ask: What type of client (juvenile) can our program serve? Will the program serve youths who need inpatient or outpatient substance abuse treatment services? Ongoing planning and objective risk/ needs assessment screening are crucial to this process in order to determine the type of client to be placed into the program.

Second, the creation of a comparison group is vital if we are to attribute specific intervention effects to a specific drug court program. A comparison group refers to a group of individuals who have eligibility markers, primarily demographics and risk/need indicators, similar to those of drug court participants. Because of administrative and sometimes ethical constraints on assignment, individuals placed on juvenile probation caseloads often serve in comparison groups, as they tend to have similar criminal and drug use histories as well as similar demographic characteristics. A complicating factor is the extent to which comparable interventions are received across groups. Statistical verification of impact is enhanced when the range and intensity of interventions provided in the comparison group is modest relative to the program group. In many juvenile systems in particular, relatively rich intervention services are available even in the "standard" protocol of probation (e.g., drug testing and substance-abuse treatment services, although typically not judicial monitoring). The impact of the intervention program, especially in resource-rich jurisdictions, becomes harder to discern under such circumstances.

The use of comparison groups allows for the direct comparison of change in outcome measures between the two groups (i.e., drug court participants and traditional juvenile probationers). Without such comparisons, changes identified in the treatment group (drug court participants) may not be attributed to the drug court program but, rather, to youths' natural maturation, changing social conditions, or a variety of other factors.

The "what" of evaluation refers to the most important outcomes anticipated as a consequence of the program, with effective evaluations assessing changes in key outcome indicators. For drug courts, the two key indicators of success are reduced criminality and abstinence from use of chemical substances (alcohol and illicit drugs). The "when" of evaluation refers to the temporal measurement of key indicators. In order to effectively isolate intervention effects between groups, the collection of data should be made during three time periods: pre-program (generally retrospectively), in-program, and post-program. Post-program measures may also address the duration of any positive effects and anticipated challenges (e.g., criminal recidivism, relapse patterns for substance use) to those effects.

The bulk of the extant research regarding drug courts addresses one central question: "Do drug courts work?" Researchers and evaluators alike have attempted to answer this question over the last decade or so and, as a result, there is a growing literature to draw upon. Most of this literature is regrettably atheoretical and lacks key elements of evaluation design—all this leading to mixed conclusions about the effectiveness of drug courts (Belenko 2001). Here we review four of the more recent juvenile drug court studies that attempt to address the who, what, and when questions of program evaluation.

Rodriguez and Webb employed a quasi-experimental design to examine the Maricopa County, Arizona, juvenile drug court, which targets youths age 13–16 1/2 who "reside in zip codes that produce the highest percentage of drug referrals to the juvenile court" (2004:295). The program comprises three phases and is a minimum of nine months in length.[2] Drug court participants were compared with individuals sentenced to probation (comparison group). Through their analysis, the authors found that drug court participants, overall, had lower rates of subsequent delinquency than nonparticipants. They also found that as the length of time spent in the drug court program increased, however, the number of delinquent offenses committed by the participants actually increased. Moreover, they found no significant differences in marijuana use among drug court participants and comparison group members; it is also interesting to note that drug court participants were nearly three times more likely to test positive for cocaine than were nonparticipants. Rodriguez and Webb suggest a potential explanation for these findings: youths involved in drug court for long periods of time will have increased exposure to other drug-abusing peers, which may create a social environment that exacerbates drug abuse.

Gilmore, Rodriguez, and Webb (2005) also employed a quasi-experimental design to examine the Maricopa County program. In this study, the experimental or treatment group comprised the first 114 participants in the juvenile drug court (enrolled between October 1997 and December 2000). The comparison group comprised a random sample of 100 (out of 204 total) youths deemed inappropriate for drug court and thus sentenced to standard probation. This was the only study we found that attempted to apply a social science theory of behavioral change to drug court evaluation, in this case, social control theory, which focuses on the strength of an individual's bonds to specific groups and institutions (i.e., family, school, peers, employment) that affect his or her propensity to engage in delinquent activity (see Chapter 11). Thus, Gilmore, Rodriguez, and

Webb sought to answer three research questions: (1) What is the effect of drug court treatment and social bonds on delinquent behavior while juveniles are in treatment? (2) What is the effect of drug court treatment and social bonds on program completion? (3) Is the effect of drug court on delinquent behavior and program completion mediated by social bonds?

Gilmore. Rodriguez, and Webb found no statistically significant differences between the treatment and comparison groups with regard to the number of delinquent complaints. They also found that drug court participants were more likely to test positive for drug and alcohol use and to be discharged from the program as unsuccessful. Gilmore, Rodriguez, and Webb also noted that drug court was unable to positively affect offenders' social bonds and that the "juvenile justice system will have a difficult time addressing serious substance abuse and delinquency with drug courts if such bonds" are not amenable to programmatic change (2005:306).

The third study is that of Applegate and Santana (2000), who examined the Juvenile Substance Abuse Treatment Court (JSATC) in Orange County, Florida, which targets first-time through fourth-time nonviolent offenders under the age of 18 who reside in the county.[3] In this research, the authors sought to answer three questions: (1) What characteristics predict whether clients graduate from treatment or fail in the program? (2) What effects do drug courts have on the youths' overall level of social and psychological functioning? (3) What effect do drug courts have on criminal recidivism rates?

In order to answer these questions, Applegate and Santana compared drug court graduates with participants who were unsuccessfully discharged from the JSATC program and concluded that three demographic characteristics significantly predicted successful completion: longer participation in treatment, race (nonblack), and family background of a "good" attitude toward treatment. With regard to changes in participants' level of social and psychological functioning, the authors note that participants who successfully completed the JSATC program and those who were enrolled in school at the time of program entry had significantly greater increases in overall levels of family, school, and peer functioning.[4] The recidivism rate for JSATC graduates was 7.1 percent as compared to 21.1 percent for those participants who were unsuccessfully discharged. Moreover, the average length of time to recidivism was significantly higher for program graduates as compared to unsuccessfully discharged participants (134.5 days and 88 days, respectively).

The fourth study is that of Sloan, Smykla, and Rush (2004), who compared the criminal recidivism rates of Adolescent Substance Abuse Program (ASAP) participants and Jefferson County Juvenile Drug Court Program (JCJDCP) participants in Birmingham, Alabama. The ASAP began in 1993 and was phased out when the JCJDCP began in 1995. The JCJDCP is a postadjudicatory program that consists of four phases and is a minimum of one year in length.[5] Comparisons were made between all participants unsuccessfully discharged from the drug court between January 1, 1996, and December 31, 1999, and a random sample of juveniles unsuccessfully discharged from the ASAP between January 1, 1994, and December 31, 1995 (prior to the implementation of the JCJDCP). The researchers concluded that there were no significant differences in the recidivism patterns of the two groups.

▪ The Midwest Juvenile Drug Court Program

Research Design
We now turn our attention to the MJDCP, which has been in operation since 1998 and is part of a county justice system that has been at the forefront of the drug court movement since 1992. The juvenile drug court program is one of three drug courts in Midwestern County (the other two are separate adult men's and women's programs). All three program structures operate closely to the key components laid out by the National Association of Drug Court Professionals, which are "benchmarks . . . describing the very best practices, designs, and operations of drug courts" (1997:3).

The MJDCP has clearly established policies and procedures for eligibility, and its operation and key outcomes have been evaluated both internally by program staff and by an external evaluation team since its inception. Eligibility for the drug court program is determined by program staff and includes the following criteria: (1) The youth has been formally referred to family court for adjudication on a delinquency petition, and (2) the youth scores a 2–4 on a substance abuse screening tool that indicates the level of drug/alcohol use (2 = use, 3 = abuse, 4 = chemical dependency).

The MJDCP is a post-adjudicatory program, with youths entering it only *after* being found legally guilty in juvenile court. All participants receive a substance abuse assessment and individualized treatment plan that guides their participation through the program. The MJDCP consists of four phases spanning a minimum of nine months in length. Phases 1–3 are each 12 weeks in length; Phase 4, which functions as aftercare, varies in length depending on participants' needs (as put forth in the treatment plan). Participants transition from one phase to the next after demonstrating "progress" for 10–12 weeks. Progress refers to the extent to which youths achieve certain benchmarks stipulated in the program, such as continued abstinence, no contact with law enforcement, progression in substance abuse treatment, and completion of other educational or vocational classes. Participants in the aftercare phase meet with a family therapist who is responsible for assessing whether or not a participant is capable of functioning on his or her own. Participants successfully completing Phase 4 graduate from the program.

While enrolled in the MJDCP, participants engage in a myriad of activities, including weekly meetings with family interventionists, random drug testing, individual counseling sessions, parent education groups (for parents/guardians of program participants), school, and biweekly status review hearings with drug court personnel and the drug court judge. During the status review hearings, which take place in juvenile court with the drug court team, juvenile client (and family), and the drug court judge, each participant discusses his or her progress in the program and receives positive or negative sanctions as a result. Positive sanctions refer to rewards that tend to reinforce good behavior—such as verbal praise from the judge, gift certificates, phase promotion, reduced drug testing and reporting, and program graduation. Negative sanctions refer to punishments that function to dissuade negative behavior—such as verbal admonishment from the judge, required written essays focusing on negative behavior, community service hours, increased drug testing and reporting, and short- and long-term detention. All decisions within the program are made by the drug court team, which includes family interventionists, substance abuse treatment providers, prosecution and defense counsel, a court coordinator, and a judge.

The data presented in this chapter are from the Year 9 evaluation report of the MJDCP that covers the period between January 1, 1998, and September 30, 2006. This time frame provides for a unique opportunity to assess the long-term effects of the program. For the purposes of evaluation, a control group was created at the inception of the program to allow for comparison of differences in the outcome measures, that is, subsequent criminality. All youths were assessed prior to adjudication to ascertain their risk/needs. After this assessment, they were assigned (not randomly) to either the drug court program, comparison group, or other juvenile justice programs as deemed appropriate.[6] At the end of Year 9, there were 233 youths in the treatment group and 183 in the comparison group. Our evaluation also included a one-year post-program follow-up, however, so those who were still in the program at the end of Year 9 or who had been out of the program for less than a year were excluded from the evaluation, reducing the size of the sample used in this study to 183 for the treatment group and 123 for the comparison group.

Before turning to the data, it is important to note three limitations of the study. First, this research focuses on one juvenile drug court program in a medium-size Midwestern city. As discussed earlier, although there is some agreement on the principles around which drug courts should operate, there is a substantial variety in the way these principles are operationalized and monitored (see Sloan and Smykla 2003). Consequently, the results should not be generalized to the population of juvenile drug courts. Second, it remains unclear as to whether the comparison group chosen for this research allows meaningful comparisons to be made insofar as the selection of treatment participants *explicitly targets those with more severe substance abuse dependency problems*. To the extent that substance abuse and criminal activity are related—a core supposition of drug courts in the first place—this creates a substantial bias against discernible program effects. Third, the available data at the time of this writing do not allow for a theoretical informed assessment of why the MJDCP does or does not work. We address this limitation further in the concluding section of the chapter.

■ Results

Demographic Characteristics of Participants
The appendix at the end of this chapter provides the breakdown of the demographic characteristics of the youths in the treatment and comparison groups for the Year 9 evaluation by age, race/ethnicity, and household income. The data do not reveal substantive differences between the groups that would affect the evaluation. Once again, the most substantively significant difference between the treatment and comparisons groups is that the former includes youths with more severe substance abuse dependency problems.

Retention Rates
We calculated retention rates in the MJDCP by dividing the number of participants who graduated or were still active in the program by the number of participants who had ever been in the program. Participants' status was then divided into three categories: (1) graduates, (2) unsuccessful terminations, and (3) those still active in the program. Of the 233 participants ever in the drug court program, 33.0 percent (N = 77) graduated, 53.2 percent (N = 124) were discharged, and 13.7 percent (N = 32) were still active in the program at the end of Year 9. The overall retention rate (graduates and those still in the program at Year 9) is 47 percent, which is lower than the national retention rate of 68 percent (Drug Court Clearinghouse and Technical Assistance Project 2001).[7] The comparison of retention rates is problematic, however, because drug courts vary as to the degree of voluntary participation, the longevity of the programs, and the criminal and substance abuse histories of the participants. As noted earlier, the MJDCP recruits participants with more extensive substance abuse problems, which contribute to the lower rates of retention.

Subsequent Drug Use
One key indictor of drug court program success is, of course, reduced substance use, which is measured in the MJDCP via drug testing. Although drug tests were not administered to the comparison group, an examination of use among drug court participants is an important part of the evaluation.

All participants were required to submit to random drug tests,[8] and Figure 26.1 describes the percent of participants for all nine years who tested positively. These data are arranged by the phases through which incidences of drug use is expected to decline—a decline that is indicated in the data. Among the

Figure 26.1 Drug Testing by Phase

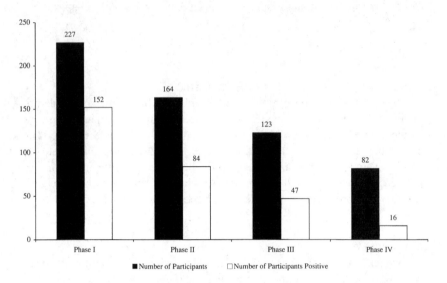

participants in Phase I, 67 percent had at least one positive test; among the participants in Phase II, 51 percent had a least one positive test; among the participants in Phase III, 38 percent had at least one positive test; and among the participants in Phase IV, 19.5 percent had at least one positive test.

Subsequent Criminality

We used two general measures of subsequent criminality to examine drug court effectiveness. First, we calculated the average *crime rates* (total, misdemeanors, and felonies) of the treatment and comparison groups across the three stages of evaluation—the pre-program stage (one year prior to the program), the in-program stage, and the post-program stage (one year following the program)—by dividing the number of *adjudicated crimes* (i.e., total, misdemeanors, and felony convictions) committed by participants in the respective groups by the number of individuals in each group (see Figure 26.2). Second, we calculated the average *recidivism rate* by dividing the number of *adjudicated individuals* in each group by the number of individuals in each group.[9] For example, 151 of the 183 individuals in the treatment group were adjudicated for a crime during the pre-program period (a recidivism rate of 0.83), and 100 out of 123 individuals in the comparison group were adjudicated (a recidivism rate of .81) (see Figure 26.3).

Figure 26.2 compares the respective crime rates of the treatment and comparison groups across the three stages of evaluation. The comparison group

Figure 26.2 Crime Rate Comparison

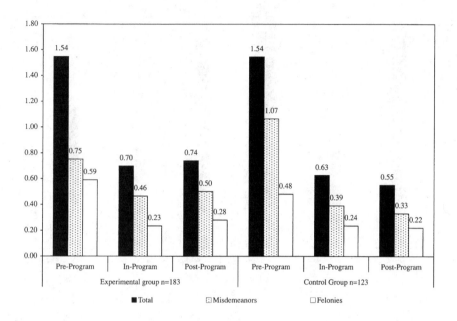

showed a continual decline across all three periods of evaluation (1.54 pre-program, .63 in-program, and .55 post-program for the total rate). The treatment group showed a decline between the pre-program and in-program periods (1.54 total pre-program rate, and .70 total in-program rate), but a slight increase in the post-program period (.74 total crime).

The recidivism rates for the treatment and comparison groups are displayed in Figures 26.3. Both groups showed a decline between the pre-program and in-program recidivism rates (.83 to .38 for the treatment group total rate, and .81 to .35 for the comparison group total rate), but increases thereafter (the post-program total rate for the treatment group increased to .74, and the post-program total rate for the comparison group increased to .55). As with the crime rates shown in Figure 26.2, the treatment group had a higher recidivism rate during the post-program period than the comparison group, a result consistent with prior research that found that drug courts are not particularly effective.

▨ Discussion and Implications

Earlier we proposed that reduced criminality and substance use were two key indicators of success for drug court programs. Our data show that participants in the MJDCP did achieve declines in positive testing for drug use from one phase to the next, as well as reductions in adjudicated crime and recidivism

Figure 26.3 Recidivism Rate Comparison

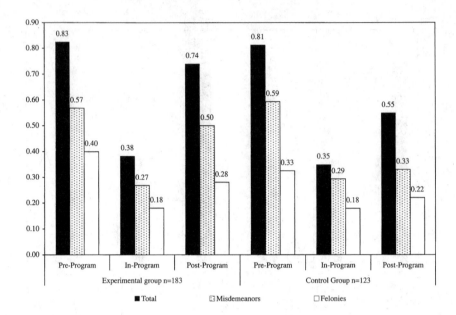

from the pre-program period to the period after participation. In this respect, our evaluation indicates that the MJDCP is a successful program, at least in the short term. Long-term positive effects are less clear, however, as crime and recidivism rate comparisons between the experimental drug court participants and the comparison group showed little difference. Moreover, post-program rates were actually higher for the experimental group.

That said, we want to emphasize that the null findings in previous research on juvenile drug courts, as well as our own, do not mean that we think that drug courts should be abandoned. This is especially true in the case of the MJDCP because the experimental group was not only "nonrandom" but was explicitly designed to include youths with the highest levels of substance abuse dependence. This purposeful selection bias is programmatically sensible but, again, hampers evaluation via group comparisons.[10] Nevertheless, the evaluation has been used as an incentive for program staff to revisit the program to find ways of improving both its operation and evaluation.

Moreover, our intention here is not only (or even primarily) to evaluate the quality and worth of the MJDCP program, but rather to use the program to demonstrate the complexity of addressing those questions. Evaluation research almost always operates in the absence of classic experimental controls. As such, we are exposed to a variety of measurement and interpretation problems.

Such problems must be explicitly recognized and embraced if the basic evaluation questions of quality and worth are to be approached. Some of these challenges may be mitigated by more explicit attention to the classic operational questions—"who" is to be evaluated and in comparison to whom, "what" effects are important to evaluate and can they be fairly and consistently measured, and "when" should these effects be measured to provide useful feedback to decisionmakers in the programs and in the constituencies that may support those programs? But the other basic question, raised earlier, is the theory question: What is and should be the role of substantive theory in evaluating juvenile drug courts? It is primarily to this theory question that we now turn.

Scriven notes that within the field of program evaluation, researchers are typically concerned with establishing the quality and worth of a program "in whole or in part, at the request of some client or clients, and for the benefit of some audience. To do this we do *not* need to know how the programs work or why they fail to work, or even what their components are. . . . The professional imperative of the evaluator is to evaluate; anything else is icing on the cake" (1999:521–522; emphasis added). The upshot of Scriven's observation is that most evaluation research lacks theoretical substance, and as such, it is all too often at variance with social scientists' interest in not just describing social reality but in explaining it and using that explanation to predict future outcomes. Over the past several generations of scientists, the very notion of scientific explanation has revolved around this distinction (see Hempel and Oppenheim 1948; Nagel 1979; Salmon 1989). If science has a heart, its heart is clearly explanatory. Explanation in science, as elsewhere, can be oriented toward prediction, debunking, and even emancipation, all of which are thought to be rooted first in understanding. That said, to understand means more than to observe outcomes and pronounce them good, bad, or indifferent—this is evaluation plus.

So in what ways is this explanatory impetus essential to, or even compatible with, the heart of evaluation? In the standard account, the argument for a theoretically grounded explanation would stress its ability to support prediction and generalization. This potential is only available, however, if four conditions hold true.[11] First, the theory must be well specified as to how it operates and under what conditions. It must, in other words, provide a coherent (if not complete) account of relevant change. Second, these specifications must be capable of adequate operationalization, that is, reasonable measures of the key specifications of the theory are possible. Third, this operational form of the theory must have been implemented with integrity in the empirical site under investigation. Fourth, there must be substantial agreement or consensus that the theory provides a likely and powerful explanation for the kind of change that is at issue.[12] We take Scriven's (1999) argument to mean that these conditions do not generally occur in evaluation research settings.

Let us examine more closely the case *for* and *against* theory[13] in the evaluation of juvenile drug courts. The argument for theory is so obvious that it typically remains unexpressed. Simply, although it may be worthwhile to evaluate the merit of a particular juvenile drug court at a particular time, our real interest is in improving that program and offering lessons for other current or potential programs. These practical goals are in addition to our disciplinary interests in understanding for its own sake and in order to weigh the relative merit of alternative understandings (theory testing and development). All of these goals require more than a "black box" approach to program evaluation. The black box approach refers to the tendency in evaluations to focus on *external* rather than *internal* processes in evaluating success. External measures refer to the outcomes produced as a result of participating in juvenile drug court (e.g., decreased criminal recidivism, increased abstinence, improved quality of life). Internal measures, on the other hand, refer to the processes that together make up the drug court program and thus (or at least it is believed) contribute to the external measures (e.g., length and level of therapeutic counseling available, presence of and interaction with the drug court judge throughout the program). Drug courts are based on the assumption that these internal processes make some contribution to the external outcomes. At present, however, most drug court evaluations tend to focus exclusively on external measures, largely ignoring the internal processes. We argue that this practice is problematic because, given the dearth of information about internal processes, we actually know very little about why drug courts work the way they do.

It is important to realize that the need for theory-dependent drug court evaluation is generally assumed even when it is not explicit. The rhetoric of federal and other recent funding for drug courts, for example, has embraced the logic of the "demonstration grant"—the ability to learn something in the local site that can be instructive in other sites. The internal validity of the outcomes at the local site and the external validity of those results to other sites are both theory dependent.

Again, the first condition for a theory-dependent evaluation is the availability of a well-specified theory. What are the candidates in juvenile drug court research? As our literature review showed, the "16 key principles" are usually called on to support identification of the program as a drug court in the first place. These components approach but do not comprise a theory in the usual social science sense. The components basically define a working drug court but do not really tell us why or how drug courts should be expected to change young people's behavior. In the traditional view, the core of a theory is precisely this insight as to the mechanism of change—that is what we mean by explanation. The legal theory of therapeutic jurisprudence may indeed similarly qualify as a legal theory. It explains why and how laws and procedures should be structured in particular ways to pursue principles of treatment rather than punishment, but it fails markedly as an explanation of treatment-based change itself; it simply encourages treatment. Why and how that treatment, judicial review, or programmatic approach should effect change in clients remains, precisely, a black box.

It is therefore not an exaggeration to say that juvenile drug courts have not been coherently theorized from a social science perspective. At the same time, it is fairly clear that there are several perfectly coherent theories that could be sensibly developed for juvenile drug courts. As we noted earlier, in our review of Gilmore, Rodriguez, and Webb's (2005) research, social control theory may be an appropriate candidate. Although Gilbert, Rodriguez, and Webb found little empirical support for the effects of social bonds on criminal recidivism or substance use outcomes, we strongly suspect that this study was not a fair test of those theories because the third condition (as discussed above) was not met, that is, the program they evaluated was not designed around or faithful to the theory from which the indicators of bonds were derived.

On the other hand, our own work is centered on developing versions of social learning theory as applied to drug courts (see Chapter 7). Briefly put, differences in delinquent and nondelinquent groups are understood in terms of youths' internalization of cultural norms/values and subjects' definitions of right versus wrong and acceptable versus unacceptable behavior. Indicators of social reinforcements (rewards and punishment) and attempts at resocialization could be readily collected and easily incorporated in drug court evaluations.

There are other candidates for theoretical informed drug courts as well,[14] and this raises a question regarding the fourth condition outlined above—the need for theoretical consensus. At this time, it is not at all clear that there is a consensus regarding a candidate for a theory of juvenile drug courts that one would really expect to powerfully and robustly explain results. This is not to say that such a theory is not possible, but we have yet to spend sufficient time and effort in developing this consensus. This is a substantial problem since much of the empirical side of social science is fragmented and insufficiently oriented to careful replication. Nonetheless, the key point for evaluation is that in the absence of that consensus, theory-based evaluation is at best distracting from the sufficiently challenging work of establishing the merit or worth of a program. At worst, it encourages focus on tests of statistical significance for parameters in negligibly interesting models (Sloan, Smykla, and Rush 2004), which essentially entails "teaching to a test" that no one really believes is worth passing.

In spite of our critique, we firmly believe that juvenile drug courts should remain an important dispositional option in the juvenile justice system. The existing evaluation research may be unimpressive, but it has been sufficient to encourage a growing number of jurisdictions to experiment with this alternative to incarceration and search for ways to make drug courts more effective. But unless and until a persuasive theoretical basis for drug court outcomes is posited and built into the structure of a well-monitored program, theory-driven evaluation will remain an afterthought.

Appendix Treatment and Comparison Group Demographics

	Treatment Group (N = 233)		Comparison Group (N = 183)	
Age	%	N	%	N
12	0.4	1	1.6	3
13	3.0	7	9.8	18
14	18.9	44	19.7	36
15	32.2	75	30.1	55
16	41.2	96	28.4	52
17	3.9	9	9.8	18
18	0.4	1	.5	1
Race/ethnicity				
White, non-Hispanic	60.5	141	47.5	87
African American	34.3	80	46.4	85
Hispanic	2.6	6	4.4	8
Multiracial	2.6	6	1.6	3
Sex				
Male	83.3	194	73.8	135
Female	16.7	39	26.2	48
Household income[a]				
$0–9,999.99	8.3	12	5.0	3
$10,000–19,999.99	27.6	43	35.0	21
$20,000–29,999.99	21.2	33	31.7	19
$30,000–39,999.99	21.2	33	10.0	6
$40,000–49,000	10.9	17	3.3	2
$50,000 or more	11.5	18	15.0	9

Note: a. Income data were only available for 156 of the MJDCP members and 60 comparison group members. The percentages are based upon these figures.

▦ Notes

1. The approved Human Subjects Institutional Review Board Protocol for this research required that the specific location not be disclosed because of the "sensitive" nature of the topic. Hence, MJDCP is a pseudonym.

2. During Phase I (8–12 weeks), participants attend weekly status hearings, meet with probation officers, and are drug tested a minimum of three times per week. Participants and their parents also attend individual and family classes. In order to transition to Phase II, participants must complete all phase requirements and submit 12 consecutive clean urine screens. During Phase II, participants attend bimonthly status hearings, engage in 8–12 weeks of treatment, and are drug tested a minimum of two times per week. In order to transition to Phase III, participants must successfully complete treatment and continue to submit negative urine screens. During Phase III (transitional/aftercare phase), participants attend monthly status hearings and are drug tested a minimum of one time per week. In order to graduate from the program, participants must successfully complete program objectives and continue to submit negative urine screens.

3. Potential participants and their parent(s) are interviewed by the drug court case manager to determine their attitudes toward treatment and their appropriateness for the program. Participants deemed appropriate begin outpatient substance abuse treatment,

which lasts an average of six months. "The length of stay in the treatment program depends upon the individual's identified course of care and his or her progress through three phases of increasing responsibility." In addition to attending treatment, participants are required to do the following: "observe a curfew, meet regularly with a case manager, appear in court for case reviews with a supervising judge, and abide by all state, local, and federal laws" (Applegate and Santana 2000:286). Participants successfully completing the program have their charges either dismissed or reduced.

4. Applegate and Santana employed the Children's Global Assessment Scale to measure the level of family, school, and peer functioning.

5. While in Phase I (three months), participants are placed on intensive probation supervision, which includes electronic monitoring and random home visits by the supervising probation officer. Participants are randomly drug tested two times per week (minimum) and are required to attend treatment, complete the "Drug-Free" curriculum, and participate in a drug prevention group one time per week (six weeks in length). Moreover, the parents/guardians of Phase I participants must also attend and complete a series of parenting classes. While in Phase II (three months), participants are stepped down to "medium" probation supervision (electronic monitoring device is removed) and randomly drug tested every other week. While in Phase III (three months), participants are stepped down to "minimum" probation supervision and randomly drug tested. Moreover, Phase III program participants have to appear in court one time per month. While in Phase IV (three months), participants are randomly drug tested but only need to appear in court at the time of graduation.

6. Drug relapse data were not collected for the comparison group because drug tests are not routinely administered to this group. In a few instances, participants were moved from the comparison group to the treatment group. These participants were excluded from the evaluation.

7. The median number of in-program days for the treatment group was 304, whereas the median number of in-program days for the comparison group was 320. The mean number of days for the treatment group was 339, whereas the mean number of days for the comparison group was 441.

8. It is important to note three data collection issues related to drug testing. First, if a participant was discharged or was in the middle of a phase at the end of the evaluation year (September 30, 2006), data were collected from the time he or she entered that phase until the date he or she was discharged or until the end of the evaluation year; although the participant had not yet completed the phase, the information was included in the evaluation of that phase. Second, the evaluation did not have complete drug testing information for six participants, reducing the size of the sample to 227. Third, in a few cases the date of the drug test was indicated as having taken place outside of the scope of the program, perhaps due to a data entry error. These cases were excluded from the analysis.

9. When calculating recidivism rates and making comparisons across groups, it is imperative that the time frames being utilized have been standardized. With this in mind, the time frames for the treatment group were operationalized as follows. First, the pre-program time period is the one year prior to MJDCP entry. Second, the in-program time period is the length of time a participant spent in the MJDCP. Third, the post-program time period is the one year following discharge from the MJDCP. Moreover, for the comparison group, the time periods were operationalized as follows: First, the pre-program time period is the one year prior to being placed on probation supervision; second, the in-program time period is the length of time a participant spent under probation supervision; third, the post-program time period is the one year following discharge from probation supervision.

10. In ongoing work, we are attempting to account for this bias through more complex statistical analyses (see also Minor, Hartmann, and Davis 1990).

11. This chapter outlines only the most basic dimensions of this debate, using the juvenile drug court area to illustrate. A fuller treatment of the issues and particularly of their foundations and implications (e.g., evolving conceptions of scientific explanation, the problematic role of causality, the role of levels of explanation, and the importance of reductionism and emergence) is in preparation.

12. The first and fourth conditions may appear to be the same but are not. The first requires only that the theory is internally sensible, that its parts relate to each other in a reasonable way. The fourth condition requires that this theory is a sensible explanation for X, that its application to X should explain much of the interest in X. Some quite coherent theories would simply not really be expected to matter much in some applications.

13. This is a reference to *Against Method* by Lakatos and Feyerabend (1999). These two philosophers of science famously disputed the necessity for intersubjectively accepted rules and procedures of method as against a supposedly anarchic approach.

14. Deterrence/rational choice and labeling theories could also be applied. The former asserts that if drug court participants are cognizant of the negative impact their addiction has had on their lives and the consequences associated with program violations, they will be less likely to relapse or engage in law-violating activities (see Introduction to Part 3 and Chapter 6). Labeling theory proposes that labeling individuals as "deviant" may result in these persons internalizing the label and acquiring a negative self-image; drug courts could attempt to resocialize participants and encourage them to establish a new self-image (see Introduction to Part 4 and Chapter 13). Attempts at integrating theoretical perspectives may also prove useful (see Barak 1998; Elliott, Ageton, and Cantor 1979; Elliott, Huizinga, and Ageton 1985). Remember, however, that for any of these theoretical perspectives to frame an evaluation, the ability of the program to implement theoretically important characteristics, as well as the payoff of these characteristics on recidivism, must be explicitly assessed.

■ References

Applegate, Brandon K., and Steven Santana. 2000. "Intervening with Youthful Substance Abusers: A Preliminary Analysis of a Juvenile Drug Court." *Justice System Journal* 21:281–300.

Barak, Gregg. 1998. *Integrating Criminologies.* Boston: Allyn and Bacon.

Belenko, Steven. 2001. "Research on Drug Courts: A Critical Review 2001 Update." *National Drug Court Institute Review* 1:1–60.

Belenko, Steven, and Richard Dembo. 2003. "Treating Adolescent Substance Abuse Problems in the Juvenile Drug Court." *International Journal of Law and Psychiatry* 26:87–110.

DeMatteo, David, Douglas B. Marlowe, and David S. Festinger. 2006. "Secondary Prevention Services for Clients Who Are Low Risk in Drug Court: A Conceptual Model." *Crime and Delinquency* 52:114–134.

Drug Court Clearinghouse and Technical Assistance Project. 1996. *Juvenile Drug Courts: Preliminary Assessment of Activities Underway and Implementation Issues Being Addressed.* Washington, DC: American University.

———. 1998. *Looking at a Decade of Drug Courts.* Washington, DC: American University.

———. 2001. *Juvenile Drug Court Activity Update: Summary Information.* Washington, DC: American University.

Einstadter, Werner J., and Stuart Henry. 2006. *Criminological Theory: An Analysis of Its Underlying Assumptions.* Oxford: Rowman and Littlefield.

Elliott, Delbert S., Suzanne S. Ageton, and Rachelle J. Cantor. 1979. "An Integrated Theoretical Perspective on Delinquent Behavior." *Journal of Research in Crime and Delinquency* 16:3–27.

Elliott, Delbert S., David Huizinga, and Suzanne S. Ageton. 1985. *Explaining Delinquency and Drug Use.* Beverly Hills, CA: Sage.

Gilmore, Anna S., Nancy Rodriguez, and Vincent J. Webb. 2005. "Substance Abuse and Drug Courts: The Role of Social Bonds in Juvenile Drug Courts." *Youth Violence and Juvenile Justice* 3:287–315.

Goldkamp, John S. 1994. "Miami's Treatment Drug Court for Felony Defendants: Some Implications of Assessment." *Prison Journal* 74:110–166.

Hartmann, David J. 2002. *Evaluation of the Michigan Drug Court Grant Program: Executive Summary.* Kalamazoo, MI: Kercher Center for Social Research.

Hempel, Carl G., and Paul Oppenheim. 1948. "Studies in the Logic of Explanation." *Philosophy of Science* 15:135–175.

Hora, Peggy F. 2002. "A Dozen Years of Drug Treatment Courts: Uncovering Our Theoretical Foundation and the Construction of a Mainstream Paradigm." *Substance Use and Misuse* 37:1469–1488.

Hora, Peggy F., William G. Schma, and John T. Rosenthal. 1999. "Therapeutic Jurisprudence and the Drug Treatment Court Movement: Justice System's Response to Drug Abuse and Crime in America." *Notre Dame Law Review* 74:439–537.

Huddleston, C. West, Douglas B. Marlowe, and Rachel Casebolt. 2008. *Painting the Current Picture: A National Report Card on Drug Courts and Other Problem-solving Courts in the United States.* Washington, DC: US Department of Justice.

Lakatos, Imre, and Paul Feyerabend. 1999. *Against Method.* Chicago: University of Chicago Press.

Logan T. K., William Hoyt, and Carl Leukefeld. 2001. "A Statewide Drug Court Needs Assessment: Identifying Target Counties, Assessing Readiness." *Journal of Offender Rehabilitation* 33:1–25.

Marlowe, Douglas B. 2003. "Integrating Substance Abuse Treatment and Criminal Justice Supervision." *Science and Practice Perspectives* 2:4–14.

McGee, Charles M., John Parnham, Thomas T. Merrigan, and Michael Smith. 1998. "Applying Drug Court Concepts in the Juvenile and Family Court Environments: A Primer for Judges." Prepared for the 1995 Drug Court Symposium at American University under Sponsorship of the State Justice Institute.

Miller, J. Mitchell, Holly Ventura Miller, and J. C. Barnes. 2007. "The Effect of Demeanor on Drug Court Admission." *Criminal Justice Policy Review* 18:246–259.

Minor, Kevin I., David J. Hartmann, and Stephen Davis. 1990. "Preserving Internal Validity in Correctional Evaluation Research: The Biased Assignment Design as an Alternative to Randomized Designs." *Journal of Contemporary Criminal Justice* 6:216–225.

Nagel, Ernest. 1979. *The Structure of Science: Problems in the Logic of Scientific Explanation.* Indianapolis, IN: Hackett Publishing.

National Association of Drug Court Professionals. 1997. *Defining Drug Courts: The Key Components.* Washington, DC: Drug Courts Program Office, Office of Justice Programs, US Department of Justice.

———. 2008. *Drug Court Grant Receives a 50% Increase in Funding;* available at http://www.nadcp.org/.

National Center on Addiction and Substance Abuse. 2004. *Criminal Neglect: Substance Abuse, Juvenile Justice, and the Children Left Behind.* New York: Columbia University.

National Drug Court Institute. 2003. *Juvenile Drug Court Strategies.* Washington, DC: US Department of Justice.

———. N.d. "Drug Courts: A National Phenomenon"; available at http://www.ndci.org (accessed March 25, 2008).

Office of Justice Programs. 1999. "Attorney General Reno Announces Funds to Continue Successful Drug Court Program." Washington, DC: US Department of Justice.

Roberts, Marilyn, Jennifer Brophy, and Carolyn Cooper. 1997. "The Juvenile Drug Court Movement." Office of Juvenile Justice and Delinquency Prevention Fact Sheet 59; available at http://www.ncjrs.org.

Rodriguez, Nancy, and Vincent J. Webb. 2004. "Multiple Measures of Juvenile Drug Court Effectiveness: Results of a Quasi-experimental Design." *Crime and Delinquency* 50:292–314.

Salmon, Wesley C. 1989. *Four Decades of Scientific Explanation.* Minneapolis: University of Minnesota Press.

Scriven, Michael. 1999. "The Fine Line Between Evaluation and Explanation." *Research on Social Work Practice* 9:521–524.

Senjo, Scott R., and Leslie A. Leip. 2001. "Testing and Developing Theory in Drug Court: A Four-part Logit Model to Predict Program Completion." *Criminal Justice Policy Review* 12:66–87.

Sloan, John J., and John O. Smykla. 2003. "Juvenile Drug Courts: Understanding the Importance of Dimensional Variability." *Criminal Justice Policy Review* 14:339–360.

Sloan, John J., John O. Smykla, and Jeffrey P. Rush. 2004. "Do Juvenile Drug Courts Reduce Recidivism? Outcomes of Drug Court and Adolescent Substance Abuse Program." *American Journal of Criminal Justice* 29:95–115.

Snyder, Howard N. 2005. *Juvenile Arrests 2003.* Washington, DC: US Department of Justice.

Whiteacre, Kevin W. 2004. "Denial and Adversity in a Juvenile Drug Court." *International Journal of Drug Policy* 15:297–304.

———. 2007. "Strange Bedfellows: The Tensions of Coerced Treatment." *Criminal Justice Policy Review* 18:260–273.

Appendix:
Note on Statistical Techniques

THE ARTICLES IN THIS BOOK THAT UTILIZE QUANTITATIVE TECHNIQUES, though sophisticated in method, have been chosen for their accessibility to students. Nonetheless, we think it would be helpful to include a brief explanation of some of the statistical techniques employed in six of the chapters for those students who may not yet have taken a statistics or research methods course.

In Chapter 4, "Gangs, Drugs, and Delinquency in a Survey of Urban Youth," Finn-Aage Esbensen and David Huizinga use **factor analysis** and **cluster analysis** to identify different types of neighborhoods from which to select respondents for their survey. Factor analysis is a technique that researchers use to identify underlying patterns (factors) that are common to a set of interrelated variables. Cluster analysis is a similar technique, but it portrays results in the form of a graph or picture that looks something like the branches of a tree and that indicates which variables are similar to or different from one another.

In Chapter 5, "The Impact of Sex Composition on Gangs and Gang Member Delinquency," Dana Peterson, Jody Miller, and Finn-Aage Esbensen use **chi-square tests** and **t-tests** to ascertain whether there are significant differences between gangs with varying compositions of male and female members. There are technical issues at stake in deciding which test is most appropriate to use with particular types of data, but both essentially measure whether or not differences between groups are greater than would be expected by chance.

In Chapter 7, "Social Learning Theory, Drug Use, and American Indian Youths: A Cross-Cultural Test," L. Thomas Winfree, Curt Griffiths, and Christine Sellers use **multiple regression** to analyze survey data. Multiple regression allows researchers to better understand the relationship between a dependent variable and a set of independent variables. The effect of each independent variable is isolated by simultaneously controlling for (or taking into account) the effect of the other independent variable. Winfree, Griffiths, and Sellers use this technique to measure the effects that various social learning variables (independent variables) have on the alcohol and marijuana use (dependent variables) of American Indian and Caucasian youths. Only independent values with values (B [unstandardized] coefficients and Beta [standardized] coefficients) that are statistically significant can be said to have meaningful effects on delinquency.

In Chapter 11, "Family Relationships and Delinquency," Stephen Cernkovich and Peggy Giordano use several techniques to analyze the association between family relationships and delinquency. The survey they administered to their respondents presented them with a series of statements with which they were asked to indicate agreement or disagreement; the survey items use a five-point **Likert scaling** format ranging from "strongly agree" to "strongly disagree." Cernkovich and Giordano also use factor analysis (see Chapter 4) to identify common patterns in these responses, which they analyze by means of several statistical techniques, among them **analysis of variance.** Analysis of variance allows researchers to determine whether the variation between *different* groups is greater (to a statistically significant degree) than the variation *within* each group. Only if the between-group variation is greater than the within-group variation can the researcher conclude that the groups differ with respect to the variables under consideration. In this case, Cernkovich and Giordano are interested in ascertaining whether youths who are more or less strongly bonded or attached to their parents are more or less prone to delinquency. Cernkovich and Giordano also use **correlation** and multiple regression techniques to analyze their data. A correlation is a simple measure of association between one variable and another, whereas multiple regression allows for the simultaneous consideration of several independent variables (see Chapter 7). **Mutlicollinearity** can be a problem in regression analysis when the independent variables are highly associated, making it difficult to accurately assess their separate effects on the dependent variable.

In Chapter 15, "Juvenile Involvement in Occupational Delinquency," John Paul Wright and Francis Cullen use a form of multiple regression analysis known as **ordinary least squares** (OLS) to analyze the relationship between several independent variables and occupational delinquency. The technical difference between OLS and other regression techniques need not concern us here; for our purposes the logic is the same, as is the problem of multicollinearity (see Chapters 7 and 11).

Finally, in Chapter 25, "Viable Options: Intensive Supervision Programs for Juvenile Delinquents," William Barton and Jeffrey Butts use various techniques, such as analysis of variance to determine whether the program outcomes of youths receiving varying sentencing dispositions (in-home program commitments versus state commitments) are significantly different (see Chapter 11). In their analysis they also adjust for a statistical phenomenon known as **regression to the mean,** which in lay terms refers to the "law of averages." In this case, it means that lower preprogram self-reported delinquency scores will tend to be higher at the postprogram stage, and higher preprogram scores will tend to be lower at the postprogram stage.

Index

Abbot, Grace, 34
Abortion, 74(n5), 201, 212, 404
Addams, Jane, 11
Adler, Freda, 72
Adolescent subcultures, 352, 369–391; adolescent status and social type metaphors, 370–386; band students, 388(n11); benefits of delinquent behavior, 387; and bullying, 223–224; community perceptions of, 372; in correctional institutions, 510–518, 519(n10); "country" types ("farmers," "hicks," etc.), 383, 386; defined/described, 369; derogatory names, 374, 379–382; drug-using groups, 377, 380, 385, 386; and gang wannabes, 381–382, 386; and gangs, 377, 381, 386; intellectual groups ("nerds," "geeks," etc.), 372–373, 377, 382–383, 386–387; intermediary groups, 382–386; names and characteristics 1950s–1970s, 373–376; "NINs," 389(n15); and parochial schools, 385–386; "punks," "heavy metalers," "goths," etc., 377, 384–385; and race/ethnicity, 375; and religious background, 385; and sexuality, 388(n7); "skaters," 377, 385, 386; "skinheads," 389(n14); and social class, 370–376, 378–380; socialite groups ("jocks," "preppies," etc.), 372–373, 377–379, 386, 388(n7); special education students, 388(n12); streetcorner groups ("druggies," "dirtballs," etc.), 372–375, 377, 379–382; "theater freaks," 388(n8). *See also* Gangs; Peer groups

Adolescent Substance Abuse Program (ASAP; Birmingham, AL), 548–549
Adoption studies, 130–131
Adult criminal court, transfer of serious cases to, 454, 470–471
"Affectional discipline," 30
African American youth, 472(n3); community acceptance of gang members, 448; and community-based corrections, 525–535; and Denver Youth Study, 85; and disposition of cases, 467–468, 470, 472(n3); disproportionate arrest rate, 68–69, 464–465; and dropout risk factors, 276–277, 292; and drug trade, 395–397, 410; economic bifurcation of black communities, 318(n17), 411; family circumstances of, 469; and family interactions, 247–249, 256–258; and gang membership, 85, 112, 395–399, 402, 448; and IQ, 132; names for adolescent subcultures, 375, 381; and police, 410, 464–466, 479–482; and positive functions of gangs, 398–399; and provision of opportunity programs, 304; and school disciplinary practices leading to dropout, 278–292, 293(n7). *See also* Urban neighborhoods
Age of juvenile delinquents: age-graded gangs in Chicago, 436; and alcohol/drug use by Native American vs. Caucasian youth, 170–174; changing attitudes of maturing delinquents (maturational reform), 139, 445–446; and Denver Youth Study, 85–86; and family interactions, 251–252; and

565

gang membership, 85–86; life stages of delinquent youth, 394–395; and police assessment of suspicion, 480; schools' informal expulsion of overage "troublemakers," 288–291; and sex composition of gangs, 111–112; statistics on age and crime, 66–68; and transfer of cases to adult criminal court, 470
Ageton, Suzanne S., 69–70
Agnew, Robert, 221–222, 339, 341
Akers, Ronald L., 140, 143(n4), 164–165
Alabama: Birmingham drug court programs, 548–549
Albuquerque, NM: gangs in, 398
Alcohol use: and adolescent subcultures, 378; and affluent law-violating youth groups, 356–358, 363–364; drug and alcohol use by Native Americans vs. Caucasian youth as test of social learning theory, 161–176; gang vs. nongang involvement, 86–87; and lower-class law-violating youth, 361; and Native American culture, 163–164, 174; as status offense, 167
Alinsky, Saul, 301–302
Allen, Emile Anderson, 318(n16), 404(n2)
Allen, F. A., 41
Allen, Nathan, 15
Allen, Stephen, 10
Altgeld, John Peter, 31
Anderson, Elijah, 318(n17), 410–412, 416, 425–428
Andrews, D. A., 137, 459, 460(n6)
Anomie, 220
Anomie-opportunity theory, 221, 227(n4), 234–235, 303–305, 317(n7)
Apache Indians, 163
Applegate, Brandon K., 548
Apprenticeship, 2
Arizona: Phoenix gangs, 398; Maricopa County drug court program, 547
ASAP. See Adolescent Substance Abuse Program
Asian youth, 132, 375, 381, 396
Astor, Mrs. William, 10
Athletics: and adolescent subcultures, 371, 377–379, 386; and affluent law-violating youth, 358; bullying by jocks, 223–224; and lower-class law-violating youth, 362–363, 367
Attachment, and social control theory, 163, 164, 232, 242–243, 312
Auto theft/"borrowing," 183, 185–187
Autonomic nervous system (ANS) disorders, 129
Avanites, Thomas M., 67

Baby boom, 67
Bachman, Jerald G., 330, 332
Bahr, Stephen, 168
Barton, William, 523–539
Beccaria, Cesare, 138
Becker, Howard, 434
Behaviorism, 136–137, 139–140, 459. See also Social learning theory
Belief, and social control theory, 163, 164, 232
The Bell Curve (Herrnstein and Murray), 132
Bennett, Andy, 416
Bennett, Susan, 313
Bentham, Jeremy, 138
Berger, Ronald: on adolescent subcultures, 352, 369–391; on community organization, 234, 297–322; on legal and extralegal factors in authorities' decisionmaking, 457, 463–475; on school shooters, 142, 219–227; on urban street gangs, 393–406
Binder, Arnold, 455–456, 464, 467
Binet, Alfred, 131
Biological theories of crime, 15–16, 128–133, 142–143(nn 1,2)
Birth control, 15, 37, 200, 403–404
Black, Donald, 413
Blalock, Hubert M., 104, 108, 115, 119
Blau, Peter M., 102–104, 108, 112, 115, 119
Blazak, Randy, 225, 375
Bloods (gang), 397
Blumstein, Albert, 67, 70, 464
Boostrom, Ronald L., 310
Bordua, David, 240
Bortner, M. A., 460, 470
Bowditch, Christine, 275–296
Bowen, Louise, 11
Bowker, Lee H., 199

Boys, 211–215, 437–438; benefits of delinquent behavior as bonding mechanism for affluent youth, 387; cultural dilemma of supervision vs. youths' needs for independence, 448; and disposition of cases, 468–469; and family interactions, 246–258; and gang demographics in Denver Youth Study, 85; and gang vs. nongang delinquency, 86–88; pimping, 233, 268–271; and sexual relations in gangs, 200, 211–215, 400–404; teen fatherhood, 211, 404; and workplace delinquency, 334–337. *See also* Gangs, sex composition of; Identity, male; Law-violating youth groups; Pimping; Police-juvenile interactions; Social class; Values, street culture; *specific ethnic groups*

Brace, Charles Loring, 10, 12, 14

Brain abnormalities, 130

Braithwaite, John, 326, 460

Breed v. Jones, 456

Brockway, Zebulon R., 19, 20

Brown, Brooks, 223–224

Bruce, Dickson D., 455–456

Brunson, Rod K., 105, 120

Bullying, and school shooters, 142, 219–227

Burgess, Robert L., 165

Burkett, Steven R., 235(n2)

Burris-Kitchen, Deborah J., 400–401

Busing, and diffusion of gangs, 398

Butts, Jeffrey, 523–539

Bynum, Jack E., 369

Cage, Robin J., 60(n5)

California: community tolerance of gang violence, 434; prison-based "scared straight" programs, 149; San Diego gangs, 396–397; San Francisco girl gangs, 402. *See also* Los Angeles, CA

Campbell, Anne, 84–85, 93, 142, 369, 401

Canter, Rachelle J., 241

CAP. *See* Chicago Area Project

Carpenter, Cheryl, 139, 141, 183–197

Carpenter, Mary, 19

Carter, Timothy J., 468

Cauffman, Elizabeth, 328

Causes of Delinquency (Hirschi), 71, 232

Causes of delinquent behavior, 127–229; biological explanations, 15–16, 128–133, 142–143(nn 1,2); community reinforcement of deviance, 368; contact with corrupt adults, 28, 130–131; and cultural bias in theories of crime and delinquency, 162, 176(n1); environmental toxins, 130; intelligence and delinquency, 131–133; lack of opportunities for conventional status attainment, 409; and low self-control, 130, 327, 331, 334–337, 340, 341; and probation system, 38–40; psychological explanations, 133–137; routine activities approach to crime, 317(n12); twin and adoption studies, 130–131. *See also* Anomie-opportunity theory; General strain theory; Labeling theory; Social control theory; Social learning theory; Social structure, as contributing factor in delinquency; Strain theory

Cavan, Sherri, 499(n1)

Cernkovich, Stephen A., 72–73, 231, 232, 239–262, 400

Chambliss, William, 351, 355–368, 466

Champbell, Anne, 399

Chesney-Lind, Meda, 106, 466

Cheung, Paul, 469–470

Chicago, IL: community tolerance of gang violence, 433–451; drug trade and Puerto Rican gangs, 395; girl gangs, 402; positive functions of gangs, 398–399; Sampson et al. study of collective efficacy and crime, 317(n6); Shaw and McKay study on high crime areas, 74(n3); street code of personal honor in, 352; widespread nonresident gang membership, 397

Chicago Area Project (CAP), 52, 60(n6), 299–302, 314, 446

Child labor, 11–12

Childhood: changing concepts of, 2–3; colonial America, 2–3; connection between prostitution and early childhood experiences, 271–274; ideal child concept, 3; Middle Ages, 1–2; modern era, 1–2; and Progressive Era reformers' assumptions about children and morality, 39–40. *See also*

Adolescent subcultures; Causes of delinquent behavior; Family interactions; Schools

Children's Aid Society, 10

Child-saving movement, 3, 4, 9–25; and changes in economic and social institutions, 10–12; crime prevention ideas, 15–16; elite support for, 11; images of crime and delinquency, 14–17; and juvenile court system, 17–22; and reformatory system, 19–22; supporters of, 12–14

Cicourel, Aaron V., 277, 478–479

Classic strain theory, 221

Clelland, Donald, 468

Cleveland, OH, 264, 271–272

Clinton, Bill, 544

Clothing, 207–208, 413. See also Adolescent subcultures

Cloward, Richard A., 306, 341, 520(n25)

Cockerham, William C., 177(n8)

Cohen, Albert K., 71, 200, 221

Cohen, Stanley, 57

Collective efficacy, 302, 317(n6)

Colonial America, 2–3

Colorado: legislation on legal responsibility of adults, 28. See also Columbine high school; Denver Youth Study

Columbine high school, 219–220, 223–227, 375–376

Colvin, Mark, 314

Commitment, and social control theory, 164, 177(n4), 232

Communication between parents and children, 242, 253; difference between instrumental and intimate communication, 246; instrumental communication, 246–258; intimate communication, 246–257; self-report survey questions, 259–260

Communities, inner-city. See Urban neighborhoods

Communities, suburban. See Suburban and rural communities

Community organization for prevention of delinquency, 234–235, 297–322, 434; and anomie-opportunity theory, 303–305; Chicago Area Project (CAP), 52, 60(n6), 299–302, 314, 446; collective efficacy, 302, 317(n6); combined offender-oriented and victim prevention strategies, 311–313, 315; comprehensive community action projects of the 1960s, 305–309; descendants of CAP in the 1960s, 303–309; difficulties in recruiting neighborhood leadership, 312; examples of sponsored youth activities, 300–301; Job Corps, 304–305, 317(n8); locality development approach, 234, 298–302, 306–310; mentor programs, 315; Mobilization for Youth (MFY), 52, 234, 306–308; Neighborhood Anti-Crime Self-Help Program (NASP), 311–313; Neighborhood Youth Corps, 304–305; provision of opportunity programs (Job Corps, etc.), 304–305, 314, 317(n8); resistance of relatively closed institutions (schools, etc.) to outside scrutiny/input, 312; social action approach, 234, 298–299, 306–309, 314; social planning approach, 234, 298–299, 304–310, 314; Spergel's identification of strategies, 317(n4); territorial conflicts caused by victim prevention emphasis, 310; victim prevention programs, 309–313; Violent Juvenile Offender Research and Development Program (VJORDP), 311–312

Community tolerance of gang violence, 352, 433–451; "awareness contexts," 434; black gang members accepted by community, 448; and formal social occasions, 437, 442–445; gang members as relatives and friends, 433, 434, 440–443, 447–449; Hispanic/Latino gang members accepted by community, 433–451; honor, violence, and etiquette, 437–439; negative tolerance, 433, 434; negotiated character of moral judgments, 435; outsiders' intolerance of gang violence, 446–447; positive tolerance, 433, 434, 440; relations between gangs and nongang youth, 439–440; tolerance and negotiated order, 434–435; transition from order to disorder, 443–446; white gang members as social outcasts, 448

Community-based corrections, 52–53, 56–59, 458, 523–539; cost savings of, 458, 532–534, 538(n6); evaluation of, 525–526; program activities, 526–528; recidivism rates, 458, 523, 528–532, 538(n7). *See also* Probation

Comprehensive Youth Training and Community Involvement Program (CYTCIP), 524–535, 537(n1)

Conflict between parents and children, 260. *See also* Family interactions

Conflict theory of society, 5

Conklin, John E., 67

Connell, R. W., 222

Consent decree, 455

Constitutional rights of youth, 50–51, 454–457, 460(n4)

Cooley, Charles, 16

Corporate capitalism, 10–12, 17

Correctional institutions, 501–522; bifurcation in clientele (future hardened criminals vs. tractable troubled youth), 57; and bureau-cratization vs. individualization, 520(n20); community-based alternatives to, 458; comparison of punitive custodial institutions and rehabilitative community-based programs, 57, 501–522; convict code, 415, 501–502; drift toward punitive, exclusionary programs, 57; effective-ness compared to intensive probation programs, 523–539; indigenous origins vs. direct importation models of inmate social structure, 501–502; informal vs. formal collaboration between staff and inmates, 517–518, 521(n26); and informing, 513–516; inmate alienation, 510–511; inmate leaders, 515, 517, 520–521(nn 25,26); inmate perceptions of staff and inmates, 511–512; inmate subcultures and social structure, 501–502, 510–518; inmate violence and exploitation, 502–503, 510–518; "pains of imprisonment," 502, 510–512; problems with, 54, 57; recommen-dations for, 53, 57–59, 517–518; recruitment of incarcerated gang members into organized crime, 396; relationship between staff ideology

and program characteristics, 509–510; "scared straight" programs, 138–139, 149–159; separation of status offenders from delinquents, 51; social back-ground of inmates, 502; social control strategies, 505–509, 513–515, 517–518, 519(n10), 520–521(nn 25,26); success of group-oriented rehabili-tative treatment, 141, 458, 501, 517–518; types of institutions based on organizational goals and strategies of treatment, 503–512; verbal assaults ("ranking") and social control, 519(n10); and XYY males, 129. *See also* Houses of refuge; Reformatory system

Corsaro, William A., 387

Cottage system, 4, 19–20

Counseling: detached street workers, 300–301, 306; lack of counseling resources in schools, 291, 293(n10); Progressive Era judges as doctor-counselors, 18

Counter-denunciation as defensive strategy during court proceedings, 493–499

Court system. *See* Judges; Juvenile drug courts; Juvenile justice system

Crack cocaine, 396–397, 410

Crespo, Manuel, 293(nn 14,18)

Crime and delinquency: and affluent law-violating youth groups, 356–358; and age of offenders, 66–68; crimes as "payback," 413, 422–423, 425–426; decline of crime rate in the 1990s, 67–68, 74–75(nn 5,6); and definitions that encourage law violation (social learning theory/differential association theory), 140–141; and differing treat-ment of male and female offenders, 468–469; expansion in definition of delinquency, 33–35; gang vs. nongang delinquency, 86–92; and gender, 71–74, 85, 93–94, 114–118; images of in the Progressive Era, 14–17; inflated statistics due to a few high-frequency offenders, 70; and lower-class law-violating youth, 360–361; National Youth Survey categories, 70; and official vs. self-report data, 69; onset of behavior (primary deviance),

75(n7), 232, 233; prevalence vs. incidence of offending, 70, 86, 87; rise of crime rate in the 1960s and 1970s, 67; and social control theory, 232; statutory definitions of "delinquency," 18; and techniques of neutralization, 184; *Uniform Crime Reports* categories, 65–66; victim prevention programs, 309–313; white-collar crime, 74(n4), 323–324, 326–327, 339; workplace as domain of delinquency, 324–327. *See also* Causes of delinquent behavior; Demographics; Gangs; Law-violating youth groups; Prevention of delinquency; Recidivism rates; Status offenses; Victimization; Violence; *specific crimes*

Crime and Punishment (Dostoevsky), 39
Criminal anthropology, 129
Criminology. *See* Causes of delinquent behavior
Crips (gang), 397
Crofton, Walter, 19
Crutchfield, Robert D., 240
Cullen, Francis, 132–133, 235, 323–349
Curry, G. David, 105–106
Curtis, Lynn A., 311, 313
Custodial institutions. *See* Correctional institutions
Cyberbullying, 387(n2)
CYTCIP. *See* Comprehensive Youth Training and Community Involvement Program

Dalgard, Odd Steffen, 130
Dana, Reverend Malcolm, 36
Dannefer, Dale, 464
Darwin, Charles, 128
Davidson, Laura A., 170
Dawley, David, 318(n19)
DeFina, Robert H., 67
Definitions that encourage law violation (social learning/differential association theory): and choice of targets, 140–141, 143(n3); and drug use in Native American vs. Caucasian youth, 161–176
DeMatteo, David, 546
Demographics: in Denver Youth Study, 71, 84–86, 93–94; overview of

measurement and social distribution of delinquency, 65–77; statistics on class and delinquency, 68–70; statistics on race/ethnicity and delinquency, 68–70; statistics on sex composition of gangs, 111; US census data on general population, 68

Denver Youth Study (DYS), 70–71, 79–98; demographic results, 71, 84–86, 93–94; instability of gang membership, 88; and policy recommendations, 95; research methodology, 80–84; results on gang delinquency vs. nongang delinquency, 86–92; and temporal ordering of gang membership and delinquent activity, 80, 88, 94–95, 98(n12); text of self-reporting survey, 96–97

Dependent children, defined, 453
Detention/preventive custody, 29–30, 454
Deterrence, 138–139; certainty of punishment (rather than swiftness or severity) as greatest deterrent, 138; and informal sanctions (shame, embarrassment, family disapproval), 139; and juvenile drug courts, 560(n14); prison-based "scared straight" programs, 138–139, 149–158
Detroit, MI. *See* Wayne County, MI
DeVall, Kristen, 459, 541–562
Differential association theory, 139–140, 143(n4); and drug use by Native American vs. Caucasian youth, 141, 161–176
Differential definitions, 165–166, 168–169. *See also* Definitions that encourage law violation
Differential reinforcement, 140, 165
Disposition of cases: and assessments about parental control, 478–479; and assessments of "trouble," 487–489, 499(n1); and attitude of offender, 479; defined/described, 455; "delinquent" designation based on factors unrelated to specific offense, 478; factors in discretionary decisionmaking, 467–470, 487–490; and magnitude of offense, 478; and prior contacts with police, 478–479; race, class, and gender variations in outcomes,

467–469, 472(n3); and urban vs. rural courts, 472(4). *See also* Correctional institutions; Judges; Juvenile drug courts; Probation; Treatment of juvenile delinquents

Disrespect. *See* Respect/disrespect

Doerner, William G., 460(n4)

Domestic violence, 213–214

Donahue, John J., 74(n5)

Dostoevsky, Feoder, 39

Drive-by shootings, 443

Dropouts and "pushouts," 276, 288–291, 292(n2)

Drug courts. *See* Juvenile drug courts

Drug trade, 394; diminishing life chances of drug-selling youth, 395; as easiest employment opportunity in inner cities, 410; and gang girls' views on criminality, 209; gang vs. nongang involvement, 86–87, 90–91; and gangs, 395–398; and organized crime, 395–396; and "payback" crimes, 189–190, 196; and territorial conflicts, 203, 410

Drug use: and adolescent subcultures, 380, 385, 386; disparity in arrest rates for white and nonwhite youth, 464–465; gang vs. nongang involvement, 86–87, 90–91; girls' perception of difference between "use" and "addiction," 208–209; marijuana use by Native American vs. Caucasian youth, 161–176; National Youth Survey categories, 70

Due process rights of youth, 454–457, 460(n4)

Dugdale, Richard, 15

Durkeim, Émile, 220, 232, 303, 317(n7)

DYS. *See* Denver Youth Study

Economic Opportunity Act (1964), 304, 306

Economics: and anomie-opportunity theory, 221, 303–305; and child-saving movement, 10–12; correlation between economic growth and declining crime rates, 67; and differing visibility of affluent vs. lower-class groups, 364–366; girls' rejection of poverty by reckless spending, 207; materialistic attitudes

of youth, 325, 333–337, 341–342; policy recommendations, 314–316; recognition of role in criminal behavior, 16; Shaw and McKay study on high crime areas in Chicago (1942), 74(n3); "underground economy," 233, 263–274; youths as consumers, 325, 372

Ectomorph body type, 129

Eder, Donna, 387

Education, 304, 306, 308, 317(n9). *See also* Schools

Ego, 134

Eisenhower Foundation, 312–313

Elliott, Delbert S., 69–70, 95, 464

Emerson, Robert, 457–458, 487–500

Empey, Lamar, 52

Employment: availability of low-paid service economy jobs, 325; comprehensive community action projects of the 1960s, 305–309; correlation between delinquency and availability and quality of jobs, 318(n16), 326–327; correlation between delinquency and youth employment, 325–326; disjunction between gang girls' aspirations and available opportunities, 207; disjuncture between culturally approved goals and available opportunities, 221, 303; disjuncture between job training and supply of available jobs, 309, 314; drug trade as best employment opportunity, 410; negative effects on adolescents, 325, 327; policy recommendations, 314–316; provision of opportunity programs of the 1960s (Job Corps, etc.), 304–305, 314, 317(n8); statistics on teen employment, 325, 328; and teen mothers, 206–207. *See also* "Underground economy"; Workplace delinquency

Endomorph body type, 129

England, Ralph W., 369

English common law, 3, 6(n1)

"Enhancement" model of delinquent behavior, 95

Environmental toxins, 130

Erickson, Maynard, 52

Erlanger, Howard S., 318(n19), 449(n4)

Esbensen, Finn-Aage, 70–71, 74, 79–126
Eugenics, 15, 133
Evans, Mrs. Glendower, 21

Fagan, Jeffrey, 84, 94, 106, 312, 412, 470
Family circumstances: and authorities' assessments about parental control, 478–479; colonial America, 2–3; and discretionary decisionmaking in the juvenile justice system, 469; inadequacy of broken/unbroken home dichotomy, 240–241; Middle Ages, 1–2; modern era, 1; and *parens patriae* doctrine, 47; Progressive Era reformers' assumptions about, 37–38; relative importance of quality of life factors vs. broken/unbroken home variable, 243, 247–248, 258; stepfamilies, 247–249, 252–254; and teen parents, 206–207; and workplace delinquency, 332, 334–337
Family Court Act (1962), 51
Family interactions, 231–233, 239–262; and achievers in at-risk communities, 233; and "awareness contexts," 434; caring and trust, 245–249, 257; communication, 242, 248–258; conflict, 246–258; connection between prostitution and early childhood experiences, 271–274; control and supervision, 245, 247–258; counter-denunciation following parents' complaints against children, 497–498; domestic violence, 213–214; family disapproval as deterrent, 139; gang members as "good sons," 441–442, 445, 449; gang threats to family members, 444; and girl gang members, 401; identity support, 245, 248–258; importance of family honor, 441, 448–449, 449(n3); intimate communication, 246–248; and maternal employment, 241; neglect of family variables in early studies, 240; parental disapproval of peers, 248–258; psychological presence of parents, 242; and race/ethnicity, 247–249, 256–258; reciprocal relationship of delinquency and negative interactions, 246–247;

relative importance of family interaction variables, 254–256; relative importance of quality of life factors vs. broken/unbroken home variable, 243, 247–248, 258; and social control theory, 232, 242–243, 258; in stepfamilies, 247–249, 252–254; and tolerance of children's gang activity, 434, 440–443, 448–449; and workplace, 332. *See also* Parents
Fare v. Michael C., 456
Fathers: connection between prostitution and early childhood experiences, 271–274; stepfathers, 247–249, 252–254; teen fathers, 211, 404. *See also* Family interactions
Feld, Barry, 457, 458, 471, 501–522
Felt, Jeremy, 11
Feminism, 12–13, 23(n21), 72. *See also* Identity, female
Ferdinand, Theodore N., 5–6, 45–60, 460
Festinger, David S., 546
Feyerherm, William, 469
Fighting: and achieving status in street culture, 214–215, 411–414, 438–440; characteristics of gang fights, 442–443; and community perceptions of lower-class law-violating youth, 360; in correctional institutions; distinction between upholding honor and gaining a reputation for toughness, 440, 441; and formal social occasions, 437, 442–445; and girls, 200, 214–215, 399, 401, 403; justified by counter-denunciation, 494; settings for fights, 442–445; and violent crime, 394; youths' attempts to avoid, 445. *See also* Gang violence; Values, street culture; Violence
Figlio, Robert M., 68
Figueria-McDonough, Josephina, 72
Finckenauer, James O., 150–153, 156
Fire, playing with, 195
Firestone, Shulamith, 23(n21)
Fishbein, Diane, 133
Florida: Orange County drug court program, 548
Fobes, Catherine, 317(n8)
Folks (gang), 397
Fort, Jeff, 396
Fort Wayne, IN: gangs, 400–401

Fort Worth, TX: Porterfield self-report survey (1943), 69
Foster care, 32
Freudian psychology, 134–135
Frith, Simon, 416

Gang delinquency: delinquency and number of years of membership, 89–90; delinquency following departure from the gang, 88, 92; distinguished from group delinquency, 351–352; and drug trade, 395–398; gang girls' views on criminality, 209–210; gang vs. nongang delinquency, 86–92, 97(n1); impact of sex composition, 101–123; and organized crime, 395–396; policy recommendations, 95; reduced gang activity during protest actions, 318(n19); temporal ordering of gang membership and delinquent activity, 80, 88, 94–95, 98(n12); theories of delinquency, 95
Gang membership: and adolescent subcultures, 381–382; age of joining, 85–86; age-graded gangs in Chicago, 436; core vs. peripheral membership, 87, 112; demographics in Denver Youth Study, 84–86, 93–94; diffusion of gangs and nonresident gang membership, 398; "emerging" gang cities, 97(n3), 397–398; gang wannabes, 398; multigenerational membership, 394; nonresident gang membership, 397, 398; and race/ethnicity, 393; reasons for joining gangs, 394, 396, 397, 401; recruitment of incarcerated gang members into organized crime, 396; and social class, 393; spread of gangs to smaller communities, 398; temporal ordering of gang membership and delinquent activity, 80, 88, 94–95, 98(n12); transitory nature of membership, 70–71, 88, 94. See also Girls as gang members; specific ethnic groups
Gang Resistance Education and Training (G.R.E.A.T.) program, 74, 101, 108–109, 122(n6)
Gang violence, 433–451; changing attitudes of maturing gang members, 445–446; as extension of honor, 437–438, 440; and formal social occasions, 437, 442–445; girls' views on gang warfare, 209; outsiders' intolerance of, 446–447; police patrol of neighborhood boundaries in order to stop gang wars, 480–481
Gangs: boy-girl interactions in, 212–215, 400–404; as community institutions with positive functions as well as negative, 398–399; community tolerance of, 394, 398–399; definition in Denver Youth Study, 82–83; gang cohesiveness/organization, 396; gang members as "good sons," 441–442, 445, 449; gangs in the 1920s, 393–394; lack of parental options for controlling gang youth, 445–446, 448–449; mutual dependency of members viewed as weakness, 446; "near gangs," 83; negative community perceptions of, 351; and nongang youth, 439–440, 445; and sexual relations, 211–215, 400–404; stereotypes about, 94. See also African American youth; Denver Youth Study; Girls as gang members; Hispanic/Latino youth; Law-violating youth groups; Police-juvenile interactions; White youth
Gangs, sex composition of, 74, 101–123; Blalock's majority group power approach, 104, 108, 115, 119; Blalock's minority group threat hypothesis, 104, 119, 472(n1); Blau's group proportion approach, 102–104, 108, 112, 115, 119; Denver Youth Study results, 71, 85, 93–94; gang characteristics and activities, 113–118; gang types based on sex composition, 75(n9), 103–108, 110; and girls' experiences as gang members, 106–107, 120; Kanter's group proportion/tokenism approach, 103–104, 108, 112, 115, 119; low delinquency rates in single-gender gangs, 120–121, 123(nn 12,15); and male control of entry, 123(n14); Peterson et al. study results, 111–121; statistics on gang composition, 111, 400
Gangsta rap, 408, 414, 417, 426, 428. See also Rap music

Gault, Gerald, 455–456

Geis, Gilbert, 327, 455–456

Gender: and alcohol/drug use by Native American vs. Caucasian youth, 170–174; and disposition of cases, 468–469; and family interactions, 246–258; gender bias, 60(n5); gender socialization, 71–72; gender theory and school shooters, 142, 222–223; impact of sex composition of gangs, 101–123; and police decisionmaking, 466; sex composition of gangs in Denver Youth Study, 71, 85, 93–94. *See also* Boys; Girls; Girls as gang members; Identity, female; Identity, male

General strain theory, 142, 220–222, 225–227

Genetic influences on behavior, 129–131, 143(n2)

Gill, Kimveer, 226

Gilmore, Anna S., 547–548, 557

Giordano, Peggy C., 72–73, 120, 231, 232, 239–262, 400

Girard, Stephen, 10

Girard College, 10

Girls: and birth control/pregnancy, 200, 271, 403–404; delinquent youth sent away to other relatives, 204–205; derogatory names for, 388(n7); and disposition of cases, 468–469; and double standard of behavior, 204, 401, 466; and family interactions, 246–258; and fighting, 399, 401; girls constituting a majority of arrests in prostitution, shoplifting, and running away, 72; greater supervision of, 448; impact of sex composition of gangs, 101–123; initial exclusion of girls from Job Corp opportunities, 317(n8); masculinity-liberation theory of criminality, 72; and misogyny in rap music, 428; and police interactions, 466; sexual abuse, 266–267, 272–273, 401; teen motherhood, 200, 201, 206–207, 210–211, 403–404; temporal ordering of gang membership and delinquent activity, 98(n12); and verbal assaults, 519(n10); women's shame reflecting on male family members, 449(n3); and workplace

delinquency, 334–337. *See also* Gangs, sex composition of; Girls as gang members; Identity, female; Police-juvenile interactions; Prostitution; Values, street culture; *specific ethnic groups*

Girls as gang members, 201, 206–207, 214, 399–404; auxiliary female gangs, 401–402; boy-girl interactions, 211–215, 400–404; and delinquency, 399–400; and drug addiction, 208–209; and femininity, 200, 210–215, 400–404; and fighting, 200, 214–215, 401, 403; gang demographics in Denver Youth Study, 71, 85, 93–94; gang experiences as liberating vs. injurious, 106; and gang fights, 443; gang initiation rituals, 402; and gang vs. nongang delinquency, 86–88; girls' perceptions of their parents, 213–214; lack of opportunity in mainstream society, 401; and *marianismo,* 213–215; need for violent reputation in order to avoid victimization, 214–215, 401; and passivity, 211–212; and physical abuse, 213–214; physical appearance, 200, 207–208, 403; reasons for joining gangs, 401; role in gangs ignored in early studies, 93; romantic disputes with rival girls, 214, 403; self-definition by rejection through social talk (gossip, put downs), 142, 199–218; and sexual relations, 200, 211–215, 400–404; social workers' perceptions of inappropriate gender roles, 200; spending habits, 207; and techniques of neutralization, 201; views on criminality, 209–210

Glaser, Barney, 434

Glassner, Barry, 141, 183–197

Goldman, Nathan, 479

Goldston, Stephen E., 315

Gordon, Milton, 162

Goring, Charles, 143(n1)

Gossip and put downs, 142, 199–218

Gottdiener, Mark, 375

Gottfredson, Michael R., 327, 331, 332, 340

Gould, E. R. L., 16

Gove, Walter R., 240

Grady, Elizabeth, 70
G.R.E.A.T. program. *See* Gang
  Resistance Education and Training
  (G.R.E.A.T.) program
Gregory, Paul, 459, 541–562
Griffiths, Curt, 141, 161–181
Group-oriented rehabilitative treatment,
  141, 458, 501, 508–509, 511, 517–518
Growing Up Poor (Williams and
  Kornblum), 233, 263–274
Guardian Angels, 310
Gubrium, Jaber F., 415
Guns, 195, 410, 412, 421–422, 443. *See
  also* School shooters
Gutek, Barbara A., 120

Hagan, John, 316, 372
Hagedorn, John M., 381, 397, 404
Haldeman, Harry, 11
Handler, Joel, 18
Harris, Eric, 219–220, 223–227, 227(n7),
  375
Hartmann, David, 459, 541–562
Hasenfeld, Yeheskel, 469–470
Hathaway, Starker R., 135
Hawkins, J. David, 237
Hazard, Geoffrey C., Jr., 40
Head Start, 317(n9)
Henderson, Joel H., 310
Henrotin, Ellen, 11
Hernstein, Richard, 132
Heroin, 208
Hewitt, John, 201, 435
Hill, Matthew Davenport, 19
Hindelang, Michael J., 69
Hirschi, Travis: on delinquent
  predisposition, 332; on demographics
  and serious vs. minor offenses, 69;
  and intimate communication, 246; on
  low self-control, 331, 340; on religion
  and delinquency, 235(n2); social
  control theory and family interactions,
  232, 242–243; and studies of Native
  American youth, 163–164; on white-
  collar crime, 327
Hispanic/Latino youth: boy-girl
  interactions, 211–215; community
  tolerance of gang violence in Chicago
  Chicano community, 433–451; and
  Denver Youth Study, 85; and domestic
  violence, 213–214; and dropout risk

factors, 276, 292; and drug trade, 395,
  396; and gang membership, 85, 394,
  397; girl gangs, 402; girls' self-
  definition by rejection through social
  talk (gossip, put downs), 199–218;
  importance of image of "purity"
  before marriage, 200, 212; names for
  adolescent subcultures, 375, 380–381;
  and police patrols of neighborhood
  boundaries, 481; and sex composition
  of gangs, 112; street code of personal
  honor, 352, 437–438; and teen
  parents, 404
History of juvenile justice and
  delinquency, 1–63; and biological
  explanations for delinquency, 128–
  133; change in focus of correctional
  efforts, 33, 53; colonial America, 2–3;
  early charitable institutions, 10–11;
  early laws on trials of minors, 17;
  expansion in definition of delinquency,
  33–35; gangs in the 1920s, 393–394;
  goals of Progressive Era reformers,
  32–33, 36; ideal child concept, 3; and
  Johnson administration, 52; juvenile
  court movement, 27–43; Middle Ages,
  1; nineteenth century, 3–4, 46–49;
  post–World War II criticisms of
  juvenile justice system, 50–54;
  Progressive Era, 4, 9–22, 27–43; and
  rational-choice theory, 138; treatment
  and prevention programs of the 1960s
  and 1970s, 51–53. *See also* Legislation
Hobbies. *See* Involvement, and social
  control theory
Hoffman, Lois Wladis, 241
Hoge, Dean, 293(n11)
Holstein, James A., 414–415
Homicide: and community tolerance of
  gang violence, 435–436, 439;
  distinction between upholding honor
  and gaining a reputation for toughness,
  441; and prevalence of guns, 410;
  statistics on, 449(n2). *See also* Gang
  violence; School shooters; Violence
Hora, Peggy F., 544
Horowitz, Irving L., 434
Horowitz, Ruth, 204, 214, 352, 433–451
Hough district of Cleveland, OH, 264,
  271–272
Houses of refuge, 3–4, 28, 34, 38, 57

Hovland, Arild, 156–157
Huff, C. Ronald, 393
Huizinga, David, 70–71, 79–100, 464

Id, 134
Ideal child concept, 2–3
Identity, female: femininity and gang membership, 200, 210–215, 400–404; gender socialization, 71–72; girls' self-definition by rejection through social talk (gossip, put downs), 142, 199–218; *marianismo,* 213–215. *See also* Adolescent subcultures
Identity, male: degradations to masculine identity and school shooters, 142, 219–227; and displays of material wealth, 409, 413; and displays of toughness, 352, 409, 412, 438; and fathering children, 404; gender socialization, 71–72; lack of opportunities for conventional status attainment in inner-city communities, 409; mutual dependency viewed as weakness, 446; necessity of accepting offers of sex, 214; separation of gang identity from workplace identity, 437–438; and sexual activity, 214, 388(n7), 389(n18), 403, 404, 413; and symbolic inter-action, 139–140; and verbal agility, 371, 409. *See also* Adolescent subcultures
Identity support, 245–259
Illegal service crimes, defined, 70
Illinois: Division of Youth Services, 302; juvenile code of 1899, 1, 49
Imitation, and social learning theory, 140, 165
Immigrants, 37, 203–206, 393
Incidence of offending (individual offending), distinguished from prevalence, 70, 86, 87
Index crimes (Part I offenses), described, 65
Industrial Revolution, 10–12, 46–47
Infanticide, 1
Informal disposition of cases, 454–457. *See also Parens patriae* doctrine
Inner-city neighborhoods. *See* Urban neighborhoods
In re Ellery, 51
In re Gault, 454–456

In re Lavette, 51
In re Winship, 456
Insiders Crime Prevention program, 155–156
Instrumental communication, 246
Intake stage of juvenile justice system, 454, 467
Intensive Probation Unit (IPU), 524–535
Internet, 387(n2)
Involvement, and social control theory, 163, 232
IPU. *See* Intensive Probation Unit
IQ test, 131–133

Jankowski, Sanchez, 396
JCJDCP. *See* Jefferson County Juvenile Drug Court Program
Jefferson County Juvenile Drug Court Program (JCJDCP), 548–549
Jensen, Gary F., 177(n2)
Jilek-Aall, Louise, 162
Job Corps, 304–305, 317(n8)
Job Training Partnership Act, 315
Joe, Karen A., 106
Johnson, Bruce, 141, 183–197
Johnson, David, 468–469
Johnson, Lyndon, 52, 60(n9), 303
Johnson, Richard E., 168, 177(n6), 253
Jones, Richard S., 414
JSATC. *See* Juvenile Substance Abuse Treatment Court
Judges, 457–458, 487–500; assessment of "trouble," 487–489, 499(n1); assessments of juvenile's moral character, 489–490; and counter-denunciation as defensive strategy, 493–499; court's refusal to acknowledge complaints of unfair treatment by police, 498–499; as doctor-counselors in Progressive Era court system, 18; elected vs. appointed judges, 470; factors in discretionary decisionmaking, 467–470; and juvenile drug courts, 543, 544; outcomes of cases, 488–489; personal characteristics of, 30, 50; and pressure from referral agency to "do something," 469–470, 489; role in juvenile court system, 30–32; and seriousness of offenses, 488; and total denunciation of

delinquent youth, 490–493. *See also*
Juvenile drug courts
Juvenile Awareness Project, 150–152,
156
Juvenile Court Act (1899), 17
Juvenile delinquents: bifurcated
population of offenders, 48, 57;
constitutional rights of, 50–51,
454–457, 460(n4); "delinquent"
designation based on factors unrelated
to specific offense, 478; delinquents
distinguished from status offenders
and dependent children, 51, 453;
interviews of teenagers involved in
underground economy, 263–274; lack
of parental options for controlling
delinquent youth, 445–446, 448–449;
moral character of, 489–493; social
construction of "troublemakers" in
school, 283–284. *See also* Age of
juvenile delinquents; Boys; Causes of
delinquent behavior; Crime and
delinquency; Demographics; Gangs;
Gender; Girls; Law-violating youth
groups; Police–juvenile interactions;
Race/ethnicity; Social class; Values,
street culture; *specific ethnic groups*
Juvenile drug courts, 459, 541–562;
Birmingham program (Alabama),
548–549; defined/described, 542–543;
and deterrence/rational choice theory,
560(n14); distinguished from
traditional models of criminal justice,
542–543; funding, 545; and labeling
theory, 560(n14); Maricopa County
program (Arizona), 547–548; Midwest
Juvenile Drug Court Program, 541,
549–560; Orange County program
(Florida), 547–548; program
evaluation, 545–549, 555–557; and
recidivism, 547–549, 551–558; and
social control theory, 547–548, 557;
and social learning theory, 557;
strategies of, 543–545; therapeutic
jurisprudence, 544–545
Juvenile justice system: and attorneys,
457, 470–471, 491; change in focus of
correctional efforts, 33, 53; and
Chicago Area Project, 301; consent
decree, 455; contrast to adult criminal
court, 17, 30; courtroom procedure,

17, 30–31, 454–455; detention/
preventive custody, 29–30, 454; due
process rights of youth, 50–51,
454–457, 460(n4); and emerging
school systems of the late eighteenth
and early nineteenth centuries, 46–47;
English common law, 3, 5, 6(n1);
factors in discretionary decisionmaking, 457–471; formal and
informal disposition of cases, 31–32,
454–457; gender biases, 51; and
Illinois juvenile code of 1899, 1, 49;
importance of prior record, 469;
intake stage, 29, 454, 467; investigation of cases, 29; origins and early
institutions, 3, 46–49; overview of
contemporary system, 453–461;
post–World War II criticisms of
juvenile justice system, 50–54;
preference for home rehabilitation,
31–32, 38; and pressure from referral
agency, 469–470, 489; privacy issues,
31; Progressive Era, 17–22, 27–43;
racial discrimination, 51; repetitive
pattern of reform and decay, 57–58;
role of judges, 30–32; role of
probation officer, 29; separation of
child from adult offenders, 28; stages
of juvenile justice, 453–455; transfer
of cases to adult criminal court, 454,
470–471. *See also* Correctional
institutions; Crime and delinquency;
Disposition of cases; Identity, female;
Identity, male; Juvenile drug courts;
Parens patriae doctrine; Police;
Police-juvenile interactions;
Prevention of delinquency; Probation;
Recidivism rates; Treatment of
juvenile delinquents
Juvenile Substance Abuse Treatment
Court (JSATC), 548

Kanter, Rosabeth Moss, 103–104, 108,
112, 115, 119, 120
Karmen, Andrew, 459
Katz, Jack, 226
Katz, Michael, 20
Kelling, George L., 75(n6)
Kent v. U.S., 454, 456
Kimmel, Michael S., 223
Kinkel, Kip, 227(n2)

Kirchheimer, Otto, 20
Kitsuse, John I., 277
Klebold, Dylan, 219–220, 223–227, 227(n7), 375
Klein, Donald, 315
Klein, Malcolm W., 53, 97(n1), 101, 199, 351, 466
Kobrin, Solomon, 53
Konrad, Alison M., 102
Korn, Richard, 493
Kornblum, William, 233, 263–274
Kringlen, Einar, 130
Krisberg, Barry A., 302, 472(n5)
Ksander, Margret, 141, 183–197
Kubrin, Charis, 352, 407–432
Kunitz, Stephen J., 162

Labeling theory: and arrest rates, 69; defined/described, 277–278; differing perceptions of youth offending based on social class, 351, 355–368; and juvenile drug courts, 560(n14); and primary vs. secondary deviance, 75(n7), 287; relative vs. absolute labeling effects, 236(n3); and schools, 233–234, 275, 277–278, 282–285
LaFree, Gary, 67
Larkin, Ralph, 223–227, 373, 376
Lathrop, Julia, 11, 34
Latino youth. See Hispanic/Latino youth
Laub, John H., 339, 468
Lauderback, David, 402
Lavrakas, Paul J., 313
Law-violating youth groups, 351–352; adult careers of affluent vs. lower-class youth, 366–367; affluent youth offenders and school, 355–356; defined/described, 352; delinquent behavior of affluent youth in Chambliss's study, 355–359, 363–364; delinquent behavior of lower-class youth in Chambliss's study, 359–364; delinquent youths as part of "respectable" society, 355; differing perceptions of youth offending based on social class, 351, 355–368, 372; differing visibility of affluent vs. lower-class groups, 364–365; gang delinquency distinguished from group delinquency, 351–352; lower-class youth offenders and school, 362–363;

and perceptions about "seriousness" of offenses, 363–364; police interactions and social class, 357–359, 360–362. See also Gangs
Lead exposure, 75(n6), 130
Ledonne, Danny, 227(n9)
Legislation: early laws on juvenile cases, 27–28; early laws on trials of minors, 17; Economic Opportunity Act (1964), 304, 306; expansion in definition of delinquency, 33–35; Family Court Act (1962), 51; Illinois juvenile code (1899), 1, 49; Job Training Partnership Act, 315; Juvenile Court Act (1899), 17; on legal responsibility of adults, 28; on separation of status offenders from delinquents, 51; Violent Crime Control and Law Enforcement Act (1994), 544
Leiber, Michael J., 472(n3)
Leip, Leslie A., 542
Lemert, Edwin, 435
Letchworth, William, 19, 21
Levitt, Steven D., 67, 74(n5)
Levy, Jerrold E., 162
Lindsey, Ben, 17, 28, 30, 36, 39, 50
Lions (Chicago gang), 436–449
Lishner, Denise, L., 237
Locality development, 234, 299, 314; Chicago Area Project (CAP) as example of, 299–302; comprehensive community action projects of the 1960s, 305–309; conflicts between locality development and social planning, 310; defined/described, 298; dilemmas of strategy, 302; Neighborhood Anti-Crime Self-Help Program (NASP), 311–313; and victim prevention programs, 309–310
Lofland, Lyn, 433
Lombroso, Cesare, 15, 128–129, 142–143(n1)
Longclaws, Lyle, 163
Lopez, Lou, 97(n3)
Los Angeles, CA: changes in gang characteristics due to drug trade, 396; community treatment program, 52; multigenerational Chicano gangs, 394; nonresident gang membership in Chicano gangs, 397; and origins of rap music, 408

Loughlin, Julia, 141, 183–197
Louisville, KY, 263
Low-income communities. *See* Urban
    neighborhoods
Lubove, Roy, 36
Lundman, Richard, 138

Mack, Julian, 18, 33
Maconochie, Alexander, 19
Mahler, Matthew, 223
Majority group power theory, 104, 108,
    115, 119
Makkai, Toni, 326
Malone, Donna, 375
Mann, Coramae Richey, 465
Marcos, Anastasios M., 168
Marianismo, 213–215
Marijuana. *See* Drug trade; Drug use
Marlowe, Douglas B., 542, 546
Masculinity-liberation theory of female
    criminality, 72
Mass media: focus on violence at
    suburban/rural schools, 220; and
    gangs, 398; glorification of violence,
    220; and social learning theory, 140;
    television as principal source of
    outside influence, 207
Massachusetts: Department of Youth
    Services, 55–58; early laws on
    juvenile cases, 27–28; study of
    correctional institutions, 505–521;
    successful treatment programs, 55–58
Materialism: material wealth as status
    symbol, 409, 413; materialistic
    attitudes and workplace delinquency,
    331–337, 341–342; youths as
    consumers, 325, 372
Maturational reform, 139, 445–446
Matza, David: on maturational reform,
    139; on techniques of neutralization,
    140–141, 183, 201, 493–494; on
    thrill-seeking activities, 389(n18);
    on verbal assaults, 519(n10)
Maxson, Cheryl L., 97(n1), 101
May, Philip A., 162–163
McCarthy, John, 293(n11)
McClearly, Richard, 521(n25)
McCorkle, Lloyd, 493
McGarrell, Edmund F., 467
McKay, Clifford, 60(n6)
McKay, Henry D., 299–300

McKiever v. Pennsylvania, 456
Measures of delinquent activity, 65–77
Mednick, S., 129
Menard, Scott, 95
Meridian, MS, 264–265
Merten, Don, 370
Merton, Robert, 303, 317(n7)
Mesomorph body type, 129
Messerschmidt, James W., 400
Messner, Steven F., 342
MFY. *See* Mobilization for Youth
MHS. *See* Michigan Human Services,
    Inc.
Michigan: cost savings of community-
    based corrections, 458, 523–539;
    Michigan Human Services, Inc.
    (MHS), 524–535; Michigan Reforma-
    tory Visitation program, 153–155
Michigan Human Services, Inc. (MHS),
    524–535
Middle Ages, 1
Midwest Juvenile Drug Court Program
    (pseudonym), 541, 549–560
Miller, Jerome, 151–152
Miller, Jody, 74, 101–126
Miller, Walter B., 352, 379
Milner, Murray, Jr., 382, 386, 388(n11)
Milwaukee, WI: gangs in, 397–398
Minnesota Multiphasic Personality
    Inventory, 135
Minority group threat hypothesis, 104,
    119, 472(n1)
Mississippi: school shooters, 219
Mobilization for Youth (MFY), 52, 234,
    306–308
Model Cities program, 304
Monachesi, Elio, 135
Moore, Joan W., 201, 397, 400–402, 404
Moral values. *See* Values, mainstream;
    Values, street culture
Mothers: girls' rejection of perceived
    passivity of their mothers, 213–214;
    maternal employment, 241; teen
    motherhood, 200, 201, 206–207,
    210–211, 403–404. *See also* Family
    interactions; Parents
Muncer, Steven, 369
Murray, Charles, 132

NASP. *See* Neighborhood Anti-Crime
    Self-Help Program

National Drug Court Institute, 543–544
National Evaluation of the Gang Resistance Education and Training program, 108–109
National Youth Survey (NYS), 70, 331
Native American youth: and acculturation, 162–163; and definitions that encourage law violation, 141, 161–176; and differential association theory, 141, 161–176; and diffusion of gangs, 398; and disposition of cases, 472(3); drug and alcohol use by Native Americans vs. Caucasian youth as test of social learning theory, 161–176; names for adolescent subcultures, 375; parenting styles, 163–164, 174; and social integration, 163; and suicide, 163
Navajo Nation, 163, 398
"Near gangs," 83
"Negotiated order" approach to organizations, 277–278
Neighborhood Anti-Crime Self-Help Program (NASP), 311–313
Neighborhood Youth Corps, 304–305
Neutralization, techniques of, 140–141, 143(n3), 183–197; appeals to higher loyalties, 141; condemnation of the condemners, 140–141; denial of injury, 140, 183–184, 194–195; denial of responsibility, 140; denial of the victim, 140, 183–184, 187–190, 195; and female gang members, 201
Nevin, Rick, 75(n6)
New Jersey: prison-based "scared straight" programs, 150–153
New Jersey v. T.L.O., 456
New York: Family Court Act (1962), 51; Thornberry et al. study of high-risk youth in Rochester, 94–95
New York City: delinquent youth in Brooklyn neighborhoods, 394–395; girls in gangs, 199–218, 399; Mobilization for Youth, 52, 234, 306–308; pimping and prostitution in, 266–269; prison-based "scared straight" programs, 149
Nicknames for subcultures. *See* Adolescent subcultures
Nihilism, 428, 430(n7)
Nixon, Richard, 53

Nondelinquent youth: achievers in at-risk communities, 233. *See also* Family interactions; Schools
Non-index crimes (Part II offenses), described, 65
Norland, Stephen, 241
Norway: "scared straight" program, 156–157
Nurge, Dana, 105
Nye, F. Ivan, 240, 241
NYS. *See* National Youth Survey

Office of Economic Opportunity, 306
Oglala Sioux, 174
Ohlin, Lloyd, 306, 308
Orenstein, Peggy, 402
Organizational sociology: Blalock's majority group power theory, 104, 108, 115, 119; Blalock's minority group threat hypothesis, 104, 119, 472(n1); Blau's group proportion approach, 102–104, 108, 112, 115, 119; impact of sex composition of gangs, 101–123; Kanter's group proportion/tokenism approach, 103–104, 108, 112, 115, 119–120. *See also* Labeling theory
Organized crime, 395
Orphanages, 10

Padilla, Felix, 395
Palmer, Mrs. Potter, 11
Palmer, Ted, 53
Parens patriae doctrine, 5, 6(n1), 17, 455; and different juvenile court philosophies, 469; and due process rights of youth, 456; English common law, 5; and fairness, 50–51; and origins of juvenile justice system, 46–48; and successful programs, 59; undermined by ineffective treatment programs, 53–54
Parents, 248–258; authorities' assessments about parental control, 478–479; beliefs about employment of adolescents, 325; connection between prostitution and early childhood experiences, 271–274; counter-denunciation following parents' complaints against children, 497–498; criminality of, 143(n4); cultural

dilemma of supervision vs. youths' needs for independence, 448; delinquent youth sent away to other relatives, 204–205, 448; and domestic violence, 213–214; girls' rejection of perceived passivity of their mothers, 213–214; interactions with schools, 281–282, 285–287; lack of options for controlling gang youth, 444–445, 448–449; and materialistic attitudes of youth, 342; maternal employment, 241; parenting styles of Native Americans, 163–164, 174; psychological presence of, 242; and social control theory, 232, 242–243, 258; stepparents, 247–249; teen parents, 200, 201, 206–207, 210–211, 403–404; tolerance of children's alcohol consumption, 163–164; tolerance of children's gang activity, 434, 440–445, 448–449; unhealthy prenatal and postnatal practices, 130–131. *See also* Family interactions

Parolees, and Chicago Area Project, 301, 302

Part I, Part II offenses (*UCR* categories), 65

Pattillo-McCoy, Mary, 411

Peer groups: coworker delinquency, 323, 327, 330, 333–340; and differential association theory, 139–140, 143(n4); and lack of adult supervision in socially disorganized communities, 300; and lack of alternative activities in urban neighborhoods, 409; need for spending money in order to achieve higher status, 325, 372; and negative work environments, 323, 327; parental disapproval of peers, 248–258, 260; and religion, 235(n2); and social disorganization theory, 234; and social learning theory, 331; workplace as social domain, 325. *See also* Adolescent subcultures; Differential association theory; Gangs; Law-violating youth groups; Social learning theory; Values, street culture

Peirce, Bradford Kinney, 21

Pennsylvania. *See* Philadelphia, PA

People (gang), 397

Perrow, Charles, 53

Personal agency, 235(n1)

Personality factors in delinquency, 135–136; coping strategies, 222; emotional reactions to strain, 222; low self-control, 136, 222, 327, 331, 334–337, 340, 341

Persons in Need of Supervision (PINS), 51

Peterson, Dana, 74, 101–126, 400

Philadelphia, PA: fighting as status-building mechanism, 412; Wolfgang et al. birth cohort study, 68

Phoenix, AZ: gang activity in, 398

Piliavin, Irving, 457, 477–486

Pimping, 233, 268–271

PINS. *See* Persons in Need of Supervision

Platt, Anthony, 4–5, 9–25, 35

Ploeger, Matthew, 332

Police: antagonism between police and local residents, 310, 410; assessments of situations of suspicion, 479–482; different organizational styles of departments, 466–467; greater surveillance in lower-class areas due to residents' lack of access to private space, 465; legal and extralegal factors in decisionmaking, 457, 463–467; patrols of boundaries of neighborhoods, 480–481; preference for social planning approaches, 310; recognition of danger spots, 480; residents' unwillingness to cooperate with due to fear of retaliation, 425; residents' unwillingness to cooperate with due to upholding family honor, 449; self-help crimes in areas lacking effective authoritative agents, 413; and victim prevention programs, 310; views on gang violence, 446–447

Police-juvenile interactions, 477–486; and affluent law-violating youth, 357–359; challenges to police authority/avoiding loss of face, 483–485, 486(n12); and demeanor of juvenile, 359, 365–366, 465, 479, 483; and gender of offenders, 466; and lower-class law-violating youth, 360–362, 464–466; outcomes of interactions, 483–485; and prior contacts with police, 478–479; and probation officers, 484; and racial bias, 464–466; and situations of suspicion, 479–482; suspects provoked into resisting arrest, 485; suspicion triggered by individual attributes, 481; and trivial charges, 484

Policy recommendations, 88, 234, 314–316. *See also* Correctional institutions; Prevention of delinquency; Treatment of juvenile delinquents

Pollock, V., 129

Polsky, Howard, 519(n10)

Pope, Carl E., 469

Porterfield, Austin L., 69

Porterfield self-report survey (1943), 69

Poverty, 74(n3), 206–208. *See also* Economics; Social class; Urban neighborhoods

Pregnancy, 200, 403–404

President's Committee on Juvenile Delinquency and Youth Crime, 306–307

Press, Andrea, 429(n2)

Prevalence of offending, distinguished from incidence, 70, 86, 87

Prevention of delinquency: and abortion, 74(n5); "broken windows" strategy, 75(n6); and child-saving movement, 15–16; combined offender-oriented and victim prevention strategies, 311–313, 315; and decline of crime rate in the 1990s, 74–75(nn 5,6); difficulties of evaluating programs, 315–316; and expansion of state intervention, 35–36; late nineteenth-century ideas, 15; mentor programs, 315; and Neighborhood Anti-Crime Self-Help Program (NASP), 311–313; prevention programs of the 1960s and 1970s, 51–53; and rise of juvenile court system, 17–19; victim prevention programs, 309–313; and Violent Juvenile Offender Research and Development Program (VJORDP), 311–312. *See also* Community organization for prevention of delinquency; Deterrence; Policy recommendations; "Scared straight" programs

Primary deviance, 75(n7), 233

Privacy issues, 31

Probation: home-based intensive probation services, 458, 523–539; personal characteristics of probation officers, 40; and police-juvenile interactions, 484; probation officers and child placement, 32; and Progressive Era, 36, 38–40; successes of, 52–53; unofficial probation, 33

Progressive Era, 4; and the awareness of class differences, 38; change in focus of correctional efforts, 33; and changes in economic and social institutions, 10–12; characteristics of reformers, 37; expansion in definition of delinquency, 33–35; goals of Progressive Era reformers, 32–33, 36; images of crime and delinquency, 14–17; juvenile court movement, 27–43; legislation on legal responsibility of adults, 28; penal reform, 16; reformers' assumptions about children and morality, 39–40; separation of child from adult offenders, 28; views on the humanitarian treatment of children, 35; and women's philanthropic work, 12–13, 37. *See also* Child-saving movement

Property crimes: and denial of injury, 183–184, 194–195; and differing treatment of male and female offenders, 468–469; and life stages of delinquent youth, 394–395; National Youth Survey categories, 70; and transfer of cases to adult criminal court, 470; and XYY males, 129. *See also* Theft; Vandalism

Prostitution, 217(n5), 233, 263–274; and childhood experiences, 271–274; and double standard, 271; and gang girls' views on criminality, 209; girls constituting a majority of arrests, 72; loss of ties with family and friends, 271; negative experiences in the workplace and the allure of the underground economy, 270–271; and pregnancy, 271; and sexual abuse, 266–267, 272–273; and street values, 270–271

Provo, UT: community treatment program, 52

Psychological approach to delinquency, 133–137; applications of psychological approaches, 137; behaviorism, 136–137, 139–140, 459; and female gang members, 199; Freudian psychology, 134–135; low self-control, 136, 327, 331, 334–337, 340, 341; and school shootings, 220. *See also* Identity, female; Identity, male; Social learning theory; Social psychology of delinquency; Treatment of juvenile delinquents

Pueblo Indians, 163

Puerto Rican youth: and aggression, 214–215; drug trade and Puerto Rican gangs, 395; girls' self-definition by rejection through social talk (gossip, put downs), 199–218; importance of image of "purity" before marriage, 200, 212; and teen parenthood, 211–212. *See also* Hispanic/Latino youth

Punishment: and differential reinforcement, 140; perceptions of, 138–139, 153; and rational-choice theory, 138; social control strategies of correctional institutions, 505–509. *See also* Correctional institutions; Deterrence; Disposition of cases; Prevention of delinquency; Probation; Schools; Treatment of juvenile delinquents

Puritans, 2

"Pushouts," 276, 288–291, 292(n2)

Quadagno, Jill, 317(n8)

Quicker, John, 400

Quinceañeras, and gang violence, 437, 442–445

Race/ethnicity: and anomie-opportunity theory, 303; and cultural bias in theories of crime and delinquency, 162, 176(n1); and Denver Youth Study, 84–85; differences between white and black urban neighborhoods, 411; and discretionary decisionmaking in the juvenile justice system, 467–468; and disposition of cases, 467–468, 472(n3); and disproportionate arrest rates, 68–69; and dropout risk factors,

276–277; drug use by Native American vs. Caucasian youth as test of social learning theory, 161–176; and family interactions, 247–249, 256–258; and gangs of the 1920s, 393; and girls' self-definition, 203–206; and inflated statistics due to a few high-frequency offenders, 70; and labeling theory, 69; names for adolescent subcultures, 375, 380–381; and police interactions, 464–466; racial discrimination, 60(n5); and sex composition of gangs, 111–112; statistics on race/ethnicity and delinquency, 68–70; and workplace delinquency, 333–337. *See also specific ethnic groups*

Rafter, Nicole Hahn, 129

Rahway State Prison, 150–153, 156

Rap music, 352, 401, 407–432; constitutive perspective, 414–415; and construction of violent social identity, 418–426; criminal records of rap artists, 429(n4); and cultural codes, 426–429; gangsta rap, 408, 414, 417, 426, 428; guns in, 421–422; and inner-city context, 409–411; lyrics making light of the street code, 430(n8); and mainstream culture, 428; misogyny in, 428; nihilism in, 428, 430(n7); and normative climate of violence, 408–409, 415–416; origins of, 408; and recording industry, 429(n5); and respect/disrespect, 411–414, 422–426; situational and situated meaning of lyrics, 416; and social control, 409, 410, 413; and social identity, 408–409, 411–416, 426; and street code, 408–409, 411–416, 418–426; violence portrayed as social control, 422–423

Rape, 217(n3), 482, 494–495, 515

Rational-choice theory, 138–139, 560(n14)

Reagan, Ronald, 53

Reasons, Charles E., 176(n1)

Recidivism rates, 458, 559(n9); intensive probation vs. more costly placements, 458, 523, 528–532, 538(n7); and juvenile drug courts, 547–549, 551–558, 559(n9)

Reformatory system, 3–4, 19; cottage

system, 4, 19–20; diverse nature of institutions, 48; and emerging school systems, 47; ideology and methods of, 20–21; Progressive Era, 19–22; reformatory distinguished from traditional penitentiary, 19. *See also* Correctional institutions; Houses of refuge

Reintegrative shaming, 460, 461(n7)

Religion, 235(n2), 301

Respect/disrespect: acquiring respect through a violent reputation, 411–414, 418–426; and crimes as "payback," 188–189, 413, 422–423, 425–427; distinction between upholding honor and gaining a reputation for toughness, 440, 441; personal honor, violence, and etiquette in Chicago Chicano community, 437–438; and testing/challenging, 423–424, 437–440, 445; types of disrespect, 423

Restitution, 459–460, 461(n7)

Restorative justice movement, 461(n7)

Riis, Jacob, 14

Robbins, Susan P., 163, 177(n3)

Robinson, Cyril D., 395, 396

Rochester, NY: Thornberry et al. study of high-risk youth, 94–95

Rodriguez, Nancy, 547–548, 557

Roe v. Wade, 74(n5)

Roper v. Simmons, 456

Rose, Tricia, 416

Rosenfeld, Richard, 342

Rosenthal, John T., 544

Rothman, Jack, 298

Roughnecks (lower-class law-violating youth group in Chambliss's study), 351, 359–368

Routine activities approach to crime, 317(n12)

Ruggiero, Mary, 325–326

Rusche, Georg, 20

Rush, Jeffrey P., 548–549

Ryerson, Ellen, 5, 27–43

Saints (affluent law-violating youth group in Chambliss's study), 351, 355–359, 363–368

Saints (gang), 398–399

Samenow, Stanton E., 137

Sampson, Robert J., 302, 317(n6), 339, 465, 468

San Antonio, TX: girl gangs in, 402

San Diego, CA: gangs in, 396–397

San Francisco, CA: community tolerance of gang violence, 434; girl gangs in, 402

Sanborn, Frank, 19

Sanders, William B., 393, 396, 397

Sandman Ladies (gang), 201–217

Santana, Steven, 548

Scandinavia, 51

"Scared straight" programs, 138–139, 149–159; ineffectiveness of, 138–139, 153, 155–157; Michigan Reformatory Visitation program, 153–155; Rahway State Prison program, 150–153, 156; Ullersmo Prison project (Norway), 156–157; Virginia State Penitentiary program, 155–156

Scarpitti, Frank R., 472(n3)

Schall v. Martin, 456

Scheuble, Laurie K., 468–469

Schlossman, Stephen L., 30, 35, 38, 302

Schma, William G., 544

Schmidt, Jennifer A., 325

Schneider, Barbara, 325

School shooters, 142, 219–227; and bullying, 223–225; Columbine high school, 219–220, 223–227, 375–376; and gender theory, 222–223; and general strain theory, 220–222, 225–227; psychological explanations, 220; shootings in the 1990s, 219; shootings in the 2000s, 226; and video games, 226, 227(n9)

Schools, 279–293, 371; adolescent subcultures in, 370–389; and affluent law-violating youth, 355–356, 358–359; bullying ignored by adults, 224–225; cheating on tests, 358; and Chicago Area Project, 301; conflict between school and family obligations, 290–291; correlation between school commitment/GPA and workplace delinquency, 331, 333–337; disciplinary practices leading to dropout, 276–292; dropout risk factors, 276, 291–292; dropouts, voluntary vs. involuntary, 276–277; and erosion of bonds between youths and society, 275;

exclusion of "troublemakers" through informal expulsion, 276, 288–291; and extended period of adolescence, 1; failure to distinguish gang and nongang youth, 447; fewer resources in low-income communities, 132; and gang members, 445; goal of discipline policies, 288, 293(n12); influence of student's past record in interpreting meaning of misconduct, 283–285, 293(n11); interactions with parents, 281–282, 285–287; and labeling theory, 233–234, 275, 277–278; lack of counseling resources, 291, 293(n10); and low IQ, 132; and lower-class law-violating youth, 358–359, 362–363; policy recommendations, 234; predatory students, 223–225, 227(n7); and reformatory system, 20; resistance to outside scrutiny, 312; rise of compulsory education, 12, 17, 46–47; strain derived from rules and regimentation of school, 221; strain of school failure, 221; suspension for offenses threatening school's authority rather than safety, 282, 283, 293(n7); teachers' avoidance of community events, 447; teachers' lack of understanding of honor and violence connection, 447; teachers' views on gang violence, 446–447; and teen parenthood, 211; tracking system, 132, 293(n18); and transformation from primary to secondary deviance, 233; vandalism as retaliation against, 188–189, 221. *See also* Athletics; Correctional institutions
Schulenberg, John, 330, 332
Schutt, Russell K., 464
Schwartz, Gary, 370
Schwendinger, Herman, 370–375, 378
Schwendinger, Julia, 370–375, 378
Scriven, Michael, 555
Secondary deviance, 75(n7), 233, 278, 287
Sedlak, Michael W., 302
Seductions of Crime: Moral and Sensual Attractions of Doing Evil (Katz), 226
Self-control: low self-control as contributing factor in delinquency, 136, 327, 331, 334–337, 340, 341

Self-efficacy, 235(n1), 315
Self-esteem, 236(n3); masculine gender strain and school shooters, 222–223; and "payback" crimes, 189; and violent reputation, 411–414. *See also* Identity, female; Identity, male
Self-report studies of delinquency, 239–262; and age of offenders, 66–67; Cernkovich and Giordano's family interactions study, 232, 239–262; discrepancies in official vs. self-report data, 69–70; and drug use by Native American vs. Caucasian youth, 166–174; and labeling theory, 69; Porterfield study (Fort Worth, TX), 69. *See also* Denver Youth Study
Sellers, Christine S., 140, 141, 143(n4), 161–181
Sellin, Thorsten, 68
Seminole Indians, 164
Senjo, Scott R., 542
Senna, Joseph J., 4
Sentences. *See* Disposition of cases; Judges; Treatment of juvenile delinquents
Serotonin, 130
Sex: and adolescent subcultures, 388(n7), 389(n18); gang girls perceived as promiscuous, 200, 212; sexual relations in gangs, 200, 211–215, 400–404; status gained from sexual activity, 388(n7), 389(n18), 403, 404, 413. *See also* Identity, female; Identity, male; Prostitution
Sex composition of gangs. *See* Gangs, sex composition of
Sex Girls (gang), 201–217
Sexual abuse, 266–267, 272–273, 401
Shaming. *See* Reintegrative shaming
Shaw, Clifford R., 299–300, 302
Shaw, Henry, 60(n6)
Shelden, Randall G., 466
Shelden, William H., 129
Shoplifting, 72, 185, 188, 209
Short, James, 448
Siegel, Larry J., 4
Sikes, Gini, 402
Single-parent homes. *See* Family circumstances
Sisters in Crime (Adler), 72
Skinner, B. F., 136

Skolnick, Jerome H., 393–394, 396, 466
Sloan, John J., 548–549
Slums. *See* Urban neighborhoods
Smith, Douglas A., 169–170
Smith, Mrs. Perry, 11
Smykla, John O., 548–549
Snitching: disrespect through, 423; informing in correctional institutions, 513–516
Social action, 234, 298–299, 314; and Alinsky, 301–302; comprehensive community action projects of the 1960s, 305–309; conflicts between social action and locality development/social planning, 307–309; defined/described, 299; limitations of, 314; and reduced gang activity, 318(n19)
Social bonds with society. *See* Social control theory
Social class: and adolescent status and social type metaphors, 370–376, 378–380; and anomie-opportunity theory, 303; and antagonism between police and local residents, 310, 410; and authorities' assessments about parental control, 478–479; and child-saving movement, 9–22; and conflict theory of society, 5; demeanor of affluent vs. lower-class offenders upon confrontation, 359, 365–366, 465; and discretionary decisionmaking in the juvenile justice system, 467–468; disjuncture between culturally approved goals and available opportunities, 221, 303; economic bifurcation of black communities, 318(n17), 411; and environmental toxins, 130; and family involvement, 233; and images of crime in the Progressive Era, 14–17; and IQ, 131–132; and labeling theory, 69, 368; loss of self-efficacy in economically marginal communities, 315; middle-class values and Progressive Era goals, 36–38; and nineteenth-century education system, 12; and parents' interactions with schools, 286–287; perceptions of youth offending based on social class, 351, 355–368; police interactions with affluent youth, 357–359; police interactions with lower-class youth, 360–362, 464–466,

477–486; and poor prenatal and early childhood care, 130; Shaw and McKay study on high crime areas in Chicago, 74(n3); social disorganization theory, 234, 236(n4), 299–302, 409; statistics on class and delinquency, 68–70; strategies of negotiating the school system based on social class, 355–356, 358–359; and territorial conflicts caused by victim prevention emphasis, 310; visibility of affluent vs. lower-class groups, 364–365. *See also* Schools; Suburban and rural communities; Urban neighborhoods; Values, mainstream; Values, street culture
Social control theory: and causal order of negative interactions and delinquency, 246–247; culture-bound quality of, 164; elements of social bonds, 232, 243; and family inter-actions, 232, 242–243, 258; and juvenile drug courts, 547–548, 557; and results of Denver Youth Study on gang membership, 95; social control strategies of correctional institutions, 505–509, 513–515, 517–518, 519–521(nn 10,25,26); and studies of Native American youth, 163–164; and Violent Juvenile Offender Research and Development Program (VJORDP), 312; violent social control portrayed in rap music, 409, 410, 413, 422–423
Social Darwinism, 14–16
Social disorganization theory, 234, 236(n4), 299–302, 409
Social learning theory: and correctional interventions, 137, 141, 459; defined/described, 139–142, 165; and drug use by Native American vs. Caucasian youth, 141, 161–176; and group-based rehabilitative interventions, 141; and juvenile drug courts, 557; and results of Denver Youth Study on gang membership, 95; and sex composition of gangs, 120; summary of empirical research, 143(n4); and techniques of neutralization, 140–141, 143(n3); and Violent Juvenile Offender Research and Development Program (VJORDP), 312; and workplace delinquency, 326,

331, 339. *See also* Differential association theory

Social planning model of community organization, 234, 314; comprehensive community action projects of the 1960s, 305–309; conflicts between locality development and social planning, 310; defined/described, 298–299; limitations of, 304–305, 314; and police, 310; and provision of opportunity programs, 304–305, 314

Social psychology of delinquency, 137–229; delinquents' perspectives on the role of the victim, 141–142, 183–197; and deterrence, 138–139, 149–157; and drug and alcohol use by Native Americans vs. Caucasian youth, 161–176; and gang girls' self-definition, 199–218; gender theory, 142, 222–223; general strain theory, 142, 220–222, 225–227, 303, 339; overview of approaches, 137–142; and rational-choice theory, 138–139; and school shooters, 142, 219–227; social learning theory and symbolic inter-action, 139–142. *See also* Causes of delinquent behavior; Values, street culture

Social structure, as contributing factor in delinquency, 16, 28; family inter-actions, 231–233; schools, 233–234, 275–296; sex composition of gangs, 101–123; underground economy, 263–274; workplace, 235, 323–349. *See also* Community organization for prevention of delinquency; Correc-tional institutions; Organizational sociology; Social class; Social disorganization theory; Suburban and rural communities; Urban neighborhoods

Social welfare programs: comprehensive community action projects of the 1960s, 305–309; Progressive Era reforms, 10–12; provision of opportunity programs of the 1960s (Job Corps, etc.), 304–305; and sense of alienation of aid recipients, 315; and teen parents, 206, 211

Society: and general strain theory, 142, 220, 221; lack of genuine commitment to reducing inequality, 316; social bonds with, 232, 235(n2), 242–243, 275. *See also* Community organization for prevention of delinquency; Religion; Schools; Suburban and rural communities; Urban neighborhoods; Values, mainstream; Values, street culture

Society for the Reformation of Juvenile Delinquents, 10

Spencer, Herbert, 14

Spergel, Irving A., 317(n4)

St. Louis, MO: crimes as "payback," 413

Stark, Rodney, 235(n2)

State agencies: and failure of treatment programs, 54; and locality develop-ment projects, 302; recommendations for successful programs, 60(n7); and social planning programs, 304–305; successful programs in Massachusetts and Utah, 55–58. *See also* Social welfare programs; *specific states*

Status offenses, 5, 19; and alcohol use by Native American vs. Caucasian youth, 167–168, 174–176; defined/described, 5, 453; and discretionary decisionmaking in the juvenile justice system, 469; more severe treatment of female status offenders, 466; National Youth Survey categories, 70; resurgence of, 59–60(n1); separation of status offenders from delinquents, 51

Steffensmeier, Darrell J., 66, 318(n16), 404(n2)

Steinberg, Laurence, 328

Stephenson, Richard M., 472(n3)

Stepparents, 247–249, 252–254

Stokes, Randall, 201, 435

Stoneall, Linda, 398

Storvall, Elisabet, 156–157

Strain theory, 303, 339; classic strain theory, 221; distinction between classic and general strain theory, 221–222; general strain theory and school shooters, 142, 220–222; and school failure, 221; and school rules/regimentation, 221

Strauss, Anslem, 434

Street, David, 53

Street values. *See* Values, street culture

Strodtbeck, Fred, 448

Stubbs, George W., 50

Stutz, Eric, 226

Subcultures of adolescents. *See*
Adolescent subcultures

Suburban and rural communities:
differing perceptions of youth
offending based on social class, 351,
355–368; drug and alcohol use by
Native Americans vs. Caucasian
youth, 161–176; media attention on
violence at suburban schools, 220;
negative perceptions of gangs, 351;
school shooters, 142, 219–227

Suicide, 163, 220, 223, 227(n8)

Sullivan, Mercer L., 394–395

Superego, 134

Supervision of youth, 204–205, 260,
300, 448. *See also* Family interactions

Suspension from school, 279–293

Sutherland, Edwin, 139–140, 323–324,
326, 339

Sutton, John, 47

Swaddling, 2

Sykes, Gresham M., 140–141, 183, 201,
389(n18), 493–494

Symbolic interaction, 139–140

Tappan, Paul, 50

TCAEP. *See* Tri-Cities Adolescent
Employment Survey

Techniques of neutralization. *See*
Neutralization, techniques of

Television. *See* Mass media

Tennessee: study on juvenile involvement in occupational delinquency,
323–349; Tri-Cities Adolescent
Employment Survey (TCAEP), 328

Texas: Porterfield self-report survey
(1943), 69

Theft: and "careless victims," 143(n3),
184–187; and disrespect through
victimization, 423–425; effectiveness
of precautions against, 184; expropriation of property in correctional
institutions, 514, 516; inappropriate
victims, 190–192; and life stages of
delinquent youth, 394–395; and lower-
class law-violating youth, 360–361;
and "payback" crimes, 188–189;
victim's actions leading to negation
or escalation of harm, 192–194

Therapeutic community treatment
model, 508–509

Therapeutic jurisprudence, 544–545

Thomas, Charles, 60(n5)

Thompson, William E., 369

Thornberry, Terence, 94–95

Thornton, William E., 460(n4)

Thrasher, Frederic, 393

Thurston, Henry, 37

Token economy, 137

Tokenism, 103–104, 119, 120, 177(n8).
See also Gangs, sex composition of

Tracking system in schools, 132,
293(n18)

Training schools. *See* Correctional
institutions

Transportation, and differing visibility of
affluent vs. lower-class law-violating
groups, 364–365

Treatment of juvenile delinquents:
community programs, 52–53, 56–59;
ethical problems in biological
interventions, 133; intensive probation
vs. other placements, 523–539;
nonstate programs, 54; perception
that treatment does not work, 53;
post–World War II criticisms of
juvenile justice system, 50–54; and
Progressive Era, 38–40; reasons for
failure, 54–55; recommendations for
successful programs, 53, 55–59,
517–518; reintegrative shaming, 460,
461(n7); and restitution, 459–460,
461(n7); and social learning theory/
behaviorism, 137, 141, 459; treatment
programs of the 1960s and 1970s,
51–53; victim-offender mediation,
461(n7). *See also* Community-based
corrections; Correctional institutions;
Disposition of cases; Group-oriented
rehabilitative treatment; Juvenile
drug courts; Juvenile justice system;
Probation; "Scared straight"
programs

Tri-Cities Adolescent Employment
Survey (TCAEP), 328

Truancy, 5, 355–368; conflict between
school and family obligations,
290–291; successful strategies among
affluent youth, 355–356, 358, 359. *See
also* Schools

Tuthill, Richard, 50
Twin studies, 130–131

UCR. *See Uniform Crime Reports*
Ullersmo Prison project (Norway), 156–157
"Underground economy," 263–274. *See also* Drug trade; Pimping; Prostitution
Uniform Crime Reports (*UCR;* FBI), 65–66
Upward Bound, 304
Urban neighborhoods: active street life and visibility of offenders, 465; characteristics of, 299, 409–411; and child-saving movement, 9–10; differences between white and black urban neighborhoods, 411; and Industrial Revolution, 46–47; lack of opportunities for conventional status attainment, 409; police patrol of neighborhood boundaries, 480–481; poor police-community relations, 310, 410, 425, 449; poor quality of schools in low-income neighborhoods, 132; poverty and social unrest, 9–10; and rap music, 352, 409–411; self-help crimes in areas lacking effective authoritative agents, 413; Shaw and McKay study on high crime areas in Chicago, 74(n3); street code and neighborhood subculture, 352, 411–414; territorial conflicts over drug trade, 410; tolerance of children's gang activity, 352, 433–451. *See also* Community organization for prevention of delinquency; Community tolerance of gang violence; Social class; Social disorganization theory; *specific ethnic groups*
US Supreme Court cases, 454–456, 460(n4)
Utah, 52, 55–56

Values, mainstream: and informal sanctions (shame, embarrassment, family disapproval), 139; middle-class values and Progressive Era goals, 36–38; and offenders' techniques of neutralization (denial of responsibility, etc.), 140–141
Values, street culture, 352, 422–424;
delinquents' perspectives on the role of the victim, 141–142, 183–197; distinction between upholding honor and gaining a reputation for toughness, 440, 441; and guns, 412; masculine code of honor and response to shame and humiliation, 225–226; mutual dependency viewed as weakness, 446; personal honor, violence, and etiquette in Chicago Chicano community, 437–438; and prostitution, 270–271; and rap music, 352, 407–432; resisting victimization, 424–425; and respect/disrespect, 188–189, 222–223, 411–414, 418–427; snitching, 423, 425; and social identity, 408–409, 411–416, 426–427; and social structure of correctional institutions, 502–503; street code vs. Puerto Rican island values, 204–205; and testing/challenging, 423–424, 437–440; violence and crime as payback, 412–413, 422–423, 425–427. *See also* Identity, female; Identity, male; Social learning theory
Van Winkle, Nancy Westlake, 163
Vandalism: and affluent law-violating youth groups, 356–357, 363; and counter-denunciation, 496–497; and denial of injury, 183–184, 194–195; school vandalism as retaliation, 187–188, 221
Vaughan, Dianna, 327
Venkatesh, Sudhir Alladi, 398
Verbal assaults ("ranking"), 519(n10)
Vernonia School District v. Acton, 456
Victim prevention programs, 309–313
Victimization, 141–142, 183–197, 501; bullying, 223–225; "careless" victims, 143(n3), 184–187, 196; in correctional institutions, 502–503, 510–518; "deserving" victims, 187–190, 196; disrespect through, 423–425; and drug trade, 189–190; and failure to fight back, 222, 515; inappropriate victims, 190–192; self-report surveys, 66–67; and techniques of neutralization, 140–141, 143(n3), 183–197; victimless crime, 194–195, 209; victim's actions leading to negation or escalation of harm, 192–194

Victim-offender mediation, 461(n7)
Video games, 226, 227(n9)
Vinter, Robert D., 53
Violence: acquiring respect through a
  violent reputation, 411–414, 418–426;
  in correctional institutions, 502–503,
  510–518; domestic violence, 213–214;
  gang violence as extension of honor,
  437–438, 440; and low serotonin
  levels, 130; National Youth Survey
  categories, 70; and payback, 412–413,
  425–427; prevalence of guns, 410,
  412; and social control, 409, 410, 413,
  505–509, 513–515; strategies for
  avoiding harm to the "innocent,"
  190–192; territorial conflicts over
  drug trade, 203, 410; transition from
  order to disorder, 443–446; victim's
  actions leading to negation or
  escalation of harm, 192–194; and
  video games, 226, 227(n9). See also
  Community tolerance of gang
  violence; Fighting; Gang violence;
  School shooters; Social control theory
Violent Crime Control and Law
  Enforcement Act (1994), 544
Violent Juvenile Offender Research and
  Development Program (VJORDP),
  311–312
Virginia State Penitentiary, 155–156
VJORDP. See Violent Juvenile Offender
  Research and Development Program
Voight, Lydia, 460(n4)
Volavka, J., 129

Waiver hearings on transfer of cases to
  adult criminal court, 454, 470–471
War on drugs, 464
War on poverty, 52, 303
Warr, Mark, 120
Warren, Bruce O., 235(n2)
Warren, Marguerite, 53
Watkins, S. Craig, 429(n5)
Wax, Rosalie H., 163–164, 174
Wayne County, MI: intensive probation
  program, 523–539
Webb, Vincent J., 547–548, 557
Weddings, and gang violence, 437,
  442–445
Weis, Joseph G., 69, 374

Welfare state. See Social welfare
  programs
Werthman, Carl, 457, 477–486
Westley, William, 484–485, 486(n12)
Wey, Hamilton, 15
White youth: and Denver Youth Study,
  85; derogatory names for adolescent
  subcultures, 388(n10); and disparity in
  drug arrest rates, 464–465; and
  disposition of cases, 467–468, 472(3);
  drug use by Native American vs.
  Caucasian youth as test of social
  learning theory, 161–176; and family
  interactions, 247–249, 256–258;
  and gang membership, 85; and
  sex composition of gangs, 112;
  white gang members as social
  outcasts, 448
White-collar crime, 74(n4), 323–324,
  326, 339
Wieder, Lawrence D., 415
Wilkinson, Deanna, 412
Williams, Terry, 233, 263–274
Wilson, James Q., 75(n6), 308, 472(n2)
Wilson, William J., 318(n17)
Wines, Enoch, 17, 19, 21
Wines, Frederick, 49
Winfree, Thomas, 141, 161–181
Wisconsin: Milwaukee gangs, 397–398;
  potential school shootings, 226; study
  of adolescent subcultures, 376–386,
  388(n7)
Wolfgang, Marvin, 68
Women: and child-saving movement,
  12–13; and Progressive Era
  philanthropy, 37. See also Girls;
  Girls as gang members; Identity,
  female; Mothers
Wooden, Wayne S., 225, 375
Woodham, Luke, 219, 226, 227(n1)
Workplace delinquency, 33, 235,
  323–349; "amplification" effect of
  workplace delinquency, 33, 335–336;
  characteristics of jobs, 326, 330;
  coworker delinquency, 323, 327, 330,
  333–340; and family background, 332,
  334–337; and gender, 334–337;
  hypotheses about, 332–333; and low
  self-control, 327, 331, 334–337, 340,
  341; and materialistic attitudes,

331–337, 341–342; negative experiences and the allure of the underground economy, 270–271; and negative work environments, 323, 327, 330, 334–341; and previous delinquency, 330–331, 333–340; quality of jobs, 326, 327, 339; and school commitment/GPA, 331, 333–337; self-selection into negative environments, 337–338, 340–341; separation of gang identity from workplace identity, 437–438; as social domain for adolescents, 340; and social learning theory, 326, 331, 339; "spill over" effect of employment, 333, 336, 339–340; types of crimes, 329–330; white-collar crime, 323–324, 326–327, 339; workplace as social domain for adolescents, 325
Wright and Cullen study, 328–345
Wright, John Paul, 235, 323–349

XYY chromosome syndrome, 129

Yablonsky, Lewis, 83
Yochelson, Samuel, 137
Youth Services Bureaus (Johnson administration), 60(n9)

Zey-Ferrell, Mary K., 326
Zimring, Franklin, 67, 74(n5)

About the Book

THIS NEW ANTHOLOGY OFFERS A COMPREHENSIVE OVERVIEW OF THE essential topics in juvenile delinquency and justice. The selections encompass both landmark scholarship and cutting-edge research to expose students to a wide range of theoretical and methodological approaches. Thematic section introductions and editors' notes provide context and draw attention to how a sociological perspective can deepen understanding of the topics at issue.

The text:

- uses compelling ethnographic studies to capture student interest
- addresses current concerns such as school shooters, occupational delinquency, gangsta rap, and drug courts
- highlights issues of race/ethnicity, gender, and class
- emphasizes critical approaches to adolescent subcultures and gang delinquency
- includes quantitative articles selected for their accessibility

The result is a lively and substantive grounding in the field.

Ronald J. Berger is professor of sociology at the University of Wisconsin–Whitewater. His most recent books include *Crime, Justice, and Society: An Introduction to Criminology* (now in its 3rd edition) and *Wheelchair Warrior: Gangs, Disability, and Basketball.* **Paul D. Gregory** is assistant professor of sociology at the University of Wisconsin–Whitewater. He has been a probation officer and drug court evaluator and serves on the board of directors of the Wisconsin Association of Treatment Court Professionals.